Lecture Notes in Computer Science

For information about Vols. 1–4289
please contact your bookseller or Springer

Lecture Notes in Computer Science 4394

Commenced Publication in 1973
Founding and Former Series Editors:
Gerhard Goos, Juris Hartmanis, and Jan van Leeuwen

Alexander Gelbukh (Ed.)

Computational Linguistics and Intelligent Text Processing

8th International Conference, CICLing 2007
Mexico City, Mexico, February 18-24, 2007
Proceedings

 Springer

Volume Editor

Alexander Gelbukh
National Polytechnic Institute (IPN)
Center for Computing Research (CIC)
Col. Nueva Industrial Vallejo, 07738, DF, Mexico
E-mail: gelbukh@gelbukh.com

Library of Congress Control Number: 2007920471

CR Subject Classification (1998): H.3, I.2.7, I.7, I.2, F.4.3

LNCS Sublibrary: SL 1 – Theoretical Computer Science and General Issues

ISSN   0302-9743
ISBN-10   3-540-70938-X Springer Berlin Heidelberg New York
ISBN-13   978-3-540-70938-1 Springer Berlin Heidelberg New York

Springer is a part of Springer Science+Business Media

springer.com

© Springer-Verlag Berlin Heidelberg 2007
Printed in Germany

Typesetting: Camera-ready by author, data conversion by Scientific Publishing Services, Chennai, India
Printed on acid-free paper   SPIN: 12020966   06/3142   5 4 3 2 1 0

Preface

CICLing 2007 (www.C ICLing.org) was the 8th Annual Conference on Intelligent Text Processing and Computational Linguistics. The CICLing conferences are intended to provide a wide-scope forum for discussion of both the art and craft of natural language processing research and the best practices in its applications.

This volume contains the papers accepted for oral presentation at the conference. The conference also featured a poster session; full papers accepted for the poster session were published elsewhere—see information on the website. Since 2001 the CICLing proceedings have been published in Springer's Lecture Notes in Computer Science series, as volumes 2004, 2276, 2588, 2945, 3406, and 3878.

A total of 179 papers by 468 authors from 34 countries were submitted for evaluation, see Tables 1 and 2. Each submission was reviewed by at least two independent Program Committee members. This volume contains revised versions of 53 papers by 157 authors from 19 countries selected for inclusion in the conference program. The acceptance rate was 29.6%.

Table 1. Statistics of submissions and accepted papers by country or region

Country or region	Authors Subm	Accp	Papers[1] Subm	Accp	Country or region	Authors Subm	Accp	Papers[1] Subm	Accp
Afghanistan	1	2	1	1	Lithuania	2	2	1	1
Algeria	2	–	1	–	Mexico	29	10	10	3
Australia	5	–	2	–	Poland	1	1	1	1
Brazil	10	2	4.66	1	Portugal	4	–	1.33	–
Canada	11	5	6	2	Romania	4		3	–
China	86	20	30.4	5.73	Russia	1	1	0.33	0.33
Cuba	6	–	1.66	–	Saudi Arabia	1	–	0.5	–
Egypt	1	–	0.5	–	Singapore	1	–	0.33	–
Finland	2	2	0.66	0.66	South Africa	2	–	1	
France	12	8	5.33	3.33	Spain	50	31	16	9.66
Germany	8	–	4	–	Switzerland	1	–	1	–
Hong Kong	15	14	4.6	3.6	Thailand	2	–	0.66	–
India	8	–	4	–	Tunisia	6	3	2.5	1
Iran	1	–	1	–	Turkey	6	3	3	1
Israel	7	3	3	2	United Arab Emirates	1	–	0.5	–
Japan	34	5	12	1.66	United Kingdom	21	5	8.5	2.5
Korea, South	88	18	29.5	5	United States	39	22	17	7.5
					Total:	*468*	*157*	*179*	*53*

[1] Counted by authors. E.g., for a paper by 3 authors, 2 from Mexico and 1 from USA, we added $\frac{2}{3}$ to Mexico and $\frac{1}{3}$ to USA.

Table 2. Statistics of submissions and accepted papers by topic[2]

Accepted	Submitted	Topic
19	40	Statistical methods
12	45	Information extraction
10	32	Other
10	23	Machine translation
9	39	Information retrieval
9	16	Syntax and chunking
8	15	Morphology and POS tagging
7	26	Clustering and categorization
7	24	Knowledge representation
7	21	Word sense disambiguation
6	28	Lexical resources
5	10	Theories and formalisms
4	32	Semantics
4	28	Text mining
4	12	Parsing algorithms
3	11	Text generation
2	14	Summarization
2	14	Natural language interfaces
2	5	Spell checking
2	3	Anaphora resolution
1	4	Discourse
0	7	Speech processing

[2] According to the topics indicated by the authors. A paper may be assigned to more than one topic.

The volume features invited papers by Gregory Grefenstette of the Commissariat à l'Énergie Atomique, France, Kathleen McKeown of Columbia University, USA, and Raymond Mooney of the University of North Texas at Austin, who presented excellent keynote lectures at the conference. Publication of extended full-text invited papers in the proceedings is a distinctive feature of CICLing conferences. What is more, in addition to presentation of their invited papers, the keynote speakers organized separate vivid informal events, which is also a distinctive feature of this conference series.

The following papers received the Best Paper Awards and the Best Student Paper Award, correspondingly:

1st Place: Enhancing Cross-Language Question Answering by Combining Multiple Question Translations, by Rita M. Aceves-Pérez, Manuel Montes-y-Gómez and Luis Villaseñor-Pineda;

2nd Place: Characterizing Humour: An Exploration of Features in Humorous Texts, by Rada Mihalcea and Stephen Pulman;

3rd Place: Text Categorization for Improved Priors of Word Meaning, by Rob Koeling, Diana McCarthy, and John Carroll;

Student: Expert vs. Non-expert Tutoring: Dialogue Moves, Interaction Patterns and Multi-Utterance Turns, by Xin Lu, Barbara Di Eugenio, Trina C. Kershaw, Stellan Ohlsson, and Andrew Corrigan-Halpern.

The Best Student Paper was selected from papers where the first author was a full-time student. The authors of the awarded papers were given extended time for their presentations. In addition, the Best Presentation Award and the Best Poster Award winners were selected by a ballot among the attendees of the conference.

Besides its high scientific level, one of the success factors of CICLing conferences is their excellent cultural program. CICLing 2007 was held in Mexico, a wonderful country rich in culture, history, and nature. The participants of the conference had a chance to see the solemn 2000-years-old pyramids of the legendary Teotihuacanas, a monarch butterfly wintering site where the old pines are covered with millions of butterflies as if they were leaves, a great cave with 85-meter halls and a river flowing from it, Aztec warriors dancing in the street in their colorful plumages, and the largest anthropological museum in the world; see photos at www.CICLing.org.

I would like to thank all those involved in the organization of this conference. In the first place these are the authors of the papers constituting this book: it is the excellence of their research work that gives value to the book and sense to the work of all other people involved. I thank the Program Committee members for their hard and very professional work on reviewing so many submissions in a short time. Very special thanks go to Manuel Vilares and his group, Rada Mihalcea, and Ted Pedersen for their invaluable support in the reviewing process.

The entire submission, reviewing, and selection process, as well as putting together the proceedings, was supported for free by the EasyChair system (www.EasyChair.org); I express my gratitude to its author Andrei Voronkov for his constant support and help. I also express my most cordial thanks to the members of the local Organizing Committee for their considerable contribution to making this conference become a reality, and to our sponsoring organization—the Center for Computing Research (CIC) of the National Polytechnic Institute (IPN), Mexico—for hosting the conference. Last but not least, I deeply appreciate the Springer staff's patience and help in editing this volume—it is always a great pleasure to work with them.

December 2006   Alexander Gelbukh

Organization

CICLing 2007 was organized by the Natural Language and Text Processing Laboratory of the Center for Computing Research (CIC, www.cic.ipn.mx) of the National Polytechnic Institute (IPN), Mexico.

Program Chair

Alexander Gelbukh

Program Committee

Eneko Agirre
Christian Boitet
Igor Bolshakov
Ted Briscoe
Nicoletta Calzolari
Kenneth Church
Dan Cristea
Barbara Di Eugenio
Gregory Grefenstette
Catalina Hallett
Yasunari Harada
Diana Inkpen
Nancy Ide
Alma Kharrat
Adam Kilgarriff
Richard Kittredge
Sandra Kuebler
Aurelio Lopez Lopez
Bernardo Magnini
Igor Mel'čuk
Rada Mihalcea
Ruslan Mitkov
Raymond Mooney
Masaki Murata

Vivi Nastase
Olga Nevzorova
Nicolas Nicolov
Sergei Nirenburg
Constantin Orasan
Ted Pedersen
Viktor Pekar
Fuji Ren
Fabio Rinaldi
Vasile Rus
Ivan Sag
Franco Salvetti
Serge Sharoff
Grigori Sidorov
Thamar Solorio
Carlo Strapparava
John Tait
Linda C. Van Guilder
Felisa Verdejo
Karin Verspoor
Manuel Vilares Ferro
Marilyn Walker
Yorick Wilks
Deniz Yuret

Award Committee

Alexander Gelbukh
Eduard Hovy
Rada Mihalcea

Ted Pedersen
Yorick Wiks

Additional Referees

Mohamed Abdel Fattah
Mustafa Abusalah
Iñaki Alegria
Miguel A. Alonso
Muath Alzghool
Bogdan Babych
Fco. Mario Barcala Rodríguez
Francesca Bertagna
Razvan Bunescu
Hiram Calvo
Tommaso Caselli
Simon Clematide
Víctor Manuel Darriba Bilbao
Richard Evans
Marcello Federico
Milagros Fernández Gavilanes
Corina Forascu
Davide Fossati
Oana Frunza
Olac Fuentes
Carlos Gómez Rodríguez
Jorge Graña Gil
Aminul Islam
Assad Jarrahian
Rohit Kate
Shih-Wen Ke

Steve Legrand
Xin Lu
Fernando Magán Muñoz
David Martinez
Carmén Carlota Martínez Gil
Ben Medlock
Miguel Angel Molinero Alvarez
Monica Monachini
Matteo Negri
Jong-Hoon Oh
Paulo Pinheiro da Silva
Juan Otero Pombo
Octavian Popescu
Oana Postolache
Christoph Reichenbach
Francisco Ribadas Pena
Claudia Soria
Aitor Soroa
Rajen Subba
Alberto Tellez Valero
Jesus Vilares Ferro
Andreas Vlachos
Philipp Wetzler
Yuk Wah Wong
Wajdi Zaghouani

Organizing Committee

Hiram Calvo Castro
Virginia Contreras Hernández
César Guzmán Rentería
Yulia Ledeneva

Raquel López Alamilla
Martin Haro Martínez
Oralia del Carmen Pérez Orozco
Sulema Torres Ramos

Website and Contact

The website of CICLing conferences is www.CICLing.org. It contains information on the past CICLing events and satellite workshops, abstracts of all published papers, photos from all CICLing events, and video recordings of some keynote talks, as well as the information on the forthcoming CICLing event. Contact: gelbukh@cicling.org, gelbukh@gelbukh.com; more contact options can be found on the website.

Table of Contents

Computational Linguistics Research

Lexical Resources

Corpus-Based Knowledge Acquisition

Morphology and Part-of-Speech Tagging

Named Entity Recognition and Temporal Expression Treatment

Word Segmentation, Sentence Splitting, and Chunking

Grammar Formalisms and Syntax

Word Sense Disambiguation and Discrimination

Semantics

Humor and Emotion Analysis

Intelligent Text Processing Applications

Machine Translation

Natural Language Generation and Intelligent Tutoring Systems

Information Retrieval

Question Answering

Text Summarization and Information Extraction

Text Categorization and Clustering

Spell-Checking

Integration of Linguistic Resources for Verb Classification: FrameNet Frame, WordNet Verb and Suggested Upper Merged Ontology

Ian C. Chow[1] and Jonathan J. Webster[2]

[1] Department of Chinese, Translation and Linguistics
City university of Hong Kong, Tat Chee Avenue, Kowloon, Hong Kong
ianchow@cityu.edu.hk
[2] The Halliday Centre for Intelligent Applications of Language Studies
City University of Hong Kong, Tat Chee Avenue, Kowloon, Hong Kong
ctjjw@cityu.edu.hk

Abstract. The work described in this paper was originally motivated by the construction of a lexical semantic knowledge base for analysis of Ideational Metafunction of language in Systemic Functional Grammar and the Generalized Upper Model ontology. The work involves mapping FrameNet Frames with Ideational Meanings and instantiating WordNet Verb as the meaning evoking linguistic elements. As the work evolved, the developed method has allowed the assignment of sense-tagged WordNet verb to FrameNet Lexical Units of each Frame. The task is achieved by linking FrameNet Frames with SUMO (Suggested Upper Merged Ontology) concepts. We describe our method of mapping which reuses and integrates linkages between WordNet, FrameNet and SUMO. The generated verb list is furthered examined with WordNet::Similarity, a semantic similarity and relatedness measuring system.

1   Introduction

Verb classification is a useful resource for semantic analysis and cognitive linguistics research. Categorization of semantically-related verbs renders assistant in understanding of the meaning construal of natural language in clause level. NLP tasks involving event recognition, discourse polarity analysis and semantic role labeling (SRL) require semantically-related verbs lists for clause pattern and participant role identification.

It is apparent that verb classification is heavily relied by clausal semantic analysis. In view of this, we aim at constructing a lexical semantic resource consists of comprehensive sense-tagged verb lexicons in addition with clause level knowledge.

Rather than start from scratch, we reuse and integrate available resources including WordNet[8], FrameNet[15] and Suggested Upper Merged Ontology (SUMO)[16]. WordNet provides intensive lexical coverage with semantic links among them but lacks information in clausal semantics. FrameNet identifies clause patterns, semantic role, verb argument structure and examples but a lower lexical coverage. SUMO is a non-linguistic upper ontology which has been mapped with WordNet [17]. SUMO is

A. Gelbukh (Ed.): CICLing 2007, LNCS 4394, pp. 1 – 11, 2007.

taken as an interface between FrameNet and WordNet in order to extend the integration of the two linguistic resources.

2 Background and Motivation

The work described in this paper was originally motivated by constructing a verb classification for Ideational Metafunction analysis in Systemic Functional Grammar (SFG). Systemic Functional Grammar [9] is a theory centered on the notion of language function. According to Systemic Functional Grammar, there are three *metafunctions* of language: Ideational Metafunction, Interpersonal Metafunction and Textual Metafunction.

Verb classification is crucial for Ideational Metafunction analysis. Ideational Metafunction can be seen as the construal of an experience, in the other words, the encoding of a happening or an event. The notion focuses on that a clause consists of a *Process* and some *Participants*, i.e. "who did what to whom". Process, the verbal group, acts as the nucleus of a clause determining the type of experience construed. There are four major process types: Material (construe doing & happening), Mental (construe processes of sensing & perception), Verbal (the processes of saying) and Relational (construe attributive relation between participants).

Systemic Functional Grammar has been computationally formalized into an ontology, Generalized Upper Model (GUM). GUM [3] defined concepts of SFG Ideational Metafunction but lacks lexical information. The ultimate goal of this work is to instantiate verbs to GUM concepts denoting different process types.

The four SFG process types represent four verb categories. Comparing with other verb classifications such as WordNet, VerbNet, FrameNet and Levin's verb list, the SFG verb classification is much more generic and meta. Thus, the goal of constructing a SFG verb list can therefore achieved by the techniques in ontology reuse and knowledge base mapping rather than starting from scratch. FrameNet's *Frame* although is "too fine-grained" with respect to the types of happening *construal* in Ideational Metafunction, its notation is highly compatible for mapping with the four meta SFG categories on the basis that both Frames and Process are denoting an event scenario. In FrameNet, verbs which can evoke a Frame are defined in the Frame's Lexical Units list (LU), which means such verb categorization is motivated by semantic relatedness rather than syntactic similarity. Moreover, Frames in FrameNet are organized hierarchically, although it has a fine-grained categorization, the defined subclass "is-a" relations aid the mapping of Frames with Processes.

However, the verb coverage of FrameNet's LU is not rich enough. The intensive lexical coverage of WordNet is rather attractive for linguistic analysis. There were various works of mapping WordNet with FrameNet (e.g. [4] [6] [14] [18] [21]). Depending on their intended goal, the mapping focuses on particular set of Frames or FrameNet defined LU, thus, a large number of WordNet verbs were not linked with FrameNet. In order to categorize as much verbs from WordNet as possible, previous WordNet FrameNet Mapping is taken as learning data, we determine an ontology-aided algorithm to automatically populate verb synsets from WordNet into the word list (Lexical Units, LU) of FrameNet Frame. Figure 1 depicts the framework of the project.

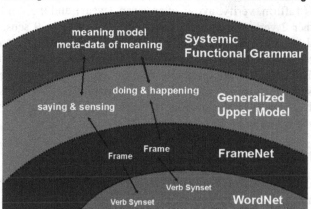

Lexicogrammar – A semantic resource for ideational meaning

Fig. 1. The framework of mapping knowledge bases of different linguistic strata

3 Extension of FrameNet Verb Coverage

A bottom-up knowledge base engineering methodology is applied to construct the lexical semantic resource represented in Figure 1. The primary attention is therefore focused on linking WordNet verbs to FrameNet LU. There are several works done on this area [4], [6], [21]. Our principle is to apply the relations links in WordNet to generate verb candidates for expanding the FrameNet LU and at the same time rely on the FrameNet declared LU which is semantic relatedness motivated. We applied Shi & Mihalcea's [21] mapping (hereafter, FnWnMap) which is verb focused. Verbs in FrameNet LU are tagged with WordNet sense. Taking the mapping as a learning data, we defined several ways of extending the LU verb coverage with WordNet.

3.1 Direct Retrieval – WordNet Synset

WordNet is an extremely large lexical database covers a vast number of English nouns, adjectives, verbs and adverbs. Lexical data are organized into synonym sets, named synset. Each synset carries a concept shared by its included synonyms. There are different relations defined among the synsets including hypernym, hyponym entailment, antonym and etc.

The first extension of LU verb coverage is straightforward. Since all lexemes in the same synset share the same concept, if one of them is capable of evoking a Frame, all lexemes in the same synset is capable of evoking the same Frame due to the synonym relations. By means of the sense-tagged information defined from FnWnMap, for each verb in a Frame's LU, we retrieve its belonged synset and map the whole synset to the frame, i.e. populated all synonyms in the synset to the LU.

For example, the LU of the Frame "STATEMENT" includes a verb "assert". FnWnMap has tagged two senses for it: "to declare or affirm solemnly and formally as true;..." and 'state categorically". The synset carries the former sense includes another 7 verbs {affirm, verify, avow, aver, swan, swear} and the synset of the latter sense has another 2 verbs {asseverate, maintain}. All of these 9 sense-tagged verbs are thus populated into the LU of "STATEMENT". Unsurprisingly, some of these discovered verbs have been defined in the FnWnMap, for instances "affirm", "aver" and "avow". This supports our principle of verb synonyms share the same synset concepts possess the same frame-evoking capability. The synset retrieving methodology has increased the number of verb sense mapping to 7900 from the defined 3652 verb sense in FnWnMap.

3.2   WordNet Relation Links and Frame as Domain

The second extension of verb coverage takes a Frame as a domain and applies the relation links among synsets in WordNet. As the FnWnMap has tagged the WordNet sense of the verb in each Frame's LU, a list of Frame-specific synsets can be retrieved. Next, we retrieve a set of related synsets which are directly related to each of these Frame-specific synsets as mapping candidates. Unlike other WordNet FrameNet Mapping which focuses on particular types of relation links, all relation links defined in WordNet are taken into account [6] to generate the set of candidate synsets because every type of links (hypernym, troponym, entailment, etc.) does represent a semantic similarity or relatedness.

All of the domain-specific synsets have a certain semantic similarity - the same frame-evoking semantics. In addition, the WordNet organized synsets as a semantic network by different semantic links. Thus, the Frame-specific synsets together with the candidates form a small lexical semantic network as shown in Figure 2.

We designed 2 different algorithms for automatic identification of appropriate candidate synsets for mapping to the LU of domain Frame:

1. Map candidate synsets with a high affinity to the domain Frame.
2. Link the domain Frame with SUMO concept.
   Retrieve SUMO concepts mapped with WordNet synsets.
   Map domain Frame with Candidate synsets which mapped to the Frame linked SUMO.

3.3   Affinity of Candidate Synsets with Domain Frame

This algorithm relies on the semantic relatedness defined by WordNet relation links. Some candidate synsets have more connection links with the verb synsets residing within the Frame domain. This implies that these candidates have a high affinity to the domain and thus are selected to be mapped into the Frame LU [6]. A threshold value is set for the number of connection links representing the affinity of the synsets to the domain. Preliminary test on random selected frames show that that setting the threshold value as greater than 1 is precise enough to draw appropriate synsets to the domain Frame LU. The pseudo-code of the algorithm is shown below Figure 2.

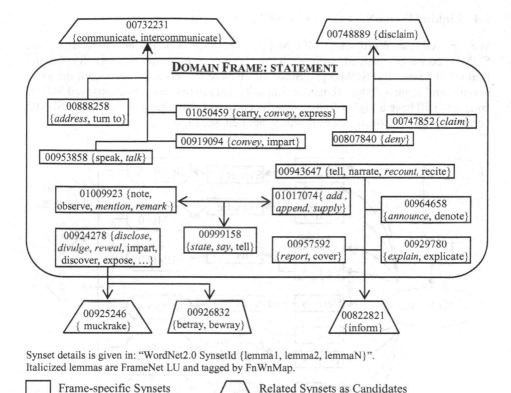

Synset details is given in: "WordNet2.0 SynsetId {lemma1, lemma2, lemmaN}".
Italicized lemmas are FrameNet LU and tagged by FnWnMap.

☐ Frame-specific Synsets   ⬡ Related Synsets as Candidates

Fig. 2. A portion of domain-specific synsets and related synsets of STATEMENT Frame

For each Frame F
  Retrieve all F related synsets into a set $SYN_F = \{S_1, S_2, \ldots S_n\}$
  For each $S_n \in SYN_F$,
    $S_{nn} = DirectRelatedSynset(S_n)$, $S_{nn} \in CandSyn_F$.
  $CandSyn_F = \{S_{1a}, S_{1b}, \ldots S_{1x}, S_{2a}, S_{2b}, \ldots S_{2x}, S_{3a}, S_{3h}, \ldots S_{3n}, S_{na}, S_{nb}, \ldots S_{nx}\}$,
  For each $S_{nn} \in CandSyn$
    If S_{nn} has number of relation links > 1
    Then map S_{nn} as F related synsets, populate lexemes in S_{nn} into F's LU

In figure 2, three synsets, {communicate, intercommunicate} with connection links of 4, {disclaim} with connection links 2 and {inform} with connection links of 5, are drawn and mapped to the Frame STATEMENT as their new sense-tagged LU.

In fact, a recursive methodology may be applied so as to increase the number of synset mapping. However, this will definitely decrease the precision of the mapping because the candidate synsets retrieved in each recursion will be more semantically distant to the domain.

3.4 Linking FrameNet Frame with SUMO Concept

We applied the WordNet-SUMO Mapping [17] (WNSumoMap) to retrieve the SUMO concepts mapped with each of the domain-specific synsets for linking FrameNet Frame and SUMO [7]. Since all of these synsets are drawn from the same domain and share a certain semantic similarity and relatedness, some retrieved SUMO concepts will have a higher frequency of occurrences than the others. A list of SUMO concepts with their occurrences is thus generated, see Figure 3.

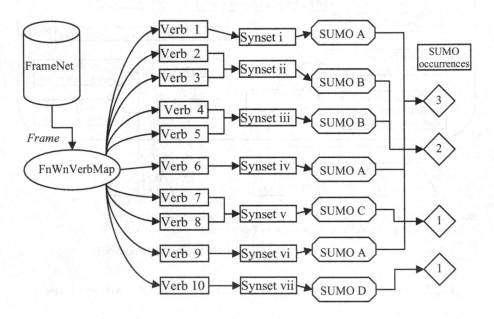

Fig. 3. The relational network of FrameNet Frames, WordNet Synsets and SUMO Concepts

A statistical distribution analysis [18] is proceeded to categorize the listed SUMO concepts according to degree of prominence for Frame Mappings. The linking of Frames and SUMO concepts is classified into three types according to the standard distribution:

1. Core SUMO concepts have an occurrence with a positive standard score greater or equal to 1 in the distribution of the occurrence.
2. Peripheral SUMO concepts have an occurrence with a positive standard score between 0 and 1 in the distribution of the occurrence.
3. Irrelevant SUMO concepts have an occurrence with a negative standard score in the distribution.

The higher the occurrence of a SUMO concept, the more prominent is it to the Frame. It should be remarked that it is a relational linkage between FrameNet Frames and SUMO concepts *but neither* a mapping of equivalence *nor* subclass mapping. The retrieved SUMO concepts are world concept of the verb synsets but not the Frame.

The Core linkage defined above can be stated as "The lexical realization of the SUMO concepts is highly capable of evoking the Frame" or represented in F-Logic, an ontology engineering program code, as a parameterized relation:

```
SUMO[evoke@(Core)->Frame]. Frame[evokeBy@(Core)->SUMO].
```

In fact, if a Frame is to be mapped to SUMO as equivalence or subclass, it is likely to be mapped with the concept PROCESS.

In many cases, the mappings are unproblematic. Frames with more mapped verbs yield reliable and satisfying SUMO mappings. On the basis of statistical analysis and automatic knowledge acquisition, larger learning data returns better result. A small number of Frames possessing relatively small number of FnWnMap synsets poses a null result. For instances the JUSTIFYING Frame, it has only five FnWnMap synsets returned and each of them was mapped with different SUMO Concepts: &%Arguing+, &%Communication+, &%Process+, Stating+ and &%Reasoning+. A standard deviation of zero is found due to their equal occurrences. In such case, the equivalence of occurrences means all of them possess the same weight in the distribution, therefore we categorize all of the SUMO concepts as Peripheral SUMO to the Frame implying that neither of the SUMO concepts are Core nor Irrelevant to the frame.

Candidate synsets mapped with the Frame Core SUMO concept is determined as appropriate synsets to be populated into the Frame LU list. The designed algorithm is supported by WordNet semantic relations in drawing candidate and the consistency of the frame-evoking semantics between the mapped synsets and candidates interfaced by SUMO world concepts. The frame-evoking semantics is, however, determined by statistical distributional prominence rather than philosophical and semantic mappings. Thus, to achieve a reliable resulting extended Frame LU, only Frame Core SUMO concepts is taken in the automatic learning process. The establishment of the Frame Peripheral SUMO concept is for loosening the selection criteria which is not suggested for the automatic machine mapping but serves as an aid for case by case human mapping.

The pseudo-code of the algorithm is shown below:

For each Frame F, as defined in previous code:
    $SYN_F = \{S_1, S_2, \dots S_n\}$
For each $S_n \in SYN_F$,
    $Sumo_n = SUMO(S_n)$, $Sumo_n \in FrameSUMOS_F$
    Core F SUMO = $Sumo_n$ with standard score >=1 in FrameSUMOS$_F$
    Periph SUMO = $Sumo_n$ with standard score >=0 & <1 in FrameSUMOS$_F$
    Irrel F SUMO = $Sumo_n$ with standard score <0 in FrameSUMOS$_F$
CandSyn$_F$ = $\{S_{1a}, S_{1b}, \dots S_{1n}, S_{2a}, S_{2b}, \dots S_{2n}, S_{3a}, S_{3b}, \dots S_{3n}, S_{na}, S_{nb}, \dots S_{nn}\}$
If $SUMO(S_{nn})$ = Core F SUMO
Then populate lexemes in S_{nn} into F's LU

Table 1 shows the data of the STATEMENT Frame. It has 94 FnWnMap verbs belonged to 75 synsets. These 75 synsets are mapped with 30 different SUMO concepts. It yields three Core SUMO concepts: Communication+, Stating+ and Stating= and one Peripheral SUMO concept: Expressing+.

Table 1. SUMO concepts statistical distribution of the STATEMENT Frame

SUMO Concepts	Occurrences	Standard Score	Frame SUMO Mappings Types
Arguing+	1	-0.456	IRRELEVANT
BodyMotion+	2	-0.168	IRRELEVANT
Committing+	1	-0.456	IRRELEVANT
Communication+	12	2.706	CORE
ContentDevelopment+	2	-0.168	IRRELEVANT
Declaring+	2	-0.168	IRRELEVANT
Declaring=	2	-0.168	IRRELEVANT
Disseminating+	2	-0.168	IRRELEVANT
Disseminating=	1	-0.456	IRRELEVANT
EmotionalState+	1	-0.456	IRRELEVANT
Expressing+	3	0.119	PERIPHERAL
ExpressingDisapproval+	1	-0.456	IRRELEVANT
IntentionalProcess+	1	-0.456	IRRELEVANT
IntentionalPsychologicalProcess+	1	-0.456	IRRELEVANT
Lecture=	2	-0.168	IRRELEVANT
LinguisticCommunication+	2	-0.168	IRRELEVANT
Publication+	1	-0.456	IRRELEVANT
Questioning+	1	-0.456	IRRELEVANT
ReligiousProcess+	2	-0.168	IRRELEVANT
Requesting=	2	-0.168	IRRELEVANT
Speaking+	2	-0.168	IRRELEVANT
Speaking=	1	-0.456	IRRELEVANT
Stating+	16	3.855	CORE
Stating=	9	1.843	CORE
Supposing+	1	-0.456	IRRELEVANT
Testifying=	1	-0.456	IRRELEVANT
Translating=	1	-0.456	IRRELEVANT
agent+	1	-0.456	IRRELEVANT
refers=	1	-0.456	IRRELEVANT
Arguing+	1	-0.456	IRRELEVANT

4   Data Evaluation

Linking an upper ontology (generic world concepts) to a domain-specific linguistic resources (frame-semantics) base on statistical analysis of concept distribution is a novel mapping approach. In order to evaluate the precision of our data, the FnWnMap defined frame-mapped synsets are taken as the golden standard, we applied a word sense similarities and relatedness measuring system, WordNet::Similarity[19], to determine the semantic relatedness between the SUMO interfaced mapped synsets with the golden standard.

WordNet::Similarity (WNS) [19] provides 6 similarity measures and 3 relatedness measures which uses WordNet information including path lengths for various WordNet relations (hypernym, meronym, etc.) and overlap among glosses and examples, semantic density, information content, depth of is-a hierarchy to determine the degree of relatedness of a pair of given words. Giving a pair of words, WNS can return a relatedness score according to the measure type chosen.

For each Frame, we create a set of pairs $P_F = L_i \times L_j$, i j, where L are the lexemes from all of the frame-mapped synsets defined by the FnWnMap and P_F is inputted to WNS. The mean score MEAN$_F$ and the standard deviation STDEV$_F$ is computed from the result scores. These values represent the average semantic relatedness between lexemes appropriate to the domain Frame and the tolerable deviation to this average relatedness respectively. The two scores are then used to evaluate the semantic relatedness of the list of lexemes generated by the SUMO interfaced mapping results.

Similarly, for each Frame, and for each lexeme drawn by SUMO interfacing is paired with the list of lexemes defined by FnWnMap. The set of pair, Psumo = V x L$_i$, where V is each SUMO mapped lexeme and L are the FnWnMap lexemes, is fed to WNS. From the returned set of scores, the mean score MEAN$_V$ is computed and then compared with the MEAN$_F$. IF the MEAN$_V$ value is lower than one negative STDEV$_F$ of MEAN$_F$, the semantic relatedness of lexeme V is evaluated as insufficiently semantically related to the Frame and is out-classified for mapping with the Frame.

Preliminary experimentation confirmed that the *lesk* [20] measure provided the most accurate results [14] among the nine measures in WNS. There is another reason for designating the *lesk* measure for the evaluation. It is because *lesk* assigns relatedness score by gloss overlaps of the pair of the two senses and the senses of other words linked to the pairs, for instances the first word and the related word of second and vice versa, overlaps scoring can also be made between gloss-gloss, example-gloss or gloss-example. In the other words, weight is given to the information content overlaps rather than path length measurement. As mentioned, the SUMO interfaced mapping is supported by WordNet semantic links in drawing candidates. Bias will occur if the scoring measure focuses on path length.

In FnWnMap, there are 313 Frames with 3652 verbs sense-tagged mapped. The above lexical coverage extension is performed to all of the Frames. Number of new lexeme yielded from our mapping varies among Frames due to the different number of sense-tagged learning data. For example, the Multi-Link and SUMO-interfacing extension together generates 263 new WordNet sense-tagged verb lexemes mapped to the STATEMENT Frame, 23 in the ATTACK Frame and 123 in the GIVING Frame.

4.1 Evaluation Result

The evaluation result is satisfying. There are 7359 new WordNet sense-tagged lexemes drawn. 1772 of them are recalled by the multi-WordNet links extension, 6121 are recalled by the SUMO interfacing extension and 534 were recalled by both. It is predictable that the verbs recalled by both extension methodologies possess the highest precision rate, 99.63%, by the WNS evaluation. The precision of SUMO interfaced mapping scores a very high precision rate as well, 99.17%. The Multi-WordNet links mapping also has an acceptable rate of 97.18%, see table 2.

Table 2. Precision of new verb-sense mapping evaluated by WordNet::Similaritiy

FrameNet WordNet Mapping Extension Methodology	Mapped Verb Sense	Out-classified by WNS *lesk* measure	Precision Rate
Multi-WordNet-links	1772	50	97.18%
SUMO interfacing	6121	51	99.17%
Multi-WordNet-links and SUMO interfacing	534	2	99.63%
Overall verb recruitment	7359	99	98.65%

5 Conclusion

On the basis of available linguistic resources, ontologies and different mappings and linking between these knowledge bases, building a task-oriented semantic resource can be achieved by techniques of information reuse and integration. Non-linguistic ontology like SUMO can be applied for interfacing between linguistic resources. Mapping or linking ontology and linguistic database is generally established by conceptual mapping which is an intensive work involves philosophic, semantic and axiomatic issues. Under an evaluation based on semantic relatedness, the work shed lights on the role of statistical distribution analysis in mapping between linguistic knowledge base and ontology. Manual evaluation of these sense-tagged verb mapping is expensive but worth as not only due to the product knowledge base but also evaluating the statistical mapping approach.

A relative larger lexical semantic knowledge base is generated. The extended verb classification serves as a more useful resource for various semantic analysis tasks. It is significant that the work constructs a usable sense-tagged inventory for NLP, as suggested by [14], this would contribute the future of automatic WSD.

Continuing the work of building a Systemic Functional Grammar lexical semantic knowledge base, similar approach shall be applied in exploiting mapping FrameNet Frame with Generalized Upper Model concepts of CONFIGURATION which denotes event happenings based on not only to the semantic of experience construal but also the lexico-grammar of language as in the Systemic Functional Grammar Ideational Lattice [9]. WordNet sense-tagged lexical instantiation will at the same time be a portion of the final outcome linguistic resource.

References

1. Bateman, John A. "Upper modeling organizing knowledge for natural language processing." *In 5th International Workshop on Natural Language Generation.* June, 1990, Pittsburg. PA. (1990)
2. Bateman, John A. "The Theoretical Status of Ontologies in Natural Language Processing" in *the Proceedings of the workshop on 'Text Representation and Domain Modelling – Ideas from Linguistics and AI'.* Berlin. (1991)
3. Bateman, John A, Renate Henschel, Fabio Rinaldi. Generalized Upper Model 2.0, On-line publication at I1-OntoSpace: http://www.ontospace.uni-bremen.de/twiki/bin/view/Main/LinguisticOntology (2005)
4. A. Burchardt, K. Erk, and A. Frank. "A WordNet Detour to FrameNet" In Sprachtechnologie, mobile Kommunikation und linguistische Resourcen., vol. 8, Computer Studies in Language and Speech, H.-C. S. Bernhard Fisseni, Bernhard Schröder and Petra Wagner, Ed. Frankfurt am Main: Peter Lang, pp. 408-421. (2005)
5. Charles J. Fillmore, Christopher R. Johnson, and Miriam R.L. Petruck. "Background to FrameNet" International Journal of Lexicography 16: 235-250 (2003)
6. Chow, Ian C. & Wong, Tak Ming. "Axiomatizing Relational Network for Knowledge Engineering - Exploring WordNet and FrameNet". In Proceedings of *The 2006 IEEE International Conference on Information Reuse and Integration.* Hawaii, USA. pp. 262-267 (2006)

7. Ian C Chow, Jonathan J Webster. "Mapping FrameNet and SUMO with WordNet Verb: Statistical Distribution of Lexical-Ontological Realization," *Proceedings of the Fifth Mexican International Conference on Artificial Intelligence (MICAI'06)*. Mexico City, Mexico. IEEE CS press. pp. 262-268 (2006)
8. Fellbaum, Christiane. WordNet An Electronic Lexical Database MIT Press. Cambridge. (1998)
9. Halliday, MAK & Matthiessen ,Christian MIM. Construing experience through meaning. New York: Continuum. (1993)
10. Levin, Beth. English Verb Class and Alternations: A Preliminary Investigation. Chicago: University of Chicago Press. (1993)
11. Maedche , Alexander D. Ontology learning for the semantic Web Kluwer Academic Publishers. London. (2002)
12. McCarthy, Diana. Using semantic preferences to identify verbal participation in role switching alternations. *In Proceedings of ANLP-NAACL 2000*, pages 256–263, Seattle, WA. (2000)
13. Merlo and Stevenson. "Automatic Verb Classification Based on Statistical Distribution of Argument Structure", Computational Linguistics, 27:3, pp. 373--408. (2001)
14. Ide, N. Making Senses: Bootstrapping Sense-tagged Lists of Semantically-Related Words. In Gelbukh, Alexander (Ed.), *Computational Linguistics and Intelligent Text*, Lecture Notes in Computer Science, Springer. (2006).
15. Ruppenhofer, J., Ellsworth, M., Petruck, M.,, Johnson, C. FrameNet II: Theory and Practice. On-line publication at http://framenet.icsi.berkeley.edu/ (2006)
16. Niles, I., and Pease, A. Towards a Standard Upper Ontology. *In Proceedings of the 2nd International Conference on Formal Ontology in Information Systems (FOIS-2001)*, Chris Welty and Barry Smith, eds, Ogunquit, Maine, October 17-19. (2001)
17. Niles, I., and Pease, A. "Linking Lexicons and Ontologies: Mapping WordNet to the Suggested Upper Merged Ontology", *Proceedings of the IEEE International Conference on Information and Knowledge Engineering*. pp. 412-416 (2003)
18. Oltramari, A. "LexiPass methodology: a conceptual path from frames to senses and back" Proceedings of *the Fifth international conference on Language Resources and Evaluation, LREC*. (2006)
19. Pedersen, T., Patwardhan, S , Michelizzi, J.: WordNet::Similarity - Measuring the Relatedness of Concepts. *Proceedings of the Nineteenth National Conference on Artificial Intelligence* pp.1024-1025 (2004)
20. Banerjee, S., Pedersen, T.: Extended gloss overlaps as a measure of semantic relatedness. *Proceedings of the Eighteenth International Joint Conference on Artificial Intelligence* pp. 805–810 (2003)
21. Shi, L., Mihalcea, R.: Putting Pieces Together: Combining FrameNet, VerbNet and WordNet for Robust Semantic Parsing. *Computational Linguistics and Intelligent Text Processing*, 6th International Conference Proceedings. Lecture Notes in Computer Science, Vol. 3406. Springer, Berlin Heidelberg New York pp. 100-111 (2005)
22. SUMO. The Suggested Upper Merged Ontology. http://www.ontologyportal.org/
23. Webster, Jonathan J & Chow, Ian C. "Mapping WordNet to a Relational Network", *Proceedings of IEEE Natural Language Processing and Knowledge Engineering*, WuHan, pp. 718-722 (2005)

French EuroWordNet
Lexical Database Improvements

Christine Jacquin, Emmanuel Desmontils, and Laura Monceaux

Lina, Laboratoire d'Informatique Nantes Atlantique
2 rue de la Houssinière
BP92208, 44322 Nantes Cedex 03
France
{christine.jacquin,emmanuel.desmontils,laura.monceaux}@univ-nantes.fr

Abstract. Semantic knowledge is often used in the framework of Natural Language Processing (NLP) applications. However, for some languages different from English, such knowledge is not always easily available. In fact, for example, French thesaurus are not numerous and are not enough developed. In this context, we present two modifications made on the French version of the EuroWordnet Thesaurus in order to improve it. Firstly, we present the French EuroWordNet thesaurus and its limits. Then we explain two improvements we have made. We add non-existing relationships by using the bilinguism capability of the EuroWordnet thesaurus, and definitions by using an external multilingual resource (Wikipedia [1]).

1 Introduction

The interest of using semantic knowledge in the context of NLP systems has been widely shown in the state of the art, mainly in the context of applications dedicated to English language [2]. In fact, for these kinds of applications, the semantic knowledge is often coming from thesaurus like WordNet [3]. For European language such as Dutch, German, French, Italian, Czech, ... a multilingual thesaurus named EuroWordNet exists [4]. This thesaurus is designed according to the English WordNet thesaurus developed by the University of Princeton. However, the parts of the thesaurus dedicated to languages others than the English one are often not enough complete according to concepts and relationships. Some versions (for example, the French EuroWordnet Thesaurus) do not contain any definitions associated to concepts. Moreover, for some languages like French, the thesaurus does not evolved because no research group are still working in order to update the thesaurus and to continue the work initiated fifteen years ago. The presented paper proposes some ways on how to improve existing EuroWordnet Thesaurus by exploiting its multilingual property and external multilingual resources. The language used to illustrate our approach is the French one. But this can be applied on other languages. Precisely, in this paper, we explain, on the one hand, how to add relationships between concepts by using the English part of the EuroWordNet thesaurus. And on the other hand, we present the process

A. Gelbukh (Ed.): CICLing 2007, LNCS 4394, pp. 12–22, 2007.

for adding definitions to concepts which is based on the use of the multilingual encyclopedia: Wikipedia.

2   EuroWordNet: Presentation and Limits

EuroWordNet is a multilingual thesaurus composed of several European languages like Dutch, German, French, Italian, Czech... This thesaurus is designed according to the English WordNet thesaurus developed by the University of Princeton [3]. This latter is based on psycholinguistics works and computer-science works on human lexical memory. The aim of this thesaurus is to provide a conceptual search in a dictionary and therefore to organize lexical information according to words meanings. Nouns, verbs, adjectives or adverbs are represented by synsets (sets of synonyms) which are linked together by semantic relationships like the subsumption relationship (hypernymy/hyponymy) or the whole/part relationship (meronymy/holonymy). Each monolingual thesaurus is independant and uses its own lexicon and its own relationships. However, each thesaurus is linked to each others by an interlingual index (ILI). The index is thus used as switching language which makes it possible to pass from one language to another one. However, it is necessary to keep in mind that some concepts belonging to a language do not necessarily exist in another one: the best covered language according to relationships and concepts is the English language. Moreover, for some languages (like French), concepts definitions are missing. Like for the WordNet thesaurus, the EuroWordNet thesaurus presents some design problems for an use by NLP applications. In this latter, links between parts of speech and domain information (for example) are often non-existent. For the French part, a small set of structured concepts have been built concerning the data-processing domain, but this set is rather restricted and especially the concepts are practically not linked to each others (it is a very flat hierarchy). Furthermore, despite a weak level of polysemy in WordNet (more or less 18%), the necessity to disambiguate words is a recurrent problem (78% of words have more than one meaning in a corpus like Semcor) [5]. For example, the word *break* is associated to 63 senses. This quite important natural polysemy of texts and a too fine granularity do not facilitate the use of this thesaurus in NLP applications [6], [7].

3   Improvement Made to the Relationships

In a nutshell, the available version of EuroWordNet at the initial state is not enough complete to be used to significantly improve NLP applications. The first problems we solve is linked to the accessibility of this database and the update of the relationships.

3.1   An Usable Database

Buying the EuroWordNet thesaurus, we have a tool («Periscope») which makes it possible the interrogation of the thesaurus stored in a database in a proprietary format. Conversely, no library (API) makes it possible to interface this database with another application. We only have structured text files, which contain various concepts, synsets and relationships. These files, after a small study, can seem easy to treat. However, these files are not always consistent. For example, the concepts occurences are not all coded under the same format (many transcription errors...). In order to be able to use the EuroWordNet database in our applications, a long and tedious work has been necessary to recover the data. Firstly, we have parsed and have corrected the provided text files. Then, the data were stored in a PostgreSQL [8] database and a Java API has been developed to interface the application and the database.

By using the database, we still noted some number of problems closely related to the design of the French EuroWordNet thesaurus.

3.2   Update of the Semantic Relationships

Studying the thesaurus with our API, we have discovered that some relationships were missing. For instance, the word «citronnier» ("lemon tree" in English) was present in the French thesaurus but was orphan. Indeed, it was not attached to any concept. It should have been connected by the hypernymy/hyponymy relationship to the concept *«arbre fruitier»* (*"fruit tree"*) which really exists in the thesaurus. Our first goal was to use the bilingual property of EuroWordNet (switching from a language to another one by the way of the interlingual index) in order to add relationships belonging to a thesaurus into another one which does not contain these relationships. However, we keep in mind that, for a theoretical point of view, this process is not satisfactory: a concept does not necessarily decline itself in the same way from a language to another one. For this problem, [9] have enunciated the Hierarchy Preservation Principle which allows them to automatize the import of most of the semantic relations from WordNet into their Romanian EuroWordnet. They have proved that this principle is right for relationship such as hypernym/hyponym, holonym/meronym, cause/effect ... Thus, we have adopted this principle too. In addition, as we do not manipulate a lot of data, we have verified them manually. As result, while checking manually the added data, we have validated all the updates proposed by our process.

The process used for updates made on the hypernymy/hyponymy relationship is detailed in the next algorithm. We use the transitivity property of this relationship to perform these updates.

> **For Each** EuroWordNet's concept c in a source language (French in our case) **Do**
>> - select the corresponding synset s in the target language (English in our case)
>> - **If** s exists **Then**
>>> - select the nearest hyperonym h from the synset s which has a correspondence in the source language
>>> - **If** h exists and h is not a hypernym of c in the source language **Then**
>>>> - add a relationship between h and c in the source language

End If
End If
End For Each

The results are shown in table 1. By using the algorithm described above, 70 missing hypernym relationships were added. This is actually a low rate knowing that the number of hypernymy relationships belonging to the French EuroWord-Net is 22757 (71958 in the English one). This shows that for the existing concepts and for the hypernymy/hyponymy relationship, the French thesaurus designers achieved a rather complete work. For the other transitive relationships, we re-iterated the same process. For those which did not support this property, we simply bound a concept to another one if the two concepts exist in the source language and if a relationship found in target language did not exist in source language. For the meronymy relationship, 218 relationships were added to the 1418 present in the initial French thesaurus (17530 in English). Moreover, by studying these results, we noted many inconsistencies in the provided text files. For the other relationships (such as near-antonym, has-subevent...), 562 relationships were added to the 1408 which exist in the French thesaurus (69920 in English).

Table 1. Results concerning the relationships update in the French EuroWordNet

	Concepts	Hypernymy relationships	Meronymy relationships	Other relationships
English language	91143	71958	17530	69920
French language	22737	22757	1418	1408
French added relationships		70	218	562

We thus notice that, on the one hand few hypernymy/hyponymy relationships were added, but on the other hand a consequent number of other relationships could be found. Therefore, the initial thesaurus was rather complete concerning the subsumption relationship. The solution to increase the number of these re-lationships is thus either to acquire them starting from texts as [10], or to use external resources to add concepts and then to re-use the treatment that we explained at the beginning of this paragraph to define new relationships.

4   Inserting Definitions into EuroWordNet Thesaurus

In many NLP applications, and in particular in question answering applications, taking into account definitions of words in the search of the answer to a question is very useful. This strategy is largely exploited by question answering systems dedicated to English language, which use the WordNet definitions [11] [12]. In fact, these definitions coming from thesaurus make it possible to guide the pro-cess of answer search, and, in addition, can contain the answer. Unfortunately, a major problem arises for the French language: it exists few or no resources of this type giving access to such definitions.

4.1 Wikipedia

For few years, a happy initiative has been born which makes it possible the development in the form of wiki of a free encyclopedia on Internet: Wikipedia [1]. In this context, people can contribute by writing pages relating to various subjects and can integrate them into the encyclopedia [1]. Furthermore, this information source, which moves every day, becomes a base of study for various scientific communities [14] [15].

When a request containing one word (simple or complex) is submitted to Wikipedia, the answer consists of a page which can be of various type:

– If there is only one sense indexed in the encyclopedia relative to the submitted word, a page that we name *definition page* is shown. With the help of a suitable filtering of HTML code, we are able to recover the first paragraph of the page which can be considered as a definition of the word for a given sense.
– If the word refers to different senses, a page which we name *homonymous page* is shown with an enumeration of all the senses indexed in the encyclopedia and for each sense a hypertext link which leads to a definition page relating to this given sense.
– If the term does not belong to Wikipedia a specific page is shown.

Another interesting characteristic is that Wikipedia is a multilingual encyclopedia. By using hypertexts links, an user can navigate from a page written in a langage to another one written in an other language (if the link exists). For instance, when the word "bicycle" is submitted to the English Wikipedia, a page relating to this word is shown and it is possible to read similar pages written in other languages (French, German, Turkish...). It should be noted that for languages other than English, the link towards the page in English generally exists but, the reverse is not always true !

4.2 Definition Extraction in French Language

Our first idea was based on the exploitation of both Wikipedia and French EuroWordNet in order to extract definitions. For each French EuroWordNet's concepts, the corresponding synset list is provided to Wikipedia. Then, all pages corresponding to these synsets are retrieved from the Web. The most probable definition is then determined by the use of a similarity measure. After experiments, it appeared that, French EuroWordNet thesaurus has not a sufficient coverage. In fact, numerous terms included in definition do not belong to the

---

[1] It is of course necessary to keep in mind the problem of the validity of information. But, one can see the article of the Nature review [13] which shows that Wikipedia's articles are almost as relevant as those from the Britannica encyclopedia !

thesaurus. The definition discrimination criteria is not efficient and leads to wrong results. Indeed, some definitions are wrong classified, only because some terms included in the definition do not belong to the thesaurus.

In order to take into account these last observations, we then decided to exploit the multilingual capacity of Wikipedia and EuroWordNet. We first present the definition extraction process and the results obtained. This process is based, on the one hand on the better coverage of English EuroWordNet and Wikipedia than their French version and on the other hand of their ability to switch from a language to another one. Firstly, we associate an English Wikipedia's definition to an English EuroWordNet's synset. Our approach is rather similar to that describes in [16]. In this work, the authors use a similarity measure mainly based on the Vector Space Model, in order to associate WordNet's synset to Wikipedia's entries. In our case, we use a similarity measure based on Wu and Palmer Measure [17] which takes into account the concepts involved in the WordNet's and Wikipedia's definitions, the Wordnet's hypernyms and synonyms. Afterwards, we use the WordNet's and the Wikipedia's multilingual property to associate a French definition to a French synset.

4.3 General Process

The process is shown through the algorithm below:

For Each concept in target language **Do**
    - **If** the equivalent English concept exists in EuroWordNet **Then**
        - submit each element of the synset to English Wikipedia encyclopedia
        - retrieve the associated pages
        For Each candidate definition **Do**
            - compute the similarity beetween the definition coming from English EuroWordNet and the candidate definition
        End For Each
        - determine the most probable candidate definition
        - **If** the page containing the selected candidate definition exists in the target language **Then**
            - extract the definition from the page written in target language
            - update the concept definition in target language
        End If
    End If
End For Each

Thus, the aim is to extract concept definition from English Wikipedia and then, if the page and the link exist, to obtain, from French Wikipedia, the symmetrical definition in French language. For a given concept and in order to determine the most probable definition, we use a similarity measure. It measures the similarity between a concept definition coming from English EuroWordNet and the candidate definitions coming from the English Wikipedia. Definitions are represented like term (simple noun phrase) sets which belong to them[2]. Calculating the similarity between two definitions is the same thing as calculating the similarity between two terms sets. The used similarity is related to that of [18] who have defined a similarity between two concept sets. Their measure is derived from the Wu et Palmer's measure which is shown in formula 1 where c is the most specific subsumer of c_1 and c_2, $depth(c)$ is the number of edges from c to the taxonomy root, and $depth_c(c_i)$ with i in $\{1,2\}$ is the number of edges from c_i to the taxonomy root through c. Wu and Palmer propose a similarity measure related to the edge distance in the way it takes into account the most specific subsumer of the two concepts, characterizing their commonalities, while normalizing in a way that accounts for their differences.

$$s_{wp}(c_1, c_2) = \frac{2 * depth(c)}{depth_c(c_1) + depth_c(c_2)} \qquad (1)$$

This measure is less effective than the Resnik's measure [19] but is better than the traditional edge-counting measure.

But, in our context, Resnik's measure is difficult to apply. In fact, it needs the determination of semantic concept frequencies that we do not have (this means manual semantic tagging applies on large corpora)

[18] have extended the Wu and Palmer's measure for calculating the similarity between two concepts sets C and C' respectively of n and m elements. The equation dedicated to this measure is given below.

$$sim_{Concept}(C, C') = \frac{1}{2}\left(\frac{1}{n}\sum_{i=1}^{n}\max_{j \in [1,m]} s_{wp}(c_i, c'_j)\right. \qquad (2)$$

$$\left. +\frac{1}{m}\sum_{j=1}^{m}\max_{i \in [1,n]} s_{wp}(c'_j, c_i)\right)$$

We determine the similarity between two definitions which are represented by two terms set. We first define the similarity $sim(t, t')$ between two terms t and t' in this manner:

Given that C and C' are two concept sets which represent respectively t and t' and which comprise n and m elements (this means that C and C' are respectively the set of possible meanings of t and t').

$$sim(t, t') = \max_{i \in [1,n] j \in [1,m]} s_{wp}(c_i, c'_j) \qquad (3)$$

The similarity between two terms is the maximum of the Wu and Palmer's similarity between concepts which can be represented by these terms. We then define in the same manner, the similarity between c and a term t which is the label of n concepts by:

$$sim_{conceptTerm}(c, t) = \max_{i \in [1,n]} s_{wp}(c, c_i) \qquad (4)$$

---

[2] Noun phrases are detected after lemmatization and part-of-speech tagging of definitions.

Finally, we define the similarity between two sets of terms T et T' whose cardinality are respectively n and m by:

$$Sim(T, T') = \frac{1}{n+1}(\sum_{i=1}^{n} \max_{j\in[1,m]} sim(t_i, t'_j)$$

$$+ \max_{i\in[1,p]j\in[1,m]} sim_{conceptTerm}(h_i, t'_j)) \qquad (5)$$

We explained how we have defined our measure which is based on that of [18]. On the one hand, we have replaced Wu and Palmer's similarity $s_{wp}(c_i, c'_j)$, which is dedicated to two concepts, by the similarity concerning two terms $sim(t_i, t'_j)$. On the other hand, we do not take into account, in a symmetrical manner in the calculus, the similarity between two term sets. In fact, we highlight the first set of terms. Indeed, the first term set corresponds to terms belonging to definitions coming from the English EuroWordNet and the second one represents a candidate definition coming from Wikipedia.

We have made this choice because definitions coming from EuroWordNet are concise and often those coming from Wikipedia are more detailed. This fact implies that this calculated similarity is more representative of this notion. In fact, our similarity measure calculates the concept covering degree between the EuroWordNet's definition and the Wikipedia's candidate definitions. In this evaluation, taking into account the opposite covering degree leads to have less discriminated result values[3].

We can notice that concept hypernyms h_i belonging to a definition are also used in the similarity calculus. But we only take into account hypernyms distant at most of three edges from a concept hierarchy root. The English EuroWordNet's definitions are sometimes concise and the addition to them of some hypernyms, close to the concepts (excepted those too general), helps to determine the correct Wikipedia's definition which often contains terms related to these hypernyms.

4.4 Results Analysis

We perform our process on 1000 EuroWordNet's concepts which are present in the English and French database. The results are shown in table 2. The concepts are mainly relative to concrete objects and organisms. This choice was made on the one hand because, in the context of question answering systems, the question focus often represents a concrete concept (for definitional queries). On the other hand, we must not forget that Wikipedia is an encyclopedia, thus it contains few definitions associated to abstract concepts close to root elements of the EuroWordNet thesaurus. We have made an experiment with concepts concerning acts (defense,...) and we do not obtain satisfactory

---

[3] The size difference of the two sets of concepts implies that the covering degree, between the concepts set linked to a Wikipedia's candidate definition and the concepts set of the EuroWordNet's definition, is often weak.

results. Indeed, these abstract terms are practically never defined for themselves but are declined according to the various domains where they can appear and their use in these various domains. For treating these kinds of terms, we should preferably use dictionary knowledge rather than encyclopedia knowledge.

Table 2. Experiments results concerning 1000 concepts present in English EuroWordNet

	1 Sense	<= 5 Senses	> 5 Senses	No Existence	Total
Label(s) in English Wikipedia	584	157	203	56	1000
Label(s) in French Wikipedia	486	124	112		722
Error determination or weak similarity (< 0,5)	56	12	22		90

We notice that for 1000 concepts belonging to French and English EuroWordNet, 56 among them have no labels in Wikipedia. This is rather few, but this shows the good coverage of English Wikipedia encyclopedia that day after day increases. 58% of concepts (584), correspond to only one meaning in Wikipedia (this means that, for their label sets and by the way of Wikipedia, we can access to one and only one definition page). For 10% of them (56), the similarity calculated between the English EuroWordNet's definition and the Wikipedia's definition is weak (< 0,5). After analysis, we notice that these problems are coming from the fact on the one hand that some EuroWordNet's definitions are not complete and are succinct and on the other hand that a definition is only represented by the simple noun phrases which belong to it. In some cases, it would be very important to take also into account verbs and adjectives. For example, in the case of concepts representing acts, an act can be expressed by a noun or by a verbal form.

15 % of concepts (157) are associated to 1 to 5 meanings and for approximately 8% (12) of them, the process does not have linked the correct definition to them. 20 % of concepts (203) are linked to more than 5 meanings coming from Wikipedia (some have more than 20 meanings associated to them) and for 11% of them (22), the process does not have linked the correct definition to them. The wrong results are coming from the same problem encountered in the case of the single definition, or from the fact that definitions are not present in the term set proposed.

Concerning the definition extraction process for French language, we can see that the more the number of meaning is high, the more definitions present in French pages decrease. The explanation is that some definitions are directly extracted from French *homonym pages* (no definition page will be still written) and the equivalent to these pages does not obviously exist for French language.

5   Conclusion

In this article, we have presented works relating to the improvement of the Eu-roWordNet thesaurus with an aim of being used in question answering systems for French language. Indeed, this thesaurus presents a weak coverage concerning the number of concepts and the number of relationships compared to its English version. Moreover, the definitions relating to the concepts are not available in French version. First and foremost, we have described a process to increase the number of relationships in French language by using the bilingual property of EuroWordNet and its capacity to switch from a language to another one. Com-pared to the number of existing concepts for French language, we added few subsumption relationships. This means that for the greater part of the concepts, the designers's work was rather thorough and exhaustive. However, we added a consequent number of other relationships (meronymy...) which are missing in the initial thesaurus. Therefore, to increase the number of these relationships, it will be necessary, either to acquire them directly from texts like [10], or to use external resources to add concepts to the French version by applying the treat-ment which we have presented in part 3.2 of this article. We have also presented a process based on Wikipedia for acquiring definitions. It is based on the multi-lingual property of EuroWordNet thesaurus and of Wikipedia encyclopedia, and on a similarity measure between definitions. To improve the results, we are now working, on the exploitation of metalanguage patterns [20] to help the process to choose the correct definition when several definitions with close similarity coef-ficients are candidates. We have used these results in the CLEF 2006 evaluation campaign [21] dedicated to the French language. The obtained results concerning definitional queries were improved by the use of these EuroWordNet's updates. We plan to participate to the multilingual campaign (French-English). We just began a work concerning concepts inserting into the French EuroWordNet also based on the use of Wikipedia. Finally, our process for enriching a thesaurus is not dependant of a particular language. It can be extended to other European languages which do not have a large coverage of relationships and no definitions related to concepts in their own thesaurus.

References

1. Wikipedia: http://en.wikipedia.org/wiki/. (2006)
2. Gonzalo, J., Verdejo, F., Chugur, I., Cigarran, J.: Indexing with wordnet synsets can improve text retrieval. In: Proceeding of the workshop on Usage of Wordnet for NLP, ACL-98. (1998) 38–44
3. Miller, G.: Wordnet: an online lexical database. In: International journal of lexi-cography. Volume 3. (1990) 235–312
4. Vossen, P. In Publishers, K.A., ed.: EuroWordnet - A multilingual database with lexical semantic networks. (1998)
5. Loupy, C.D.: Managing synonymy and polysemy in a document retrieval system using wordnet. In: Proceedings of Creating and Using Semantic for Information Retrieval and Filtering Workshop, LREC. (2002)

6. O'Hara, T., Mahesh, K., Niremburg, S.: Lexical acquisition with wordnet and the mikrokosmos ontology. In Harabagui, S., ed.: COLING-ACL conference: Use of WordNet in Natural Language Processing Systems. (1998) 94–101
7. Hanks, P., Pustejovsky, J.: A pattern dictionnary for natural language processing. In: Revue Française de Linguistique Appliquée, numéro spécial sur les dictionaires. (2005) 63–82
8. PostGreSQL: http://www.postgresqlfr.org/. (2006)
9. Tufi, D., Cristea, D.: Methodological issues in building the romanian wordnet and consistency checks in balkanet. In: Proceedings of the LREC special Workshop on WordNets. (2002) 35–41
10. Morin, E., Jacquemin, C.: Automatic acquisition and expansion of hypernym links. In Kluwer, ed.: Computers and the Humanities (CHUM). (2005) 363–396
11. Moldovan, D., Pascal, M., Harabagiu, S., Surdeanu, M.: Performance issues and error analysis in an open-domain question answering system. In transactions on information systems, A., ed.: Journal on Very Large Databases. Volume 21. (2003) 133–154
12. Saggion, H., Gaizauskas, R., Hepplz, M., Roberts, I., Greenwood, M.: Exploring the performance of boolean retrieval strategies for open domain question answering. In: Proceeding of the Workshop on Information Retrieval for Question Answering, SIGIR (2004)
13. Butler, D., Hogan, J., Hopkin, M., Peplow, M., Simonite, T.: Online article from the nature review. In: http://www.nature.com/news/2005/051212/full/438900a.html. (2005)
14. Inex: http://inex.is.informatik.uni-duisburg.de. (2005)
15. Wiqa: http://ilps.science.uva.nl/wiqa. (2005)
16. Ruiz-Casado, M., Alfonseca, E., Castells, P.: Automatic assignment of wikipedia encyclopedic entries to wordnet synsets. In LNCS, S.V., ed.: Proceedings of Advances in Web Intelligence, AWIC'05. (2005) 380–386
17. Wu, Z., Palmer, M.: Verb semantics and lexical selection. In: the 32nd annual meeting of the association for computational linguistics. (1994) 133–138
18. Halkidi, M., Nguyen, B., Varlamis, I., Vazirgiannis, M.: Thesus: Organising web document collections based on link semantics. In transactions on information systems, A., ed.: Journal on Very Large Databases. Volume 12. (2003) 320–332
19. Resnik, P.: Semantic similarity in a taxonomy: an information based measure and its application to problems of ambiguity in natural language. In: Journal of artificial intelligence research. Volume 11. (1999) 95–130
20. Pearson, J. In Compagny, J.B.P., ed.: Terms in context. (1998)
21. Clef06: Cross language evaluation campaign. In: http://www.clef-campaign.org/. (2006)

Building a Large-Scale Commonsense Knowledge Base by Converting an Existing One in a Different Language

Yuchul Jung[1], Joo-Young Lee[2], Youngho Kim[1], Jaehyun Park[2], Sung-Hyon Myaeng[1,*], and Hae-Chang Rim[2]

[1] School of Engineering, Information and Communications University,
119, Munjiro, Yuseong-gu, Daejeon, 305-732, Korea
{enthusia77, yhkim, myaeng}@icu.ac.kr
[2] Department of Computer Science and Engineering, Korea University 1,
5-ka, Anam-dong, Seongbuk-Gu, Seoul 136-701, Korea
{jylee, jhpark, rim}@nlp.korea.ac.kr

Abstract. This paper describes our effort to build a large-scale commonsense knowledge base in Korean by converting a pre-existing one in English, called ConceptNet. The English commonsense knowledge base is essentially a huge net consisting of concepts and relations. Triplets in the form of Concept-Relation-Concept in the net were extracted from English sentences collected from volunteers through a Web site, who were interested in entering common-sense knowledge. Our effort is an attempt to obtain its Korean version by utilizing a variety of language resources and tools. We not only employed a morphological analyzer and existing commercial machine translation software but also developed our own special-purpose translation and out-of-vocabulary handling methods. In order to handle ambiguity, we also devised a noisy concept filtering and concept generalization methods. Out of the 2.4 million assertions, i.e. triplets of concept-relation-concept, in the English ConceptNet, we generated about 200,000 Korean assertions so far. Based on our manual judgments of a 5% sample, the accuracy was 84.4%.

1 Introduction

This paper describes a hybrid English-Korean Machine Translation (E-K MT) method for making a Korean ConceptNet (K-ConceptNet) based on English ConceptNet [1]. ConceptNet is an easily usable, freely available commonsense knowledge base and natural-language-processing toolkit which supports many practical textual-reasoning tasks over real-world documents including topic-gisting, affect-sensing, analogy-making, and other context-oriented inferences. The knowledge base is a semantic network presently consisting of over 1.6 million assertions of commonsense knowledge covering the spatial, physical, social, temporal, and psychological aspects of everyday life. The Open Mind Common Sense (OMCS) Project [2] started common

---

* Corresponding Author.

A. Gelbukh (Ed.): CICLing 2007, LNCS 4394, pp. 23 – 34, 2007.

sense knowledge gathering with the help of the general public from the year 2000. As of today, the knowledge base consists of over 729,000+ sentences that were inputted from a template-based web interface; it uses strict templates to make it easier to parse the sentences into the forms used in ConceptNet. As part of the OMCS project, ConceptNet [1] was developed based on the OMCS knowledge.

By applying a set of automatic processes (such as extraction, normalization, and relaxation) to the semi-structured English sentences of the OMCS corpus, ConceptNet corpus was generated. ConceptNet's semantic network can be visualized like Fig. 1. For example, concepts can be represented in semi-structured English by composing a verb (e.g. 'drink') with a noun phrase ('coffee') or a prepositional phrase ('in morning')

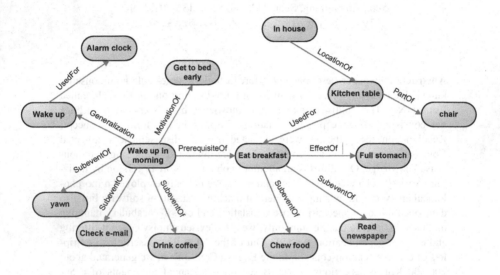

Fig. 1. ConceptNet's semantic network of commonsense knowledge, excerpt from [1]

Among the many avenues we should explore with ConceptNet is an investigation on its usefulness across cultural boundaries. First of all, it is not so clear whether the granularity of the concept nodes and the types of the 20+ relationships in ConceptNet are appropriate for commonsense computing in a country using a different language. On the flip of the coin is that ConceptNet is not immediately usable for most practical applications in Korea because they involve texts in the Korean language. Although a variety of interesting ideas have been proposed for using ConceptNet, it is not clear whether they are applicable to problems in the Korean context. If the original ConceptNet is "translated" into Korean, promising commonsense applications can appear in the Korean language domain. Besides, the existence of the knowledge base in two different languages would be in and of itself useful for applications across the two cultural boundaries.

As an effort to understand the effects of different culture and language within the common sense semantic network of OpenMinds, the GlobalMind[1] project, a multilingual OMCS, has been launched. Currently, a web site is available with an OMCS style knowledge input interface and a visual browser for word inference involving English, Korean, Japanese, and Chinese languages. Our K-ConceptNet construction effort and the GlobalMind project are complementary to each other.

Given the needs, the first task to be embarked on is "Translating" ConceptNet in English to Korean. However, the size of over 1.6 million assertions in ConceptNet makes the task of translation a formidable one, if it is done manually. Although our approach, a combined method which uses a commercial E/K translation S/W (EasyMan E/K translator[2]) and our rule-based translation module for translation, does not produce perfect translation results, it is imperative to employ the method that will at least help reducing the cost of translation. Actually, the commercial E/K translation software produces a large number of mistranslations – awkward or incorrect translations – because it does not take advantage of the OpenMind's strict template nor they generate Korean sentences with the structure of the template. To fill up the chasm, we have developed a rule-based translation module that can handle English ConceptNet corpus driven from OMCS sentences. Our manual evaluation of 5% sample among 200,000 E-K translated results shows a reasonably high accuracy of about 84.4%.

2 The Method

Ideally speaking, Korean ConceptNet should be built from a Korean OpenMind corpus. That is, collecting Korean commonsense knowledge from Korean people is probably the most natural way. Before launching an OMCS style web-site to build a Korean OpenMind corpus, we wanted to investigate the potential of a method for automatically building Korean ConceptNet using already existing English Concept-Net. The result can be combined with common sense knowledge directly obtained by running a Web site.

Researchers attempted to construct a Korean WordNet using exsiting WordNet [3] and Korean MRD [4]. In addition, Moon [5] used hypernym information of a Korean dictionary in combination with Korean translation of the English WordNet. A manual pruning was done during the noun construction for accuracy. However, this approach is very complex and time-consuming because it requires lots of manual pruning processes that rely on linguists' vocabulary. Another research for constructing a Korean WordNet based on the English WordNet [6] used a bilingual dictionary to link the senses of Korean nouns to the synsets of English WordNet. They built several heuristics for word sense disambiguation (WSD) and combined each heuristic with a decision tree. The approach achieved over 90% of accuracy.

The nature of user-inputted commonsense sentences, OMCS [2], is quite different from that of WordNet. Thus, existing approaches of Korean WordNet construction are

---

[1] GlobalMind Web Site: http://globalmind.media.mit.edu
[2] EasyMan E/K translator: http://www.clickq.com/

not directly applicable to Korean ConceptNet construction. In addition, there exists no comparable resource to the best of our knowledge.

Our approach has some unique procedures compared to the previous Korean WordNet construction approaches because the coverage of translation is beyond simple nouns; a concept in English ConceptNet can be a noun, compound-noun, phrase, or number.

As in Fig. 2, our approach is divided into largely three parts.

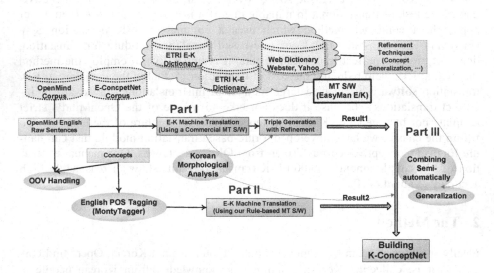

Fig. 2. Overall Architecture

(1) Part I: Translating the English OpenMind corpus into Korean, and converting the result to Korean ConceptNet

This part uses commercially available machine translation (MT) software, EasyMan E/K translator, to translate English OpenMind raw sentences (e.g. "*Ants are social insects*"). After the E-K translation phase, triples (first order logic style) are generated to be compared with the results of the second part described below (e.g. *<Is-A> <"개미/NNG">,<사회/NNG+적/XSN+ 이/VCP+ㄴ/ETM 곤충/NNG>* where the second argument corresponds to "ant" and the third to "social insect".)

(2) Part II: Translating the English ConceptNet into a Korean ConceptNet

The second part is based on the ConceptNet-specific rule-based MT software implemented by us. About 130 rules for E-K translation have been extracted based on our elaborate analysis of the ConceptNet corpus. Simply speaking, the translation follows English translation patterns that most Korean people would agree. The rules can perform English-Korean translation based on part-of-speech (POS) tagged information as in Table 1, and they cover more than 95.2% of the whole English ConceptNet corpus. We implemented this because the commercial MT software generated too many incorrect translation results in the target language.

(3) Combing the results of Part I and Part II
The results of the two translation approaches are combined by an algorithm that includes concept generalization. The purpose of the algorithm is to generalize the results of the first and second parts into a more acceptable Korean ConceptNet.

Because OpenMind sentences have words not found in dictionaries (we call them "out-of-vocabulary (OOV) words"), which are usually broken words or newly coined words, they have been handled through our auto-correction word list (pairs of frequently occurring typos and their correct expressions) and a Web dictionary. Since the corpus is in a highly structured short sentence form, and the first sense among the senses of an ambiguous word is correct, we hypothesized that we would have relatively clean translations compared to other texts such as news paper, novel, etc.

2.1 Translating the English OpenMind Using a Commercial MT Software

This part is an attempt to reuse a large amount of commonsense knowledge in English OpenMind and build Korean ConceptNet. We generate Korean translation of the sentence in English OpenMind and subsequently Korean ConceptNet from it. Before selecting EasyMan as our E/K MT software that shows the best translation result, we tested three E/K MT software packages: EasyMan, EnGuide4.0, and Smartran5.0. Although translated sentences are not always complete, we assume that triplets in Korean can be extracted through a set of procedures as follows.

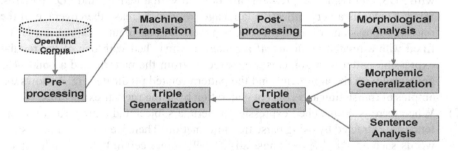

Fig. 3. Concept Generation after MT Translation [Part I]

Fig. 3 shows the overall process of OpenMind translation and concept generation. Because machine translation is still an active research area awaiting a breakthrough, English-Korean translation results of OpenMind have many incorrect sentences. Our simple experiment reveals that the errors are mostly caused by complex sentences, which include those with double quotation marks and long sentences. To alleviate these problems, the OpenMind sentences were preprocessed by the following schemes.

- If a sentence length (number of words in a sentence) is greater than N (currently, N = 30), we remove that sentence. Basically, the goal of OpenMind translation approach is not converting whole OpenMind but gathering as many correct, appropriate Korean sentences as possible. Therefore it is better to reject sentences that may generate translation errors than to achieve 100% coverage.
- Sentences beginning with some specific patterns are not meaningful because they were collected by prompting users with fill-in-the-blank templates to restrict the structure of sentences. The repeating patterns are removed in the translation results. For example, the first part before the colon in the sentence, *"Things that are often found together are: water, people, boat,"* is a template, and only the part after that is extracted and translated.

The Korean sentences generated from the translation process are tagged with part of speech (POS) and then parsed using [7] and [8]. Because of translator errors, some of the translated Korean sentences have a grammatically invalid or awkward structure. In the parsing step, those sentences that have a paring failure are dropped.

Similar to ConceptNet, the concepts of K-ConceptNet are generated from the sentences by using regular expressions, POS information, and syntactic structure information. The difference is that ConceptNet uses shallow paring (chunking) information, whereas K-ConceptNet uses full parsing information. Since the Korean language has free word order unlike English, it is hard to analyze the relationship between two arguments that are extracted from a sentence by using chunking information only.

The procedure for creating a concept from a Korean sentence is as follows:

(1) Pre-defined regular expressions are applied to a sentence. The sentence is tagged with POS, and regular expressions are defined with a lexicon and POS patterns. Since Korean is a very inflective language, we can increase the coverage of the regular expressions by using the POS patterns. Each regular expression is defined with a related predicate. If a sentence is matched with one of the regular expression patterns, arguments are extracted from the pattern, and a concept is generated with the arguments and the pattern-related predicate. Fig. 4 shows examples of translation and concept generation by using regular extractions.

(2) When there is no matched expression pattern, a subject and a predicate of a sentence are extracted by using parse tree information. Then, we remove unnecessary words such as '대부분의(almost all)', '어떤(some, certain)' from each subject and predicate that were extracted, and create a concept with the remained part.

(3) In the next step, created concepts are generalized by word replacement. For example, we replace words like '당신(you)' and '우리(we)' by a general word '사람(person)'.

2.2 Translating the English ConceptNet with Heuristic Translation Rules

The second part is to translate the predicates in English ConceptNet into Korean predicates. Because the OpenMind corpus were already generalized, parsed, and optimized into predicates in English ConceptNet [1], we translate these predicates

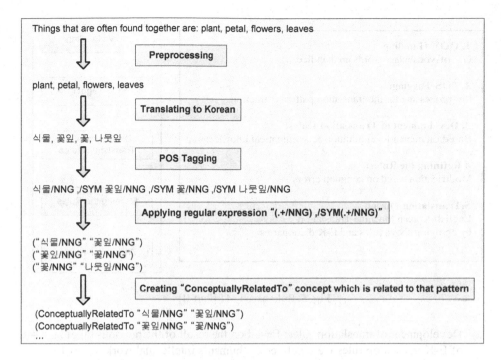

Fig. 4. An Example for Concept Generation

into Korean for building Korean ConceptNet. To implement our rule-based machine translation (MT) E/K software for Korean ConceptNet building, we have designed the following 5-step procedures (Fig. 5). This is facilitated by the intuition that existing concepts within English ConceptNet are words which can be directly translated by using English-Korean dictionary, simple phrases, or sentences that are interpretable using POS tagged pattern (e.g. "bike," "falling off a bike," and "you get hurt," respectively).

(1) OOV handling: Only the two major types of OOV problems (broken words and newly coined words) were considered because a complete OOV handling requires too much of time-consuming manual efforts. In the current work, about 42.5% (4,430) of the whole OOV words (10,425), which were identified based on ETRI E/K dictionary, have been corrected automatically by using the OneLook dictionary[3], Online Webster dictionary[4], and Yahoo Web E/K dictionary[5].

(2) POS tagging: We chose MontyTagger[6], a rule-based part-of-speech tagger based on Eric Brill's transformational-based learning POS tagger [9] which uses a Brill-compatible lexicon and rule files. Through the POS tagging process based on MontyTagger, we could build a base-line for starting a MT.

---

[3] http://www.onelook.com/
[4] http://www.webster-dictionary.org/
[5] http://kr.dic.yahoo.com/search/eng/
[6] http://web.media.mit.edu/~hugo/montytagger/

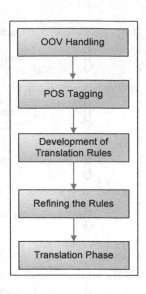

OOV Handling

POS Tagging

Development of
Translation Rules

Refining the Rules

Translation Phase

1. OOV Handling
Out-of-vocabulary words are handled.

2. POS Tagging:
Pre-processing for the translation pattern extraction

3. Development of Translation Rules:
Based on human-level intuition & grammatical knowledge

4.Refining the Rules:
Modification based on common errors

5.Translation Phase:
English-Korean Machine Translation
by applying above rules and E-K dictionaries

Fig. 5. Rule-based MT [Part II]

(3) Development of translation rules: Based on the result of the previous tagging, a set of E-K translation rules were defined by human's intellectual work. As in Table 1, about 95.2% of the concepts were covered by about 130 translation rules.

(4) Refining the rules: Although a set of translation rules has been developed, there is a potential for POS tagging errors. After checking hundreds of manual POS pattern checking, we have revised the errors to minimize rule-based translation errors.

(5) Machine translation of sentences: By using a machine readable E-K dictionary, which is previously developed by ETRI for a general MT system, we have translated 95.2% of the English concepts in the English ConceptNet. A sample of translation results are shown in Table 2.

2.3   Combining Two Translation Results

To combine the translated Korean concepts that were generated separately by the commercial MT software and our rule-based MT, we have employed a morphological analyzer [7] and heuristics for concept generalization.

For example, if a word 'diagram' is translated to '그림/NNG (picture)' by our rule-based MT module and to '도표/NNG (figure)' by the commercial MT software, this kind of conflict should be resolved. In the subsequent generalization process, we used word in the synonym list is extracted from Korean WordNet[10] manually. The synonym list contains 50 pairs of synonym words.

In addition, we remove *josa* , which is a case marker in Korean, playing a role of function word like a preposition or a particle. For example, in a phrase '사람의 손(hand of a person)', the *josa* '의' corresponds to a preposition 'of'. Basically,

Table 1. Extracted POS Patterns of English Concepts

No.	Pattern	Example	Count	Accumulated Ratio	Num. of Concept (*)
1	NN/	dog	25,506,691	51.603%	2,550,691
2	JJ/NN/	social insect	403,140	59.758%	2,953,831
3	NN/NN/	george washington	320,010	66.233%	3,273,841
4	VB/	fly	285,844	72.016%	3,559,685
5	VB/NN/	hold thing	167,418	75.403%	3,727,103
6	NN/POS/NN	person 's way	123,588	77.903%	3,850,691
7	JJ	small	59,268	79.102%	3,909,959
8	CD/NN/	4 person	58,467	80.285%	3,968,426
...	...	...	...	...	...
30	VB/NN/POS/NN/	carry person 's lunch	9,513	89.591%	4,428,406
31	JJS/NN/	biggest lizard	9,464	89.782%	4,437,870
32	NN/CD/	january 2000	8,717	89.958%	4,446,587
...	...	...	...	...	...
91	VBP/RB/VB/	do not eat	1,757	94.255%	4,458,986
92	VB/IN/NN/POS/NN/	fit in person 's garage	1,742	94.291%	4,660,728
...	...	...	...	...	...
127	CD/POS/NN/	one 's environment	1,058	95.250%	4,708,141
128	VB/NN/POS/NN/IN/NN	lose person 's car under sofa	1,043	95.271%	4,709,184

(*) This means the number of concepts with a duplicate counting permitted.

Table 2. Translation Results

(OMCS raw sentence id, Predicate, Concept_A, Concpet_B, f=x, i=y)
(1, IsA, "dog/NN", "mammal/NN", f=24, i=3)
➔ (1, IsA, "개", "포유 동물", f=24, i=3)
(90169, CapableOf, "cat/NN", "eat/VB", f=0, i=14)
➔ (90169, CapableOf, "고양이", "먹다", f=0, i=14)
(294455, ConceptuallyRelatedTo, "person/NN 's/POS finger/NN", "use/NN", f=2, i=0)
➔ (294455, ConceptuallyRelatedTo, "사람의 손가락", "사용-", f=2, i=0)
(301670, LocationOf , "in/IN school/NN", "in/IN chemistry/NN lab/NN", f=1, i=0)
➔ (301670, LocationOf, "학교에", "화학실험실에", f=1, i=0)
(340531, UsedFor, "finger/NN", "play/VB guitar/NN", f=1, i=0)
➔ (340531, UsedFor, "손가락", "기타를 연주하다", f=1, i=0)
(728883, ConceptuallyRelatedTo, "gas/NN", "temperature/NN and/CC pressure/NN", f=0, i=1)
➔ (728883, ConceptuallyRelatedTo, "가스", "기온 그리고 압력", f=0, i=1)

* Concept_A and Concept_B are tagged respectively by using MontyTagger.
* f counts the number of times a assertion is uttered in the OMCS corpus
* i counts how many times an assertion was inferred during smoothing phase

'사람의 손' and '사람 손(person hand)' have the same meaning in Korean, and by removing the *josa*, we can combine them. As a result, we have built 200,000 E-K translated assertions.

3   Manual Evaluations of E-K Translated Concepts

An evaluation of the translation quality was carried out with randomly selected 5% of the E-K translation results consisting of 200,000 K-ConceptNet assertions. Each translation is graded by one of the four ranks (described below) by two graduate students, who are Korean native speakers, and their grading measures are given below:

[A] Perfect: No problems in translation. The meaning of the sentence is very clear and no grammatical error of word translation exists.
[B] Good: Easily understandable translation with a minor grammatical error.
[C] Acceptable: The meaning of the sentence can be understood only after several times of reading.
[D] Nonsense: Hard to understand or very ambiguous translation with many errors

Table 3. Translation Accuracy

Category	Rank	Num. of Concepts	Percentage
Good	A	4841	50.07%
	B	1873	19.37%
	C	1446	14.96%
Bad	D	1508	15.60%
Total	A+B+C+D	9668	100%

From this evaluation, we obtained the accuracy of 84.4% assuming that D is a failure (Table3). Based on our analysis the translation errors were due to the lack of context information, insufficient coverage of translation rules, or word sense ambiguities. During the evaluation, the evaluators looked at the English raw sentences of English

Table 4. K-ConceptNet Examples used in Evaluation

(OMCS raw sentence id, Predicate, Concept_A, Concpet_B, f=x, i=y)
ID:1 [dogs are mammals]
P1: (1, IsA, "개/NNG", "포유/NNG+류/XSN", f=1, i=0)
CN: (1, IsA "dog/NN" "mammal/NN" "f=24;i=3;")
P2: (1, IsA, "개/NNG", "포유/NNG 동물/NNG", f=24, i=3)

ID:169263 [Something you find at a museum is statuary]
P1: (169263, LocationOf, "조각/NNG", "박물관/NNG", f=1, i=0)
CN: (169263 LocationOf "statuary/NN" "at/IN museum/NN" "f=1;i=0;")
P2: (169263 LocationOf "조소/NNG" "박물관/NNG+에서/JKB" "f=1;i=0;")

ID: 728866 [uncles are part of a family]
P1: (728866, PartOf, "가족/NNG", "아저씨/NNG", f=1, i=0)
CN: (728866, IsA "uncle/NN" "part/NN of/IN family/NN" "f=1;i=0;")
P2: (728866 IsA "아저씨/NNG" "가족/NNG+의/JKG 부분/NNG" "f=1;i=0;")

* P1: Result of Part I, P2: Result of Part2, and CN: English ConceptNet sentence
* Concept_A and Concept_B are tagged respectively by using Korea University's morphological analyzer which follows 21 Sejong tag set.
* f counts the number of times a assertion is uttered in the OMCS corpus
* i counts how many times an assertion was inferred during smoothing phase

OpenMind, derived English ConceptNet triples, and its translation as well. Table 4 is selected examples that are used in the evaluation.

4 Concluding Remarks and Future Work

We proposed a method for building a Korean ConceptNet by translating English ConceptNet and the original OMCS sentences. The method combines two different sources of translation evidence, i.e., translations from commercial MT software and from a rule-based MT approach. In addition, several NLP techniques have been incorporated, such as OOV handling, POS tagging, automatic rule refinement, morphological analysis, and concept generalization. Finally, based on the challengeable approach, we generated 200,000 K-ConceptNet assertions with reasonably high accuracy and time efficiency.

Through our experiments, we developed a firm belief that our approach can be adoptable to the development of ConceptNet in other languages if machine readable language resources are available and translation patterns from English to the target language can be easily extractable. Although detailed pre-processing and post-processing should be differentiated according to the languages, the overall approach can be generally applied language-independently without too much manual work.

For future work, we have a plan to integrate our work with Korean language part of GlobalMind to extract commonsense knowledge automatically from the Web. For further extension of ConceptNet, we are interested in extracting commonsense knowledge from the existing World Wide Web because a great deal of commonsense is contained in those semi-structured or free text web pages.

For the robustness of Korean ConceptNet, we still need further helps from the general public. As a way to build & evaluate Korean commonsense knowledge, we have launched a web-site[7] where our machine translated results are opened to everybody who access to the web page. Anyone can evaluate existing E-K translated concepts by looking at the original English sentences and participate in inputting corrected commonsense knowledge in Korean.

References

1. Liu, H., and Singh, P.: ConceptNet – A Practical Commonsense Reasoning Tool-kit. BT Technology Journal, (2004), 211-226.
2. Singh, P., Lin, T., Mueller, E. T., Lim, G., Perkins, T., and Li Zhu, W.: Open Mind Common Sense: Knowledge acquisition from the general public. *Proc. of the 1st Int. Conf. on Ontologies, Databases, and Applications of Semantics for Large Scale Information Systems*, (2002), 1123-1237.
3. C. Fellbaum.: WordNet, *an electronic lexical database*. MIT Press, (1998)
4. Hangeul Society: *Urimal Korean Unabridged Dictionary*, Eomungag, (1997) (in Korean)
5. Moon, Y. J.: Methodology and Techniques for the Design of Korean Noun WordNet. *Proc. of the Natural Language Processing Pacific Rim Symposium*, (1997), 465-469

---

[7] Korean ConceptNet Web Site: http://k-conceptnet.icu.ac.kr

6. Lee, C. K., *et al.*: Automatic WordNet mapping using word sense disambiguation. *Proc. of Joint SIGDAT Conference on EMNLP/VLC,* (2000), 142-147.
7. Lee, D.-G.: Probabilistic Models for Korean Morphological Analysis and Part-of-Speech Tagging. Ph. D. thesis, Korea University, (2005).
8. Park, S.-Y.: Probabilistic Feature-based Parsing Model for Korea Syntactic Analysis. Ph. D. thesis, Korea University, (2005).
9. Brill, E.: Some advances in rule-based part of speech tagging. *Proc. of the 20th National Conf. on Artificial Intelligence*, (1994), 722-727.
10. Jung, Y.I., Yoon, A.-S., and Kwon, H.-C.: Disambiguation Based on Wordnet for Transliteration of Arabic Numerals for Korean TTS, *Proc. of Computational Linguistics and Intelligent Text Processing (CICLing)*, (2006), 366-377.

Conquering Language: Using NLP on a Massive Scale to Build High Dimensional Language Models from the Web

Gregory Grefenstette

Commissariat à l'Energie Atomique, CEA LIST, SRCI, BP 6,
92265 Fontenay aux Roses Cedex, France
Gregory.Grefenstette@cea.fr
http://www-list.cea.fr/gb/index_gb.htm

Abstract. Dictionaries only contain some of the information we need to know about a language. The growth of the Web, the maturation of linguistic processing tools, and the decline in price of memory storage allow us to envision descriptions of languages that are much larger than before. We can conceive of building a complete language model for a language using all the text that is found on the Web for this language. This article describes our current project to do just that.

1 Introduction

Linguistics has long been a descriptive science. From early prescriptive grammars of Sanskrit, Greek and Latin, through the elaboration of glosses in the middle ages, to the comparison of language families starting in the mid eighteenth century, down to the interest in computational grammars from the mid twentieth century until now. Man has tried to describe the interesting and difficult in language. In the last part of the twentieth century, computers were added into the mix, exploiting large hand tagged text collections, first the Brown and Lancaster corpora, and finally the British National Corpus, with its 100 million words of hand corrected, part-of-speech tagged text. But even this computational linguistics research is ultimately based on the descriptions and choices made by the compilers of the hand tagged corpora. This first round of descriptive linguistics research has led to the creation of large language resources: large lexicons for morphological analysis, training text for part of speech taggers, and robust grammars for analyzing large quantities of text. We are now ready to enter into a second round of linguistics, in which the descriptions of language will no longer be based on manual effort of description, but in which complete descriptions of language use and behavior can be automatically acquired and stored. We can now move from the question *What do we know about language?* to the question *What do we do now that we know everything about a language?*

The convergence of three different phenomena allows us to consider that it is now possible to know everything we want to know about every word in every written language. These three phenomena, which have all appeared in the last decade, are

A. Gelbukh (Ed.): CICLing 2007, LNCS 4394, pp. 35–49, 2007.

1. the maturity of the linguistic processing tools mentioned above.
2. the continuing explosion of cheap computing power and storage possibilities
3. the arrival of the internet, bringing free access to enormous quantities of text

Exploiting all three will allow us to see linguistics and language differently.

In this paper, we present our first attempts to create a full description of a language, to conquer the language, in some sense, by extracting and treating as much of the presence of the language on the Web as possible. The paper is divided into the following sections. First we describe how we know how much language is available for a given language, and we show how to gather basic statistics for the words in the language. Next, in Section 3, we detail the process for extracting language modeling information from the internet, estimating the time necessary for generating the entire model. In Section 4, we show some potential applications of the extracted model. This is followed by a description of related research and a conclusion.

2 Estimating Language Presence

Before we begin deriving a given language model, we must ask whether we have access to enough text to build a complete model for that language. How much text is enough text? We cannot say. But let us take as a minimum the number of 100 million words, the number of words in the largest hand corrected, annotated corpus created for English, the British National Corpus. Suppose that we want to make a language model for Danish, or Basque, or Catalan. Do we at least have 100 million words of these languages available to us through a search engine? We tried to answer this question for a number of languages starting in 1996. Before 2002, search engines such as AltaVista displayed occurrence counts for each query word as well as the global page count for the query.[1] When this real count was available it was possible to estimate the total number of words indexed for language by probing search engines with common words for a language, that each had a known frequency for that language. Details of this estimation are given in [1]. Results from our last estimation of language volumes, using data graciously obtained from Yahoo, gave the following estimates seen below in Table 1. The volume of text available through search engines for all of these languages was growing over the three year period from 2001 to 2004, doubling or more for most languages. In all cases the raw number of words available for these languages is greater than the number of words available in the British National Corpus[2]. The numbers given in this table are

---

[1] This page count is the only information returned by search engines today. And even this page count is no longer an actual page count, but only an estimation of the number of pages containing the query words. Currently search engines calculate actual page counts on a sample database and extrapolate to the total number of pages they have indexed. See Jean Veronis's blog for a discussion of this estimate. http://aixtal.blogspot.com/2005/02/web-googles-missing-pages-mystery.html

[2] Of course, the British National Corpus is marked up in a variety of ways: part of speech tags, dates published, speakers, etc. Internet text has less and more disparate metatags, if any.

also only a lower bound on the number of words available, because other pages of text exist for all of these languages on pages not crawled by the reference search engine, either because of its crawling policy, or because the text is available on the Hidden Web through search form interfaces (such as MedLine's search interface) and not as static pages that can be downloaded and crawled. See [2] for accessing more text in the Hidden Web. We can thus presume that, for many of the languages present on the Web, we have a sufficient quantities of text from which to build languages models.

	Word count estimate 2001	Word count estimate 2004
Basque	55,340,000	148,776,424
Estonian	98,066,000	208,739,164
Croation	136,073,000	188,527,817
Catalan	203,592,000	1,206,027,725
Finnish	326,379,000	826,416,488
Danish	346,945,000	1,684,667,584
Czech	520,181,000	1,008,251,069
Dutch	1,063,012,000	3,333,039,454
French	3,836,874,000	13,648,627,968
German	7,035,850,000	16,583,288,838
English	76,598,718,000	145,959,354,990

Fig. 1. Language estimates for a few European languages in 2001 and 2004. The number of words available on the Internet doubled or more for most of these languages in this period. All of the languages have more than 100 million words, the number of words in the British National Corpus.

Now let us suppose that we begin with a full list of words for the language, excluding proper nouns and technical terms. Such lists can be obtained by generating all word forms using a morphological analyzer, or from other sources, such as the Ispell data files for the language [3].

In the rest of this paper, we will use French as a sample language, though the results should be the same for any other non agglutinative language.[3] Beginning with a list of French word forms generated by the LIMA system [4], we have a list of 400,000 French word forms to model, generated from just under 100,000 lemmas. For example the lemma *chien (dog)* produces two words in the word form list *chien* and *chiens*. The verb *aimer (to love)* produces all the conjugated forms *aime, aimes, aimons, aimez*, etc. Though verbs generate many word forms, nouns usually only generate two in French so the average number of word forms per lemma here is about 4.

---

[3] Even agglutinative languages such as Finnish and Hungarian can be used, if one accepts a restriction on the number of letters any word in the word list generated, or used. Though, in this case, the number of word forms will be in the millions rather than the hundreds of thousands.

We take this word list, and as a first step in building a language model for French, we gather counts of the number of web pages that each word appears in. Since it is relatively common for a given word in languages with common historical roots to share word forms (for example, both English and French use the word form *relations* among thousands of other cognates), we need some way to restrict searching ambiguous words to obtain counts specific to our target language. Though most search engines allow the searcher to restrict their search to pages in one of a number of specified languages, we decided not to use this option for two reasons. One, we do not know what language identification algorithm [5][6] the search engines use for deciding whether a page is written in a given language, these algorithms being unpublished and unevaluated. Second, we wanted to develop a technique for all web languages, not restricted to those on a search engine list.[4] In order to restrict the count of pages to pages written in French, we decided to add on a number of common French words as "anchors" for any query, the idea being that a page that contains our search word AND these anchor words is probably in French. We chose the following anchor words in French: {*et, le, la, que, pour*}. So when we want to query the web for the number of pages that contain the word *relations*, for example, we build the following search query:

"relations" "et" "le" "la" "que" "pour"

For English, we would a query like:

"relations" "the" "with" "and" "in" "of"

Of course, in either case, it is possible to retrieve pages with the above queries that are neither in French, nor in English. And also, we know that we will be missing some French pages that contain the word *relations* but which do not contain one of the five anchor words. To test the presence of these "anchor" words in a known language corpus, we took a list of documents from the TREC information retrieval campaigns. In the French TREC corpus, there are 62,464 documents with more than 200 words. 12,031 of these documents (19%) do not contain all five of the French anchor words we used. For English, using a set of 13,856 documents with more than 200 words from the corpora in TREC, we found 1359 documents (10%) that did not contain the English anchor words given above. As the length of the document increases, the percentage of documents that do not contain the anchor terms decreases. Since we are looking to construct a language model for the whole language, we are more interested in longer documents, using this anchor technique provides counts that are probably inferior, but in a systematic way, to the real counts of words, and tend to return longer documents.

If we run the query *"relations" "et" "le" "la" "que" "pour"* on Google on a given day, we find 3,880,000 pages that contain all six words. If we run the query

---

[4] For example, Google allows the user to search in 36 languages. The restriction of search results to a given language should not be confused with the option to use different languages in the search interface. Google provides more than 115 interface languages.

"relations" without the anchor words on Google but with the "Search French pages" option activated, then we get 4,600,000 result pages. If we run the same queries on AllTheWeb, the result page says that there are 12 million pages with the anchor words and 18 million for *"relations"* (without the anchors) in the AlltheWeb French documents[5]. We see that these numbers are a rough approximation. Jean Veronis explains that these numbers must be taken with precaution (see footnote 1 above). Here, though, we through caution to the wind, since we are not interested in exact number but only relative magnitudes, and we continue to collect page counts for each of the 400,000 French words using this anchoring technique. This harvesting can be done over a period of 400 days using, for example, the Google search API which allows a user to send 1000 queries a day. If this API is spread over more than one machine and more than one user, then the searches may be parallelized. Other search engines provide other means for sending batched queries. After a certain number of days, the first element of the language model can be acquired: the relative frequencies of all the words for a language on the web (under the unknown indexing bias of the search engine used). This step has been performed for a large subset of French words in the Lexique project [7], and can be downloaded from www.lexique.org.

héliastes	445	hélicoïdes	275
hélice	211000	hélicon	1910
hélices	121000	héliconienne	9
hélichryses	10	héliconiens	10
héliciculture	842	hélicons	108
hélicicultures	7	hélicoptère	723000
hélicier	48	hélicoptères	535000
héliciers	14	hélicos	65200
hélico	143000	héligare	73
hélicoïdal	13800	héligares	8
hélicoïdale	13700	hélio	17300
hélicoïdales	1150	héliocentrique	3380
hélicoïdaux	8680	héliocentriques	482
hélicoïde	421	héliocentrisme	1980

Fig. 2. A subset of the French lexicon with sample page counts from a search engine. These are the page counts we acquired for pages containing the given word and the following anchor words "le" "la" "et" "que" "pour", used to *anchor* the page in French.

A sample of the type of word counts, using anchor words, can be seen in Figure 2. If we retain up to one hundred URLs for each of the 400,000 French word forms, we

---

[5] On both search engines, if we search for *relations la la que et pour* with the "English Only" language option activated we still get hundreds of thousands of documents back, though the snippets look obviously French. This is one more reason why we do not want to trust the unknown language identification methods of search engines.

gather about 5 million unique URLs that cover the entire French lexicon as a basis for creating our language model.

3 Extracting Language Modeling Information

Once we are convinced that we have enough text for the language, and we have its full list of words (surface forms), we can begin to build the model of the language as shown in the previous section. While collecting information about the frequency of each word, we can also collect a seed list of URLs for each word. We are not interested here in indexing the web, that is, associating URLs to each word in the lexicon, but rather collecting examples of word usage. Nonetheless, we do have to perform a crawl of a large portion of the web. Each page retrieved then has to be treated by language specific natural language processing tools (for example [8]) to extract data to feed the model. This section describes all these steps.

3.1 Fetching Web Pages and Character Encoding

When we collect text for non English languages, text encoding becomes a problem to face. Both HTML and XHTML markups provide tags for specifying the character set used in a web page:

```
<meta http-equiv="Content-Type" content="text/html; char-
                  set=UTF-8">
     <?xml version="1.0" encoding="ISO-8859-1"?>
```

But in practice we find that we could not always trust human encoding of this attribute. We sometimes have to test and discover the actual character encoding ourselves. This encoding detection can be done in conjunction with language identification [9] or separately. We performed it separately. For encoding, we implemented a simple system that takes as input a URL, fetches the HTML of this URL using the UNIX command *wget*, and then extracts the encoding found in the HTML metatags. If the ecnoding tag is found, we use the UNIX command *recode* to transform the character encoding specified into UTF8, which is the input code expected by our natural language processing tools. However, we noticed in dealing with French web text, that pages specified as using the iso-8859-1 character set (the most common encoding for Western European languages) were often actually encoded in UTF-8 (the new standard). We modified our fetching program so that when HTML pages specify this encoding, we re-check using the UNIX command *file* which identifies the type and encoding of a file. If *file* finds that the file is in UTF, we replace the encoding specified in the HTML text. If no charset is specified, we suppose that it is written in iso-8859-1 which is the most common for French. Obviously, if we were to treat another language instead of French, this strategy would have to be adapted. Just as knowledge about the best anchor words to use is needed for a new language, we also have to know the most common encoding for each language[6].

---

[6] See http://www.cs.tut.fi/~jkorpela/chars.html for a tutorial on character set encodings.

3.2 Extracting Text from Web Pages

Once we have recoded the fetched web page into UTF-8, we use another command *lynx*[7] that formats a web page for a line-based (teletype) device. This command was useful in the first days of the Web in the early 1990's when line-based computer terminals were still present, and it is still useful for browsing the web in *xterm* windows, and is still maintained to accurately parse web pages. For web text processing, the *dump* argument to *lynx* is particularly useful since it extracts only the visible text from a web page, eliminating all the HTML markup and dealing with issues such as frames. Since *lynx* relies heavily on specified character set encodings, we pass it as input our wget-fetched and UTF-8 re-encoded HTML that we are sure is in UTF-8, as described in the last section, rather than the raw URL. *lynx* also provides a formatted listing of all the outgoing URL links found in a web page which is useful for finding new pages, in addition to our seed URLs.

3.3 Language Identification and Web Crawling

Beginning with the seed URLs for each word in the language, we first verify that we have not already treated this URL by comparing it to a list of already seen URLs. If the URL is new, we apply the text extraction steps specified in the last two sections[8]. It is still possible that the input file is not really in the language that we are interested in modelling. The URL may have been found because it contained a target-language word and all of the anchor words, but still be in a different source language. For this reason, we submit the extracted text to a language identifier. Language identifiers use characteristic sequence of letters or short words [6] to guess which language a text is written in. We use the language identifier of the LIMA natural language processing system, and reject the page if the most likely language is not the one we are interested in, French in this paper.

When a text has been identified as being in French, we also extract all the outgoing links from the page and add them to a list of new pages to browse. The two lists of seen URLs and new URLs are the basis of any web crawler [11].

Having implemented this simple crawler for extracting French text using a full French lexicon, anchor words, and language identification, we find that about 75% of the URLs that we access produce useful text. The remaining 25% of the URLs fail for one of the following reasons:

☐ Page no longer exists, or timeout in accessing the page. Using *wget*, we give each URL 3 seconds to respond.
☐ No text on page. Page only contains images, or pointers to other pages.
☐ Text not in French, according to our language identifier

We found that each French URL successfully retrieved reveals, on average, 6 new URLs to explore. The average size of a retrieved web page converted into text is 8000 bytes.

---

[7] http://lynx.isc.org/ is the lynx homepage.
[8] We do not consider the problem of different pages with the exactly same content. Studies performed by [10] found an incidence of less than 5% of exact page matches with different URLs during a collect of web pages.

3.4 Natural Language Processing

For each French text gathered, we apply the LIMA natural language processor [4] to extract the elements of the language model we want to create. Our linguistic analysis[9] performs tokenization, morphological analysis, part-of-speech tagging, and dependency extraction, creating an analysis graph that can be traversed to extract many different types of output. We extract the following elements for each word:

☐ the lemmatized form of the word
☐ the syntactic dependency relations involving the word
☐ the normalized noun phrases, in LIMA format (lemmas, stopwords[10] removed)
☐ the words and phrases found in a window of 5, and 10 non stopword words
☐ named entities found in a window of 20 words around each word.

For example, from the text.

```
Vérifiez encore l'angle du robinet et serrez les bou-
lons
(verify once again the spigot angle and tighten the nuts)
```

we extract the lemmatized words:

```
vérifier, angle, robinet, serrer, boulon
```

the dependency relations:

```
COMPDUNOM(robinet,angle)    noun-modifier(spigot,angle)
COD_V(angle,vérifier)       verb_object(verify angle)
COD_V(boulon, serrer)       verb_object(tighten nut)
```

the normalized noun phrase:

```
angle_robinet (spigot angle)
```

the words and phrases found in a window of words around each word. Each lemma in this two column list is listed with another lemma that is found 2 (non-stop) words or concepts before or after the word :

```
vérifier angle              robinet serrer
vérifier angle_robinet      robinet boulon
angle vérifier              serrer angle_robinet
angle angle_robinet         serrer robinet
angle robinet               serrer boulon
robinet angle               boulon robinet
robinet angle_robinet       boulon serrer
```

---

[9] Linguisitic analysis tools can be found at http://www.alphaworks.ibm.com/tech/lrw/ and http://www.gate.ac.uk/download/

[10] A stopword is a function word such as an article, preposition, etc; that is not usually indexed in information retrieval systems. http://www.ranks.nl/tools/stopwords.html provides pointers to lists of stopwords Catalan, Czech, Danish, Dutch, English, French, German, Hungarian, Italian, Norwegian, Polish, Portuges , Spanish, and Turkish.

Similarly, we extract the lemmas and phrases in a window of 5 words before and after each word, as well as the named entities (predefined categories of phrases such as the names of persons, organizations, and locations, see [12]) that are found up to 10 words before or each word.

3.5 Processing Output and Example

This output generates a lot of data for each page treated. For an average size page of 8 Kb of text, 300 Kb of output data is produced. We are examining efficient ways of storing this data that we are currently collecting from the Web for the 5 million seed URLs for French. Time estimations on the subset we have treated are that we can produce output for 400 URL per hour on one PC (Intel Xeon, CPU 3.40GHz, 2Mb cache), with fetching and converting the text for a URL only accounting for a small part of the time, and the linguistic processing and extraction from the results graph accounting for the rest. This means that we can treat 1 million URL in 100 days. Data extraction is independent for each URL, so that process can be parallelized. And we are currently planning to move to a parallel machine.[11]

The final language model for each word will depend on the amount of text treated. As more of the web is covered, the models will reach a web-biased stasis. And we hope that the results approach some satisfying model of language for the applications we will sketch below.

In the meantime, we can show some preliminary, anecdotal results. After treating a sample of around 30,000 URLs, we find the following type of information for a common word like *avion (airplane)*

Common verbal patterns for *avion (airplane,plane)* with their frequencies:

```
COD_V( avion , prendre ) (737)    take an airplane
SUJ_V( avion , décoller ) (115)   airplane takes off
SUJ_V( avion , atterrir ) (82)    airplane lands
COD_V( avion , fabriquer ) (80)   build an airplane
COD_V( avion , voir ) (75)        see a plane
SUJ_V( avion , survoler ) (74)    plane flies over
SUJ_V( avion , aller ) (73)       plane goes
SUJ_V( avion , arriver ) (68)     plane arrives
SUJ_V( avion , voler ) (61)       plane flies
COD_V( avion , reprendre ) (59)   take plane again
COD_V( avion , détourner ) (59)   hijack plane
COD_V( avion , piloter ) (56)     fly a plane
SUJ_V( avion , venir ) (54)       plane comes
COD_V( avion , utiliser ) (54)    use a plane
COD_V( avion , abattre ) (54)     shoot down a plane
```

---

[11] We are planning to move to the TERA-10 supercomputer. This CEA LIST machine, made by Bull, is composed of 4352 Intel Montecito dual-core processors (8704 cores), connected together by a Quadrics high-performance interconnection network and can perform 50 tera-flops (50,000 billion operations per second).

Common phrases involving *avion(airplane,plane)* as a modifier

```
billet_avion (671)        airplane ticket
accident_avion (95)       airplane accident
pilote_avion (76)         airplane pilot
détournement_avion (67)   airplane hijacking
descente_avion (66)       airplane landing
voyage_avion (58)         airplane trip
vol_avion (57)            airplane flight
place_avion (47)          airplane seat
passager_avion (46)       airplane passnger
bruit_avion (45)          airplane noise
crash_avion (40)          airplane crash
retard_avion (39)         plane delay
```

Common phrases involving *avion(airplane,plane)* as a head of the phrase:

```
avion_ligne (178)         commercial plane
avion_combat (92)         combat plane
avion_militaire (83)      military plane
avion_petit (81)          small plane
avion_chasse (80)         fighter plane
avion_premier (75)        first plane
avion_transport (51)      transport airplane
avion_réaction (43)       jet airplane
avion_civil (43)          civilian airplane
avion_américain (43)      American plane
avion_privé (38)          private plane
avion_hélice (34)         propeller plane
```

If we consider the words found in a window of 5 words before or after *avion (airplane)* in these web pages, we get a list that begins with

```
prendre (2602), billet (2580), pouvoir (2392), faire
(2186), aller (1864), aéroport (1820), vol (1510), de-
voir (1324), voir (1118), arriver (970), pilote (950),
passager (894), ...
```

But since we know the relative frequency of each word for French as seen in section 2, it is more interesting to look at the words that are most strongly associated with *avion (plane)*, rather than seeing those that are most common, as given above. For this we can now calculate the mutual information, as suggested by [13], of each neighboring word and *avion (plane)*, since we know how many times the word appears on the web in French, and how many times it is found with our target word (*avion*) in the web pages we have treated. The first two hundred most strongly associated words with *avion(plane)* from these URLS are

```
abattre accident acheter aile aimer air aller altitude
amener américain annoncer apparaître appareil appeler
aérien arme armée aéroport arrivé arrivée arriver ar-
rêter attendre atterrir atterrissage avancer aviation
bagage bateau billet bombe bord bruit bus cabine cargo
chambrer char chasse ciel civil combat commencer com-
mercial compagnie complet construire continuer con-
trôleur crash croire décider déclarer décollage dé-
coller demander descendre descente destination devoir
diriger distance dormir départ déplacement détourné
détournement détourner détruire effectuer embarquement
embarquer emmener empêcher ennemi entendre environ es-
cale essayer exister expliquer exploser explosion fa-
briquer faillir faire finir flotte frapper gêner heure
hélice hélicoptère horaire hôtel indestructible
indiquer israélien laisser lâcher léger maintenance
manquer marcher matin matériau militaire missile monder
monter moteur navire noir nuit observer occuper parler
passager passeport passer payer penser perdre permettre
petit pilotage pilote piloter piste plaire porter pou-
voir prendre provenance prévoir équipage quitter réac-
tion radar ramener rappeler rater reconnaissance re-
garder rejoindre remplir rentrer repartir reprendre
rester retard revenir rouler route réserver russe sau-
ter sembler sentir serpent siège séjour sol sommer sor-
tir suivre survoler taire taxi étayer température ten-
ter terroriste tomber toucher tour tourner trafic train
trajectoire transport transporter utiliser véhicule
vitesse voisin voiture vol volant voler vouloir voyage
voyager
```

This set of words may change as more text is extracted for this word (*avion*) though we can imagine that many of the words will still be very strongly associated with the concept.

Now imagine that we have these common phrases, and syntactic patterns, and 'clouds' of strongly associated words (that also have frequencies associated with them that are not shown above) for each of the 100,000 lemmas of French, as we plan to have at the end of the first year of this project in 2007. What can we do with information? We will sketch some of the uses of this vast language model in the next section.

4 Possible Applications

The uses of a language model are varied. The model that we are building will provide the relative frequency of all language phenomena for the complete set of 100,000 French lemmas in our lexicon, up to the dimension of the Web that we treat. In information retrieval, relative frequency (in the guise of inverse document frequency) is one key statistic of word importance that has long been used [14]. Rarer word get more weight than more common words in ranking documents. With this model, we will have the relative frequency of all words, and later of all phrases. In parsing, information on lexical associations has been used to resolve structural ambiguities [15][16] but never based on complete explicit language statistics from the web, though the implicit web statistics have been used [17].

For other language applications, such as machine translation and speech understanding, the benefits of having a web-sized model of language are even more evident. Implicit web statistics have been shown to be useful in choosing the right translations of noun phrases [18], translating and transliterating proper names [19][20]. For example, if one wants to translate the English phrase *tighten the nut* into French, it is useful to know that *serrer le boulon (tighten the nut [for a bolt])* is more common on the web than *serrer la noix(tighten the nut [to eat])*.

For speech-to-text, current systems make errors such as the following which comes from output produced by one of the leading systems in the world:

> *Text spoken:* le pape est apparu très fatigué il a célébré l' eucharistie le dernier repas du christ mais il a renoncé au lavement des pieds *(the pope appeared very tired. he celebrated the eucharist, the last meal of christ, but he renounced performing the washing of the feet.)*

> *Output of Speech-to-Text:* le pape est apparu très fatigué il a célébré le péristyle le dernier repas du christ et mais il a renoncé au lavement didier *(the pope appeared very tired. he celebrated the* **peristyle***, the last meal of christ, but he renounced performing the washing of* **didier***.)*

Both interpretations, the true and the erroneous, are available inside the speech-to-text system, but the current language models that these systems are based upon ngrams sequences of words and analysis can break down when unseen sequences appear. In our explicit model of all the words in the language, we will have statistics about the common dependency relations such as

```
SUJ_V (eucharistie, célébrer) celebrate eucharist
NNPREP (pied, lavement) noun-modifier(feet,washing)
```

These elements of the language model will allow us to prefer more common interpretations of speech streams and produce more likely translations of speech into text. In addition, storing statistics about dependency relations rather than exact word sequences will provide more robust speech recognition, since new utterances involving known dependencies (but maybe different modifiers) will still be recognizable.

There are many other language applications that use Web data to extract knowledge about language and about the world. Some examples are detecting affect and opinion [21], gathering world knowledge about visual aspects [22], or gathering more general world knowledge [23]. But all these techniques current use the implicit language model on the web and must generate queries and probe the Web for word statistics rather than using an explicit linguistic model, as suggested in our project and in [24].

5 Related Research and Conclusion

Google announced in the summer of 2006 that it has extracted all sequences of 5 words appearing more than 40 times in over 1 trillion words of running text[12] that it has indexed. This ngram language model is being distributed through the Linguistic Data Consortium on 6 DVDs[13]. There are 1.1 billion sequences with their frequencies listed in this data. Their own research has shown that the more data you apply to tasks such as machine translation, the larger the language models, the better the results.

It is obvious that online dictionaries are not the answer to the problem of creating the next generation of language models. Dictionaries contain descriptions of the extraordinary, what a person might need to know about a word or phrase, whereas the computer, for its language understanding, needs to know the ordinary: what words are found in what patterns, what other words are to be found nearby. We are now at a point where it is possible to extract all this information on a very large scale from the sum of what humanity is publishing on the web, creating a very language model as could only have been dreamed of a few years ago. Once this modelling is done for individual words, the next step is to do it for all the lexical structures, with one entry for each multiword noun phrase (for example, performing the same analysis as is shown above with *avion(plane)* for *billet-avion (plane ticket))* and for each syntactic dependency pair. This extraction of a multiword model of language is another level of complexity but it is also feasible with current linguistic processing techniques and current computing power.

Acknowledgements

This research is funded in part by the European Network of Excellence "Multimedia Understanding through Semantics, Computation and Learning" MUSCLE (EU contract FP6-507752); and partly through a grant from the Fondation Jean-Luc Lagardere.

References

1. Grefenstette, G., Nioche, J.. Estimation of English and non-English language use on the WWW. In Proceedings of RIAO (2000)
2. Ipeirotis, P. G., Agichtein, E., Jain, P., and Gravano, L.: To search or to crawl?: towards a query optimizer for text-centric tasks. In Proceedings of the 2006 ACM SIGMOD international Conference on Management of Data (Chicago, IL, USA, June 27 - 29, 2006). SIGMOD '06. ACM Press, New York, NY, (2006) 265-276
3. Nemeth, L., Tron, V., Halacsy, P., Kornai, A., Rung, A., Szakadat, I. Leveraging the open source ispell codebase for minority language analysis, In Fir:st Steps in Language Documentation for Minority Languages: Computational Linguistic Tools for Morphology, Lexicon and Corpus Compilation, Proceedings of the SALTMIL Workshop at LREC, (2004) 56–59.

---

[12] This list of 5-grams (sequences of five words) is available on 6 DVDs through the LDC.. http://www.ldc.upenn.edu/Catalog/nonmem_agree/Web_1T_5gram_V1_User_Agreement.html. is providing it free for research institutions and universities.

[13] http://webspace.isi.edu/mt-archive/MTS-2005-Och.pdf

4. Besançon, R., de Chalendar, G., Ferret, O., Fluhr, C., Mesnard, O., Naets, H.:. Concept-Based Searching and Merging for Multilingual Information Retrieval: First Experiments at CLEF 2003. Proceedings of CLEF (2003) 174-184.
5. Cavnar, W. B., Trenkle, J. M.: N-gram based text categorization. In Proceedings of SDAIR-94, 3rd Annual Symposium on Document Analysis and Information Retrieval, Las Vegas, NV, (1994) 161-175
6. Grefenstette, G.: Comparing two language identification schemes. In Proceedings of the Third International Conference on the Statistical Analysis of Textual Data (JADT'95), Rome, December 11-13 (1995) 263-268
7. New, B., Pallier, C., Brysbaert M., Fer L.: Lexique 2 : A New French Lexical Database. Behavior Research Methods, Instruments, & Computers, Volume 36, Number 3, (2004) 516-524
8. Cunningham, H.., "GATE: A Framework and Graphical Development Environment for Robust NLP Tools and Applications," *Proc. 40th Anniversary Meeting Assoc. for Computational Linguistics* (ACL 2002), Assoc. for Computational Linguistics, East Stroudsburg, Pa., (2002)
9. G-I. Kikui. Identifying the coding system and language of on-line documents on the internet. In Proceedings of the 16th International Conference on Computational Linguistics (COLING) (1996)
10. Berland, S., Grabar, N. : Assistance automatique pour l'homogénéisation d'un corpus Web de spécialité. In Actes des 6èmes Journées internationales d'analyse statistique des données textuelles, JADT 2002, Saint-Malo (2002)
11. Heydon, A., Najork, M.: Mercator: A scalable, extensible Web crawler, World Wide Web, v.2 n.4, (1999) 219-229
12. Sundheim, B.: Overview of results of the MUC-6 evaluation. In Sixth Message Understanding Conference (MUC-6): Proceedings of a Conference held in Columbia, Maryland, November 6-8, (1995) 13-32
13. Church, K. W. and Hanks, P.: Word association norms, mutual information, and lexicography. *Comput. Linguist.* 16, 1 (Mar. 1990), 22-29
14. Hiemstra. D.: A probabilistic justification for using tf.idf term weighting in information retrieval. International Journal on Digital Libraries, 3(2): (2000) 131-139
15. Hindle, D. and Rooth, M:. Structural ambiguity and lexical relations. In Computational Linguistics, 19(1), the MIT Press (1993) 103-120
16. Merlo P., Crocker M. W., Berthouzoz C.: Attaching multiple prepositional phrases: Generalized Backed-off Estimation. In Cardie C. and Weischedel, R. editors, Proceedings of the second conference on Empirical Methods in Natural Language Processing, EMNLP-97, (1997). 149-155
17. Nakov, P., Hearst, M.: Using the Web as an implicit training set: Application to structural ambiguity resolution. In: Proceedings of HLT-EMNLP, Vancouver, British Columbia, Canada (2005) 835–842
18. Grefenstette, G.: The World Wide Web as a resource for example-based machine translation tasks. In Proceedings of the ASLIB Conference on Translating and the Computer, London (1998)
19. Yiping Li and G. Grefenstette. Translating Chinese idiographic characters via corpus and web validation. In CORIA'2005, Grenoble, France, March 9-11, 2005
20. Qu, Y., Grefenstette, G.: Finding Ideographic Representations of Japanese Names Written in Latin Script via Language Identification and Corpus Validation In Proc. of ACL (2004) 184-191.

21. Turney, P.D., Littman, M.L.: Measuring praise and criticism: Inference of semantic orientation from association, ACM Transactions on Information Systems (TOIS), 21 (4), (2003) 315–346
22. Grefenstette, G.:The Color of Things: Towards the automatic acquisition of information for a descriptive dictionary in Revue Française de Linguisitque Appliquée, vol X-2 1386-1204, (2005) 83-94
23. Cimiano, P., Staab, S.: Learning by googling, ACM SIGKDD Explorations Newsletter, v.6 n.2, p.24-33, December (2004)
24. Kilgarriff, A.: Linguistic search engine. In Kiril Simov, editor, Shallow Processing of Large Corpora: Workshop Held in Association with Corpus Linguistics 2003, Lancaster, England. (2003)

On Heads and Coordination
in Valence Acquisition

Adam Przepiórkowski

Institute of Computer Science
Polish Academy of Sciences,
Warsaw, Poland
adamp@ipipan.waw.pl
http://nlp.ipipan.waw.pl/~adamp/

Abstract. The aim of this paper is to present the design of a partial syntactic annotation of the IPI PAN Corpus of Polish [22] and the corresponding extension of the corpus search engine Poliqarp [25,12] developed at the Institue of Computer Science PAS and currently employed in Polish and Portuguese corpora projects. In particular, we will argue for the need to distinguish between, and represent both, syntactic and semantic heads, and we will sketch the representation of coordination, the area traditionally controversial both in theoretical and in computational linguistics. The annotation is designed in a way intended to maximise the usefulness of the resulting corpus for the task of automatic valence acquisition.

1 Introduction

1.1 Motivation and Outline

Treebanks are resources often used for the automatic acquisition of linguistic and natural language processing (NLP) knowledge such as frequencies of particular constructions or phrase types, syntactic valence or collocational information.[1]

The aim of this article is to present the design of a treebank to be used specifically for the purposes of automatic valence acquisition,[2] where both morphosyntactic and lexico-semantic selectional requirements will be learned. For this reason, it is necessary to identify both the syntactic head (for morphosyntactic valence constraints) and the semantic head (for lexico-semantic selectional restrictions) of any construction. Section 2 shows that semantic heads cannot be deduced automatically from the syntactic structure. But if both the syntactic and the semantic head are annotated for any constructions, then the unsolved question of the headedness of coordinate structures becomes even more pressing; a possible solution is proposed in section 3.

The treebank mentioned above will be built in two stages. First, a partial treebank will be constructed with the help of shallow grammars which will identify NPs, PPs, and other possible verbal dependents. No attempt will be made

---

[1] This article is an extended and corrected version of [23].

[2] But, no doubt, this resource will turn out to be useful also for many other purposes.

A. Gelbukh (Ed.): CICLing 2007, LNCS 4394, pp. 50–61, 2007.

at constructing the full structure of a clause at this stage. That resulting information will be used to automatically construct a preliminary valence dictionary (cf. [24] and [7] for recent relevant experiments on Polish). The second stage will consist in the manual construction of full parses for clauses, possibly on the basis of the results of automatic deep parsing (with the use of the valence dictionary created in the first stage).

This paper reports on work within the first stage. After discussing the syntactic/semantic head distinction in §2 and coordination in §3, we propose an XML representation for such annotation in §4 and, in §5, we describe a conservative extension of the query language used by the Poliqarp search engine that takes advantage of such grammatical annotation. The remainder of this section briefly presents the current status of the IPI PAN Corpus of Polish, which constitutes the empirical basis for the planned treebank, and Poliqarp, the search tool used to query the corpus.

1.2 The IPI PAN Corpus

The IPI PAN Corpus of Polish ([22]; http://korpus.pl/), presently the only morphosyntactically annotated large corpus of Polish, was first made available for search in June 2004. The whole corpus contains over 250 million segments (over 200 million orthographic words; punctuation marks count as separate segments and some orthographic words are split into smaller segments for good linguistic reasons described in [26,27]). Recently, a source (XML) version of a subcorpus containing 100 million segments has been made available to the public for non-commercial research purposes.[3] Unique features of this corpus include a carefully designed and documented morphosyntactic tagset and the inclusion of all possible morphosyntactic interpretations, in addition to those chosen by the tagger as correct in the given context. The corpus is XML-encoded according to (slightly modified) XCES [11] specifications.

1.3 Poliqarp

Poliqarp is an indexing and searching tool developed in the same project as the IPI PAN Corpus, but it was designed as a universal corpus management tool: the tagset may be specified externally and the internal character coding is UTF-8, so the tool could be used for any corpus of any language.[4] A stable version 1.0 of Poliqarp was made available to the community under the GNU GPL licence (cf. http://korpus.pl/index.php?page=poliqarp).

The syntax query of Poliqarp is based on that of CQP [5], but it contains some unique features. One of the most interesting is that one may refer both to all morphosyntactic interpretations given by the morphological analyser and to the disambiguated interpretations; for example, the query '[case~acc & case=gen]' may be used to find those forms which were tagged as genitive but which may, in

---

[3] See http://korpus.pl/index.php?page=download for details.

[4] It has been used recently for the Portuguese corpus developed by António Branco's group in Lisbon, [1], cf. http://lxcorpus.di.fc.ul.pt/.

other contexts, be analysed as accusative. Moreover, since some contexts do not provide sufficient information to fully disambiguate a form, Poliqarp allows to distinguish between certain and uncertain information. For example, the query '[case=gen]' may be used to search for any forms whose disambiguated interpretation (possibly one of many, if the tagger could not narrow down interpretations to one) is genitive, while '[case==gen]' finds those forms that have a unique (certain) genitive interpretation.[5]

See [22] for a detailed description of the tagset and the query language.

2   Distinguishing Syntactic and Semantic Heads

It is well known that valence must be expressed both at the syntactic and at the semantic level; a verb (or any predicate) may refer to the morphosyntactic (e.g., part of speech, case) or the lexico-semantic (e.g., volition, humanness) properties of its argument. For this reason, both the syntactic head and the semantic head of a potential dependent must be made available to the valence acquisition algorithm.[6]

In many cases syntactic heads are also semantic heads, as in the majority of noun phrases, but there are exceptions. In many cases, the syntactic structure of a construction allows one to automatically deduce the semantic head, as in the case of the English determiner+noun NPs, where the noun is always the semantic head, although the determiner may be taken to be the syntactic head, but again there are exceptions. For these reasons it is necessary to explicitly represent both the syntactic head and the semantic head in a treebank.

One area where it is very difficult to automatically recognise the semantic head on the basis of syntax only is the domain of numeral and nominal phrases in Polish. In Polish, numerals are a morphosyntactic rather than a semantic class; when in subject position, they exhibit a special agreement pattern with the verb, which occurs in the 'default' 3rd person singular neuter form rather than in the form which would agree with the noun. For example 'Five books lay on the table' would be translated into *Pięć książek*-GEN.FEM.PL *leżało*-3RD.NEUT.SG *na stole* (lit.: 'five books lay on table') rather than **Pięć książek*-GEN.FEM.PL *leżały*-3RD.FEM.PL *na stole*. It is commonly assumed that numerals are the syntactic

---

[5] Let us mention, for completeness, that the query '[case~~gen]' would find all forms which are unambiguously genitive, regardless of context, i.e., forms whose all possible interpretations are genitive.

[6] Note that this distinction is understood here, roughly, as approximating Mel'čuk's distinction between the morphological and syntactic dependency on one hand, and the semantic dependency on the other hand (cf. [16] for a summary and references), rather than as in Head-driven Phrase Structure Grammar (HPSG) [19,20], where so-called adjuncts are always semantic heads because they are semantic functors. The notion of *semantic head* corresponds to the notion of "useful head" in [31] or "lexical head" used interchangably with "semantic head" in [8]. A distinction between syntactic heads and semantic heads was already known by the modistic grammarian Radulphus Brito (c. 1300), cf. [6].

heads of such numeral constructions [29,21], while the nouns are semantic heads. On the other hand, the noun is both the syntactic and the semantic head in a noun phrase. However, there are number-denoting lexemes which are clear morphosyntactic nouns, e.g., *tuzin* 'dozen', where it is the complement of the syntactic head noun that should be analysed as the semantic head, and there are also lexemes such as *tysiąc* 'thousand' which are morphosyntactically ambigous between the numeral and the nominal interpretation. In fact, various measure phrases are widely discussed cases of the syntactic/semantic head mismatch in various languages, cf., e.g., [35] for English and [31] for French, with a broader spectrum of such mismatches in nominal phrases, involving phrases like *part of the room, herd of wildebeest, kind of fish, bout of the flu* and *her jerk of a husband*, discussed in [8] and [9].

Another area where syntax does not pre-determine semantic headedness are adjectival phrases: there is a subset of (syntactically) adjectival phrases, called elective phrases, as in *największy z chłopców* '(the) biggest of boys', where the semantic head is actually the noun argument of the proposition *z* 'of' subcategorised for by the comparative or superlative form of the adjective (*największy* 'biggest' in this example).

More examples can be given of Polish constructions whose purely morphosyntactic makeup does not determine the semantic headedness. For this reason, if a treebank is to be useful in applications such as exhaustive valence extraction, it must explicitly encode both kinds of headedness.

3   Coordination

Coordination is one of the most controversial areas in theoretical linguistics. In particular, it is far from clear what should count as the head in coordinate constructions. Postulating the existence of two possibly different heads makes things even worse: while many syntactic theories take the conjunction to be the syntactic head, it clearly is not the semantic head. In fact, each conjunct should be treated as a semantic head.

This is exactly the stance that we adopt here: since — assuming that a coordinated structure has a semantic head — all conjuncts should be treated as heads, we will assume that coordinations are actually multi-headed structures, with each conjunct providing a syntactic head and a corresponding semantic head.

This decision is also dictated by valence acquisition considerations: in cases of coordination of unlike categories [28], the coordinate structure provides evidence for two syntactically different valence frames of the same verb. For example, the sentence *Opowiadał o Wenecji i że musi tam wrócić* '(He) was saying about Venice and that (he) must return there' (from [13]) is grammatical only because the verb OPOWIADAĆ ('talk', 'say') may be combined either with a prepositional phrase headed by the preposition O or with a clause headed by the complementiser ŻE. This evidence would be missed, or at least it would have to be reached via much more complicated reasoning, if the conjunction or just one of the conjuncts were taken to be the syntactic head.[7]

Note that this treatment of coordination makes coordinate structures essentially multi-headed, as in [3] (or, in a way, as in [33] and in a mediaeval modistic grammar [6], where a coordinate structure is not a phrase in its own right, but the verb has a direct relation to each of the conjuncts), unlike in modern linguistic theories, which often analyse coordination as head-argument constructions, either by postuling that coordinate constructions are headed by the first conjunct (e.g., [16]), or that they are headed by conjunction (e.g., [30]). We believe that the cases of coordination of unlike categories, such as mentioned above, while providing practical reasons for the treatment of coordinate structures as multi-headed in the context of a valence acquisition project, also constitute a strong evidence for such a multi-headed theoretical linguistic analysis of coordination.[8]

The final argument for this treatment of coordination comes from the design of the query syntax to be discussed in §5.

4   XML Representation

Each text in the IPI PAN Corpus of Polish currently consists of three XML files: `header.xml`, containing metadata, `text.xml`, validated by the (slightly modified) `xcesDoc.dtd` from the XCES (XML Corpus Encoding Standard; [11]) specification, containing the text itself with some structural annotation, and `morph.xml`, validated by the (slightly modified) `xcesAna.dtd`, containing morphosyntactic annotation.

Each `morph.xml` is sequence of `<tok>` elements grouped into sentences (`<chunk type="s">` elements), which are in turn grouped into paragraphs (`<chunk type="p">` elements). A three-segment fragment of a `morph.xml`, translated as 'for (the) Częstochowa steel-mill', is given below:[9]

```
<tok id="tA10">
<orth>dla</orth>
<lex disamb="1"><base>dla</base><ctag>prep:gen</ctag></lex>
</tok>
```

---

[7] It should be noted that the coordination of unlike categories is systematically (if not textually) common in Polish, e.g., [32,13] discusses various other cases of coordination involving an NP and a clause, [14] discusses many cases of coordination involving an NP and a PP, [21] gives examples of coordination of NPs of different cases, etc.

[8] An alternative theory that can easily account for such data is an ellipsis-based theory of (apparent) non-constituent coordination of [2]. In general, HPSG is perhaps unique among contemporary theories in directly addressing various difficult problems of coordinate structures and proposing explicit solutions.

[9] As mentioned above, all morphosyntactic interpretations are retained for each segment, but the one that the tagger ruled as correct is marked with the '`disamb="1"`' attribute.

```
<tok id="tA11">
<orth>Huty</orth>
<lex disamb="1"><base>huta</base><ctag>subst:sg:gen:f</ctag></lex>
<lex><base>huta</base><ctag>subst:pl:nom:f</ctag></lex>
<lex><base>huta</base><ctag>subst:pl:acc:f</ctag></lex>
<lex><base>huta</base><ctag>subst:pl:voc:f</ctag></lex>
</tok>
<tok id="tA12">
<orth>Częstochowa</orth>
<lex disamb="1"><base>częstochowa</base>
                <ctag>subst:sg:nom:f</ctag></lex>
</tok>
```

This is a PP syntactically headed by the preposition *dla* with the named entity NP headed by *Huty* 'steel mill' modified by the proper name *Częstochowa*. Accordingly, there are two constructions here: the NP headed both syntactically and semantically by *Huty*, and the PP, syntactically headed by *dla* and semantically headed by the semantic head of the NP, i.e., by *Huty*.

For the partial annotation stage of the treebank building, we propose a simple standoff annotation consisting of sequence of `<group>` elements containing the information of the extent of the construction (the attributes `from` and `to`), of the syntactic and semantic head (`synh` and `semh`) and of the type of the construction (PG for prepositional group and NG for nominal group):

```
<group from="tA10" to="tA12" synh="tA10" semh="tA11" type="PG"/>
<group from="tA11" to="tA12" synh="tA11" semh="tA11" type="NG"/>
```

Note that both the syntactic head and the semantic head are tokens (segments) rather than constructions. Since, for each (non-coordinate) construction, the syntactic head is a lexical item, this phrase structure representation can actually be easily translated into dependency representation, in the spirit of [18]. Moreover, instead of saying that the semantic head is the NP argument of the preposition, we are saying that the semantic head of the PP is the semantic head of the NP argument of the PP. This way each construction can be almost (see below) exhaustively characterised by two lexical items within that construction.[10]

The XML representation is more complicated in case of coordination phrases. Such constructions will be marked as groups of `type="Coordination"`, without the `synh` and `semh` attributes, but containing groups of `type="Conjunction"`, as well as groups of `type="Conjunct"`, representing particular conjuncts. For example, assuming that the phrase *zarówno Ratyzbona, jak i Tybinga* 'both Regensburg and Tübingen' is tokenised into 6 segments (*zarówno, Ratyzbona, ,, jak, i, Tybinga*) with `id` values from `t1` to `t6`, the partial syntactic annotation may look as follows:

---

[10] Note that, while we assume that the syntactic head is an immediate constituent of the construction, the semantic head can be deeply embedded, as in the constructed example *[dla [pięciu [największych [z [tych hut]]]]]*, 'for five biggest of these steelmills', semantically headed by *hut*.

```
<group from="t1" to="t6" type="Coordination"/>
<group from="t1" to="t1" synh="t1" semh="t1" type="Conjunction"/>
<group from="t2" to="t2" synh="t2" semh="t2" type="Conjunct"/>
<group from="t3" to="t5" synh="t5" semh="t5" type="Conjunction"/>
<group from="t6" to="t6" synh="t6" semh="t6" type="Conjunct"/>
```

All (headed; see below) conjuncts provide heads for the whole coordinate structure. Each `group` of `type="Conjunct"` may consist either of a single token (as in the example above), in which case the values of the attributes `from`, `to`, `synh` and `semh` are equal to the `id` of that token, or it may consist of a `group` (simple or coordinate), in which case the values of these attributes are the same as the values of that group. This in particular means that, when one of the conjuncts is a coordinate structure itself, this conjunct will have no `synh` and `semh` attributes, as in the following representation corresponding to the English *either A and B, or C*. Assuming that this construction is tokenised into 7 segments, the representation of such an embedded coordination will be as follows:

```
<group from="t1" to="t7" type="Coordination"/>
<group from="t1" to="t1" synh="t1" semh="t1" type="Conjunction"/>
<group from="t2" to="t4" type="Conjunct"/>
<group from="t2" to="t4" type="Coordination"/>
<group from="t2" to="t2" synh="t2" semh="t2" type="Conjunct"/>
<group from="t3" to="t3" synh="t3" semh="t3" type="Conjunction"/>
<group from="t4" to="t4" synh="t4" semh="t4" type="Conjunct"/>
<group from="t5" to="t6" synh="t6" semh="t6" type="Conjunction"/>
<group from="t7" to="t7" synh="t7" semh="t7" type="Conjunct"/>
```

Any immediate constituent of a coordinate phrase which is neither of the two `types` above (`Conjunction` or `Conjunct`) is assumed to be a parenthetical, i.e., not the actual part of the coordinate construction.

5   Extending the Poliqarp Query Language

Poliqarp provides a rich query language with two levels of regular expressions: over strings and over segment specifications,[11] but it currently does not make it possible to query a corpus for syntactic representation. It is *not* our aim to extend Poliqarp to a full fledged syntactic query tool; such tools exist, notably the tools created within the TIGER project ([15]; http://www.ims.uni-stuttgart.de/projekte/TIGER/). In fact, we have created an XSLT stylesheet converting syntactic information in the format given above (but ignoring the semantic head information) into the TIGER XML format.

However, such general treebank search tools have various restrictions, and the Poliqarp extension described here aims at complementing these tools. One particular restriction of the TIGER tools that the representation described above

---

[11] For example, the query '[orth="a{2,}.*[bB]"]{3,}' could be used to search for sequences of at least three segments whose orthographic form starts with at least two as and ends with a small or capital b.

violates is that each node may only have one incoming edge.[12] While the representation above assumes (although it does not enforce) that any given token may be a syntactic head of at most one construction, many constructions may share the same semantic head, as in the example cited in fn. 10 above.

5.1 Simple Constructions

Each segment specification in the Poliqarp query language is a brackets-enclosed combination of constraints connected by logical connectives; for example the following specifies a nominal or adjectival segment whose gender is not feminine:[13] '[(pos=noun | pos=adj) & gend!=f]'. Each constraint is an attribute-value specification, where the attribute is either pos (part of speech), a grammatical category (e.g., gend or case), orth (orthography) or base (the lemma).

Queries for syntactic constructions have a similar syntax, but they use a different repertoire of attributes, non-overlapping with the attributes used to specify segments. Two main attributes to be used for querying for syntactic groups are: type and head. The attribute type refers to the values of the XML attribute type, so '[type=Coordination]' will find coordinated constructions, while '[type="[PN]G"]' will find prepositional and nominal groups.

The syntax of values of the attribute head differs from that of the other attributes; its values must be enclosed in a double or a single set of square brackets, as in: '[head=[...][...]]' or '[head=[...]]'. In the first case, the first brackets specify the syntactic head and second brackets specify the semantic head, as in the following query which may be used to find elective constructions: '[head=[pos=adj][pos=noun]]'.

In the second case, the content of the single brackets specifies both the syntactic head and the semantic head and, additionally, makes the requirement that they be the same segment. This means that the queries '[head=[case=gen] [case=gen]]' and '[head=[case=gen]]' have a slightly different semantics: the first will find syntactic groups where the two heads may be different or the same, but they must be genitive; the second will find groups with the two heads being necessarily the same genitive segment.

The usefulness of such queries may be illustrated with a query for verbs which co-occur with dative dependents denoting students; the first approximation of such a query may look like this: '[pos=verb][head=[case=dat] [base=student]]'. This query will find not only dative nominal groups headed by a form of STUDENT, but also dative numeral groups whose main noun is a form of STUDENT, appropriate dative adjectival elective groups, etc.

Two additional attributes are introduced as syntactic sugar: synh and semh. The specification 'synh=[...]' is fully equivalent to 'head=[...][]', i.e., it puts a constraint on the syntactic head only, while the specification 'semh=[...]' is fully equivalent to 'head=[][...]', i.e., no constraint on the syntactic head is given.

---

[12] There is a special mechanism for adding a second edge, e.g., in order to represent control.

[13] A shorter equivalent query is: '[pos="noun|adj" & gend!=f]'.

It may seem that, given the possibility to specify the syntactic head of the construction, the attribute type is redundant; in fact, we are not currently aware of cases where the specification 'type="PG"' or 'type="NG"' could not be replaced by an appropriate reference to the grammatical class (part of speech) of the syntactic head. However, the type attribute is useful for finding constructions which are not defined by their heads, for example, *oratio recta* constructions, and — as we will see below — it is also useful for dealing with coordinate structures.

5.2   Coordination

In §3 we presented the view that coordinate structures are best treated as multi-headed, with each conjunct coming with its own set of syntactic/semantic heads. Given that constructions may have multiple syntactic/semantic head pairs, we give the existential import to specifications like '[head=[...][...]]', '[head=[...]]', '[synh=[...]]' and '[semh=[...]]'. That is, a query like '[head=[pos=noun]]' will find nominal groups, as well as coordinate groups containing at least one nominal conjunct. The query can be constrained to simple nominal groups or to coordinate constructions by adding an appropriate type specification, e.g., '[head=[pos=noun] & type="NG"]' should only find simple nominal groups.

This existential semantics of head specifications can be taken advantage of in finding coordinations of unlike categories, as in the query '[synh=[case=gen] & synh=[case=acc]]', which may find coordinate phrases with a genitive and an accusative conjunct.[14]

On the other hand, the drawback of this query semantics is that it does not make it possible to find fully homogeneous coordinate structures, with the exclusion of heterogeneous structures mentioned above; i.e., there is currently no way to say that *all* syntactic/semantic head pairs should satisfy a certain requirement. However, the analogy between segment specifications and syntactic group specifications suggests an immediate solution to this problem, namely, allowing an additional operator '==' for head specifications, which enforces the universal treatment of the specification. So, just like the query '[case==gen]' can be used to search for segments whose all disambiguated interpretations are genitive (cf. §1.3), '[synh==[pos=noun] & type="Coordination"]' will find coordinate phrases whose all conjuncts are syntactically nominal groups.

Note that it is theoretically possible that some conjuncts do not have immediate heads; one such situation is illustrated in §4 (p. 56), where the conjunct which is an immediately embedded coordinate structure does not have the attributes synh and semh. Another such situation may theoretically arise when one of the conjuncts is an *oratio recta* group. In such cases, even if all the other, headed, conjuncts are nominal, the whole coordinate construction will not be identified by the query '[synh==[pos=noun] & type="Coordination"]'. However, with the use of the negation operator '!', it is possible to formulate a query

---

[14] Such mixed coordination is possible in Polish in cases where the genitive is actually a partitive genitive realisation of an accusative requirement.

that will find coordinate constructions whose all *headed* conjuncts are nominal, e.g.: '[synh!=[pos!=noun] & type="Coordination"]'. This query translates into: find a construction of type="Coordination" such that no conjunct can be characterised as having a non-nominal syntactic head; this targets exactly syntactically nominal and headless conjuncts.

6 Conclusion

Although there exist treebanks which contain interesting semantic information, the tectogrammatical level of Prague Dependency Treebank [4] being a good example, to the best of our knowledge few treebanks contain the explicit distinction between syntactic and semantic heads, the Sinica Treebank [10] being the only exception we are aware of. However, both heads must be identified in the process of automatic valence acquisition, as well as in other applications.[15]

This paper gave some rationale for the explicit encoding of such a distinction in a partial treebank of Polish and showed how to implement this encoding: we described how to conservatively extend the XCES encoding to syntactic groups marked with both kinds of heads, and how to conservatively extend the syntax query of Poliqarp to take advantage of this information. Moreover, we proposed a treatment of coordination as multi-headed constructions, and proposed further corresponding extensions of the XML scheme and the Poliqarp query syntax.

The proposal outlined above contains some controversial features, e.g., the identification of heads as segments, i.e., always leaves in the syntactic tree, and the specific treatment of coordination with each conjunct (with the exception of headless conjuncts) bringing its own set of syntactic/semantic heads. However, we feel that ideas presented here are ripe for the community review.

References

1. Florbela Barreto, António Branco, Eduardo Ferreira, Amália Mendes, Maria Fernanda Nascimento, Filipe Nunes, and João Silva. Open resources and tools for the shallow processing of Portuguese: The TagShare project. In *Proceedings of LREC 2006*, 2006.
2. John Beavers and Ivan A. Sag. Coordinate ellipsis and apparent non-constitutent coordination. In Stefan Müller, ed., *Proceedings of the HPSG04 Conference*, pages 48–69, Stanford, CA, 2004. CSLI Publications.
3. Leonard Bloomfield. *Language*. Holt, New York, 1933.
4. Alena Böhmová, Jan Hajič, Eva Hajičová, and Barbora Hladká. The Prague Dependency Treebank: Three-level annotation scenario. In Anne Abeillé, ed., *Treebanks: Building and Using Parsed Corpora*, pages 103–127. Kluwer, Dordrecht, 2003.
5. Oli Christ. A modular and flexible architecture for an integrated corpus query system. In *COMPLEX'94*, Budapest, 1994.

---

[15] For example, in text retrieval, e.g., [17], in the identification of grammatical relations, e.g., [34], etc.

6. Michael A. Covington. A 700-year-old argument for a syntactic transformation. http://www.ai.uga.edu/mc/trans700.html.

7. Jakub Fast and Adam Przepiórkowski. Automatic extraction of Polish verb subcategorization: An evaluation of common statistics. In Zygmunt Vetulani, ed., *Proceedings of the* 2nd Language & Technology Conference, pages 191–195, Poznań, Poland, 2005.

8. Charles J. Fillmore, Collin F. Baker, and Hiroaki Sato. Seeing arguments through transparent structures. In *Proceedings of LREC 2002*, pages 787–791, Las Palmas, Canary Islands, Spain, 2002. ELRA.

9. Charles J. Fillmore, Christopher R. Johnson, and Miriam R.L. Petruck. Background to FrameNet. *International Journal of Lexicography*, 16(3):235–250, 2003.

10. Chu-Ren Huang, Chen Keh-Jiann, Chen Feng-Yi, Chen Keh-Jiann, Gao Zhao-Ming, and Chen Kuang-Yu. Sinica treebank: Design criteria, annotation guidelines, and on-line interface. In *Proceedings of 2nd Chinese Language Processing Workshop (Held in conjunction with the 38th Annual Meeting of the Association for Computational Linguistics, ACL-2000)*, pages 29–37, Hong Kong, 2000.

11. Nancy Ide, Patrice Bonhomme, and Laurent Romary. XCES: An XML-based standard for linguistic corpora. In *Proceedings of the Linguistic Resources and Evaluation Conference*, pages 825–830, Athens, Greece, 2000.

12. Daniel Janus and Adam Przepiórkowski. Poliqarp 1.0: Some technical aspects of a linguistic search engine for large corpora. In Jacek Waliński, Krzysztof Kredens, and Stanisław Goźdź-Roszkowski, eds., *The proceedings of Practical Applications of Linguistic Corpora 2005*, Frankfurt am Main, 2006. Peter Lang. To appear.

13. Krystyna Kallas. *Składnia współczesnych polskich konstrukcji współrzędnych.* Wydawnictwo Uniwersytetu Mikołaja Kopernika, Toruń, 1993.

14. Iwona Kosek. *Przyczasownikowe frazy przyimkowo-nominalne w zdaniach współczesnego języka polskiego.* Wydawnictwo Uniwersytetu Warmińsko-Mazurskiego, Olsztyn, 1999.

15. Wolfgang Lezius. TIGERSearch — ein Suchwerkzeug für Baumbanken. In Stephan Busemann, ed., *Proceedings der 6. Konferenz zur Verarbeitung natürlicher Sprache (KONVENS 2002)*, Saarbrücken, 2002.

16. Igor A. Mel'čuk. Levels of dependency in linguistic description: concepts and problems. In Vilmos Àgel, Ludwig Eichinger, Hans-Werner Eroms, Peter Hellwig, Hans-Jürgen Heringer, and Henning Lobin, eds., *Dependenz und Valenz: Ein Internationales Handbuch Der Zeitgenösischen Forschung*, pages 188–229. De Gruyter, Berlin, 2003.

17. Christof Monz and Maarten de Rijke. Tequesta: The University of Amsterdam's texual question answering system. In *Proceedings of Tenth Text Retrieval Conference (TREC-10)*, pages 513–522, 2001.

18. Joakim Nivre. Theory-supporting treebanks. In Joakim Nivre and Erhard Hinrichs, eds., *Proceedings of the Second Workshop on Treebanks and Linguistic Theories (TLT2003)*, pages 117–128, Växjö, Norway, 2003.

19. Carl Pollard and Ivan A. Sag. *Information-Based Syntax and Semantics, Volume 1: Fundamentals.* Number 13 in CSLI Lecture Notes. CSLI Publications, Stanford, CA, 1987.

20. Carl Pollard and Ivan A. Sag. *Head-driven Phrase Structure Grammar.* Chicago University Press / CSLI Publications, Chicago, IL, 1994.

21. Adam Przepiórkowski. *Case Assignment and the Complement-Adjunct Dichotomy: A Non-Configurational Constraint-Based Approach.* Ph. D. dissertation, Universität Tübingen, 1999.

22. Adam Przepiórkowski. *The IPI PAN Corpus: Preliminary version.* Institute of Computer Science, Polish Academy of Sciences, Warsaw, 2004.
23. Adam Przepiórkowski. On heads and coordination in a partial treebank. In Jan Hajič and Joakim Nivre, eds., *Proceedings of the TLT 2006,* pages 163–174, Prague, 2006.
24. Adam Przepiórkowski and Jakub Fast. Baseline experiments in the extraction of Polish valence frames. In Mieczysław A. Kłopotek, Sławomir T. Wierzchoń, and Krzysztof Trojanowski, eds., *Intelligent Information Processing and Web Mining,* Advances in Soft Computing, pages 511–520. Springer-Verlag, Berlin, 2005.
25. Adam Przepiórkowski, Zygmunt Krynicki, Łukasz Dębowski, Marcin Woliński, Daniel Janus, and Piotr Bański. A search tool for corpora with positional tagsets and ambiguities. In *Proceedings of LREC 2004,* pages 1235–1238, Lisbon, 2004. ELRA.
26. Adam Przepiórkowski and Marcin Woliński. A flexemic tagset for Polish. In *Proceedings of* Morphological Processing of Slavic Languages, *EACL 2003,* pages 33–40, Budapest, 2003.
27. Adam Przepiórkowski and Marcin Woliński. The unbearable lightness of tagging: A case study in morphosyntactic tagging of Polish. In *Proceedings of the LINC-03, EACL 2003,* pages 109–116, 2003.
28. Ivan A. Sag, Gerald Gazdar, Thomas Wasow, and Steven Weisler. Coordination and how to distinguish categories. *Natural Language and Linguistic Theory,* 3:117–171, 1985.
29. Zygmunt Saloni and Marek Świdziński. *Składnia współczesnego języka polskiego.* Wydawnictwo Naukowe PWN, Warsaw, 4th (changed) edition, 1998.
30. Petr Sgall, Eva Hajičová, and Jarmila Panevová. *The Meaning of the Sentence in Its Semantic and Pragmatic Aspects.* Reidel, Dordrecht, 1986.
31. Max Silberztein. Finite-state description of the French determiner system. *French Language Studies,* 13:221–246, 2003.
32. Marek Świdziński. Realizacje zdaniowe podmiotu-mianownika, czyli o strukturalnych ograniczeniach selekcyjnych. In Andrzej Markowski, ed., *Opisać słowa,* pages 188–201. Dom Wydawniczy Elipsa, 1992.
33. Lucien Tesnière. *Éléments de Syntaxe Structurale.* Klincksieck, Paris, 1959.
34. Rebecca Watson, John Carroll, and Ted Briscoe. Efficient extraction of grammatical relations. In *Proceedings of the Ninth International Workshop on Parsing Technology,* pages 160–170, Vancouver, British Columbia, 2005. Association for Computational Linguistics.
35. Abby Wright and Andreas Kathol. When a head is not a head: A constructional approach to exocentricity in English. In Jonh-Bok Kim and Stephen Wechsler, eds., *Proceedings of the 9th International Conference on Head-Driven Phrase Structure Grammar,* pages 373–389. CSLI Publications, Stanford, CA, 2003.

Chinese Terminology Extraction Using Window-Based Contextual Information

Luning Ji, Mantai Sum, Qin Lu, Wenjie Li, and Yirong Chen

The Department of Computing, The Hong Kong Polytechnic University
Hong Kong, China
{cslji, 02116279d, csluqin, cswjli, csyrchen}@comp.polyu.edu.hk

Abstract. Terminology extraction is an important work for automatic update of domain specific knowledge. Contextual information helps to decide whether the extracted new terms are terminology or not. As extraction based on fixed patterns has very limited use to handle natural language text, we need both syntactical and semantic information in the context of a term to determine its termhood. In this paper, we investigate two window-based context word extraction methods taking into account of syntactic and semantic information. Based on the performance of each method individually, a hybrid method which combines both syntactical and semantic information is proposed. Experiments show that the hybrid method can achieve significant improvement.

Keywords: Chinese terminology, terminology extraction, window-based contextual word, termhood, unithood.

1 Introduction

The rapid development of science and technology in different technology domains has generated so many new theories, new materials, and new technologies, which in turn has created many new concepts. Existing domain specific knowledge needs to be updated constantly for more efficient and effective access. Manual updating method which relies on domain experts simply cannot cope with such rapid change. Thus, automatic terminology extraction is getting more attention in recent years.

This paper presents a prototype system for automatic extraction of new terms considering unithood and verification of them as terminology (terms in a specific domain) through the examination of window-based contextual information which judges the termhood of these candidate terms [9]. *Unithood* refers to the degree of strength that a string forms a valid term. *Termhood* refers to the degree at which a linguistic unit is related to or more straightforwardly represents domain specific concepts. When a candidate string has both these two characteristics, it is considered a terminology in the specific domain. The work in this paper is conducted for Chinese in the area of information technology domain. However, the techniques developed in this project could be applicable to other domains and other languages in principle.

The obvious difference between Chinese and Latin based languages such as English is that Chinese does not have word delimiters. Therefore, word segmentation is considered a necessary prerequisite to natural language applications for Chinese including

A. Gelbukh (Ed.): CICLing 2007, LNCS 4394, pp. 62–74, 2007.

terminology extraction. No matter how previous work has achieved very good performance on Chinese word segmentation, segmentation ambiguity is unavoidable. In this paper, a hybrid method using statistical information of both the internal and contextual relationships of candidate strings is applied after word segmentation. It helps to find back the wrongly-segmented terms and form the candidate term list for further verification. To achieve a better recall, we do not restrict the lengths and patterns of candidate strings.

For terminology verification which is the main focus of this paper, we make use of window-based contextual information. The hypothesis is that if a reasonable amount of its neighbouring words are domain specific, the new term must also belong to the specific domain and thus is a terminology, except some most-commonly used auxiliary words such as "的(of)". Two window-based approaches based on contextual information syntax and semantics are proposed. After evaluating the merits and problems of each approach, a hybrid approach is designed to combine both the syntactic and semantic information.

The rest of this paper is organized as follows. Section 2 gives a brief description of related work. Section 3 describes the algorithm design for term extraction and verification in detail. Section 4 presents the experiments and evaluations. The hybrid approach is introduced in Section 4. Section 5 is the conclusion.

2 Related Work

Previous researches have focused on the extraction of terminology through the calculation of termhood. The most commonly used measurement for termhood measurement is Term Frequency Inverse Document Frequency (*TFIDF*). *TFIDF* calculates the termhood by combining word frequency with a document and word occurrence within a set of documents in a specific domain. However, classical measures such as TFIDF are so sensitive to term frequencies that they fail to avoid very frequent non-informative words. Hisamitsu [16] used the baseline method for defining the representative-ness of a term. The document set which contains all the documents is labeled as D_0. Documents that contains the term T is labeled as $D(T)$. If a term is topic specific, all the terms in $D(T)$ should probably have different distributions in D_0. However, the baseline method cannot handle some "background noise", that is words which are irrelevant to T yet occur in $D(T)$. Chang [8] proposed a statistical model for finding domain specific words. He defined Inter-Domain Entropy (*IDE*) by acquiring normalized relative frequencies of occurrence of terms in various domains. Terms whose IDE are above a threshold are unlikely to be associated with certain domains.

All these above mentioned techniques pay attention to the distribution of a term occurring within a domain or across domains. The contextual information they investigate is derived at the document level, i.e. the information of different documents or across different domains. However, few work have been done on the contextual information more specifically and more directly within the sentence of a candidate term. We believe that the closer the contextual information to the term, the closer their relationship to the term especially semantically.

Furthermore, most previous research work is conducted for Latin-based languages such as English. However, the lack of word delimiters in written Chinese takes additional efforts in candidate term extraction. It is also necessary to handle problems caused by word segmentation and PoS tagging if they are to be used.

3   Algorithm Design

Our system contains three major modules, namely *Pre-Processing*, *Candidate Term Extraction*, and *Terminology Verification*.. Automatic new term extraction uses unithood as its measurement and terminology extraction uses termhood as the measurement for candidate terms.

3.1   The Preprocessing Module

The preprocessing module includes word segmentation, Part-of-Speech tagging (PoS), frequency count and garbage string filtering to obtain candidate word strings.

As mentioned in the Introduction Section, word segmentation is the prerequisite for Chinese text. In this work, we also need to have grammatical tag such as noun, verb, adjective and etc for syntactic and semantics analysis. So firstly we apply word segmentation and PoS tagging to the selected Chinese corpus.

Secondly, we apply the PatTree structure [4] on the segmented corpus to extract all the lexical patterns without restriction on pattern length. Using the PatTree structure, all possible character strings with their frequency counts are maintained. Candidate list is built with frequency larger than certain threshold and sorted by word length. We consider word length as a factor in statistic measurements in the next step. To maintain a good recall with consideration of the data sparseness problem, the threshold is set to 2 meaning that only strings occur twice or more are taken as candidate terms.

Although we do not restrict the lexical patterns of terms, some common non-term patterns which are considered as garbage strings are detected and filtered out by a stop-word list, such as "我的(mine)","在香港(in Hong Kong)", "当上课(when having class)", "桌子上(on the table)", "完成了(finished)". Because it is unlikely to be an independent term when these stop words are at certain specific positions, such as at the beginning or at the end. Besides, personal names tagged as "nr" are not the targets in this project and also filtered out here.

3.2   Automatic Term Extraction

Two kinds of statistic-based measurements are used to estimate the soundness of an extracted string being a word [14]: the internal measurement and the contextual measurement. Our work analyzes both internal and external factors during the process of term extraction.

Internal measurement estimates the soundness by the internal associative strength between constituents of the item [14]. We use the *Significance Estimation Function (SEF)* shown in formula (1) to measure the internal association. *SEF* is used to judge if a pattern c is more complete in semantics than its substrings a and b where $a \subset c$ and $b \subset c$. It works especially well for multi-character terms, compared to other commonly-used approaches such as Mutual Information.

$$SEF = \frac{f(c)}{f(a) + f(b) - f(c)} \tag{1}$$

where c ($c = C_1 C_2 C_3 \ldots C_n$) is a lexical pattern to be estimated, a ($a = C_2 C_3 C_4 \ldots C_n$) is the longest right substring, and b ($b = C_1 C_2 C_3 \ldots C_{n-1}$) is the longest left substring. $f(a)$, $f(b)$ and $f(c)$ are the frequency of string a, b and c, respectively.

The value of *SEF* is between 0 and 1. A larger *SEF* indicates that patterns a and b tend to occur together in the text. Thus c is more complete in semantics than either a or b. *SEF* equals to 1 means a and b only occur as substring of c. A candidate string is accepted as a term if its internal associative strength is larger than a given threshold.

The external measurement estimates the soundness by the dependency of the item on its context of the candidate string [14]. We apply the *C*-value measure shown in formula (2) to calculate the external strength [7][11]. The *C*-value is given as follows:

$$
C\_value(c) = \begin{cases} \log_2 |c|\, f(c) & c \text{ is not nested} \\ \log_2 |c|\, (f(c) - \dfrac{1}{P(T_C)} \sum_{b \in T_c} f(b)) & c \text{ is nested} \end{cases}
\tag{2}
$$

Where c is the candidate string, $|c|$ is the number of words in string c, $f(c)$ is the frequency of occurrence of c in the corpus, T_c is the set of extracted candidate terms that contain c, $P(T_c)$ is the number of these longer candidate terms. *C*-value aims to get more accurate terms, especially those nested terms, such as the word "计算"(calculate) can be an independent term, yet it can also be contained in another term "计算机" (computer).The *C*-value method also has enhancement in non-nested terms because it put a term length into consideration. Formula (2) shows that the more often a candidate string occurs alone and the longer its size, the higher the *C*-value. The more often a candidate string occurs as a substring, the lower its value is. Besides, the more the number of longer strings in which the candidate string occurs, the higher its value [7]. Simply put, a larger value implies a more likely term. Let us take word "贝叶斯"(Bayes) as another example. Although the internal measurement of "贝叶斯" is very high, its *C*-value is low, since "贝叶斯" always occurs as a substring of the words "贝叶斯定理"(Bayes' Theorem), "贝叶斯算法"(Bayes Algorithm) or "贝叶斯决策"(Bayes Decision). That is to say, the word "贝叶斯" (Bayes) is less likely to be an independent term. In our term extraction model, only candidates with both the internal and external measurements larger than certain thresholds are considered as valid terms.

3.3 Terminology Verification

Terminology verification is the main focus of this paper. Three different approaches to extract window-based contextual information are proposed. The main idea is to make use of the neighbouring words within a reasonable window size of the candidate terms. The hypothesis is that if a reasonable amount of its neighbouring words are domain specific, the terms must also be domain specific and thus is terminology.

As the Chinese corpus is segmented with PoS tags, the neighbouring words carry two aspects of information: the words themselves, which carry their semantic information and PoS tags which carry the syntactic information. Both semantic and syntactic information of the contextual words make contributions on terminology verification. The first approach uses the semantic approach to extract the semantic information of window-based contextual words through a domain knowledge base. The second approach applies the syntactic structure of valid terminology contextual words for validation. After reviewing the pros and cons of these two approaches, a third hybrid approach which combines both the statistical and syntactic information is proposed. Details of the hybrid approach will be discussed in Section 4.

3.3.1 The Semantic Approach

The first approach uses a statistical method to extract semantic information of the neighbouring words within the observing window through existing domain knowledge base (*DKB*). If the majority of the neighbouring words already appear in an existing DKB, the candidate term is considered a valid terminology in that domain. Suppose we have a sentence containing the new extracted term "蓝牙(Bluetooth)" in the sentence "蓝牙是一个开放性的、短距离无线通信技术标准。 (Bluetooth is the standard on an open, short-distance wireless communication technology.) " and we do not know whether "蓝牙(Bluetooth)" belongs to IT domain. If we already know that its neighbouring words "无线(wireless)", "通信技术(communication technology)" are both typical terminology in IT domain. It is very likely that "蓝牙(Bluetooth)" is also a terminology in the IT domain. Details of the actual DKB used in the experiment will be discussed in Section 4.

Three parameters are needed when designing an algorithm in this approach:

Table 1. Parameters for the Semantic approach

Parameter Name	Explanation
Window Size	Maximum length of context words to be extracted both forwards and backwards of the candidate, 5 is used
Frequency of Occurrence	Threshold value of the number of occurrence of the context word
Percentage in DKB	Threshold value of the percentage of the context words occurred in the DKB

Details of the algorithm are shown below:

```
Input: candidate term list from the output of the Term Extraction Module;
Output: terminology list
Method:
    For each candidate term in candidate term list: {
        Locate all the occurrences of this candidate term from the corpus
        For each occurrence {
            Extract its neighbouring words within the Window Size
            Collect the frequency information of every neighbouring word}
        For each neighbouring word (frequency > Frequency of Occurrence){
            Calculate the percentage of neighbouring words found in DKB}
        If (percentage of neighbouring words > the Percentage in DKB) {
        Output the candidate term as terminology}}
```

The three parameters have different extents of influence to the final results. The smaller the window size is, the closer relationship between the candidate and the context words. Since the context words with very low frequency of occurrence are considered noise data, the higher threshold value of frequency reduces the effect of the noise data. The minimum percentage of occurrence in the knowledge base justifies the relevance of the candidate term to the domain. The higher the percentage required, theoretically, the higher the relevancy of the candidate terms to the domain.

Only the context words within one sentence can be considered as meaningful context to the candidate terms. We define one sentence as a set of words which form a grammatically complete statement, and the boundary of sentences is separated by ", 。 ! ? ". Besides, we use full word matching when checking the context words with the knowledge base.

3.3.2 The Syntactic Approach

The second approach makes use of the PoS information of the candidate term itself and its neighbouring words to help verify the terminology. In this approach, we mainly use the PoS tagging information to generate and build the syntactic rule structure for both the candidate term itself and its neighbouring words. For example, we find out that, if a terminology is a noun (tagged as n), it is mostly likely to be followed by a verb and noun, tagged by the pattern "$v+n$". By applying the valid patterns for both candidate term itself and its neighbouring words, we can positively identify the candidate term as a valid terminology.

In this approach, there are two parameters to be considered:

Table 2. Parameters of the syntactic approach

Parameter Name	Explanation
Rule Length	Length of syntactic rules for checking the context of the candidate terms both forwards and backwards
Rule Number	Number of rules used for checking (start from using the most frequent rule)
Rule Frequency	Threshold value of frequency of selected rules

The two parameters *Rule Length* and *Rule Number* have different effects. The *Rule Length* controls the checking range of context, which should be within the *Window Size* in this approach. The longer the *Rule Length*, the more context words will be considered, thus the more precise the extraction is. The *Rule Number* limits the number of rules applied. More rules means more chances for the terms to be matched. The sequence of matched rule is according to their frequency in the learning phase.

Details of the algorithm are listed in two phases below:

Use a list of terminology which is deemed correct in its domain. Each entry is a terminology which may have multiple words and every word has PoS information.

Input: a *terminology list* with PoS tags, *segmented corpus*; *candidate term list*
Output: extracted terminology list
Method:
Training:
      For each record in the *terminology list* {
          Record the frequency of syntactic pattern of it PoS tagging}

For each acquired syntactic pattern of terminology P_i {
    If (freq(P_i) > *Rule Frequency*){
        Keep the syntactic pattern in *valid terminology pattern set S_t*}}
For each item in the *valid terminology pattern set* {
    For each terminology T_j{
        Find its pattern in the valid terminology pattern set
        Locate all the O_k occurrences of T_j in *segmented corpus*
        For each O_k of T_j {
            Collect the frequency of syntactic patterns of T_j 's neighbors
            within *Rule Length*}}}
Keep syntactic patterns of neighbors in valid neighbouring pattern set S_n
(Number of Rules = *Rule Number*)
Testing:
    For each candidate term in *candidate term list*{
        Match its PoS tags with the valid terminology patterns in S_t
        Keep the matched candidate terms T_m}
    For each matched term T_m {
        Match its neighbouring words with valid patterns in S_n
        Keep the matched terms as valid terminology}

During the implementation and experiment phase, we analyze each rule pattern of terminology separately. In the evaluation phase, we combine the results of all patterns together to calculate the overall precision and recall.

4 Experiment and Discussion

The corpus used contains 16 papers of 1,500,000 characters selected from Chinese IT journals from 1998 to 2000. They cover popular topics in IT domain, such as electronics, software engineering, telecom, and wireless communication. The DKB used in this work has a simple structure with only one term a line and a total of 288,000 I.T. terms from the Institute of Computational Linguistics, Peking University.

We apply a Unicode-based adaptive segmenter [12]. The same as most other segmentors used nowadays, this is a general purpose segmenter which is not tailored for a specific domain. Its ability to deal with unknown or new words in certain specific domain is limited. Even though the internal and external measurements help to find back these wrongly-segmented words, the propagated errors caused by segmentation to terminology extraction still exist and cannot be avoided.

The performances are evaluated in terms of precision (P), recall(R) and F-measure (F). For evaluation purpose, we have manually collected and recorded all the correct terminology from the selected corpus as the standard answers beforehand. A total of 3,438 correct terminology are recorded as standard answer for 100% recall. In order to avoid subjectivity problem when we measure the final results as well as the preparation of standard answers, two research students did the manual work independently and consolidated with verification.

4.1 Performance of the Two Approaches

Two sets of experiments are conducted for each of the two approaches. We set a different value to one parameter at one time, to show the contribution of each parameter.

4.1.1 The Semantic Approach

In the following two experiments, different sets of *Frequency of Occurrence* and *Percentage in DKB* were tested and the corresponding results are shown in the following tables. *Window Size* is always fixed to 5.

- **Experiment 1:** Change *Frequency of Occurrence* (*Percentage in DKB* = 40%)

Table 3. Performances of different frequencies in the Semantic Approach

Freq	Number of Extracted Term	Number of Correct Terms	P(%)	R(%)	F(%)
2	2660	931	35.0	27.1	30.5
4	1035	508	49.1	14.8	23.1
6	591	320	54.1	9.3	15.9

- **Experiment 2:** Change *Percentage in DKB* (*Frequency of Occurrences* = 2)

Table 4. Performances of different percentages in the Semantic Approach

Percentage	Number Of Extracted Terms	Number of Correct Terms	P(%)	R(%)	F(%)
40	2660	931	35.0	27.1	30.5
75	2441	889	36.4	25.9	30.3
100	1852	704	38.0	20.5	26.6

Table 3 shows that increasing the threshold frequency of context words can increase precision, in spite of the significant drop of recall, which also leads to a decrease of F-measure. The frequency of 2 gives the best performance according to *F-measure*. The cause for recall to drop to 9.3% when frequency = 6 is the data sparseness, as the corpus size is quite small. So, we fix *Frequency of Occurrences* to 2 in the second test. From **Table 4**, we can see that increasing the percentage requirement of matching the DKB makes the precision higher with a lower recall. Comparatively, the lowest percentage gives the best performance in terms of *F-measure*.

To conclude, when window size is 5, frequency is 2 and percentage is 40%, we achieve the best performance (30.5% of *F-measure*) in the semantic approach.

4.1.2 The Syntactic Approach

After learning and generating rule patterns of terminology itself, we focus on the six most frequent patterns: "*n+n*", "*n*", "*nx+n*", "*vn+n*", "*v+n*" and "*n+n+n*". Those patterns whose occurrences are below 50 are not considered as valid patterns. For each term pattern, the contextual syntactic patterns with both backward and forwards direction are extracted and up to five rules for each rule length are recorded. For the contextual word rules, we set the threshold of frequency to 10. Due to the limitation of this paper, detailed contextual rules are not shown for each term pattern (See Appendix 2, 3 for reference). The following two tables show the performance results with different parameter values.

• **Experiment 3:** Change *Rule Length* Only (*Rule Number* = 5)

Table 5. Performances of different *Rule Lengths* in the Syntactic Approach

Rule Length	Number Of Extracted Terms	Number Of Correct Terms	P(%)	R(%)	F(%)
2	561	314	56.0	9.0	15.5
3	250	152	60.8	4.4	8.2
4	80	57	71.3	1.3	3.3

• **Experiment 4:** Change *Rule Number* Only (*Rule Length* = 2)

Table 6. Performances of different rule numbers in the Syntactic Approach

Rule Number	Number Of Extracted Terms	Number Of Correct Terms	P(%)	R(%)	F(%)
2	369	207	56.1	6.0	10.8
3	474	263	55.5	7.6	13.4
5	561	314	56.0	9.0	15.6

It is significant that the *Rule Length* of two gives the best performance comparatively as shown in **Table 5** according to *F-measure*. When the *Rule Length* increases to four, the *F-measure* drops heavily to about 3%. This is because the longer the rule length is, the more restrictive and harder to match the candidate terms. To the opposite, in **Table 6**, the more rules are provided for matching, the better recall can be achieved while maintaining the precision. From the above two experiment results, we can conclude that it can get the best performance using the syntactic approach when Rule Length is set to two with five contextual rules provided.

However, compared to the semantic approach, we can find that the syntactic approach get very low recall on the whole although a very significant increase on precision. The reason is that we make the rule selection much stricter. In order to increase the precision of the syntactic approach, we set a high threshold for filtering some noise pattern, which also filtered out some valid patterns. Some patterns and rules have very low frequency during the learning process, especially for the longer patterns. Besides, the error of PoS tags also leads to the low recall.

4.2 The Hybrid Approach

As mentioned above, the contextual words carry both semantic and syntactic information, which are represented by both the word and its PoS tagging. The introduced two approaches consider each aspect independently. From the experiments results of the two approaches, we find out that the semantic approach can get a better recall while the syntactic approach achieves a better precision. Naturally, we want to build a hybrid method taking into both data to achieve the best *F*-measure. The following gives the formula for the hybrid approach:

$$Score = p * 10 * \frac{\sum Freq\ (cwkb\ )}{Freq\ (c)} + RL * \frac{\sum (b(RV\ ) + f\ (RV\ ))}{Freq\ (c)} \quad (3)$$

where p is the percentage of the context words occurred in the DKB; $cwkb$ is the context words that occur in the DKB; c is the candidate term with certain pattern; $Freq(c)$ is the frequency of c ; RL is the rule length applied for matching; RV is the score of the applied rules. E.g., if the candidate term meets the first rule among total 5 rules, RV is 5; 4 if meets the second rules; $b(RV)$ is the rule value of matched backward rules; $f(RV)$ is the rule value of matched forward rules

Formula (3) takes into consideration of both semantic information and syntactic information. Different weights about two aspects are tested and finally we have Formula (3) as our final combination approach representation.

Applying formula (3) to the same data set, we get the performance results of the hybrid approach shown in Table 7, with the parameter - *Rule Length* equals to the window size. We set the threshold of Score as 5 according to the experiences.

- **Experiment 5:** Change *Rule Length* Only

Table 7. Performances of different *Rule Lengths* in the Hybrid Approach

Rule Length	Number Of Extracted Terms	Number Of Correct Terms	P (%)	R (%)	F (%)
2	1445	982	68.0	28.6	40.3
3	1514	1018	67.2	29.6	41.1
4	1538	1045	67.9	30.4	42.0

As our expectation, from **Table 7**, we can see that the hybrid approach not only increases the precision but also maintain the recall, which directly leads to better *F-measure*. That is because we take advantages of both the semantic and the syntactic approaches. It keeps not only some low frequency terms (which is filtered out in the semantic approach), but also some terms with irregular tagging (which is filtered out in the syntactic approach).

As we mentioned in the related work, the differences between our work and other algorithms which also made use of contextual information are, we did our work on the contextual information at a more micro level around the candidate term within one sentence. In order to prove that the contextual information we focus on can perform better, we also select a baseline *–Lexicon Set Algorithm (LSA)* [3] for comparisons. [Chen Yirong, 3] represented that LSA made use of the classified domain corpora

Table 8. Performances of Different Approaches

Approach	Extracted Terms	Correct Terms	P(%)	R(%)	F(%)
Baseline (LSA)	566	283	50.0	8.2	14.1
Semantic	2660	931	35.0	27.1	30.5
Syntactic	561	314	56.0	9.0	15.5
Hybrid	1538	1045	67.9	30.4	42.0

information to verify the domain specificity. By subtracting the extracted terms from general domain corpus, the extracted terms from specific domain are domain-specific. **Table 8** shows the comparison results.

Table 8 shows the comparison results of the three approaches proposed in this paper with the baseline - Lexicon Set Algorithm (LSA) [3]. The same data set and standard answer are applied to these four approaches. It is obvious that all of our approaches perform better than the baseline according to the *F*-measure. Although the precision of baseline exceeds the approach of the semantic one, its recall has a large deduction. Among the four approaches, the hybrid approach has the best performance.

5 Conclusion

This paper presents a prototype system for terminology extraction for Chinese within a context window within a sentence. For terminology verification, two approaches – the semantic and the syntactic approach are introduced. In the semantic approach, neighbouring words are checked against a domain knowledge base to verify a terminology. In the syntactic approach, we apply the syntactical patterns of terminology itself and rules for its neighbouring words to the candidate terms.

Experiments show that the semantic approach can get better recall (27.1%) and syntactic approach can achieve a better precision (71.3%). A hybrid approach which combines both the semantic and syntactic information show that the hybrid approach achieves the best *F*-measure, not only maintains a good precision but also a good recall. Compared with close related work, we achieve significant improvement.

Due to the limited time, the work was conducted on a relatively small corpus and the extended corpus can help to reduce data sparseness problem.

Acknowledgements. The project is supported by the HK Polytechnic University funded project B-Q824 with account number RGBN and account number RGED.

References

1. Beatrice Daille, "Study and Implementation of Combined Techniques for Automatic extraction of terminology" , in P. Resnik and J. Klavans (eds) The Balancing Act: Combining Symbolic and Statistical Approaches to Language, MIT Press, p 49-66, 1996.
2. E. Milios, Y. Zhang, B. He, and L. Dong. "Automatic Term Extraction and Document Similarity in Special Text Corpora". In *Proc. of the 6th Conf.e of the Pacific Association for Computational Linguistics*, pages 275-284, Halifax, NS, Canada, August 22-25, 2003.
3. Chen Yirong, Lu Qin, Li Wenjie, Sui Zhifang,Ji Luning , "A Study on Terminology Extraction Based on Classified Corpora", LREC2006
4. Chien, L.F. "Pat-tree-based adaptive keyphrase extraction for intelligent Chinese information retrieval". *Information Processing and Management,1999* vol.35 pp.501-521
5. E. Frank, G. W. Paynter, I. H. Witten, C. Gutwin and C. G. Nevill-Manning. "Domain-specific keyphrase Extraction", *In Proc. of 16th Int. Joint Conf. on Artificial Intelligence IJCAI-99, 1999, pp. 668-673.*
6. Hiroshi Nakagawa and Tatsunori Mori. A simple but powerful automatic term extraction method. In *the Proc. of the 2nd Int. Workshop on Computational Terminology*, Taipei,Taiwan, August 31, 2002. pp. 29-35.

7. Ismail Fahmi , "C-value method for multi-word term extraction", In seminar in Statistics and Methodology, May 23, 2005
8. Jing-Shin Chang, "Domain Specific Word Extraction from Hierarchical Web Documents: A First Step Toward Building Lexicon Trees from Web Corpora", in Proc. of the Fourth SIGHAN Workshop on Chinese Language Learning,2005 pp. 64-71
9. Kageura, K. and Umino, B. "Methods of automatic term recognition: a review". *Terminology* 3(2), 259-289, 1996.
10. Katerina T. Frantzi, "Incorporating Context Information for the Extraction of Terms". In Proc. of *ACL/EACL '97*, pages 501-503, Madrid, Spain, July 1997
11. K.T. Frantzi and S. Annaniadou, "Extracting nested collocations", In the Proc. Of COLING'96, pp. 41-46 (1996)
12. Qin Lu, Shiu-tong Chan, Baoli Li and Shiwen Yu, "A Unicode-based Adaptive Segmenter", *Journal of Chinese Language and Computing 14 (3):221-234,2004*
13. Schone, P., Jurafsky D. "Is knowledge-free induction of multiword unit dictionary headwords a solved problem?": *In Proc. of EMNLP 2001.*
14. Shengfen Luo, Maosong Sun. "Two-Character Chinese Word Extraction Based on Hybrid of Internal and Contextual Measures": *Proc. of the Second SIGHAN Workshop on Chinese Language Processing, July 2003, pp. 24-30.*
15. SUI Zhifang CHEN Yirong, "The Research on the automatic Term Extraction in the Domain of Information Science and Technology", in Proc. of *the 5th East Asia Forum of the Terminology*, 2002
16. T. Hisamitsu and Y. Niwa. "A measure of term representativeness based on the number of co-occurring salient words", *In Proc. of the 19th COLING, 2002.*

Appendix 1: Distribution of Top 10 Patterns of Correct Terminology

Syntactic Pattern	Frequency	Syntactic Pattern	Frequency
n+n	342	n+n+n	57
N	330	n+v	50
nx+n	224	n+vn	48
vn+n	162	v+v	28
v+n	117	n+v+n	24

Appendix 2: Contextual Rules for Pattern "n"

Window Size	Direction	Contextual Word Rules
2	Backward	"v+u","v+v","n+u","v+n","n+vn"
2	Forward	"u+n","vn+n","u+vn","v+v","n+v"
3	Backward	"d+v+v","v+v+vn","n+c+n","n+u+vn","v+u+n"
3	Forward	"u+vn+n","u+n+v","u+n+n","n+u+vn","vn+u+n"
4	Backward	"n+n+c+n","n+vn+n+u","m+q+vn+vn", "v+p+n+u","d+v+u+n"
4	Forward	"n+u+vn+n","n+c+n+n","vn+n+u+n", "d+v+m+q","n+n+n+a"

Appendix 3: Contextual Rules for Pattern "v+n"

Window Size	Direction	Contextual Word Rules
2	Backward	"n+u","v+v","n+b","d+v","n+v"
2	Forward	"u+vn","u+n","v+v","n+v","b+v"
3	Backward	"n+n+b","d+a+u","u+n+u","v+u+n","v+f+b"
3	Forward	"b+v+n","n+vn+u","u+n+v","v+v+v","u+vn+n"
4	Backward	"v+u+n+u","v+d+a+u","ng+n+n+b", "n+vn+u+h","v+k+v+v"
4	Forward	"n+vn+u+a","n+v+b+v","c+v+n+v", "c+b+b+n","f+v+ng+v"

Baby-Steps Towards Building a Spanglish Language Model

Juan C. Franco and Thamar Solorio

University of Texas at El Paso
El Paso, TX, 79912
{jcfranco, tsolorio}@utep.edu

Abstract. Spanglish is the simultaneous use, or alternating of both, traditional Spanish and English within the same conversational event. This interlanguage is commonly used in U.S. populations with large percentages of Spanish speakers. Despite the popularity of this dialect, and the wide spread of automated voice systems, currently there are no spoken dialog applications that can process Spanglish. In this paper we present the first attempt towards creating a Spanglish language model.

1 What Is Spanglish?

Spanglish has existed for a long time, but has not been formally recognized as a language, nor has it been classified as a particular linguistic phenomenon. This interlanguage is more of a continuum of the mix between English and Spanish. From a linguistic point of view, it is difficult to decide what to consider Spanglish. It is debatable whether to consider Spanglish as an interlanguage, a pidgin, or a creole language. An interlanguage is a language that is often spoken between linguistic borders [1]; Spanglish does not fit this category, as it is also spoken in areas where no such borders exist, New York City being an example of this. A pidgin is a communication system created when people communicate despite their lack of knowledge in the other language [1]; this might explain its origin, but it certainly does not apply to its use, as most of the Spanglish speakers are bilingual. A creole language originates when a community adopts a pidgin as their primary source for communication [1]; a fragment of Spanglish speakers fall under this category since they cannot use traditional English or Spanish because of lack of proper training, but this cannot be generalized to all the Spanglish speakers, a large percentage of Spanglish speakers are bilingual who can express themselves in either of the traditional languages.

The origins of Spanglish in the U.S. are attributed, to a large extent, to socio-historical circumstances. The Mexican-American war, which according to history, started with the annexation of Texas to the U.S., resulted in Mexico ceding the territories of California and New Mexico to the U.S. in the mid eighteen hundreds. For many years Spanish speakers were going back and forth across these regions maintaining contact with English speakers. Many years later, the U.S. experienced a considerable immigration from Spanish speaking countries

A. Gelbukh (Ed.): CICLing 2007, LNCS 4394, pp. 75–84, 2007.

like Mexico, Cuba, Venezuela, Colombia and even Spain. In recent years, the flow of immigrants from Spanish speaking countries has not ceased to occur. In addition to this, the constant contact among the border cities between the U.S. and Mexico certainly has had influence on the proliferation of Spanglish.

In this paper we report results from building a Language Model (LM) with a small Spanglish corpus we collected. To the best of our knowledge, we are the first attempting to build a LM for Spanglish. Such LM is one of the first steps towards advancing the state-of-the-art regarding the automated processing of interlanguages, an achievement that will open the road for exploring interesting research avenues and applications. A good example is the possibility for building an automated speech recognizer for spoken dialog systems capable of processing requests from Spanglish speakers. We present here evaluation results of the language model, and although they show the language model to be weak, the results are promising. We will continue working on gathering more data to improve the corpus. However, the corpus already represents a valuable asset for deeper analysis of bilingualism. It will allow a statistical analysis that can support a formal characterization of Spanglish. The next section describes some of the most salient features of Spanglish.

2   Linguistic Features of Spanglish

In the linguistic, sociolinguistic, psychology, and psycholinguistic literature, bilingualism and the inherent phenomena it exhibits has been studied for nearly a century [7,8,11,12,13,16,20]. Despite the numerous previous studies of linguistic characteristics of bilingualism, there is not a clear consensus on the use of concepts related to the language alternation patterns in bilingual speakers. The alternation of languages within a sentence is known as code-mixing, but it has also been refereed as intrasentential code-switching, and intrasentential alternation [1,10,18]. Alternation across sentence boundaries is known as intersentential code-switching, or just code-switching. Yet there is another alternation mode defined as borrowing, which consists on adopting words, or idiomatic expressions, of a foreign language, usually modifying the original word, or expression, to suit the grammar or morphology of the receiving language [19].

In this paper we present Ardila's classification of Spanglish characteristics into two groups: shallow and deep phenomena. From his definition, shallow phenomena encompass code-mixing and code-switching; these are the linguistic features of Spanglish that can be easily spotted by humans. In contrast, deep phenomena includes, among other things, the transformation of Spanish to approximate English; the transformations can be so subtle that they are harder to detect, even for speakers of traditional Spanish, and include false cognates, also known as false friends. For our research purpose we are interested mostly in shallow phenomena of Spanglish, thus, the following subsections are focused on this type of features. The interested reader can find more information regarding the deep phenomena in [1].

2.1 Code-Switching

Code-switching is defined as the change of language from one sentence to the following, or when starting a new topic. That is, the speaker starts an utterance in a given language, then switches to the other, and continues his/her utterance in the other language. What is very interesting about code-switching is that most speakers don't even notice when they are changing tongues [6]. It is likely that this is due to the speaker being more focused on expressing an idea, and in the process of formulating an accurate expression of that idea they make use of the known vocabulary in the two languages.

Toribio states that, " ... code-switched forms are context-bound, practiced by bilinguals for bilinguals" [21]. This might explain why most English speakers are unaware of the existence of Spanglish, which in turn explains partially why Spanglish has received little to no attention by linguistic researchers. A common misconception of code-switching is the belief that it is just random mixtures of languages, when in fact, " ... it is rule-governed and systematic, demonstrating the operation of underlying grammatical restrictions" [21]. Spanglish speakers, however, don't receive instruction on how to code-switch, they just use it. Toribio published a study where she defines syntactic rules governing Spanglish; these rules however, have not been validated by a statistical analysis. The lack of a good quality Spanglish corpus makes difficult to perform such a study.

2.2 Borrowing

Borrowing refers to the situation in which a sentence is composed by all words, but one, from the same language. The borrowed word can be one that is commonly used in the other language, thus it is retrieved first. Also, the word might be borrowed from the other language because there is no equivalence of meaning in the first language. There are other language alternations that can also be considered as borrowing, these are explained somewhere else [1,19].

2.3 Code-Mixing

In contrast to code-switching, when the change of language occurs at the end of sentences, or topics, in code-mixing the change of language is present within the same sentence. That is, a sentence might begin in one language, and then switch and end in the other [1].

2.4 Examples of Shallow Phenomena

Table 1 presents examples illustrating each of the linguistic features described above. Now that we described the salient linguistic features of Spanglish, and presented the motivation behind our work, we give a brief introduction to language models. Then, we will continue this paper with the description of the data collected, and the results of testing the LM developed. Examples of the linguistic phenomena described above is shown in Table 1.

Table 1. Examples of some of the linguistic phenomena present in Spanglish

Linguistic Phenomenon	Example
code-switching	*Le dejé un mensaje en la contestadora.* She called me back and...
	(I left a message on the answering machine. She called me back and...)
borrowing	*Vámonos al* mall.
	(Lets go to the mall)
code-mixing	I need to tell her *que no voy a poder ir*
	I need to tell her that I won't be able to make it

3   Language Models

Language models are statistical models of word sequences. LMs can assign probabilities to sequences of words. The way LMs estimate the probability of a word sequence W with length n is by looking back in history to the previous words. More specifically, the probability of a word sequence W, denoted as $p(W)$ can be approximated as follows:

$$p(W) = \prod_{i=1}^{n} p(w_i | w_1, \ldots, w_{i-1}) \qquad (1)$$

Since it would be difficult to find a corpus from which we can reliably estimate all the terms $p(W)$, we approximate them using a shorter history. Then Equation 1 becomes:

$$p(W) = \prod_{i=1}^{n} p(w_i | w_{i-2}, w_{i-1}) \qquad (2)$$

for a trigram model. Since we are using a history of $n - 1$ words, this is also called an n-gram language model. LMs need a corpus appropriate for the target task in order to estimate, as accurately as possible, the probability of observing sequences of words. But for any corpus of finite size, there will always be unobserved events from which the language model will assign a zero probability. In such cases we can use smoothing, or discounting techniques, to assign a non-zero probability to these events. The language model we build in this work uses the Good-Turing discounting method [9]. To determine the quality of a LM we can use two measures from information theory that are commonly used for speech recognition and many other NLP tasks: entropy and perplexity. In this context, entropy measures how well an n-gram grammar matches a corpus. This measure is defined in equation 3.

$$H(x) = - \sum_{x \in X} p(x) log_2 p(x) \qquad (3)$$

where x is a random variable over the set of words, X, in the vocabulary of the model, and $p(x)$ refers to the probability of observing word x. Perplexity is an estimate of the branching factor of the recognition task, it measures the complexity of a text source from the point of view of the recognizer [14]. The perplexity of a given LM is computed as 2^H, where H is the entropy measure described above. Both perplexity and entropy are estimated over a separate test text. LMs have been used successfully in many NLP problems. Some examples are speech recognition, hand-writing recognition, text classification, augmentative communication for the disabled, and spelling error detection [3,15].

4   Data Collection

A Spanglish conversation was the basis for building the corpora. The conversation was recorded between three staff members of a southwestern university of the United States. The volunteers were recorded during their lunch break and were instructed to ignore as much as possible the fact that they were being recorded. It is clear that at the beginning of the recording session the subjects were very self conscious, but after a few minutes they ignored the recorder and started talking spontaneously. The three speakers come from a highly bilingual background. Two of the speakers were raised in Mexico, and they moved to the U.S. in their early adulthood. The third speaker was born and raised in the U.S. but started learning Spanish when she moved to a border city as a teenager.

This recording session has around 40 minutes of continuous speech. The conversation ranges over four topics and shows the casual interaction of Spanglish speakers. The vocabulary of the transcription has a total of 1,516 different word forms. This transcription and the audio file are freely available for research purposes[1].

One of the major problems faced during this project is that the current corpus is far too small, thus it has a very limited vocabulary. It also contains incomplete sentences, due to overlapping and stuttering segments of speakers within the source audio file. All of these factors prevent the the corpus from being ideal for training. A language model will need a corpus size in the order of several thousands, or even millions, of words to estimate more accurately the probability of the n-grams. However, this is just a first approximation, as more data become available we can retrain the language model and achieve better results.

5   Tools of the Trade

We describe in this section the software tools we used, first in the task of transcribing the Spanglish conversation, and then in the development of the language model. For the transcription task we used Transcriber, a free distribution

---

[1] By contacting the authors.

software program that facilitates the manual annotation of speech. This program features a user-friendly graphical user interface (GUI) for segmenting speech recordings and is ideal for transcribing long speech files. More information and access to download the tool can be found in [2]. For the LM we used the CMU-Cambridge Statistical Language Modeling (SLM) toolkit [5]. This toolkit is a practical component for the creation and evaluation of language models; among the functionality provided with this tool are the generation of word frequency lists and vocabularies, word n-gram counts, vocabulary counts, n-gram-related statistics, various back-off n-gram language models, out-of-vocabulary (OOV) rate, n-gram-hit ratios, distribution of back-off cases, annotation of test data with language scores, and perplexity and entropy calculation [5].

An additional program that was used is the Universal Text Imitator (UTI) [22] , which is a program that serves as an all-purpose text generator targeted to generate sentences approximating the style and content of any given document. UTI works in conjunction with the Charniak parser to build a probabilistic context-free grammar, then it generates sentences by traversing the grammar. This tool can also by used in combination with the SML toolkit.

6   Test Phase and Results

There were two tests phases for this project. One involved using the SML toolkit to generate a language model and evaluating it, and the other one consisted of having UTI build a grammar and generate random sentences with such model. The results of both experiments are discussed below.

6.1   SML Test

We divided the transcription file into a training file and testing file, 85% of the original transcription was used for training and the remaining 15% was used for testing. Then, we input to the SML toolkit the training file and we generated several n-gram models. After the language models were trained, we used the test file to measure the entropy and perplexity of the different models. We performed different tests by varying the frequency threshold of the vocabulary. Table 2 presents the results of these experiments.

We can see that the best results were obtained with the 2-gram and 3-gram models, both showing very similar results. This was not surprising as we know that 3-gram models are still the state-of-the-art on speech recognizers [14]. For a vocabulary domain, such as the one from the conversation, these numbers are not bad. However, they represent an optimistic view of what would be achieved in real situations, where the speakers, and the topics, would be different from the ones in this conversation.

Table 2. Perplexity (P) and entropy (E) for the random sentence generation with different n-grams, where three types of vocabulary files were created; one with the top 3000 words (-top 3000), and with words repeated at least 5 (-gt 5) and 2 times (-gt 2)

2-gram model	-top 3000	-gt 5	-gt 2	3-gram model	-top 3000	-gt 5	-gt 2
P	99.16	49.96	66.40	P	100.17	49.40	66.48
E	6.63	5.64	6.05	E	6.65	5.63	6.05

4-gram model	-top 3000	-gt 5	-gt 2	5-gram model	-top 3000	-gt 5	-gt 2
P	102.66	49.79	69.19	P	104.01	50.95	71.73
E	6.68	5.64	6.11	E	6.67	5.67	6.16

6.2   UTI Test

The language model generated by the SML toolkit and a training text, were used by the UTI to generate the probabilistic context-free grammar. Then, a total of 220 sentences were produced for the experiments. For analyzing the resulting sentences generated by UTI, we categorize them into coherent sentences, semi-coherent and incoherent sentences. We grouped as coherent the sentences generated that "make sense", that is, sentences that we believed could have been uttered by humans. Semi-coherent phrases are those that sound weird, or are not likely to be used by humans, but they have the syntax of either of the traditional languages. A semi-coherent phrase can be turned into a coherent phrase by substituting a word in the sentence to another word with the same part of speech. Lastly, incoherent phrases are those that don't resemble human-like sentences. Table 3 presents a summary of the results on these experiments.

Table 3. Results of generating sentences using the UTI. Column label **S** stands for Spanish, column **E** for English, and column labeled **Spg** for Spanglish. Coherent sentences are grammatical sentences that sound human like; semi-coherent sentences are grammatical sentences that do not make sense, but by a simple replacement of words with the same part-of-speech they can be turned into coherent sentences; incoherent sentences are ungrammatical sentences that are not likely to be uttered by humans.

N-gram Model	Coherent				Semi-Coherent				Incoherent
	S	E	Spg	Total	S	E	Spg	Total	
2-gram	1.81%	4.09%	1.81%	7.71%	0.90%	2.27%	3.63%	6.80%	85.45%
3-gram	2.27%	5.00%	4.54%	11.81%	0.90%	3.18%	4.54%	8.62%	79.54%
4-gram	0.90%	5.00%	1.81%	7.71%	0.45%	3.18%	1.36%	4.99%	86.81%
5-gram	0.45%	5.00%	1.36%	6.81%	0.90%	1.36%	1.36%	3.62%	89.54%

For the random sentence evaluation, the bigram and trigram models worked better than the other models that were used. Although the sentences generated by the UTI software were obtained with the help of a context-free grammar file, it is evident from Table 3 that the model that produced the majority of Spanglish phrases was the 3-gram model.

Table 4. Examples of the random sentences generated by the UTI

Coherent sentences:
- *Como muy convinced.* (Like very convinced.)
- *I dije, you know.* (I said, you know.)
- *Y the first girl.* (And the first girl.)
- *So, they know your entire body through thirty- de esos.* (So, they know your entire body through thirty of those.)
- *En the parade.* (At the parade.)
Semi-coherent sentences in Spanglish:
- *I dije you was little.* (I told you was little.)
- *I call a las cinco, and I had to go y to sign him.* (I call at five and I had to go and to sign him.)
- *Le dije, it didn't volunteer we to a notary about a moment.* (I told him/her, it didn't volunteer we to a notary about a moment.)
Incoherent sentences:
- *Tonto no iban gonna grabando.* (Fool they were not gonna record.)
- *Remind upstairs the gusta que.* (Remind upstairs the like that.)
- *Digo, you called fue dando antibiotics, you, and, also, to the.* (I mean, you called was giving antibiotics, you, and, also, to the.)

Table 4 shows some of the sentences generated by the UTI software. We show only Spanglish-like sentences, although the grammar also generated several sentences in English and a few of them in Spanish. Spanish phrases were generated only with the bigram model. It is observed that within the corpus, the use of English dominated, possibly explaining the lack of Spanish output sentences.

7 Final Remarks

The term Spanglish has existed for several decades now, but the negative connotation associated with it in the past, or as Nash wrote, slightly derogatory label [17], has changed in recent years; the ever-increasing number of Spanglish speakers, as well as the raise in sensitivity, and understanding of bilingualism, has contributed to the fact that newer generations do not consider the word as a derogative one, but simply as the best label so far to describe the very interesting phenomenon of the long interaction between English and Spanish.

According to projections from the U.S. Census Bureau by 2050, one out of every four people in the U.S. will be Hispanic [4]. Currently, the Hispanic population of the U.S. is the largest minority, and is a powerful consumer base that is being neglected by automated voice systems unable to handle their speaking preferences. Hispanics have contributed towards an increase in the amount of call traffic where automated voice systems are used. Unfortunately these calls end up being transferred to the human operator after several failed attempts from the system to parse the utterances of the frustrated caller.

Extending automated voice systems with Spanglish LM and acoustic models is a must for large companies searching to increase their Hispanic market. This will be a relevant advance for state-of-the-art ASR systems, and the experience of achieving this goal for Spanglish can shed light into the advancement of the automated recognition of other interlanguages. It is also important to remark that once we have an ASR system for Spanglish, we can then focus on applications of higher level NLP tasks including intelligent tutors for second language learners, summarization and topic segmentation for security, and writing assisting tools for Spanglish speakers, to name a few. Our research effort is the first step towards opening this research road.

8 Current and Future Work

There is a large list of exciting research paths that arise as a result of this work. We provide here a short description of what is currently under way, and things we want to explore in the near future.

- In order to come up with a more reliable language model, more Spanglish resources are needed. Future audio conversation recordings are currently being planned. In addition, we are currently looking at ways to gather written Spanglish samples, like e-mails, chat forums, or blogs.
- We are also working in a statistical analysis of the structure of Spanglish. Our goal is to develop a parser for Spanglish. This will allow to focus on other higher level NLP tasks dealing with Spanglish.
- We are also planning to experiment with the prediction of code-switching points by using prosodic and syntactic features. If we can predict when a change of language is very likely, then it would be possible to divide the Spanglish utterances into fragments belonging to either of the traditional languages, which in turn can be processed by existing tools.

Acknowledgements

We thank the National Science Foundation for supporting this work under grant 0080940, and the data transcription under award IIS-0415150. We would also like to thank Olac Fuentes and the reviewers of this paper for their useful comments.

References

1. Alfredo Ardila. Spanglish: An anglicized spanish dialect. *Hispanic Journal of Behavioral Sciences*, 27(1):60–81, 2005.
2. Claude Barras, Edouard Geoffrois, Zhibiao Wu, and Mark Liberman. Transcriber: development and use of a tool for assisting speech corpora production. *Speech Communication*, 33(1–2), 2001. Software downloaded from http://trans.sourceforge.net/en/download.php.

3. Chris Brockett, William B. Dolan, and Michael Gamon. Correcting esl errors using phrasal smt techniques. In *Proceedings of the 21st International Conference on Computational Linguistics and 44th Annual Meeting of the Association for Computational Linguistics*, pages 249–256, Sydney, Australia, July 2006. Association for Computational Linguistics.
4. U.S. Census Bureau. U.s. interim projections by age, sex, race, and hispanic origin, 2004. Retrieved August 30, 2006 from http://www.census.gov/ipc/www/usinterimproj/.
5. Philip R. Clarkson and Ronald Rosenfeld. Statistical language modeling using the cmu-cambridge toolkit. In *Proceedings ESCA Eurospeech 1997*, 1997.
6. Elena M. de Jongh. Interpreting in Miami's federal courts: Code-switching and Spanglish. *Hispania*, 73(1):274–78, March 1990.
7. S. Ervin and C. Osgood. Second language learning and bilingualism. *Journal of abnormal and social phsychology, supplement 49*, pages 139–146, 1954.
8. Aurelio M. Espinosa. Speech mixture in New Mexico: the influence of English language on New Mexican Spanish. *H. Stevens and H. Bolton, eds., The Pacific Ocean in history*, pages 408–428, 1917.
9. I. J. Good. The population frequencies of species and the estimation of population parameters. *Biometrika*, 40:16–264, 1953.
10. François Grosjean. *Life with Two Languages: An Introduction to Bilingualism*. Harvard University Press, 1982.
11. John J. Gumperz. Linguistic and social interaction in two communities. In John J. Gumperz, editor, *Language in social groups*, pages 151–176, Stanford, 1964. Stanford University Press.
12. John J. Gumperz. Bilingualism, bidialectism and classroom interaction. In *Language in social groups*, pages 311–339, Stanford, 1971. Stanford University Press.
13. John J. Gumperz and Eduardo Hernandez-Chavez. *Cognitive aspects of bilingual communication*. Oxford university Press, London, 1971.
14. Frederick Jelinek. *Statistical Methods for Speech Recognition*. The MIT Press, 1998.
15. Daniel Jurafsky and James H. Martin. *Speech and Language Processing: An Introduction to Natural Language Processing*. Prentice Hall, 2000.
16. John M. Lipski. Code-switching and the problem of bilingual competence. In M. Paradis, editor, *Aspects of bilingualism*, pages 250–264, Columbia, SC, 1978. Hornbeam.
17. Rose Nash. Spanglish: Language contact in Puerto Rico. *American Speech*, 45(3/4):223–233, 1970.
18. Shana Poplack. Sometimes I'll start a sentence in Spanish y termino en español: toward a typology of code-switching. *Linguistics*, 18(7/8):581–618, 1980.
19. Shana Poplack, David Sankoff, and Chris Miller. The social correlates and linguistic processes of lexical borrowing and assimilation. *Linguistics*, 26(1):47–104, 1988.
20. David Sankoff. *Social aspects of multilingualism in New Guinea*. Ph.D. thesis, McGill University, 1968.
21. Almeida Jacquline Toribio. Spanish/english speech practices: Bringing chaos to order. *International Journal of Bilingual Education and Bilingualism*, 7(2–3):133–155, 2004.
22. Sam Wintermute. The universal text imitator, October 2006. Software downloaded from http://www-personal.umich.edu/~swinterm/nlpproj/.

Latent Variable Models
for Causal Knowledge Acquisition

Takashi Inui[1], Hiroya Takamura[2], and Manabu Okumura[2]

[1] Integrated Research Institute,
Tokyo Institute of Technology
4259, Nagatsuta, Midori-ku, Yokohama, 226-8503, Japan
inui@iri.titech.ac.jp
[2] Precision and Intelligence Laboratory,
Tokyo Institute of Technology
4259, Nagatsuta, Midori-ku, Yokohama, 226-8503, Japan
takamura@pi.titech.ac.jp, oku@pi.titech.ac.jp

Abstract. We describe statistical models for detecting causality between two events. Our models are kinds of latent variable models, actually expanded versions of the existing statistical co-occurrence models. The (statistical) dependency information between two events needs to be incorporated into causal models. We handle this information via latent variables in our models. Through experiments, we achieved .678 F-measure value for the evaluation data.

1 Introduction

One of the bottlenecks in developing natural language understanding systems is the prohibitively high cost of building a comprehensive common-sense knowledge base. For example, in question-answering systems [9] and dialogue systems [1], acquiring a great deal of knowledge about *causal relations* or *causality* between events is one central issue.

The causal relations are assumed to be a subclass of general dependency relations between two events although there are various kinds in them (see, for example, [10,11] and [22]). Therefore, causal models need to capture the dependency information between the two events. There are two approaches for automatic causal knowledge acquisition; these approaches capture the dependency information in a different manner:

- cue-phrase-based approach, for example, Girju [8], and Terada [24],
- probabilistic approach, for example, Chang et al. [2].

The former approach is based on cue phrases such as "because" and "since". This approach captures the dependency information between two events directly using cue phrases. However, these cue-phrase-based methods have a low coverage problem because these methods cannot treat event pairs without cue phrases. In fact, Inui et al. [15] investigated what amount of causal relation instances (event pairs holding a causal relation) are present with/without cue phrases in text. In their investigation, they reported that only approximately 30% of causal relation instances have a cue phrase. This

A. Gelbukh (Ed.): CICLing 2007, LNCS 4394, pp. 85–96, 2007.

result suggests that in order to develop knowledge acquisition methods for causal relations with high coverage, we must deal with linguistic expressions with no explicit cue phrases as well as those with cue phrases.

On the other hand, the latter, probabilistic approach constructs statistical models and captures the dependency information between two events by co-occurrence statistics indirectly. The statistical models can treat both event pairs with and without cue phrases; in other words, the models are independent of cue phrases. As a result, these models in the probabilistic approach can achieve higher coverage of causal knowledge acquisition than cue-phrase-based methods.

In the probabilistic approach, Chang et al. [2] proposed a statistical model. It goes without saying that their model can treat both event pairs with and without cue phrases. However, Chang's model has a problem. Since their model is based on the Naive Bayes assumption, capturing the dependency information between two events is hard in the model. To solve this problem, in this paper, we describe new statistical models for detecting causality between two events. Our models are kinds of latent variable models, actually expanded versions of the statistical co-occurrence models proposed by Hofmann et al. [13]. We handle the dependency information between two events given as an input pair via latent variables.

To estimate our models, in addition to co-occurrence information of event pairs, we used a small set of triplets consisting of event pairs with class labels indicating whether an event pair holds causality or not. From the viewpoint of machine learning community, one can see a set of triplets (event pairs with class labels) as a labeled dataset, and a set of plain event pairs as an unlabeled dataset. To deal with both labeled and unlabeled dataset, we used a semi-supervised learning algorithm based on the Expectation-Maximization algorithm.

The rest of the paper is organized as follows. In Section 2, we describe previous work. In Section 3, we explain our models as well as basic models for comparison. Next, we report on our experimental results in Section 4. We summarize the paper in Section 5.

2   Related Work

Some methods of automatic causal knowledge acquisition have been developed [7,16,8,24,14,25,2].

Girju [8] proposed a method for extracting noun phrase pairs expressing a causal relation from English text based on cue phrases. She used WordNet [6] as semantic constraints for selecting candidate pairs. Terada [24] proposed a similar method for extracting causal expressions. Terada applied a sequential pattern mining algorithm [21] to get semantic constraints instead of WordNet. Terada's model is language independent because it needs no language dependent knowledge resources such as WordNet. Inui et al. [14] classified verb phrase pairs co-occurring with cue phrases using Support Vector Machines [27]. Khoo et al. [16] acquired causal knowledge with manually created lexico-syntactic patterns specifically for the MEDLINE text database [26]. These studies are cue-phrase-based approaches.

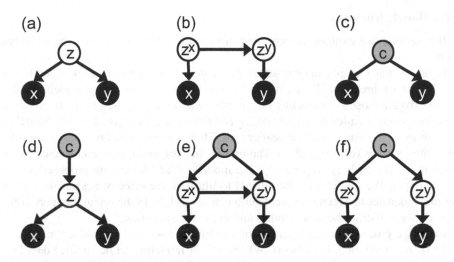

Fig. 1. Graphical representations of statistical dependencies of models. The random variables X and Y represent cause events and effect events, respectively (observed). The variable C represents class label (partially observed), and Z, Z^X, and Z^Y are latent variables (unobserved).

Torisawa [25] proposed a statistical model for acquiring causal knowledge from text. Torisawa focused on verb phrase pairs in Japanese newspaper articles, and constructed a statistical causal model using an unsupervised learning algorithm. In our research, we used both labeled and unlabeled data with a semi-supervised learning algorithm. The difference that we found in experiments pertaining to knowledge acquisition performance between two learning algorithms (unsupervised vs. semi-supervised) is discussed in Section 4.3.

Chang et al. [2] adopted a combination of the Naive Bayes classifier and the Expectation Maximization algorithm. Chang's model is learned in a semi-supervised fashion. Unfortunately, as mentioned in Section 1, Chang's model has a problem. Although we need to incorporate the (statistical) dependency information between two events into causal models, capturing this information by Chang's model is hard because their model is based on the Naive Bayes assumption. However, we handle dependency information via latent variables in our models; they are expanded versions of the statistical co-occurrence models. The details are described in the next section.

3   Statistical Models for Causal Knowledge Acquisition

Suppose that a pair $\langle x, y \rangle$ represents an event pair, c represents an actual value of class variable $C \in \{0, 1\}$, and a triplet $\langle x, y, c \rangle$ represents a labeled sample. Our purpose in this research is to develop statistical models for detecting whether an event pair holds a causal relation ($c = 1$) or not ($c = 0$), given a set of labeled data $D^l = \{\langle x, y, c \rangle_1, ..., \langle x, y, c \rangle_{|D^l|}\}$ and a set of unlabeled data $D^u = \{\langle x, y \rangle_1, ..., \langle x, y \rangle_{|D^u|}\}$.

3.1 Model Structures

In this section, we explain the proposed models for detecting causality between two events.

Figure 1 shows graphical representations of statistical dependencies of several models. The upper three models, (a), (b), and (c), are well-known existing models. Models (a) and (b) are those for modeling of co-occurrence data proposed by Hofmann et al. [13]. Model (a) is called an aspect model, and (b) is called a product model. Model (c) is a variant of the Naive Bayes classifier [18]. These three models are bases of the other remaining models (d), (e), and (f). The models (d), (e), and (f) are constructed by expanding (a), (b), and (c), respectively. The models (d) and (e) are our proposed models in this paper. The model (f) is introduced to illustrate the effectiveness of incorporating dependencies between two events into causal models. In the remaining part of this section, we will describe these models and their characteristics.

First, we give simple explanations of models (a) and (b) to introduce models (d) and (e). As mentioned, models (a) and (b) are for modeling co-occurrence data [13]. Here, in the graphical representations in Figure 1, node X represents a random variable corresponding to cause events, and node Y represents a random variable corresponding to effect events. Nodes Z, Z^X, and Z^Y represent latent variables. Each state of the latent variables of Z, Z^X, and Z^Y can be interpreted as semantic clusters consisting of some similar events. This means that latent variables enable parameter smoothing to reduce the data sparseness problem. In addition, we can see from Figure 1-(a) and Figure 1-(b) that latent variables incorporate dependencies between two events, that is, a cause event and an effect event, into the models. In model (a), dependencies between the two events are incorporated implicitly via one latent variable. On the other hand, in model (b), dependencies between the two events are incorporated explicitly via two latent variables (as indicated by the arrow from Z^X to Z^Y).

Although both (a) and (b) can treat as an input the set of event pairs D^u ($\{\langle x, y \rangle_1, ..., \langle x, y \rangle_{|D^u|}\}$), these two models cannot treat a set of triplets including class label D^l ($\{\langle x, y, c \rangle_1, ..., \langle x, y, c \rangle_{|D^l|}\}$). Therefore, we expand models (a) and (b) to (d) and (e) to make D^l an input. We call (d) the extended aspect model (or shortly *Class-Asp*) and (e) the extended product model (or shortly *Class-Pro*). Our models (d) and (e) not only include two advantages (parameter smoothing and incorporation of dependencies between two events) as well as (a) and (b), but also can incorporate the information of class variable C into themselves. Obtaining the actual value of C in all event pairs is practically impossible due to the high cost of manual annotation of class information. Therefore, we use both D^u and D^l for training. For that purpose, we apply a semi-supervised learning algorithm based on the Expectation-Maximization algorithm [5] to estimate model parameters. The details of the parameter estimations are described in the next section.

Additionally, we introduce model (f) by expanding (c) to reveal the role of latent variables in (d) and (e). Model (c) is a variant of the Naive Bayes (NB) classifier, a 2-term Naive Bayes classifier [1] [18]. Model (f) is easily derived from (c) by adding

---

[1] In fact, in a similar fashion to models (d) and (e), class variable c is partially observed in our setting. Therefore, a semi-supervised learning algorithm is applied to estimate parameters of model (c). See [19] and also Section 3.2 for details on parameter estimation.

two latent variables Z^X and Z^Y to random variables X and Y of model (c), as shown in Figure 1. We call model (f) the Latent Naive Bayes (LNB) based on what Zhang et al. [28] created. Note here that while the shape of the model structure of (f) is very similar to that of (d) and (e), their statistical characteristics are quite different. While dependency information between two events is taken into consideration in model (d) and (e), no dependency information is taken into consideration in model (f). The effect of incorporating dependencies between the two events is examined in Section 4.

3.2   Model Estimation

In this section, we explain the method of parameter estimation of models. Although we introduced six models in the previous section, here we explain only (e) extended product model due to space limitations. For the remaining five models, we applied a similar parameter estimation procedure. We expect that one could easily assume the parameter estimation method is used for the remaining models.

Suppose in Figure 1-(e) that the random variables X and Y represent cause events and effect events, respectively, that the variable C represents a class variable, and that Z^X and Z^Y are latent variables. The generative probability of x, y, z^x, z^y, c is represented by equation (1):

$$P(x, y, z^x, z^y, c) = P(x|z^x)P(y|z^y)P(z^x|c)P(z^y|z^x, c)P(c). \tag{1}$$

We use the Expectation-Maximization (EM) algorithm [5] to estimate the model parameters. According to the theory of the EM algorithm, we can increase the likelihood of the model with latent variables by iteratively increasing the Q-function. The Q-function (i.e., the expected log-likelihood of the joint probability of complete data with respect to the conditional posterior of the latent variables) is represented by equation (2):

$$Q(\theta) = \sum_{x_i} \sum_{y_j} \sum_{c_m} N_{x_i y_j c_m} \sum_{z_k^x} \sum_{z_l^y} \{ \bar{P}(z_k^x, z_l^y | x_i, y_j, c_m)$$
$$\times \log P(x_i|z_k^x)P(y_j|z_l^y)P(z_k^x|c_m)P(z_l^y|z_k^x, c_m)P(c_m) \}$$
$$+ \sum_{x_i} \sum_{y_j} N_{x_i y_j} \sum_{z_k^x} \sum_{z_l^y} \sum_{c_m} \{ \bar{P}(z_k^x, z_l^y, c_m | x_i, y_j)$$
$$\times \log P(x_i|z_k^x)P(y_j|z_l^y)P(z_k^x|c_m)P(z_l^y|z_k^x, c_m)P(c_m) \}. \tag{2}$$

Here, θ denotes the set of the new parameters. $N_{x_i y_j c_m}$ denotes the frequency of a triplet $\langle x_i, y_j, c_m \rangle$ in D^l. $N_{x_i y_j}$ denotes the frequency of a pair $\langle x_i, y_j \rangle$ in D^u. $\bar{P}(\cdot)$ represents the probability computed using the current parameters.

The E-step (expectation step) corresponds to a simple posterior computation. The formulas can be represented by equation (3) and equation (4):

$$\bar{P}(z_k^x, z_l^y | x_i, y_j, c_m) =$$
$$\frac{P(x_i|z_k^x)P(y_j|z_l^y)P(z_k^x|c_m)P(z_l^y|z_k^x, c_m)P(c_m)}{\sum_{z_k^x} \sum_{z_l^y} P(x_i|z_k^x)P(y_j|z_l^y)P(z_k^x|c_m)P(z_l^y|z_k^x, c_m)P(c_m)}, \tag{3}$$

$$\bar{P}(z_k^x, z_l^y, c_m | x_i, y_j) =$$

$$\frac{P(x_i|z_k^x)P(y_j|z_l^y)P(z_k^x|c_m)P(z_l^y|z_k^x, c_m)P(c_m)}{\sum_{z_k^x}\sum_{z_l^y}\sum_{c_m}P(x_i|z_k^x)P(y_j|z_l^y)P(z_k^x|c_m)P(z_l^y|z_k^x, c_m)P(c_m)}. \tag{4}$$

For deriving update rules in the M-step (maximization step), we use a simple Lagrange method for this optimization problem. We obtain update rules equation (5) to equation (9):

$$P(c_m) = \frac{\sum_{x_i}\sum_{y_j}\{N_{x_iy_jc_m} + N_{x_iy_j}\sum_{z_k^x}\sum_{z_l^y}\bar{P}_B\}}{\sum_{x_i}\sum_{y_j}\sum_{c_m}\{N_{x_iy_jc_m} + N_{x_iy_j}\sum_{z_k^x}\sum_{z_l^y}\bar{P}_B\}}, \tag{5}$$

$$P(x_i|z_k^x) = \frac{\sum_{y_j}\{\sum_{c_m}N_{x_iy_jc_m}\sum_{z_l^y}\bar{P}_A + N_{x_iy_j}\sum_{z_l^y}\sum_{c_m}\bar{P}_B\}}{\sum_{x_i}\sum_{y_j}\{\sum_{c_m}N_{x_iy_jc_m}\sum_{z_l^y}\bar{P}_A + N_{x_iy_j}\sum_{z_l^y}\sum_{c_m}\bar{P}_B\}}, \tag{6}$$

$$P(z_k^x|c_m) = \frac{\sum_{x_i}\sum_{y_j}\{N_{x_iy_jc_m}\sum_{z_l^y}\bar{P}_A + N_{x_iy_j}\sum_{z_l^y}\bar{P}_B\}}{\sum_{x_i}\sum_{y_j}\sum_{z_k^x}\{N_{x_iy_jc_m}\sum_{z_l^y}\bar{P}_A + N_{x_iy_j}\sum_{z_l^y}\bar{P}_B\}}, \tag{7}$$

$$P(y_j|z_l^y) = \frac{\sum_{x_i}\{\sum_{c_m}N_{x_iy_jc_m}\sum_{z_k^x}\bar{P}_A + N_{x_iy_j}\sum_{z_k^x}\sum_{c_m}\bar{P}_B\}}{\sum_{x_i}\sum_{y_j}\{\sum_{c_m}N_{x_iy_jc_m}\sum_{z_k^x}\bar{P}_A + N_{x_iy_j}\sum_{z_k^x}\sum_{c_m}\bar{P}_B\}}, \tag{8}$$

$$P(z_l^y|z_k^x, c_m) = \frac{\sum_{x_i}\sum_{y_j}\{N_{x_iy_jc_m}\bar{P}_A + N_{x_iy_j}\bar{P}_B\}}{\sum_{x_i}\sum_{y_j}\sum_{z_l^y}\{N_{x_iy_jc_m}\bar{P}_A + N_{x_iy_j}\bar{P}_B\}}, \tag{9}$$

where,

$$\bar{P}_A = \bar{P}(z_k^x, z_l^y | x_i, y_j, c_m),$$

$$\bar{P}_B = \bar{P}(z_k^x, z_l^y, c_m | x_i, y_j).$$

These steps are iteratively computed until convergence. If the difference in the values of the Q-function before and after an iteration decrease below threshold, we regard it as converged.

In the actual EM computation, we use the tempered EM [12] instead of the standard EM already explained, because the tempered EM can avoid an inaccurate estimation of the model caused by "over-confidence" in computing the posterior probabilities. In the tempered EM, one can adjust the confidence of a currently estimated probability value by hyper-parameter β. We performed experiments described later with all the values of β in $\{1.0, 0.9, 0.8, 0.7, 0.6, 0.5\}$. Furthermore, too much influence by unlabeled data sometimes deteriorates the model estimation. Therefore, we introduce another hyper-parameter λ following Nigam et al. [19]. The λ acts as a weight on unlabeled data. For the extended product model, unlabeled training samples in D^u are weighted by multiplying the second term of (2) by λ. We performed experiments described later with all the values of λ in $\{1.0, 0.1, 0.001, ..., 1 \times 10^{-7}\}$. Details on the hyper-parameters β and λ can be obtained in previous respective studies [12,19].

3.3   Causality Detection

In this section, we describe how to detect causality between two events using the models described. First, we describe a method for causality detection for four models in which class variable C is incorporated: (c) NB, (d) Class-Asp, (e) Class-Pro, and (f) LNB. After that, we describe a method for causality detection for the remaining models, (a) and (b).

For models (c), (d), (e), and (f), given an event pair $\langle x, y \rangle$, causality between the input events is detected using the formula

$$\hat{c} = argmax_{c_m} P(c_m | x, y). \tag{10}$$

Actually, the concrete calculating formulas for $P(c_m | x, y)$ differ. For example, the formula corresponding to (e) is equation (11):

$$P(c_m | x, y) = \frac{\sum_{z_k^x} \sum_{z_l^y} P(x | z_k^x) P(y | z_l^y) P(z_k^x | c_m) P(z_l^y | z_k^x, c_m) P(c_m)}{\sum_{z_k^x} \sum_{z_l^y} \sum_{c_m} P(x | z_k^x) P(y | z_l^y) P(z_k^x | c_m) P(z_l^y | z_k^x, c_m) P(c_m)}. \tag{11}$$

Equation (10) cannot be applied to models (a) and (b) because these two models do not have class variable C. We apply another procedure to (a) and (b). When an input event pair $\langle x, y \rangle$ is given, we first calculate the degree of co-occurrence of $\langle x, y \rangle$ with point-wise mutual information (PMI) [3]:

$$PMI(x, y) = log \frac{P(x, y)}{P(x) P(y)}. \tag{12}$$

Then, we set a threshold σ for PMI and detect causality of input pair $\langle x, y \rangle$ depending on the relationship between PMI and σ:

$$\langle x, y \rangle \text{ holds} \begin{cases} \text{causality} & \text{if } PMI(x, y) \geq \sigma \\ \text{no causality} & \text{otherwise.} \end{cases}$$

4   Experiments

We conducted two experiments in order to demonstrate that our proposed models with a class variable and latent variable(s) provide promising results for automatic causality detection between two events. First, we describe general settings of the experiments in Section 4.1. After that, we report our experimental results in Section 4.2 and Section 4.3.

4.1   Settings

We used triplets extracted from an annotated corpus created by Inui et al. [15] as labeled dataset D^l. In this corpus, causal relation information was added to social aspect domain articles of the Mainichi newspaper [17], written in Japanese. The articles include content mainly with respect to accidents, troubles, and other occurrences in our life. The following are example event pairs holding causal relations:

(1) a. hidoi yakedo-wo ou — byohin-he hakobu,

   (*to get a serious burn — to be transferred to the hospital*)

   b. tabemono-ga nodo-ni tumaru — shinu.

   (*to choke on food — to die*)

We extracted 200 positive and 200 negative samples (event pairs) from this corpus. To guarantee the reliability of the data used for the experiments, we selected positive samples that more than one annotator have judged as holding causal relations, and selected negative samples that no annotators have judged as holding causal relations. All the events in the 400 samples were represented in the form of verb phrases. We observed that only 4 samples in 200 positive samples co-occur with cue phrases "tame" and "node" (the same meaning as "because" and "since" in English) in the articles. Remember that the existing cue-phrase-based methods can treat only 4 samples, but they cannot treat all remaining samples well.

Usually events are represented with more than one word, typically represented with a verb phrase, such as the above. Fortunately, we observed in our preliminary analysis of text articles included in the corpus that *causality of a verb phrase (VP) pair tends to depend only on verb pair information in the VP pair if the VP pair has a syntactic dependency relation between two verbs*[2]. From this observation, in this work, we treat only verb information to reduce the complexity of model structures by estimating the statistical models described in Section 3. For example, suppose that the following sample S, in which the verb pair has a syntactic dependency relation, is in the dataset.

S. ⟨ tabemono-ga nodo-ni tumaru, shinu ⟩
   (*to choke on food*)   (*to die*)

In this case, we generated the following verb pair T from S and used it to estimate the models.

T. ⟨ tumaru, shinu ⟩
   (*to choke (on something))* *(to die)*

Naturally, some exceptions occur. In future work, we have to make precise modeling of events involving both the verb and information pertaining to the argument.

As unlabeled dataset D^u, we used verb pairs extracted from the same newspaper articles as those of D^l. All verb pairs in D^u have syntactic dependency relations between two verbs. We observed that only approximately 5% of samples in D^u co-occur with cue phrases "tame" and "node" in the articles. To investigate the effectiveness of unlabeled data, we used three different amounts of unlabeled data (100 samples, 1,000 samples, and 10,000 samples).

---

[2] This tendency would be language dependent.

Table 1. Results of model comparison (F-measure)

# of labeled samples	# of unlabeled samples	Incorporation of Dependencies			
		No		Yes	
		(c) NB	(f) LNB	(d) Class-Asp	(e) Class-Pro
320	0 (pure-supervised)	.298	.533	.319	**.583**
	100 (semi-supervised)	.328	.569	.588	**.610**
(=400 × 4/5)	1,000 (semi-supervised)	.459	.595	**.644**	.641
	10,000 (semi-supervised)	.623	.631	.677	**.678**

We employed 5-fold cross validation for the evaluation. The evaluation measure is an F-measure calculated with the following formulas.

$$F = 2RP/(R + P)$$
$$R = |A \cap B|/|A|$$
$$P = |A \cap B|/|B|$$

A = set of event pairs holding causal relations

B = set of event pairs detected by a model as holding causal relations

4.2 Results(1): The Effectiveness of Incorporating Dependencies Between Two Events into Causal Models

First, we compared four models: (c) NB, (d) Class-Asp, (e) Class-Pro, and (f) LNB to demonstrate the effectiveness of incorporating dependencies between two events into causal models. Each model incorporates the class variable C into itself. The results are shown in Table 1. Each row represents the F-measure values obtained using different sizes of the unlabeled data. In particular, the first row (size of the unlabeled data = 0) shows the results obtained in an entirely (pure) supervised fashion, while other rows show the results obtained in semi-supervised fashion. The best result for each row is indicated in bold-faced type. As mentioned in Section 3.2, we have to set two hyper-parameters β and λ to estimate model parameters. We attempted several combinations of β and λ and empirically set these values so that each model obtains the best result. Automatic hyper-parameter optimization will be addressed in the future.

Table 1 clarifies that the F-measure value of model (c) NB is lower than those of (d) Class-Asp, (e) Class-Pro, and (f) LNB. The main difference in (c) from (d), (e), and (f) is that the model may or may not include latent variable(s). Model (c) includes no latent variables. However, models (d), (e), and (f) include one or two latent variable(s). Based on these results, we found that the latent variable(s) contribute to causality detection. Furthermore, models (d) and (e) outperform model (f). As stated in Section 3.1, while dependency information between two events is taken into consideration in models (d)

Table 2. Advantage of class variable

	Model	F-measure
without class variable	(a) Aspect	.638
	(b) Product	.641
with class variable	(d) Class-Asp	.730
	(e) Class-Pro	.829

and (e) via latent variable(s), no dependency information between the two events is taken into consideration in model (f). Therefore, incorporating dependencies between two events into models is effective.

We can see that causal models were successful when used in a semi-supervised fashion. Since the first row of Table 1 shows lower performance than the others, entirely (pure) supervised learning did not work as well as compared with semi-supervised learning. The performance of causality detection increases as the amount of unlabeled data increases.

4.3   Results(2): The Effectiveness of Class Labels

Next, we examined the effectiveness of class variable C. For that purpose, we compared (d) Class-Asp with (a) Aspect and (e) Class-Pro with (b) Product. Note here that the models (d) and (e) have a class variable C and these models are obtained in semi-supervised fashion, while the models (a) and (b) have no class variables and these models are obtained in un-supervised fashion.

As mentioned in Section 3.3, for the models (a) Aspect and (b) Product, we have to set a threshold σ for PMI. We set σ and calculated the F-measure as follows. We measured every F-measure value corresponding to σ by changing the threshold value σ. Then, the best F-measure value for each model was obtained. The results are shown in the first row of Table 2. To achieve fair comparisons, we also defined a threshold υ for $P(\hat{c}|x, y)$ in which the class $\hat{c}$ was obtained by equation (10) for the models (d) Class-Asp and (e) Class-Pro. We reserved final outputs for input pairs if $P(\hat{c}|x, y) \leq \upsilon$. We measured every F-measure value corresponding to υ by changing the threshold value υ for $P(\hat{c}|x, y)$. Then, the best F-measure value for each model was obtained. The results are shown in the second row of Table 2. We used 10,000 samples as unlabeled data for training in each model.

Table 2 demonstrates that although little labeled data was used, the class variable provides us with the useful information for causality detection.

4.4   Examples

Finally, we show some examples of event pairs holding causal relations obtained by the Class-Pro model in Figure 2. (The samples are represented in English for readers. However, we actually used Japanese text.) Each pair in Figure 2 was not included in our labeled dataset. Our models demonstrate great potential for causality detection of unknown event pairs.

CAUSE		EFFECT
a railcar hits a falling stone	—	*it is derailed*
someone jumps in front of a train	—	*(s)he dies*
a car is driven on the sidewalk	—	*it hits a person*
a car strays into the opposite traffic lane	—	*it crashes into other cars*
a company runs out of money	—	*it goes bankrupt*

Fig. 2. Examples of event pairs holding causal relations obtained by Class-Pro model

5   Conclusion

In this paper, we described models for detecting causality between two events extracted from text. Our models are expanded versions of statistical co-occurrence models. Our experiments demonstrate that models with a class variable and latent variable(s) provide promising results for automatic causality detection between two events.

The following issues will need to be addressed to refine our models.

– We constructed causal models only with verb information to reduce the complexity of model structures. However, we have to develop methodology for precise modeling of events to create more accurate knowledge acquisition methods for causal relations.
– We focused on causal relations between two events independent of some other events around them. However, events in the same context (or environment) are generally assumed to be mutually dependent. Therefore, we should extend causal models to treat *causal chains*. Using the framework of Bayesian networks [20,4] would be one possible approach for constructing statistical models for causal chains from text, such as the one made by [23].

References

1. James F. Allen. *Recognizing intentions from natural language utterances. In M. Brady and R.C. Berwick (Eds.), Computational models of discourse.* MIT Press, 1983.
2. Du-Seong Chang and Key-Sun Choi. Causal relation extraction using cue phrase and lexical pair probabilities. In *Proceedings of the 1st International Joint Conference of Natural Language Processing (IJCNLP-2004)*, pages 61–70, 2004.
3. Kenneth W. Church and Patrick Hanks. Word association norms, mutual information, and lexicography. In *Proceedings of the 27th. Annual Meeting of the Association for Computational Linguistics (ACL-1989)*, pages 76–83, 1989.
4. Gregory Cooper, David Heckerman, and Christopher Meek. A Bayesian approach to causal discovery. Technical report, Microsoft Research Advanced Technology Division, Microsoft Corporation, Technical Report MSR-TR-97-05, 1997.
5. Arthur P. Dempster, Nan M. Laird, and Donald B. Rubin. Maximum likelihood from incomplete data via the EM algorithm. *Journal of the Royal Statistical Society, Series B*, 34:1–38, 1977.
6. Christiane Fellbaum. *WordNet: An Electronic Lexical Database.* The MIT Press, 1998.

7. Daniela Garcia. COATIS, an NLP system to locate expressions of actions connected by causality links. In *Proceedings of The 10th European Knowledge Acquisition Workshop*, pages 347–352, 1997.
8. Roxana Girju. Automatic detection of causal relations for question answering. In *Proceedings of Annual Meeting of the Association for Computational Linguistics, Workshop on Multilingual Summarization and Question Answering - Machine Learning and Beyond*, 2003.
9. Roxana Girju and Dan Moldovan. Mining answers for causation questions. In *Proc. The AAAI Spring Symposium on Mining Answers from Texts and Knowledge Bases*, 2002.
10. Jerry. R. Hobbs. Coherence and co-reference. *Cognitive Science*, 1:67–82, 1979.
11. Jerry. R. Hobbs. On the coherence and structure of discourse. Technical report, Technical Report CSLI-85-37, Center for The Study of Language and Information, 1985.
12. Thomas Hofmann. Unsupervised learning by probabilistic latent semantic analysis. *Machine Learning Journal*, 42(1):177–196, 2001.
13. Thomas Hofmann and Jan Puzicha. Statistical models for co-occurrence data. Technical Report AIM-1625, Artificial Intelligence Laboratory, MIT, 1998.
14. Takashi Inui, Kentaro Inui, and Yuji Matsumoto. What kinds and amounts of causal knowledge can be acquired from text by using connective markers as clues? In *The 6th. International Conference on Discovery Science*, volume 2843 of *Lecture Notes in Artificial Intelligence*, pages 180–193. Springer-Verlag, 2003.
15. Takashi Inui and Manabu Okumura. Investigating the characteristics of causal relations in Japanese text. In *Proceedings of Annual Meeting of the Association for Computational Linguistics, Workshop on Frontiers in Corpus Annotation II: Pie in the Sky*, pages 37–44, 2005.
16. Christopher S. G. Khoo, S. Chan, and Y. Niu. Extracting causal knowledge from a medical database using graphical patterns. In *Proceedings of The 38th. Annual Meeting of The Association for Computational Linguistics (ACL-2000)*, pages 336–343, 2000.
17. Mainichi. Mainichi Shimbun CD-ROM version, 1995.
18. Tom Mitchell. *Machine Learning*. McGraw-Hill, 1997.
19. Kamal Nigam, Andrew K. McCallum, Sebastian Thrun, and Tom M. Mitchell. Text classification from labeled and unlabeled documents using EM. *Machine Learning*, 39(2/3): 103–134, 2000.
20. Judea Pearl. *Causality: Models, Reasoning, and Inference*. Cambridge Universiy Press, 2000.
21. Jian Pei, Jiawei. Han, Behzad Mortazavi-Asi, Helen Pinto, Qiming Chen, Umeshwar Dayal, and Mei-Chun Hsu. PrefixSpan: mining sequential patterns efficiently by prefix projected pattern growth. In *Proceedings of 1st. Conference of Data Enginnering (ICDE-2001)*, pages 215–226, 2001.
22. James Pustejovsky. *The Generative Lexicon*. MIT Press, 1995.
23. Olivia Sanchez-Graillet and Massimo Poesio. Acquiring bayesian networks from text. In *Proceedings of the 4th International Conference on Language Resources and Evaluation (LREC-2004)*, pages 955–958, 2004.
24. Akira Terada. *A Study of Text Mining Techniques Using Natural Language Processing*. PhD thesis, Tokyo Institute of Technology, 2003.
25. Kentaro Torisawa. An unsupervised learning method for commonsensical inference rules on events. In *Proceedings of the Second CoLogNet-ElsNET Symposium*, pages 146–153, 2003.
26. U.S. National Library of Medicine. The MEDLINE database, 2001. See also, http://www.ncbi.nlm.nih.gov/PubMed/.
27. Vladimir N. Vapnik. *The Nature of Statistical Learning Theory*. Springer, 1995.
28. Nevin L. Zhang, Thomas D. Nielsen, and Finn V. Jensen. Latent variable discovery in classification models. *Artificial Intelligence in Medicine*, 30(3):283–299, 2004.

Finite-State Technology
as a Programming Environment

Shuly Wintner

Department of Computer Science, University of Haifa, 31905 Haifa, Israel
shuly@cs.haifa.ac.il

Abstract. Finite-state technology is considered the preferred model for representing the phonology and morphology of natural languages. The attractiveness of this technology for natural language processing stems from four sources: modularity of the design, due to the closure properties of regular languages and relations; the compact representation that is achieved through minimization; efficiency, which is a result of linear recognition time with finite-state devices; and reversibility, resulting from the declarative nature of such devices.

However, when wide-coverage grammars are considered, finite-state technology does not scale up well, and the benefits of this technology can be overshadowed by the limitations it imposes as a programming environment for language processing. This paper focuses on several aspects of large-scale grammar development. Using a real-world benchmark, we compare a finite-state implementation with an equivalent Java program with respect to ease of development, modularity, maintainability of the code and space and time efficiency. We identify two main problems, *abstraction* and *incremental development*, which are currently not addressed sufficiently well by finite-state technology, and which we believe should be the focus of future research and development.

1   Introduction

Finite-state technology (FST) denotes the use of finite-state devices, such as automata and transducers, in natural language processing (NLP). Since the early works which demonstrated the applicability of this technology to linguistic representation [1,2,3], FST is considered adequate for describing the phonological and morphological processes of the world's languages [4,5]. Even non-concatenative processes such as circumfixation, root-and-pattern morphology or reduplication, were shown to be in principle implementable in FST [6,7].

The utility of FST for NLP was emphasized by the implementation of several toolboxes which provide extended regular expression languages and compilers which convert expressions to finite-state automata and transducers. These include *INTEX* [8]; *FSM* [9], which is a unix-based set of programs for manipulating automata and transducers; *FSA Utilities* [10], which is a freely available, Prolog implemented system; and *XFST* [5], which is a commercial package assumed to be the most suitable for linguistic applications by providing the most expressive language.

A. Gelbukh (Ed.): CICLing 2007, LNCS 4394, pp. 97–106, 2007.

The benefits of FST for NLP stem from several properties of finite-state devices:

True representation: Following the pioneering work of Johnson [1], it is now clear that the kind of phonological and morphological rules that are common in linguistic theories can be directly implemented as finite-state relations. The implementation of linguistically motivated rules in FST is therefore straightforward and direct [11].

Modularity: The closure properties of regular languages and relations provide various means for combining regular expressions, supporting a variety of operations on the languages these expressions denote. For example, closure under *union* facilitates a separate development of two grammar fragments which can then be directly combined in a single operation. The most useful operations under which transductions are closed is probably *composition*, which is the central vehicle for implementing *replace rules* [3,11].

Compactness: Finite-state automata can be minimized, guaranteeing that for a given language, an automaton with a minimal number of states can always be generated. Toolboxes can apply minimization either explicitly or implicitly to improve storage requirements.

Efficiency: When an automaton is deterministic, recognition is optimally efficient (linear in the length of the string to be recognized). Automata can always be determinized, and toolboxes can take advantage of this to improve time efficiency.

Reversibility: Finite-state automata and transducers are inherently declarative: it is the application program which either implements recognition or generation. In particular, transducers can be used to map strings from the upper language to the lower language or vice versa with no changes in the underlying finite-state device.

These benefits encouraged the development of several large-scale morphological grammars for a variety of languages, including some with complex morphology such as German, French, Finnish, Turkish, Arabic and Hebrew.

The main claim of this paper, however, is that finite-state technology is still inferior to its alternatives when the development of large-scale grammars is concerned. This claim is supported by a realistic experiment defining a sophisticated morphological task, both using FST (section 2) and with a direct implementation in Java of the same grammar (section 3). We compare the two approaches in section 4 along several axes. The conclusion (section 5) is the identification of two main Achilles Heels in contemporary technology: the lack of *abstraction* mechanisms and the computational burden of incremental changes. We believe that these two issues should be the focus of future research in finite-state technology.

2   A Motivating Example

In order to evaluate the scalability of finite-state technology we consider, as a benchmark, a large-scale task: accounting for the morphological and orthographic phenomena of Hebrew, a natural language with non-trivial morphology. Clearly, languages with simple morphology (e.g., English) do not benefit from FST approaches, simply because it is so inexpensive to generate and store all the inflected forms. It is only when relatively complicated morphological processes are involved that the benefits of FST become apparent, and Hebrew is chosen here only as a particular example; the observations reported in section 4 are valid in general, for all similar tasks.

Hebrew, like other Semitic languages, has a rich and complex morphology. The major word formation machinery is root-and-pattern, where roots are sequences of three (typically) or more consonants and patterns are sequences of vowels and, sometimes, also consonants, with "slots" into which the root's consonants are inserted. After the root combines with the pattern, some morpho-phonological alterations take place, which may be non-trivial. The combination of a root with a pattern produces a *lexeme*, which can then be inflected in various forms. Inflectional morphology is highly productive and consists mostly of suffixes, but sometimes of prefixes or circumfixes. The morphological problems are amplified by issues of orthography. The standard Hebrew script leaves most of the vowels unspecified. Furthermore, many particles, including prepositions, conjunctions and the definite article, attach to the words which immediately follow them. As a result, surface forms are highly ambiguous.

The finite-state grammar which we used as a benchmark here is HAMSAH [12], an XFST implementation of Hebrew morphology. The grammar is obtained by composing a large-scale lexicon of Hebrew (over 20,000 entries) with a large set of rules, implementing mostly morphological and orthographic processes in the language. As the lexicon is developed independently [13] and is represented in XML, it must be converted to XFST before it can be incorporated in the grammar. This is done by a set of Perl scripts which had to be specifically written for this purpose. In other words, the system itself is not purely finite-state, and we maintain that few large-scale systems for morphological analysis can be purely finite-state, as such systems must interact with independently developed components such as lexicons, annotation tools, user interfaces etc.

A specialized set of rules implements the morphological processes which apply to each major part of speech. For example, figure 1 depicts a somewhat simplified version of the rule which accounts for the *wt* suffix of Hebrew nouns. This rule makes extensive use of composition (denoted by '.o.') and replace rules ('->' and '<-'). The effect of this rule is dual: on the surface level, it accounts for alterations in the concatenation of the suffix with the stem (e.g., *iih* becomes *ih*, *wt* changes to *wi* and a final *h* or *t* are elided); on the lexical level, it changes the specification of *number* from *singular* to *plural*.

The rule should be read from the center outwards. The variable **noun** denotes the set of all lexical items whose part of speech is noun; by default, these nouns are singular masculine. In XFST, a set of words is identified with with the identity transduction which relates each word in the set with itself. The first composition on top of the **noun** transduction selects only those nouns whose **plural** attribute is lexically specified as **wt** (other nouns may be lexically specified for a different plural suffix). Of those, only the ones whose **number** attribute is **singular** are selected. Then, the value **singular** in the lexical (upper) string is replaced by **plural** in the context of immediately following the attribute **number**. In the surface (lower) language, meanwhile, a set of compositions operators takes care of the necessary orthographic changes, and finally, the plural suffix *wt* is concatenated to the end of the surface string.

```
define pluralWTNoun [
 [
  [ plural <- singular || number _ ]
  .o. $[number singular]
  .o. $[plural wt]
  .o. noun
  .o. [ i i h -> i h || _ .#. ]
  .o. [ i t -> i || _ .#. ]
  .o. [ w t -> w i || _ .#. ]
  .o. [ [h|t] -> 0 || _ .#. ]
 ] [ 0 .x. [w t] ]
];
```

Fig. 1. XFST account of plural nouns

This rule is a good example of how a single phenomenon is factored out and accounted for independently of other phenomena: the rule refers to lexical information, such as 'number' or 'plural', but completely ignores irrelevant information such as, say, gender. However, it also hints at how information is manipulated by regular expressions. Since finite-state networks have no memory, save for the state, all information is encoded by strings which are manipulated by the rules. Thus, a simple operation such as changing the value of the *number* feature from *singular* to *plural* must be carried out by the same replace rules which account for the changes to the surface form. Furthermore, there is no way to structure such information, as is common in programming languages; and there is no way to encapsulate it.

3   An Alternative Implementation

We re-implemented the HAMSAH grammar directly as a Java program. The method we used was *analysis by generation*: we first generated all the inflected forms induced by the lexicon and store them in a database; then, analysis is simply a database lookup. It is common to think that for languages with rich morphology such a method is impractical. While this may have been the case in the past, contemporary computers can efficiently store and retrieve millions of inflected forms. Of course, this method would break in the face of an infinite lexicon (which can easily be represented with FST), but for most practical purposes it is safe to assume that natural language lexicons are finite.

To separate linguistic knowledge from processing code as much as possible, our Java implementation uses a database of *rules*, which are simple string transductions intended to account for simple (mostly morpheme boundary) morphological and orthographic alterations. When generating inflected forms, the program identifies certain conditions (e.g., a plural suffix *wt* is to be attached to a noun). It then looks up this condition in the rule database and retrieves the action to apply, depending on the suffix of the input string. An example of the rule database, with alterations pertaining to the suffix *wt* (cf. figure 1), is depicted in figure 2. For most morphological processes, solutions such as this can accurately stand for linguistic rules of the form depicted in figure 1.

When input ends in: *iih it   wt h, t* default
Replace it by: *ih i   wi* ε
Then add: *wt wt wt wt   wt*

Fig. 2. Direct account of plural nouns

Note that rules such as the one depicted in figure 2 are *generation* rules, and must not be confused with the kind of ad-hoc rules used at run time for, e.g., stemming. They fully reflect the linguistic knowledge encoded in finite-state replace rules. Granted, the example rule is simplistic, and more complex phenomena require more complicated representation, but since most of morphology takes place along morpheme boundaries, this is a reasonable representation.

The morphological analyzer was obtained by directly implementing the rules and applying them to the lexicon. The number of inflected forms (before attaching prefixes) is 473,880 (over 300,000 of those are inflected nouns, and close to 150,000 are inflected verb forms). In addition to inflected forms, the analyzer also allows as many as 174 different sequences of prefix particles to be attached to words; separation of prefixes from inflected forms is done at analysis time. The direct implementation is equivalent to the finite-state grammar: this was verified by exhaustively generating all the inflected forms with each of the systems and analyzing them with the other system.

4   Comparison and Evaluation

Having described the XFST benchmark grammar and its direct Java implementation, we now compare the two approaches along several axes. It is important to emphasize that we do not wish to compare the two systems, but rather the methodology. In particular, we chose XFST as it is one of the most efficient, and certainly the most expressive, FST toolbox available. A recent comparison of XFST with the FSA Utilities package [14] shows that the latter simply cannot handle grammars of the scale of HAMSAH. The following is a list of issues in which finite-state technology turned out to be problematic compared with the alternative; in the next section we focus on issues that we believe should be given more attention in future research on FST. All experiments were done on a dual 2GHz processor Linux machine with 2.5Gb of memory.

Truthfulness. One of the assets of FST is that it allows for a very accurate implementation of linguistic rules. However, a good organization of the software can provide a clear separation between linguistic knowledge and processing in any programming environment, so that linguistic rules can be expressed concisely and declaratively, as exemplified in figure 2.

Reversibility. A clear advantage of FST is that grammars are fully reversible. However, with the analysis by generation paradigm the same holds also for a direct implementation: the generator is directly implemented, and the analyzer is implemented as search in the database of generated forms.

Expressivity. Here, the disadvantages of finite-state technology as a programming environment are clear. Programming with finite-state technology is very different from programming in ordinary languages, mainly due to the highly constrained expressive power of regular relations (programmers sometimes feel that they are working with their hands tied behind their backs). While FST can theoretically account for non-concatenative processes, existing toolboxes provide a partial, and sometimes overly complicated, solutions for such problems. Sometimes a trans-regular operation is called for, and many other times the constrained expressivity of regular relations is too limiting.

Portability. XFST is a proprietary package with three versions available for three common operating systems. Other finite-state toolboxes are freer; FSA is open source, but as we noted earlier it simply cannot cope with grammars the size of HAMSAH. FSM is available for a variety of Unix operating systems, as a binary only, whereas INTEX is distributed as a Windows executable. In contrast, a Java implementation can be delivered to users with all kinds of (contemporary) operating systems and hardware, and is optimally portable. The practical portability limitations directly hamper the utilization of finite-state technology in practical, commercial systems.

Abstraction. Large-scale morphological grammars tend to be extremely *non-modular*. Each surface string is associated, during its processing, with a lexical counterpart which describes its structure. The lexical string is constantly rewritten by the rules, as in figure 1. Due to the inherent sequentiality of strings, all the information which is associated with surface strings is encoded sequentially. In particular, adding a piece of information (e.g., adding the feature *gender* to an existing grammar which did not specify this property) requires a change in all the rules which account for this information; there is no way to abstract away from the actual implementation of this information, and the grammar developer must be consistent with respect to where this information is specified (i.e., whether it precedes or follows information on *number*).

Since information cannot be encapsulated and the language provides no abstraction mechanisms, collaborative development of finite-state grammars is difficult. All grammar developers must be aware of how information is represented at all times. Furthermore, since the only data type is strings, debugging becomes problematic: very few errors can be detected at compile time.

In contrast, a direct Java implementation benefits from all the advantages of developing in an object-oriented environment. For example, the modules which inflect nouns and adjectives inherit from the same module, accounting for all *nominals*, which in turn inherits from a general module of inflection rules.

Collaborative development. A different facet of modularity has to do with the qualifications of the grammar developers. In order to take advantage of the full power of XFST, grammar developers must be simultaneously trained linguists and experienced programmers. With a direct implementation, a true interdisciplinary collaboration is enabled where a linguist can be in charge of characterizing the linguistic phenomena (and building the rule database) and a programmer can be responsible only for the actual implementation.

Maintenance. A by-product of the non-modularity of FST grammars is that maintaining them is difficult and expensive. It is hard to find a single person who is knowledgeable in all aspects of the design, and any change in the grammar is painful. This must be added to the poor compile-time performance, which again hampers maintainability.

Compile-time efficiency. A major obstacle in the development of XFST grammars is the speed of compilation. As is well known, many of the finite-state operators result in huge networks: theoretically, composition of networks of m and n states yields a network with $O(m \times n)$ states, and replace rules are implemented using composition. This leads to temporary networks which are sometimes larger than the available memory, requiring disk access and thereby slowing compilation down dramatically. While automata can always be minimized, this is not the case for transducers [15].

Theoretically, it is very easy to come up with very small regular expressions whose compilation is intractable. For any integer $n > 2$, there exists an n-state automaton A, such that any automaton that accepts the complement of $L(A)$ needs at least 2^{n-2} states [16]. An example of an XFST expression whose compilation time is exponential in n is: `~[ [a|b]* a [a|b]^n b [a|b]* ]`. In practice, the complete Hebrew grammar is represented, in XFST, by a network of approximately 2 million states and 2.2 million transitions. Compiling the entire network takes over 48 minutes and requires 3Gb of memory.

Compilation time is usually considered a negligible criterion for evaluating system performance. However, when developing a large-scale system, the ability to make minor changes and quickly re-make the system is crucial. With XFST, modification of even a single lexical entry requires at least an intersection of (the XFST representation of) this entry with the network representing the rules which apply to it. As a concrete example, adding a single two-character proper name (which does not inflect) to the lexicon increased the size of the network by 9 states and 10 arcs, but took almost three minutes to compile. Adding a two-character adjective resulted in the addition of 27 states and 30 arcs, and took about the same time.

In the direct implementation, modification of a single lexical entry requires generation of all inflected forms of this entry, which takes a fraction of a second; the time it takes to generate k lexical entries is proportional to k and is independent of the size of the remainder of the system. The analysis program is not altered.

To summarize the differences, figure 3 shows the time it takes to compile a network when k lexical entries are modified, for three values of k, corresponding to the number of adjectives, adverbs and the size of the entire lexicon. This time is compared with the time it takes to generate all inflected forms of these sub-lexicons in the analysis by generation paradigm.

#items	360 (adverbs)	1,648 (adjectives)	21,400 (all)
FST	13:47	13:55	48:12
Java	0:14	3:59	30:34

Fig. 3. Compilation/generation times (in minutes) when some lexical items change

Run-time efficiency. While finite-state automata guarantee linear recognition time, this is not the case with transducers, which cannot always be determinized [17]. Even when a device can be determinized, the determinization algorithm is inefficient (theoretically, the size of the deterministic automaton can be exponential in the size of its non-deterministic counterpart).

As it turns out, storing a database of half a million inflected forms (along with their analyses) is inexpensive, and retrieving items from the database can be done very efficiently. We experimented with two versions: one uses MySQL as the database and the other loads the inflected forms into a hash table. In this latter version, most of the time is spent on loading the database, and retrieval time is negligible.

We compared the performance of the two systems on four tasks, analyzing text files of 10, 100, 1,000 and 10,000 tokens. The results are summarized in figure 4, and clearly demonstrate the superiority of the direct implementation. In terms of memory requirements, XFST requires approximately 57Mb of memory, whereas the Java implementation uses no more than 10Mb. This is not a significant issue with contemporary hardware.

5   Discussion

We compared the process of developing a large-scale morphological grammar for Hebrew with finite-state technology with a direct implementation of the morphological rules in Java. Our conclusion is that finite-state technology remains superior to its alternatives with respect to the true representation of linguistic knowledge, and is therefore more adequate for smaller-scale grammars, especially those whose goal is to demonstrate specific linguistic phenomena rather than form the basis of large practical systems. However, viewed as a programming

#Tokens	10	100	1,000	10,000
FST		1.25	2.40	12.97	118.71
Java+MySQL	1.24	3.04	8.84	44.94
Java+Hash	5.00	5.15	5.59	7.64

Fig. 4. Time performance of both analyzers (in seconds)

environment, FST suffers from severe limitations, the most significant of which are lack of abstraction and difficulties in incremental processing.

Abstraction is the essence of computer science and the key to software development. Working with regular expressions and developing rules which use strings as the only data structure does not leave much space for sophisticated abstraction. Several works attempt to remedy this problem. XFST itself provides a limited solution, in the form of *flag diacritics* [5]. These are feature-value pairs which can be added to the underlying machines in order to add limited memory to networks; a similar solution, which is fully worked-out mathematically, is provided by *finite-state registered automata* [7]. These approaches are too low-level to provide the kind of abstraction that programmers have become used to. A step in the right direction is the incorporation of feature structures and unification into finite-state transducers [18], and in particular the recent proposal to use typed feature structures as the entities on which such transducers operate [19]. More research is needed in order to fully develop this direction and incorporate its consequences into a finite-state based grammar development framework.

The problem of incremental grammar development, exemplified in figure 3, can also be remedied by incorporating some recent theoretical results, in particular in incremental construction of lexicons [20,21], into an existing framework. Ordinary programming languages benefit from decades of research and innovation in compilation theory and optimization. In order for finite-state technology to become a viable programming environment for natural language morphology applications, more research is needed along the lines suggested here.

Acknowledgments. This work was funded by the Israeli Ministry of Science and Technology, under the auspices of the Knowledge Center for Processing Hebrew. The research was supported by a grant from the Israel Internet Association. I am very grateful to Shlomo Yona for implementing the XFST grammar and to Dalia Bojan for implementing the Java system. Kemal Oflazer provided useful comments on an earlier version of this paper. I also wish to thank Yael Cohen-Sygal, Alon Itai, Nurit Melnik and Shira Schwartz for their help. The views expressed in this paper as well as all remaining errors are, of course, my own.

References

1. Johnson, C.D.: Formal Aspects of Phonological Description. Mouton, The Hague (1972)
2. Koskenniemi, K.: Two-Level Morphology: a General Computational Model for Word-Form Recognition and Production. The Department of General Linguistics, University of Helsinki (1983)

3. Kaplan, R.M., Kay, M.: Regular models of phonological rule systems. Computational Linguistics **20** (1994) 331–378
4. Roche, E., Schabes, Y., eds.: Finite-State Language Processing. Language, Speech and Communication. MIT Press, Cambridge, MA (1997)
5. Beesley, K.R., Karttunen, L.: Finite-State Morphology: Xerox Tools and Techniques. CSLI, Stanford (2003)
6. Beesley, K.R.: Arabic morphology using only finite-state operations. In Rosner, M., ed.: Proceedings of the Workshop on Computational Approaches to Semitic languages, Montreal, Quebec, COLING-ACL'98 (1998) 50–57
7. Cohen-Sygal, Y., Wintner, S.: Finite-state registered automata for non-concatenative morphology. Computational Linguistics **32** (2006) 49–82
8. Silberztein, M.: Dictionnaires électroniques et analyse automatique de textes : le système INTEX. Masson, Paris (1993)
9. Mohri, M., Pereira, F., Riley, M.: The design principles of a weighted finite-state transducer library. Theoretical Computer Science **231** (2000) 17–32
10. van Noord, G., Gerdemann, D.: An extendible regular expression compiler for finite-state approaches in natural language processing. In Boldt, O., Jürgensen, H., eds.: Automata Implementation. Number 2214 in Lecture Notes in Computer Science. Springer (2001)
11. Karttunen, L.: The replace operator. In: Proceedings of the Annual Meeting of the Association for Computational Linguistics. (1995) 16–23
12. Yona, S., Wintner, S.: A finite-state morphological grammar of Hebrew. Natural Language Engineering (Forthcoming)
13. Itai, A., Wintner, S., Yona, S.: A computational lexicon of contemporary Hebrew. In: Proceedings of The fifth international conference on Language Resources and Evaluation (LREC-2006), Genoa, Italy (2006)
14. Cohen-Sygal, Y., Wintner, S.: XFST2FSA: Comparing two finite-state toolboxes. In: Proceedings of the ACL-2005 Workshop on Software, Ann Arbor, MI (2005)
15. Mohri, M.: Minimization algorithms for sequential transducers. Theoretical Computer Science **234** (2000) 177–201
16. Holzer, M., Kutrib, M.: State complexity of basic operations on nondeterministic finite automata. In: Implementation and Application of Automata (CIAA '02). (2002) 151–160
17. Mohri, M.: Finite-state transducers in language and speech processing. Computational Linguistics **23** (1997) 269–312
18. Zajac, R.: Feature structures, unification and finite-state transducers. In: FSMNLP'98: The International Workshop on Finite-state Methods in Natural Language Processing, Ankara, Turkey (1998)
19. Amtrup, J.W.: Morphology in machine translation systems: Efficient integration of finite state transducers and feature structure descriptions. Machine Translation **18** (2003) 217–238
20. Daciuk, J., Mihov, S., Watson, B.W., Watson, R.E.: Incremental construction of minimal acyclic finite-state automata. Computational Linguistics **26** (2000) 3–16
21. Carrasco, R.C., Forcada, M.L.: Incremental construction and maintenance of minimal finite-state automata. Computational Linguistics **28** (2002) 207–216

Morphological Disambiguation of Turkish Text with Perceptron Algorithm

Haşim Sak[1], Tunga Güngör[1], and Murat Saraçlar[2]

[1] Dept. of Computer Engineering,
Boğaziçi University, Bebek, 34342, Istanbul, Turkey
{hasim.sak,gungort}@boun.edu.tr
[2] Dept. of Electrical and Electronic Engineering,
Boğaziçi University, Bebek, 34342, Istanbul, Turkey
murat.saraclar@boun.edu.tr

Abstract. This paper describes the application of the perceptron algorithm to the morphological disambiguation of Turkish text. Turkish has a productive derivational morphology. Due to the ambiguity caused by complex morphology, a word may have multiple morphological parses, each with a different stem or sequence of morphemes. The methodology employed is based on ranking with perceptron algorithm which has been successful in some NLP tasks in English. We use a baseline statistical trigram-based model of a previous work to enumerate an n-best list of candidate morphological parse sequences for each sentence. We then apply the perceptron algorithm to rerank the n-best list using a set of 23 features. The perceptron trained to do morphological disambiguation improves the accuracy of the baseline model from 93.61% to 96.80%. When we train the perceptron as a POS tagger, the accuracy is 98.27%. Turkish morphological disambiguation and POS tagging results that we obtained is the best reported so far.

1 Introduction

Morphological disambiguation problem can be stated as finding the correct morphological parses of the words in a text given all the possible parses of the words. The parses can be obtained by using a morphological parser such as [1]. The morphological parsing of a word may result in multiple parses of that word due to the ambiguity in the root words and the morphemes, and the complex morphophonemic interaction between them ordered according to the morphotactics. Even to decide the part-of-speech tagging of a word, we may need to disambiguate the parses if they have different part-of-speech tags for the final derived word forms.

The agglutinative or inflective languages such as Turkish, Czech, Finnish, and Hungarian impose some difficulties in language processing due to the more complex morphology and relatively free word order in sentences when compared with languages like English. The morphemes carry syntactic and semantic information that is called morphosyntactic and morphosemantic features, respectively.

A. Gelbukh (Ed.): CICLing 2007, LNCS 4394, pp. 107–118, 2007.

Morphological disambiguation problem for these morphologically productive languages can also be considered as morphosyntactic tagging in analogy to part-of-speech tagging in other languages. The morphological disambiguation of text in these languages is required for further natural language processing tasks such as syntax parsing, word sense disambiguation, semantic parsing and analysis, language modeling for speech recogniton, etc. to be accomplished.

There have been generally two approaches to part-of-speech tagging. The rule-based approaches employ a set of hand-crafted linguistic rules that use the context information of a word to constrain the possible part-of-speech tags [2] or to assign a part-of-speech tag to that word [3]. These disambiguation rules can also be learned using transformation-based learning approach [4]. The statistical approaches select the most likely interpretation based on the estimation of statistics from unambiguously tagged text using a Markov model [5] or a maximum-entropy model [6] or ambiguously tagged text using a hidden Markov model [7].

The morphosyntactic tagging of agglutinative or inflective languages is more difficult due to the large number of tags. An exponential probabilistic model has been employed to tagging of the inflective language Czech [8]. Several constraint-based methods for morphological disambiguation in Turkish have been applied [9,10]. A trigram-based statistical model has also been used in morphological disambiguation of Turkish text [11]. This model has also been used in this work as a baseline and will be discussed in later sections. A recent work has employed a decision list induction algorithm called Greedy Prepend Algorithm (GPA) to learn morphological disambiguation rules for Turkish [12].

The voted or averaged perceptron algorithms that have been previously applied to classification problems [13] have also been adapted very successfully to common NLP tasks such as syntax parsing of English text [14] and part-of-speech tagging and noun phrase chunking [15].

In this paper we describe the application of ranking with perceptron algorithm to morphological disambiguation of Turkish text. We use a baseline trigram-based model of a previous work to enumerate n-best candidates of morphological parse sequences of sentences. We then apply the perceptron algorithm to rerank the n-best list using a set of features. In the following sections, we first state the morphological disambiguation problem formally and describe the baseline model. We then present the perceptron algorithm and the features incorporated in the model. We conclude with the experiments and results.

2   Morphological Disambiguation

Turkish is an agglutinative language with a productive inflectional and derivational morphology. The complex morphology of Turkish allows thousands of word form to be constructed from a single root word using inflectional and derivational suffixes. The morphological parsing of a word may result in multiple interpretations of that word due to this complex morphology. Morphological disambiguation problem can be stated as finding the correct morphological parses of the words in a text given all the possible parses of the words.

The example below shows the multiple interpretations for the Turkish word
`alın` with their parses as output from a Turkish morphological analyzer [1] and
their English gloss.

```
alın+Noun+A3sg+Pnon+Nom (forehead)
al+Adj^DB+Noun+Zero+A3sg+P2sg+Nom (your red)
al+Adj^DB+Noun+Zero+A3sg+Pnon+Gen (of red)
al+Verb+Pos+Imp+A2pl ((you) take)
al+Verb^DB+Verb+Pass+Pos+Imp+A2sg ((you) be taken)
alın+Verb+Pos+Imp+A2sg ((you) be offended)
```

As can be seen, some of the parses have different root words and have unrelated morphological features due to the complex morphology of Turkish. These
ambiguities mostly can be resolved using the contextual information, however
the relatively free word order of Turkish also poses some difficulties in the sense
that the limited context information cannot resolve the ambiguities. Some of the
ambiguities can only be solved using semantic or discourse knowledge.

2.1   Representation

Agglutinative or inflective languages encode more information than just part-of-
speech tag in a word thanks to the more complex morphology. The morphemes
that constitute a word carry syntactic and semantic information that is called
morphosyntactic and morphosemantic features, respectively. For morphological
disambiguation, we need to determine all the syntactic morphological features of
a word. Therefore morphological disambiguation can be called morphosyntactic
tagging in analogy to part-of-speech tagging. We will use the same representation
for the tags by Hakkani-Tür et al. in [11] where the full morphological parses of
the words including the root words and their morphological features are treated
as their morphosyntactic tags. An example that shows one of the morphological
parses of the word `alın` consisting of the root word and some morphological
features seperated using derivational boundary marker ^DB is given below.

```
al+Adj^DB+Noun+Zero+A3sg+P2sg+Nom (your red)
```

Due to the productive inflectional and derivational morphology, the vocabulary size of Turkish can be very large. The large vocabulary size causes data
sparseness problem and large number of out-of-vocabulary words when the word
forms are considered as the units in a statistical model. This large vocabulary
also prevents us from storing all the words and their possible tags in a lexicon. To alleviate the data sparseness problem and the inability of constructing a
word form lexicon, they split the morphological parse of a word to its root and
a sequence of inflectional groups (IGs) using derivational boundaries as shown
below.

$$root + IG_1{}^\frown DB + IG_2{}^\frown DB + ...^\frown DB + IG_n$$

In this way, instead of considering the morphological parse as a single unit,
the inflectional groups can be treated as distinct units. As an example, the

above morphological parse can be written as a sequence of the root al and two inflectional groups.

al+[Adj]+[Noun+Zero+A3sg+P2sg+Nom]

2.2 Problem Definition

In this section, we formally define the morphological disambiguation problem using the representation of morphological parses described in the previous section. The problem can be stated as follows: given a sequence of words $W = w_1^n = w_1, w_2, \ldots, w_n$, find the corresponding sequence of morphological parses $T = t_1^n = t_1, t_2, \ldots, t_n$ of the words. Using the Bayesian approach, this can be formulated as follows:

$$\arg\max_T P(T|W) = \arg\max_T \frac{P(T)P(W|T)}{P(W)}$$
$$= \arg\max_T P(T)$$

We can get rid of the $P(W)$ since it is constant for all morphological parses of the word and we can take $P(W|T)$ as equal to 1, since given the morphological parses we can uniquely determine the sequence of word forms assuming no morphological generation ambiguity. Therefore the problem has been reduced to finding the most probable parse sequence given all the possible parse sequences for a sentence.

2.3 Methodology

The problem of finding the most likely parse sequence given all the possible parse sequences for a sentence can be solved by estimating some statistics over the parts of the parses on a training set and choosing the most likely parse using the estimated parameters. This approach has been applied in trigram-based statistical model of Hakkani-Tür et al. in [11] using the root and inflectional groups as the units of the model to alleviate the data sparseness problem as described above. However this approach has not given competitive results for Turkish when compared to the POS tagging of English. The performance of their morphological disambiguation system is 93.95%. When their system is used as a POS tagger by considering the last POS tag assigned to the word in its parse, the performance is 96.07%.

Using their trigram-based model to assign probabilities to trigram parse sequences, we decoded an n-best list of candidate parses for a sentence using the Viterbi algorithm. Then we applied the perceptron algorithm to rank the candidates. The averaged or voted perceptron that we used for ranking has been applied successfully to a range of NLP tasks by Collins and Duffy in [14,15]. We chose the perceptron method since it is very flexible in features that can be incorporated in the model and the parameter estimation method is very easy and just requires additive updates to a weight vector. This is also the first application of the perceptron algorithm to morphological disambiguation as far as we know. In the next sections we describe the baseline model and perceptron algorithm.

3   Baseline Trigram-Based Model

Trigram-based probabilistic model of Hakkani-Tür et al. in [11] has been used as a baseline to enumerate n-best candidate parses with the Viterbi algorithm. Their method breaks up the morphosyntactic tags at each derivation boundary into groups of morphosyntactic features consisting of POS tag of the derived form and a sequence of inflectional features as described above. A simple trigram model is estimated from the statistics over the groups of morphosyntactic features (called inflectional groups).

Using a trigram tagging model and representing morphosyntatic tag t_i as a sequence of root form plus inflectional groups $(r_i, IG_{i,1}, \ldots, IG_{i,n_i})$, we can write $P(T)$ as follows:

$$P(T) = \prod_{i=1}^{n} P(t_i | t_{i-2}, t_{i-1})$$

$$= \prod_{i=1}^{n} P((r_i, IG_{i,1}, \ldots, IG_{i,n_i})|$$

$$(r_{i-2}, IG_{i-2,1}, \ldots, IG_{i-2,n_{i-2}}),$$

$$(r_{i-1}, IG_{i-1,1}, \ldots, IG_{i-1,n_{i-1}}))$$

To estimate $P(T)$, they have made some assumptions: The first assumption is that a root word depends only on the roots of the previous two words. The second assumption is that the presence of IGs in a word only depends on the final IGs of the two previous words. These two assumptions lead to their first model which they report as giving the best results. This is the model that we used for the baseline model in this work.

Using these assumptions, $P(T)$ can be written as:

$$P(T) = \prod_{i=1}^{n} (P(r_i | r_{i-2}, r_{i-1})$$

$$\prod_{k=1}^{n_i} P(IG_{i,k} | IG_{i-2,n_{i-2}}, IG_{i-1,n_{i-1}}))$$

We estimated the individual probabilities using the standard n-gram probability estimation methods from a morphologically disambiguated training set. Then we constructed a second order Markov model of the candidate morphological parses using the estimated morphosyntactic tag trigram probabilities for a sentence, and finally we used the Viterbi algorithm to decode the n-best candidates with their likelihoods.

4   Perceptron Algorithm

We have replicated the perceptron algorithm from Collins (see [15]) in Figure 1. This algorithm estimates the parameter vector $\bar{\alpha}$ using a set of training examples. The algorithm makes multiple passes (denoted by T) over the training examples.

Inputs: Training examples (x_i, y_i)
Initialization: Set $\bar{\alpha} = 0$
Algorithm:
For $t = 1 \ldots T, i = 1 \ldots n$
$\quad$ Calculate $z_i = \arg \max_{z \in \mathbf{GEN}(x_i)} \Phi(x_i, z) \cdot \bar{\alpha}$
$\quad$ **If** $(z_i \neq y_i)$ **then** $\bar{\alpha} = \bar{\alpha} + \Phi(x_i, y_i) - \Phi(x_i, z_i)$
Output: Parameters $\bar{\alpha}$

Fig. 1. A variant of the perceptron algorithm from Collins (see [15])

For each example, it finds the highest scoring candidate among all candidates using the current parameter values. If the highest scoring candidate is not the correct one, it updates the parameter vector $\bar{\alpha}$ by the difference of the feature vector representation of the correct candidate and the highest scoring candidate. This way of parameter update increases the parameter values for features in the correct candidate and downweights the parameter values for features in the competitor. The morphological disambiguation problem as formulated above can be used with this algorithm as follows:

- The training examples are the sentence $x_i = w_{[1:n_i]}^i$ and the morphological parse sequence $y_i = t_{[1:n_i]}^i$ pairs for $i = 1 \ldots n$, where n is the number of training sentences and n_i is the length of the i'th sentence.
- The function $\mathbf{GEN}(x_i)$ maps the input sentence to the n-best candidate parse sequences using the baseline trigram-based model.
- The representation $\Phi(x, y) \in \Re^d$ is a feature vector, the components of which are defined as $\Phi_s(w_{[1:n]}, t_{[1:n]}) = \sum_{i=1}^{n} \phi_s(t_{i-2}, t_{i-1}, t_i)$, where $\phi_s(t_{i-2}, t_{i-1}, t_i)$ is an indicator function for a feature that depends on the current morphosyntactic tag (morphological parse) and the history of the previous two tags. Then the feature vector components $\Phi_s(w_{[1:n_i]}, t_{[1:n_i]})$ are just the counts of the local features $\phi_s(t_{i-2}, t_{i-1}, t_i)$. For example one feature might be:

$$\phi_{100}(t_{i-2}, t_{i-1}, t_i) = \begin{cases} 1 \text{ if current parse } t_i \\ \quad \text{is al+Verb+Pos} \\ \quad +\text{Imp+A2pl and} \\ \quad \text{previous parse } t_{i-1} \\ \quad \text{interpretation} \\ \quad \text{is a pronoun} \\ 0 \text{ otherwise} \end{cases}$$

- The expression $\Phi(x, y) \cdot \bar{\alpha}$ in the algorithm is the inner product $\sum_s \alpha_s \Phi_s(x, y)$.

We used the "averaged parameters" to apply the method to the test examples since the averaged parameters are more robust to noisy or unseperable data [15]. The estimation of parameter values from training examples using the algorithm in Figure 1 is the same. The only difference is that we make a simple modification to the algorithm to sum the parameter values for each feature in a vector after each training example and the algorithm returns the averaged parameters γ by dividing this sum vector by the total number of examples used to update the vector. With this setting, the perceptron algorithm learns an averaged parameter vector γ that can be used to choose the most likely candidate morphological parse sequence of a sentence using the following function:

$$F(x) = \arg \max_{y \in \mathbf{GEN}(x)} \Phi(x,y) \cdot \gamma$$

$$= \arg \max_{y \in \mathbf{GEN}(x)} \gamma_0 \Phi_0(x,y) + \sum_{s=1}^{d} \Phi_s(x,y)\gamma_s$$

where γ_0 is a weighting factor for the log probability $\Phi_0(x,y)$ assigned to the parse sequence by the baseline model. This parameter is found emprically as explained in the later sections.

Convergence theorems for the perceptron algorithm applied to tagging and parsing problems are given in [15].

5   Experiments

5.1   Data Set

We used a morphologically disambiguated Turkish corpus of about 950,000 tokens (including markers such as begin and end of sentence markers). Alternative ambiguous parses of the words are also available in the corpus as output from a morphological analyzer. This data set was divided into a training, development, and test set. The training set size is about 750,000 tokens or 45,000 sentences. The development set size is about 40,000 tokens or 2,500 sentences. The test set size is also about 40,000 tokens or 2,500 sentences. The training set was used to train the baseline trigram-based model and for the parameter estimation in perceptron algorithm. The development set was used to tune some of the parameters in the perceptron algorithm. The final tests were done on the test set.

5.2   Features

In the perceptron algorithm for morphological disambiguation we used a feature set that takes into account the current morphosyntactic tag (parse) and the history of the previous two tags. The set of features that we included in the model is shown in Table 1. In this table IG_i is the sequence of the inflection groups of the i'th morphosyntactic tag in the sentence. $IG_{i,j}$ is the j'th inflection group of the i'th morphosyntactic tag in the sentence. n_i is the number of inflection groups in the i'th morphosyntactic tag in the sentence.

Table 1. Features used for morphological disambiguation

Gloss	Feature
Trigram	(1) $r_{i-2}IG_{i-2}, r_{i-1}IG_{i-1}, r_iIG_i$
Bigram	(2) $r_{i-2}IG_{i-2}, r_iIG_i$
	(3) $r_{i-1}IG_{i-1}, r_iIG_i$
Current parse	(4) r_iIG_i
Previous parse and current IGs	(5) $r_{i-1}IG_{i-1}, IG_i$
Two previous parse and current IGs	(6) $r_{i-2}IG_{i-2}, IG_i$
Root trigram	(7) r_{i-2}, r_{i-1}, r_i
Root bigram	(8) r_{i-2}, r_i
	(9) r_{i-1}, r_i
Root unigram	(10) r_i
IGs Trigram	(11) IG_{i-2}, IG_{i-1}, IG_i
IGs Bigram	(12) IG_{i-2}, IG_i
	(13) IG_{i-1}, IG_i
IGs Unigram	(14) IG_i
for $j = 1 \ldots n_i$	(15) $IG_{i-2,n_{i-2}}, IG_{i-1,n_{i-1}}, IG_{i,j}$
n-grams using last IG of two previous	(16) $IG_{i-2,n_{i-2}}, IG_{i,j}$
parse and IG of current parse	(17) $IG_{i-1,n_{i-1}}, IG_{i,j}$
	(18) $IG_{i,j}$
for $j = 1 \ldots n_i - 1$	(19) $IG_{i,j}IG_{i,j+1}$
bigrams of IGs in current parse	
(local morphotactics)	
for $j = 1 \ldots n_i$	(20) $j, IG_{i,j}$
IG and its position from the begining	
Current parse is a proper noun and	(21) $PROPER$
it starts with capital letter	
Number of IGs in current parse	(22) $\#IG_i$
Current parse is a verb and	(23) $ENDSINVERB$
it ends sentence	

5.3   Optimal Parameter and Feature Selection

The free parameters in the perceptron algorithm are the number of iterations T and the weighting factor for the log probability $\Phi_0(x, y)$ assigned to the parse sequence by the baseline model. To optimize these parameters we ran the perceptron algorithm over the training set with varied parameters and tested on the development data to compare the results with different parameter values. We found that $T = 5$ iterations with $\gamma_0 = 0.0$ gives the best configuration for the parameters. The optimal weighting factor found to be 0.0 can be reasoned that the baseline model performance is comparatively very low and discarding the baseline log probability is better in this case.

We also did some experiments to select a subset of features that is optimal in terms of the accuracy of morphological disambiguation. The greedy algorithm that we used starts with no feature selected. Then it chooses the feature that

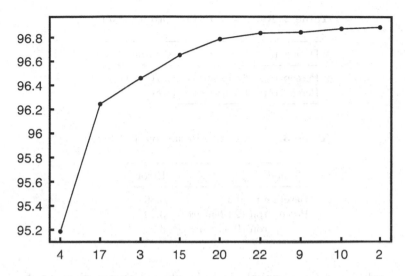

Fig. 2. Accuracy with respect to features added

improves the accuracy on the development set most. It continues in this manner with the remaining features until no feature increases the accuracy. Figure 2 shows the selected 9 features (4, 17, 3, 15, 20, 22, 9, 10, 2 - in this order) (see Table 1 for features referenced by these numbers) and the performance improvement when features are added.

5.4   Results

We first used the baseline trigram-based model to decode 50-best parses of each sentence in the data set. The training set was split to 5 portions and for each portion the baseline model was trained on the other 4 portions and that portion was decoded using the learned model. The development and test set was decoded using the baseline model trained with all the data in the training set. The baseline model also returns the log probability for each 50-best parses.

The baseline model performed with an accuracy of 93.61% on the test set. The perceptron algorithm was trained using the 50-best parse decodings of the training set. The parameter tuning was done using the 50-best parse decodings of the development set. The final test was done on the test set. Table 2 gives the accuracy results for the perceptron algorithm. The accuracy of the perceptron algorithm on the test set is 96.76% when all the 23 features are used and it is 96.80% when the 9 features (4, 17, 3, 15, 20, 22, 9, 10, 2) selected by the greedy method that we described above are used. The greedy method is effective in eliminating the non-discriminative features and hence increasing the runtime performance of the algorithm by reducing feature vector dimensions. For a comparision of the perceptron performance over the baseline model, see Table 3. The perceptron algorithm provides about 50% error reduction over the baseline model.

Table 2. Ranking with Perceptron Results

Data set	Accuracy(%)
Perceptron (23 features)	96.76
Perceptron (9 features)	96.80

Table 3. Comparative Results on Test Set

Method	Error(%)
Baseline model	6.39
Perceptron (23 features)	3.24
Perceptron (9 features)	3.20

Error analysis for the morphological disambiguation experiment with 9 features shows that in 35% of errors (about 1.1% of all words) the root of the word is incorrectly decided. In 40% of errors the root is correct but its part of speech is incorrectly decided. In 17% of this case, the POS tag of the root is incorrectly decided as a noun in place of adjective. In 11%, noun should be pronoun, in 9% adjective should be noun, in 7% noun should be postposition, in 7% adjective should be determiner, in 5% noun should be adverb, in 5% adjective should be adverb and in 4% adverb should be adjective. In 25% of errors, root and its part of speech are correct but some inflection group is incorrect. In 16% of this case, a noun such as `kitabı` meaning in accusative case "the book" is incorrectly decided as a noun in nominative case meaning "his/her book". In 12%, the reverse is true. In 9%, the words that are derived from a verb using past participle suffix like `sevdiği` (beloved) is incorrectly labeled as adjective or noun.

We also ran the perceptron algorithm on a manually disambiguated small test set of 958 tokens to compare our results with Yüret and Türe in [12]. They have used the same train set in our experiments and tested on this small set. The comparative results can be seen in Table 4. The relatively inferior performance of the perceptron algorithm on this set can be explained by the small size of the test set and limited accuracy of the semi-automatically disambiguated train set.

The Turkish morphological disambigution performance using the perceptron algorithm (96.80%) is very close to the English part-of-speech tagging performance using the perceptron algorithm (97.11%) and maximum-entropy model (96.72%) as given in [15]. For a better comparison, when we consider the part-of-speech tag of the word as given in the morphological parse of the word as the part-of-speech tag of the last derived form, the performance goes up to 98.19%. When we trained the perceptron to do POS tagging using the same 9 features used in the morphological disambiguation, the accuracy increased to 98.27%.

Table 4. Comparative Results on Manually Tagged Test Set of 958 tokens

Method	Accuracy(%)
Baseline model	95.48
GPA (Yüret and Türe, 2006)	95.82
Perceptron (23 features)	96.28
Perceptron (9 features)	95.93

Table 5. Turkish POS tagging performance

POS tagger	Accuracy(%)
Baseline model	95.67%
Baseline model as reported in (Hakkani-Tür et al., 2002)	96.07%
MD perceptron (9 features)	98.19%
POS perceptron (9 features)	98.27%

The POS tagger performance for Turkish using perceptron algorithm is compared with the Turkish POS tagger performance as reported by Hakkani-Tür et al. in [11] in Table 5. We also presented our test result for the baseline model of Hakkani-Tür et al. on our test set in this table to make the comparison fair.

6   Conclusions

We presented an application of the perceptron algorithm to the morphological disambiguation of Turkish text. We used the Viterbi algorithm and a baseline trigram model to enumerate 50-best parses of a sentence. Then we ranked the candidates using the averaged perceptron algorithm. The perceptron algorithm provided about 50% error reduction over the baseline model. We found that a small set of features seems to be effective in morphological disambiguation of Turkish text. We also trained a perceptron for Turkish POS tagging which gives 98.27% accuracy. Turkish morphological disambiguation and POS tagging accuracy that we obtained is the best reported so far.

Acknowledgements

This work was supported by the Boğaziçi University Research Fund under the grant number 06A102 and partially supported by TUBITAK BIDEB 2211. The authors would like to thank Kemal Oflazer and Deniz Yüret for providing us the data set to conduct morphological disambiguation experiments.

References

1. Oflazer, K.: Two-level Description of Turkish Morphology. Literary and Linguistic Computing **9(2)** (1994) 137–148
2. Karlsson, F., Voutilainen, A., Heikkila, J., Anttila A.: Constraint Grammar-A Language-Independent System for Parsing Unrestricted Text (1995)
3. Brill, E.: A Simple Rule-Based Part-of-Speech Tagger. Proceedings of Third Conference on Applied Natural Language Processing, Trento, Italy (1992)
4. Brill, E.: Transformation-Based Error-Driven Learning and Natural Language Processing: A Case Study in Part-of-Speech Tagging. Computational Linguistics (1995)
5. Church, K. W.: A stochastic parts program and noun phrase parser for unrestricted text. Proceedings of Second Conference on Applied Natural Language Processing, Austin, Texas (1988)
6. Ratnaparkhi, A.: A Maximum-Entropy Model for Part-of-Speech Tagging. Proceedings of the emprical methods in natural language processing conference (1996)
7. Cutting, D., Kupiec, J., Pealersen, J., Sibun, P.: A practical part-of-speech tagger. Proceedings of Third Conference on Applied Natural Language Processing, Trento, Italy (1992)
8. Hajič, J., Hladká, B.: Tagging inflective languages: prediction of morphological categories for a rich, structured tagset. Proceedings of COLING-ACL Conference (1998)
9. Oflazer, K., Tür, G.: Combining Hand-crafted Rules and Unsupervised Learning in Constraint-based Morphological Disambiguation. Proceedings of the ACL-SIGDAT Conference on Empirical Methods in Natural Language Processing, Philadelphia, PA, USA (1996)
10. Oflazer, K., Tür, G.: Morphological Disambiguation by Voting Constraints. Proceedings of ACL/EACL, The 35th Annual Meeting of the Association for Computational Linguistics, Madrid, Spain (1997)
11. Hakkani-Tür, D. Z., Oflazer, K., Tür, G.: Statistical Morphological Disambiguation for Agglutinative Languages. Computers and the Humanities **36(4)** (2002)
12. Yüret, D., Türe, F.: Learning Morphological Disambiguation Rules for Turkish. Proceedings of HLT-NAACL (2006)
13. Freund, Y., Schapire, R. E.: Large Margin Classification using the Perceptron Algorithm. Machine Learning **37(3)** (1999) 277–296
14. Collins, M., Duffy, N.: New Ranking Algorithms for Parsing and Tagging: Kernels over Discrete Structures, and the Voted Perceptron. Proceedings of ACL (2002)
15. Collins, M.: Discriminative Training Methods for Hidden Markov Models: Theory and Experiments with Perceptron Algorithms. Proceedings of EMNLP (2002)

Part-of-Speech Tagging Using Word Probability Based on Category Patterns

Mi-young Kang[1], Sung-won Jung[1,2], Kyung-soon Park[3], and Hyuk-chul Kwon[1,2]

[1] Pusan National University, Korean Language Processing Laboratory, Department of Computer Science Engineering,
[2] Pusan National University, Center for U-Port IT Research and Education
[3] Nara Info Tech co., ltd
Jangjeon-dong, Geumjeong-gu, 609-735, Busan, Korea
{kmyoung,swjung,hckwon}@pusan.ac.kr, reallywhat@gmail.com

Abstract. This paper focuses on part-of-speech (POS, category) tagging based on word probability estimated using morpheme unigrams and category patterns within a word. The word-N-gram-based POS-tagging model is difficult to adapt to agglutinative languages such as Korean, Turkish and Hungarian, among others, due to the high productivity of words. Thus, many of the stochastic studies on Korean POS-tagging have been conducted based on morpheme N-grams. However, the morpheme-N-gram model also has difficulty coping with data sparseness when augmenting contextual information in order to assure sufficient performance. In addition, the model has difficulty conceiving the relationship of morphemes within a word. The present POS-tagging algorithm (a) resolves the data-sparseness problem thanks to a morpheme-unigram-based approach and (b) involves the relationship of morphemes within a word by estimating the weight of the category of a morpheme in a category pattern constituting a word. With the proposed model, a performance similar to that with other models that use more than just the morpheme-unigram model was observed.

1 Introduction

Interpretation of the lexical category of parts of speech (POS) is crucial to understanding the exact syntactic structure of a sentence. Most of the previous stochastic work on POS-tagging has been adapted to English, in which the basic syntactic units are words, and in which many content and function words consist of single morphemes[1][3][10]. By contrast, words are morphologically complex in many languages in which agglutinative morphology is predominant, for example Hungarian and the Turkic languages. Korean, as a member of the latter group, can be analyzed into *several morpheme strings* that include different parts of speech. Chains of suffixes are attached to the ends of nominal and verbal stems, and these determine most of the grammatical relationships. Therefore, there is a data-sparseness problem in adapting the word N-gram model to Korean POS-tagging, which problem makes such adaptation difficult. Thus many of the stochastic studies on Korean POS-tagging

A. Gelbukh (Ed.): CICLing 2007, LNCS 4394, pp. 119–130, 2007.

have been performed based on the morpheme N-gram model. However, the morpheme N-gram model also has difficulty coping with data-sparseness when augmenting contextual information in order to assure sufficient performance. Furthermore the model has difficulty conceiving the relationship of morphemes within a word.

Therefore, this paper aims to implement a POS-tagging model that (a) resolves the data-sparseness problem by following a morpheme-unigram-based approach and (b) involves the relationship of morphemes within a word by estimating the word probability based on the category pattern constituting a word. To that end, this paper is organized as follows. Section 2 discusses previous N-gram models adopted for POS-tagging and adapted to Korean language characteristics. Section 3 describes the POS-tagging system that considers the morpheme unigram and its weight in the category pattern constituting a word, Section 4 discusses the experiments, and Section 5 offers concluding comments.

2 N-Gram POS-Tagging Models and Korean Language Characteristics

2.1 Word N-Gram Is Not of Practical Use for Korean

Most stochastic tagging methods have been developed for English, in which the basic syntactic units are words, and in which many content and function words consist of single morphemes[1][3][10]. However, word-N-gram information is not of practical use for Korean, because of the data sparseness resulting from Korean's typological characteristics: (a) the free-word-order tendency in sentences and (b) the remarkable productivity of the Korean word due to the predominance in Korean of agglutinative morphology. A Korean sentence tolerates a certain level of *free word-order*: words, which are delimited by spaces, in the sentence in (1) can be ordered in the various ways shown in (2), among many other potential orderings, except for some cases in which the violation of local syntactic dependency produces ungrammatical sentences, such as in (2)d and (2)e.[1]

na+neun # sigi+leul # jal # majchu+l # su # iss+eoss+da. <NPP "I" + JX> # <NNG"time" + JKO> # <MBG "well"> # <VV "to meet"+ETM> # <NNBG "ability"> # <VV "to have"+EP+EF+PNT>[2] "I could meet the deadline well."   (1)

---

[1] Some local syntactic constraints do exist in Korean, even though Korean is a free-word-order language. For example, a bound noun should always follow a modifier or a noun; a modifier should always precede a noun, and an auxiliary verb follows main verbs, among others. However, this paper will not discuss in detail the local syntactic constraints, because the main interest is to discuss POS-tagging using the word-probability-based category pattern within a word.

[2] We have adopted the Revised Romanization of Korean, released on 4 July 2000 by the South Korean Ministry of Culture and Tourism. Also, see Appendices 1 and 2 for symbols and abbreviations and for the Korean POS tags.

a. sigi+leul # na+neun # jal # majchu+l # su # iss+eoss+da. <NNG "time" + JKO> # <NPP "I" + JX> # <MBG "well"> # <VV "to meet"+ETM> # <NNBG "ability"> # <VV "to have"+EP+EF+PNT>

b. na+neun # jal # sigi+leul # majchu+l # su # iss+eoss+da. <NPP "I" + PX> # <MBG "well"> # <NNG "time" + JKO> # <VV "to meet"+ETM> # <NNBG "ability"> # <VV "to have"+EP+EF+PNT>

c. sigi+leul # jal # majchu+l # su # iss+eoss+da # na+neun. <NNN "time" + PCO> # <MBG "well"> # <VV "to meet"+ETM> # <NNBG "ability"> # <VV "to have"+EP+EF> # <NPP "I" + JX+PNT>   (2)

d. * na+neun # sigi+leul # jal # su # majchu+l # iss+eoss+da. <NPP "I" + JX> # <NNG "time" + JKO> # <MBG "well"> # <NNBG "ability"> # <VV "to meet"+ETM> # <VV "to have"+EP+EF+PNT>

e. * na+neun # sigi+leul # jal # majchu+l # iss+eoss+da#su. <NPP "I" + JX> # <NNG "time" + JKO> # <MBG "well"> # <VV "to meet"+ETM> # <VV "to have"+EP+EF> # <NNBG "ability"+PNT>

2.2 Morphotactic Constraints Within a Korean Word and Previous Alternatives

Contrary to this liberty in word order, there exist *strict morphotactic constraints* within a word. Most words in a Korean sentence are polymorphic, composed of several morphemes that have different parts of speech, (e.g., in (1) *na+neun*, *sigi+leul*, *majchu+l*, and *iss+eoss+da*. In polymorphemic words, the suffixations are subject to strict morphotactic control. The following conjugations of the verb *majch* <VV "to catch"> show that the size of a word varies according to productive morphological concatenation, and that the concatenation is strictly ordered.

a. majchu+da <VV "to catch"+EF>
b. majchu+eoss+da <VV "to catch"+EP+EF>
c. majchu+eoss+da+lago < VV "to catch"+EP+EF + EQ>   (3)
d. majchu+eoss+da+lago+neun < VV "to catch"+EP+EF+EQ+JX>

In consideration of the above Korean typological characteristics, many of the stochastic studies on Korean POS-tagging have been based on stochastic morpheme information extracted from corpora [5][6][7] (See Table 2). However, in considering only morpheme-level stochastic information, Korean POS-tagging precision is poor. Most of those studies used from *morpheme bigram* to *morpheme trigram* in maximum, whereas the ideal morpheme-*N*-gram order should follow the number of morphemes in a word in order to involve recognition of word. Introducing a variability of morpheme-*N*-gram order according to word length (the number of morphemes) is quasi-impossible, because the number of categories in a Korean word can vary from 1 to 7 according to the experimental results using our training data (see Table 3).

Thus the main challenge in those morpheme-N-gram approaches is now how to integrate word-concept- and word-level information. Among several alternatives, we can find a hybrid model that combines rule- and stochastic-based approaches as well as a model that includes a new parameter. The former conceives word-level information by applying rules. The model uses, first, an ordinary HMM model employing bi-gram tag transition probability and morpheme-lexical probability.

$$T^* = \mathrm{argmax}_T \prod_{i=1}^{n} \mathrm{Pr}(t_i \mid t_{i-1})\, \mathrm{Pr}(m_i \mid t_i)$$

t: tag; m: morpheme; T^*: optimal tag sequence that maximizes the forward Viterbi scores   (4)

Second, it introduces error-correction rules at the word level. The error-correction rules, which correct HMM tagging errors, are automatically learned [5]. The latter model introduces a new parameter for considering word-level context, that is, word-boundary P, in (5), below [7].

$$T(w_{1,n}) = \mathrm{argmax}_{c_{1,u}, m_{1,u}} \mathrm{Pr}(c_{1,u}, m_{1,u} \mid w_{1,n})$$

$$\approx \mathrm{argmax}_{c_{1,u}, m_{1,u}} \mathrm{Pr}(c_{1,u}, p_{2,u}, m_{1,u})$$

$u\ (\ n)$: No. of morphemes in a sequence corresponding to the given word sequence; c: a morpheme-unit tag; m: a morpheme; p: transition probability (a transition across a word boundary or a transition within a word)   (5)

In the model $\wedge (C_{[s](K:J)}, M_{[s](L:I)})$, the word-spacing, word boundary, $[s]$ can be considered for both tag probability and morpheme probability. The probability of a current morpheme tag c_i conditionally depends on both the previous K tags and the previous J morphemes, and the probability of the current morpheme m_i conditionally depends on the current tag and the previous L tags as well as the previous I morphemes. The model shows the best performance by considering both trigrams of tags and morphemes $\wedge (C_{[s](2:2)}, M_{[s](2:2)})$ and the transition probability according to word spacing in both the tags and the morphemes.

However, neither of the two alternatives considers the relationship between morphemes within a word. In the following sections, we propose our alternatives, the POS-tagging model based on the category pattern, which allows word recognition through considering the relationship between morphemes within a word, while using only morpheme unigram information.

3   Korean POS-Tagging Using Word Probability Based on Category Patterns

This section proposes our alternative, POS-tagging model that considers only morpheme unigrams and their weight in a category pattern constituting a word.

3.1   Application of Category-Pattern-Based Model to Bayesian Models for POS-Tagging

Our alternative model is based on the Bayesian model, which is used in most studies on POS-tagging. The Bayesian model, when applied to POS-tagging, aims to select the most likely POS-tag sequence for a given sentence, as in (6).[3]

---

[3] The notation of Charniak *et al.* (1993) was adopted for our description.

$$\arg\max_{t_{1,n}} P(t_{1,n} \mid w_{1,n})$$

$$= \arg\max_{t_{1,n}} \frac{P(w_{1,n} \mid t_{1,n})P(t_{1,n})}{P(w_{1,n})}$$

$$= \arg\max_{t_{1,n}} P(w_{1,n} \mid t_{1,n})P(t_{1,n})$$

N = sentence length (i.e. the No. of words); $w_{i,i+m}$ = the words occurring at position i through $i+m$ (alternative notations: $w_i...w_{i+m}$); $t_{i,i+m}$ = the tags $t_i...t_{i+m}$ for $w_i...w_{i+m}$ (6)

The following two assumptions are formulated in order to reduce parameters in Equation (6), which are estimated from the training corpus.

Assumption 1. Words are independent of each other.
Assumption 2. A word's identity depends on only its POS-tag (category).

In Section 2 we saw that in Korean the free-word order is predominant. Based on this characteristic, we assume the independence of each word category.

Assumption 3. Tags are independent of each other.

Adopting Assumptions 1 to 3, Equation (6) is reformulated as Equation (7):

$$p(w_{1,n} \mid t_{1,n})p(t_{1,n}) = \prod_{k=1}^{n} p(w_k \mid t_k)p(t_k)$$

$$= \prod_{k=1}^{n} \frac{p(w_k, t_k)}{p(t_k)} p(t_k) = \prod_{k=1}^{n} p(w_k, t_k)$$

w_k = k^{th} word in a sentence
t_k = the category tag of w_k
$w_k t_k$ = w_k that are tagged as t_k (7)

As we described in the above sections, most Korean words are not monomorphemic, contrary to a language such as English. Most Korean words are composed of morpheme strings. Each morpheme, as a part of a word, refers to a grammatical category (i.e., the POS; see APPENIX 2). Morphemes are strictly ordered according to their category in a particular category pattern (*cp*) in a word.

Definition 1. Words are analyzed according to their constituent morphemes.
Definition 2. A morpheme constitutes a particular category pattern in a word alone, or with other morpheme(s).

To apply these morphotactic constraints, let *CP* be the set of possible category patterns we could find within a Korean word. The word w_k is composed of $mc_{k,1}...$ $mc_{k,\mu}$, related to cp_j, an element of *CP*, as shown in (8).

$$CP = \{cp_1, \cdots, cp_\beta\}, cp_j = cp_{j,1} \cdots cp_{j,v},$$

$$if\ (w_k = m_{k,1}...m_{k,\mu}\ and\ mc_{k,1} \cdots mc_{k,\mu} = cp_j)$$

$$then\ mc_{k,i} = cp_{j,i}$$

$mc_{k,i}$ = Category of the ith morpheme in w_k
cp_j = Category pattern of $mc_{k,1}...mc_{k,\mu}$ that constitutes w_k (8)

Within a word, each morpheme is constrained under a strict category pattern. Therefore, if we can find the appropriate parameter for including the category pattern, we do not need, while maintaining Assumption 4, to augment the morpheme-N-gram order.

Assumption 4. Morphemes in a word are independent of each other when they belong to a category pattern.

Following Definitions 1, 2 and Assumption 4, Equation (7) is reformulated as Equation (9).

$$if \ (w_k = m_{k,1} \ldots m_{k,\mu} \ and \ t_k = mc_{k,1} \cdots mc_{k,\mu} = cp_j)$$

$$then \ \prod_{k=1}^{n} p(w_k, t_k) = \prod_{k=1}^{n} p(w_k, cp_j) = \prod_{k=1}^{n} \prod_{i=1}^{\mu} p(m_{k,i}, mc_{k,i})$$

$$= \prod_{k=1}^{n} \prod_{i=1}^{\mu} p(m_{k,i}, cp_{j,i})$$

μ = Total No. of morphemes in w_k.
$m_{k,i} = i^{th}$ morpheme in w_k.   (9)

3.2 Parameter Training and POS Assigning

To determine the correlation among individual morpheme categories in a word w_k, we use an indirect method based on Assumption 5, while excluding category patterns in which only a single morpheme appears.

Assumption 5. A morpheme participates as a category in a category pattern with a particular power.

According to Assumption 5, morphemes constitute a word under a particular category pattern, cp_j, with a correlation between those morphemes in the pattern. A morpheme probability within a category pattern is estimated according to its category power in the category pattern.

Category power training proceeds by comparing (a) the observed probability of a real word, which is estimated by its relative frequency, and (b) the estimated word probability based on the morpheme probability weighted according to its category power in the category pattern of the word. The latter should be in direct proportion to the observed probability of a real word.

$$p(w_k, cp_j) = \prod_{i=1}^{\mu} p(m_{k,i}, cp_{j,i}) \approx \prod_{i=1}^{\mu} p(m_{k,i}, cp_{j,i})^{wcp_{j,i}}$$

$wcp_{j,i}$ = Weight (i.e. Power) of the individual category, $cp_{j,i}$, in category pattern cp_j.   (10)

Collecting training data. To fit the parameter of category power $wcp_{j,i}$ in a category pattern, *real-word lists according to each category pattern cp_j* (CPWL) were extracted from the corpora (Table 1), which lists were tagged with POS tags using a rule-based tagging system with a precision of 97.20%. A total of 667 types of CPWL containing more than 50 words were extracted. Each CPWL was sorted by word-frequency rank, and sample word-list data sets per category pattern for training

(SCPWLs) were constructed by selecting one word every 10 words from each CPWL in order to save time during training. When the number of words in the CPWL was less than 1,000 words (about 414 CPWLs in all), they were all sampled in SCPWLs. (For an illustration of the process of parameter fitting, see Fig. 2).

Parameter fitting. The optimum parameters according to each pattern cp_j were fitted by applying a simulated annealing algorithm to those training-sample data sets. The *hill-climbing algorithm* was adopted in order to fit the parameters. However, the *hill-climbing algorithm* was less economical than *simulated annealing* because it always chose the parameters with the best value, and thus could possibly become trapped in a local maximum, thus requiring many restarts. In contrast, the simulated annealing algorithm tolerated the choosing of the worst value and was thus protected from any effect of *local maxima*. The parameter-fitting training algorithm shown in (11) adjusted $wcp_{j,(1...n)}$ so as to minimize the mean of the error between the observed probability of a word, $p(w_k, cp_j)$, and the word probability estimated from the morpheme probability, which was weighted with a category weight, $wcp_{j,(1...n)}$, in the category pattern cp_j. The number of categories in a category pattern of a Korean word, can vary from 1 category to 10 categories, according to the experimental results using our training data (See Table 1). Thus from 1 parameter to a maximum of 7 parameters are trained according to the category pattern.

$$ErrorMean\ (cp_j) = \left[\sum_{\gamma=1}^{Tcp_j}\left|p(w_\gamma, cp_j) - \prod_{i=1}^{\mu}p(m_{\gamma,i}, cp_{j,i})^{wcp_{j,i}}\right|\right]\Big/Tcp_j$$

$$if\ mc_{\gamma,1}\cdots mc_{\gamma,\mu} = cp_j, \underset{wmcp_{j,i}}{arg\ min}\left(\left[\sum_{\gamma=1}^{Tcp_j}\left|p(w_\gamma, cp_j) - \prod_{i=1}^{\mu}p(m_{\gamma,i}, cp_{j,i})^{wcp_{i,i}}\right|\right]\Big/Tcp_j\right) \quad (11)$$

Tcp_j = Total No. of training category patterns (cp_j); $w_\gamma = \gamma^{th}$ word in the Tcp_j

POS assigning using morpheme unigrams and category power. Our aim was to obtain the optimal tag list for a sentence. Thus, applying the parameters trained by (11), our POS-tagging model using morpheme unigrams and category power can be refined as the following.

$$EP(w_k, cp_j) = \begin{cases} if\ mc_{k,1}\cdots mc_{k,\mu} = cp_j = t_k & \prod_{i=1}^{\mu}p(m_{k,i}, cp_{j,i})^{wcp_{j,i}} \\ otherwise & 1/Tw \end{cases} \quad (12)$$

$$t_{i,n} = \underset{t_{i,n}}{arg\ max}\prod_{k=1}^{n}EP(w_k, t_k) \quad (13)$$

Patterns containing a single category, such as *NNG, MBG, NNBG, MDG, NPP,* and *IC*, corresponded exactly to a word. Thus, whereas they were not considered in our training of the category weights of the morpheme, they were assigned a relative frequency as a word probability without a weighted probability of a morpheme. Patterns such as *<NNBU + ETN + JKO>* and *<VV + EF + EP + ETN>* (i.e. those of less than 50 words), among others, rarely appeared; thus it was rather difficult to train parameters. In addition, unknown patterns are possibly encountered. A fixed value,

1.0/total No. of words, was assigned to $EP(w_k, cp_j)$ by considering them to have appeared once over the total number of training words.

4   Experimentation and Application

The present tagging model using word probability based on category patterns (TMWPCP) was trained and tested on data shown in Table 1. The training corpus was composed of two years' worth of newspaper articles and of three years' worth of news broadcasting scripts. The evaluation data were randomly extracted from one year's worth of newspaper articles from another newspaper.

Table 1. The training and test data suite

	Training Corpus	Evaluation Data
Size in No. of Words	34,090,673	32,503

Table 2. The precision of the TMWPCP compared to other models (in %)

	Model	Precision
Lee S.H. (1995)	HMM (morpheme unigram)	93.60
Lee G.B *et* *al.* (1997)	HMM (morpheme unigram) + Error Correction Rule	94.90
Lee S.Z. *et* *al.* (2000)	HMM (morpheme trigram, category trigram) + Word Boundary	96.97
	Joint Independence (morpheme bigram, category bigram) + Word Boundary	96.95
TMWPCP	Morpheme Unigram + Category Weight	96.08
	Morpheme Unigram + Korean Local Syntactic Dependency Rule	97.53

According to the comparison of the evaluation results, shown in Table 2, we can understand that although the category-pattern-based tagging model uses only unigram, it shows almost the same performance as the models based on more than unigram. The TMWPCP clearly outperforms any other simple unigram models. It slightly underperforms compared with the bigram- or trigram-based HMM model; however, that model uses too many histories, whereas our model uses just *current morpheme probability* and *its category weight*. Also, the TMWPCP introduces the word-recognition concept. Thus it implies Korean morphotactic contraints within a word. However, it neglects local syntactic constraints in Korean such as those we saw in Section 2. With the application of about 20 local syntactic dependency rules, the system showed a 1.45% improvement.

We estimated the coverage of the 667 category patterns (i.e. SCPWLs), which are set with the trained parameters, by measuring them in 30% blocks from 100% to 10%, and then in 1% blocks from 10% to 0%. Figure 1 shows no significant precision decrease between 100% and 7% of words in SCPWLs. Seven percent of words in SCPWLs contained about 50 different category patterns. The coverage of category patterns is depicted in Fig. 1. As shown, the model using zero percent of category patterns with category weight corresponds to the simple morpheme-unigram model that uses the relative frequency of morpheme unigrams. Because the system uses only morpheme unigrams and category weight-value, already it does not demand a significant memory size; however, if we can reduce the size of parameter lists, it would further help implementation in embedded systems.

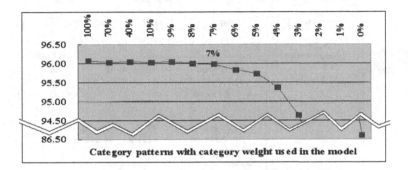

Fig. 1. Coverage of category patterns

The sample cases of the optimum parameters for the patterns containing more than one morpheme, per different number of parameters, are shown in Table 3. Those trained parameters are applied for POS-tagging of morpheme strings within a word.

Table 3. Sample of optimum parameters on cp_j

Rank	IntraCP (cp_w)	Parameters							Error Mean	Error Standard Deviation
		$wcp_{j,1}$	$wcp_{j,2}$	$wcp_{j,3}$	$wcp_{j,4}$	$wcp_{j,5}$	$wcp_{j,6}$	$wcp_{j,7}$		
1	NNG+JKO	0.90	0.78						1.30E-06	7.42E-06
...	...	...	...	...	...	...	...	...	...	...
130	VA+ETN+JKO	0.67	0.33	1.00					6.00E-07	4.06E-06
498	NNG+ETN+JKO	0.38	1.00	1.00					5.19E-08	6.66E-08
...	...	...	...	...	...	...	...	...	...	...
12	VV+EP+EF +PNT	0.63	0.42	0.59	0.41				1.12E-06	2.20E-05
...	...	...	...	...	...	...	...	...	...	...
18	NNV+XSV+EP+ EF+ PNT	0.52	0.16	0.64	0.45	0.52			7.60E-07	6.21E-06
...	...	...	...	...	...	...	...	...	...	...
188	MDQ+NNBU +COP+EP+EF+ PNT	0.38	0.59	0.13	0.06	0.45	0.33		2.53E-07	1.16E-06
...	...	...	...	...	...	...	...	...	...	...
611	MDQ+NNBU+XSU +COP+EP+EF+ PNT	0.40	0.10	0.04	0.18	0.76	0.08	0.16	5.43E-08	4.57E-08

Fig. 2 demonstrates the process of the POS-tagging of the word 여기는 [yeogineun] in sentence (14).

yeogi+neun # uri+ga # jinael # gos+i+bnida.

<NPD"this" + JX> # <NPP"we"+JKS > # <VV "to stay"+ETM> # <NNG   (14)
"place"> # <COP "to be"+EF> # <PNT> "This is where we are going to stay"

The algorithm (12) selects the category pattern *NPD+JX*, which returns the maximum value for the candidate morpheme strings within the word in question.

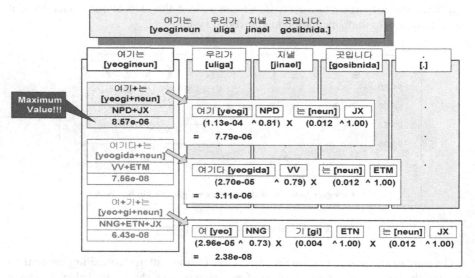

Fig. 2. Application

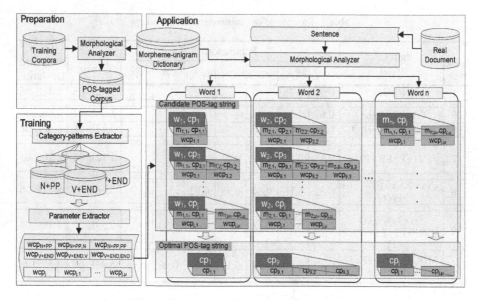

Fig. 3. The process of system implementation

5 Conclusions and Further Work

This paper suggested a new Korean POS-tagging model, TMWPCP, that uses morpheme unigrams and word probability based on category patterns. We showed that a morpheme participates as a category in a category pattern with a particular power for constituting a word in Korean. In the result, although TMWPCP used only morpheme unigrams and not more, we obtained a similar precision to those obtained in previous studies. The TMWPCP (a) is robust in assigning POS for unseen Korean words and (b) could be applicable to the other languages with agglutinative morphology, because it is constructed on the basis of morpheme unigrams and the recognition of inner-word structure simply by training the category power. However, we need to investigate further in order to find the optimal algorithm that can apply local syntactic dependency to the TMWPCP without requiring local syntactic dependency rules.

Acknowledgements. This work was supported by the National Research Program under Grant M10400000332-06J0000-33210.

References

1. Brill, E.: A simple rule-based part of speech tagger. Proceedings of the third conference on Applied natural language processing (1992), 152-155.
2. Charniak, E., Hendrickson, C., Jacobson, N., Perkowitz, M.: Equations for part-of-speech tagging. Proceedings of the Eleventh National Conference on Artificial Intelligence (1993), 784-789.
3. Cutting, D., Kupiec, J., Pedersen, J., Sibun, B.: A practical part-of-speech tagger. Proceedings of the third conference on Applied natural language processing (1992), 133-140.
4. Hakkani-Tür, D.Z., Oflazer, K. Tür, G.: Statistical Morphological Disambiguation for Agglutinative Languages. Proceedings of Computational Linguistics (2000), 285-291.
5. Lee, G.B., Cha, J.W., Lee, J.H.: Hybrid POS tagging with generalized unknown-word handling. Proceedings of the 2nd international workshop on information retrieval with Asian languages (1997), 43-50.
6. Lee, S.H.: A Korean part-of-speech tagging system with handling unknown words. Master's thesis from Korea Advanced Institute of Science and Technology (1995)
7. Lee, S.Z., Tsujii, J.I., Rim, H.C.: Hidden Markov Model-Based Korean Part-of-speech Tagging Considering High Agglutinativity, Word-Spacing, and Lexical Correlativity. Proceedings of the 38th Annual Meeting on Association for Computational Linguistics (2000), 384-391.
8. Manning, C.D., Schütze, H.: Foundations of Statistical Natural Language Processing. MIT Press (2000).
9. Oflazer, K., Kuruöz, İ.: Tagging and Morphological Disambiguation of Turkish Text. Applied Natural Language Processing Conference (1994), 144-149.
10. Weischedel, R., Meeter, M., Schwartz, R., Ramshaw, L., Palmucci, J.: Coping with ambiguity and unknown words through probabilistic models. Computational Linguistics (1993), 359-382.

Appendix

1. Symbols and abbreviations

Symbols and abbreviations	Tag
#	space (word bound)
+	morphological bound
*	ungrammatical form
< >	POS tag(s) and/or its meaning between " "

2. The categories (POS-tags) of Korean morphemes[†]

Category	Tag	Category	Tag
General noun	NNG	Vocative postposition	JKV
Verbal noun	NNV	Quotation postposition	JKQ
Adjectival noun	NNA	Adjunctive postposition	PX
Proper noun	NNP	Connective postposition	PC
General Bound noun	NNBG	General ending	EF
Numeral bound noun	NNBU	Pre-ending	EP
Personal pronoun	NPP	Conjunctive ending	EC
Demonstrative pronoun	NPD	Modifier ending	ETM
Cardinal number	NRC	Nominalization ending	ETN
Ordinal number	NRO	Quotation ending	EQ
Verb	VV	General prefix	XPG
Adjectival verb	VA	Numeral prefix	XPU
Auxiliary verb	VX	plural suffix	XSP
Copula	COP	General suffix	XSG
General modifier	MDG	Numeral suffix	XSU
Numeral modifier	MDQ	Modifier suffix	XSM
General adverb	MBG	Verbalization suffix	XSV
Connective adverb	MBC	Adjectivation suffix	XSA
Interjection	IC	Foreign word	SCF
Subjective postposition	JKS	Chinese character	SCD
Objective postposition	JKO	Unit symbol	SCU
Modifier postposition	JKM	Currency unit	SCC
Adverb postposition	JKB	Punctuation	PNT[‡]

[†]The size of a POS-tag set in Korean varies by study: it ranges from 25 tags to 65 tags. However, the number of tags changes according to whether or not punctuation marks are included; whether or not a casual distinction of postposition is applied; and whether or not alphanumeric-symbol tags are specified.

[‡]The category 17 punctuation tags are grouped in PNT.

Handling Conjunctions in Named Entities

Robert Dale[1] and Paweł Mazur[1,2]

[1] Centre for Language Technology, Macquarie University,
NSW 2109, Sydney, Australia
{rdale, mpawel}@ics.mq.edu.au
[2] Institute of Applied Informatics, Wrocław University of Technology
Wyb. Wyspiańskiego 27, 50-370 Wrocław, Poland
Pawel.Mazur@pwr.wroc.pl

Abstract. Although the literature contains reports of very high accuracy figures for the recognition of named entities in text, there are still some named entity phenomena that remain problematic for existing text processing systems. One of these is the ambiguity of conjunctions in candidate named entity strings, an all-too-prevalent problem in corporate and legal documents. In this paper, we distinguish four uses of the conjunction in these strings, and explore the use of a supervised machine learning approach to conjunction disambiguation trained on a very limited set of 'name internal' features that avoids the need for expensive lexical or semantic resources. We achieve 84% correctly classified examples using k-fold evaluation on a data set of 600 instances. Further improvements are likely to require the use of wider domain knowledge and name external features.

1 Introduction

Named entity recognition consists of identifying strings in a text that correspond to named entities, and then classifying each such named entity string as being of a specific type, with typical categories being Company, Person and Location. The range of named entity categories to be identified is usually application dependent.

Introduced for the first time as a separately evaluated task at the Sixth Message Understanding Conference in 1995 (see, for example [1,2]), named entity recognition has attracted a considerable amount of research effort. Initially handled with hand crafted rules (as, for example, in many of the participating systems in MUC-6 and MUC-7) and later by means of statistical approaches (see [3,4]), the state-of-the-art provides high performance for named entity identification and classification both for specific domains and for language- and domain-independent systems.

However, our experience with existing software tells us that there are still some categories of named entities that remain problematic. In particular, relatively little work has explored the disambiguation of conjunctions appearing in named entity strings. Resources such as an appropriate domain lexicon or relevant semantic knowledge might allow a system to emulate a human's ability to determine that a string like *Seshasayee Paper and Boards Limited* is a single company name; but in the absence of such resources, the string could just as easily be interpreted as two separate names. Determining the correct interpretation is clearly important for any application which relies

A. Gelbukh (Ed.): CICLing 2007, LNCS 4394, pp. 131–142, 2007.

on named entity extraction. We are interested in how such interpretations can be arrived at relatively cheaply, and particularly without recourse to expensive-to-construct resources, so as to allow for rapid development in new domains.

The significance of this kind of ambiguity depends, of course, on the extent to which the phenomenon of conjunctions in named entities is widespread. Our current work focuses on a corpus of 13000 company announcements released through the Australian Stock Exchange: these are documents provided by companies in order to meet both continuous and periodic disclosure requirements, in which we want to track mentions of companies and individuals across time.

From this corpus, we selected 45 documents at random; in these documents, there were a total of 545 candidate named entity strings, of which 31 contained conjunctions. This informal sampling suggests that conjunctions appear, on average, in around 5.7% of candidate named entity strings; however, in some documents in our sample, the frequency is as high as 23%. For comparison, in the MUC-7 evaluation data, the proportion of candidate named entity strings containing conjunctions is 4.5%. The documents in our corpus have some features that are not necessarily typical for other corpora. In particular, texts in this domain frequently have some of the characteristics of legal documents, where many sometimes apparently arbitrary elements are given initial capitals. Therefore, we might expect some specific domains, such as those dealing with accountancy and law, to have a higher density of names involving conjunctions. These frequencies are sufficient to suggest that the seeking of an appropriate means of handling conjunctions is a worthwhile and important pursuit.

The paper is structured as follows. In Section 2, we provide a characterisation of the problem to be addressed, and in Section 3 we summarise some related work. In Section 4, we describe the data used in our experiments, the name-internal text features used as attributes for classification, and the data encoding used to encode the features into a feature vector. Then, in Section 5, we discuss how we determined a baseline for our experiments, and describe the machine learning algorithms we used. Section 6 provides a discussion of the evaluation scheme we adopted, and an overview of the results achieved in the experiments. Section 7 presents details of what went wrong by analysing misclassified examples from our data set. Finally, in Section 8, we present a discussion of possible directions in which the approach described here could be further developed.

2   Problem Description

An examination of the candidate named entity strings appearing in our corpus reveals four distinct uses of the conjunction, as exemplified in the following examples:

1. Oil and Gas Ltd
2. Agfa and Fuji
3. John and Mary Smith
4. Company Secretary Resignation and Appointment

In example (1), we have a single named entity that happens to contain an internal conjunction; in example (2), we have a conjunction of two distinct named entities; and in examples (3) and (4), we have conjunctions that, from a linguistic perspective, contain a form of ellipsis, so that one conjunct is incomplete on its own, but can be completed using information provided in the other conjunct. Correspondingly, we distinguish four categories of candidate named entity strings containing conjunctions.

Name Internal Conjunction (NI): This category covers those cases where the candidate named entity string contains one named entity, where the conjunction is part of the name. Some examples from our corpus: *Publishing and Broadcasting Limited, J B Were & Son, Hancock and Gore,* and *Acceptance and Transfer Form.*

Name External Conjunction (NE): This category covers those cases where the conjunction serves to separate two distinct named entities. Some examples from our corpus: *Italy and Central Europe, Hardware & Operating Systems, Mr Danny Fisher and Mr Don Wilson,* and *American Express and Visa International.*

Right-Copy Separator (RC): This category of conjunction separates two named entities, where the first is incomplete in itself but can be completed by copying information from the right-hand conjunct. This is perhaps most common in conjunctions of proper names, as in *John and Mary Smith,* but appears in other contexts as well. Some examples from our corpus: *State and Federal Government, Eastern and Western Australia,* and *General & Miscellaneous Equipment.*

Left-Copy Separator (LC): This is similar to the above category, but instead of copying information from the right-hand conjunct, to complete the constituent named entities we need to copy information from the left conjunct. Examples in our corpus: *Gas Supply and Demand, Financial Statements and Reports, Hospital Equipment & Systems, J H Blair Company Secretary & Corporate Counsel.*

Conceptually, we might view the last two categories as subtypes of the more general category **Copying Separator**; however, we keep the two categories separate since the process of reconstructing the unelided conjuncts is different in each case.

Our approach to the problem of determining the type of a conjunction in a candidate named entity string is to use a machine-learned classifier. We are particularly interested in seeing how far we can address the task using only limited knowledge sources: in the work described here, we restrict ourselves to very limited gazetteers that contain the most frequent proper nouns that appear in our corpus, and to the use of so-called 'name-internal' properties (i.e., characteristics of the candidate string itself, rather than of its surrounding context). Using only limited gazetteers maximises portability; considering only name internal properties will make it easier to see the impact of subsequently adding contextual information. Perhaps more importantly with regard to the specific data we are dealing with, we find many candidate strings appearing in typographic contexts such as tables where the relevant local context can be hard to determine, if it exists at all; in such cases, all we can rely on are the name-internal features.

3   Related Work

One of the first approaches to named entities containing conjunctions is reported in [5]. This work dealt with only two categories of conjunctions (those we have termed Name Internal and Name-External), but also considered the use of commas as conjunctions.

Their solution was based on heuristics using the syntactic number of the verb used with the candidate named entity string and the number of conjuncts in the expression (a large number suggests a Name External conjunction). The reference to name-external syntactic information here means that this approach would not work for much of our data, which is contained in tables.

Coates-Stephens [6] describes the FUNES system, developed for the acquisition of proper names and their descriptions from free text. This work covers all four categories of conjunction that we have identified; the solution is based on the identification of the syntactic number or keywords in a candidate named entity string or in its description, for example in apposition.

McDonald's Sparser [7] uses hand-written rules that make use of name-internal and name-external features of candidate named entity strings; The approach produces nearly 100% correct results on a selected sublanguage for "Who's News" articles from the Wall Street Journal, but McDonald notes that a new implementation would be required in order to apply the approach to a more diverse set of texts.

Mikheev et al. [8] suggested the strategy of examining the preceding document context to identify candidate conjuncts that should be considered as separate named entities. Mikheev et al. mention this approach being part of their system used in the MUC-7 competition, but no data is reported on the accuracy of this kind of heuristic; in our experience, there are many cases where there are no antecedent mentions that can be used in this way. Furthermore, in the MUC-7 data Left- and Right-Copy categories are not distinguished from Name-Internal.

In more recent work of relevance, we would point to the novel approach to segmentation described in [9]. Using multilabel classification, it is possible to tag overlapping and non-contiguous segments. However, to our knowledge there are no available results to indicate how well this approach would work for the conjunction disambiguation problem. Other work [10] has used the presence of a conjunction as a feature in machine-learning-based NER, but it is unclear what benefits were gained by introducing this feature.

More generally, of course, the processing of conjunctions has been a focus of interest in linguistics; in particular, Categorial Grammar (see, for example, [11]) provides a sophisticated treatment of the syntax of conjunctions.

4   Experimental Setup

4.1   Corpus and Data Preparation

The focus of our project is a data set from the Australian Stock Exchange (ASX). This data set consists of a large number of company announcements: for a variety of regulatory reasons, listed companies provide around 100000 documents to the ASX each year, and the ASX subsequently makes these available to users via the web. For more information about the documents in this corpus, and a discussion of our general approach to processing them, see [12].

The corpus used for our research consisted of a 13460 document sub-corpus drawn from a larger corpus of company announcements from the ASX. The documents range in length from 8 to 1000 lines of text.

Table 1. Example distributions in categories

NI	NE	RC	LC	Sum
185	350	39	26	600
30.8%	58.3%	6.5%	4.3%	100%

Evaluation data was prepared as follows. For our purposes, we define a candidate named entity string to be any sequence of words with initial capitals and one embedded conjunction. We also allowed these strings to contain the lowercased preposition *of* and the determiners *a, an,* and *the*. Candidate named entity strings from sentences written completely in uppercase or with every word being initcapped (i.e., strings in 'title case') were ignored. Using a Perl script, we extracted 10925 candidate named entity string instances from our corpus, corresponding to 6437 unique forms. From the set of unique forms, we randomly selected 600 examples for our test data set. In a small number of cases, problems arising from typographic features such as ASCII formatted tables caused us to manually correct some individual strings. An example of the need for such correction is demonstrated by the candidate extracted string *Name of Entity Hancock & Gore Limited*, where it turns out that *Name of Entity* is a label in a list, and *Hancock & Gore Limited*, being a company name, is the value of that label; however, in our data, the text extraction process has caused the separating formatting to be lost, resulting in the two strings being concatenated. In this case we remove *Name of Entity* from the string extracted by our Perl script, on the assumption that a smarter text extraction technique would be able to interpret the layout more accurately.

The resulting set of strings was then annotated using a set of small gazetteers listing common person names, company names, locations and other elements that are frequent in our corpus and related to our tagset, which is described in the next section.[1]

The categories of the conjunctions in the candidate named entity strings were assigned by a human annotator. Table 1 presents the distribution of evaluation instances across the four conjunction categories introduced above.

4.2 The Tag Set

We developed a 16-tag tag set, presented in Table 2, to annotate the tokens in our corpus of candidate named entity strings. Most of the tags, such as Loc, Org, GivenName, AlphaNum, Dir, and PersDesig, are the same as those used by many other named entity recognizers; some, however, are specific to our needs. The Son tag is used to annotate tokens whose surface form is either *Son* or *Sons*: these occur relatively often in company names (as, for example, in *A Davies & Sons Pty Ltd*), and are a strong indicator of the Name Internal Conjunction category. The Of and Det tags are used to mark the preposition *of* and the determiners *the, a* and *an*, irrespective of casing. Finally, Init-Capped is used to annotate any tokens that do not belong to the other categories, or which are ambiguous between those categories.

---

[1] This is part of our strategy for fast deployment in a new domain, where a seed lexicon is constructed from the most frequent words that contain initial capitals.

Table 2. The tagset used for text annotation

No	Tag	Meaning	No	Tag	Meaning
1	Loc	The name of a location	9	CompDesig	A company designator
2	Org	The name of an organization	10	Son	*Son(s)*
3	GivenName	A person's given name	11	Dir	A compass direction
4	FamilyName	A person's family name	12	AlphaNum	An alphanumeric expression
5	Initial	An initial in the range A-Z	13	Month	The name of a month
6	CompPos	A position within a company	14	Of	Preposition *of*
7	Abbrev	Abbreviation	15	Det	Determiners *the, a, an*
8	PersDesig	A person designator	16	InitCapped	Unrecognized initcapped token

Table 3. The popularity of tags in annotated data

Tag	Occurrences	Percentage	Tag	Occurrences	Percentage
InitCapped	925	42.24	Of	76	3.47
Loc	245	11.19	Abbrev	73	3.33
Org	175	7.99	PersDesig	39	1.78
FamilyName	164	7.49	Det	31	1.42
CompDesig	138	6.30	Dir	12	0.55
Initial	108	4.93	Son	7	0.32
CompPos	99	4.52	Month	6	0.27
GivenName	89	4.06	AlphaNum	3	0.14

We also recognize multi-word elements where there is no ambiguity (for example, in the case of unambiguous person, location and company names). For example, although the company name *Australia and New Zealand Banking Group Limited* is not in our gazetteer, *New Zealand* as a country name is, and so this string is recognized as a sequence of tokens whose types are marked as Loc and Loc Org CompDesig; here the second Loc tag corresponds to the pair of tokens *New Zealand*.

We refer to the sequence of tags assigned to a particular string as a **pattern**. A pattern also indicates the conjunction type present in the string, as determined through the human annotation; so, for the example above, the complete pattern is ⟨Loc and Loc Org CompDesig, Internal⟩.

Table 3 presents the number of tags of each type used to annotate our data set; in total there were 2190 tags assigned over the 600 candidate named entity strings, for an average of 3.65 tags per instance.

Notably, a significant number of the tokens are tagged as simply being of type Init-Capped; this is in keeping with our deliberate use of small gazetteers, and is likely to be the case in any domain where new names are constantly being introduced.

4.3   Encoding

For the purposes of machine learning, we encode each pattern in the following way. We create an attribute for each of the 16 tag types for each of the left and right sides of a conjunction, for a total of 32 attributes. The attributes are of integer type with values $\{0, 1\}$, thus signaling either the presence or absence of a token of that type anywhere within either conjunct. We also introduce an additional binary attribute, ConjForm, for encoding the lexical form of a conjunction in the string: 0 denotes &; 1 denotes *and*.

With each data instance there is associated a categorical ConjType attribute with the values {Internal, External, Right-Copy, Left-Copy}; this is used to encode the actual category of the conjunction in the string.

5   The Algorithms

5.1   Baseline

It is quite common to determine a baseline using the 0-R algorithm, which simple predicts the majority class [13]. On our data set, with this approach we get a baseline accuracy of 58.33%. However, we have found that with the 1-R algorithm, described in [14], we obtain a better-performing model based simply on the lexical form of the conjunction:

```
IF ConjForm='&' THEN PredCat←Internal
IF ConjForm='and' THEN PredCat←External.
```

This very simple rule provides a baseline of 69.83%.

5.2   Classifiers

The experiments were conducted using the WEKA toolkit [13]. This provides implementations of several machine learning algorithms, along with the data structures and code needed to perform data input and output, data filtering, and the evaluation and presentation of results.

After some initial exploration using a variety of algorithms for supervised machine learning available in WEKA, we chose the following: the Multilayer Perceptron (see [15]), two lazy algorithms (IBk and K*; see [16] and [17] respectively), and three tree algorithms: Random Tree (an algorithm for constructing a decision tree that considers K random features at each node), Logistic Model Trees (see [18]) and J4.8 (see [19]). We also include here the results for Naïve Bayes and Sequential Minimal Optimization (see [20]), given the popularity of these methods in the field.

6   Results

6.1   Evaluation Scheme

For evaluation, we used the k-fold method with $k = 10$, so that our data set of 600 examples was divided into ten folds by random selection of instances from the original data set. Then, for each of the folds, the classification models were built on the remaining 540 examples and tested on the held-out fold. The sum of correctly classified examples for all folds is the final result. There are some side effects of this evaluation approach, which we mention in Section 7; however, it still makes more sense to use this approach for our small data set of 600 examples, than artificially dividing this set into even smaller training and test data sets.

Table 4. Results for k-fold evaluation

Algorithm	Correctly classified (out of 600)
IBk	84.00% (504)
Random Tree	83.83% (503)
K*	83.50% (501)
SMO	82.33% (494)
Mult. Perc.	82.17% (493)
LMT	81.17% (487)
J4.8	79.50% (477)
Naïve Bayes	70.67% (424)
Baseline	69.83% (419)

Table 5. Detailed accuracy by category of a conjunction for results of IBk classifier

Category	Precision	Recall	F-Measure
Name Internal	0.814	0.876	0.844
Name External	0.872	0.897	0.885
Right-Copy	0.615	0.410	0.492
Left-Copy	0.800	0.462	0.585
weighted mean	0.834	0.840	0.833

Table 6. Confusion matrix for IBk

Name Internal	Name External	Right Copy	Left Copy	→ classified as ↓
162	28	6	3	Name Internal
18	314	17	11	Name External
4	6	16	0	Right Copy
1	2	0	12	Left Copy

6.2   Classification Results

Table 4 presents the results achieved in the experiments. All algorithms scored above the baseline, though Naïve Bayes, with the worst result, was very close to the baseline.

The best classifier turned out to be IBk, the K-nearest neighbours algorithm. The precision, recall and F-measure for this case are presented in Table 5. Table 6 provides a confusion matrix with the desired and actual classification of examples. The best results are for Name Internal and Name External conjunctions. The low results for Right- and Left-Copy Separator conjunction types are mainly because of low recall for these categories: 0.410 and 0.462, respectively. This is most likely caused by the fact that there are very few examples of these categories: 6.5% and 4.3%, respectively (see Table 1).

We used the χ^2 test for equality of distributions and a significance level of 90% to check whether the difference between the result of IBk and other algorithms is statistically significant; on this basis, we find that only the difference between the IBk algorithm and the Random Tree algorithm is no greater than chance.

It is interesting to note that the relatively simple Random Tree algorithm scored so highly. We tried different values for its parameter K, the number of randomly chosen attributes to be considered at each node. The result presented in the table is for $K = 22$; for the default $K = 1$, the algorithm correctly classified 490 examples.

7   Analysis

7.1   Conjunction Category Indicators

A statistical analysis of the data reveals some strong conjunction category indicators.

For the Name External these are:

- a Month tag in the left conjunct (as in *September and December*);
- a Comp-Desig or Abbrev tag in the left conjunct (as in *Alliance Technology Pty Ltd and Suco International* or *NLD and BRL Hardy*); but there are exceptions: *JP Morgan Investment Management Australia Ltd and Associates, Association of Mining & Exploration Companies* and *ASX Settlement and Transfer Corporation*, which are all Name Internal;
- a Month or PersDesig tag in the right hand conjunct (as in *February and March* or *Mr R L Hanwright & Mrs M J Hanwright*; and
- a GivenName, Dir or Abbrev tag in the right hand conjunct, although there are exceptions: *Beaches and Quay West Brisbane* and *SMDS and ATM WANS* (both are of the Right-Copy Separator type).

The presence of a Son tag is a strong indicator of a Name Internal conjunction.

7.2 Error Analysis

We have demonstrated that with supervised machine learning over a simple set of features, we achieve a classification error rate of 16–18%. We now provide some discussion of the classification errors made by the best-performing learner, the IBk algorithm.

InitCapped: Of the 96 misclassified examples, 38 (39.58%) consist of a pattern consisting entirely of InitCapped tags. In such cases, classification ends up being determined on the basis of the ConjForm attribute: if the value is &, then the conjunction is classified as being Name Internal, and if its value is *and*, the conjunction is classified as being Name External. Consequently, the following examples are misclassified: *Victorian Casino and Gaming Authority*, *Coal Handling and Preparation Plan*, *Gas Supply and Demand Study*, and *Explanatory Memorandum & Proxy Form*.

At the same time, there were 96 InitCapped-only patterns that were classified correctly; this means that out of all 134 InitCapped-only patterns 71.64% were classified correctly, which is quite consistent with the previously-discussed baseline.

There were also another 11 misclassified instances consisting mainly of InitCapped tags along with some other tags; examples of these are: *Australian Labor Party and Independent Members* ⟨Loc InitCapped Org and InitCapped InitCapped⟩, *Association of Mining & Exploration Companies* ⟨CompDesig Of InitCapped & InitCapped InitCapped⟩ and *Securities and Exchange Commission* ⟨InitCapped and InitCapped Org⟩.

Long Patterns: Two misclassified instances were represented by relatively long patterns: for example, *Fellow of the Australian Institute of Geoscientists and The Australasian Institute of Mining*, represented by the 12-tag pattern ⟨CompPos Of Det Loc Org Of InitCapped and Det Loc Org Of InitCapped⟩.

Other Interesting Cases: There were two cases of misclassified strings whose patterns themselves contained more common patterns as subsequences; in these cases, the information in the larger pattern was not insufficient to override the pull of the embedded pattern. One example is the string *WD & HO Wills Holdings Limited*: being the name of a company, here the conjunction is Name-Internal, with the pattern ⟨Initial Initial & Initial Initial FamilyName CompDesig⟩. However, this is incorrectly classified as containing a Right-Copy Separator conjunction, as is the case in the constituent pattern ⟨Initial Initial & Initial Initial FamilyName⟩.

The string *Wayne Jones and Topsfield Pty Ltd*, which in reality involves a Name External conjunction, was classified as Name Internal. We would note here that, in the absence of additional contextual information, conjunctions of person names and company names are often ambiguous even for humans.

Another related highly ambiguous type of example corresponds to the pattern ⟨FamilyName and FamilyName⟩, which can either be a conjunction of two person names or just one company name.

We also note here the impact of the k-fold evaluation approach. Since a new model is built for each fold, it turns out that the IBk classifier assigned category Name Internal to instances of the pattern ⟨InitCapped and InitCapped Org⟩ in one case, but assigned Right-Copy in another case. Consequently, both *Federal and State Government* (Right-Copy), being in one fold, and *Securities and Exchange Commission* (Name Internal), being in another fold, were misclassified.

Other Observations: There are also some cases which we expected to be handled easily, but which turned out to be problematic. For example, *D J Carmichael Pty Limited and Kirke Securities Ltd* was classified as Name Internal, although it contains company designators in both conjuncts and the form of conjunction is *and*. Similarly, the string *Department of Transport and Department of Main Roads* (with the pattern ⟨Org Of Init-Capped and Org Of InitCapped InitCapped, External⟩) was classified as Name Internal.

Finally, there are around 15–20 examples for which it is difficult to provide a clear explanation for misclassification along the lines of the cases above; in these cases, the major issue is the classifier's ability to generalize the rules (which is not necessarily due to a deficiency in the algorithm, but perhaps due to the simple tagset we use).

8   Conclusions and Future Work

We have presented the problem of conjunction disambiguation in named entities and defined four categories of conjunction in candidate named entity strings. We defined the problem as one of classification and showed that it can be handled well using supervised machine learning algorithms and a limited set of name-internal features.

Given the similarity in results for most of the different machine-learned classifiers we used, we conclude that a significant improvement of results lies in a richer feature selection rather than in choice of the classifier. This conclusion is also supported by the fact that some examples are difficult for a human to classify without wider context or domain knowledge.

A number of issues arise in the work reported here as candidates for future work. We have restricted ourselves to candidate strings which contain a single conjunction; however, there are of course cases where multiple conjunctions appear. One category consists of examples like *Audited Balance Sheet and Profit and Loss Account*, where again the kinds of syntactic ambiguity involved would suggest a more syntactically-driven approach would be worth consideration. Another category consists of candidate named entity strings that contain commas as well as lexicalised conjunctions.

A rudimentary analysis of frequently occurring n-grams in our corpus makes it clear that some strings containing conjunctions appear frequently. For example, in our corpus there are 296 occurrences of the string *Quarter Activities and Cashflow Report*,[2] making it the most frequent 5-gram. Moreover, there are another 34 occurrences of this string with the conjunction & in place of *and*, and another six strings with the variant spelling *Cash Flow*. In any real application context, it would make sense to filter out these common cases via table lookup before applying a machine learning process to classify the remaining conjunctions. This kind of preprocessing could identify frequent strings containing either Name Internal or Name External conjunctions. Another form of preprocessing could involve the analysis of abbreviations: for example, in the string *ASX Settlement and Transfer Corporation (ASTC)*, the abbreviation *ASTC* could be used to decide that the preceding conjunction has the category Name Internal.

More generally, there are three directions in which we might move in order to further improve performance.

First, we can always use larger gazetteers to reduce the number of tokens that can only be tagged as InitCapped. This, of course, has a cost consequence; in current work, we are exploring how performance on this task improves as larger numbers of frequent name elements from the corpus are incorporated into the gazetteers. Another consequence of extending gazetteers is the problem of the same token being in two or more gazetteers, for example Location and FamilyName. A naive approach would be to assign these tokens the catch-all InitCapped tag, but since this is what we want to avoid, we could also assign all the ambiguous tags and indicate this fact in the feature vector. This would require a redesign of the feature vector.

Second, we can make more sophisticated use of the name internal properties of the candidate string. This includes, as noted above with regard to the *Exchanges* example, taking account of the syntactic number of the constituent tokens. Armed with a part of speech tagger, we could also attempt heuristic chunking of the candidate strings which might assist in determining conjunction type; and a resource like WordNet might be used to identify terms with shared superordinates, as in the *Paper and Boards* example.

Third, we can extend the learning process to take account of contextual features. As noted earlier, there are cases where the local context cannot be easily determined, but in many cases local syntactic information such as the number of an associated verb can serve to distinguish the type of conjunction being used. However, as demonstrated here, it is already possible to achieve a high level of accuracy without recourse to name external features; as we noted earlier, this is important in our domain, where names often appear in tables, making local context unavailable.

Acknowledgements

We acknowledge the support of the Capital Markets Cooperative Research Centre in carrying out this work. The work was carried out while the second author was a visiting scholar at Macquarie University. The final version of this paper was prepared while the second author was a guest researcher at DFKI, Saarbrücken.

---

[2] This appears frequently as a substring of longer expressions like *First Quarter Activities and Cashflow Report*, *Second Quarter Activities and Cashflow Report*, and so on.

References

1. Grishman, R., Sundheim, B.: Design of the MUC-6 Evaluation. In: Sixth Message Understanding Conference (MUC-6): Proceedings of a Conference held in Columbia, Maryland, November 6-8, 1995, Los Altos, Ca., Morgan Kaufmann (1995)
2. Grishman, R., Sundheim, B.: Message Understanding Conference-6: A Brief History. In: COLING 1996 Volume 1: The 16th International Conference on Computational Linguistics, Los Altos, Ca., Morgan Kaufmann (1996)
3. Sang, E.F.T.K.: Introduction to the CoNLL-2002 Shared Task: Language-Independent Named Entity Recognition. In Roth, D., van den Bosch, A., eds.: Proceedings of the 6th Conference on Natural Language Learning, Taipei, Taiwan (2002) 155–158
4. Sang, E.F.T.K., Meulder, F.D.: Introduction to the CoNLL-2003 Shared Task: Language-Independent Named Entity Recognition. In Daelemans, W., Osborne, M., eds.: Proceedings of the 7th Conference on Natural Language Learning, Edmonton, Canada (2003) 142–147
5. Rau, L.F.: Extracting company names from text. In: Proceedings of the Seventh Conference on Artificial Intelligence Applications, IEEE (1991) 189–194
6. Coates-Stephens, S.: The analysis and acquisition of proper names for the understanding of free text. Computers and the Humanities **V26** (1992) 441–456
7. McDonald, D.D.: Internal and external evidence in the identification and semantic categorization of proper names. In: B. Boguraev and J. Pustejovsky, editors, Corpus processing for lexical acquisition, pages 21–39. (1996)
8. Mikheev, A., Grover, C., Moens, M.: Description of the LTG System Used for MUC-7. In: Proc. of MUC-7 Conf. (1998)
9. McDonald, R., Crammer, K., Pereira, F.: Flexible text segmentation with structured multilabel classification. EMNLP (2005)
10. Solorio, T.: Improvement of Named Entity Tagging by Machine Learning. Technical Report CCC-04-004, Coordinacin de Ciencias Computacionales (2004)
11. Steedman, M.: Dependency and Coordination in the Grammar of Dutch and English. Language **61** (1985) 523–568
12. Dale, R., Calvo, R., Tilbrook, M.: Key Element Summarisation: Extracting Information from Company Announcements. In: Proc. of the 17th Australian Joint Conf. on AI, 7th-10th Dec. 2004, Australia. (2004)
13. Witten, I.H., Frank, E.: Data Mining: Practical machine learning tools and techniques. Morgan Kaufmann, San Francisco (2005)
14. Holte, R.C.: Very simple classification rules perform well on most commonly used datasets. Machine Learning **11** (1993) 63–91
15. Rojas, R.: Neural networks: a systematic introduction. Springer-Verlag New York, Inc., New York, NY, USA (1996)
16. Aha, D.W., Kibler, D., Albert, M.K.: Instance-based learning algorithms. Mach. Learn. **6** (1991) 37–66
17. Cleary, J.G., Trigg, L.E.: K*: An Instance-based Learner Using an Entropic Distance Measure. In: Proceedings of the 12th International Conference on Machine Learning, Morgan Kaufmann (1995) 108–114
18. Landwehr, N., Hall, M., Frank, E.: Logistic Model Trees. Machine Learning **59(1/2)** (2005) 161–205
19. Quinlan, J.R.: C4.5: programs for machine learning. Morgan Kaufmann Publishers Inc., San Francisco, CA, USA (1993)
20. Platt, J.C.: Fast training of support vector machines using sequential minimal optimization. In: Advances in Kernel Methods: Support Vector Learning, Cambridge, MA, USA, MIT Press (1999) 185–208

ANERsys: An Arabic Named Entity Recognition System Based on Maximum Entropy

Yassine Benajiba, Paolo Rosso, and José Miguel Benedí Ruiz

Dpto. Sistemas Informáticos y Computación (DSIC),
Universidad Politécnica de Valencia, Spain
{ybenajiba, prosso, jbenedi}@dsic.upv.es

Abstract. The task of Named Entity Recognition (NER) allows to identify proper names as well as temporal and numeric expressions, in an open-domain text. NER systems proved to be very important for many tasks in Natural Language Processing (NLP) such as Information Retrieval and Question Answering tasks. Unfortunately, the main efforts to build reliable NER systems for the Arabic language have been made in a commercial frame and the approach used as well as the accuracy of the performance are not known. In this paper, we present ANERsys: a NER system built exclusively for Arabic texts based-on n-grams and maximum entropy. Furthermore, we present both the specific Arabic language dependent heuristic and the gazetteers we used to boost our system. We developed our own training and test corpora (ANERcorp) and gazetteers (ANERgazet) to train, evaluate and boost the implemented technique. A major effort was conducted to make sure all the experiments are carried out in the same framework of the CONLL 2002 conference. We carried out several experiments and the preliminary results showed that this approach allows to tackle successfully the problem of NER for the Arabic language.

1 Introduction

We carried out a research on the Arabic language NLP tools and resources in general (corpora, gazetteers, POS taggers,etc). This led us to the conclusion that in comparison with other languages Arabic misses lexical resources, especially free resources available for a research purposes.

Some of the most important resources that any language requires are the NER systems which allow to identify proper names in an open-domain text. The study of English and French newspapers proved that these entities represent 10% of the articles [1]. Many are the tasks which rely on the huge quantity of information NER systems may provide: Information Extraction (IE), Information Retrieval (IR), Question Answering (QA), text clustering, etc. In the sixth Message Understanding Conference (MUC-6)[1] the NER task was defined as three sub-tasks: ENAMEX (for the proper names), TIMEX (for temporal expressions) and

---

[1] http://cs.nyu.edu/cs/faculty/grishman/muc6.html

A. Gelbukh (Ed.): CICLing 2007, LNCS 4394, pp. 143–153, 2007.
© Springer-Verlag Berlin Heidelberg 2007

NUMEX (for numeric expression). The first sub-task is the one we are concerned about. ENAMEX was defined as the extraction of proper names and classification of each one of them as: (i) Organization (named corporate, governmental, or other organizational entity); (ii) Location (name of politically or geographically defined location) or (iii) Person (named person or family). Not many are the available corpora for the NER task. For instance, in the CONLL 2002 conference[2] the available corpora were only for the Chinese, English, French, Japanese, Portuguese and Spanish languages [2]. This is the reason why we had to build our own corpora to carry out this work. It is our intention to make the corpora available in order to share it with other researchers interested in carrying out a comparative work on the NER task in Arabic. It is important to point out that some companies have built Arabic NER systems for comercial ends: Siraj[3] (by Sakhr), ClearTags[4] (by ClearForest), NetOwlExtractor[5] (by NetOwl) and InxightSmartDiscoveryEntityExtractor[6] (by Inxight). Unfortunately, no performance accuracy nor technical details have been provided and a comparative study of the systems is not possible.

Two are mainly the techniques which were used to build NER systems for the Arabic. They are based, respectively, on the use of a set of keywords and special verbs as triggers and a set of rules to extract the proper names [3], and second using a high precision morphological analysis [4].

With respect to language-independent NER systems, many are the research works which were done: in the shared task of the CONLL 2002 and CONLL 2003[7] for testing the English, Spanish and Dutch corpora, most of the best participants used a maximum entropy approach [5][6][7][8], whereas some others preferred to combine morphological and contextual evidence [8]. Moreover, in [9] very good results were obtained using a character level n-gram model and in [10] a comparison made between the HMM (F-measure of 31.87) and the maximum entropy (55.77) (additional features and a collection of first names as external source allow to increase the F-measure, respectively, up to 84.24 and 85.61). Finally, in the NAACL/HLT 2004[8], a NER system based on maximum entropy for the English, Chinese and Arabic languages [11], obtained F-measure 68.5 for Arabic and 68.6 for Chinese. The Arabic corpus used to carry out the experiments had 166.8k tokens, and it was obtained from ACE Evaluation (September 2003), now it is held now by the Language Data Consortium[9] (LDC) and it is not freely accessible. Furthermore, a text segmentation technique was used for the Arabic text to reduce data sparseness mainly because Arabic is a highly inflected language[10]. Thus, through the above study of the different systems we

---

[2] http://www.cnts.ua.ac.be/conll2002/ner/
[3] http://siraj.sakhr.com/
[4] http://www.clearforest.com/index.asp
[5] http://www.netowl.com/products/extractor.html
[6] http://www.inxight.com/products/smartdiscovery/ee/index.php
[7] http://www.cnts.ua.ac.be/conll2003/ner/
[8] http://www1.cs.columbia.edu/~pablo/hlt-naacl04/
[9] http://www.ldc.upenn.edu/
[10] http://corporate.britannica.com/nlt/arabic.html

found out that the technique that mainly proved to be efficient for the NER task is the maximum entropy.

The rest of this paper is structured as follows. In the second section of this paper we will focus on the Arabic NER systems. Moreover, the details about Arabic inflections will be given. Section Three will describe with more details the maximum entropy approach. Section Four is dedicated to show the data sets we built to carry out our experimental work. Finally, in the fifth section we present the results of our preliminary experiments, whereas in the sixth section we draw some conclusions and discuss future works.

2   Named Entity Recognition in Arabic

The earlier mentioned language-independent NER systems which participated in the CONLL conference used a general approach based on the common character-istics to all languages. When working with the Arabic language, some important characteristics need to be taken into account:

(i) a character may have up to three different forms, each form corresponds to a position of the character in the word (beginning, middle or end).

(ii) Arabic does not have capital letters; this characteristic represents a con-siderable obstacle for the NER task because in other languages capital letters represent a very important feature;

(iii) it has long vowels and short vowels, but short vowels are not used any-more in newspapers and this fact introduces a quite high ambiguity in texts (disambiguation using these short vowels is not possible);

(iv) and finally, it is a language with very complex morphology because it is highly inflectional.

The last characteristic is the most important for a NER perspective. The Arabic language is highly inflectional because the general form of a word is:

Prefix(es) + Stem + Suffix(es)

The number of prefixes and suffixes might be 0 or more. Affixes are added to the stem to obtain the needed expression. For instance, a simple example would be: the word *"manzil"* in Arabic means *"house"* and *"almanzil"* is *"the house"*. This example shows how an Arabic word may be translated in two words. A more complicated example would be, for instance, the word *"wasayaktoubounaha"* which means *"and they will write it"*. If we write this word in the general form introduced above it would be:

wa + sa + ya + "ktoub" + ouna + ha

For a NER perpective, this peculiarity of the Arabic language will is a great obstacle because it causes data sparseness.

In the NER system described in [3], a set of rules and keywords was used in order to extract proper names (the problem of data spareseness was not mentioned in the paper). In [11] the authors emphasized this problem and they used an algorithm of text segmentation (introduced in[12]). This algorithm is based on a n-gram language model, and it computes the morpheme trigram probabilities. In order to do so, they have used a manually segmented corpus; it was reported that the algorithm gives an accuracy of 97%. It is important to emphasize that such algorithm is not easy to implement since it requires a large manually segmented corpus for training.

In the ANERsys we take into consideration the data sparsness problem. Instead of performing a text segmentation we use an heuristic method which takes into consideration only prefixes.

3   The Maximum Entropy Approach

The Maximum Entropy (ME) technique has been successful not only in the NER task but in many other NLP tasks [15][16][17]. Let introduce the ME approach through a simple example. Let us consider the following sentence taken from the Aljazeera English newspaper[11]:

"Sudan's Darfur region remains the most pressing humanitarian problem in the world, the Food and Agriculture Organisation says."

We need to classifiy the word *"Darfur"* as one of the following four classes: (i) *Pers*: proper name of a *Person*; (ii) *Loc*: proper name of a *Location*; or (iii) *Org*: proper name of an *Organization*; (iv) *O*: not a proper name. If we consider that we do not have any information about the word then the best probability distribution is the one which assigns the same probability to each of the four classes. Therefore, we would choose the following distribution:

$$p(O) = p(Pers) = p(Loc) = p(Org) = 0.25 \tag{1}$$

because it is the one that less introduces biases of all the possible distributions. In other words, it is the distribution that maximizes the entropy (In this section we mean by "The best probability distribution" the distribution that minimizes the Kullback-Leibler[12] distance measure to the real probability distribution).

Let suppose instead that we succeeded in obtaining some statistical information from a training corpus and that 90% of the words starting with a capital letter (and not being the first word of the sentence) are proper names. Thus, the new probability distribution would be:

$$p(O) = 0.1 \quad \text{and} \quad p(Pers) = p(Loc) = p(Org) = 0.3 \tag{2}$$

This example briefly shows how a maximum entropy classifier performs. Whenever we need to integrate additional information it calculates the best distribution which is the one that maximizes the entropy. The idea behind this approach

---

[11] http://aljazeera.net

[12] http://ar.wikipedia.org/wiki/Kullback-Leibler_divergence

is that the best distribution is obtained when we do not use any other information but the one we had in the training phase, and if no information is available about some classes, the rest of the probability mass is distributed uniformly between them.

In the example, we managed to make the probability distribution calculations because we considered a reduced number of classes, and we also took into consideration simple statistical information about the proper names (generally called *"context information"*). Unfortunately, this is never true for the real cases where we usually have a greater number of classes and a big range of context information. Therefore, a manual calculation of the probability distribution is not possible. Thus, a robust maximum entropy classifiers model is needed. The exponential model proved to be an elegant approach for the problem which uses various information sources, as the following equation illustrates:

$$p(c|x) = \frac{1}{Z(x)} * exp(\sum_i \lambda_i.f_i(x,c)) \tag{3}$$

Z(x) is for normalization and may be expressed as:

$$Z(x) = \sum_{c'} exp(\sum_i \lambda_i.f_i(x,c')) \tag{4}$$

Where c is the class, x is a context information and $f_i(x,c)$ is the i-th feature. The features are binary functions indicating how the different classes are related to one or many context information, for example:

$f_j(x,c)= 1$ if $word(x)=$ *"Darfur"* and $c=B-LOC$, 0 otherwise.

To each feature there is an associated weight λ_i since each feature is related to a class and thus it may have a bigger or a lower influence in the classification decision for one class or another. The weights are estimated using the General Iterative Scaling (GIS) algorithm, which ensures convergence on the correct weights after a number of iterations [14].

From a general viewpoint, building a maximum entropy classifier consists of the following steps:

(i) by means of observation and experiments to determine a list of characteristics about the context in which named entities usualy appear (generaly not as simple because some of these information proved not to be so useful and it needs to be replaced; therefore, we might return to this step several times to optimise this list);

(ii) to estimate the different weights λ_i using the GIS algorithm.

(iii) to build a classifier which basically computes for each word the probabilities to be assigned to each of the considered classes: $p(B - PERS|w_i)$, $p(I - PERS|w_i)$, etc. using the ME formula and then assigning the class with the highest probability to this word.

The feature set we used to implement ANERsys is described in detail in the fifth section.

4   The Developed Resources

As we have mentioned in the introduction, it is not possible to find free Arabic corpora oriented to the NER task. Therefore, we have decided to build our own corpora: for training and test. Moreover, we have built also gazetteers to test the effect of using external information sources on the system. It is our intention to make available theses resources on the web in order to ease the further research activity of the NER task in Arabic. Following, we present the main characteristics of the developed resources:

4.1   ANERcorp[13]: Two Corpora for Training and Test

As reported in the CONLL 2002, the annotated corpora should contain the words of the text together with the correspondent type. The same classes that were defined in the MUC-6 (organization, location and person) were used in the corpora; "Miscellaneous" is the single class that was added for Named Entities which do not belong to any of the other classes. Therefore, any word on the text should be annotated as one of the following tags:

B-PERS : The Beginning of the name of a PERSon.
I-PERS : The continuation (Inside) of the name of a PERSon.
B-LOC   : The Beginning of the name of a LOCation.
I-LOC   : The Inside of the name of a LOCation.
B-ORG : The Beginning of the name of an ORGanization.
I-ORG   : The Inside of the name of an ORGanization.
B-MISC : The Beginning of the name of an entity which does not belong to any
               of the previous classes (MISCellaneous).
I-MISC   : The Inside of the name of an entity which does not belong to any of
               the previous classes.
O   : The word is not a named entity (Other).

In CONLL, it was also decided to use the same format for the training file for all the languages, organising the file in 2 columns: the first column for the words and the second one for the tags. Figure 1 shows extracts from the CONLL 2002 English training corpus and from the training Arabic ANERcorp we developed:

With respect to the CONLL 2002, we have not built three corpora for the Arabic (one for training, another for a first test which consists of fixing parameters and a last one for the final test) but just two corpora (for training and testing). Before, we performed a text normalisation in order to avoid high data sparseness effects. For instance, because of the peculiarity of the language, if no normalisation is performed on the corpus we could find the word *"Iran"* written in two different ways. Unfortunately, the normalisation of the Arabic text is not carried out in a unique way, but looking at the TREC 2001[14] and 2002[8] Arabic/English Cross Lingual IR it is mostly done replacing few characters by an

---

[13] http://www.dsic.upv.es/~ybenajiba
[14] http://trec.nist.gov/

with O	فرانكفورتB-LOC
Del B-PER	, O
Bosque I-PER	اعلنO
in O	اتحادB-ORG
the O	صناعةI-ORG
final O	السياراتI-ORG
years O	فيO
of O	
the O	المانياB-LOC
seventies O	امسO
in O	الاولO
Real B-ORG	انO
Madrid I-ORG	
. O	

Fig. 1. Extracts from the English training corpus used in CONLL 2002 and the training Arabic ANERcorp

equivalent one. This gave good results for IR systems but it does not seem to be convenient for a NER task because it would cause a loss of valuable information needed to extract the proper names. Therefore, to customise the normalisation definition to our case, in ANERcorp we only reduced the different forms, for instance, of the character "A" in just one form.

Finally, we would like to mention that the ANERcorp consists of 316 articles. We preferred not to choose all the articles from the same type and not even from the same newspapers in order to obtain a corpus as generalised as possible. In the following table we present the ratio of articles extracted from each source:

Table 1. Ratio of sources for the extracted article

Source	Ratio
http://www.aljazeera.net	34.8%
Other newspapers and magazines	17.8%
http://www.raya.com	15.5%
http://ar.wikipedia.org	6.6%
http://www.alalam.ma	5.4%
http://www.ahram.eg.org	5.4%
http://www.alittihad.ae	3.5%
http://www.bbc.co.uk/arabic/	3.5%
http://arabic.cnn.com	2.8%
http://www.addustour.com	2.8%
http://kassioun.org	1.9%

ANERcorp contains 150,286 tokens and 32,114 types which makes a ratio of tokens to types of 4.67. The Proper Names are 11% of the corpus. Their distribution along the different types is as follows:

Table 2. Ratio of phrases by classes

Class	Ratio
PERSon	39%
LOCation	30.4%
ORGanization	20.6%
MISCellaneous class	10%

4.2 ANERgazet[15]: Integrating Web-Based Gazetteers

ANERgazet consists of three different gazetteers, all built manually using web resources:

(i) *Location Gazetteer*: this gazetteer consists of 1,950 names of continents, countries, cities, rivers and mountains found in the Arabic version of wikipedia[16];

(ii) *Person Gazetteer*: this was originally a list of 1,920 complete names of people found in wikipedia and other websites. Splitting the names into first names and last names and omitting the repeated names, the list contains finally 2,309 names;

(iii) *Organizations Gazetteer*: the last gazetteer consists of a list of 262 names of companies, football teams and other organizations.

5 Experiments and Results

In order to carry out some experiments we have trained and tested the ANERsys with, respectively, 125,000 and 25,000 tokens of ANERcorp. Furthermore, we used the following feature set which we estimated useful after several experiments (*wi* is the word to classify, *wi-1* is the word appearing before *wi-1* and *wi+1* the word appearing after):

(i) *wi* appears right after a bigram (w_{i-2}, w_{i-1}) or before a bigram (w_{i+1}, w_{i+2}): where (w_{i-2}, w_{i-1}) and (w_{i+1}, w_{i+2}) are elements of a list of bigrams (compiled in the training phase) which usually proper names appear near to;
(ii) *wi* mostly appears in the training phase tagged as class c;
(iii) *wi* is not a stop word (a list of 1650 stop words has been prepared for this feature);
(iv) the class of the previous word is *ci-1*;
(v) *wi*, *wi-1* or *wi+1* are elements of a gazetteer.

We used the *YASMET*[17] software to compute the weights λ_i. First, we used the baseline script[18] to tag each word of the test using a model which consists only of assigning the class which most frequently was assigned to it in the training corpus. And second, we used ANERsys to tag the same test corpus in order

[15] http://www.dsic.upv.es/~ybenajiba

[16] http://ar.wikipedia.org

[17] http://www.fjoch.com/YASMET.html

[18] http://www.cnts.ua.ac.be/conll2002/ner/bin/baseline.txt

to be able to estimate the performance of ANERsys. Furthermore, in order to have a CONLL-like framework, we used the same evaluation software[19]. This evaluation script, accepts as input a file of three columns: the first column contains the words, the second the reference tags and the third the guessed tags. At output it gives the precision, recall and F-measure of each class. Table Three shows the baseline results, whereas Table 4 and 5 illustrate, the performance of ANERsys with and without, respectively, using ANERgazet.

Table 3. Baseline of the ANERcorp test corpus

Baseline	Precision	Recall	F-measure
Location	75.71%	76.97%	76.34
Misc	22.91%	34.67%	27.59
Organisation	52.80%	33.14%	40.72
Person	33.84%	14.76%	20.56
Overall	**51.39%**	**37.51%**	**43.36**

Table 4. ANERsys performance (without using ANERgazet) on the ANERcorp test corpus

ANERsys	Precision	Recall	F-measure
Location	82.41%	76.90%	79.56
Misc	61.54%	32.65%	42.67
Organisation	45.16%	31.04%	36.79
Person	52.76%	38.44%	44.47
Overall	**62.72%**	**47.58%**	**54.11**

Table 5. ANERsys performance (using ANERgazet) on the ANERcorp test corpus

ANERsys	Precision	Recall	F-measure
Location	82.17%	78.42%	80.25
Misc	61.54%	32.65%	42.67
Organisation	45.16%	31.04%	36.79
Person	54.21%	41.01%	46.69
Overall	**63.21%**	**49.04%**	**55.23**

6   Conclusions and Future Works

This paper presents ANERsys, a NER system oriented to the Arabic language, together with ANERcorp and ANERgazet, the resources which were devoloped in the context of the implementation of the system.

In order to carry out the NER task a maximum entropy approach was employed. ME proved to be a convenient solution for the NER task thanks to its

---

[19] http://bredt.uib.no/download/conlleval.txt

feature-based model, and it helped to raise 12 points above the baseline without using any POS-tag information or text segmentation. We investigated also the possibility of integrating web-based gazetteers but we found out that the use of gazetteers does not improve significantly the performance of the system. The same conclusion is supported also by [10], whereas other works [13] showed the contrary. We do not believe that the results did not improve much becuase of the small size of the gazetteers; even so we plan to investigate further this issue.

The main difference observed between the location entities and entities of other classes show that the quality of the system depends mainly on the events seen in the training data because location entities tend to appear in a more regular context than the other entity classes. For this reason, we are planning to increase the ANERcorp training and test corpora in order to obtain better results. In this work we used an ad-hoc method to cope with the data spareseness problem due to the nature of the Arabic language. We plan in the next future to use a more robust algorithm to perform a text segmentation before we train the system. Furthermore, we consider to POS-tag our training and test corpora because it will be a very important feature for a good quality NER system.

Acknowledgments

The research work of the first author was supported partially by MAEC - AECI. We would like to thank the MCyT TIN2006-15265-C06-04 research project for partially funding this work.

References

1. Friburger, N., Maurel, D.: Textual Similarity Based on Proper Names. *(MFIR'2002) at the 25 th ACM SIGIR Conference*, Tampere, Finland, 2002, pp. 155–167.
2. Beth M. Sundheim.: Overview of results of the MUC-6 evaluation. In *Proceedings of the 6th Conference on Message understanding*, November 06-08, 1995, Columbia, Maryland.
3. Abuleil, S., Evens, M.: Extracting Names from Arabic text for Question-Answering Systems. *Computers and the Humanities*, 2002 - Springer.
4. Maloney, J., and Niv, M.: TAGARAB, A Fast, Accurate Arabic Name Recognizer Using High-Precision Morphological Analysis. In *Proceedings of the Workshop on Computational Approaches to Semitic Languages*, 1998.
5. Bender, O., Och, F. J., Ney, H.: Maximum Entropy Models For Named Entity Recognition. In *Proceedings of CoNLL-2003*. Edmonton, Canada, 2003.
6. Hai L. Chieu, Hwee T. Ng: Named Entity Recognition with a Maximum Entropy Approach. In *Proceedings of CoNLL-2003*. Edmonton, Canada, 2003.
7. Curran, JR. and Clark, S.: Language Independent NER using a Maximum Entropy Tagger. In *Proceedings of CoNLL-2003*. Edmonton, Canada, 2003.
8. Cucerzan, S. and Yarowsky, D.: Language Independent Named Entity Recognition Combining Morphological and Contextual Evidence. In *Proceedings, 1999 Joint SIGDAT Conference on Empirical Methods in NLP and Very Large Corpora*, pp. 90–99.

9. Klein, D., Smarr, J., Nguyen, H., Christopher D. Manning: Named Entity Recognition with Character-Level Models. In *Proceedings of CoNLL-2003*. Edmonton, Canada, 2003.

10. Malouf, R.: Markov Models for Language-Independent Named Entity Recognition. In *Proceedings of CoNLL-2003*. Edmonton, Canada, 2003.

11. Florian, R., Hassan, H., Ittycheriah, A., Jing, H., Kambhatla, N., Luo, X., Nicolov, N. and Roukos, S.: A Statistical Model for Multilingual Entity Detection and Tracking. In *Proceedings of NAACL/HLT*, 2004.

12. Lee, Y.-S., Papineni, K., Roukos, S., Emam, O., Hassan, H.: Language Model Based Arabic Word Segmentation. In *Proceedings of the 41st Annual Meeting of the ACL*. pp. 399–406. Sapporo, Japan.

13. Carreras, X., Marquez, L., and Padro, L.: Named Entity Extraction Using AdaBoost. In *Proceedings of CoNLL 2002 Shared Task*, Taipei, Taiwan, September 2002.

14. Ratnaparkhi, A.: A Simple Introduction to Maximum Entropy Models for Natural Language Processing. *Technical Report IRCS-97-08, University of Pennsylvania, Institute for Research in Cognitive Science*.

15. Amaya, F. and Benedi, J.M.: Improvement of a Whole Sentence Maximum Entropy Language Model Using Grammatical Features. *Association for Computational Linguistics*, Toulouse, France, 2001, pp. 10-17.

16. Fleischman, M., Kwon, N., Hovy, E.: Maximum Entropy Models for FrameNet Classification. In *Proceedings of the 2003 Conference on Emprical Methods in Natural Language Processing*, 2003, pp. 49-56.

17. Rosenfeld, R.: A Maximum Entropy Approach to Adaptive Statistical Language Modeling. *Computer Speech and Language*, 10:187228, 1996.

Applying Machine Learning to Chinese Entity Detection and Tracking

Donglei Qian[1,2], Wenjie Li[1], Chunfa Yuan[2], Qin Lu[1], and Mingli Wu[1]

[1] Department of Computing
The Hong Kong Polytechnic University, Hong Kong
{csdlqian, cswjli, csluqin, csmlwu}@comp.polyu.edu.hk
[2] Department of Computer Science and Technology
Tsinghua University, China
qdl05@mails.tsinghua.edu.cn, cfyuan@mail.tsinghua.edu.cn

Abstract. This paper presents a Chinese entity detection and tracking system that takes advantages of character-based models and machine learning approaches. An entity here is defined as a link of all its mentions in text together with the associated attributes. Entity mentions of different types normally exhibit quite different linguistic patterns. Six separate Conditional Random Fields (CRF) models that incorporate character N-gram and word knowledge features are built to detect the extent and the head of three types of mentions, namely named, nominal and pronominal mentions. For each type of mentions, attributes are identified by Support Vector Machine (SVM) classifiers which take mention heads and their context as classification features. Mentions can then be merged into a unified entity representation by examining their attributes and connections in a rule-based coreference resolution process. The system is evaluated on ACE 2005 corpus and achieves competitive results.

1 Introduction

The Chinese Entity Detection and Tracking (CEDT) task is motivated by the ACE program, which aims at developing automatic content extraction technologies to support automatic processing of human languages. The CEDT task is more complicated than the conventional Named Entity Recognition (NER) task in terms that the concept of entity is redefined and consequently becomes more integrated. According to the ACE guidelines, an entity is defined as an object or set of objects in the world. All the references to an entity are called mentions [1]. A mention is either named, which corresponds to the named entity in traditional NER task, or non-named, which is further categorized into nominal and pronominal. Furthermore, not only the extent but also the head of each mention must be identified. The extent refers to as the whole noun phrase including both modifier (phrase) and head (phrase). The sample entity structures are illustrated in Figure 1, where each mention has a TYPE attribute associated with. The type indicates whether the mention is named (NAM), such as 布什, nominal (NOM), such as 布什州长, or pronominal (PRO), such as 自己.

A. Gelbukh (Ed.): CICLing 2007, LNCS 4394, pp. 154 – 165, 2007.

Example sentence

[[布什] 州长] 返回了 [[自己] 的农场]

[Governor [Bush]] returned to [[his] farm]

Detected entities and mentions

Entity 1 {

  Mention 1 {布什 (Extent 布什 Head 布什)},

  Mention 2 {布什州长 (Extent 布什州长 Head 州长)},

  Mention 3 {自己 (Extent 自己 Head 自己)}}

Entity 2 {

  Mention 1 {自己的农场 (Extent 自己的农场 Head 农场)}}

Fig. 1. The upper part is an annotated sentence from the ACE training corpus, and the lower part lists entities and mentions together with the extents and heads detected in the sentence

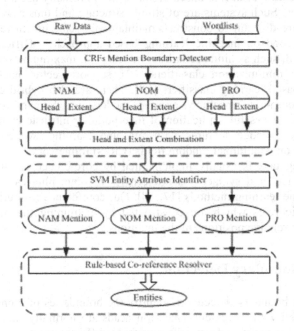

Fig. 2. CEDR system overview. Three sub-tasks are boxed off by dotted rectangles.

The CEDT task is to detect all the mentions in the source texts, merge them into the entities and determine the associated attributes of the mentions and entities. In this paper, we divide the whole task into three sub-tasks, i.e. mention boundary detection, entity attribute identification and coreference resolution, as they are shown in Figure 2. The boundaries of three different types of mentions are detected separately. Three detectors are built on Conditional Random Fields (CRFs) framework. The entity attribute identifier is a set of Support Vector Machine (SVM) based classifiers. For coreference resolution, a rule-based approach is applied by integrating the mention (entity) attribute and mention relative position information.

The remainder of the paper is organized as follows. Section 2 reviews the related work on entity detection and tracking. Sections 3 to 5 then details the three parts of our CEDT system respectively. Section 6 presents the evaluation results. Finally, Section 7 concludes the paper.

2   Related Work

Entity Detection and Tracking (EDT) is important for many natural language processing tasks, such as information extraction and machine learning. Conferences like MUC, CoNLL and ACE are aimed to develop EDT technology.

The EDT task can be divided into two parts: entity detection and tracking. Both entity detecting and tracking technologies can be categorized into rule-based and machine learning-based approaches.

For entity detection task, rule based systems [8, 9] normally use a large number of hand-crafted rules. Such systems are of simple structure and thus easy to understand. However, they are difficult to construct, maintain and scale up. In recent years, the research has focused on machine learning based approaches. Different algorithms have been applied, such as hidden Markov models [11], maximum entropy classifiers [12], robust risk minimization classifiers [13], support vector machine [14], and transformation based learning classifiers [10]. There are also hybrid entity detection systems that incorporate machine learning models and human knowledge [15]. Motivated by the successful application of incorporating intrinsic entity features and external word knowledge features with machine learning, we build our entity detection system on conditional random fields (CRFs) framework.

Entity tracking task is usually implemented by coreference resolution. One can make use of lexical and syntactic characteristics of noun phrases [16], or employ statistical machine learning methods [17, 18]. Our coreference resolution is based on a set of heuristic rules which are constructed by examining the mention (entity) attributes and the relative positions of the mentions.

3   Mention Boundary Detection

We implement a boundary detector to identify the boundaries of mention heads and extents. Compared with the extents, mention heads are normally shorter and exhibit more significant linguistic features with respect to different mention types. Head and extent boundaries are detected separately so that at least the high accuracy with head detection can be expected. Then heads and extents are combined together to form whole mentions. During the combination, head and extent boundaries constrain each other. This provides a second chance for those wrongly detected boundaries to be corrected. On the other hand, the mentions of different types have different frequently used character lists and exhibit distinct linguistic patterns. It makes suitable to detect named, nominal and pronominal mention boundaries separately. According to the above mentioned reasons, we build six separate models to detect extents and heads of named, nominal and pronominal mentions.

3.1 Character-Based Model Combined with Word Knowledge

Mention boundary detection task in Chinese is arguably more difficult than in English due to two problems. First, Chinese does not use blank spaces or any other delimiters to indicate word boundaries. Both character and word can be used as basic language unit in boundary detection task. Although word-based models contain word segmentation information which is useful for boundary detection, they are heavily affected by word segmentation errors, and may cause more severe data sparseness problem when applying statistical-based approaches. Based on these observations, we build a character-based model to avoid segmentation error propagation problem. Practically, without using segmentation information, the boundary detection task can be recognized as a variant of word segmentation task [6]. Second, no capitalization features can help the detection of names. In English language, proper nouns, such as person names and place names, are ordinarily capitalized. But this is not the case in Chinese. Our choice is to make use of certain wordlists to complement name recognition.

3.2 Boundary Detection with Conditional Random Fields

Conditional Random Fields (CRF) [2] is a framework for sequential segmenting and labeling. It has shown significant effectiveness in many classical natural language processing tasks, such as shallow parsing [3], Chinese word segmentation [4] and named entity recognition [5]. Compared with other sequential labeling approaches, like hidden Markov models and maximum entropy Markov models, CRF is more advanced in relaxing strong independence assumptions and handling labeling bias problems. So CRFs can easily incorporate large arrays of arbitrary, non-independent features to solve sequential problems.

The boundary detection task can be described as a sequential labeling problem. Since our models are character-based, we assign to each character in the sequence with a label indicating whether the token is the beginning, inside or outside of a mention.

3.3 Character-Based N-Gram Features and Wordlist-Based Features

Though CRF prescribes no restrictions on the number of the features it uses, we must consider the tradeoff between the training time and the set of features. The most efficient way is to include the most significant features of each character which can contribute the most to the boundary detection under the limited hardware and software resources. Following seven character-based N-gram features are shared among three types of mentions and are deemed as the basic features (where index 0 indicates the current character, and indices $n/-n$ indicate the characters n positions to the right or left of the current character, $n=1$ or 2).

Character uni-gram features: $\{c_{-2}, c_{-1}, c_0, c_1, c_2\}$
Character bi-gram features: $\{c_{-1}c_0, c_0c_1\}$

Besides, we introduce certain specific features based on external wordlists to detect named and pronominal mentions.

For named mention detection, we construct three wordlists, namely Chinese surname list (i.e. List 1), country and capital city list (i.e. List 2), and China province and city list (i.e. List 3). Features based on the three wordlists are defined as follows.

> Surname uni-gram feature: {sur0}
> Place name bi-gram features: {$p_{-1}p_0$, p_0p_1}

For pronominal mention detection, a pronoun list (i.e. List4) is used. The feature is

> Pronoun hybrid feature: {pro}

Table 1 shows the features and their corresponding values.

Table 1. Specific features and corresponding functions used in named and pronominal mention boundary detection

Feature	Value	Description
sur_0	in	c_0 is in List 1
	out	otherwise
$p_{-1}p_0/p_0p_1$	in	$c_{-1}c_0/c_0c_1$ is a substring of a term in List 2 or List 3
	out	otherwise
pro	bi0	$c_{-1}c_0$ is in List 4
	bi1	c_0c_1 is in List 4
	uni	c_0 is in List 4
	none	otherwise

3.4 Head and Extent Combination

When mention heads and extents are detected separately, their boundaries are sometimes inconsistent. In other words, the extent and the head of the same mention might be overlapped due to incorrect boundaries identified. According to the task specification, each head corresponds to exactly one extent while an extent may have one or more heads at the same time. We apply the following heuristic rules to combine heads with extents:

> If no head is found inside an extent, we recognize the extent as a redundant one and ignore it by whole;
> If a head is isolated (no extent is found to cover or overlap the range of the head), we make the head itself be the corresponding extent;
> If a head overlaps an extent, we expand the extent range and make it cover the whole head.

4 Entity Attribute Identification

Type and class attributes are additional information used to characterize the entities. In ACE, entities are categorized into the following seven types: person, organization, Geo-political entity, location, facility, vehicle and weapon. They are further divided into four classes: specific referential, generic referential, negatively quantified and underspecified.

Since each mention belongs to exactly one entity, the mentions therefore naturally inherit the type and class attributes from the entities they belong to. Here we use ENTITY-TYPE and ENTITY-CLASS to indicate the inherited attributes. Besides, each mention also has its own TYPE attribute, which has been obtained in mention boundary detection task. The overall attribute structure for an entity is shown in Figure 3.

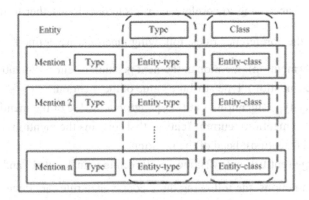

Fig. 3. Entity and mention attribute hierarchical structure. Mentions inherit the attributes from the corresponding entities.

We introduce how to identify ENTITY-TYPE and ENTITY-CLASS attributes for each mention in this section. These two attributes are used later in coreference resolution to help finding out relevant mentions and linking them into entities.

We consider the attribute identification task as a classification problem. Support Vector Machine (SVM) is a supervised machine learning methods used for classification and regression. It has been successfully used in natural language processing and text categorization [7] etc. It is suitable for the problems with sparse instances and is able to incorporate a large number of arbitrary features. Since basic SVM classifiers only conduct binary classification tasks, we use one-against-the-rest approach to solve the multi-class problem. Named, nominal and pronominal mentions are classified all together by two separate SVM-based classifiers. Each classifier classifies the detected mentions by ENTITY-TYPE or ENTITY-CLASS. Characters in mention heads and their context are taken as features in the classifiers in a bag-of-character representation. The features at different position (on the boundaries of a mention, within a mention or within the context of a mention) have different impacts on mention attribute classification. The assigned values are listed in Table 2.

Table 2. Features and assigned values depending on feature importance (c_0 - c_n indicates the mention head)

Position	Feature	Value
Boundary of a head	c_0, c_n	1
Inside a head	c_1 - c_{n-1}	0.8
Context of a head	$c_{-2}, c_{-1}, c_{n+1}, c_{n+2}$	0.5

5 Coreference Resolution

Once mentions are detected and their attributes are identified, coreference resolution is applied to link all coreferent mentions. Mentions are considered as coreferent when they refer to the same entity. The rule-based coreference resolution mainly uses two kinds of information, i.e. mention attributes and mention relative positions.

At first, each mention is recognized as an independent entity. Then, we check each pairs of "entities" according to coreference rules to decide whether to merge them or not.

To formalize the coreference rules, following functions are defined.

- next (mention): mention at the next position of current mention in the text.
- type (mention): type attribute value of the mention.
- entity-type (mention): entity-type attribute value of the mention.
- entity (mention): current "entity" that contains the mention.
- head (mention): head of the mention.
- merge (entity1, entity2): merge all mentions in "entity1" and "entity2".

Given these functions, the following three coreference rules are devised.

Rule 1
next (mention1) = mention2 $\land$ type (mention2) = PRO $\land$ entity-type (mention1) = entity-type (mention2) $\Rightarrow$ merge (entity (mention1), entity (mention2))
Rule 2
type (mention1) = type (mention2) $\land$ $\neg$ (type (mention2) = PRO) $\land$ entity-type (mention1) = entity-type (mention2) $\land$ head (mention1) = head (mention2) $\Rightarrow$ merge (entity (mention1), entity (mention2))
Rule 3
next (mention1) = mention2 $\land$ ((type (mention1) = NOM $\land$ type (mention2) = NAM) $\lor$ (type (mention1) = NAM $\land$ type (mention2) = NOM)) $\land$ entity-type (mention1) = entity-type (mention2) $\Rightarrow$ merge (entity (mention1), entity (mention2))

Rule 1 corefers the PRO mention to the mention before it, Rule 2 corefers the NAM/NOM mentions of the same mention head and Rule 3 corefers the neighboring NAM and NOM mentions of the same ENTITY-TYPE.

6 Experimental Results

The dataset used in our experiments is provided by the Linguistic Data Consortium for ACE 2005 Chinese evaluation task. Table 3 shows the basic statistics. For evaluation, the dataset is divided into a training set of 506 texts (80% of all) and a testing set of 127 texts (20% of all). The mention boundary detection task and entity attribute identification task are evaluated separately. These are followed by a complete system evaluation according to ACE entity detection and recognition evaluation standard.

Table 3. Data statistics for Chinese

Source Type	Character	Text
Newswire	121797	238
Broadcast News	120513	298
Weblogs	65681	97
Total	307991	633

6.1 Mention Boundary Detection Results

In the mention boundary detection task, head and extent of each mention are detected separately. Table 4 presents the head and extent boundary detection results. From the result, we have got the following findings. For each type of mention, the performance of head detection is higher than extent detection. PRO head and extent detection have best performances while NOM extent detection performs the worst among all.

Table 4. Mention head and extent boundary detection results for named (NAM), nominal (NOM) and pronominal (PRO) mention s

	Precision (%)	Recall (%)	F1-measure (%)
NAM Head	77.68	70.58	73.96
NAM Extent	75.38	67.79	71.38
NOM Head	79.73	73.56	76.52
NOM Extent	62.61	53.09	57.46
PRO Head	91.44	91.75	91.60
PRO Extent	89.14	89.60	89.37

Mentions that do not include modifiers have the same head and extent boundaries. Our statistics on the ACE 2005 dataset shows that about 90% of NAM and PRO mentions have same head and extent boundaries, while only 40% of NOM mentions' head and extent boundaries are the same. This shows that NOM mentions are generally more complicate in its forms than NAM and PRO mentions. Both the significant difference between head and extent detection performance and the extreme low performance of NOM extent detection demonstrate that modifiers in mentions may blur the linguistic feature of entity mentions. PRO head and extent have highest F1-measure. This is certainly because that most characters occurred in PRO heads come from a small set of Chinese pronouns which is used as additional feature during PRO boundary detection process.

Mention heads and extents are combined after their boundaries detected separately. Since head and extent boundaries may overlap, we use several reasoning rules to perform the combination, as presented in Section 3.4. Table 5 lists the mention detection result after combination. F1-measure of NOM mentions is relatively lower due to the worse performance of NOM extent detection.

Tabel 5. Mention boundary detection results after head and extent combinition

Type	Precision (%)	Recall (%)	F1-measure (%)
NAM	77.74	71.61	74.55
NOM	59.33	52.86	55.91
PRO	89.00	89.77	89.39

Table 6. Mention boundary detection results for separated boundary detection system

	Manual	Model	Match	Precision (%)	Recall (%)	F1-measure (%)
Head	6482	5989	4792	80.01	73.93	76.85
Extent	5892	5218	3715	71.20	63.05	66.88
Combined	5892	5395	3808	70.58	64.63	67.48

Table 7. Mention boundary detection results for unified boundary detection system (baseline system)

	Manual	Model	Match	Precision (%)	Recall (%)	F1-measure (%)
Head	6482	6120	4936	80.65	76.15	78.34
Extent	5016	4548	3082	67.77	61.44	64.45
Combined	5016	4544	3097	68.16	61.74	64.79

The entire system performance is listed in Table 6. In order to evaluate the effectiveness of this boundary detection mechanism, we build a baseline system which detects all types of mentions at once. Here this system is called unified boundary detection system and the system performance is listed in Table 7. The Manual and Model columns represent the number of mention boundaries annotated in dataset and system output respectively, and the Match column represents the number of matched boundaries between dataset and system output. According to the mention annotation rule, some extents may be included in others. These nested extents can not be represented and labeled at the same time due to our sequential labeling model. For example, in Figure 1, the extent "自己" is nested in the other extent "自己的农场", and only one of them can be detected in our sequential labeling model. Since unified boundary detection system includes more nested extents than separated boundary detection system, the total Manual extent number is comparatively smaller. As a result, the correctly detected extent boundary in unified boundary detection system is less than separated boundary detection system, i.e. 3097 vs. 3808.

Comparing the performances of the two systems, we get the following observations. (1) The head detection F1-measure of unified system is higher than separated system. According to the sequential labeling model, once a sequence of characters is labeled as a head, the characters could not be labeled as part of another head. So the correctly labeled heads provide implied segmentation information. The unified model contains more heads than separated model, which lead to a higher head detection performance. (2) The extent detection F1-measure of separated system is higher than unified system. This is quite obvious since there are more nested extents in unified system. (3) The combined mention detection F1-measure of separated system is higher than unified system. Benefiting from our combination strategy, the performance of combined mention detection is better than extent detection. However, the extent detection performance is of decisive importance. In sum, detecting different types of mentions separately is an effective mechanism for enhancing mention boundary detection performance.

6.2   Entity Attribute Identification Results

Attribute identification relies on a set of SVM-based classifiers. Each classifier is used to classify the ENTITY-TYPE or ENTITY-CLASS attribute of NAM, NOM or PRO mentions. In order to evaluate the performance of entity attribute identification system, we run the system on true mentions extracted from the ACE dataset instead of the mentions detected by our mention boundary detection system. Table 8 presents the classification results of all six classifiers. All the results are acceptable. However, it is possible to introduce more linguistic features to improve the classification accuracy.

Table 8. ENTITY-TYPE and ENTITY-CLASS attributes classification results

Type	Entity-type Accuracy (%)	Entity-class Accuracy (%)
NAM	86.9264	99.8543
NOM	88.5542	81.2936
PRO	81.7869	88.6598

6.3   Entity Tracking Results

The coreference result is not evaluated separately. Instead, we evaluate the performance of the entire CEDT system with ACE Entity Detection and Recognition (EDR) evaluation tool.

The EDR evaluation tool measures the correctness of system's output entity tokens. An entity token is considered to be correctly recognized only if all of its mentions detected and corresponding attributes extracted correctly. The EDR value in Table 9 is a normalized value with different cost parameters assigned to different types of mention. The performance of the system is evaluated with the following three ACE criteria. (1) false alarm, i.e. the spurious entities output by the system; (2) miss, i.e. the entities missed by the system; and (3) error i.e. the entities detected but misrecognized by the system. Besides, the precision, recall and F1-measure give the result which measured for all entities and mentions independent of their types. Table 10

Table 9. Entity tracking results according to ACE evaluation

EDR Value	Precision (%)	Recall (%)	F1-measure (%)
58.1	69.7	63.0	66.2

Table 10. ACE Chinese EDR evaluation results in three domains

	Overall	Broadcast News	Newswire	Weblogs
Best	69.2	70.5	69.6	65.0
Our System	58.1	58.4	58.7	56.6
Worst	43.8	44.1	48.0	30.1

compares the scores of our system with the official results of the best and worst ACE 2005 Chinese EDR participating systems. Our system is evaluated on the ACE 2005 corpus and the result shows it performs competitive.

Table 11 presents the total number and EDR value of each type of entity. Our system detects seven types of entities, namely person (PER), organization (ORG), Geo-political entity (GPE), location (LOC), facility (FAC), vehicle (VEH) and weapon (WEA). Among all types, the GPE value is the best. It is because we use external place name lists during mention boundary detection task. The FAC and WEA values are comparatively low due to the small number of samples in training dataset. The PER value is also low. Since we simply use a surname list for PER mention, it is not sufficient compared to the variety of characters used in Chinese names. We consider introducing additional wordlists as a complement to improve the performance.

Table 11. Entity tracking result listed by entity type

Entity Type	Entity Number	EDR Value
FAC	231	38.4
GPE	596	70.8
LOC	196	59.9
ORG	684	57.6
PER	1108	53.3
VEH	75	60.3
WEA	46	35.9

Another limitation of our system is that the current coreference resolution is not efficient; especially it can not resolve the pronominal mention coreference problem accurately. The coreference resolution is an important part in entity tracking and is useful in natural language understanding areas. We will further investigate coreference resolution in the future.

7 Conclusion

In this paper, we present a Chinese entity detection and tracking system. The system is separated into three sub-tasks, mention boundary detection, entity attribute identification and coreference resolution. The first two tasks apply machine learning approaches while the last task is based on heuristic rules. In our system, the named, nominal and pronominal entity mentions are detected separately with their respective word knowledge based features. The experimental results show that the system achieved a competitive performance in the CEDT task.

Acknowledgments

The work presented in this paper was supported partially by Research Grants Council of Hong Kong under grant number CERG PolyU5181/03E, and partially by National Natural Science Foundation of China under grant number 60573186.

References

1. Linguistic data consortium (LDC): ACE (Automatic Content Extraction) Chinese annotation guidelines for entities. Version 5.5. (2005)
2. John Lafferty, Andrew McCallum, and Fernando Pereira: Conditional random fields: probabilistic models for segmenting and labeling sequence data. In: International Conference on Machine Learning of ICML-2001. (2001)
3. Fei Sha and Fernando Pereira: Shallow parsing with conditional random fields. In: Proceedings of Human Language Technology of NAACL-2003. (2003)
4. Huihsin Tseng, Pichuan Chang, Galen Andrew, Daniel Jurafsky, and Christopher Manning: A conditional random field word segmenter, In: Proceedings of SIGHAN Workshop on Chinese Language Processing. (2005)
5. Wenliang Chen, Yujie Zhang, and Isahara, Hitoshi: Named entity recognition with conditional random fields. In: Proceedings of the Fifth SIGHAN Workshop on Chinese Language Processing. (2006) 118-121
6. Yuchieh Wu, Jiechi Yang, and Qianxiang Lin: Description of the NCU Chinese word segmentation and named entity recognition system for SIGHAN Bakeoff 2006. In: Proceedings of the Fifth SIGHAN Workshop on Chinese Language Processing. (2006) 209-212
7. Thorsten Joachims: Text categorization with support vector machines: learning with many relevant features. In: Proceedings of ECML-98, 10th European Conference on Machine Learning. (1998)
8. Ralph Grishman and Beth Sundheim: Design of the muc-6 evaluation. In: Proceedings of MUC-6. (1995)
9. George R. Krupka and Kevin Hausman: Description of the NetOwl TM extractor system as used for MUC-7. In: Proceedings of the MUC-7. (1998)
10. Yaqian Zhou, Changning Huang, Jianfeng Gao, and Lide Wu: Transformation based Chinese entity detection and tracking. In: Proceedings of International Joint Conference on Natural Language Processing. (2005) 232-237
11. Daniel M. Bikel, Richard Schwartz, and Ralph M. Weischedel: An algorithm that learns what's in a name. In: the Machine Learning Journal Special Issue on Natural Language Learning. (1999)
12. Dan Klein, Joseph Smarr, Huy Nguyen, and Christo-pher D. Manning: Named entity recognition with character-level models. In: Proceedings of CoNLL-2003. (2003)
13. Honglei Guo, Jianmin Jiang, Gang Hu, and Tong Zhang: Chinese named entity recognition based on multilevel linguistic features. In: Proceedings of IJCNLP-2004. (2004)
14. Hongqiao Li, Changning Huang, Jianfeng Gao and Xiaozhong Fan: The use of SVM for Chinese new word identification. In: Proceedings of IJCNLP2004. (2004)
15. Youzheng Wu, Jun Zhao, and Bo Xu: Chinese named entity recognition model based on multiple features. In: Proceedings of HLT/EMNLP. (2005) 427-434
16. Hobbs, Jerry R.: Resolving pronoun references. In: Lingua, Vol. 44. (1978) 311-338
17. Wee Meng Soon, Daniel Chung Yong Lim, and Hwee Tou Ng: Machine learning approach to coreference resolution of noun phrases. In: Computational Linguistics. (2001) 521-544
18. Xiaoqiang Luo, Abe Ittycheriah, Hongyan Jing, Nanda Kambhatla, and Salim Roukos: A mention-synchronous coreference resolution algorithm based on the bell tree. In: Proc. of the 42nd Annual Meeting of the Association for Computational Linguistics. (2004) 135-142

Evaluation of an Automatic Extension of Temporal Expression Treatment to Catalan*

E. Saquete, P. Martínez-Barco, and R. Muñoz

Grupo de investigación del Procesamiento del Lenguaje y Sistemas de Información
Departamento de Lenguajes y Sistemas Informáticos. Universidad de Alicante
Alicante, Spain
{stela,patricio,rafael}@dlsi.ua.es

Abstract. This paper presents the automatic extension to Catalan of a knowledge-based system for the recognition and normalization of temporal expressions, called TERSEO, and originally developed for Spanish but automatically extended to English and Italian using the automatic translation of the existing temporal models. Besides, when an annotated corpus for the new language is also available, the translation is combined with the extraction of new expressions from this annotated corpus. Experimental results demonstrate how, while still adhering to the rule-based paradigm, the development of automatic rule translation procedures allowed us to minimize the effort required for porting to new languages obtaining quite good results in evaluation. Relying on such procedures, and without any manual effort or previous knowledge of the target language, TERSEO recognizes and normalizes temporal expressions in different languages. For the Catalan extension, only the automatic translation of the Spanish temporal model was used, due to the lack of other resources. However, after extending TERSEO to Catalan following this procedure good results (76% precision and 77% recall for recognition) were obtained.

1 Introduction

The computational analysis of time is a challenging problem, as the needs of applications based on information extraction techniques expand to include varying degrees of time stamping and temporal ordering of events and/or relations within a narrative. Recently, there are a growing interest in this matter as can be proved by some recent international conferences and workshops, such as TIME 2006[1], ARTE 2006[2] or Time Expression Recognition and Normalization Workshop (TERN 2004[3]). Significant progress has been made in these meetings,

---

* This paper has been supported by the Valencian Community Government, project GV06/028: "Tratamiento bilingüe valenciano-castellano de preguntas temporales complejas en los sistemas de búsqueda de respuestas".

[1] http://www.cs.brandeis.edu/ jamesp/time2006/
[2] http://www.timeml.org/acl2006time/
[3] http://timex2.mitre.org/tern.html

A. Gelbukh (Ed.): CICLing 2007, LNCS 4394, pp. 166–174, 2007.

leading to developing a de facto standard for a specification language for events, temporal expressions and their ordering (TimeML [1]).

Moreover, the NLP community has focused their efforts in breaking the language barrier hampering their applications in real use scenarios. Such a strong interest towards multilinguality is demonstrated by the growing number of international conferences putting systems' multilingual/cross-language capabilities among the hottest research topics. Among these, for instance, the European Cross-Language Evaluation Forum[4] (CLEF) is a successful evaluation campaign which aims at fostering research in different areas of multilingual information retrieval. At the same time, in the temporal expressions recognition and normalization field, systems featuring multilingual capabilities have been proposed. Among others, [4], [11] and [5] emphasized the potentialities of such applications in different information retrieval related tasks.

Systems that treat temporal information are based on knowledge or on machine learning. In spite of the good results obtained in the *recognition* task, *normalization* by means of machine learning techniques still shows relatively poor results with respect to rule-based approaches, and still remains an unresolved problem.

The difficulty of porting systems to new languages (or domains) affects both rule-based and machine learning approaches. With rule-based approaches [9,2], the main problems are related to the fact that the porting process requires rewriting from scratch, or adapting to each new language, large numbers of rules, which is a costly and time-consuming process. Machine learning approaches [10,3], on the other hand, can be extended with little human intervention through the use of language corpora. However, the large annotated corpora that are necessary to obtain high performance are not always available. In this paper we describe how a procedure that builds temporal models for new languages, starting from previously defined ones is applied to a language with good results. While still adhering to the rule-based paradigm, its main contribution is the proposal of a simple, but effective, methodology to automate the porting of a system from one language to another. To accomplish this, we take advantage of the architecture of an existing system developed for Spanish (TERSEO, see [8]), where the recognition model is language-dependent but the normalizing procedure is completely independent. In this way, the approach is capable of automatically learning the recognition model, adjusting the set of normalization rules.

The paper is structured as follows: Section 2 provides a short overview of TERSEO and the previous extensions of this system to other languages; Section 3 describes the automatic extension of the system to a new language (Catalan) using automatic translation of the expressions; Section 4 presents the procedure to automatically develop a corpus in Catalan language using a previously annotated corpus in Spanish and it shows the results of evaluation experiments performed on this new extension and the comparison with other extensions previously performed, and finally some conclusions are presented.

---

[4] http://www.clef-campaign.org/

2   History of TERSEO Extensions

At first, TERSEO was developed in order to automatically recognize temporal expressions (TEs) appearing in a Spanish written text, and normalize them according to the temporal model proposed in [6], which is compatible with TimeML annotation standard for temporal expressions [1].

The different modules of the system are shown in Figure 1. The first step of the system (recognition) includes a pre-processing with a POSTagger of the input texts, which are tagged with lexical and morphological information that are given as input to the recognition parser. This parser is implemented using an ascending technique (chart parser) and is based on a temporal grammar.

Once the parser has recognized the TEs in an input text, they are resolved by the normalization unit, which updates the value of the reference according to the date they refer to, and generates the TIMEX2 tags for each expression. The normalization unit uses an inference engine in order to resolve all the temporal expressions. This inference engine exploits a centralized unit (TER-ILI unit) that contains a set of general resolution rules. Unlike the rules used in the recognition phase, the resolution rules are language independent and will be common for all the sets of temporal expressions in any multilingual extension of TERSEO.

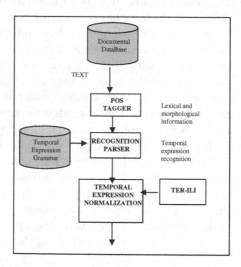

Fig. 1. Graphic representation of the TERSEO architecture

After this, TERSEO was extended to other languages with the automatic building of temporal models for new languages starting from previously defined ones, so as to overcome the problems that are inherent in the rule-based paradigm. With the rule-based approach, the porting implies a big effort due to the necessity of rewriting rules from scratch.

In a first experiment, for English language, the model was obtained automatically from the Spanish one, through the automatic translation of the Spanish temporal expressions into English. The resulting system for the recognition and normalization of English TEs obtained good results both in terms of precision (P) and recall (R) [7].

In the case of Italian, we developed a new procedure which exploits on one hand both the Spanish and the English models already available, translating them to Italian and, on the other hand, an Italian corpus (I-CAB corpus, as part of the ONTOTEXT project[5] funded by the Provincia Autonoma di Trento) annotated with temporal expressions in order to extract new temporal expressions that were not previously obtained by the translation of models to this language. These two approaches were combined to extract the Italian model. The reason for considering Spanish and English models in automatic translation is the fact that they complement each other: on the one hand, the Spanish model was obtained manually and showed high precision values in detection (88%); on the other hand, although the English model showed lower precision results in detection (77%), the on-line translators from English to Italian perform better than translators from Spanish to Italian.

3   Extension to Catalan

For the Catalan extension, and due to the restrictions in resources, only the Spanish Temporal model was used as input, because there is no automatic translator from English to Catalan. Moreover, there is no annotated corpora in Catalan in order to extract more temporal expressions from it, so the Catalan temporal expressions were obtained only through the automatic translation from the Spanish ones. The full process is presented in Figure 2.

In depth, two steps were followed in the extension of TERSEO sytem to Catalan:

- Step 1: Recognition Rule Collection. In this step, all the Catalan recognition rules are obtained. For this language, these new temporal expressions are obtained using an automatic translator.
- Step 2: Resolution Rule Assignment. The normalization rule for the new Catalan temporal expressions will be the same as its equivalent in Spanish, due to the fact that the resolution rules are language independent and they are the same for all the languages in our system.

Moreover, Step 1 of this process is divided in three phases:

1. Automatic translation of the recognition rules. For this phase, the Spanish temporal recognition rules are used as input, and they will be translated to Catalan using an automatic translator called Internostrum[6]. This translator is able to translate from Spanish to Catalan. Due to the fact that there is no machine translator from English to Catalan or Italian to Catalan, neither the recognition rules in English nor the recognition rules in Italian could be used as input for the extension of the system.

---

[5] http://tcc.itc.it/projects/ontotext
[6] http://internostrum.com/

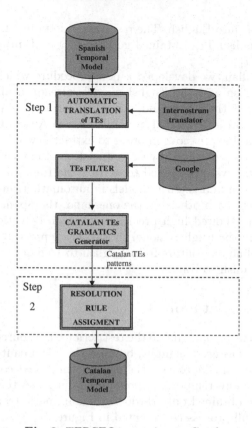

Fig. 2. TERSEO extension to Catalan

2. Temporal expressions filtering. In order to avoid wrong translations of the temporal expressions Google was used as a filtering resource, removing those not found in the searching of the expression.
3. TE Generalization. In this phase, the TEs Gramatics Generator uses the morphological and syntactical information from the collected TEs, using a POStagger as a resource, to generate the grammatical rules that generalize the recognition of the TEs.

4   Evaluation of the New Extension

4.1   Corpus Development

For the evaluation of this new extension, it is necessary to have a Catalan corpus that was both plain and annotated with TIMEX2 tags. Due to the fact that there is no such corpus nowadays, we decided to automatically translate the Spanish manually annotated corpus using the Internostrum translator because this translator preserve the original tags and it is able to only translate the plain text from Spanish to Catalan.

The original Spanish corpus, that was previously used to evaluate the Spanish system as well, consist of a set of 100 articles from a Spanish newspaper that was manually annotated using the TimeML specification. Therefore, after the automatic translation, a new corpus with another 100 articles in Catalan was also available. Only, a manual rapid and shallow review it was necessary to correct some possible mistakes generated by the automatic translator.

4.2   Results

Using the new corpus built for our Catalan extension, the system was evaluated and, apart from precision, recall and f-measure, the following metrics were used:

- CORR: This value is increased when two items are identical.
- INCO: This value is increased when two items are not identical.
- MISS (non detected):This value is increased when a existing temporal expression was not detected by the system.
- SPUR (spurious): This value is increased if the system returns a temporal expression that is not annotated in the gold standard as a temporal expression.
- POS: Number of references that contribute to the final result.
  POS = CORR + INCO +MISS
- ACT: The number of references that the system treats and returns.
  ACT = CORR + INCO + SPUR

Table 1. Metrics examples

GOLD STANDARD	TERSEO	RESULT
<TIMEX2 VAL="2006-12-02"> ahir < /TIMEX2>	<TIMEX2 VAL="2006-12-02"> ahir < /TIMEX2>	CORR
<TIMEX2 VAL="2006-12-02"> ahir < /TIMEX2>	<TIMEX2 VAL="2006-12-03"> ahir < /TIMEX2>	INCO
<TIMEX2 VAL="2006-12-02"> ahir < /TIMEX2>	–	MISS
–	<TIMEX2 VAL="PXY"> anys < /TIMEX2>	SPUR

In the next Table 2, the results of this metrics are shown:

As it can be observed in the results, they are quite successful taking into account that only few hours were required to obtain the Catalan temporal model using the Spanish one as input. The same platform that was developed for the English extension has been used in this case, changing only the translator resource. Best results are obtained in recognition, but the attributes VAL and ACNHOR_DIR have obtained quite good results as well.

Table 2. Results for the systems in Catalan

tag	pos	act	corr	inco	miss	spur	prec	rec	F
TIMEX2	433	436	334	1	98	101	0.766	0.771	0.769
ANCHOR_DIR	51	47	29	6	16	12	0.617	0.569	0.592
ANCHOR_VAL	51	47	14	21	16	12	0.298	0.275	0.286
TEXT	433	436	190	145	98	101	0.436	0.439	0.437
VAL	331	334	209	122	0	3	0.629	0.631	0.629

Besides, a comparison of the results of the F-Measure of the TIMEX2 attribute for the four languages of TERSEO (Spanish, English, Italian and Catalan) is presented in Figure 3.

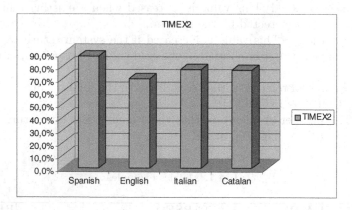

Fig. 3. Comparison of TERSEO between languages

As it can be seen in the Figure, the results for Catalan are quite similar to the Italian extension, and only 11% of loss in F-Measure compared to the Spanish one, that was manually obtained. In contrast, the process to obtain the Catalan temporal model was completely automatic, very simple and rapid with our procedure. Due to the fact that Catalan is quite similar to Spanish, good results were expected.

5   Conclusions

In this paper, a new automatic extension of a rule-based approach to TEs recognition and normalization has been presented. The procedure is based on building temporal models for new languages starting from previously defined ones. This procedure is able to fill the gap left by machine learning systems that, up to date, are still far from providing acceptable performance on this task.

The same procedure was previously used to extend the system to English and Italian. In this case, the automatic extension of the system has been performed to Catalan language, and due to the lack of other resources, only the automatic translation from the Spanish temporal model to Catalan could be used. This fact made the process very simple and fast also.

However, as results illustrate, the proposed methodology (even though, as it is expected, with a lower performance with respect to language-specific systems) is effective solution for a rapid and automatic porting of an existing system to new languages.

The results of the automatic extended languages are quite successful compared with the results obtained by the system in Spanish, where rules were manually obtained. In Catalan, an F-Measure of around 77 % was obtained in the evaluation of the TIMEX2 attribute.

As a future work, it would be interesting trying to extend the system to non Latin languages, such as Chinese, Arabic and so on, in order to see if the designed platform is working well with this kind of languages or if, on the contrary, something needs to be tuned to obtain a good performance of the system.

References

1. L. Ferro, L. Gerber, I. Mani, B. Sundheim, and G. Wilson. Tides.2005 standard for the annotation of temporal expressions. Technical report, MITRE, 2005.
2. E. Filatova and E. Hovy. Assigning time-stamps to event-clauses. In ACL, editor, *Proceedings of the 2001 ACL Workshop on Temporal and Spatial Information Processing*, pages 88–95, Toulouse,France, 2001.
3. G. Katz and F. Arosio. The annotation of temporal information in natural language sentences. In ACL, editor, *Proceedings of the 2001 ACL Workshop on Temporal and Spatial Information Processing*, pages 104–111, Toulouse,France, 2001.
4. T. Moia. Telling apart temporal locating adverbials and time-denoting expressions. In ACL, editor, *Proceedings of the 2001 ACL Workshop on Temporal and Spatial Information Processing*, Toulouse,France, 2001.
5. M. Negri and L. Marseglia. Recognition and normalization of time expressions: Itc-irst at tern 2004. Technical report, ITC-irst, Trento, 2004.
6. E. Saquete. *Temporal information Resolution and its application to Temporal Question Answering*. Phd, Departamento de Lenguages y Sistemas Informáticos. Universidad de Alicante, June 2005.
7. E. Saquete, P. Martínez-Barco, and R. Muñoz. Evaluation of the automatic multilinguality for time expression resolution. In *DEXA Workshops*, pages 25–30. IEEE Computer Society, 2004.
8. E. Saquete, R. Muñoz, and P. Martínez-Barco. Event ordering using terseo system. *Data and Knowledge Engineering Journal*, page (To be published), 2005.
9. F. Schilder and C. Habel. From temporal expressions to temporal information: Semantic tagging of news messages. In ACL, editor, *Proceedings of the 2001 ACL Workshop on Temporal and Spatial Information Processing*, pages 65–72, Toulouse,France, 2001.

10. A. Setzer and R. Gaizauskas. On the importance of annotating event-event temporal relations in text. In LREC, editor, *Proceedings of the LREC Workshop on Temporal Annotation Standards, 2002*, pages 52–60, Las Palmas de Gran Canaria,Spain, 2002.

11. G. Wilson, I. Mani, B. Sundheim, and L. Ferro. A multilingual approach to annotating and extracting temporal information. In ACL, editor, *Proceedings of the 2001 ACL Workshop on Temporal and Spatial Information Processing*, pages 81–87, Toulouse,France, 2001.

A Generalized Approach to Word Segmentation Using Maximum Length Descending Frequency and Entropy Rate

Md. Aminul Islam, Diana Inkpen, and Iluju Kiringa

School of Information Technology and Engineering,
University of Ottawa, Ottawa, ON, Canada, K1N 6N5
{mdislam, diana, kiringa}@site.uottawa.ca

Abstract. In this paper, we formulate a generalized method of automatic word segmentation. The method uses corpus type frequency information to choose the type with maximum length and frequency from "desegmented" text. It also uses a modified forward-backward matching technique using maximum length frequency and entropy rate if any non-matching portions of the text exist. The method is also extendible to a dictionary-based or hybrid method with some additions to the algorithms. Evaluation results show that our method outperforms several competing methods.

1 Introduction

Word segmentation is an important problem in many natural language processing tasks; for example, in speech recognition where there is no explicit word boundary information given within a continuous speech utterance, or in interpreting written languages such as Chinese, Japanese and Thai where words are not delimited by white-space but instead must be inferred from the basic character sequence. We differentiate the terms *word breaking* and *word segmentation*. Word breaking refers to the process of segmenting known words that are predefined in a lexicon. Word segmentation refers to the process of both lexicon word segmentation and unknown word or new word[1] detection. Automatic word segmentation is a basic requirement for unsupervised learning in morphological analysis. Developing a morphological analyzer for a new language by hand can be costly and time consuming, requiring a great deal of effort by highly-specialized experts.

In databases, word segmentation can be used in schema matching to solve semantic heterogeneity, a key problem in any data sharing system whether it is a federated database, a data integration system, a message passing system, a web service, or a peer-to-peer data management system [16]. The name of an element in a database typically contains words that are descriptive of the element's semantics. N-grams

---

[1] New words in this paper refer to out-of-vocabulary words that are neither recognized as named entities or factoids, nor derived by morphological rules. These words are mostly domain-specific and / or time-sensitive.

A. Gelbukh (Ed.): CICLing 2007, LNCS 4394, pp. 175–185, 2007.

have been shown to work well in the presence of short forms, incomplete names and spelling errors that are common in schema names [10].

Also, extracting words (word segmentation) from a scanned document page or a PDF is an important and basic step in document structure analysis and understanding systems; incorrect word segmentation during OCR leads to errors in information retrieval and in understanding the document.

One of the common approaches involving an extensive word list combined with an informed segmentation algorithm can help achieve a certain degree of accuracy in word segmentation, but the greatest barrier to accurate word segmentation is in recognizing unknown words, words not in the lexicon of the segmenter. This problem is dependent both on the source of the lexicon as well as the correspondence between the text in question and the lexicon. Fung and Wu [11] reported that segmentation accuracy is significantly higher when the lexicon is constructed using the same type of corpus as the corpus on which it is tested.

The term *maximum length descending frequency* means that we choose maximum length n-grams that have a minimum threshold frequency and then we look for further n-grams in descending order based on length. If two n-grams have same length then we choose the n-gram with higher frequency first and then the n-gram with next higher frequency if any of its characters are not a part of the previous one. If we follow this procedure, after some iterations, we can be in a state with some remaining character(s) (we call it *residue*) that is not matched with any type in the corpus. To solve this, we use the *leftMaxMatching* and *rightMaxMatching* algorithms presented in Section 3 along with entropy rate.

This paper is organized as follow: Section 2 presents a brief overview of the related work. The proposed method is described in Section 3. A walk-through example of the method is presented in Section 4. Evaluation and experimental results are discussed in Section 5. We address the potential applications of the proposed method and conclude in Section 6.

2 Related Work

Word segmentation methods can be roughly classified as either dictionary-based or statistically-based methods, while many state-of-the-art systems use hybrid approaches. In dictionary-based methods, given an input character string, only words that are stored in the dictionary can be identified. The performance of these methods thus depends to a large degree upon the coverage of the dictionary, which unfortunately may never be complete because new words appear constantly. Therefore, in addition to the dictionary, many systems also contain special components for unknown word identification. In particular, statistical methods have been widely applied because they use a probabilistic or cost-based scoring mechanism rather than a dictionary to segment the text [12].

A simple word segmentation algorithm is to consider each character a distinct word. This is practical for Chinese because the average word length is very short, usually between one and two characters, depending on the corpus [11], and actual words can be recognized with this algorithm. Although it does not assist in task such as parsing, part-of-speech tagging, or text-to-speech systems [24], the character-as-word segmentation algorithm has been used to obtain good performance in Chinese information retrieval, a task in which the words in a text play a major role in indexing.

One of the most popular methods is *maximum matching* (MM), usually augmented with heuristics to deal with ambiguities in segmentation. Another very common approach to word segmentation is to use a variation of the *maximum matching algorithm*, frequently referred to as the *greedy algorithm*. The greedy algorithm starts at the first character in a text and, using a word list for the language being segmented, attempts to find the longest word in the list starting with that character. If a word is found, the maximum-matching algorithm marks a boundary at the end of the longest word, then begins the same longest match search starting at the character following the match. If no match is found in the word list, the greedy algorithm simply segments that character as a word and begins the search starting at the next character. A variation of the greedy algorithm segments a sequence of unmatched characters as a single word; this variant is more likely to be successful in writing systems with longer average word lengths. In this manner, an initial segmentation can be obtained that is more informed than a simple character-as-word approach. As a demonstration of the application of the character-as-word and greedy algorithms, consider an example of "desegmented" English, in which all white spaces has been removed: the "desegmented" version of the text *the most favourite music of all time* would thus be *themostfavouritemusicofalltime*, Applying the character-as-word algorithm would result in the useless sequence of tokens *t h e m o s t f a v o u r i t e m u s i c o f a l l t i m e*, which is why this algorithm only makes sense for languages such as Chinese. Applying the greedy algorithm with a "perfect" word list containing all known English words would first identify the word *them*, since that is the longest sequence of letters starting at the initial *t* which forms an actual word. Starting at the *o* following *them*, the algorithm would then find no match. Continuing in this manner, *themostfavouritemusicofalltime* would be segmented by the greedy algorithm as *them o s t favourite music of all time*. A variant of the maximum matching algorithm is the *reverse maximum matching* algorithm, in which the matching proceeds from the end of the string of characters, rather than the beginning. In the foregoing example, *themostfavouritemusicofalltime* would be segmented as *the most favourite music o fall time* by the reverse maximum matching algorithm. Greedy matching from the beginning and the end of the string of characters enables an algorithm such as *forward-backward matching*, in which the results are composed and the segmentation optimized based on the two results [7].

Many unsupervised methods have been proposed for segmenting raw character sequences with no boundary information into words [1, 2, 4, 5, 8, 14, 15]. Brent [1] gives a good survey of these methods. Most current approaches are using some form of EM to learn a probabilistic speech-or-text model and then employing Viterbi decoding procedures [19] to segment new speech or text into words. One reason that EM is widely adopted for unsupervised learning is that it is guaranteed to converge to a good probability model that locally maximizes the likelihood or posterior probability of the training data. For the problem of word segmentation, EM is typically applied by first extracting a set of candidate multi-grams from a given training corpus [8], initializing a probability distribution over this set, and then using the standard iteration to adjust the probabilities of the multi-grams to increase the posterior probability of the training data. Somewhat similar tasks of segmenting words into morphemes, where methods use minimal length description were shown to give good results [13].

Saffran et al., [21] proposed that word segmentation from continuous speech may be achieved by using transitional probabilities (TP) between adjacent syllables A and B, where, $TP(A \rightarrow B) = P(AB)/P(A)$, with $P(AB)$ being the frequency of B following A, and $P(A)$ the total frequency of A. Word boundaries are postulated at local minima, where the TP is lower than its neighbors.

In corpus-based word segmentation, there is either no explicit model learnt, as when neural networks [20] or lazy learning [6] are used, or the derived models are less sophisticated and do not use any abstractions of the word constituents found in data [3, 17]. Using annotated corpora greatly facilitates learning. However, there are situations in which one is interested in Unsupervised Learning (UL), that is, from unannotated corpora. Motivation for UL can vary from purely pragmatic, such as the high cost or unavailability of annotated corpora, to theoretical, when language is modelled as yet another communication code within the framework of Information Theory [22].

3   Proposed Method

Let $S = l_1 l_2 l_3 \ldots l_m$ denotes a text of m consecutive characters without any space in between them for which we need to segment and $C = \{c_1, c_2, \ldots, c_\tau\}$ denotes a large corpus of text containing τ words (tokens). Also, let $T^p = \{t_1, t_2, \ldots, t_p\}$ be the set of all (p) unique words (types) which occur in the corpus C and $T^f = \{f_1, f_2, \ldots, f_p\}$ be the set of frequencies of all the corresponding types in T^p i.e. f_x is the frequency of type t_x. Unlike the corpus C, which is an ordered list containing many occurrences of the same words, T^p is a set containing no repeated words. Again, let n be the maximum length of any possible words in the segmented words list where n m and $N^p = \{l_1, l_2, .., l_n, l_1 l_2, l_2 l_3, .. , l_1 l_2.. l_n, \ldots\}$ be the set of all possible n-grams where $\eta = |N^p|$ is the total number of n-grams in N^p. We can also consider N^p as $N^p = \{w_1, w_2 \ldots, w_\eta\}$. And $N^f = \{f_1', f_2' \ldots, f_\eta'\}$ be the set of frequencies of all the corresponding n-grams of N^p taken from T^f, i.e. f_x' is the frequency of w_x. To get rid of the noise types of the corpus, we assign a set of minimum frequencies for each possible length from 1 to n to be considered as a valid word. $M^f = \{\alpha_1, \alpha_2 \ldots, \alpha_n\}$, where α_x is the minimum frequency required to be a valid word of length x. The steps of the method are as follows:

Step 1: Sort all the elements of N^p in descending order based on length (in characters). Again sort in descending order for same length words of the sorted N^p (say $\overline{N^p}$) based on the frequencies of N^f. For each element in $\overline{N^p}$ do the next steps:

Step 2: If $S \neq \emptyset$ and the current maximum length n-gram (say w_n) in $\overline{N^p}$ satisfies $f_n' \geq \alpha_{|w_n|}$ and $w_n \in S$ (i.e., $S \cap w_n = w_n$) then add w_n to segmented word list, S' (i.e., $S' \leftarrow S' \cup w_n$) and remove w_n from S (i.e., $S \leftarrow S \setminus w_n$) and add a blank space as a boundary mark.

Step 3: If $S \neq \emptyset$ and not all elements in $\overline{N^p}$ are done then update w_n by the next maximum length n-gram from $\overline{N^p}$ and go to step 2.

Step 4: Rearrange all the words of S' in accordance with S. If $S = \emptyset$, then output S' and exit. Otherwise, for each remaining chunks[2], r in S call *matchResidue(r)*, output S' and exit.

Algorithm *matchResidue*

Input: r, S'

1.   // Take the prefix word, w_{n-1} and suffix
2.   // word, w_n of r from S' according to the
3.   // would be position of r in S'.
4. $S' \leftarrow S' \setminus w_{n-1}$
5. $S' \leftarrow S' \setminus w_n$
6. $S_t \leftarrow w_{n-1} \cup r \cup w_n$
7.   // $S_t = \{l_1 l_2 l_3 \ldots l_m\}$, where m is the length of S_t
8. $S_t' \leftarrow leftMaxMatching(S_t)$
9. $S_t'' \leftarrow rightMaxMatching(S_t)$
10. **if** ($|S_t'| > |S_t''|$)
11. $S' \leftarrow S' \cup S_t''$
12. **elseif** ($|S_t'| < |S_t''|$)
13. $S' \leftarrow S' \cup S_t'$
14. **else**
15.   find a $x \in \{S_t', S_t''\}$ for which entropy
16.   rate $\dfrac{1}{|x|} \sum\limits_{i=1}^{|x|} \log_2 (f_i)$ is maximum
17. $S' \leftarrow S' \cup x$
18. **end**

Output: S'

Algorithm *leftMaxMatching*

// n is the maximum length of any possible valid words in S_t and $n \leq m$

Input: S_t

1. **while** $S_t \neq \emptyset$ **do**
2. $N^p \leftarrow \{l_1, l_1 l_2, l_1 l_2 l_3 \ldots, l_1 l_2 \ldots l_n\}$
3.   i.e., $N^p \leftarrow \{w_1, w_2 \ldots, w_n\}$
4. $N' \leftarrow \{f_1', f_2' \ldots, f_n'\}$
5. $M' \leftarrow \{\alpha_1, \alpha_2 \ldots, \alpha_n\}$
6. $i \leftarrow 1$
7.   **while** ($i \leq n$ && $i \leq m$)
8.   **if** ($f_i' \geq \alpha_i$)
9. $max \leftarrow i$
10.   **end**
11.   increment i

---

[2] A single chunk may contain one or more characters.

```
12.        end
13.        S'_t ← S'_t U w_max
14.        S_t ← S_t \ w_max
15. end
Output: S'_t
```

Algorithm *rightMaxMatching*
// n is the maximum length of any possible valid words in S_t and $n \leq m$
Input: S_t
```
1. while S_t ≠ Ø do
2.        N^p ← {l_m, l_{m-1}l_m, l_{m-2}l_{m-1}l_m, ..,
3.              l_{m-n}l_{m-n+1}... l_m}
4.        i.e., N^p ← {w_1, w_2 ..., w_n}
5.        N^f ← {f'_1, f'_2 ..., f'_n}
6.        M^f ← {α_1, α_2..., α_n}
7.        i←1
8.        while ( i ≤ n && i ≤ m )
9.            if ( f'_i ≥ α_i )
10.              max ← i
11.           end
12.           increment i
13.        end
14.        S'_t ← S'_t U w_max
15.        S_t ← S_t \ w_max
16. end
Output: S'_t
```

4   A Walk-Through Example

As a demonstration of the application of the proposed algorithms, consider the same example of "desegmented" English text, S = {*themostfavouritemusicofalltime*}. We have used the BNC[3] (British National Corpus) to calculate T^p and T^f. let, n=10 be the maximum length[4] of all possible words in S and M^f = {1000, 500, 50, 16, 15, 12, 10, 3, 2, 2}. Table 1 shows the sorted n-grams, $\overline{N^p}$ and their frequencies, N^f for this specific example.

For each element w_n (say, *favourite*) in $\overline{N^p}$,
Step 2: w_n satisfies $f'_n \geq \alpha_{|w_n|}$ as $4671 \geq 2$ and w_n is a substring of S.
S'={*favourite*} and S = {*themost musicofalltime*}.
Step 3: Not all elements in $\overline{N^p}$ are done, update w_n = {*alltime*} and go to step 2.
Step 2: doesn't satify $f'_n \geq \alpha_{|w_n|}$ as 6<10 though w_n is a substring of S.

---

[3] http://www.natcorp.ox.ac.uk/
[4] Though in BNC, the length of the longest valid word is 34.

Table 1. Sorted n-grams and their frequencies (the right-hand side continues the table)

$\overline{N^p}$	N^f	$\overline{N^p}$	N^f	$\overline{N^p}$	N^f	$\overline{N^p}$	N^f
favourite	4671	tfa	2	hem	305	ll	233
alltime	6	of	3052752	sic	292	ri	230
favour	6805	it	1054552	mus	269	ou	151
musico	10	he	641236	emu	247	ic	132
music	15134	me	131869	ico	95	vo	93
vouri	1	us	80206	uri	46	ur	77
them	167457	co	17476	fal	44	tf	11
time	164294	th	16486	ofa	36	a	2179299
most	98276	st	15565	mos	36	i	873059
fall	11202	al	7299	fav	33	l	59
item	3780	fa	2172	tem	31	c	46
rite	293	em	1641	emo	20	t	21
allt	28	os	1005	ost	18	s	19
emus	14	te	831	rit	13	e	17
musi	3	si	658	ite	11	r	14
hemo	3	mo	639	usi	8	h	12
emos	2	ti	615	ime	6	f	10
the	6057315	im	576	cof	5	v	9
all	282012	lt	485	avo	5	m	8
our	93463	av	291	lti	4	o	5
tim	3401	mu	276	vou	3	u	3

Step 3: Not all elements in $\overline{N^p}$ are done, update $w_n = \{favour\}$ and go to step 2.

Step 2: Condition fails as w_n is not a substring of S.

Step 3: Not all elements in $\overline{N^p}$ are done, update $w_n = \{musico\}$ and go to step 2.

Step 2: Condition fails as w_n does not satisfy $f_n' \geq \alpha_{|w_n|}$ as 10<12.

Step 3: Not all elements in $\overline{N^p}$ are done, update $w_n = \{music\}$ and go to step 2.

Step 2: w_n satisfies $f_n' \geq \alpha_{|w_n|}$ as 15134   15 and w_n is a substring of S.

$S' = \{favourite, music\}$ and
$S = \{themost\ ofalltime\}$.

We will only show the step 2 of all the remaining elements in $\overline{N^p}$ that satisfy the conditions.

Step 2: $w_n = \{them\}$, $S' = \{favourite, music, them\}$ and $S = \{ ost\ ofalltime\}$.
Step 2: $w_n = \{time\}$, $S' = \{favourite, music, them, time\}$ and $S = \{ ost\ ofall \}$.
Step 2: $w_n = \{fall\}$, $S' = \{favourite, music, them, time, fall\}$ and $S = \{ ost\ o \}$.

Step 4: Rearrange $S' = \{ them, favourite, music, fall, time\}$ and $S \neq \emptyset$, so call **matchResidue**(ost) and then **matchResidue**(o).

Case 1: matchResidue(ost) is called
$S' = S' \setminus \{ w_{n-1}, w_n \}$

$S' = \{\ them, favourite, music, fall, time\}\backslash\{\ them, favourite\ \}$
  $= \{music, fall, time\}$
$S_{t_i} = \{themostfavourite\}$
$S_t' = \{them, os, t, favourite\} \leftarrow leftMaxMatching(themostfavourite)$
$S_t'' = \{the, most, favourite\} \leftarrow rightMaxMatching(themostfavourite)$
As $|S_t'| > |S_t''|$, $S' = \{music, fall, time\}$ U S_t''
i.e., $S' = \{the, most, favourite, music, fall, time\}$

Case 2: matchResidue(o) is called
$S' = S' \backslash\{\ w_{n-1}, w_n\ \}$
$S' = \{the, most, favourite, music, fall, time\}\backslash\{\ music, fall\ \}$
  $= \{the, most, favourite, time\}$
$S_{t_i} = \{musicofall\}$
$S_t' = \{music, of, all\} \leftarrow leftMaxMatching(\ musicofall)$
$S_t'' = \{mus, ico, fall\} \leftarrow rightMaxMatching(\ musicofall)$
As in this case $|S_t'| = |S_t''|$, we need to find whether S_t' or S_t'' maximizes the entropy rate,
$\dfrac{1}{|x|}\sum_{i=1}^{|x|}\log_2(f_i)$, where $x \in \{S_t', S_t''\}$. The entropy rate for S_t' is (13.89 + 21.54 +
18.11) / 3 and for S_t'', (8.07 + 6.57 + 13.45) / 3. So, $S' = \{the, most, favourite, time\}$ $\cup$
S_t', as $\dfrac{1}{|S_t'|}\sum_{i=1}^{|S_t'|}\log_2(f_i) > \dfrac{1}{|S_t''|}\sum_{i=1}^{|S_t''|}\log_2(f_i)$. Finally, $S' = \{the, most, favourite, music,$
$of, all, time\}$.

5   Evaluation and Experimental Results

An obstacle to high-accuracy word segmentation is that there are no widely accepted guidelines for what constitutes a word; therefore, there is no agreement on how to "correctly" segment a text in a "desegmented" language. Native speakers of a language do not always agree about the "correct" segmentation, and the same text could be segmented into several very different (and equally correct) sets of words by different native speakers. Such ambiguity in the definition of what constitutes a word makes it difficult to evaluate segmentation algorithms that follow different conventions, as it is nearly impossible to construct a "gold standard" against which to directly compare results [7]. As shown in [23], the rate of agreement between two human judges on this task is less than 80%.

  The performance of word segmentation is usually measured using *precision* and *recall*, where recall is defined as the percent of words in the manually segmented text identified by the segmentation algorithm, and precision is defined as the percentage of words returned by the algorithm that also occurred in the hand-segmented text in the same position. In general, it is easy to obtain high performance for one of the two measures but relatively difficult to obtain high performance for both. *F-measure* (*F*) is the geometric mean of *precision* (*P*) and *recall* (*R*) and expresses a trade-off between those two measures. These performance measures are defined as follows:

$$P = TP / (TP + FP)$$
$$R = TP / (TP + FN)$$
$$F = (1 + \beta)PR / (\beta P + R)$$
$$= 2PR / (P + R), \text{ with } \beta = 1 \text{ such that } precision \text{ and } recall \text{ weighted equally.}$$

For instance, if the target segmentation is "we are human", and the model outputs "weare human", then precision is 1/2 ("human" out of "weare" and "human", recall is 1/3 ("human" out of "we", "are", and "human") and F-measure is 2/5.

We used the type frequency from BNC and tested our segmentation method on part of the Brown corpus. Specifically, we converted a portion of the corpus to lowercase letters and removed all white space and punctuation. We used 285K characters, 57904 tokens as our test data. We obtained 84.28% word precision rate, 81.63% word recall rate, and 82.93% word F-measure.

In a second test, we used the type frequency from BNC and tested our segmentation method on the Brown corpus to make sure that we test on different vocabulary from the training data. This insures that some of the word in the test set were not previously seen (out-of-vocabulary words). There were 4,705,022 characters and 1,003,881 tokens in the Brown corpus. We obtained 89.92% word precision rate, 94.69% word recall rate, and 92.24% word F-measure. The average number of tokens per line could be the reason for obtaining better result when we tested on the Brown corpus, as 8.49 and 16.07 are the average number of tokens per line in the Brown corpus and the BNC corpus, respectively.

One of the best known results on segmenting the Brown corpus is due to Kit and Wilks [15] who use a description-length gain method. They trained their model on the whole corpus (6.13M) and reported results on the *training* set, obtaining a boundary precision of 79.33%, a boundary recall of 63.01% and boundary F-measure of 70.23%. Peng and Schuurmans [18] trained their model on a subset of the corpus (4292K) and tested on *unseen* data. After the lexicon is optimized, they obtained 16.19% higher recall and 4.73% lower precision; resulting in an improvement of 5.2% in boundary F-measure. De Marcken [9] also used a minimum description length (MDL) framework and a hierarchical model to learn a word lexicon from raw speech. However, this work does not explicitly yield word boundaries, but instead recursively decomposes an input string down to the level of individual characters. As pointed out by Brent [1], this study gives credit for detecting a word if any node in the hierarchical decomposition spans the word. Under this measure [9] reports a word recall rate of 90.5% on the Brown corpus. However, his method creates numerous chunks and therefore only achieves a word precision rate of 17%. Christiansen *et al.* [5] used a simple recurrent neural network approach and report a word precision rate of 42.7% and word recall rate of 44.9% on spontaneous child-directed British English. Brent and Cartwright [2] used a MDL approach and reported a word precision rate of 41.3% and a word recall rate of 47.3% on the CHILDES collection. Brent [1] achieved about 70% word precision and 70% word recall by employing additional language modeling and smoothing techniques. Peng and Schuurmans [18] obtained 74.6% word precision rate, 79.2% word recall rate, and 75.4% word F-measure on the Brown corpus. A balance of high precision and high recall is the main advantage of our proposed method. However, it is difficult to draw a direct comparison between these results because of the different test corpora used by different authors.

Fig. 1 summarizes the result of different methods, which are tested on the Brown corpus based on precision, recall and F-measure. Though all the methods in Fig. 1 use the Brown corpus, the testing data sets in the Brown corpus are not exactly the same.

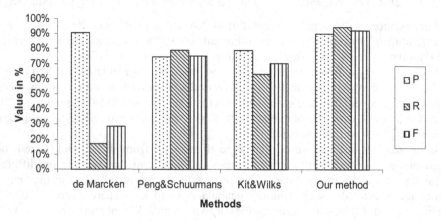

Fig. 1. Test result on the Brown corpus

6 Conclusion and Future Work

Actually the uses of *maximum length descending frequency* and entropy rate can effectively distill special terms and proper nouns when the corpus covers a huge collection of both domain-dependent and domain-independent words, and it can effectively avoid statistical errors on shorter strings which belong to a longer one. However, names are not always easy to exploit and contain abbreviations and special characters that vary between domains. This method can be used to address this issue, an important step of schema matching in databases. Top choices search engines segment the 'desegmented' part from a search text only if the 'desegmented' part contains two to three words. Even the popular search engine Google segments a 'desegmented' part of search text consisting of only two words and fails to provide any search result when the search text consists of more than two 'desegmented' words. Experimental results show that our method can segment words with high precision and high recall. Future directions also involve integrating the current algorithm into a larger system for comprehensive and context-based word analysis.

References

1. Brent, M.: An efficient, probabilistically sound algorithm for segmentation and word discovery. *Machine Learning* 34, (1999) 71–106
2. Brent, M. and Cartwright, T.: Distributional regularity and phonotactics are useful for segmentation. *Cognition* 61, (1996) 93-125
3. Brill, E.: Some advances in transformation-based part of speech tagging. In: *Proc. of the Twelfth National Conference on Artificial Intelligence*, AAI Press/MIT Press, (1994) 748–753

4. Christiansen, M. and Allen, J.: Coping with Variation in Speech Segmentation. In *Proceedings of GALA 1997: Language Acquisition: Knowledge Representation and Processing*, (1997) 327-332
5. Christiansen, M., Allen, J. and Seidenberg, M.: Learning to Segment Speech Using Multiple Cues: A Connectionist Model. *Language and Cognitive Processes* 13, (1998) 221-268
6. Daelamans, W., van den Bosch, A. and Weijters, A.: IGTree: Using trees for compression and classification in lazy learning algorithms. *Artificial Intelligence Review, 11*, (1997) 407–423
7. Dale, R., Moisl, H. and Somers, H.: *Handbook of Natural Language Processing*. Marcel Dekker, Inc. New York (2000) 22-26
8. Deligne, S. and Bimbot, F.: Language Modeling by Variable Length Sequences: Theoretical Formulation and Evaluation of Multigrams. In *Proceedings ICASSP* (1995)
9. de Marcken, C.: The Unsupervised Acquisition of a Lexicon from Continuous Speech. *Technical Report AI Memo No. 1558, M.I.T., Cambridge, Massachusetts* (1995)
10. Do, H.H. and Rahm, E.: COMA – A System for Flexible Combination of Schema Matching Approaches. In *VLDB* (2002)
11. Fung, P. and Wu, D.: Improving Chinise tokenization with linguistic filters on statistical lexical acquisition. *Fourth Conference Applied Natural Language Processing*, Stuttgart (1994) 180-181
12. Gao, J., Li, M., Wu, A. and Huang, C.-N.: Chinese word segmentation and named entity recognition: a pragmatic approach. *Computational Linguistics*, 31(4) (2005)
13. Gelbukh, A., Alexandrov, M. and Han, S.Y.: Detecting Inflection Patterns in Natural Language by Minimization of Morphological Model. In *CIARP 2004*, LNCS 3287, (2004) 432-438
14. Hua, Y.: Unsupervised word induction using MDL criterion. In *Proceedings ISCSL2000*, Beijing (2000)
15. Kit, C. and Wilks, Y.: Unsupervised Learning of Word Boundary with Description Length Gain. In *Proceedings CoNLL99 ACL Workshop*. Bergen (1999)
16. Madhavan, J., Bernstein, P., Doan, A. and Halevy, A.: Corpus-based Schema Matching. In *International Conference on Data Engineering (ICDE-05)* (2005)
17. Mikheev, A.: Automatic rule induction for unknown word guessing. *Computational Linguistics*, 23(3) (1997) 405–423
18. Peng, F. and Schuurmans, D.: A Hierarchical EM Approach to Word Segmentation, In *Proceedings of the Sixth Natural Language Processing Pacific Rim Symposium (NLPRS 2001)* Tokyo, Japan. (2001) 475-480
19. Rabiner, L.: A Tutorial on Hidden Markov Models and Selected Applications in Speech Recognition. In *Proceedings of IEEE*, 77(2) (1989)
20. Rumelhart, D.E. and McClelland, J.: On learning the past Tense of English verbs. In *Parallel distributed processing* Vol. II, Cambridge, MA: MIT Press (1986) 216–271
21. Saffran, J.R., Newport, E.L. and Aslin, R.N.: Word segmentation: The role of distributional cues. *Journal of Memory and Language 35*, (1996) 606–621
22. Shannon, C.E. and Weaver, W.: *The mathematical theory of communication*. Urbana: University of Illinois Press (1963)
23. Sproat, R., Shih, C., Gale, W. and Chang, N.: A stochastic finite-state word-segmentation algorithm for Chinese. *Computational Linguistics*, 22(3) (1996) 377–404
24. Sproat, R., Shih, C., Gale, W. and Chang, N.: A stochastic word segmentation algorithm for a Mandarin text-to-speech system. *32nd Annual Meeting of the Association for Computational Linguistics*, Las Cruces, NM (1994) 66-72

Tagging Sentence Boundaries in Biomedical Literature

Weijian Xuan, Stanley J. Watson, and Fan Meng

Molecular and Behavioral Neuroscience Institute and Department of Psychiatry
University of Michigan, Ann Arbor, Michigan 48109
mengf@umich.edu

Abstract. Identifying sentence boundaries is an indispensable task for most natural language processing (NLP) systems. While extensive efforts have been devoted to mine biomedical text using NLP techniques, few attempts are specifically targeted at disambiguating sentence boundaries in biomedical literature, which has a number of unique features that can reduce the accuracy of algorithms designed for general English genre significantly. In order to increase the accuracy of sentence boundary identification for biomedical literature, we developed a method using a combination of heuristic and statistical strategies. Our approach does not require part-of-speech taggers or training procedures. Experiments with biomedical test corpora show our system significantly outperforms existing sentence boundary determination algorithms, particularly for full text biomedical literature. Our system is very fast and it should also be easily adaptable for sentence boundary determination in scientific literature from non-biomedical fields.

1 Introduction

High throughput experiment approaches, such as genome-wide or organism-wide expression profiling studies, significantly enrich biomedical literature and at the same time, make computer-based literature mining almost a necessity in biomedical research. Since most of the experiment results are still summarized and presented in free text format, automated methods for extracting relevant information in Medline as well as full length text literature can be very helpful for the understanding of biological significance of high throughput results. The Medline database [1] already contains over 16 million citations, and more than half a million new records were added into the Medline database last year. In addition, the availability of full length papers in electronic format has also greatly improved in the last decade. Out of 19448 journals included in the PubMed, 5426 journals provide online access of full length papers in electronic format. The extensive access to full length papers as well as abstracts provides unprecedented opportunities for understanding the biomedical significance of high throughput data through computer-based literature mining. In deed, extensive efforts have been devoted to develop literature mining systems that aim at mining important entities, experimental evidences, interactions, hypothesis and other domain knowledge from free text.

One of the common features of text mining systems is the incorporation of NLP techniques. Many NLP techniques, such as part-of-speech (POS) taggers [2], sentence

A. Gelbukh (Ed.): CICLing 2007, LNCS 4394, pp. 186–195, 2007.

alignment [3] and text segmentation [4], require that texts have already been segmented into sentences. In the Information Retrieval (IR) field, recent researches have taken the sentence as the frame/conceptual unit for the identification of true term dependencies [5] and the evaluation of pairwise sentence similarity [6]. In practice, isolating sentences is a prerequisite for virtually any syntactic analysis of text corpus.

Sentence Boundary Disambiguation (SBD) may appear to be an easy task. In reality, however, achieving high accuracy for the purpose of literature mining is not a trivial problem due to the ambiguity of punctuation marks. For example, while an exclamation point or a question mark is almost always indicating the end of a sentence, the most frequently used period is very ambiguous. A period can signal a decimal point, a sentence boundary, an abbreviation, or even an abbreviation at a sentence boundary. In about 6 million Medline abstracts we investigated, about 33% of the periods are ambiguous.

There are already some reports on identifying sentence boundaries in general English literature. The first class of approaches for SBD uses rule-based methods. Cherry and Vesterman [7] implemented the UNIX STYLE program that recognized sentence boundaries mainly through a short list of abbreviations and a lexicon of known words. Aberdeen at al [8] developed a sentence splitting module containing 75 abbreviations and over 100 regular expression rules written in Flex. There are also two Perl modules (http://www.cpan.org), Text::Sentence and Lingua::EN::Sentence, designed for the SBD purpose using regular expressions.

Machine learning algorithms are used in the second class of approaches. They basically utilize features of context words surrounding the ambiguous punctuation mark and treat the sentence tagging task as a classification problem. The Wall Street Journal (WSJ) corpus and the Brown corpus are usually used for the evaluation of various SBD solutions. Palmer and Hearst [9] presented a system, SATZ, for SBD task. They used POS information of context words. Nevertheless, they found the SBD task and POS tagging is a chicken and egg problem. To circumvent this problem, they utilized prior probabilities of POS assignments, as opposed to definite POS assignments, as contextual information. They achieved around 99% accuracy on the WSJ corpus. Humphrey and Zhou [10] described a feed-forward neural network to disambiguate periods, but did not report the accuracy of their results. Stamatatos et al [11] presented a simplified version of Transformation Based Learning theory for the automatic extraction of rules for the SBD task. Mikheev [12] tackled the SBD task through a variation of POS tagging framework. They claimed 0.8% and 1.2% error rate on WSJ and Brown corpus, respectively. Reynar and Ratnaparkhi [13] applied a maximum entropy approach to the problem. They presented a trainable model that requires no hand-crafted rules, lexicon, POS tags, or domain knowledge. Their method achieved 98.8% accuracy on the WSJ corpus and 97.9% on the Brown corpus.

Given the high accuracy of aforementioned methods, it would seem that the SBD problem has largely been solved. However, these approaches were not designed to deal with the SBD problem in biomedical literature thus some of their assumptions and methods are not appropriate for biomedical texts. For example, a common postulation in rule-based approaches stipulates if the word immediately before an ambiguous period is a single uppercase letter then the period does not denote a full-stop. Nevertheless, in molecular biology literature, a lot of gene/protein names end with a single uppercase letter, e.g. *cyclin F*, and it is common to have such gene names at the end of a sentence. The performance of machine learning approaches highly depends on the quality, the content and even the size of the training corpus. Generating an appropriate corpus that covers most of the unique issues in biomedical literature for effective training purpose requires considerable human effort. Furthermore, in biomedical literature, there are much more unknown words and abbreviations than in general domain. As a result, none of these methods perform well on biomedical corpora.

In this paper, we present an efficient method for tagging sentence boundaries in biomedical literature using a combination of heuristic and statistical strategies. Our method does not require part-of-speech taggers or training procedures. Experiments with both Medline abstracts and full length papers show the accuracy of our method is significantly better than existing systems on biomedical corpora. Our program is also very fast and it allows the on-the-fly processing of biomedical literature. The program is available upon request, and the online evaluation version is available at: http://brainarray.mbni.med.umich.edu/sbd.asp.

2   Methods

In this section, we will first describe the special features of biomedical text related to the SBD problem and then present our solution.

2.1   Special SBD Issues in Biomedical Literature

After a comprehensive investigation of characteristics of sentence boundaries in biomedical literature, we identified several unique features that differentiate biomedical literature from regular English text for the SBD task.

1. Abbreviations

It is well known that biological and medical literature contain considerable number of abbreviations. For example, *E.coli, i.c.v., N. lactamdurans, Hs.1259, M.HsaIIP, C. elegans, H2B.1B, S. pombe*, etc. Large amount of abbreviations containing period(s) is one of the major sources of errors in sentence boundary determination of existing SBD programs.

2. Proper names

In biomedical field, especially in molecular biology, there are a lot of domain-specific proper names, e.g. gene/protein names. They can be in various case forms, i.e., uppercase, lowercase, capitalized or mixed forms, e.g., *A2MP* and *hA2aR*. It's not uncommon to begin a sentence with lowercased proper names such as, "*hKv beta 3 was* ...", "*p230 also includes* ..." and "*hRCE1 activity was* ...".

In regular English corpus, when an abbreviation is followed by a period and the word following a period is number or lowercased word, then the period does not denote a sentence boundary [12]. Apparently, this assumption does not hold in biomedical literature, as we have a large amount of abbreviations appear at the end of sentences and lowercased proper names frequently show up at the beginning of sentences.

3. Lack of naming convention

Unlike general English literature, biomedical text contains a large amount of compound words not recorded in regular dictionaries. The lack of naming convention has led to the naming "chaos" and the same concept can be expressed in many different ways. This situation significantly degrades the results of classic POS taggers. As a result, SBD algorithms based on POS taggers will obtain less accuracy on biomedical corpora than on general corpora.

4. Complex citations

Biomedical text corpus usually contains citations. These citations consist of, among others, author names and journal/conference names. These names often appear in the form of abbreviation (e.g., "*Acta Physiol. Pol. 1975, 26 (1): 1-11.*", "*Roe. Li, Z., Xia, L., Lee, L. M., Khaletskiy, A., Wang, J., Wong, J. Y. C. and Li, J-J.*", and "*M. Fransen, P.P. Van Veldhoven, S. Subramani, Biochem. J. 340 (1999) 561-568*"). Even in Medline abstracts, various forms of citations appear frequently. Existing SBD algorithms were not designed to handle such citations effectively.

5. Conversion problem

Another problem we identified in Medline records or full text papers is that the conversion from either PDF or HTML to text format, or the generation of text using Optical Character Recognition (OCR) may produce erroneous results. For example, "$Ang\ I{\cdot}mL^{-1}{\cdot}h^{-1}$" may become "*Ang I. mL(-1). h(-1)*", and "*1.5-3.0 mM*" may become "*1 . 5-3 . 0 mM*" after format conversion.

In general, these issues are more significant in full length papers since more abbreviations, citations, alternative descriptions are used than those in Medline abstracts. The diversity as well as the subtleness of these unique features makes machine learning approaches inefficient for achieving high accuracy in SBD for biomedical literature, unless significant efforts can be devoted for tagging large volumes of error-free training corpus from different areas of biomedical research. Consequently, we believe that the rule-based approach is more suitable for the SBD task on biomedical literature.

2.2 Rule-Based Approach for Biomedical Literature SBD

Based on the above analysis, we developed a set of heuristic rules to deal with unique issues for sentence boundary determination in biomedical literature. These rules are combined with resources derived from statistical analysis of biomedical literature for higher accuracy. We implemented our approach in Perl.

1. Potential sentence boundaries

In our system, we consider the ".", "?", "!" as potential sentence terminals. While there are also cases where the ":" and ";" may signal the end of a sentence, the frequency of their occurrence are negligible. For biomedical text, we found it is sufficient only to consider cases where ".", "?", "!" are immediately followed by spaces or punctuation marks.

We first split the text at all potential boundaries, and use a series of rules to disambiguate the punctuation marks. Multiple adjacent fragments are concatenated if the punctuation marks between them do not signal a sentence terminal.

2. Resources for abbreviation and author names

Several existing knowledge bases in biomedical domain can be utilized for the SBD task. We extracted all abbreviations that contain periods (excluding decimal points) from Unified Medical Language System (UMLS) [14] and the Entrez Gene database [15]. A total of 14746 compound abbreviations were extracted from these resources. We counted the frequency of every bigram, i.e., words immediate before and after a period. For example, "*S. cerevisiae*", which occured 41 times in UMLS and Entrez Gene as a sub-string of compound terms. In addition, we manually constructed a list of 31 commonly used abbreviations, e.g. *Dr., Prof.*

In order to better discriminate abbreviations associated with author names, we pulled out 320347 unique last names from over 12 million Medline citation records. Furthermore, we also compiled a list of 1223 tokens that potentially represent biomedical measuring units, e.g. *mM, ng, kb, mol, kDa*. Meanwhile, we compiled a list of 25143 common English words from expanded UNIX spelling dictionary. While these lists may never be complete, they are fairly comprehensive and can be easily integrated into our system. Such a collection of frequently used abbreviations in biomedical domain noticeably helps the disambiguation process.

3. Sub-section segmentations

We manually constructed a short list of 76 common words and their plural forms that are often used as a concise sub-title in an abstract. Some examples from this list are *Aim, Background, Case, Comment, Conclusion, Design, Discussion, Guideline, Introduction, Method, Objective, Patient, Site*, etc. If a potential sentence split in the first step contains only a capitalized word in this list, it indicates the beginning of a sub-section. Using such patterns, we are able to not only split sentences but also accurately segment the document into semantically coherent sub-sections.

4. Sequential groups

It's common to find abstracts that contain multiple facts, e.g. assumptions, procedures, or results. For clarity and simplicity, these facts are usually grouped into sequential sentences by numbering "*1., 2., 3., ...*", "*A., B., C., ...*", "*I., II., III., ...*". A special algorithm was developed to identify such sequential groups. We first scan the document to detect potential sequential groups. We consider a target paragraph contains sequential groups if it consists of more than two consecutive Arabic numbers, English or Roman numerals, in increasing order. The identification of sequential sentences helps the disambiguation of sentence boundaries, particularly when there are multiple ambiguous abbreviations in a sentence.

5. Embedded segmentations

Some punctuation marks, including quotation marks, round brackets "*()*", and square brackets "*[]*", are usually used to enclose textual material, or to classify or group text. Multiple statements enclosed by these punctuation marks are semantically coherent. For example, in the sentence "*The AMPK gene from rat has recently been cloned [Carling et al., J. Biol. Chem. 269 (1994) 11442-11448].*", a citation is enclosed by square bracket thus multiple periods in this passage indicate abbreviations rather than sentence stops.

6. Abbreviation extraction

While we constructed a large resource for biomedical abbreviations, it is impossible to include all abbreviations in our resource since new abbreviations are showing up from time to time. To dynamically identify abbreviations, we make use of three types of document- and corpus-level statistics: unigrams/bigrams, surface clues and templates.

For each period, except those denote decimal points, we consider the word immediately before it as a unigram. As mentioned previously, a bigram is defined as the word immediately before the period together with the word right after the period. We extract unigrams and bigrams in each document, excluding those that contain words included in our compiled list of common English word. Unigrams and bigrams occur frequently in corpus are likely to be abbreviations in the domain of a given corpus. Unigrams and bigrams occur frequently only in a subset of documents are potentially field-specific abbreviations.

There are also surface clues we can use for high confidence dynamic abbreviation identification. For example, when a word is followed by a period and then a comma, the corresponding word must be an abbreviation. Conversely, when a word is followed by a period in some places but not by any punctuation marks in other contexts in the same document, it suggests that this word is usually not an abbreviation. When this occurs, it indicates that the period followed by this word signals a sentence terminal.

For the high frequency abbreviations extracted from corpus-wide statistics, we also examine the features of their suffix, i.e. the characteristics of the word following it, for the purpose of generating templates useful for increase the accuracy of dynamic abbreviation identification.

For example,

- Abbreviations often followed by a numeral, e.g. *Jan., No.*
- Abbreviations often followed by a lowercased word, e.g. *i.e., vs.*
- Abbreviations often followed by a capitalized proper name, e.g. *Prof. Fred, Dr. La*

7. Citation identification

Biomedical literature frequently quotes other publications in the middle or at the end of sentences. Many journals use citation formats that contain author name initials and/or journal/conference abbreviations. Consequently, periods in citations are a major source of sentence boundary ambiguity.

We found the following citation patterns frequently occur in biomedical literature: (1) Quotations in parenthesis or brackets. (2) Numbers including publication dates, journal volume/issues, and page numbers; single letter initials. (3) Last name for multiple authors. (4) Journal abbreviations that are often composed of multiple adjacent short words, e.g. *"Natl. Acad. Sci."*.

To enhance the accuracy of the identification of journal titles, we extracted 3610 unique journal abbreviations from titles of 5748 journals that covered by ISI Journal Citation Report [16].

We consider a phrase as citation if it satisfies two or more of the above patterns. Periods within citations will not be treated as signals for the termination of a sentence.

8. Handling Medline conversion error

We found two main problems in the process of generating Medline records from journal publications. One is the conversion from superscript in formatted journal publications to regular characters in plain text and the conversion of middle dot symbol to period, i.e. "·" to ".". This type of errors can be identified based on the observation that the superscripts are often enclosed by parentheses, which are added during their conversion into regular character. In addition, in biomedical domain superscripts are usually digits or used mainly for expressing measuring units. For example, "*Ang I ·mg of tissue^{-1}· h^{-1}*", is usually converted to "*Ang I. mL(-1). h(-1)*". Once such patterns are detected immediately before and after a period, it indicates the occurrence of a dot symbol instead of a full sentence stop.

The second problem is the insertion of spaces between digits and decimal points. If there is one single space both before and after a period, and the word before and after the space are both digits or measuring units or short symbols with case variations, it signals that a conversion problem rather than a sentence boundary. For example, "*ADP.P$_i$*" may become "*ADP . Pi*", and "*0.75 mM*" may become "*0 . 75 mM*" in the Medline database.

3 Results

The maximum entropy method proposed by Reynar and Ratnaparkhi [13] is the most frequently cited work for sentence boundary determination. The maximum entropy approach does not require any supporting resources beyond the sentence-boundary annotated corpus. We therefore use their system as a benchmark in the evaluation of our method for sentence boundary determination in biomedical corpus.

For evaluation purpose, we constructed a test corpus from depression research literature by retrieving all Medline abstracts related to the keyword "*depression*". This search resulted in 101,048 abstracts. We randomly selected 500 of them as our test corpus and manually tagged sentence boundaries. In total, there are 3928 sentences in our test corpus.

We use the standard measure of precision and recall for the performance evaluation of various methods. Errors fall into two categories: (1) *false positive:* a punctuation mark that a method erroneously labels as a sentence boundary; (2) *false negative*: an actual sentence boundary that a method does not label correctly.

Since maximum entropy method requires a training corpus, we randomly selected another 1000 Medline abstracts related to depression, and we tagged sentence boundaries manually. We trained the maximum entropy system using 2000, 4000, and 6000 sentences, and obtained error rate of 2.91%, 2.02% and 2.24% respectively.

For comparison, we also evaluated two other publicly available programs: the MMTx from the National Library of Medicine [17] and the Sentence Splitter from University of Illinois (http://l2r.cs.uiuc.edu/~cogcomp). MMTx has a component for SBD. In our evaluation, we used its latest version (v2.4.B). Sentence Splitter is a program dedicated to sentence segmentation, and it is used by quite a number of NLP research groups. Table 1 is the summary of the comparison results from our test corpus. It seems all methods perform reasonably well with Medline abstracts but the error rate of our method is about one order of magnitude lower than other methods. Considering that SBD is usually a pre-processing step, even a small error rate in this phase may lead to a domino effect in some NLP applications such as identifying conceptual relationships.

Table 1. Results from the 500 Medline abstracts test corpus

Methods	Error rate	Sentence detected	False Positives	False Negatives
Our method	0.27%	3923	3	8
Maximum Entropy	2.02%	3958	56	26
Sentence Splitter	3.40%	3849	59	79
MMTx	5.03%	3928	128	76

Furthermore, full-length papers usually contain more complications than Medline abstracts. Therefore we further benchmarked the accuracy of above approaches on full-length biomedical literature. We selected 8 full-length papers in the area of molecular biology from the list of the most read papers on the PNAS website and manually tagged 1615 sentences.

Table 2 clearly demonstrates that our method outperforms other approaches in disambiguating sentence boundaries of full-length biomedical text. Other approaches have higher false positive/false negative ratio, which suggests that they tend to over-split sentences. For example, maximum entropy method generates false positive at some multi-word biomedical terms such as "*C. elegans*", and MMTx raises false positives at author names such as "*D. A. Pollen*".

Table 2. Results on the molecular biology full-length test corpus

Methods	Error Rate	Sentence Detected	False Positives	False Negatives
Our method	1.23%	1598	4	21
Maximum Entropy	6.75%	1700	111	26
Sentence Splitter	5.27%	1624	58	49
MMTx	15.6%	1686	128	76

Most of the false negatives are due to abbreviations at the end of sentences. There are also some hard-to-catch rare exceptions, such as extraneous punctuations, e.g. ellipse, dashes, and unpaired parenthesis.

Besides its accuracy, our method is also very fast. We analyzed whole Medline corpus from 1965 to July 21, 2006. There are a total of 15,995,358 citations, among which 8,325,901 have abstracts. On a PC (P4 2.8GHz) running Windows 2000, it took our system only 5.5 hours to tag sentence boundaries for the entire Medline collection.

4 Discussion

Biomedical text has some features that clearly differentiate it from text in the general genre for sentence boundary determination. By identifying these features and utilizing existing resources, we successfully developed a program that can determine sentence boundary in biomedical text with very high accuracy. In contrast, without taking note of the aforementioned features of biomedical literature, other SBD approaches were unable to achieve good performance.

We believe the accuracy of our system can be further improved by analyzing SBD errors on various biomedical sub-fields. Since our approach does not rely on any other natural language processing tools, particularly part-of-speech taggers and syntactic parsers, it significantly reduces processing overhead and achieves very good computing performance. Meanwhile, our method does not require any training procedures that are usually very time consuming. It can be easily integrated into many large biomedical literature mining systems.

Given the performance of our method, it can be used in various literature mining systems. For example, it can be used to enhance the accuracy of biomedical entity identification [18]. When sentences are isolated, it becomes easier to disambiguate entity terms. Meanwhile, some biomedical mining systems use sentence as fundamental conceptual units [19]. Segmenting text into sentences with high accuracy will thus improve the effectiveness of these systems.

Although our program is mainly targeted for the biomedical literature, it is likely to achieve good sentence boundary determination results for typical scientific literature. In fact, except for the resource for biomedical abbreviation, most of the complications specifically addressed by our program are shared by publications from different areas of scientific research. The fact that our program can incorporate abbreviation lists along with corpus-wide statistics will make the adaptation of our program for processing text from different scientific disciplines an easy task.

Acknowledgements

The authors are members of the Pritzker Neuropsychiatric Disorders Research Consortium, which is supported by the Pritzker Neuropsychiatric Disorders Research Fund L.L.C. This work is also partly supported by the National Center for Integrated Biomedical Informatics through NIH grant 1U54DA021519-01A1.

References

1. PubMed: http://www.ncbi.nlm.nih.gov/entrez, (2006)
2. Brill, E.: Transformation-Based Error-Driven Learning and Natural Language Processing: A Case Study in Part of Speech Tagging. Computational Linguistics, 21(4) (1995) 543-565
3. Brown, P.F., J.C. Lai, and R.L. Mercer: Aligning Sentences in Parallel Corpora. In Proceedings of the 29th Annual Meeting of the Association for Computational Linguistics, Berkeley, CA, USA (1991)
4. Choi, F.Y.Y.: Advances in Domain Independent Linear Text Segmentation. In Proceedings of NAACL, Seattle, WA, USA (2000)
5. Nallapati, R. and J. Allan: Capturing Term Dependencies Using a Sentence Tree Based Language Model. In Proceedings of CIKM '02 conference, McLean, VA, USA (2002)
6. Ponte, J.M. and W.B. Croft: Text Segmentation by Topic. In European Conference on Digital Libraries, Pisa, Italy (1997)
7. Cheery, L.L. and W. Vesterman: Writing Tools - The STYLE and DICTION Programs. In 4.4 BSD User's Supplementary Documents, Computer Science Research Group, Berkeley, CA, USA (1994)

8. Aberdeen, J., J. Burger, D. Day, L. Hirschman, P. Robinson, and M. Vilain: MITRE: Description of The Alembicsystem Used for MUC-6. In Proceedings of the 6th message understanding conference, Columbia, MD, USA (1995)
9. Palmer, D.D. and M.A. Hearst: Adaptive Sentence Boundary Disambiguation. In Proceedings of the 4th Conference on Applied Natural Language Processing, Stuttgart, Germany (1994)
10. Humphrey, T.L. and F. Zhou: Period Disambiguation Using a Neural Network. In International Joint Conference on Neural Networks, Washington, DC, USA (1989)
11. Stamatatos, E., N. Fakotakis, and G. Kokkinakis: Automatic Extraction of Rules For Sentence Boundary Disambiguation. In Proceedings of the Workshop in Machine Learning in Human Language Technology, Advance Course on Artificial Intelligence, Chania, Greece (1999)
12. Mikheev, A.: Tagging Sentence Boundaries. In Proceedings of NAACL, Seattle, WA, USA (2000)
13. Reynar, J.C. and A. Ratnaparkhi: A Maximum Entropy Approach to Identifying Sentence Boundaries. In Proceedings of the 5th Conference on Applied Natural Language Processing, Washington, DC, USA (1997)
14. Humphreys, B.L., D.A.B. Lindberg, S.H. M., and B.G. O.: The Unified Medical Language System: An informatics research collaboration. Journal of the American Medical Informatics Association, 5(1) (1998) 1-11
15. Pruitt, K.D. and D.R. Maglott: RefSeq and LocusLink: NCBI Gene-Centered Resources. Nucleic acids research, 29(1) (2001) 137-140
16. ISI: Journal Citation Reports. http://www.isinet.com, (2003)
17. Aronson, A.R.: Effective Mapping of Biomedical Text to the UMLS Metathesaurus: The MetaMap Program. In Proceedings of AMIA Annual Symposium, Washington, DC, USA (2001)
18. Xuan, W., S.J. Watson, H. Akil, and F. Meng: Identifying Gene and Protein Names from Biological Texts. In Proceedings of Computational Systems Bioinformatics, Stanford, CA, USA (2003)
19. Christian Blaschke, M.A.A., Christos Ouzounis, Alfonso Valencia: Automatic Extraction of Biological Information from Scientific Text: Protein-Protein Interactions. In Proceedings of the AAAI Conference on Intelligent Systems in Molecular Biology, Bethesda, MD, USA (1999)

Probabilistic Classifications with TBL

Cícero Nogueira dos Santos and Ruy L. Milidiú

Departamento de Informática, Pontifícia Universidade Católica, Rio de Janeiro, Brazil
nogueira@inf.puc-rio.br, milidiu@inf.puc-rio.br

Abstract. The classifiers produced by the Transformation Based error-driven Learning (TBL) algorithm do not produce uncertainty measures by default. Nevertheless, there are situations like active and semi-supervised learning where the application requires both the sample's classification and the classification confidence. In this paper, we present a novel method which enables a TBL classifier to generate a probability distribution over the class labels. To assess the quality of this probability distribution, we carry out four experiments: cross entropy, perplexity, rejection curve and active learning. These experiments allow us to compare our method with another one proposed in the literature, the TBLDT. Our method, despite being simple and straightforward, outperforms TBLDT in all four experiments.

1 Introduction

Since the last decade, Machine Learning (ML) has proven to be a very powerful tool to enable effective Natural Language Processing (NLP). ML has been applied to central NLP problems such as: part-of-speech tagging, word-sense disambiguation, shallow parsing and prepositional phrase attachment ambiguity resolution. Most of the more successful ML algorithms can be roughly divided into two groups: rule-based and probabilistic. One of the main advantages of the rule-based methods is that, in general, the outcome of the learning process is a small set of rules that can be interpreted by humans.

On the other hand, probabilistic algorithms have the advantage of including uncertainty measures in their outputs. These uncertainty measures are useful for situations where the application requires both the sample's classification and the classification confidence. Semi-supervised algorithms and Active Learning are methods that require the samples' classification confidence. In Semi-supervised algorithms like Co-training [1], the uncertainty measures are used to select samples where the classifier is more confident. In Active Learning, where the objective is to minimize the tagging effort, the classification confidence is used to select the more informative samples to be manually tagged.

Transformation Based error-driven Learning (TBL) is a successful symbolic machine learning method introduced by Eric Brill [2]. It has since been used for several NLP tasks, such as part-of-speech (POS) tagging [2], text chunking [3], spelling correction, portuguese noun-phrase extraction [4] and portuguese appositive extraction [5], achieving state-of-the-art performance in many of

A. Gelbukh (Ed.): CICLing 2007, LNCS 4394, pp. 196–207, 2007.

them. The classifiers generated by TBL, by default, do not produce uncertainty measures. In [6], Florian et al. propose a method that provides an uncertainty measure to TBL classifiers.

Here, we present a novel method that enables a TBL classifier to generate a probability distribution over the class labels. To assess the quality of this probability distribution, we carry out four experiments: active learning, rejection curve, perplexity and cross entropy. These experiments allow us to compare our method with the TBLDT algorithm proposed by Florian et al. [6]. Our method, despite being simple and straightforward, outperforms TBLDT in all four experiments.

The remainder of the paper is organized as follows. In section 2, we describe the TBL algorithm. In section 3, we show our proposed method. In section 4, the experimental design and the results are reported. Finally, in section 5, we present our concluding remarks.

2   Transformation Based Learning

In a classification problem setup, the application defines which feature is to be learned. This feature is represented by a set of class labels Y. For instance, in the case of part-of-speech tagging, Y is the POS tagset.

TBL uses an error correcting strategy. Its main scheme is to generate an ordered list of rules that correct classification mistakes in the training set, which have been produced by an initial guess.

The requirements of the algorithm are:

- two instances of the training set, one that has been correctly labeled with the Y's class labels, and another that remains unlabeled;
- an initial classifier, the baseline system, which classifies the unlabeled training set by trying to guess the correct class for each sample. In general, the baseline system is based on simple statistics of the labeled training set; and
- a set of rule templates, which are meant to capture the relevant feature combinations that would determine the sample's classification. Concrete rules are acquired by instantiation of this predefined set of rule templates.

The learning method is a mistake-driven greedy procedure that iteratively acquires a set of transformation rules. The TBL algorithm can be depicted as follows:

1. Starts applying the baseline system, in order to guess an initial classification for the unlabeled version of the training set;
2. Compares the resulting classification with the correct one and, whenever a classification error is found, all the rules that can correct it are generated by instantiating the templates. This template instantiation is done by capturing some contextual data of the sample being corrected. Usually, a new rule will correct some errors, but will also generate some other errors by changing correctly classified samples;

3. Computes the rules' scores (errors repaired - errors created). If there is not a rule with a score above an arbitrary threshold, the learning process is stopped;
4. Selects the best scoring rule, stores it in the set of learned rules and applies it to the training set;
5. Returns to step 2.

When classifying a new sample set, the resulting sequence of rules is applied according to its generation order.

3   Probability Estimation with TBL Classifiers

One of the TBL classifiers' disadvantages is that they make hard decisions. When a TBL rule set is applied to a sample set S, each sample $s \in S$ receives one class label $y \in Y$, $[s \leftarrow y]$. Since these hard decisions do not have an associated probability, they give no hint about the classification quality.

On the other hand, probabilistic classifiers make soft decisions by assigning to each sample a probability distribution over all possible classes. There are many situations where this kind of classification is useful. One of these situations is in pipeline systems, such as an information extractor system that performs named entity extraction on the output of a probabilistic part-of-speech tagging. Another case is the semi-supervised learning which, in general, requires uncertainty measures to select samples for which the classifier is more confident.

3.1   The Proposed Method

The method proposed in this paper enables a TBL classifier to make soft decisions. Using this method, when a TBL rule set is applied to a sample set S, each sample $s \in S$ receives a probability distribution over the class labels Y, $[s \leftarrow P(Y|s)]$, instead of a single class label $y \in Y$. The method relies in the use of the training set to estimate a probability model associated with the TBL classifier. The procedure to estimate such a probability model is based in the notion of equivalence classes.

We call an *equivalence class* a set of samples that share some specific characteristics. In this work, we use two characteristics to group the samples into equivalence classes:

– the class label assigned by the initial classifier; and
– the rules that change the samples.

Using these two information pieces, we can create two types of equivalence classes: (a) a set of samples that have the same initial class label and are changed by the same rules; or (b) a set of samples that have the same initial class label and no rules are applied to them.

For each equivalence class, we compute its probability distribution by using maximum likelihood estimation. This is done by using Eq. 1.

$$P(y|e) = \frac{count(e,y)}{count(e)} \quad \forall y \in Y \tag{1}$$

where e is an equivalence class; $count(e,y)$ is the number of samples in e whose class label is y; and $count(e)$ is the number of samples in e.

We also estimate the probability distribution of a dummy equivalence class e_p that includes all the samples in the training set. We call the distribution $P(Y|e_p)$ the *prior class labels distribution*.

The whole process used to construct the probability model associated with a TBL rule set is shown in Fig. 1. The use of the probability model can be very efficient if it is stored in a hash table. The [key, value] pairs of the hash table are formed by the equivalence classes IDs and their respective probability distributions, [*initial class label + rules applied, P(Y|e)*].

Algorithm: GenerateProbabilityModel

Input:
  − R: a TBL rule set;
  − T: the training set used in the generation of the rule set R.
Do:
  1. apply the rule set R to the training set T. For each sample $t \in T$, record the class label assigned by the initial classifier and the rules applied to it;
  2. create equivalence classes by using the information recorded in step 1;
  3. estimate the probability distribution for each equivalence class by using Eq. 1;
  4. estimate the prior class labels distribution $P(Y|e_p)$ by using Eq. 1.
Output:
  − the probability model associated with the rule set R.

Fig. 1. Algorithm used to construct a probability model associated with a TBL rule set

Probabilistic classifications using a TBL classifier and a probability model associated with it must be done as described below.

1. Classify the samples using the TBL rule set. Record, for each sample, the class label assigned by the initial classifier and the rules applied to it;
2. Using the hash table containing the probability model, assign the following items for each sample:
   − the probability distribution whose key is the initial class label of the sample and the rules applied to it; or
   − if the hash table does not contain such a key, assign to the sample the distribution $P(Y|e_p)$.

3.2 Equivalence Class Partitioning

When creating a probability model using the proposed method, some equivalence classes could be very dense, mainly the ones formed by samples that are not changed by any rule. These cases are inefficient in terms of probability estimation. In fact, if a large portion of the training set is in the same equivalence class, then the distribution assigned to it is nearly the prior class distribution. For instance, in the case of base noun-phrase identification showed in Sect. 4 almost 50% of the the training set falls in the same equivalence class.

To overcome this inefficiency, we use an *auxiliary feature* to partition the equivalence classes that are composed by samples not changed by any rule. This feature must be suitably chosen for the classification problem being solved. In the two classification problems shown in Sect. 4, we use the POS tag as the auxiliary feature. In the case of base noun-phrase identification, for instance, the densest equivalence class is partitioned into 20 new equivalence classes whose ID includes the samples' POS tag.

3.3 Smoothing

Smoothing is very useful when estimating probability models for sparse data. Smoothing deals with events that have been observed zero times and also tends to improve the accuracy of the model. In this work, we apply two smoothing techniques to the probability model generated from a TBL classifier.

Additive Smoothing. We use the *plus-delta* version [7] of the additive smoothing, which is computed by using Eq. 2.

$$P(y|e) = \frac{count(e,y) + \delta}{count(e) + \delta \cdot |Y|} \quad \forall y \in Y \qquad (2)$$

where e is an equivalence class; δ is a number between 0 and 1; $count(e,y)$ is the number of samples in e whose class labels are y; $count(e)$ is the number of samples in e; and $|Y|$ is the number of class labels.

Backoff Smoothing. The idea of this technique is to smooth a most specific estimate $P(y|e_1)$ with a less specific one $P(y|e_2)$ by computing a mixture of the two estimates [8]

$$\hat{P}_{1,2}(y|e_1) = \lambda P(y|e_1) + (1 - \lambda)P(y|e_2) \qquad (3)$$

using a mixing coefficient λ. The mixing coefficient varies between 0 and 1 according to our confidence in the first estimate. We say that the estimate $P(y|e_1)$ is most specific than $P(y|e_2)$ because the equivalence class e_1 contains less samples than e_2, and $e_1 \subset e_2$.

Given a sequence of estimates $(P(y|e_1), P(y|e_2), ..., P(y|e_k))$, where $P(y|e_1)$ is the most specific one and $P(y|e_k) = P(y|e_p)$ is the less specific one, we can recursively compute a linear combination of these estimates by

$$\hat{P}_k(y|e_k) = P(y|e_p) = P(y)$$
$$\hat{P}_i(y|e_i) = \lambda_i P(y|e_i) + (1 - \lambda_i)\hat{P}_{i+1}(y|e_{i+1}) \tag{4}$$

The estimate $\hat{P}_1(y|e_1)$ in this sequence is a linear combination of all k estimates. To compute the λ_i coefficient used in Eq. 4 we use the method described in [9]. In this method, λ_i is a function of the samples associated with the equivalence class e_i and is computed using Eq. 5.

$$\lambda_i = \begin{cases} \frac{count(e_i)}{count(e_i)+c\cdot div(e_i)} & \text{if } count(e_i) > 0 \\ 0 & \text{otherwise} \end{cases} \tag{5}$$

where $count(e_i)$ is the number of samples in e_i; c is an adjustable parameter which is tuned using held out data; and $div(e_i)$ is the number of distinct outcomes observed in e_i:

$$div(e_i) = |\{y \text{ s.t. } e_i \text{ contains at least a sample whose class label is } y\}|$$

We generate intermediary estimates in order to apply backoff smoothing to our probability model. These intermediary estimates are obtained by creating less specific equivalence classes from the ones generated in the process[1].

We partition the sample set into equivalence classes by using the following as common characteristics: the initial class label and the rules applied to the samples. We can construct less specific equivalence classes by gradually including more samples in an existing one. This is done by reducing the common information shared between the samples. To construct intermediary equivalence classes we gradually reduce the ID (initial class label and rules) of the existing one until it contains all the samples in the training set (e_p). This process is shown in the following example.

$$e_1 : ID = [y, R1, R2, R3]$$
$$e_2 : ID = [y, R1, R2]$$
$$e_3 : ID = [y, R1]$$
$$e_4 : ID = [y]$$
$$e_5 : ID = e_p$$

where ID is the set of characteristics that the samples in the equivalence class e_i have in common; y is the initial class label; and $\{R1, R2, R3\}$ are rules.

After the intermediary equivalence classes are generated, we estimate their probability distribution using Eq. 1 and then we apply backoff smoothing. In the previous example, the probability estimation $\hat{P}(Y|e_1)$ assigned to the equivalence class e_1 is a mixture of the five estimates.

3.4 Related Work

Florian et al. [6] proposed a method which enables TBL classifiers to produce soft decisions. The method involves dividing the training set into equivalence

---

[1] Described in Sect. 3.1.

classes and computing distributions over each equivalence class. The way used to divide the training set is to transform the TBL rule set into a decision tree. Once the decision tree is constructed and applied to the training set, the samples attached to the same leaf define an equivalence class. When a new sample set is to be classified, the decision tree is used.

The main difference between the method proposed here and the one of Florian et al. [6], is that we do not need to construct a decision tree. We only need to record the trace of the rules applied to each sample. Then, the rule application process remains the same. Two other differences are: (1) in [6], a further growth of the decision tree is used to partition the equivalence classes (leaves) that contains a large number of examples; and, (2) as a kind of smoothing, Florian et al. prunes the decision tree by removing the nodes that contain less examples than a given threshold.

4   Experiments

The effectiveness and quality of the proposed probabilistic extension to TBL are demonstrated by four experiments presented in this section. The experiments are performed on two tasks: text chunking and base noun phrase chunking. Text chunking consists in dividing a text into syntactically correlated of words. Base noun phrase chunking consists in recognizing non-overlapping text segments that consist of noun phrases (NPs).

The data used in the text chunking is the CoNLL-2000 corpus [10]. This corpus consists of sections 15-18 and section 20 of the Penn Treebank, and is pre-divided into 8936-sentence (211727 tokens) training set and a 2012-sentence (47377 tokens) test. This corpus is tagged with POS tags and with chunk tags. The data used in the base NP chunking is the one of Ramshaw & Marcus [3]. It is composed by the same texts as the CoNLL-2000 corpus. The difference is that the chunk tags only identify base NPs.

We have developed TBLprob which implements the probability estimation method described in Sect. 3. To compare our results with those produced by TBLDT, the method of Florian et al. [6], we use the fnTBL toolkit. fnTBL implements probability estimation using TBLDT - *conversion of TBL rules to Decision Tree.*

To perform a fair evaluation, we produce the TBL models by using only the fnTBL toolkit. Therefore, the same TBL rule sets are used to generate estimates using TBLprob and TBLDT methods. Only the Active Learning test is carried out with the rules generated by our system. The template set used in all the experiments, for both tasks, is the one proposed by Ramshaw & Marcus [3].

Tuning the smoothing parameters. The usual way of tuning the smoothing parameters is to maximize the likelihood of a held-out data set. According to Kalt [8], this is equivalent to minimizing the cross entropy of the model with a held-out set. In our case, iciency we use the *conditional cross entropy* which is defined by

$$H_c(Y|X) = - \sum_{x \in X} q(x) \cdot \sum_{y \in Y} q(y|x) \log_2 p(y|x) \tag{6}$$

where X is the test set (held-out), Y is the set of class labels, q is the probability distribution on the test set and p is the probability distribution estimated on the training set. Since the distribution $q(x)$ is unknown, we estimate the conditional cross entropy by computing an "empirical" expectation [8]:

$$H_c(Y|X) \approx \frac{-1}{|X|} \sum_{(x,y)} \log_2 p(y|x) \tag{7}$$

In our experiments, we tune the smoothing parameters by performing a 5-fold cross validation with the training set. At each cross validation iteration, the best parameter value is selected. This value is the one that minimizes Eq. 7 when the probability model using it is applied to the corresponding test set. This process is done for both tasks, text chunking and base NP chunking. Table 1 displays the mean of the best values for each test fold. These values are used in all of the following experiments.

Table 1. Best smoothing parameters by technique and task

	δ - Additive parameter	c - Backoff parameter
Text Chunking	0.05	1.0
Base NP Chunking	0.34	1.1

4.1 Cross Entropy and Perplexity

Cross entropy is typically used to measure the quality of a probability model. It takes into account the accuracy of the estimates as well as the classification accuracy of the system [6]. We utilize conditional cross entropy to compare our TBLprob estimates with the TBLDT estimates. The experiment uses Eq. 7 to estimate the cross entropy in the test set. The p distribution that appears in Eq. 7 is the one estimated by using the training set.

Perplexity is a measure closely related to cross entropy, defined as

$$P = 2^{H(Y|X)} \tag{8}$$

Table 2 presents the cross entropy and perplexity results for the various estimators. TBLprob using backoff smoothing outperforms the other schemes in both text chunking and base NP chunking. Nevertheless, the results using additive smoothing are very close to the ones using backoff.

The observed results indicate that the overall probability distribution of the TBLprob method better matches the true probability distribution. The method TBLprob without smoothing is outperformed by TBLDT only in the text

Table 2. Cross Entropy and Perplexity results for the two tasks

	Text Chunking		Base NP Chunking	
Classifier	Cross Entropy	Perplexity	Cross Entropy	Perplexity
TBLprob	0.3891	1.3096	0.1847	1.1366
TBLprob + backoff	**0.3350**	**1.2614**	**0.1668**	**1.1226**
TBLprob + additive	0.3388	1.2647	0.1672	1.1229
TBLDT	0.3818	1.3030	0.2338	1.1759

chunking task. This occurs mainly because TBLDT has a pruning factor that works as a kind of smoothing.

4.2   Rejection Curve

There are many applications where a probabilistic classifier needs to reject samples with low confidence classification. In such situations, the probability $P(y|s)$ can be used as a confidence score of the sample s to be correctly classified with the class label y. Hence, it is very useful to assess the quality of the class probability estimates of a classifier. One way to do this is to compute a rejection curve which shows the percentage of correctly classified test cases whose confidence level exceeds a given value [11]. A rejection curve that increases smoothly demonstrates that the confidence scores produced by the classifier are reliable.

We use the entropy H of the class probability distribution assigned to a sample s (Eq. 9) as a confidence measure in the construction of the rejection curve. The higher the value of H, the more uncertain the classifier is of its classification.

$$H(p(Y|s)) = - \sum_{i=1}^{|Y|} p(y_i|s) \log_2 p(y_i|s) \qquad (9)$$

The rejection curve is constructed by classifying the test set and then gradually rejecting the samples that have an entropy value greater than the current value of θ. θ takes values between the greatest entropy in the samples and 0. A point (x, y) in the rejection curve indicates that if the $x\%$ less confident samples are excluded, the remaining samples have an accuracy residual of $y\%$.

Figures 2 and 3 present the rejection curves for the text chunking and base NP chunking tasks, respectively. In both cases the TBLprob with smoothing clearly outperforms the TBLDT method at all rejection levels. In the case of text chunking, the two smoothing techniques generate classifiers with very similar behavior, producing a rejection curve that increases smoothly.

4.3   Active Learning

This section presents experimental results which show the usefulness and effectiveness of the probabilities generated by TBLprob. The experiment is to use the generated probabilities as a measure of uncertainty in an Active Learning process. The objective of the *active learning* approach is to minimize the

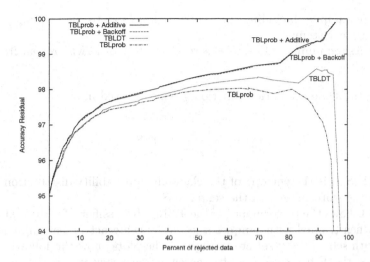

Fig. 2. Rejection curve: Text chunking

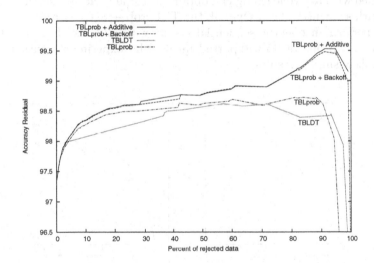

Fig. 3. Rejection curve: Base NP chunking

annotation effort by intelligently selecting the samples to be annotated. The active learning algorithm we use is the same as described in [6]:

1. Label an initial set of sentences of the corpus;
2. Train a TBL model and use the TBLProb method to obtain the class label probabilities on the rest of the corpus;
3. Choose T samples from the rest of corpus, specially the samples that optimize an evaluation function f, based on the class distribution probability of each sample;

4. Add the samples, including their correct class label to the training pool and retrain the system;
5. If the desired number of samples is reached, stop, otherwise repeat from Step 2.

We use the same evaluation function f which is used in [6]:

$$f(S) = \frac{1}{|S|} \sum_{i=1}^{|S|} H(Y|S,i) \tag{10}$$

where $H(Y|S,i)$ is the entropy of the class label probability distribution associated with the word index i in the sentence S.

Figure 4 shows the performance of the TBLprob classifier [2] for the text chunking task when trained with samples selected by using active learning and when trained with sequentially selected samples. The plots show the following information: (a) the F-measure and (b) the chunk accuracy versus the number of words in the annotated training set. Using less training data, the TBLprob classifier trained with active learning can obtain the same performance than the one trained with sequential data. Overall, the TBLprob + active learning can yield the same performance as the sequential system with 52% less data, a reduction greater than the one of 45% reported in [6]. The experiments with base NP chunking show similar results.

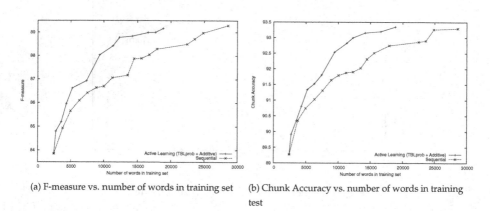

(a) F-measure vs. number of words in training set   (b) Chunk Accuracy vs. number of words in training test

Fig. 4. Performance of the TBLprob classifier versus sequential choice

5   Conclusions

In this paper, we presented TBLprob, a novel method which enables a TBL classifier to produce probabilistic classifications. We show four experiments that demonstrate the quality and the effectiveness of the proposed method. In these

---

[2] The additive smoothing ($\delta = 0.05$) is used in this experiment.

experiments, the text chunking and the base noun phrase chunking tasks were used as test cases.

The experimental results indicate that our probabilistic classifier performs at least as well as TBLDT. Moreover, using smoothing techniques, we outperformed TBLDT in our four experiments.

References

1. Blum, A., Mitchell, T.: Combining labeled and unlabeled data with co-training. In: COLT, Morgan Kaufmann (1998)
2. Brill, E.: Transformation-based error-driven learning and natural language processing: A case study in part-of-speech tagging. Comput. Linguistics **21** (1995) 543–565
3. Ramshaw, L., Marcus, M.: Text chunking using transformation-based learning. In Armstrong, S., Church, K., Isabelle, P., Manzi, S., Tzoukermann, E., Yarowsky, D., eds.: Natural Language Processing Using Very Large Corpora, Kluwer (1999)
4. Milidiú, R.L., Santos, C.N., Duarte, J.C., Renteria, R.P.: Semi-supervised learning for portuguese noun phrase extraction. In: Proceedings of 7th Workshop on Computational Processing of Written and Spoken Portuguese, Itatiaia, Brazil (2006) 200–203
5. Freitas, M.C., Duarte, J.C., Santos, C.N., Milidiú, R.L., Renteria, R.P., Quental, V.: A machine learning approach to the identification of appositives. In: Proceedings of Ibero-American AI Conference, Ribeirão Preto, Brazil (2006)
6. Florian, R., Henderson, J.C., Ngai, G.: Coaxing confidences from an old friend: Probabilistic classifications from transformation rule lists. In: Proceedings of Joint Sigdat Conference on Empirical Methods in NLP and Very Large Corpora, Hong Kong University of Science and Technology (2000)
7. Chen, S.F., Goodman, J.: An empirical study of smoothing techniques for language modeling. In Joshi, A., Palmer, M., eds.: Proceedings of the Thirty-Fourth Annual Meeting of the Association for Computational Linguistics, San Francisco, Morgan Kaufmann Publishers (1996) 310–318
8. Kalt, T.: Control Models of Natural Language Parsing. PhD thesis, University of Massachusetts Amherst (2005)
9. Collins, M.: Head-driven statistical models for natural language parsing. Computational Linguistics **29** (2003) 589–637
10. CoNLL: Shared task for computational language learning (conll). (2000)
11. Dietterich, T.G., Bakiri, G.: Solving multiclass learning problems via error-correcting output codes. Journal of Artificial Intelligence Research **2** (1995) 263–286

The Non-associativity
of Polarized Tree-Based Grammars

Yael Cohen-Sygal[1] and Shuly Wintner[2]

[1] Department of Computer Science, University of Haifa, Israel
yaelc@cs.haifa.ac.il
[2] Department of Computer Science, University of Haifa, Israel
shuly@cs.haifa.ac.il

Abstract. Polarities are used to sanction grammar fragment combination in high level tree-based formalisms such as eXtenssible Meta-Grammar (XMG) and polarized unification grammars (PUG). We show that attaching polarities to tree nodes renders the combination operation non-associative, and in practice leads to overgeneration. We first provide some examples of non-associative combination operators in existing polarity-based formalisms. We then prove that there is no other non-trivial polarity system for which grammar combination *is* associative. This property of polarities casts doubt on the usability of polarity-based grammars for grammar engineering.

1 Introduction

Development of large scale grammars for natural languages is an active area of research in human language technology. Such grammars are developed not only for purposes of theoretical linguistic research, but also for natural language applications such as machine translation, speech generation, etc. Wide-coverage grammars are being developed for various languages in several theoretical frameworks.

In this paper we focus on tree based formalisms, e.g., Tree Adjoining Grammar (TAG, [1]). A TAG consists of a number of elementary trees, which can be combined with substitution or adjunction. Several variations and extensions of TAG exist, including lexicalized TAG ([2]) and constraint-based TAG ([3]).

A wide-coverage TAG may contain hundreds or even thousands of elementary trees, and syntactic structure can be redundantly repeated in many trees ([4,5]). Consequently, maintenance and extension of such grammars is a complex task. To address these issues, several high-level formalisms were developed ([6,7,8]). These formalisms take the *metagrammar approach*, where the basic units are tree descriptions (i.e., formulas denoting sets of trees) rather than trees. Tree descriptions are constructed by a tree logic and combined through conjunction or inheritance (depending on the formalism). The set of minimal trees that satisfy the resulting descriptions are the TAG elementary trees. In this way modular construction of grammars is supported, where a module is merely a tree description and modules are combined by means of the control tree logic.

A. Gelbukh (Ed.): CICLing 2007, LNCS 4394, pp. 208–217, 2007.

The move to tree descriptions requires a mechanism to sanction only desired combinations of descriptions. To constrain undesired combinations, each node of a tree description is associated with a name and nodes with the same name must denote the same entity and therefore must be identified ([6]). The drawback of this approach is that the only channel of interaction between two descriptions is the names of the nodes. Furthermore, the names of nodes can only be used to identify two nodes, but not to disallow such an identification. To overcome these shortcomings, [9] suggest to replace node naming by a *coloring* scheme, where nodes are colored black, white or red. When two trees are unified, a black node may be unified with 0, 1 or more white nodes and produce a black node; a white node must be unified with a black one producing a black node; and a red node cannot be unified with any other node. Furthermore, a satisfying model must be *saturated*, i.e., one in which all the nodes are either black or red. In this way some combinations can be forced and others prevented.

[10] extends this mechanism by associating each node with a set of *polarity features*. A polarity feature consists of a feature, arbitrarily determined by the grammar writer, and a polarity, which can be either positive, negative or neutral. A positive value represents an available resource and a negative value represents an expected resource. Two feature-polarity pairs can combine only if their feature is identical and their polarities are opposite (i.e., one is negative and the other is positive); the result is a feature-polarity pair consisting of the same feature and the neutral polarity. Two nodes can be identified only if their polarity features can combine. A solution is a tree whose features are all neutralized.

The concept of polarities is further elaborated by [11], who defines *Polarized Unification Grammars* (PUG). A PUG is defined over a *system of polarities* $(P, \cdot)$ where P is a set (of polarities) and '$\cdot$' is an associative and commutative product over P. A PUG generates a set of finite structures over objects which are determined for each grammar separately. The objects are associated with polarities, and structures are combined by identifying some of their objects. The combination is sanctioned by polarities: objects can only be identified if their polarities are unifiable; the resulting object has the unified polarity. A non-empty, strict subset of the set of polarities, called the set of *neutral* polarities, determines which of the resulting structures are valid: A polarized structure is *saturated* if all its polarities are neutral. The structures that are generated by the grammar are the saturated structures that result from combining different structures.

PUGs are more general than the mechanisms of polarity features and coloring, since they allow the grammar designer to decide on the system of polarities, whereas other systems pre-define it. Another difference is that while in other tree based grammars, if two nodes are identified then their predecessors must be identified as well, this is not the case in PUGs. In PUGs any two objects can be identified; the only restriction on the identification of two objects is the possibility to combine their polarities.

Combination of tree-based grammar fragments with polarities is conjectured (although not proven) to be associative ([11]). In this paper we show that attaching polarities to tree nodes results in a non-associative combination operation. Practical systems which use polarities, such as XMG ([12]), suffer from overgeneration as a result of non-associativity. In section 2 we show that existing polarity schemes induce non-associative tree combination operations. Unfortunately, this is not a result of poor choice of polarities on account of existing formalisms; in section 3 we show that *any* non-trivial polarity system induces a non-associative tree combination operation. This property of polarities casts serious doubts on the usability of polarity-based grammars for grammar engineering.

2   Existing Polarity Systems

In this section we provide a few counter-examples which demonstrate the non-associativity of grammar combination in some existing grammar formalisms. In all the examples, the relation which determines how polarities combine *is* indeed associative; it is the tree combination operation which uses polarities that is shown to be non-associative.

2.1   XMG Colors

eXtensible MetaGrammar (XMG, [13,12]) is a tool for designing large scale grammars for natural languages. Following [9], XMG uses colors to sanction tree node identification. The color combination table is presented in Figure 1. W, B and R denote white, black and red, respectively, and $\perp$ represents the impossibility to combine.

$\cdot$	W	B	R
W	W	B	$\perp$
B	B	$\perp$	$\perp$
R	$\perp$	$\perp$	$\perp$

Fig. 1. Color combination in XMG

Example 1. Consider T_1, T_2, T_3 of Figure 2. The results of combining these trees in different orders are depicted in Figure 3. While $(T_1 + T_2) + T_3$ yields possible solutions, $T_2 + T_3$ has no solution and therefore the same holds for $T_1 + (T_2 + T_3)$. Notice that the solutions of $(T_1 + T_2) + T_3$ are saturated, since all the nodes in these trees are either black or red. Clearly, the combination operation with colored trees is not associative.

Example 2. Consider T_4, T_5, T_6 of Figure 4. The results of combining these trees in different orders are depicted in Figure 5. Assume that the initial set of trees is $\{T_5, T_6\}$. Adding a new tree, T_4, is expected to result in the set of $T_4 + (T_5 + T_6)$.

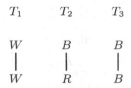

Fig. 2. Colored trees to be combined

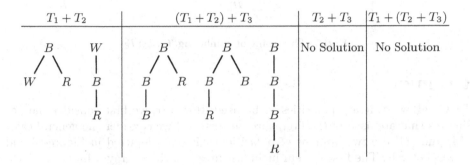

Fig. 3. The result of combining T_1, T_2, T_3

In practice, however, XMG computes all the possible combination orders, and the resulting set is $(T_4+T_5)+T_6$; observe that the resulting set overgenerates with respect to $T_4+(T_5+T_6)$. In actual grammars, where the sets of trees include hundreds of trees, the resulting solutions may include many such unexpected (and overgenerating) results. It is virtually impossible to track all the sources for such overgenerations, and therefore the maintenance of large tree-based grammars with colors is a complex, perhaps impractical task. Notice that all the intermediate and final solutions are saturated. Therefore, the saturation rule does not prevent the problem of non-associativity of colored-tree combination.

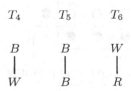

Fig. 4. Colored trees to be combined

Examples 1 and 2 sufficient for drawing the following conclusion:

Corollary 1. *Colored-tree combination is not associative.*

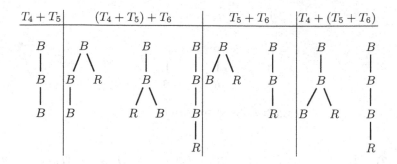

Fig. 5. The result of combining T_4, T_5, T_6

2.2 PUGs

PUGs allow arbitrary polarities to be used. However, we first consider the polarities that are used in the literature; in section 3 we consider the general case. [14] and [11] use two systems of polarities which are depicted in Figures 6 and 7, respectively. The first system includes three polarities, gray, white and black, where the neutral polarities are black and gray. A black node may be unified with 0, 1 or more gray or white nodes and produce a black node; a white node may absorb 0, 1 or more gray or white nodes but eventually must be unified with a black one producing a black node; and a gray node may be absorbed into a white or a black node. The second system extends the first by adding two more non-neutral polarities, plus and minus. The plus and minus may absorb 0, 1 or more white or gray nodes but eventually a plus node must be unified with a minus node producing a black node. The following example shows that these two operations are non-associative.

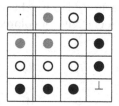

Fig. 6. A system of polarities

Example 3. Consider T_7, T_8, T_9 of Figure 8. The combination of these structures is depicted in Figure 9 (the combination is the same for both operations). Clearly $T_7 + (T_8 + T_9) \neq (T_7 + T_8) + T_9$.

Corollary 2. *PUG combination with the polarity system of either Figure 6 or 7 is not associative.*

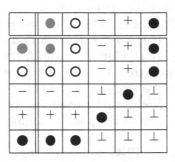

Fig. 7. A system of polarities

$$T_7 \qquad T_8 \qquad T_9$$

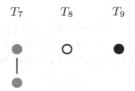

Fig. 8. Polarized trees to be combined

$$T_7 + T_8 \qquad (T_7 + T_8) + T_9 \qquad T_8 + T_9 \qquad T_7 + (T_8 + T_9)$$

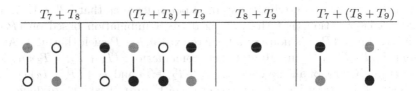

Fig. 9. The result of combining T_7, T_8, T_9

3 General Polarity Systems

In section 2 we showed that some existing polarity-based formalisms are non-associative. Unfortunately, this is not accidental; in what follows we show that the only polarity scheme that induces associative tree combination is trivial: the one in which no pair of polarities are unifiable. This scheme is useless for sanctioning tree combination since it disallows any combination.

In the sequel, if $(P, \cdot)$ is a system of polarities and $a, b \in P$, we use the shorthand notation ab instead of $a \cdot b$. $ab{\downarrow}$ means that the combination of a and b is defined and $ab{\uparrow}$ means that a and b cannot combine.

Definition 1. *A system of polarities $(P, \cdot)$ is trivial if for all $a, b \in P$, $ab \uparrow$.*

Proposition 1. *Let $(P, \cdot)$ be a system of polarities such that $|P| > 1$. If there exists $a \in P$ such that $aa{\downarrow}$ then the polarized tree combination based on $(P, \cdot)$ is not associative.*

Proof. Let $(P, \cdot)$ be a system of polarities such that $|P| > 1$ and let $a \in P$ be such that $aa\!\downarrow$. Assume toward a contradiction that the polarized tree combination based on $(P, \cdot)$ is associative. Let $b \in P$ be such that $a \neq b$ (such b exists since $|P| > 1$). Consider T_1, T_2, T_3 of Figure 10. Of all the trees in $(T_1 + T_2) + T_3$ and $T_1 + (T_2 + T_3)$, focus on trees of the structure depicted in Figure 11. All possible instantiations of these trees are depicted in Figure 12 (we suppress the intermediate calculations). Notice that these trees are only candidate solutions; they are actually accepted only if the polarity combinations occurring in them are defined.

As described in section 1 , PUG and XMG slightly differ in the way trees are combined. While in XMG, if two nodes are identified then their predecessors must be identified too, in PUG any two nodes can be identified. However, for the tree structure of Figure 11, the same sets of trees are accepted for both the XMG and the PUG approaches.

Since $aa\!\downarrow$, T_{11} is accepted as a solution of $T_1 + (T_2 + T_3)$. However, this tree is not accepted as a solution of $(T_1 + T_2) + T_3$ since $a \neq b$ and there is no tree among the possible solutions of $(T_1 + T_2) + T_3$ whose top and bottom nodes are b, a contradiction.

Proposition 2. *Let $(P, \cdot)$ be a non-trivial system of polarities such that $|P| > 1$. Then the polarized tree combination based on $(P, \cdot)$ is not associative.*

Proof. Let $(P, \cdot)$ be a non-trivial system of polarities such that $|P| > 1$. Assume toward a contradiction that the polarized tree combination based on $(P, \cdot)$ is associative. Since $(P, \cdot)$ is non-trivial, there exist $a, b \in P$ such that $ab \downarrow$. Again, consider T_1, T_2, T_3 of Figure 10 and their combinations $(T_1 + T_2) + T_3$ and $T_1 + (T_2 + T_3)$. As before, of all the trees in $(T_1 + T_2) + T_3$ and $T_1 + (T_2 + T_3)$ consider only the resulting trees having the structure of Figure 11 which are depicted in Figure 12. There are two possible cases:

1. $aa\!\downarrow$ or $bb\!\downarrow$: Then from theorem 1 it follows that the resulting tree combination operation is not associative, a contradiction.
2. $aa\!\uparrow$ and $bb\!\uparrow$: Then $(T_1 + T_2) + T_3$ has no solutions and $T_1 + (T_2 + T_3)$ has one accepted solution (T_9), a contradiction.

Proposition 3. *Let $(P, \cdot)$ be a non-trivial system of polarities such that $|P| = 1$. Then the polarized tree combination based on $(P, \cdot)$ is not associative.*

$$T_1 \qquad T_2 \qquad T_3$$

$$
\begin{array}{ccc}
b & a & a \\
| & | & | \\
a & b & a
\end{array}
$$

Fig. 10. Polarized trees to be combined

Fig. 11. A tree structure

$(T_1 + T_2) + T_3$				$T_1 + (T_2 + T_3)$			
T_4	T_5	T_6	T_7	T_8	T_9	T_{10}	T_{11}
a	b	a	a	b	a	a	b
ab	aa	bb	aa	aa	ab	aa	aa
aa	ab	aa	bb	ab	ab	bb	aa
b	a	a	a	a	a	a	b

Fig. 12. Resulting trees

Proof. Let $(P, \cdot)$ be a non-trivial system of polarities such that $P = \{a\}$. Assume toward a contradiction that the polarized tree combination based on $(P, \cdot)$ is associative. Since P is non-trivial, $aa = a$. Consider T_1, T_2, T_3, T_4 of Figure 13 and the combinations $(T_1 + T_2) + T_3$ and $T_1 + (T_2 + T_3)$. T_4 is accepted as a solution of $T_1 + (T_2 + T_3)$ but not as a solution of $(T_1 + T_2) + T_3$ (we suppress the calculations), both in the XMG and the PUG approach. Clearly $(T_1 + T_2) + T_3 \neq T_1 + (T_2 + T_3)$, a contradiction.

Corollary 3. *Let $(P, \cdot)$ be a non-trivial system of polarities. Then the polarized tree combination based on $(P, \cdot)$ is not associative.*

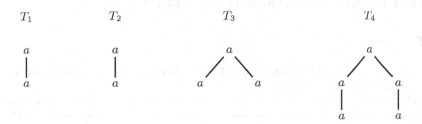

Fig. 13. Polarized trees with a single polarity

Proposition 4. *Let* $(P, \cdot)$ *be a trivial system of polarities. Then the polarized tree combination based on* $(P, \cdot)$ *is associative.*

Proof. If $(P, \cdot)$ is a trivial system of polarities then any combination of two polarized trees results in the empty set (no solutions). Evidently, polarized tree combination based on $(P, \cdot)$ is associative.

Corollary 4. *Let* $(P, \cdot)$ *be a system of polarities. Then polarized tree combination based on* $(P, \cdot)$ *is associative if and only if* $(P, \cdot)$ *is trivial.*

4 Conclusion

We showed that non-trivial systems of polarities induce non-associative tree combination operators. The practical implication of this non-associativity, at least in XMG, is overgeneration. This property of polarity-based systems most probably implies that they should not be used to sanction tree combination in grammar formalisms.

The non-associativity of polarized tree-based grammars is not a property of the polarities but rather of the combination operation and the way polarities are used by the tree combination operators. From proposition 3 it follows that even without polarities (where any two nodes can be identified), the combination is non-associative in the sense that different combination orders yield different structures. Furthermore, if two combination orders yield the same basic structures, their nodes are not necessarily associated with the same polarities, thus hampering combination associativity. The implication of this is that polarities cannot be used to guarantee associativity where it does not exist in the first place.

Polarities were associated with tree nodes to sanction tree combination in a more general way than the node naming mechanism introduced by [6]. As we show here, this renders grammar combination non-associative. A different mechanism, providing the generality of polarities but maintaining the associativity of tree combination, is required. For an example of such a mechanism, in the context of typed unification grammars, see [15].

Acknowledgments

We are grateful to Yannick Parmentier for his help. This research was supported by The Israel Science Foundation (grant no. 136/01).

References

1. Joshi, A.K., Levy, L.S., Takahashi, M.: Tree Adjunct Grammars. Journal of Computer and System Sciences (1975)
2. Schabes, Y., Abeillé, A., Joshi, A.K.: Parsing strategies with 'lexicalized' grammars: application to tree adjoining grammars. In: Proceedings of the 12th conference on Computational linguistics, Association for Computational Linguistics (1988) 578–583

3. Vijay-Shanker, K., Joshi, A.K.: Feature structure based tree adjoining grammar. In: Proceedings of the 12th conference on Computational linguistics, Association for Computational Linguistics (1988) 714–719
4. XTAG Research Group: A lexicalized tree adjoining grammar for English. Technical Report IRCS-01-03, IRCS, University of Pennsylvania (2001)
5. Abeillé, A., Candito, M.H., Kinyon, A.: FTAG: developing and maintaining a wide-coverage grammar for French. In Hinrichs, E., Meurers, D., Wintner, S., eds.: Proceedings of the ESSLLI-2000 Workshop on Linguistic Theory and Grammar Implementation. (2000) 21–32
6. Candito, M.H.: A principle-based hierarchical representation of LTAGs. In: Proceedings of the 16th conference on Computational linguistics, Copenhagen, Denemark, Association for Computational Linguistics (1996) 194–199
7. Duchier, D., Gardent, C.: A constraint-based treatment of descriptions. In: Third International Workshop on Computational Semantics (IWCS-3), Tilburg, Netherlands (1999)
8. Kallmeyer, L.: Local tree description grammars. Grammars 4 (2001) 85–137
9. Crabbé, B., Duchier, D.: Metagrammar redux. In: CSLP, Copenhagen, Denemark (2004)
10. Perrier, G.: Interaction grammars. In: Proceedings of the 18th conference on Computational linguistics, Morristown, NJ, USA, Association for Computational Linguistics (2000) 600–606
11. Kahane, S.: Polarized unification grammars. In: Proceedings of the 21st International Conference on Computational Linguistics and 44th Annual Meeting of the Association for Computational Linguistics, Sydney, Australia (2006) 137–144
12. Crabbé, B.: Grammatical development with XMG. In: Proceedings of the 5th International Conference on Logical Aspects of Computational Linguistics (LACL), Bordeaux, France (2005)
13. Duchier, D., Le Roux, J., Parmentier, Y.: The metagrammar compiler: An NLP application with a multi-paradigm architecture. In: Proceedings of the Second International Mozart/Oz Conference (MOZ 2004), Charleroi, Belgium (2004)
14. Kahane, S., Lareau, F.: Meaning-text unification grammar: modularity and polarization. In: Proceedings of the 2nd International Conference on Meaning-Text Theory, Moscow (2005) 197–206
15. Cohen-Sygal, Y., Wintner, S.: Partially specified signatures: A vehicle for grammar modularity. In: Proceedings of the 21st International Conference on Computational Linguistics and 44th Annual Meeting of the Association for Computational Linguistics, Sydney, Australia (2006) 145–152

Dependency Analysis of Clauses
Using Parse Tree Kernels

Sang-Soo Kim, Seong-Bae Park*, and Sang-Jo Lee

Department of Computer Engineering
Kyungpook National University
702-701 Daegu, Korea
{sskim,sbpark,sjlee}@sejong.knu.ac.kr

Abstract. Identification of dependency relation among clauses is one of the most critical parts in parsing Korean sentences because it generates severe ambiguities. The resolution of the ambiguities involves both syntactic and semantic information. This paper proposes a method to determine the dependency relation among Korean clauses using parse tree kernels. The parse tree used in this paper provides the method with the syntactic information, and the endings (*Eomi*) do with the semantic information. In addition, the parse tree kernel for handling parse trees has benefits that it minimizes the information loss occurred during transforming a parse tree into a feature vector, and can obtain, as a result, very accurate similarity between parse trees. The experimental results on a standard Korean data set show 89.12% of accuracy, which implies that the proposed method is plausible for the dependency analysis of clauses.

1 Introduction

The fact that Korean is a head-final and partially free word-order language leads most Korean parsers to use a dependency grammar. That is, it is the main work during parsing a sentence to identify the dependency relation between two *Eojeols*[1]. Even though Korean dependency grammar can be expressed with a few number of rules [6], the rules, in general, generates a great quantity of ambiguity. This ambiguity makes it inefficient and even impractical to parse Korean sentences. As a result, a partial parsing has become a practical alternative to a full-parsing among the natural language learning researchers.

With a successful results of partial parsers in various levels, a cascading model shows high performance in parsing Japanese [7] which shares many characteristics with Korean. In such a model, a series of machine learning techniques are applied sequentially to various subtasks of parsing such as POS tagging, text chunking, clause boundary detection, etc.

---

* Corresponding author.
[1] An *Eojeol* is a spacing unit in Korean. This is an equivalent concept to Japanese *Bunsetu*.

A. Gelbukh (Ed.): CICLing 2007, LNCS 4394, pp. 218–228, 2007.
© Springer-Verlag Berlin Heidelberg 2007

In Korean syntactic analysis, there have been also great efforts to use machine learning algorithms. In POS tagging of Korean, a hidden Markov model is a standard tool like other languages [9]. However, from text chunking, various machine learning algorithms have been used. Park et al. proposed a self-organizing n-gram model for automatic word spacing [12], and Park and Zhang applied a kind of rule learning to Korean text chunking [11]. In addition, Lee et al. used support vector machines in recognizing the boundaries of Korean clauses [8].

The recognition of clauses gets attention from not only Korean researchers but also researchers of many other languages. The representative example of this attention is the shared task of CoNLL (Conference on Natural Language Learning) in 2001 [13]. In this task, Carreras and Màrquez reported the best performance using AdaBoost with decision trees as a base learner [2]. However, in Korean, there have been, at least for our knowledge, no previous work for deciding clausal relation. The work of Lee et al. was just focused on detecting the boundaries of clauses [8]. That is, their work was to find the starting and ending points of simple Korean clauses.

This paper proposes a novel method to determine the dependency relation among simple clauses under the assumption that the clause boundaries are clearly identified. The proposed method finds the relation among clauses only using the structured information lying on parse trees and endings ('*Eomi*' in Korean).

Many machine learning algorithms applied to language learning have difficulties in handling parse trees since they have a relatively complex structure. By the way, a kernel method is a fine candidate when handling nonlinear data structures. It uses the original representation of objects rather than transforming a feature vector. In addition, it shows high performance in computing similarities of two objects by implicitly exploring the structural features of objects. Even to natural language processing (NLP), various kinds of kernel methods have been successfully applied [1,10,14] with great performance of support vector machines.

A parse tree kernel among various kernels especially gives high performance in the areas of recognizing relation in parse trees. It is a kind of convolution kernels [3], extracts hierarchical structural information from a set of parse trees, and then computes the similarity among parse trees. This method minimizes the information loss occurred during transforming a parse tree into a feature vector, and can obtain, as a result, very accurate similarity among parse trees.

The experimental results on STEP-2000 parsed corpus, one of standard parsed corpus for Korean, prove that the proposed method is good for identifying the relationship among clauses. Even though we use structural information and endings within parse trees, we obtain 89.12% of accuracy. This is the state-of-the-art performance for the task. Even better, it gives much room for improvement. When combined with the lexical information, it is expected to get higher performance.

The rest of this paper is organized as follows. Section 2 introduces the general procedure for dependency analysis of clauses and the base learning algorithms. Section 3 describes the proposed method for clausal dependency analysis based on parse tree kernels and Section 4 presents the experimental results. Finally, Section 5 draws conclusions.

2 Problem Setting

2.1 Clausal Dependency Identification

In this paper, the dependency among clauses is found by extracting the structural information represented with parse trees without any additional external knowledge. Then, dependency analysis can be considered as a classification task. Let $D = \{(\mathbf{x}_1, y_1), \ldots, (\mathbf{x}_n, y_n)\}$ be a set of training examples where $y_i \in \{-1, +1\}$ and $\mathbf{x}_i = < t_{i1}, t_{i2} >$. Here, t_{ij} is a subtree that represents a clause. The values $+1$ of y_i implies that the first clause t_{i1} is governed by the other t_{i2}. The purpose of dependency analysis from the viewpoint of machine learning is to estimate a function $f : \mathbf{x} \rightarrow y$. After the function f parameterized by θ is trained with D, the dependency y^* of an unlabeled example $\mathbf{x}$ can be determined by

$$y^* = \underset{y \in \{-1, +1\}}{\arg \max} \left(f(\mathbf{x}, \theta) = y \right).$$

The support vector machine (SVM) is one of the strongest and most widely used models for estimating f of classification tasks [4]. Assume that the training data are given as a set of $(\mathbf{X}, y), \mathbf{X} \in \mathbb{R}^n$. In the basic SVM framework, the hyperplane that separates the instance space is defined as

$$(\mathbf{w} \cdot \mathbf{X}) + b = 0, \ \mathbf{w} \in \mathbb{R}^n, \ b \in \mathbb{R}.$$

There could be the infinite number of hyperplanes that can separate correctly the training data D into two classes. The optimal one among them is the one with the largest margin. Assuming that the nearest distance from the hyperplane is 1, the margin, d can be written as

$$d = \frac{2}{||\mathbf{w}||}.$$

SVM generates a hyperplane which maximizes the margin by minimizing $||\mathbf{w}||$ under the constraint:

$$y_i[(\mathbf{w} \cdot \mathbf{X}_i) + b] \geq 1$$

for all training examples $(\mathbf{X}_i, y_i)$.

SVMs have an advantage over conventional machine learning algorithms that they show high performance independent of the dimension of feature vectors. The conventional machine learning algorithms usually require careful feature selection, which is often done heuristically or statistically. This generates in many cases an incorrect or approximate feature set for the target task. However, SVMs carry out their learning with all combination of given features without increasing computational complexity by introducing the kernel function.

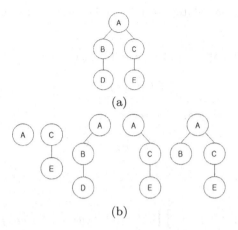

Fig. 1. (a) A parse tree, (b) Subtrees which possibly appear in the tree (a)

2.2 Parse Tree Kernels

A parse tree kernel, derived from convolution kernels, is specified for handling parse trees. In the vector representation of parse trees, each feature corresponds to a subtree that possibly appears in a parse tree. Its value is set to be the frequency of the subtree. Figure 1 illustrates an example of a parse tree and its subtrees. The explicit enumeration of all subtrees is computationally problematic since the number of subtrees in a tree exponentially increases as the size of a tree grows. Collins and Duffy proposed a method to compute the inner product of two trees without enumeration of all subtrees [3].

Let $subtree_1, subtree_2, \ldots$ be all of subtrees in a parse tree. Then, the parse tree T can be represented as a vector

$$V_T = (\#subtree_1(T), \#subtree_2(T), \ldots, \#subtree_n(T)) \tag{1}$$

where $\#subtree_i(T)$ is a frequency of $subtree_i$ in parse tree T. The inner product of two trees, T_1 and T_2 can be defined:

$$< V_{T_1}, V_{T_2} > = \sum_i \#subtree_i(T_1) \cdot \#subtree_i(T_2)$$

$$= \sum_i \left(\sum_{n_1 \in N_{T_1}} I_{subtree_i}(n_1) \right) \cdot \left(\sum_{n_2 \in N_{T_2}} I_{subtree_i}(n_2) \right)$$

$$= \sum_{n_1 \in N_{T_1}} \sum_{n_2 \in N_{T_2}} C(n_1, n_2)$$

where N_{T_1} and N_{T_2} are all of nodes in tree T_1 and T_2 respectively. An indicator function $I_{subtree_i}(n_1)$ is to be 1 if $subtree_i$ is seen rooted at node n and 0 otherwise. $C(n_1, n_2)$ is a function which is defined as

$$C(n_1, n_2) = \sum_i I_{subtree_i}(n_1) \cdot I_{subtree_i}(n_2)$$

This function can be calculated in polynomial time with the following recursive definition.

If the productions at n_1 and n_2 are different,

$$C(n_1, n_2) = 0$$

Else if both n_1 and n_2 are pre-terminals,

$$C(n_1, n_2) = \lambda \tag{2}$$

Else,

$$C(n_1, n_2) = \lambda \prod_{i}^{nc(n_1)} (1 + C(ch(n_1, i), ch(n_2, i))), \tag{3}$$

where $nc(n_1)$ is the number of children of node n_1 in the tree, $ch(n_1, i)$ is the i-th child of node n_1, and λ $(0 < \lambda < 1)$ is the decay factor for making the kernel value invariant with respect to subtree size.

This recursive algorithm is based on the fact that all subtrees rooted at a certain node can be constructed by combining the subtrees rooted at each of its children.

3   Clause Dependency Analysis with Parse Tree Kernels

3.1   Dependency Relation in Korean Clauses

In Korean, clauses can be divided into three categories: *conjunctive*, *prenominal*, and *final*. The conjunctive clauses modify other clauses, while the prenominal clauses modify noun phrases and the final clauses do nothing. Among them, the *conjunctive* and *prenominal* make dependency relation. However, only conjunctive clauses are our interest since prenominal clauses make simple relation with noun phrases.

The dependency relation made by conjunctive clauses is in general very complex, and thus it is difficult to analyze them. Consider the following sentence.

샤워실을 체육관으로 옮기고 사무실을 폐쇄하여 휴게실을 만들었다.
After the shower room was moved into the gymnasium **and** the office room was closed, a lounge was built.

It consists of three clauses as follows.

Clause A	샤워실 을 체육관 으로 옮기 고
	The shower room was moved into the gymnasium **and**
Clause B	사무실 을 폐쇄하 여
	The office room was closed **after**
Clause C	휴게실 을 만들었 다.
	A lounge was built.

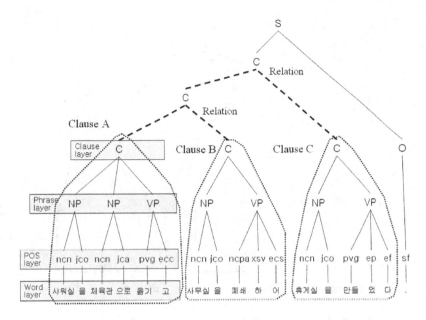

Fig. 2. An example parse tree for an example sentence

In clause A and B, the endings '*goh*' and '*yeo*' make them conjunctive clauses, while the ending '*dah*' in the clause C makes it a final clause.

Relations among clause A, B and C is shown in Figure 2. The clause A and B make a relation and are combined into a new clause. it makes a dependency with clause C. This relations can be expressed as ((A B) C). However, the relation (A (B C)) rather than ((A B) C) is also possible in general. As the number of clauses increases, there could be more ways of combining clauses. Such various relations make it difficult to parse Korean clauses in syntactic level.

3.2   Clause Representation

The dependency relation of clauses is encapsulated in a parse tree. Thus, it is critical to determine how to extract structural information from parse trees. Extracting too much information sometimes can lead to contain many uninformative and irrelevant features In addition, it may cause *data sparseness*.

The representation of clauses is defined as two kinds of problems: (i) how to determine the depth of trees, and (ii) how to organize the dependency relation. Since we consider just structural information, we use not a word layer but clause, phrase, and part-of-speech layers in a parse tree. That is, only the dotted area in Figure 3 is used in representing clauses. The reason why we exclude the word layer is that the layer may cause the curse of dimensionality via data sparseness.

In organizing dependency relation, in order to remove the uninformative tree nodes, it is possible to remove the single nodes connected to clauses [14]. In this paper, we propose two representation of parse trees as follows.

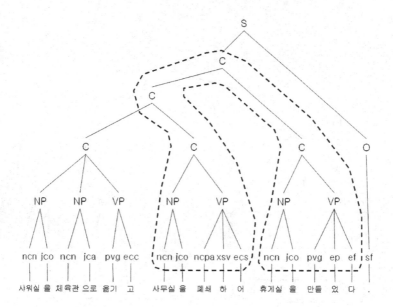

Fig. 3. An example of clause representation in a parse tree

1. Path-Enclosed Tree (PT)
   A tree is enclosed by the shortest path linking two clauses. This may include a single node as shown in Figure 4-(a). This is normal representation of parse trees.
2. Flattened Path-Enclosed Tree (FPT)
   A tree with the removal of all single nodes. The example of FTP is shown in Figure 4-(b).

3.3   Multi-class Classification

Up to now, the structural information is considered for the analysis of clausal dependency. However, the clausal dependency can not be determined only with the structural information. The semantics among clauses determines their relation in many cases. The most important information in semantics for clausal dependency is endings in the verb phrases, since the endings represent tense, modal, connection type of verb phrases, etc.

When we have n kinds of endings and m conjunctive endings ($m \leq n$), there should be $m \times n$ support vector machines to be trained. This is because the first clause should be a conjunctive clause and each support vector machine tries to determine the dependency between two clauses. That is, according to kinds of endings in principal and subordinate clauses, we model different support vector machines. This is how the semantic information is incorporated into the analysis of clausal dependency.

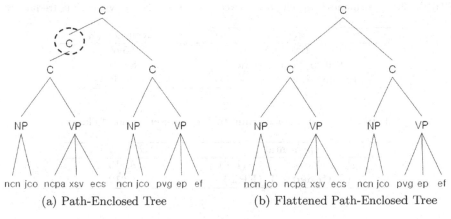

(a) Path-Enclosed Tree   (b) Flattened Path-Enclosed Tree

Fig. 4. Different representation of parse trees for clauses

Table 1. A simple statistics on the data set

Information	Training Set	Test Set
No. of sentences	6,240	694
No. of clauses	24,226	2,650
No. of prenominal and final ending clauses	15,457	1,666
No. of conjunctive clauses	8,769	984

4   Experiments

For the evaluation of the proposed method, we construct a data set derived from the parse corpus which is a product of STEP-2000 project supported by Korean government. The corpus consists of 6,934 sentences with 26,876 clauses. Table 1 shows the simple statistics on the corpus.

We split the corpus into two parts: a training set (90%) and a test set (10%). The number of clauses in a training set is 24,226, but only 8,769 are used during training SVMs. This is because our task is the relation analysis among clauses. If a parse tree represented by Equation 1 has a prenominal or final ending, it is out of our interest. When a clause has a prenominal ending, it modifies a noun phrase rather than another clause. In the same way, if it has a final ending, it does modify nothing. Thus, the training set gathers the cases where the first clause has conjunctive endings.

For all experiments below, SVM_{light} [5] is used as a classifier. We set the parameters as $C = 0.5$ and $\lambda = 0.4$. The total number of endings appearing in this corpus is 162, but we chose the endings whose frequency is larger than 10 among them. As a result, we have 117 endings used for subordinate clauses and 104 endings for principal clauses.

In encountering a clause, the most easiest way to determine the clausal dependency is, according to the characteristics of Korean language, to choose the

Table 2. Performance comparison between parse tree kernel vs. ending-frequency

Method	Accuracy (%)
Baseline	55.60
Parse Tree Kernel	**88.10**
Ending (Eomi) Frequency	56.46

Table 3. Accuracy according to the representation of clauses

Representation	Accuracy (%)
Path-Enclosed Tree (PT)	88.10
Flattened PT (FPT)	89.12

next clause as its subordinate clause. Thus, we set it as a *baseline* model. The baseline model shows just 55.60% of accuracy as shown in Table 2.

Since endings are the most important semantic information for clausal dependency analysis, it is possible to use their frequency for the task. That is, when three endings e_1, e_2 and e_3 are given, the coherence of e_1, e_2 and e_1, e_3 can be computed using their frequency in the corpus. That is, in the probabilistic notation, the probability of $P(e_2|e_1)$ can be approximated by their frequency as follows.

$$P(e_2|e_1) = \frac{f(e_1, e_2)}{f(e_1)},$$

where $f(e)$ is the frequency of e in the corpus. Thus, if $P(e_2|e_1) > P(e_3|e_1)$, then we have to set e_2 rather than e_3 as a principal clause of e_1. Table 2 shows the performance of this approach. This method gives 56.46% of accuracy, just 0.86% higher than the baseline. Therefore, from the fact that the frequency of endings results in poor performance, it is induced that the structural information contained in the parse trees plays an important role in determining the dependency analysis of clauses.

Table 3 shows the performance of the proposed method according to the clausal representation. The baseline model achieves just 55.60% of accuracy, while the proposed method reports over 88% for both representations. The fact that FPT gives slightly higher accuracy than PT implies that the single nodes in PT are irrelevant for our task. As a whole, the proposed method shows 89.12% of accuracy.

Figure 5 depicts the effect of the training examples in training support vector machines. The X-axis in this figure is the number of training examples used in learning each support vector machine, and the Y-axis is the accuracy of the support vector machine. As shown in this figure, the accuracy of support vector machines is conversely related with the number of training examples. When the number of training examples is large enough it shows high accuracy. However, with small training examples, its performance gets lower. Since each support vector machine learn the dependency for an ending pair, there could be small number of training examples for some pairs however large is the size of corpora.

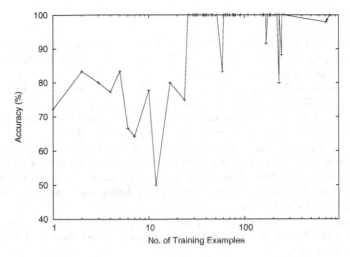

Fig. 5. The change of accuracy according to the number of training examples

It is yet an open problem how to train classifiers with the small number of training examples.

5 Conclusions

In this paper we have proposed a novel method for dependency analysis of Korean clauses. The proposed method adopted a parse tree kernel to compute the syntactic similarity among clauses, and used the endings (*Eomis*) for the semantic information. Since the dependency analysis is expressed as a classification task, the support vector machines which show the state-of-the-art performance for many NLP problems are adopted for the task.

The experimental results showed that the proposed method achieved 89.12% of accuracy, while the simple baseline method reported just 56.45%. In addition, we proved empirically that the flattened path-enclosed (FPT) way for representing parse trees is superior to the normal path-enclosed one (PT) at least in our task. While PT gave 88.10% of accuracy, FPT showed 89.12%.

The future work can be summarized into two ways. First, we will apply the proposed method to English. Since the proposed method is general enough to be applied to any language, English can be a next candidate for our method. Second, in our method, we loose the lexical information since we limit the tree up to POS layer due to data sparseness. However, the lexical information is also very important resource for our task. Therefore, we will combine the proposed method with the lexical information in the future work.

Acknowledgements

This work was supported by grant No. R01-2006-000-11196-0 from the Basic Research Program of the Korea Science & Engineering Foundation.

References

1. R. Bunescu and R. Mooney, "A Shortest Path Dependency Kernel for Relation Extraction," In *Proceedings of the Conference on Empirical Methods in Natural Language Processing*, pp. 724–731, 2005.
2. X. Carreras and L. Màrquez, "Boosting Trees for Clause Splitting", In *Proceedings of the 5th Conference on Natural Language Learning*, pp. 73–75, 2001.
3. M. Collins and N. Duffy, "Convolution Kernels for Natural Language," In *Proceedings of the 14th Neural Information Processing Systems*, 2001.
4. N. Cristianini and J. Shawe-Taylor, *An Introduction to Support Vector Machines and Other Kernel-based Learning Methods*, Cambridge University Press, 2000.
5. T. Joachims, "Text Categorization with Support Vector Machines: Learning with Many Relevant Features," In *Proceedings of the European Conference on Machine Learning*, pp. 137–142, 1998.
6. S.-S. Kang, "A Dependency Parsing Method for Head-Final Languages," In *Proceedings of the 2001 IEEE International Symposium on Industrial Electronics* pp. 69-6-699, 2001.
7. T. Kudo and Y. Matsumoto, "Japanese Dependency Analyisis using Cascaded Chunking," In *Proceedings of the 6th Conference on Natural Language Learning*, pp. 1–7, 2002.
8. H.-J. Lee, S.-B. Park, S.-J. Lee, and S.-Y Park, "Clause Boundary Recognition Using Support Vector Machines," In *Proceedings of the 9th Pacific Rim International Conference on Artificial Intelligence*, pp. 505–514, 2006.
9. S.-Z. Lee, J. Tsujii, and H.-C. Rim, "Hidden Markov Model-Based Korean Part-of-Speech Tagging Considering High Agglutinativity, Word-Spacing, and Lexical Correlativity," In *Proceedings of the 38th Annual Meeting of the Association for Computational Linguistics*, pp. 376–383, 2000.
10. A. Moschitti, "A study on Convolution Kernels for Shallow Semantic Parsing," In *Proceedings of the 42nd Annual Meeting of the Association for Computational Linguistics*, pp. 335–342 , 2004.
11. S.-B. Park and B.-T. Zhang, "Text Chunking by Combining Hand-Crafted Rules and Memory-Based Learning," In *Proceedings of the 41st Annual Meeting of the Association for Computational Linguistics*, pp. 497–504, 2003.
12. S.-B. Park, Y.-S. Tae, and S.-Y. Park, "Self-Organizing *n*-gram Model for Automatic Word Spacing," In *Proceedings of the 21st International Conference on Computational Linguistics and 44th Annual Meeting of the Association for Computational Linguistics*, pp. 633–640, 2006.
13. T. Kim Sang, F. Erik and H. Déjean, "Introduction to the CoNLL-2001 Shared Task: Clause Identification", In *Proceedings of the 5th Conference on Natural Language Learning*, pp. 53–57, 2001.
14. M. Zhang, J. Zhang, J. Su, and G.-D. Zhou, "A Composite Kernel to Extract Relations between Entities with Both Flat and Structured Features," In *Proceedings of the 21st International Conference on Computational Linguistics and 44th Annual Meeting of the Association for Computational Linguistics*, pp. 825–832, 2006.

Unsupervised Method for Parsing Coordinated Base Noun Phrases

Vasile Rus[1], Sireesha Ravi[1], Mihai C. Lintean[1], and Philip M. McCarthy[2]

[1] Department of Computer Science
[2] Department of Psychology
Institute for Intelligent Systems
The University of Memphis
373 Dunn Hall
Memphis, TN 38152
USA
{vrus, sravi1, M.Lintean, pmmccrth}@memphis.edu

Abstract. Syntactic parsing is an important processing step for various language processing applications including Information Extraction, Question Answering, and Machine Translation. Parsing base Noun Phrases is one particular parsing issue that is not handled by current state-of-the-art syntactic parsers. In this paper we present research that investigates the base Noun Phrase parsing problem. We develop a base Noun Phrase parser based on several statistical models that provide promising results on a test set of 538 base Noun Phrases. The parameters of the models are estimated from the web in the form of web counts. This makes our method unsupervised with no training data being needed.

1 Introduction

The task of syntactic parsing is valuable to many language processing applications, such as Information Extraction [6], Question Answering [20], and Machine Translation [5]. Syntactic parsing in its most general definition may be viewed as discovering the underlying syntactic structure of a sentence. The specificities include the types of elements and relations that are retrieved by the parsing process and the way in which they are represented. For example, *Treebank-style* parsers retrieve a bracketed form that encodes a hierarchical organization (tree) of smaller elements (called phrases), while *Grammatical-Relations-style(GR)* parsers explicitly output relations together with elements involved in the relation. For instance, *subj(John,walk)* explicitly marks a subject relation between *John* and *walk*.

In our operational definition, syntactic parsing is the task of discovering major phrases (e.g. noun phrases, verb phrases) in a sentence and hierarchically organizing them in a parse tree. We use the Treebank bracketing representation from [12] to represent parse trees. In the bracketed representation a tree is represented as a sequence that includes the label of the root node followed by the bracketed representation of its children. The sequence is surrounded by

A. Gelbukh (Ed.): CICLing 2007, LNCS 4394, pp. 229–240, 2007.

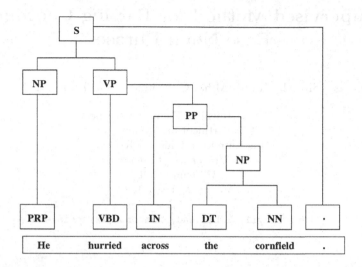

(S (NP (PRP He)) (VP (VBD hurried) (PP (IN across) (NP (DT the) (NN cornfield)))) (. .))

Fig. 1. Example of a parse tree and its corresponding bracketing representation for the sentence *He hurried across the cornfield*

parentheses/brackets. As an example, let us consider the sentence *He hurried across the cornfield*. The tree corresponding to this sentence is shown in Figure 1. Below the tree we show the corresponding bracketed representation. There is a deterministic, straightforward algorithm to map the tree in the bracketed representation and *vice versa*.

In this paper, we address the problem of base Noun Phrase (base NP) parsing, of which, little, if any, statistical research has been conducted. An early attempt is presented in [18] where a knowledge-intensive approach is used that relies heavily on lexical semantics extracted from WordNet. By contrast, our approach here is completely unsupervised; that is, no prior knowledge is needed. This makes our approach easily transferable to other languages or specific domains without extra effort or knowledge being required.

Modern parsing technologies usually do not provide a syntactic structure for base NPs. The norm [2,3] is to reduce base NPs to the head word (usually the rightmost word in the NP which provides the core meaning of the NP; e.g. the head word in *brilliant student* is *student*). Parsing base NPs is equivalent to bracketing base NPs because parsing is finding the correct bracketing in Treebank lingo. Henceforth, we will use the phrase *bracketing base NPs* to mean parsing base NPs. More generally, bracketing and parsing are also used interchangeably in this paper.

We adopt a statistical approach to the task of bracketing base NPs. A statistical approach is undertaken in two phases. First, a probability distribution is learned from a data test. Second, the probability distribution is used to predict the correct output on new data, in our case to find the correct bracketing of

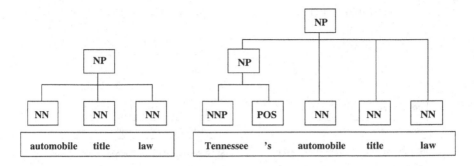

Fig. 2. Examples of two Noun Phrases (left - base NP; right - recursive NP)

a new base NP. Several issues need to be addressed: what statistical model to use, how to create the training data set, and how to estimate the probabilities and deal with sparse data. We describe our solutions to each of these issues throughout the paper.

What is a base NP? A base Noun Phrase (base NP) is a flat Noun Phrase (non-recursive). The tree on left side of Figure 2 is an example of a base NP. The example on the right is not a base NP since it contains another NP as one of its children. A base NP containing one or more nouns coordinated via a conjunction (e.g. *and*, *or*) is called a coordinated base NP. Two examples of base NPs are shown in Figure 3. Both examples can be described by the generic form *noun1 conj noun2 noun3* where the nouns can be common or proper, singular or plural. We focus on this particular type of base NPs for the rest of the paper. Usually, adjectives can be attached to nouns without losing the generality of the models presented next. Adjectives can be detected (with a part-of-speech tagger) and dropped so that complex coordinated base NPs are reduced to the previous pattern.

2 Motivation

Our work is motivated by a problem with current state-of-the-art syntactic parsers. They do not provide a syntactic structure for base NPs. The result is that all base NPs have a flat representation which makes the discovery of their meaning difficult. Similar (in terms of word categories) base NPs can have different internal structures, and consequently different meanings. In Figure 3, the same sequence of word categories, namely *noun conj noun noun*, leads to two different internal structures. The base NP on the left should be interpreted as a *player* of *soccer and tennis*, i.e. both *soccer* and *tennis* equally modify *player*. This is represented in bracketed form as *((soccer and tennis) player)*, called *left bracketing*, indicating that *soccer* and *tennis* group together before modifying *player*. The base NP on the right is interpreted as the conjunction of two concepts, *marine corps* and *navy*. This is represented in bracketed form as *((navy) and (marine corps))*, called *right bracketing*, indicating that *navy* does not mod-

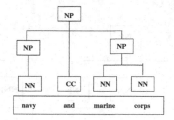

LEFT–BRACKETING

RIGHT–BRACKETING

(NP (NP (NN soccer) (CC and) (NN tennis)) (NP (NN player)))

(NP (NP (NN navy)) (CC and) (NP (NN marine) (NN corps)))

Fig. 3. Examples of two similar base NPs and their corresponding parse trees

ify *corps* at all. Knowing the correct bracketing for a base NP can help find the correct interpretation of its meaning.

The concept of *NP parsing* or *bracketing NPs* is not new in the literature. However, we argue here that it has been used misleadingly [4,?]. It is used to mean identifying any and all NPs in a sentence and not parsing the NPs to reveal their internal structure, and thus their correct meaning. A better term for this task would be *identifying NPs* or *recognizing NPs*. A related task is *NP chunking* [16] which aims at identifying only base (non-recursive) NPs. *Partial parsing* [9] is an extension of NP chunking to identify all common phrases (usually NPs, VPs - verb phrases) in a sentence without the need to generate a full syntactic parse tree which would be more expensive. Another related task is *noun compound (NC) bracketing* [15]. A noun compound is a sequence of consecutive nouns (more than two) with no other type of word in between. For a sequence of three nouns *noun1 noun2 noun3*, e.g. *liver cell antibody*, the NC bracketing decides whether to parse it as *((noun1 noun2) noun3)* - *left bracketing* or as *(noun1 (noun2 noun3))* - *right bracketing*. We argue that our task, as defined here, should carry the name of bracketing base NPs since the true meaning of bracketing is to find a syntactic structure. It is not about identifying base NPs or bigger NPs (as in [4]).

3   Previous Work

Our work relates to two major lines of research: parsing and using the web for word statistics.

3.1   Syntactic Parsing

State-of-the-art Treebank-style syntactic parsers, e.g. [2,3], simply substitute the base NP with its head word in order to simplify their task and reduce the complexity of their models. For instance, Collins [3] uses the model in Equation 1 to detect the most probable parse tree (T) given a sentence (S). Any T is viewed as a set of base NPs (B) and dependencies (D): T = (B,D). The set S is reduced to $\overline{S}$ by reducing all base NPs to their head word [11] and the dependencies (D) are only considered in the reduced sentence.

$$T_{best} = argmax_T P(T|S)$$
$$P(T|S) = P(B, D|S) = P(B|S) \times P(D|S, B) \tag{1}$$

The side effect of the simplifications is a parse tree in which base NPs are flat, with no internal structure, leaving the burden of correct interpretations for the base NPs on the users of the parser's output. Our work augments the parse trees generated by current statistical parsers by providing structure for the flat, base NPs.

3.2 Web Counts

The idea of using the web as a source of word co-occurrence counts is not new. Keller amd Lapata [8] use the web to collect frequencies for bigrams (two consecutive words) that are unseen in a given collection of texts. They retrieve counts for adjective-noun, noun-noun, and verb-object bigrams by using a search engine. Cao and Li [1] search the web to find translation candidates for a given base NP before they determine possible translations among the candidates. Nakov and Hearst [15] collect bigrams from search engines for the task of noun compound bracketing. In a similar way, we use search engines to collect much needed frequencies to estimate the parameters of our statistical models.

4 Approach and Statistical Modeling

Our general approach to the task of bracketing base NPs is to create a statistical model and use the web to extract the data necessary to estimate the parameters of the statistical model. We focus our discussion on coordinated base NPs since it is an interesting aspect of base NP parsing that has received little attention.

5 The Models

We explore three models and two approaches to computing the corresponding parameters (probabilities) for bracketing base NPs. The three models are *head-similarity* model, *adjacency* model, and *dependency* model. We use frequencies and χ^2 (Chi-Square) to estimate affinity of words in bigrams that are used to compute the parameters of the models. The adjacency and dependency models were used in similar tasks, namely noun compound bracketing [15]. The head-similarity model is completely new, and introduced here.

Let us pick generic coordinated base NPs of the form *noun1 conj noun2 noun3* based on which we discuss the models. The models are shown in Figure 4. Also, let $P(w_i \rightarrow w_j|w_j)$ be the probability of a word w_i occurring immediately before a word w_j. As a reminder, the task is to decide whether the coordinated base NP

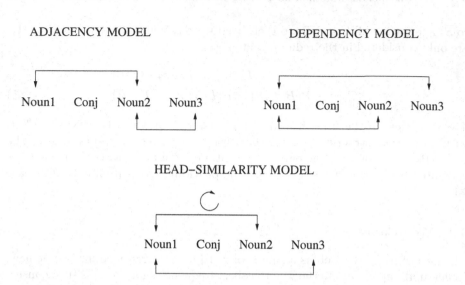

Fig. 4. Graphical representation of the three models

should be *left-bracketed, ((noun1 conj noun2) noun3)*, or *right-bracketed, (noun1 conj (noun2 noun3))*.

In this paper, we propose a new model, the *head-similarity* model, for parsing coordinated based NPs. The argument for the model is based on two observations. First, left bracketing should occur when *noun1* and *noun2* can both modify *noun3*, i.e. *noun1* and *noun2* are similar. A good example is the following base NP: *soccer and tennis player*. *Soccer* and *tennis* are similar and thus both can modify *tennis* equally. The likelihoods of *soccer player* and *tennis player* should be high in language use. In general, to check whether *noun1* and *noun2* are similar one needs to check the likelihoods of *noun1 noun3* and *noun2 noun3*. We use the web as our repository of language use from where to estimate the needed likelihoods. Second, if *noun1* and *noun3* are similar then right bracketing should be preferred. Consider the base NP *policeman and park guard*. In this case, *policeman* and *guard* are similar and thus *policeman* coordinates better with the head of *park guard*, i.e. *guard*. One way to test that *policeman* and *guard* are similar is to check the likelihoods of *park policeman* and *park guard*, i.e. check the likelihoods of *noun2 noun1* and *noun2 noun3*. To summarize, the new model decides between left and right bracketing by computing $max\{P(n_1 \rightarrow n_3|n_3) \times P(n_2 \rightarrow n_3|n_3), P(n_2 \rightarrow n_1|n_1) \times P(n_2 \rightarrow n_3|n_3)\}$. The previous formula can be reduced to the formula in Equation 2. If $P(n_1 \rightarrow n_3|n_3)$ is greater then we select left bracketing. Otherwise, we select right bracketing.

$$max\{P(n_1 \rightarrow n_3|n_3), P(n_2 \rightarrow n_1|n_1)\} \qquad (2)$$

Similar tasks, e.g. noun compound bracketing, have opted for two related models: the adjacency and dependency models. The two models are based on the affinity of different nouns in the base NP and not on the similarity of the heads of the resulting NPs as is our newly proposed model. Next, the two models are described in the context of coordinated base NPs.

The *adjacency* model checks whether *noun2 noun3* is a compound and thus coordinated with a single noun *noun1*. Using our generic coordinated base NP, the formula in Equation 3 applies. If $P(n_2 \rightarrow n_3|n_3)$ is the greater then select right bracketing. Otherwise, select left-bracketing.

$$max \{P(n_2 \rightarrow n_3|n_3), P(n_1 \rightarrow n_2|n_2)\} \qquad (3)$$

The *dependency* model compares how strongly *noun1* modifies *noun3* as opposed to *noun1* modifying *noun2*. Simply put, it computes max $\{P(n_1 \rightarrow n_2|n_2), P(n_1 \rightarrow n_3|n_3)\}$. The first term, $P(n_1 \rightarrow n_2|n_2)$, is an indicator of the strength of the association of words *noun1* and *noun2*. $P(n_1 \rightarrow n_3|n_3)$ is an indicator of the bond between *noun1* and *noun3*. If $P(n_1 \rightarrow n_3|n_3)$ is greater then do right bracketing. Otherwise, do left bracketing.

$$max \{P(n_1 \rightarrow n_3|n_3), P(n_1 \rightarrow n_2|n_2)\} \qquad (4)$$

The above models can be easily translated to coordinated base NPs of the form *noun1 noun2 and noun3*, e.g. *theater managers and owners*, by simply replacing *noun1* with *noun2* in the above formulae, *noun1* with *noun2*, and *noun3* with *noun3* (*noun3* is same), respectively.

The probabilities of the models can be approximated from the web using the maximum likelihood estimator (MLE) $P(w) = f(w)/N$; where $f(x)$ is the frequency of word w in a text collection. N is the size, in number of words, of the collection. Since we use the web as our collection, we estimate the frequency of a word w as the number of pages returned by a search engine for the query "w". We do not need to know the size N of the text collection because in our models we use conditional probabilities of the form $P(n_1 \rightarrow n_2|n_2)$ which is computed as $f(n_1, n_2)/f(n_2)$. The $f(n_1, n_2)$ term is the number of pages returned by the search engine for the exact phrase query "*noun1 noun2*".

There are other ways to measure the similarity of two words: mutual information, information gain, χ^2 (chi-square). We experiment here with χ^2, also used in [15] for bracketing noun compounds. χ^2 is a symmetric measure as opposed to the previous probabilities. However, it has been shown [8] that for noun compounds computing the probabilities in any order leads to same results. The formula for computing χ^2 is given by Equation 5.

$$\chi^2(w_i, w_j) = \frac{N(AD - BC)}{(A + C)(B + D)(A + B)(C + D)} \qquad (5)$$

In the equation, A is the frequency (#) of (w_i, w_j), B is $\#(w_i, \overline{w_j})$ - the frequency of bigrams starting with w_i and not having w_j in the next position, C is the reverse of B - $\#(\overline{w_i}, w_j)$, and D is the negation of A - $\#(\overline{w_i}, \overline{w_j})$. N, the total number of bigrams, is estimated following the method in [15] to 8 trillions. The number N = A + B + C + D comes from the assumption that Google indexes 8 billion pages and each contains about 1,000 words on average.

The other terms are estimated as in the followings: $B = \#(w_i) - \#(w_i, w_j)$, $C = \#(w_j) - \#(w_i, w_j)$, and D is estimated as N - A - B - C.

One of the major problems with statistical modeling is the lack of counts for some data, called the data sparseness problem. In our case, queries to search engines for bigrams such as "noun1 noun2" are rarely returning 0 counts (no pages). To handle the rare cases we use add-0.5 smoothing technique ([7]) which adds 0.5 to each count. If a 0 count is returned by the search engine we still have a non-zero value of 0.5 for the frequency of the corresponding query.

6   Experimental Setup and Results

In this section we describe the experiments we conducted to observe the behavior of our proposed models. We describe first how we collected the test data and the web counts. The performance of the models on the data is then presented, followed by an analysis of the errors and their sources.

We started by selecting a set of base NPs from WordNet ([14]) glosses and from the web. WordNet is a lexical database of English that organizes English words into synonymy sets, called synsets. Synsets are further interrelated via lexico-semantic relations making WordNet resembling a semantic network. Each synset in WordNet has a gloss associated with it, i.e. a definition and few usage examples. We extracted WordNet definitions and web pages related to certain topics and parsed them with Charniak's parser [2]. From parse trees the base NPs are identified by simply traversing the trees and detecting non-recursive NPs, i.e. do not have any other NPs as children. For our experiments, we only focused on coordinated base NPs. To filter out coordinated base NPs we looked for non-recursive NP nodes that expand into patterns of the form: !NN[PS] NN[PS] CC NN[PS] NN[PS] !NN[PS] (NN - comoun noun, NNP - proper noun, NNS - common noun plural, NNPS - proper noun plural). An exclamation (!) indicates the following element should not appear. By using it, we make sure we only select proper coordinated base NP, i.e. not chunks of bigger base NPs that may contain for instance noun compounds, which would only add noise to our data. For instance, the NP *almond paste and egg whites* would lead to the extraction of *paste and egg whites* had we not impose that no previous NN[PS] group should be in front of the *noun1* in the extracted coordinated base NP. The result would most likely be an ambiguous or misleading base NP. Two annotators then went over the extracted base NPs and eliminated errors (mainly caused by part of speech tagging). We also did some cleaning by eliminating base NPs with acronyms such as *S and SE Asia*. The final set contained 538 base NPs, which we call the *test data set* or simply *data set*. In order to prepare the data for automated evaluation the annotators manually bracketed the test set with correct brackets. The annotation was performed by two of the authors of this paper, and wherever a disagreement occurred a discussion took place and agreement was reached. The Kappa-statistic, a measure of inter-annotator agreement with values close to 1 meaning high agreement, is 0.911. One of our goals was to have a balanced set of data (50-50 split between left-bracketing and right-bracketing) which allows for a better comparison among different approaches. The 538 data set is a 48.2%-51.8% split between left- and right-bracketing.

6.1 Web Counts

We use the web to learn the probability distribution. The data acquisition process has three steps: (1) break the base NP into pairs of nouns and form two-noun queries to be submitted to a search engine, (2) use a search engine to obtain rough estimates for the data, and (3) extract the counts from the results page returned by the search engine. For instance, for a base NP of the form *noun1 conj noun2 noun3* we form the pairs: *noun1 noun2*, *noun1 noun3* and *noun2 noun3*. We then send each pair to Google as a phrase query (words included in quotes), e.g. "noun1 noun2", and retrieve the number of pages, or web counts, Google reports the phrase appears in. The retrieved counts are stored locally. Because we do not use training data to learn the probability distribution our approach is unsupervised.

6.2 Evaluation Measures

To evaluate the performance of our system we use standard parsing evaluation measures for Treebank-style parsers: labeled precision (LP), labeled recall (LR), and complete match. The evaluation follows a gold standard approach in which the output of a parser on the test data is compared to the correctly parsed test data. This data, or the gold standard, is obtained by manual bracketing by one or more experts (in our case, by two authors). Let us denote by a the number of correct phrases in the output from a parser for a sentence, by b the number of incorrect phrases in the output and by c the number of phrases in the gold standard for the same sentence. LP is defined as $a/(a+b)$ and LR is defined as a/c. Complete match is the percentage of test cases that have perfect (100%) LP and LR, i.e. the entire parse tree is correct. Figure 5 shows on the left a parse tree to be evaluated and on the right the corresponding correct, or gold, parse tree. The idea is to map the parse tree into a set of phrases/constituents of the form *(label, start position, end position)* where *label* is the label of an internal node of the tree and *start* and *end position* are the indices in the base NP of the leftmost and rightmost word, respectively, covered by the subtree having *label* as root. For instance, the constituent for the top NP on the tree on the right hand side in Figure 5 is (NP, 0, 3) while the constituent for its left child is (NP,0,0). We can look at each constituent as a simple way to represent a subtree in a parse tree and at the evaluation process as measuring how many subtrees in the parse tree are correct. The constituents of a gold parse tree are the correct constituents. During evaluation, if a constituent belonging to the to-be-evaluated parse tree is found among the constituents of the gold parse tree then it is counted as a correct constituent; otherwise it is counted as an incorrect constituent.

We used evalb (http://nlp.cs.nyu.edu/evalb/), a parser evaluation software, to automatically compare the output from a model with the correct bracketing of the test data set, i.e. the gold standard. Table 1 summarizes the results, showing

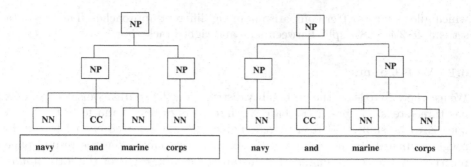

Fig. 5. Examples of a base NP to be evaluated (left tree - predicted bracketing, right tree - true bracketing)

that the adjacency model provides the best results. The head-similarity model leads to 71.82% for both Precision and Recall, and 57.73% for exact match accuracy. The figures are significantly better than the baseline shown in the first row. The dependency model was able to retrieve only 64.12% of the correct internal constituents of a base NP (recall). Of all the internal constituents of a base NP generated by the dependency model 64.12% were correct (precision). Precision and recall are equal in Table 1 because of the data type we use, coordinated base NPs of a certain pattern (*noun1 conj noun2 noun3*), and the way we represent it. The models always output 3 NPs and there are 3 NPs in the corresponding gold bracketed base NP. If the bracketing prediction is wrong 2 predicted NPs out of 3 NPs will be wrong (the top NP is always right) leading to a precision of 0.33. Similarly, only one NP (the top one) is correctly retrieved out of 3 NPs in the gold standard leading to a recall of 0.33. When the prediction is correct, the models lead to LP=LR=1.00. Averaging over a number of instances will lead to equal values for both P and R.

While the adjacency model appeared to produce the best results, closer analysis of the output suggested that this model had a bias for predicting right-bracket. Thus, the recall for right-bracket (RB) was predictably very high (90%) with a much lower precision (65%). Left-bracket (LB) results, meanwhile, were predictably less accurate (recall = 45%, precision = 79%). The head-similarity model, on the other hand, recorded weaker overall predictions (LP=55%, LR=58% for LB, LP=61%, LR=57% for RB) but roughly equal splits for those predictions (LB = 51.5%, RB = 48.5% - almost identical with the true split in the gold standard).

A quick analysis of the output for all the models allows us to draw two conclusions. First, raw counts from web could be improved by using estimation from other search engines, e.g. Yahoo and MSN's Live. Second, filter out, if possible, the results obtained and re-estimate the counts. Two filtering methods can be implemented: eliminate occurrences where words with different part of speech are reported (*guard* can be both a noun or a verb) and eliminate occurrences of pairs of nouns separated by punctuation (for instance *park/policeman* is treated as *park policeman* by Google from a search point of view).

Table 1. Results of the models on collected data (LP - Labeled Precision; LR - Labeled Recall)

Model	Performance			
	LP	LR	F-Measure	Exact Match
Baseline	66.67	66.67	66.67	50.00
Head-Sim	71.82	71.82	71.82	57.73
Adjacency	77.53	77.53	77.53	66.29
Dependency	64.12	64.12	64.12	46.18
ChiSq-HeadSim	69.71	69.71	69.71	54.56
ChiSq-Adj	77.41	77.41	77.41	66.11
ChiSq-Dep	63.75	63.75	63.75	45.62

7 Conclusion

We presented in this paper several models for bracketing coordinated base NPs. We proposed a new model, the head-similarity model, and used two other models on a data set obtained from WordNet glosses and the web. Only the head-similarity model can significantly predict both left- and right-bracketing. The estimation of the parameters of the models is based on web counts collected from a search engine which makes our method unsupervised.

References

1. Cao, Y., Li H. Base Noun Phrase Translation Using Web Data and the EM Algorithm, International Conference on Computational Linguistics (COLING), 2002
2. Charniak, E. Statistical Parsing with a context-free grammar and word statistics, Proceedings of the Fourteenth National Conference on Artificial Intelligence, Menlo Park: AAAI/MIT Press, (1997)
3. Collins, M. A New Statistical Parser Based on Bigram Lexical Dependencies. Proceedings of the 34th Annual Meeting of the ACL, Santa Cruz, CA. (1996)
4. Daume III, H., Marcu, D. NP Bracketing by Maximum Entropy Tagging and SVM Reranking Proceedings of Empirical Methods in Natural Language Processing. (2004)
5. Gildea, D., Loosely Tree-Based Alignment for Machine Translation, Proceedings of the 41th Annual Conference of the Association for Computational Linguistics, Sapporo, Japan. (2003)
6. Hobbs, Jerry R. Information Extraction from Biomedical Text, Journal of Biomedical Informatics. (2003)
7. Jurafsky, D., Martin, J. Speech and Language Processing, Prentice-Hall, 2000, ISBN: 0-13-095069-6
8. Keller, F., Lapata, M. Using the Web to Obtain Frequencies for Unseen Bigrams. Computational Linguistics 29:3, 459-484. (2003)
9. Krymolowski, Y., Dagan , I. Compositional Memory-Based Partial Parsing, in Proceedings of the Annual Meeting of the Association for Computational Linguistics (ACL), 2000, pp. 45-52. (2000)

10. Lappin, S., Leass, H. J. An Algorithm for Pronominal Anaphora Resolution. Computational Linguistics 20-4:535-561. (1994)
11. Magerman, D.M. Natural Language Parsing as Statistical Pattern Recognition, PhD Thesis, Stanford University, February, 1994
12. Marcus, M.P., Santorini, B., Marcinkiewicz, M.A. Building a Large Annotated Corpus of English: The Penn Treebank.Computational Linguistics 19-2: 313-330. (1993)
13. Markham, J., Rus, V. On the Implementation of a Baseline Part-of-Speech Tagger, Third Mid-South College Computing Conference (MSCCC-05), Oxford, Mississippi, April. (2005)
14. Miller, George A. WordNet: a lexical database for English. In: Communications of the ACM 38 (11), November, pp. 39 - 41. (1995)
15. Nakov, P., and Hearst, M. Search Engine Statistics Beyond the n-gram: Application to Noun Compound Bracketing, in the Proceedings of Ninth Conference on Computational Natural Language Learning, Ann Arbor, MI, June. (2005)
16. Ramshaw, L.A., Marcus, M.P., Text Chunking Using Transformation-Based Learning, In: "Proceedings of the Third Workshop on Very Large Corpora", Cambridge, MA, USA. (1995)
17. Rus, V. High Precision Logic Form Transformation, International Conference on Tools with Artificial Intelligence (ICTAI) 2001, November, Dallas, TX. (2001)
18. Rus, V., Moldovan, D.I. and Bolohan, O. Bracketing Compound Nouns for Logic Form Derivation, Proceedings of the FLAIRS 2002 Conference, May 2002, Pensacola, Florida
19. Sang, T.K., Erik, F. Noun Phrase Recognition by System Combination. In Proceedings of ANLP-NAACL 2000, Seattle, Washington, USA. Morgan Kaufman Publishers, pp. 50-55. (2000)
20. Voorhees, E. Overview of the TREC 2002 Question Answering Track, Proceedings of the Eleventh Text Retrieval Conference (TREC 2002). (2002)

Text Categorization for Improved Priors of Word Meaning

Rob Koeling, Diana McCarthy, and John Carroll

Department of Informatics, University of Sussex, Brighton BN1 9QH, UK
{robk,dianam,johnca}@sussex.ac.uk

Abstract. Distributions of the senses of words are often highly skewed. This fact is exploited by word sense disambiguation (WSD) systems which back off to the predominant (most frequent) sense of a word when contextual clues are not strong enough. The topic domain of a document has a strong influence on the sense distribution of words. Unfortunately, it is not feasible to produce large manually sense-annotated corpora for every domain of interest. Previous experiments have shown that unsupervised estimation of the predominant sense of certain words using corpora whose domain has been determined by hand outperforms estimates based on domain-independent text for a subset of words and even outperforms the estimates based on counting occurrences in an annotated corpus.

In this paper we address the question of whether we can automatically produce domain-specific corpora which could be used to acquire predominant senses appropriate for specific domains. We collect the corpora by automatically classifying documents from a very large corpus of newswire text. Using these corpora we estimate the predominant sense of words for each domain. We first compare with the results presented in [1]. Encouraged by the results we start exploring using text categorization for WSD by evaluating on a standard data set (documents from the SENSEVAL-2 and 3 English all-word tasks). We show that for these documents and using domain-specific predominant senses, we are able to improve on the results that we obtained with predominant senses estimated using general, non domain-specific text. We also show that the confidence of the text classifier is a good indication whether it is worthwhile using the domain-specific predominant sense or not.

1 Introduction

The fact that the distributions of word senses are often highly skewed is recognized by the word sense disambiguation (WSD) community and is often successfully exploited in WSD systems. The sense distributions can either be used as a prior in a system that collects statistical evidence from the local context of the contested word to determine the intended sense of the word, or it can be used as a back-off in those cases where the local context does not provide enough information to decide. However, manually tagging corpora with word senses is labour intensive and therefore expensive. Therefore, most researchers use the same publicly available resource, SemCor [2], to estimate word sense

A. Gelbukh (Ed.): CICLing 2007, LNCS 4394, pp. 241–252, 2007.

distributions. Despite the fact that SemCor is a fairly small corpus, it covers a reasonable range of words (and word senses) in sufficient frequencies. In WSD, the heuristic of just choosing the most frequent sense of a word is very powerful, especially for words with highly skewed sense distributions [3]. Indeed, only 5 out of the 26 systems in the recent SENSEVAL-3 English all words task [4] outperformed the heuristic of choosing the most frequent sense as derived from SemCor (which would give 61.5% precision and recall[1]). Furthermore, systems that did outperform the first sense heuristic did so only by a small margin (the top score being 65% precision and recall).

[5] have shown that information about the domain of a document is very useful for WSD. This is because many concepts are specific to particular domains, and for many words their most likely meaning in context is strongly correlated to the domain of the document they appear in. Thus, since word sense distributions are skewed and depend on the domain at hand we would like to know *for each domain of application* the most likely sense of a word.

There are, however, several problems with obtaining hand-labelled domain-specific sense-tagged data. The first being the problem of specifying the domains. There is no such thing as a standardized definition of topical domains. The definition of a domain will be dependent on user and application. People will most likely disagree on what should be considered domains, where the borders between domains lie and finally the granularity of the domain definitions. The second problem is that even if people agreed on a domain definition, producing domain-specific sense-tagged corpora would be extremely costly, since a substantial corpus would have to be annotated by hand for every domain of interest. It would be ideal if a user could specify a topical domain, collect a substantial amount of text relevant for that domain and use that corpus for estimating domain-specific sense distributions.

In response to the second problem, we proposed a method for *automatically* inducing the predominant sense of a word from raw text [6]. The method was extensively tested on domain-neutral data and we carried out a limited test of our method on text in 2 domains to assess whether the acquired predominant sense information was broadly consistent with the domain of the text it was acquired from. In a later paper, [1], we evaluated the method on domain-specific text. In order to do this, we created a sense-annotated gold-standard for a sample of words covering 2 domains (Finance and Sport) and domain-neutral data. We showed that unsupervised estimation of the predominant sense of certain words using corpora whose topical domain has been determined by hand outperforms estimates based on domain-independent text for a sample of words and even outperforms the estimates based on counting occurrences in SemCor.

However, these results were obtained using data where the domain of the documents was determined by hand. High quality high volume domain specific corpora are not always available for a given language and a given domain. In this paper we want to address some of the questions that arose from this earlier work.

---

[1] This figure is the mean of two different estimates [4], the difference being due to multiword handling.

Will our method [6] be robust enough to deal with the noise that is unavoidable if you use automatically classified text? We show, [1], that the method successfully deals with a sample of words in a domain-specific setting, however, for some applications word sense disambiguation may be required for all the words in a given text. In this paper we describe the automatic construction of domain-specific text corpora using a big newswire corpus and a text classifier. We estimate the predominant senses for all polysemous nouns (as defined in WordNet) for a number of domains. We evaluate the estimated predominant senses by 1) comparing the results with the results based on hand-classified text as presented in [1] and 2) performing a WSD task on the documents used in the SENSEVAL-2 and 3 English all-words tasks. We show that our results are very comparable with [1] and, in certain cases the domain-specific predominant sense estimates outperform those based on a domain-neutral corpus. We will look at the effect the classifier has on the success and also what the influence of corpus size is.

2   Finding Predominant Senses

We use the method described in [6] for finding predominant senses from raw text. The method uses a thesaurus obtained from the text by parsing, extracting grammatical relations and then listing each word (w) with its top k nearest neighbours, where k is a constant. Like [6] we use $k = 50$ and obtain our thesaurus using the distributional similarity metric described by [7] and we use WordNet (WN) as our sense inventory. The senses of a word w are each assigned a ranking score which sums over the distributional similarity scores of the neighbours and weights each neighbour's score by a WN Similarity score [8] between the sense of w and the sense of the neighbour that maximises the WN Similarity score. This weight is normalised by the sum of such WN similarity scores between all senses of w and the senses of the neighbour that maximises this score. We use the WN Similarity jcn score [9] since this gave reasonable results for [6] and it is efficient at run time given precompilation of frequency information. The jcn measure needs word frequency information, which we obtained from the British National Corpus (BNC) [10]. The distributional thesaurus was constructed using subject, direct object adjective modifier and noun modifier relations.

3   Creating the Domain Corpora

3.1   The GigaWord Corpus

The GigaWord English Corpus is a comprehensive archive of newswire text data that has been acquired over several years by the Linguistic Data Consortium (LDC), at the University of Pennsylvania. The data is collected from four different sources: Agence France Press English Service, Associated Press Worldstream English Service, The New York Times Newswire Service and The Xinhua News Agency English Service. The data is roughly from the years 1994 until 2002 (not every source starts and stops in the same month). The total number of documents is 4,111,240, consisting of 1,756,504 K-words. For the experiments described in this paper, we use the first 20 months worth of data of all 4 sources. There are 4 different types of documents identified in the corpus. The vast majority of the documents are of type 'story'. We are using all the data.

3.2   The Classifier

For the text classification, we adopt a previous definition of topical domains, though this could be changed in future. Since our evaluation framework and the method [6] use WN as a sense inventory, we make use of a topic domain extension for WN (WN-DOMAINS[5]). In WN-DOMAINS the Princeton English WordNet is augmented with some domain labels. Every synset in WN's sense inventory is annotated with at least one domain label, selected from a set of about 200 hierarchically organized labels. Each synsets of Wordnet 1.6 was labeled with one or more labels. The label 'factotum' was assigned if any other was inadequate. The first level consists of 5 main categories (e.g. 'doctrines' and 'social_science') and 'factotum'. 'doctrines' has subcategories such as 'art', 'religion' and 'psychology'. Some subcategories are divided in sub-subcategories, e.g. 'dance', 'music' or 'theatre' are subcategories of 'art'. We extracted bags of domain-specific words from WordNet for all the defined domains by collecting all the word senses (synsets) and corresponding glosses associated with a certain domain label. These bags of words are the blueprints for the domains and we used them to train a Support Vector Machine (SVM) text classifier using 'TwentyOne'[2]. The classifier distinguishes between 48 classes (first and second level of the WN-DOMAINS hierarchy). When a document is evaluated by the classifier, it returns a list of all the classes (domains) it recognizes and an associated *confidence score* reflecting the certainty that the document belongs to that particular domain.Selected lines of the output of the classifier are given in Figure 1.

```
<CLASSIFY_SERVER>
    <N_RESULTS>48</N_RESULTS>
        <RESULT>
            <CLASS><![CDATA[medicine]]></CLASS>
            <CONF_SCORE>0.85</CONF_SCORE>
        </RESULT>
        <RESULT>
            <CLASS><![CDATA[biology]]></CLASS>
            <CONF_SCORE>0.80</CONF_SCORE>
        </RESULT>
        .....
        <RESULT>
            <CLASS><![CDATA[artisanship]]></CLASS>
            <CONF_SCORE>0.03</CONF_SCORE>
        </RESULT>
</CLASSIFY_SERVER>
```

Fig. 1. Part of the output of the 'TwentyOne' classifier

3.3   The Domain Corpora

The 20 months worth of GigaWord corpus consists of 520501 files. Out of the 48 predefined classes, 44 are are represented in the classifier output (meaning that

---

[2] TwentyOne Classifier is an Irion Technologies product: www.irion.ml/products/ english/products_classify.html

at least one document was classified as most likely belonging to that class). The distribution of documents is, as was to be expected, very uneven. Table 1 gives an overview of the number of documents per domain.

Given the fact that we used general newswire data, it was a pleasant surprise to see so many domains well represented in the corpus. At the moment we assign a domain label to a document by simply taking the domain with the highest confidence value (the level of confidence is not considered at the moment). However, manual analysis suggests there seems to be a good case for taking the confidence level into consideration. Manual inspection of randomly selected documents suggested that documents that were assigned a confidence level under 0.74 were often assigned the wrong domain. At 0.75 the amount of noise seems to be fairly low, only to be further improved by increasing the confidence level. Evidently, the drawback of putting up a higher confidence threshold is losing data. Putting the threshold at 0.75 for the first document reduces the number of documents by some 23%. A first test using a threshold (set at 0.75) for corpus collection did not improve the results. Therefore, in the experiments in this paper we use all the data available. More experiments will be needed to explore this matter further. For the evaluation we use 6 documents from the SENSEVAL-2 and 3 English all-words tasks (see 4). The classifier assigned the domains 'art', 'medicine' and 'psychology' to the SENSEVAL-2 documents and 'politics' and 2 times 'psychology' to the SENSEVAL-3 documents. The characteristics of the 4 relevant domain corpora are given in Table 2.

Table 1. Distribution of documents over domains

Number of documents in domain	Number of domains
<500	18
500 - 1000	4
1000 - 5000	6
5000 - 10000	3
>10000	13

Table 2. Size of the domain corpora

Domain	No. of documents	No. of words
Art	11679	5729655
Medicine	14463	5644181
Psychology	44075	23748013
Politics	64106	25108055

3.4 Domain Rankings

The 4 resulting corpora were parsed using RASP [11] and the resulting grammatical relations were used to create a distributional similarity thesaurus, which in turn was used for computing the predominant senses (see 2). The only preprocessing we performed was stripping the XML codes from the documents. No other filtering was undertaken. This resulted in 4 sets of domain-dependent sense inventories. Each of them has a slightly different set of words. The words they have in common do have the same senses, but not necessarily the same estimated most frequently used sense.

4   Experiments and Evaluation

To evaluate the first sense heuristic we see how the heuristic performs on a WSD task. This simply uses the skew of the data to tag every word type with one sense. In a real application, this back off heuristic should be combined with contextual WSD information. The naive WSD system evaluation approach is a very useful one. First of all, a WSD system using only the first sense heuristic where the predominant sense is estimated using hand-annotated text is a more than decent performing participant in WSD competitions. And second, [6] have shown that unsupervised estimation of predominant senses using domain-neutral text is a good approximation of the supervised alternative. We show that if you know what topic domain you are in, you can do better with domain-specific predominant senses than with domain-neutral ones and in certain cases you might even do better than when using hand-crafted domain-neutral sense distributions. In this paper, following [1], we concentrate on the evaluation of nouns, but extending our experiment from evaluating a selected set of nouns to an all-words (nouns) task. The first experiment we perform is to take the domain rankings for the Sport and Finance domain and evaluate the predominant senses on the test data used in [1]. In the second experiment we use the senseval-2 and 3 data sets as these are standard all-words datasets available for English where automatic methods can be contrasted with information from the manually produced SemCor.

4.1   Hand-Labelled Versus Automatically Classified

The first experiment is a straightforward comparison with the results reported in [1]. The Sports and Finance corpora are collected as described in Section 3. The results reported on here are based on using 20 months of GigaWord data. The resulting Sports corpus consists of 23.6M words and the Finance corpus of 48.2M words. The main aim for this experiment is to see if the good results reported in [1] can be reproduced with automatically labelled data. Table 3 presents the best results for this experiment. It shows a small (and expected) decrease in accuracy for the Finance test set and a small (surprising) increase for the Sport test set. These results are very encouraging. Despite the decrease in precision on the Finance test set, both the BNC and the SemCor results are outperformed for both test sets.

4.2   Senseval

The purpose of Senseval is to evaluate the strengths and weaknesses of programs that can automatically determine the sense of a word in context with respect to

Table 3. WSD using predominant sens: hand-labelled (Reuters) versus automatically classified (GigaWord)

Finance		Sport	
Train	WSD Precision	Train	WSD Precision
BNC	43.3	BNC	33.2
SemCor	35.0	SemCor	16.8
Reuters Finance	49.9	Reuters Sport	43.7
GigaWord Finance	44.2	GigaWord Sport	46.1

different words, different varieties of language, and different languages. In order to do so, a number of tasks has been set up. One of the tasks is an "all-words" task. In this task every ambiguous (according to a chosen sense inventory) word-token in a text is manually annotated with the correct sense in the context where it occurred. The predicted word senses by participants are compared to the manually annotated gold-standard. Both the SENSEVAL-2 and 3 competitions had an English all-words task defined. Three documents were prepared for each edition. This total of 6 documents is what we use for evaluation.

We sent the 6 documents to the classifier to determine the topical domains. The results are given in Table 4. The classifier's first and second (between brackets) guesses are given in this table with corresponding confidence scores in the third column. The first document has a low confidence score. The document is hard to classify, even by hand. The classifier's second and third guesses ('religion' and 'architecture') are actually equally plausible. The second document is spot on (and the classifier is confident about it). The third one would manually probably be classified as 'pedagogy', but 'psychology' is plausible. The fourth document is apparently taken from a novel. This seems to confuse the classifier, which is confident that 'psychology' is the domain. The fifth document is spot on (and again, with high confidence value). The last document is a hard to classify human interest story about the aftermath of an earthquake. The classifier's first 2 guesses are relevant, but have low confidence score.

Table 4. Output of the classifier for the 6 Senseval documents

Doc.Id.	Class	Confidence Score
Se2-d00	Art (Architecture)	0.73 (0.71)
Se2-d01	Medicine (Biology)	0.85 (0.80)
Se2-d02	Psychology (Economy)	0.79 (0.72)
Se3-d000	Psychology (Economy)	0.81 (0.72)
Se3-d001	Politics (Law)	0.82 (0.77)
Se3-d002	Psychology (Earth)	0.72 (0.70)

Results. We produced separate results for the SENSEVAL-2 and 3 documents because different versions of WN were used to annotate the data. The documents in SENSEVAL-2 were annotated with WN 1.7, whilst those in SENSEVAL-3 were

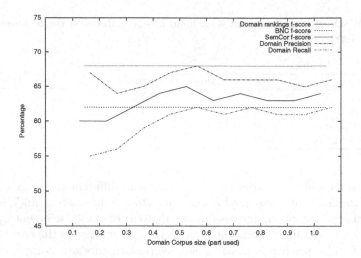

Fig. 2. Results for SENSEVAL-2: Precision, Recall and f_1-score for varying domain corpus size (percentage of available text) versus BNC (full corpus) and SemCor

annotated with WN 1.7.1. In Figure 2 we show how the results develop as a function of corpus size. Different amounts of data were available for the 3 documents involved (see table 2). In this graph we want to show how the combined results (of the 3 documents) develop if you take a certain portion of the data available for each domain. We report on f_1-score[3], Precision and Recall for predominant senses estimated using increasing portions of the domain corpora and compare them with the estimated predominant senses based on the BNC (using the whole written part of the corpus; about 90M words) and the SemCor benchmark.

There are a few interesting aspects about this figure. First of all, we can see that the overall results for the domain-based are consistently better than those from the BNC. The learning curve seems to display an upward trend, although it starts to flatten out quite early on. An interesting aspect here is the fact that Precision seems to be fairly stable from the start. It is the Recall that makes the difference for the overall f-score results. A similar, though less convincing story is told in Figure 3 for the SENSEVAL-3 results. The overall results stay slightly underneath the BNC benchmark and far away from the SemCor results. Recall is going up considerably to begin with, but flattens out quite quickly and seems to remain stable from then on.

If we look at more detail at the results, we can see that the favorable SENSEVAL-2 results are entirely due to the first and third document. The domain results for the second document starts to creep up to BNC level, but then remains there. A nice observation here is that fairly small corpora already produce nice results. The results start to be competitive at a corpus size of around the 2.5M words for the first and third document. Finally, not shown in this figure, is that the domain results for the second document also outperform the SemCor

---

[3] $F_\beta = (1 + \beta^2) * ((Prec * Recall) / (Recall + \beta^2 * Prec))$.

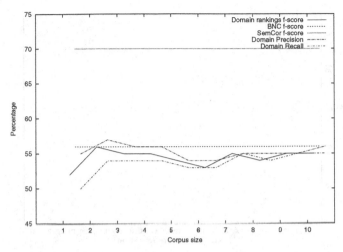

Fig. 3. Results for SENSEVAL-3: Precision, Recall and $f_1 - score$ for varying domain corpus size (percentage of available text) versus BNC (full corpus) and SemCor

results (those are slightly above the BNC results). This is not the case for the other 2 documents. They stay well below the SemCor results.

Finally the results per document in the SENSEVAL-3 data is shown in figure 5. The obvious observation here is that only the second document keeps the flag flying for the domain-specific results. The domain-specific results outperforms the BNC results comfortably, albeit still below SemCor results. The 2 Psychology documents perform poorly. Although, the first one (where the classifier was fairly confident) is significantly better than the third one (where the classifier gave a very low confidence score).

4.3   Domain Salient Words

Words that are salient to a particular domain performed particularly well in [1]. We performed an experiment to evaluate the performance if we only consider the top 1000 salient words for each domain[4]. We trimmed the list by excluding any words containing capital letters and only considered words that occurred at least 10 times in the domain corpus. Just inspecting the resulting lists of salient words proved to be interesting. The lists of 'medicine' and 'politics' salient nouns indicated immediately which domain they were for. The 'art' list did that too, but also showed quite a bit of variation (e.g. music versus painting, etc). Finally

---

[4] We computed salience as a ratio of normalised document frequencies, using the formula

$$S(w,d) = \frac{N_{wd}/N_d}{N_w/N}$$

where N_{wd} is the number of documents in domain d containing the noun (lemma) w, N_d is the number of documents in domain d, N_w is the total number of documents containing the noun w and N is the total number of documents.

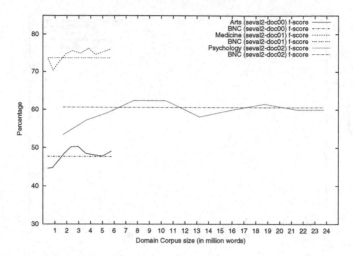

Fig. 4. Results for SENSEVAL-2: $f_1 - score$ for varying domain corpus size (in M words) versus BNC (full corpus)

the 'psychology' list was not recognizable whatsoever. It mainly consists of fairly obscure words that were not indicative of any domain in particular.

The results for this evaluation are given in Table 5. The only thing we can say about the arts document is that the coverage is low. This is unsurprising, because of the fact that it is not a clear-cut arts document. It further shows that the coverage of the medicine salient word list is very high (almost half the words of the document are covered). The results for these words is very good, but equally so for BNC and SemCor. The surprising bit is that the top 1000 salient words for the psychology domain do not have *any words* in common with the psychology document. The same thing holds for the 2 psychology documents in the SENSEVAL-3 test set. The results for the politics document are outstanding: high precision, high recall, a reasonable number of words are covered and even the SemCor results are outperformed.

5   Discussion and Future Research

The results show that for certain documents very good results can be obtained. The major factors that determine whether a document is a good candidate for using domain-specific sense priors seem to be:

- The classifier's confidence that the document belongs to a certain domain.
- Well defined and concise domains seem to be very helpful. Apparently, both the medical and the politics domain fit that bill. A good indication is the fact that a list of most salient words for that domain covers a reasonable size of the words in the document.

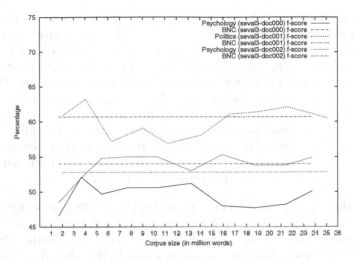

Fig. 5. Results for SENSEVAL-3: $f_1 - score$ for varying domain corpus size (in M words) versus BNC (full corpus)

The documents classified as 'psychology' suffered from several problems. The classifier seems to be too lenient towards the psychology domain. Neither one of the 3 documents classified as 'psychology' were clear-cut examples. This might mean two things. 1) the domain is inherently too broad and we are always better of using domain-neutral sense inventories, or 2) the classifier needs a tighter definition of this domain. The latter option should be easy to explore. Only including documents with a high (where 'high' needs to be specified) confidence level can be included in the domain corpus, or we could retrain the classifier with a different, more restricted bag-of-words. A first experiment with higher confidence values for including documents in a domain corpus resulted in a significant loss of data. However, we have shown that for well-defined domains only a limited amount of data is needed for good results. Certain domains (like psychology) might be more in need of tightening than others.

A testset of 6 documents is too small to draw definitive conclusions. A direct comparison with [1] taught us that we can do well with automatically created domain corpora. Even though that is a nice result, there are still many uncer-

Table 5. Evaluation results for the 1000 most salient words of each domain

Doc.Id.	Precision / BNC / SemCor	Recall / BNC / SemCor	No. Correct	No. Wrong	Not Attempted
Se2-d02	27.8 / 27.8 / 38.9	27.8 / 27.8 / 38.9	5	13	0
Se2-d00	87.8 / 87.8 / 88.8	87.8 / 87.8 / 86.4	194	27	0
Se2-d01	0 / 0 / 0	0 / 0 / 0	0	0	0
Se3-d000	0 / 0 / 0	0 / 0 / 0	0	0	0
Se3-d001	91.0 / 83.3 / 90.9	91.0 / 82.1 / 89.6	61	6	0
Se3-d002	0 / 0 / 0	0 / 0 / 0	0	0	0

tainties around how and when to use the proposed technique. We don't think that it will work on every single document. One of our objectives is to find out in which conditions this technique obtains an improved prior over one obtained from, for example, a general resource (like SemCor). The results in this paper are a firm step towards a better understanding of those conditions. There is a need for more evaluation and a good possibility is to use SemCor for this task. SemCor consists of many documents from different sources. It hosts documents from many different topic domains. As soon as we have the data for all relevant domains available (parsing the documents is the bottle neck), this will be the obvious target for experiments. It will most likely give us a better understanding of the influence of domain on the results we can expect.

Acknowledgements. This work was funded by UK EPSRC project EP/C537262 "Ranking Word Senses for Disambiguation: Models and Applications", and by a UK Royal Society Dorothy Hodgkin Fellowship to the second author. We would also like to thank Piek Vossen for giving us access to the Irion Technologies text categoriser.

References

1. Koeling, R., McCarthy, D., Carroll, J.: Domain-specific sense distributions and predominant sense acquisition. In: Proceedings of the Human Language Technology Conference and Conference on Empirical Methods in Natural Language Processing., Vancouver, Canada (2005) 419–426
2. Miller, G.A., Leacock, C., Tengi, R., Bunker, R.T.: A semantic concordance. In: Proceedings of the ARPA Workshop on Human Language Technology. (1993) 303–308
3. Yarowsky, D., Florian, R.: Evaluating sense disambiguation performance across diverse parameter spaces. Natural Language Engineering **8** (2002) 293–310
4. Snyder, B., Palmer, M.: The English all-words task. In: Proceedings of SENSEVAL-3, Barcelona, Spain (2004) 41–43
5. Magnini, B., Strapparava, C., Pezzulo, G., Gliozzo, A.: The role of domain information in word sense disambiguation. Natural Language Engineering **8** (2002) 359–373
6. McCarthy, D., Koeling, R., Weeds, J., Carroll, J.: Finding predominant senses in untagged text. In: Proceedings of the 42nd Annual Meeting of the Association for Computational Linguistics, Barcelona, Spain (2004) 280–287
7. Lin, D.: Automatic retrieval and clustering of similar words. In: Proceedings of COLING-ACL 98, Montreal, Canada (1998)
8. Patwardhan, S., Pedersen, T.: The cpan wordnet::similarity package. http://search.cpan.org/~sid/WordNet-Similarity/ (2003)
9. Jiang, J., Conrath, D.: Semantic similarity based on corpus statistics and lexical taxonomy. In: International Conference on Research in Computational Linguistics, Taiwan (1997)
10. Leech, G.: 100 million words of English: the British National Corpus. Language Research **28** (1992) 1–13
11. Briscoe, T., Carroll, J.: Robust accurate statistical annotation of general text. In: Proceedings of LREC-2002, Las Palmas de Gran Canaria (2002) 1499–1504

Case-Sensitivity of Classifiers for WSD: Complex Systems Disambiguate Tough Words Better

Harri M.T. Saarikoski[1], Steve Legrand[2], and Alexander Gelbukh[3]

[1] KIT Language Technology Doctorate School, Helsinki University, Finland
Harri.Saarikoski@helsinki.fi
[2] Department of Computer Science, University of Jyväskylä, Finland
stelegra@cc.jyu.fi
[3] Instituto Politecnico Nacional, Mexico City, Mexico
gelbukh@gelbukh.com

Abstract. We present a novel method for improving disambiguation accuracy by building an optimal ensemble (OE) of systems where we predict the best available system for target word using a priori case factors (e.g. amount of training per sense). We report promising results of a series of best-system prediction tests (best prediction accuracy is 0.92) and show that complex/simple systems disambiguate tough/easy words better. The method provides the following benefits: (1) higher disambiguation accuracy for virtually any base systems (current best OE yields close to 2% accuracy gain over Senseval-3 state of the art) and (2) economical way of building more effective ensembles of all types (e.g. optimal, weighted voting and cross-validation based). The method is also highly scalable in that it utilizes readily available factors available for any ambiguous word in any language for estimating word difficulty and defines classifier complexity using known properties only.

1 Introduction

Innumerable methods of word sense disambiguation have been tested to solve the WSD task adequately for NLP applications but no single method (e.g. classifier algorithm, configuration or ensemble, feature set or selection scheme) has been found to work superiorly for all target words. Partly because of this bias, disambiguation methods have reached a standstill [4,13]. The conclusion from this is that different disambiguation methods result in different performance results ('system bias'). In fact, differences of up to 30% in precision at word (average 5% and 3% in Senseval-2 and Senseval-3 evaluations respectively [4,13]) can take place even between state-of-the-art systems. The other way of defining this incompatibility between target words and classifying systems is that each word poses a unique set of learning problems ('word bias'). Among others [22,5,14] have showed that different classifiers for WSD have discrete but intact strong regions with regard to factors defining the word for disambiguation and the word's training contexts (e.g. number of sense-classes or number of training examples). In [6] classifier configuration through their parameters was also shown to have considerable effect on performance.

A. Gelbukh (Ed.): CICLing 2007, LNCS 4394, pp. 253–266, 2007.
© Springer-Verlag Berlin Heidelberg 2007

Optimal ensembling (OE) [17] is a method for mutually solving these two biases by attempting to redirect a learning problem (target word) to the classifier most equipped to disambiguate it. The method has been outlined in general terms in [1,3] and the such a method was suggested WSD task in [14]. More specifically, OE attempts to discover *n* base systems whose accuracies are relatively strong and whose classification profile in terms of performance is as different as possible. We call such base systems *maximally complementary*. In order to select the best base system, a machine learner is then trained with prediction factors calculated from that word and its training contexts (e.g. number of senses in the word, number of features in word training data). High prediction accuracies and resulting gains over base systems (and state of the art) using this method are reported in this paper.

Optimal ensembles have largely been neglected in WSD. This is probably because it has been believed that a single system might prove to be superior or, alternatively, because of the lack of research into factors that might predict the best system out of the ones available. In fact, large majority of WSD systems implemented so far have either been single-classifier systems (e.g. SMU system based on instance-based classifier [12]) or multi-system equal voting ensembles (e.g. JHU system a voting ensemble of six classifiers trained with the same three-feature-set input [21]). In contrast with OE, these ensembles either apply the same system for all test words (using equal or weighted voting ensemble, VE) or select best base system based on cross-validation results (CV). OE in contrast uses a handful of *a priori* factors (e.g. number of positive training examples) to select the best system for each word.

To carry out OE experiments, we have developed a meta-classifier to learn the best system for target word using two machine-learning toolkits (YALE [11], Weka [20]) and Self-Organizing Map algorithm [9] (found useful in earlier WSD experiments [8]). The aim is to learn from available WSD system scores [4,13] the rules mapping system factors (e.g. classifier algorithm, feature sets) to word and training input factors (e.g. amount of training, word grain). The output from this meta-classifier is the optimal available system for that target word which WSD systems can utilize in their building multi-system ensembles (whether they be OE, VE, CV or any other).

In this paper, we define the strength of a handful of machine learners in terms of word and training input factors. Particularly we focus on Support Vector Machines and Naive Bayes learners and investigate different configurations of those classifiers (e.g. variations of SVM complexity parameter and kernel type, NB variants with system confidence meta-knowledge and binarization of sense-classes). We present a dozen best-system prediction experiments using Senseval WSD systems and our own systems.

In the next sections, we define the case factors and system factors, outline the method in detail and present the base systems for prediction tests. Results from prediction tests follow then. Final sections are dedicated to discussion, conclusions and further research required.

2   Prediction Factors

In this section, we define the case factors that predict the best system for word and define the properties of some classifiers that help define their respective strengths.

2.1 Case Factors

Performance of best system in Senseval evaluations [4,13] degrades steadily (though not linearly) when, for example, training is decreased and word grain increased [22]. Furthermore, [22] showed that strength of different classifiers also varies with amount of training, word grain and dominant sense ratio. They showed that one system tends to be strong at low values of a case factor (i.e. at tough words) and another at high values (i.e. at easy words). For instance, a simple Transformation-Based Learner (TBL) performed better when dominant sense frequency was high (70..) and NB when it was low (0..70). Some case factors split classifiers into three regions so that one is strong at low and high values and the other at middle range. For instance, Decision List outperformed two more complex Bayesian classifiers at very low (< 5) and high (< 17) values with Bayesians outperforming it in the middle range [22]. In this paper, the system-differentiating capacity of the following factors is investigated (see also [5,6,22,14,4,13]):

Amount of training (total*) aka volume. *Totalex/totalf* is the total number of feature extracted from training data depending on the selection of feature set (e.g. some hundreds from global 1-grams, some thousands from global sequential 2-grams).

Positive/negative training (pos*,neg*). *Posex/posf* is the average number of matching training examples/features per sense *s*. *Negex/negf* is the average number of non-matching training examples / features per each non-*s*. The relationship of *total** and *pos*/neg** factors is that *totalf/totalex* set consists of subsets *posf/posex* and *negf/negex* and *domall* specifies the sense-class distribution of both training examples and features. Note also that word grain used can be counted from other factors: negex / posex + 1 or negf / posf + 1 and can therefore be omitted.

Training distribution (domall). *Domall* accounts for distribution of training to senses s_n: $s_1^2 + s_2^2 \ldots + s_n^2$.

Instance occurrences per feature (instperfeat) aka relevance. *Instperfeat* is an approximate measure of the average relevance of extracted features. An optimal feature for recognizing a sense can be defined as one occurring frequently, pointing uniquely to one sense (e.g. collocate 'steel' pointing to the crow bar sense of *bar.n*) is more facilitating than a feature pointing to several classes (e.g. word 'and' pointing to almost any sense of any word). Most features, however, are not of such high quality, occurring either too few times to occur in test instances or too many times to point to the correct sense.

Using these case factors, we can define tough words as having low-total*, low-pos*, high-neg*, low-domall and low/high instperfeat (e.g. *call.v, carry.v*) and simple words vice versa with mid-instperfeat (e.g. *oblique.n, hearth.n*) (examples from [4]).

To show the system-differentiating of case factors, we show strengths of systems based on two classifiers (SVM and NB) in 'word space' of two case factors:

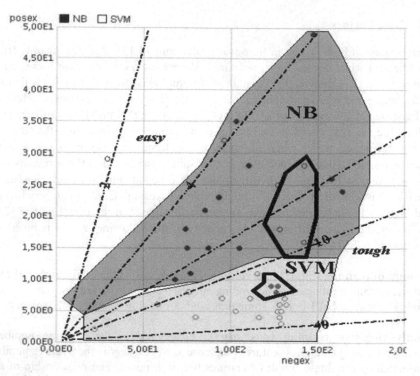

Fig. 1. Strong regions of Senseval-2 SVM/NB based systems in 'word space' of negex-posex (x,y) factors. (Plotter is provided by YALE [11]). Dots mark the words (filled = NB, unfilled = SVM). Words that lie outside linearly separable regions (i.e. most probable misclassifications) are circled. Easy words are on top left (note how at one 2-grain word SVM and NB tied) and toughness increases towards bottom right. (Posex value of *2.00E1* means average of 20 positive examples per each word sense.)

Figure 1 indicates that SVM and NB based systems occupy very different but quite linearly separable regions in negex-posex word space. We can see that SVM seems to perform well at low-posex (3 < posex < 14) and NB at high-posex half (posex > 15) while negex seems not to have as much influence. We found this relative positioning of SVM and NB to be approximately the same across different datasets and prediction tasks and also agrees with a similar experiment with the same classifiers in [5]. Interestingly, many classifier pairs tend to place in approximately those positions in word space that SVM and NB took (e.g. simple Ibk-based SMU [12] vs the more complex voting ensemble JHU [21], and TBL vs NB in [22], respectively). Some classifiers seem to handle easier words better while others tougher words.

Next we outline possible ways to define classifiers in terms of their 'complexity'.

2.2   System Factors

We exemplify some of the key differences between a handful of classifiers in terms of their respective sense decision procedures (including feature selection, weighing, evaluation and optimization strategies):

Table 1. Matrix for *adhoc* evaluation of classifier complexity. (Ibk = Instance-Based aka Nearest Neighbor Classifier, DStump = Decision Stump). (+) means that the classifier has that property (e.g. *NB-Bin+* would be NB with Bin+ property).

classifier property	SVM	NB	DTree	DStump	Ibk
Weight: performs some kind of custom weighing of features?	+	+	+	+	-
Aggreg: aggregates more than one feature (not all) per test instance to decide sense?	+	+	+/- (some)	-	+
Prior: utilizes prior sense distribution probabilities to weigh features?	-	+	-	-	-
Eval: utilizes meta-classifier's estimation of base classifier's correctness?	-	-	-	-	-
Opti: optimizes feature weights by cross-validating against training data?	+	-	-	-	-
Bin: splits n-class sense classification task into (n-1)! each vs each binary tasks?	+	-	-	-	-

This classifier matrix helps select the maximally complementary classifiers to be used as base systems in OE. We aim to prove that those differences explain why classifiers perform differently in different learning cases. The fewer positive markings (+) a classifier has, the more complex (or advanced or reflective in its decision procedure) the classifier is supposed to be. SVM is therefore proposed to be the most complex classifier of the ones compared and Ibk the simplest one with its direct comparison technique for selecting the sense of the training instance that is most similar to the test instance. Senseval system implementations of the former are UMCP [10] in Senseval-2 and IRST-kernel [13] in Senseval-3. The latter has been the base classifier with SMU [4,12] in Senseval-2 and GAMBL [13] in Senseval-3.

Specifically we focus in this paper on the differences between SVM and NB classifiers, since those have (previously been proven strong at WSD [4,13]. System matrix specifies that SVM is more 'complex' than NB in its maximization of the feature space margin by optimizing feature weights through iteration on training errors (*Opti+*), while NB makes a one-time sweep (*Opti-*) over training data and weighs features based on distribution of senses *(Prior+)* in training data. Complexity order of configurations of these and other classifiers is more difficult to estimate: for instance, whether SVM's polynomial kernel is more 'complex' than RBF kernel without knowing their performance (see [19]). In section 4, we will be looking whether the *known* system differences materialize in system performance with regard to easiness/toughness of target word and whether we can learn the complexity order of *unknown* system properties from their performance.

But first we will present the OE method in a generic WSD algorithm.

3 Optimal Ensembling Method

In this section, we integrate the OE method in a WSD algorithm (note that this method is also the setting of our prediction tests reported in the next section):

1. *Word sampling to training/testing sets.* Divide the word sample for which you have sense-tagged data (e.g. Senseval datasets [4,13]) randomly into training words (two thirds) and test words (remaining one third)[1]. Calculate case factors for all words making particularly sure that the word sample is spread equally over word space.

2. *WSD base system selection.* Select n strong candidate base systems that can be estimated as mutually complementary or opposite to each other (as defined in Table 1). Run cross-validation (CV) tests on training data and compare candidate system performance with regard to case factors. Then use these formal criteria for selection of two (or three) base systems to ensemble: (1) to ensure base systems are strong enough, select the base systems that have a relatively good overall CV accuracy at all words, (2) to ensure base systems are maximally complementary, select the base systems that provide the biggest gross gain (see Stage 4 for gross gain calculation) and (3) to ensure optimal prediction accuracy, check that the base system strong regions are relatively intact using word space visualizations (cf. Figure 1).

3. *Training and testing the predictor.* In order to make system regions more separable, remove the ties (i.e. training words where more than one selected base systems were within 1% of each other). This improves prediction accuracy considerably. Using the same training run data, use cross-validation tests or trial-and-error technique to discover the best machine learner for best-system prediction (predictor selection)[2]. Then run selected base systems on test words. (Note that in order to evaluate OE you do not necessarily have to develop or run the OE).

4. *Evaluation of predictor and OE.* Evaluate the ensemble performance from *PredictionAccuracy*GrossGain* where *PredictionAccuracy* is correct best-system-for-word predictions divided by total number of test words. *GrossGain* is the maximum gain of OE over best of its base systems resulting from a perfect system-for-word prediction for all test words. It is obtained by subtracting the all-words accuracy of OE from the all-words accuracy of its best base systems. For example, in a test set of two words, if system#1 wins over system#2 by 2% at word#1 and system#2 wins over system#1 by 4% at word#2, then gross gain is (2+4) / 2 = 3% *Net gain* is then calculated as follows: in a two-system OE with 0.80 prediction accuracy and 4.0% potential gain (gross gain), net gain is 0.80 * 4.0% = 3.2%. (We will also calculate gross gain *per word* as an alternate measure, see Discussion for justification of two measures).

5. *OE optimization.* Performance of OEs can be improved in various ways: (1) if prediction accuracy is low, either add training words or remove more tied words (e.g. words that have < 2% or < 3% difference between base systems) while still leaving enough words for learning to occur) or (2) if gross gain is low, reconfigure one of the base systems so that it complements the remaining base system(s) better.

4   Evaluation

In this section we report the best-system prediction experiments we carried out (including descriptions of the base systems, test settings and test results).

---

[1] This is the usual division for training and testing WSD systems in Senseval [4,13].

[2] We found SVM and Logistic Regression learners in their default Weka configurations [20] to generally produce the best prediction accuracies.

4.1   Test Setting

Using the method described in the previous section, we evaluated OE with systems in Senseval English lexical sample evaluations [4,13] and our own systems (separately of course). For prediction tasks with Senseval systems, we clustered systems based on the same classifier (SVM and NB). We trained best-system predictors on approximately 30-50 words (depending on the dataset and the number of removed ties, see Method) and tested the model on approximately remaining words in the dataset (typically 20-30 words).

We evaluated OEs constructed of the following types of base systems (Table 2):

Table 2. Base systems used for different optimal ensembling tasks

Dataset	Classifier	Systems [4,13]
Senseval-2	(N/A[3])	JHU [21], SMU [12], KUN [18]
	SVM	UMCP [10]
	NB	Duluth1, Duluth4 [15]
Senseval-3	SVM	IRST-kernel, nusels, TALP [13]
	NB	htsa3, CLaC1, Prob1 [13]
Custom (Senseval-2)	(N/A)	SVM [19]: c=0.1, c=1.0, c=3.0, RBF kernel NB [11], DTree [16], DStump [16,20], Ibk [1] [4]

As for our custom systems, we used SVM with polynomial kernel [19,20] varying the complexity (c) parameter from (values 0.1, 1.0 and 3.0). SVM's c parameter is crucial since it refers to the trade-off between training error and complexity of the training model [19] so that low c values prompt the SVM algorithm to build a more complex model, i.e. to iterate more over training errors. We also experimented with an alternative SVM kernel type - RBF (Gaussian based radial basis function). Though not mentioned in Table 2, we also ran a number of other types of classifiers over Senseval-2 dataset, especially two variants of NB (*NB-Bin+* and *NB-Eval+*) to compare SVM and NB strengths in their various configurations and classifier properties.

To investigate training input effects, we ran our custom systems with two contrasting types of feature sets (both from a global instance-wide window): 1-grams (i.e. collocates) that are low-volume (average at a few hundred) but high-relevance (ten instances per feature) while sequential 2-grams are high-volume (a few thousand) but low-relevance (three). These are also the two strongest feature sets for WSD [12].

4.2   Base System Complexity vs Tough / Easy Words

In this section, we will look at the ranking order of systems to confirm the effect of complexity (system properties) on different types of words (case factors).

---

[3] For reasons of focus, we are not describing the Senseval-2 systems in detail. Refer to quoted papers for details.

[4] We used default Weka [20] configurations for each of these classifiers. J48 implementation of C4.5 decision tree was used to evaluate DTree.

Table 3. Rank-based ordering of custom systems with regard to case factors and feature set. Order or classifiers has been established for each factor by comparing their performance at easy vs tough words (e.g. a classifier that is highest in totalf ranking did better than the others at tough words as defined by totalf factor). Other case factors were omitted either for showing similar ranking order (e.g. posex and posf compared to totalf) or contributing little to system differentation (e.g .neg*).

feature set	totalf	domall	instperfeat
1-grams	- c=0.1 - NB & Dtree & Ibk - c=1.0 - Dstump - RBF	- c=0.1 & c=1.0 & Dtree - NB & Ibk - Dstump - RBF	- Dtree - NB - Ibk - c=0.1 & c=1.0 & Dstump - RBF
2-grams	- c=0.1 - Ibk - Dtree & Dstump - NB - RBF	- c=0.1 - Dtree & Dstump & Ibk - NB - RBF	- Dtree - RBF - Dstump - NB & c=0.1 & c=1.0 - Ibk

Table 3 shows that strong correlation of 'complex' systems with tough words and 'simple' systems with easy words exists. For instance, SVM tends to be able to disambiguate tough words better, especially at low complexity parameter values (c=0.1). Most complex c value c=0.1 tends to perform well with tough words. Though not shown in the table, decadence of performance when increasing SVM c values (from c=0.1 toward c=3.0) is quite linear. This implies that the complexity continuum of SVM variants starts from the Gaussian RBF ('simple' system) and continues with polynomial kernel variations following the increase in values of c (complex system). Evaluating the variants of NB (NB aka NB-Prior+, NB-Bin+ and NB-Eval+), they also seem to keep their complexity order across all case factors: complex variants (NB-Bin+ and NB-Eval+) work better for tough words (almost equally well as c=0.1) and basic NB better for easier words. Such an ordering around easiness/toughness also takes place for the 'minimal pair' (DTree and DStump), differing only in the presence/absence of *Aggreg* property (i.e. DTree forms an entire decision tree, while DStump reduces that tree to a single decision node per test instance). We found the strength of Decision Stump based systems (e.g. DuluthB [15] system in Senseval-2 and in our custom batch) to be restricted to the 'easy' region of word space (top left corner in Figure 1) in contrast with its more complex ancestor Decision Tree [16] (e.g. Duluth2 [15]) which was better with tougher words (towards the center of Figure 1). Hence, it seems DTree not only seems but is also *functionally* a more complex classifier than DStump and thus suitable for tougher words. These results largely confirm the correlation of toughness and complexity.

Notably in Table 3, we find *instperfeat* (relevance) sorting the classifiers differently than the other case factors. SVM classifiers are strong in the middle range (where discriminative quality of features is highest) but DTree has risen on top (where the average instance occurrences of features is very low). We also found that while in our custom tests with little training, DTree ended 5-6% behind the best classifier, in Senseval-2 [4] DTree based systems were at a comparable level with SVM and NB based systems. In our mind, this can only be because the more volumous and relevant training input was adequate enough for DTree to be strong at tougher words and helped it to a comparable disambiguation accuracy. NB in turn was found very ineffective (no wordwins at all in custom systems batch) to deal with 2-grams (low-relevance, high-volume). It appears that NB works better, relatively speaking, when there are enough high-occurrence features to weight with prior distributions. RBF still keeps its place towards the 'easy' end even at *instperfeat* which confirms its role as an 'easy word expert'. As with DTree, 2-grams seem to agree with RBF better than 1-grams. At 2-grams, SVM's c=0.1 configuration in fact lost considerably to RBF (while both performed equally well at 1-grams).

4.3 Base System Complexity vs Best Optimal Ensembles

In this section, we will further be looking at whether the best net gains (Table 4) are obtained from the ensembling of maximally 'opposite' simple and complex systems.

Table 4. Results from applying the method on selected base systems. For two-system predictions, best prediction accuracies, gross gains and net gains (both measures) per each system batch have been bolded. (CV = selection of best system by cross-validation, VE = equal voting ensemble). All the base systems for custom OEs (3) were trained with 1-grams only. Except in (3a2) and (3a3), predictors were trained with approximately 40 words.

System batch	Optimal ensembling task (gross gain per word / per all words)	Prediction accuracy (most freq class)	Net gain per word / per all words
(1) Senseval-2	(a) JHU+SMU (8.0 / 3.8)	0.80 (0.53)	6.4 / 3.0
	(b) SMU+KUN (8.4 / 4.1)	0.82 (0.65)	6.9 / 3.4
	(c) JHU+KUN (5.5 / 2.3)	0.75 (0.71)	4.1 / 1.7
	(d) JHU+SMU+KUN (9.5 / 5.3)	0.55 (0.39)	5.2 / 2.9
	(e) SVM(N/A)+NB (5.3 / 1.6)	0.92 (0.61)	4.9 / 1.5
(2) Senseval-3	(a) htsa3+IRSTk (4.2 / 2.0)	0.82 (0.51)	3.4 / 1.7
	(b) htsa3+nusels (3.8 / 1.6)	0.70 (0.62)	2.7 / 1.2
	(c) nusels+ IRSTk (4.5 / 1.8)	0.80 (0.60)	3.6 / 1.5
	(d) htsa3+IRSTk+nusels (6.3 / 2.3)	0.55 (0.42)	3.5 / 1.3
	(e) SVM(N/A)+NB (3.2 / 0.7)	0.90 (0.68)	2.9 / 0.6
(3) Custom	(a) SVM(c=1.0)+NB (3.9 / 1.0)	-	
	(a1) single set (40 words)	0.80 (0.63)	3.1 / *0.8*
	(a2) doubled training (70 words)	0.83 (0.63)	3.2 / 0.9
	(a3) tripled training (90 words)	0.86 (0.63)	3.4 / 1.0
	(a4) VE SVM(1.0)+NB	-	1.6 / *0.5*
	(a5) CV SVM(1.0)+NB	-	3.4 / *-1.6*
	(b) SVM(c=0.1)+NB (6.0 / 1.3)	0.82 (0.53)	4.8 / 1.1
	(c) SVM(RBF)+NB (6.1 / 1.9)	0.84 (0.57)	5.0 / 1.2
	(d) SVM(c=0.1)+SVM(RBF) (5.9 / 1.5)	0.88 (0.53)	5.2 / 1.3

Results seem to confirm the hypotheses set at the beginning of this paper. OE built from maximally opposite base systems (task 3d using the complex c=0.1 variant of SVM with the simple RBF variant) has the biggest net gain over the other OEs built out of custom systems (3a-3c). We attribute this to the capacity of the complex variant for disambiguating very tough words that also provide highest net gain per word.

Notable is also that the SVM+NB ensembles (1e, 2e) tend to get the higher prediction accuracy but lower net gains than ensembles built from individual Senseval base systems (1a-d, 2a-d) in the same datasets (1 and 2). This is probably largely due to the idiosyncrasies in individual systems (with regard to training input and classifier configuration) that are by definition harder to define than base systems with known classifiers, controlled input and configuration (as in Custom systems). On the other hand, the resulting gains are low with SVM+NB ensembles because the input provided to them was probably inadequate to discriminate systems in comparison with the more 'fully trained' Senseval systems with more system variability. Also it appears that out of the classifiers evaluated for OE, SVM and NB seem to be the most complementary ones, which naturally adds to predictability between them.

High gross gains tend to correlate with high prediction accuracies and result in higher net gains. This is motivated by the fact that the regions of maximally complementary systems (i.e. ones with maximal gross gain) are easier to define by case factors and thereby ultimately predict their respective disambiguation strengths. Notice also how the more challenging three-system prediction tasks (tasks 1d and 2d) produce comparable net gains to two-system tasks (1a-1c and 2a-2c) which gives hope to reliably being able to ensemble more than two base systems. Training the predictor with more words (tasks 3a2 and 3a3) did improve prediction accuracy over single dataset training (3a1) but not very drastically. In fact, the additionally trained OE was outperformed by another system pair (c=0.1+RBF) with no extra training at all. This is evidence that even a single (Senseval or custom-generated) evaluation set is enough to predict the difference of any two *maximally complementary* base systems (almost) adequately. It should also be observed that prediction accuracies in all tasks exceed random selection baseline (0.50 in two-system tasks, 0.33 in three-system tasks) and the more challenging most frequent class baseline (*most freq class* column) which selects the most frequently winning system in training data for all test words.

5 Discussion

OE seems to produce more accurate ensembles than VE and CV ensembles when constructed of the same systems. We find conducive evidence with Senseval systems as well: for instance, DuluthC system [15] (VE of seven different systems with equal voting) ended with -2% poorer performance than its best base system. The reason for this negative net gain is probably that equal voting tends to either dilute the decisions of *very different* base systems towards average (thus ignoring that one or more of them might be more reliable in a given case) or strengthen the decision of *very similar* base systems toward their consensus decision (thus ignoring that similar classifiers let alone one single classifier cannot be right at all instances). In our experiment (3a4), VE worked almost as well as its corresponding OE (3a1) probably because SVM variant (c=1.0) and NB are neither too different (cf. close placements in Ranking table) nor too different (cf. system properties).

As to cross-validation based ensembles (CV), [1] notes that they often predict an inferior system. In our custom experiments, CV either picked low-margin winners or did not pick winners (cannot tell). This is most probably because cross-validations are run on a subset of training data, which means that the case factor values which would determine the best system (e.g. posf, negf) are then very different. Our experiment confirmed this to be true: CV task (3a5) actually resulted in negative net gain (i.e. not even exceeding base system accuracy). Also, we should note a similar result from a hybrid of CV and VE that participated in Senseval-2: JHU system [21] (using cross-validation based weighted voting of six base classifiers), finishing -1% behind its best base classifier (still finishing first in that evaluation). With such limitations, it can be very exceptional that VE or CV (or even their hybrid) would outperform their base systems. However, results indicate that OE method's base system selection (Stage 2) based on system property matrix could be utilized to select base systems (neither too different nor too similar) for VE.

We also want to specify the justification for two net gain measures (*per all words* and *per word*). The Senseval measure [4,13] for assessing WSD system accuracy uses all-words accuracy calculated from the average of per-word accuracies (or alternatively ratio of correct/incorrect guesses at all words). This basically upweighs high-accuracy (easy) words (> 90%, e.g. *hearth.n*), which do not provide the least differences between systems in OE, since easy words are usually tied by base systems. For this reason, OE net gain per *all words* is a measure (though showing superior gains over other types ensembles) that does not do justice to OE method. This is probably the reason why the two measures do not agree on the winning OE in the dataset. Calculated using the per-word measure, OE in fact provides substantial per-word net gains. For example, if we look at the accuracy for word *drive.v* in Senseval-2 by optimal ensemble (1b), it is improved by +3% from 52% to 55% over its best base system while those base systems did not differ at an easy word *dyke.n* (90% by both systems). All-words method of counting system accuracy suggests that an improvement of that +3% at some tough word (41% -> 45%) is *less valuable* than a gain of +2% at an easy word (88% -> 90%) and since datasets have a lot of easy words, even substantial improvements at tough words are diluted in all-words accuracy. For these reasons we consider net gain *per word* as a more revealing (and reliable) measure for assessing the quality of OEs.

Even per-word net gains may be unfairly low as they are quoted in results table. This is because the words where predictor predicts the best system right are more likely to be the words where one of the base systems has had the *biggest* winning margin (> 5%) and, on the other hand, the predictor is more likely to fail at words with negligible margin (< 2%). These misclassifications are also more likely to be located on the border of base system regions (see Figure 1 outliers). This 'weighting' has not been included in the net gains but for a few prediction tasks, we confirmed this *real* net gain by looking at the actual test words correctly/incorrectly predicted. Indeed, we did find that average difference between base systems in the mispredicted words was around 3% while the average difference in correct predictions was 6%. Furthermore, the higher the prediction accuracy in the task the more likely the predictor is to predict the best system of high-margin words correctly. Until we look into it, we cannot be sure *exactly* how much further net gain these corrections will bring. Nevertheless, we estimate up to +1-4% more net gain depending on the prediction task.

6   Conclusions and Future Work

We have elaborated on a method (presented formally for WSD first in [17]) for predicting the strong regions of any ensemble of WSD systems using case factors readily available for all ambiguous words in any language. WSD system accuracies seem to improve in all prediction tasks evaluated, which gives confidence that it works for any selection of base systems (for some naturally better). The economical benefit is that the method significantly reduces the need to perform computationally intensive and manually analyzed cross-validation tests for each target word separately.

Our main finding is that the simplicity/complexity of classifier's decision procedure (as defined in Table 1) correlates *very strongly* with easiness/toughness of the target word (as defined by case factors). We found that ensembling of 'opposite' systems (in terms of complexity) seems to produce the most successful optimal ensembles (as measured by both both prediction accuracy and net gain). We also found that some classifiers (Decision Trees and RBF kernel) are more sensitive to the *relevance* of features while others (complex SVM and NB variants) are more sensitive to the *volume* of feature pool. Apparently learning process in classifiers differs in terms of lower vs higher learning threshold (either based on volume or relevance), i.e. the point after which the classifier is able to conduct effective generalizations (decision rules) from the training data. Therefore, OE design requires not only the discovery of maximally complementary classifiers for the words but also the optimal matching of suitable training input to those classifiers. Therefore, we suggest that a fully-fledged OE-based WSD algorithm should start from finding the best feature set (using cross-validation based selection method specified in [12]) and then matching it with the best classifier (using OE method presented above).

The method can also be used 'in reverse', i.e. to estimate similarity of systems from their respective performance at easy vs tough words and thus providing a shortcut to discovering maximally complementary base systems for a 'definitive OE' (Stage 2). From Table 4 we see that JHU+KUN (task 1c) and htsa3+nusels (2b) systems, for example, are too similar to be ensembled optimally (shown in low prediction accuracies around 0.70). Case factors can also be used to estimate similarity of systems: e.g. Maximum Entropy or ME is another powerful classifier for WSD [13] but we found it largely overlapping with the strong region of NB in virtually all the case factors. Instead we should ensemble systems from extreme ends of the rank-based table and/or with opposite classifier properties. For this reason some classifier combinations (e.g. c=1.0+RBF or DStump+RBF) were not even considered.

Development of even more accurate (> 0.95) best-system predictors depends especially on correct weighing of the case and system factors (currently the factors are equally weighed). For instance, looking at the higher placements of DTree over NB in the rankings table, we can say that DTree's feature selection property (*Aggreg+*) outweighs NB's prior distribution property (*Prior+*). Also by running the evaluated classifiers on other more feature sets that are particularly relevant for WSD (e.g. PoS or syntactic features), we can confidently expect much more net gain without compromising prediction accuracy. Furthermore, training the predictor with more training words was also shown to increase prediction accuracy (3a1-3a3). Also, by accounting for remaining case factors (e.g. feature quality according to the number of senses it points, see also [1,3,14,17]), we believe it is possible to achieve almost perfect prediction accuracy for maximally complementary systems and to replicate comparable accuracy obtained with two-class predictions (0.90+) for three-class predictions (e.g. SVM+NB+DStump). We should note, however, that at least with Senseval systems [4,13], gross gain does not much improve after three systems.

With such strong correlations existing, more properties should be evaluated to define system complexity. For instance, there seems to be a difference between single-classifier systems (e.g. SMU [12] and KUN [18]) and multi-classifier ensembles (such as JHU [21] and CS [10]) in terms of easy vs tough words. SMU and JHU systems differed in another respect as well: cross-validation based best feature set selection routine was applied in SMU while JHU employed three static feature sets (JHU). In [5] the same type of correlation with different feature selection schemes was found in a text categorization classifier experiment: simple Information Gain (based on overlap of features between training model and test instance) performed better with easier classification cases and the more complex Binormal Separation scheme (see [5] for details) was better with tougher cases. We also want to note the positive effect of extra lexical knowledge (WordNet::Domains available at http://wndomains.itc.it/wordnetdomains.html) and unsupervised clustering of extra training contexts (British National Corpus) as utilized by top Senseval-3 system (IRSTkernel) at Senseval-3 [13]. In light of current findings, we believe simpler classifiers gradually gain ground with increased training.

For most words in most languages, the cost of acquiring enough sense-tagged examples to disambiguate all words in all targeted languages to maximum accuracy (i.e. to the point when machine learning process becomes saturated) is currently unfeasible. Therefore, we specifically want to focus on finding 'tough word experts' for the low-pos*, low-neg* region of word space. Lower grain words (high-domall) should also be focused on since most NLP applications utilizing WSD (e.g. machine translation) require a coarser grain than practiced in Senseval evaluations investigated here. For such facilitated tasks, we recommend 'simple' classifiers trained with highly relevant and rich features, possibly fueled with extra knowledge (lexical or corporal).

As a further step, we plan to evaluate the more sophisticated ('complex') classifiers (Bagging, Boosting, RandomForests, Grading etc. [20]) and their different configurations (e.g. SVM's other kernel types than polynomial and RBF) to find out whether more maximally complementary systems can be found and more net gain obtained from 'specializing', reconfiguring or traditionally ensembling those classifiers. With those additions, we expect to be able to build a highly accurate 'ultimate OE', with maximally complementary custom systems based on performance profiles of base system types divided by the natural easiness/toughness boundary.

While it has been said that classifier performance cannot be predicted, we have presented findings at least for WSD, it seems there is hope still. We believe once a slightly better prediction accuracy is achieved (> 0.95), we can directly compare other systems to each other across datasets (e.g. Senseval-2 and Senseval-3) or even across tasks (e.g. text categorization [5] and word sense disambiguation [4,13] systems) and ultimately represent the regions of all classification systems (regardless of classification task, dataset and language) in terms of the case and system factors studied in this paper. This, however, requires further research across several fields involved with machine learning based classification. At the very least, we consider this paper to be helpful in understanding why WSD classification systems based on different classifiers and inputs can achieve equal results as seen in Sensevals [4,13].

References

1. Aha, D. W. Generalizing from case studies: A case study. In Proceedings of the Ninth International Conference on Machine Learning. Morgan Kaufmann. (1992)
2. Aha, D., Kibler, D. Instance-based learning algorithms. Machine Learning. 6:37-66. (1991)

3. Bay, S. D., and Pazzani, M. J. Characterizing model errors and differences. In 17th International Conference on Machine Learning (2000)
4. Edmonds, P., and Kilgarriff, A. Introduction to the Special Issue on evaluating word sense disambiguation programs. Journal of Natural Language Engineering 8(4) (2002).
5. Forman, G., and Cohen, I. Learning from Little: Comparison of Classifiers Given Little Training. ECML'04Learning from Little: Comparison of Classifiers Given Little Training. 15th European Conference on Machine Learning and the 8th European Conference on Principles and Practice of Knowledge Discovery in Databases (2004)
6. Hoste, V., Hendrickx, I., Daelemans, W. and A. van den Bosch. Parameter optimization for machine-learning of word sense disambiguation. Journal of Natural Language Engineering, 8(4) (2002) 311-327.
7. John, G. and Langley, P. Estimating Continuous Distributions in Bayesian Classifiers. Proceedings of the Eleventh Conference on Uncertainty in Artificial Intelligence. Morgan Kaufmann, San Mateo (1995)
8. Legrand, S., Pulido JGR. A Hybrid Approach to Word Sense Disambiguation: Neural Clustering with Class Labeling. Knowledge Discovery and Ontologies workshop at 15th European Conference on Machine Learning (ECML) (2004).
9. Luo, F., Khan, L., Bastani F., Yen I-L and Zhou, J. A dynamically growing self-organizing tree (DGSOT) for hierarchical clustering gene expression profiles, Bioinformatics 2004 20(16):2605-2617, Oxford University Press. (2004)
10. Manning, C., Tolga Ilhan, H., Kamvar, S., Klein, D. and Toutanova, K. Combining Heterogeneous Classifiers for Word-Sense Disambiguation. Proceedings of SENSEVAL-2, Second International Workshop on Evaluating WSD Systems (2001) 87-90.
11. Mierswa, I., Wurst, M., Klinkenberg, R., Scholz, M. and Euler, T. YALE: Rapid Prototyping for Complex Data Mining Tasks. Proceedings of 12th ACM SIGKDD (2006)
12. Mihalcea, R. Word sense disambiguation with pattern learning and automatic feature selection. Journal of Natural Language Engineering, 8(4) (2002) 343-359.
13. Mihalcea, R., Kilgarriff, A. and Chklovski, T. The SENSEVAL-3 English lexical sample task. Proceedings of SENSEVAL-3 Workshop at ACL (2004).
14. Pedersen, T. Assessing System Agreement and Instance Difficulty in the Lexical Sample Tasks of SENSEVAL-2. Proceedings of the SIGLEX/SENSEVAL Workshop on Word Sense Disambiguation (2002).
15. Pedersen, T. Machine learning with lexical features: The Duluth approach to Senseval. In Proceedings of the Senseval-2 Workshop (2001).
16. Quinlan, R. C4.5: Programs for Machine Learning. Morgan Kaufmann Publishers, San Mateo, CA. (1993)
17. Saarikoski, H. and Legrand. S. Building an Optimal WSD Ensemble Using Per-Word Selection of Best System. In Lecture Notes in Computer Science, Volume 4225/2006, Progress in Pattern Recognition, Image Analysis and Applications, CIARP (2006)
18. Seo, H-C., Rim, H-C. and Kim, S-H. KUNLP system in Senseval-3. Proceedings of SENSEVAL-2 Workshop (2001) 222-225.
19. Vapnik, V. N. The Nature of Statistical Learning Theory. Springer (1995)
20. Witten, I., Frank, E. Data Mining: Practical Machine Learning Tools and Techniques (Second Edition). Morgan Kaufmann (2005).
21. Yarowsky, D., S. Cucerzan, R. Florian, C. Schafer and R. Wicentowski. The Johns Hopkins SENSEVAL2 System Descriptions. Proceedings of SENSEVAL-2 workshop (2002).
22. Yarowsky, D. and Florian, R. Evaluating sense disambiguation across diverse parameter spaces. Journal of Natural Language Engineering, 8(4) (2002) 293-311.

Word Clustering for Collocation-Based Word Sense Disambiguation*

Peng Jin, Xu Sun, Yunfang Wu, and Shiwen Yu

Department of Computer Science and Technology
Institute of Computational Linguistics, Peking University, 100871, Beijing, China
{jandp, sunxu, wuyf, yusw}@pku.edu.cn

Abstract. The main disadvantage of collocation-based word sense disambiguation is that the recall is low, with relatively high precision. How to improve the recall without decrease the precision? In this paper, we investigate a word-class approach to extend the collocation list which is constructed from the manually sense-tagged corpus. But the word classes are obtained from a larger scale corpus which is not sense tagged. The experiment results have shown that the F-measure is improved to 71% compared to 54% of the baseline system where the word-class is not considered, although the precision decreases slightly. Further study discovers the relationship between the F-measure and the number of word-class trained from the various sizes of corpus.

1 Introduction

Word sense disambiguation (WSD) aims to identify the intended sense of a polysemous word given a context. A typical case is the Chinese word "讲" when occurring in "讲真话" ("tell the truth") and "讲实效" ("pay attention to the actual effect"). Correctly sense-tagging the word in context can prove to be beneficial for many NLP applications such as Information Retrieval [6], [14], and Machine Translation [3], [7].

Collocation is a combination of words that has certain tendency to be used together [5] and it is used widely to attack the WSD task. Many researchers used the collocation as an important feature in the supervised learning algorithms: Naïve Bayes [7], [13], Support Vector Machines [8], and Maximum Entropy [2]. And the other researches [15], [16] directly used the collocation to form decision list to deal with the WSD problem.

Word classes are often used to alleviate the data sparseness in NLP. Brown [1] performed automatic word clustering to improve the language model. Li [9] conducted syntactic disambiguation by using the acquired word-class. Och [12] provided an efficient method for determining bilingual word classes to improve statistical MT.

This paper integrates the contribution of word-class to collocation-based WSD. When the word-based collocation which is obtained from sense tagged corpus fails,

---

* Support by National Grant Fundamental Research 973 Program of China Under Grant No. 2004CB318102.

A. Gelbukh (Ed.): CICLing 2007, LNCS 4394, pp. 267–274, 2007.

class-based collocation is used to perform the WSD task. The results of experiment have shown that the average F-measure is improved to 70.81% compared to 54.02% of the baseline system where the word classes are not considered, although the precision decreases slightly. Additionally, the relationship between the F-measure and the number of word-class trained from the various sizes of corpus is also investigated.

The paper is structured as follows. Section 2 summarizes the related work. Section 3 describes how to extend the collocation list. Section 4 presents our experiments as well as the results. Section 5 analyzes the results of the experiments. Finally section 6 draws the conclusions and summarizes further work.

2 Related Work

The underlying idea is that one sense per collocation which has been verified by Yarowsky [15] on a coarse-grained WSD task. But the problem of data spars will be more serious on the fine-grained WSD task. We attempt to resolve the data sparseness with the help of word-class. Both of them are described as follows.

2.1 The Yarowsky Algorithm

Yarowsky [15] used the collocation to form a decision list to perform the WSD task. In his experiments, the content words (i.e., nouns, verbs, adjectives and adverbs) holding some relationships to the target word were treated as collocation words. The relationships include direct adjacency to left or right and first to the left or right in a sentence. He also considered certain syntactic relationships such as verb/object, subject/verb. Since similar corpus is not available in Chinese, we just apply the four co-occurrence words described above as collocation words. Different types of evidences are sorted by the equation 1 to form the final decision list.

$$Abs(Log(\frac{\Pr(Sense_1 \mid Collocation_i)}{\Pr(Sense_2 \mid Collocation_i)})) \tag{1}$$

To deal with the same collocation indicates more than two senses, we adapt to the equation 1. For example, "上 (shang4)" has fifteen different senses as an verb. If the same collocation corresponds to different senses of 上, we use the frequency counts of the most commonly-used sense as the nominator in equation 1, and the frequency counts of the rest senses as the denominator. The different types of evidence are sorted by the value of equation 1. When a new instance is encountered, one steps through the decision list until the evidence at that point in the list matches the current context under consideration. The sense with the greatest listed probability is returned.

The low recall is the main disadvantage of Yarowsky's algorithm to the fine-grained sense disambiguation. Because of the data sparseness, the collocation word in the novel context has little chance to match exactly with the items in the decision list. To resolve this problem, the word clustering is introduced.

2.2   Word Clustering

In this paper, we use an efficient method for word clustering which Och [12] introduced for machine translation. The task of a statistical language model is used to estimate the probability $P(w_1^N)$ of the word sequence $w_1^N = w_1...w_N$. A simple approximation of $P(w_1^N)$ is to model it as a product of bi-gram probabilities: $P(w_1^N) = \prod_{i=1}^{N} p(w_i \mid w_{i-1})$. Using the word class rather than the single word, we avoid the use of the most of the rarely seen bi-grams to estimate the probabilities. Rewriting the probability using word classes, we obtain the probability model as follow:

$$P(w_1^N \mid C) := \prod_{i=1}^{N} P(C(w_i) \mid C(w_{i-1})) \bullet P(w_i \mid C(w_i)) \qquad (2)$$

Where the function C maps words to w their classes $C(w)$. In this model, we have two types of probabilities: the transition probability $P(C \mid C')$ for class C given its predecessor class C', and the membership probability $P(w \mid C)$ for word w given class C. To determine the optimal word classes $\hat{C}$ for a given number of classes, we perform a maximum-likelihood estimation:

$$\hat{C} = \arg\max_{C} P(w_1^N \mid C) \qquad (3)$$

To the implementation, an efficient optimization algorithm is the exchange algorithm [13].It is necessary to set the number of word classes before the iteration.

Two word classes are selected for illustration. First is "花生 (peanut), 大豆 (bean), 棉花 (cotton), 水稻 (rice), 早稻 (early rice), 芒果 (mango), 红枣 (jujube), 柑桔 (orange), 银杏 (ginkgo)". To the target verb "吃" (which have five senses), these nouns can be its objects and indicate the same sense of "吃". Another word class is " 灌溉 (irrigate), 育秧 (raise rice seedlings), 施肥 (apply fertilizer), 播种 (sow), 移植 (transplant), 栽培 (cultivate), 备耕 (make preparations for plowing and sowing)". Most of them indicate the sense "plant" of the target noun "小麦 (wheat)" which has two senses categories: "plant" and "seed". For example, there is a collocation pair "灌溉小麦" in the collocation list which is obtained from the sense tagged corpus, an unfamiliar collocation pair "备耕小麦" will be tagged with the intended sense of "小麦" because "灌溉" and "备耕" are clustered in the same word-class.

3   Extending the Collocation List

The algorithm of extending the collocation list which is constructed from the sense tagged corpus is quite straightforward. Given a new collocation pair exists in the novel context consists of the target word, the collocation word and the collocation type. If this specific collocation pair is found in the collocation list, we return the sense at the point in this decision list. While the match fails, we replace this collocation word with one of the words which are clustered in the same word-class to match again. The process is finished when any match success or all words in the word-class are tried. If all words in this word-class fail to match, we let this target word untagged.

For example, "讲政治"(pay attention to the politics), "讲故事"(tell a story) are ordered in the collocation list. But to a new instance "讲笑话"(tell a joke), apparently we can not match the Chinese word "笑话" with any of the collocation word. Searching from the top of the collocation list, we check that "笑话" and "故事" are clustered in the same word-class. So the sense "tell" is returned and the process is ended.

4   Experiment

We have designed a set of experiments to compare the Yarowsky algorithm with and without the contribution of word classes. Yarowsky algorithm introduced in section 2.1 is used as our baseline. Both close test and open test are conducted.

4.1   Data Set

We have selected 52 polysemous verbs randomly with the four senses on average. Senses of words are defined with the Contemporary Chinese Dictionary, the Grammatical Knowledge-base of Contemporary Chinese and other hard-copy dictionaries. For each word sense, a lexical entry includes definition in Chinese, POS, Pinyin, semantic feature, subcategory framework, valence, semantic feature of subject, semantic feature of object, English equivalent and an example sentence.

A corpus containing People's Daily News (PDN) of the first three months of year 2000 (i.e., January, February and March) is used as our training/test set. The corpus is segmented (3,719,951 words) and POS tagged automatically before hand, and then is sense-tagged manually. To keep the consistency, a text is first tagged by one annotator and then checked by other two checkers. Five annotators are all native Chinese speakers. What's more, a software tool is developed to gather all the occurrences of a target word in the corpus into a checking file with the sense KWIC (Key Word in Context) format in sense tags order. Although the agreement rate between human annotators on verb sense annotation is only 81.3%, the checking process with the help of this tool improves significantly the consistency.

We also conduct an open test. The test corpus consists of the news of the first ten days of January 1998. The news corresponding to the first three months of 2000 are used as training set to construct the collocation list. The corpus which is used to word cluster amounts to seven months PDN.

4.2   Experimental Setup

Five-fold cross-validation method is used to evaluate these performances. We divide the sense-tagged three months corpus into five equal parts. In each process, the sense labels in one part are removed in order to be used as test corpus. And then, the collocation list is constructed from the other four parts of corpus. We first use this list to tag test corpus according to the Yarowsky algorithm and set its result as the baseline. After that the word-class is considered and the test corpus is tagged again according to the algorithm described in section 3.

To draw the learning curve, we vary the number of word-class and the sizes of corpus which used to cluster the words. In open test, the collocation list is constructed from the news corresponding to the first three months of year 2000.

4.3 Experiment Results

Table 1 shows the results of close test. It is achieved by 5-fold Cross-Validation with 200 word-clusters trained from the seven months corpus. "Tagged tokens" is referred to the occurrences of the polysemous words which are disambiguated automatically. "All tokens" means the occurrences of the all polysemous words in one test corpus.

We can see the performance of each process is stable. It demonstrates that the word class is very useful to alleviate the data sparse problem.

Table 1. Results with 200 Word Classes Trained from 7 Month Corpus

	Tagged Tokens	All Tokens	Precision	Recall	F-measure
T1	2,346	4237	0.9301	0.5537	0.6942
T2	2,969	4,676	0.9343	0.5766	0.7131
T3	2,362	4,133	0.9306	0.5715	0.7081
T4	2,773	4,721	0.9318	0.5874	0.7206
T5	2,871	4,992	0.9154	0.5751	0.7046
Ave.	2,664	4,552	0.9284	0.5729	0.7081

Table 2 shows the power of word-class. B1 and B2 denote individually the baseline in close and open test. S1 and S2 show the performance with the help of word-classes in these tests. Although the precision decreases slightly, the F-measures are improved significantly. Because in open test, the size of corpus used to training is bigger while the size of corpus used to test is less compared with the corpus in open test, the F-measure is even a bit higher than in close test.

Table 2. Results of Close and Open Test

	Tagged Tokens	All Tokens	Precision	Recall	F-measure
B1	1,691	4,552	0.9793	0.3708	0.5401
S1	2,664	4,552	0.9284	0.5729	0.7081
B2	874	2,325	0.9908	0.3559	0.5450
S2	1,380	2,325	0.9268	0.5935	0.7237

5   Discussion of Results

Fig 1 presents the relationship between the F-measure and the number of word-class trained from the various sizes of corpus. The reasons for errors are also explained.

5.1 Relationship Between F-Measure with Word-Class and Corpus

When we fix the size of the corpus which is used to cluster the word-class, we can see that the F-measure is verse proportional to the number of the word classes. However in our experiments, the precision is proportional to the number of the word classes (this can not be presented in this figure). The reason is straightforward that with the augment of the word classes, there are fewer words in every word-class. So the collocation which comes from test corpus has less chance of finding the word in the decision list belonging to the same word-class.

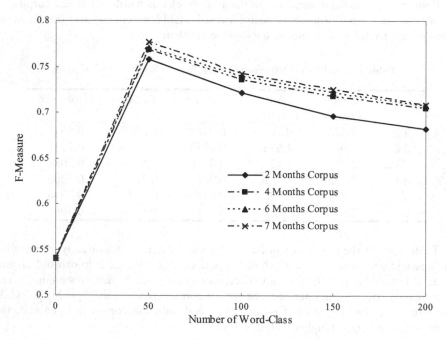

Fig. 1. F-measure at different number of word-class trained from the various sizes of corpus

When we fix the number of word classes, we can see that the F-measure increases with the size of the training corpus. This demonstrates that more data improve the system performance. But the increase rate is less and less. It shows there is a ceiling effect. That is to say, the effect on the performance will be less although more corpuses are trained for clustering the words.

5.2 Error Analysis

Unrelated words are clustered is the main cause of precision decreases. For example, there are two words "牛" (cattle) and "鞭炮" (cracker) are clustered in the same word-class. To the target word "放", "放牛" means "graze cattle" and "放鞭炮" means "fire crackers". To resolve this problem, we should pay much attention to improve the clustering results.

However, the reasonable word-classes also cause errors. Another example is "包饺子" (wrap dumpling) and "包午餐" (offer free lunch) . The word "饺子" (dumpling) and the word "午餐"(lunch) are clustered reasonable because both of them are nouns and related concepts. However, to the target polysemous word "包" , the sense is completely different: the former means "wrap" and the sense of the later is "offer free". It also explains why the WSD system benefits little from the ontology such as HowNet [4].

Although the collocation list obtained from the sense tagged corpus is extended by word classes, the F-measure is still not satisfied. There are still many unfamiliar collocations can not be matched because of the data sparseness.

6 Conclusion and the Future Work

We have demonstrated the word-class is very useful to improve the performance of the collocation-base method. The result shows that the F-measure is improved to 70.81% compared to 54.02% of the baseline system where the word clusters are not considered, although the precision decreases slightly. To open test, the performance is also improved from 54.50% to 72.37%.

This method will be used to help us to accelerate the construction sense tagged corpus. Another utility of word class is used as a feature in the supervised machine learning algorithms in our future research.

We can see that some words are highly sensitive to collocation while others are not. To the later, the performance is poor whether the word-class is used or not. We will further study which words and why they are sensitive to collocation from the perspectives of both linguistics and WSD.

References

1. Brown, P. F., Pietra, V. J., deSouza, P. V., Lai, J. C. and Mercer, R. L. Class-based N-gram Models of Natural Language. Computational Linguistics. 4 (1992) 467-479
2. Chao, G., Dyer, G.M. Maximum Entropy Models for Word Sense Disambiguation. Proceedings of the 19th International Conference on Computational Linguistics. Taipei, Taiwan (2002) 155-161
3. Dagan, D., Itai, A. Word Sense Disambiguation Using a Second Language Monolingual Corpus. Computational Linguistics. 4 (1994) 563-596
4. Dang, H. T., Chia, C., Palmer, M., Chiou, F. D., Rosenzweig J. Simple Features for Chinese Word Sense Disambiguation. Proceedings of the 19th International Conference on Computational Linguistics. Taipei, Taiwan (2002) 204-211
5. Gelbukh, A., G. Sidorov, S.-Y. Han, E. Hernández-Rubio. Automatic Enrichment of a Very Large Dictionary of Word Combinations on the Basis of Dependency Formalism. Proceedings of Mexican International Conference on Artificial Intelligence. Lecture Notes in Artificial Intelligence, N 2972, Springer-Verlag, (2004) 430-437
6. Kim, S.B., Seo, H.C., Rim, H.C. Information Retrieval Using Word Senses: Root Sense Tagging Approach, SIGIR'04, Sheffield, South Yorkshire, UK (2004) 258-265

7. Lee, H.A., Kim, G.C. Translation Selection through Source Word Sense Disambiguation and Target Word Selection. Proceedings of the 19th International. Conference on Computational Linguistics, Taipei, Taiwan (2002)

8. Lee, Y. K., Ng, H. T. and Chia, T. K. Supervised Word Sense Disambiguation with Support Vector Machines and Multiple Knowledge Sources. Proceedings of SENSEVAL-3: Third International Workshop on the Evaluating Systems for the Semantic Analysis of Text, Barcelona, Spain. (2004)

9. Li, H. Word Clustering and Disambiguation Based on Co-occurrence Data. Natural Language Engineering. 8 (2002) 25-42

10. Li W.Y., Lu Q., Li W.J. Integrating Collocation Features in Chinese Word Sense Disambiguation. Proceeding of the Fourth SIGHAN Workshop on Chinese Language Processing (2005) 87–94

11. Martin, S., Liermann, J. and Ney, K. Algorithms for Bigram and Trigram Word Clustering. Speech Communication. 1 (1998) 19-37

12. Och, F. J. An Efficient Method for Determining Bilingual Word Classes. Proceeding of the Ninth Conference of the European Chapter of the Association for Computational Linguistics. (1999) 71-76

13. Pedersen, T. A Simple Approach to Building Ensembles of Naive Bayesian Classifiers for Word Sense Disambiguation. Proceeding of the first Annul Meeting of the North American Chapter for Computational Linguistics (2000) 63–69

14. Stokoe, C., Oakes, M.P., Tait, J. Word Sense Disambiguation in Information Retrieval Revisited. Proceeding of the 26th annul International ACM SIGIR conference On research and development in Information retrieval (2003)

15. Yarowsky, D. One Sense Per Collocation, Proceeding of ARPA Human Language Technology workshop. Princeton, New Jersey (1993)

16. Yarowsky, D. Hierarchical Decision Lists for Word Sense Disambiguation, Computers and the Humanities. 1 (2000) 179–186

Lexical Constellations and the Structure of Meaning: A Prototype Application to WSD*

Aquilino Sánchez, Pascual Cantos, and Moisés Almela

Universidad de Murcia, Campus de la Merced, Facultad de Letras,
30071, Murcia, Spain
asanchez@um.es, pcantos@um.es, moisesal@um.es

Abstract. This paper presents the initial stages of a WSD system based on Lexical Constellations. The system pursues two priorities: first, minimize computational costs, and second, deal with different degrees of sense granularity. Computationally, this model has the advantage of involving relatively low-dimensional feature space, because it runs on raw contextual data. We use discriminant function analysis as it allows us to compute distances between each occurrence and each semantic class; for each meaning, we determine the location of the point (group centroids) that represents the means for all variables (collocational data) and for each case we then compute the distances (of the respective case) from each of the group centroids. Finally, we classify cases as belonging to the group (meaning) to which it is closest. The transition from coarse-grained senses to finer-grained ones can be achieved by means of reiteration of the same algorithm on different levels of contextual differentiation.

1 Introduction

The WSD community has widely admitted to working with an ill-defined notion of what is actually disambiguated. This problem is particularly reflected in two method-ological issues: (1) the establishing of sense classes and (2) the mapping of such classes onto word occurrences. As Kilgarriff (1993, 2006) has remarked, the question of where one sense ends and the next begins remains unanswered. There are no principled criteria for identifying word sense boundaries (Almela 2006: 167ff.). The problem also affects the assigning of senses to tokens. Fellbaum et al. (2005) argue that the inventory model of discrete senses is clearly not adequate for semantic annotation by human taggers.

One of the solutions to the "word sense problem" has been to give up fine-grained sense distinctions and reduce them to the immediate coarse-grained (homograph-level) discriminations. Ide and Wilks (2006) contend that most NLP tasks do not

* This research is financially supported by the Spanish Ministry of Education and Science and by the Murcian Government. The first research project (Ref.: HUM2004-00080/FILO) is funded by the Plan Nacional de Investigación Científica, Desarrollo e Innovación Tecno-lógica. The second project (00481/PI/04) is funded by Fundación Séneca, Comunidad Autó-noma de la Región de Murcia.

A. Gelbukh (Ed.): CICLing 2007, LNCS 4394, pp. 275–287, 2007.

require a fine-grained sense distinction, and that coarse-grained discrimination can be achieved with the help of reliable techniques.

However, we should consider the difference between the requirements of specific NLP tasks, on the one hand, and the goals of computational linguistics, on the other[1]. At the heart of the discussion lies the issue of *integrated/implicit* vs. *stand-alone/explicit* WSD (Agirre and Edmonds 2006). For many researchers, WSD is an intermediate task rather than an end itself. Ide and Véronis (1998: 1) explain that WSD is "necessary at one level or another to accomplish most natural language processing tasks." If WSD is conceived of as a specific component of particular applications, the collapse of fine-grained distinctions may be useful for avoiding unnecessary complications, such as the intuitive bias caused by judgements of semantic remoteness among word uses. This solution is also consistent with Kilgarriff's (1997) conclusion that the concept of a word sense does not correspond to any linguistic item, but to a task-dependent construct. In the context of NLP, it is not only unnecessary but also undesirable to divide word meaning beyond the level of granularity or refinement required by each particular application.

In the context of computational linguistics, by contrast, the exclusive input of coarse-grained senses is an oversimplification, since this strategy consists in avoiding the critical issue rather than confronting the problem, let alone resolving it. The collapse of fine-grained senses does not satisfy the demands of computational lexicography.

In turn, the main concern about word sense division is finding the adequate degree of granularity. This is a contentious issue that pervades the literature on WSD. The still unresolved question of how granular word sense division should be affects not only the design of WSD systems but also their evaluation and their comparability (Ide and Véronis 1998). Besides, the issue of granularity itself is affected by the conception of WSD as either an autonomous linguistic-computational goal or only an intermediate task-oriented application in language processing.

The motivation for our research in Lexical Constellations is to approach the issue of sense granularity afresh, without relinquishing the efficacy of supervised techniques. Our objective is not to discuss the appropriate degree of granularity for WSD systems. Nor do we attempt to adapt the lexical entry and the algorithms to a fixed degree of granularity. Rather, our main goal is to render a single WSD system capable of capturing, representing, and dealing with different degrees of granularity. Linguistically, the design of the system is informed by the semantic model of Lexical Constellations[2] (section 2), which attempts to capture successive steps or levels of

---

[1] In the literature, it has been distinguished between NLP, one the one hand, and computational linguistics, on the other. Linguistic models are applied in the field of NLP but tested and developed in the field of computational linguistics. That is to say, computational linguistics provides a formalizable framework for conducting linguistic research, whereas NLP applies formalized linguistic statements to specific practical tasks.

[2] Originally, the Model of Lexical Constellations was conceived as a way of analysing the collocational span of a node into hierarchical domains of lexical attraction (Cantos and Sánchez 2001). The technique applied was based on the comparison of relative probabilities among the collocates of the word in question. With time, we have developed the initial sketching into a model for analysing the structure of polysemy and rendered it applicable to WSD approaches. Discriminant function analysis has superseded the initial technique for assigning the collocates to groups.

sense differentiation among the contexts of a word. Computationally, this lexical model is implemented by means of reiterated applications of discriminant function analysis (section 3).

This research is being funded by two research projects. Given that neither of them has been concluded yet, we shall present here only the initial phase. In the present paper, the underpinnings of the model are sketched. We will then introduce the algorithm and comment on the case of a polysemous word in Spanish, i.e. *abuela* (grandmother). Finally, we shall outline the plans for forthcoming stages in our research projects.

2 Meaning by Constellation and WSD

The growing concern about the unit "word sense" can be linked with the generalized feeling in the WSD community that change is necessary. New issues should guide the discussion in forthcoming research. Agirre and Edmonds (2006) compare two different "routes forward." The first direction concentrates on the role of WSD in computational linguistics; the second direction focuses on the application of WSD to specific NLP tasks. The present paper follows the first direction rather than the second. Consequently, it is a must for the model to reconcile computational tractability with linguistic-theoretical adequacy.

Our WSD system elaborates upon the Firthian postulate of meaning by collocation, according to which the actual sense of a word is lexically codified in the forms of its syntagmatic environment. Thus, collocation-based semantic analysis provides an access to meaning via surface text. Computationally, the axiom of meaning by collocation has the advantage of minimizing the dimensions of the feature space. The search for disambiguating clues in context relies only on surface co-occurrence data, hence it dispenses with any kind of "deep" linguistic knowledge or enriched feature representation.

With respect to the treatment of collocation in other WSD systems, the model of Lexical Constellations contributes the following development: the correlations between contexts and senses are stepwise analysed into more and more specific domains. This hierarchy is necessary for coping with the complexities of sense-meaning correlations in real text. Linear collocational processing is not sohpisticated enough for capturing different degrees of sense granularity, i.e. for representing various levels of semantic-contextual remoteness among word uses. In other words, the standard treatment of collocation does not account for hierarchies of sense division.

In order to supersede this deficiency of standard collocational analysis, the model of Lexical Constellations applies *semantic feature activation paths*. These represent the structure of transitions from coarse to finer-grained sense classes. The hierarchies of sense remoteness are correlatives of degrees of feature differentiation among contexts.

The linguistic underpinnings of the system can be illustrated with the help of the following examples:

1) We seem to have a breed of unadventurous promoters who can only offer us the likes of Grooverider and Carl Cox, making it difficult for talented newcomers to *get the break* they deserve.

2) First of all, with regard to NAEP, the way it runs is each child takes two blocks that are 25 *minutes* long with a very *short break* in between.
3) A *short break* to The Hague, including a night's hotel *accommodation* and two nights on board ship (LACELL Corpus)[3]

In example 1, *get* refers to an 'opportunity,' while in examples 2-3, the same noun denotes a 'stop to have a rest.' Furthermore, the sense of *break* slightly varies from example 2 to 3. Both include the concept of 'a period of time,' but the former is semantically closer to the word *pause*, whereas the meaning of the latter is closer to the meaning of *holiday*. Each of these three usages is associated with specific syntagmatic profiles. Thus, the collocation *get the break* usually expresses the first sense. The collocation *short break* oscillates between the second and the third reading, depending on co-occurrence with other lexical elements. For example, forms such as *minutes* or *hours* recur in the contexts of the former sense of *short break*, whereas forms such as *accommodation* or *hotel* can be found recurrently in the contexts of the latter sense.

The difference between example 1, on the one hand, and example 2-3, on the other, is a coarse-grained one. By contrast, the difference between examples 2 and 3 is finer-grained, in that it reflects distinct sub-senses rather than separate meanings. One of the ways of accounting for these different phenomena is to include sense 1 in a different constellation than senses 2 and 3, while the latter unfold from one and the same constellation. Each constellation opens up a different semantic feature activation path. Thus, the meaning 'opportunity' does not trigger the potential features 'pause' or 'holiday.' These features are activated only by the feature 'period of time,' which belongs in the constellation of the meaning 'stop to have a rest.' The collocations *get the break* and *short break* represent different higher-level lexical constellations or hyper-domains, and the latter in turn can be decomposed into subsequent lower-level constellations or sub-domains represented by more specific collocations such as *short break* → *minutes* or *short break* → *accommodation*, respectively (see Table 1). As we progress in the semantic feature activation path from coarser to finer discriminations, each additional contextual feature unfolds from and specifies only one of the semantic domains, namely the immediately higher constellation.

The device resembles the *generative lexicon* (Pustejovski and Boguraev 1996) in one respect: it traces the extension of word meaning from underspecified senses to more specific ones. However, the model of Lexical Constellations differs from the generative lexicon in other substantial aspects. First, the knowledge for establishing sense derivation paths does not apply rule sets but is acquired basing on idiosyncratic collocational data[4]. Second, each word sense is described in terms of a prototypal

---

[3] This is a PC-installable 20.9-million word general corpus of English. The corpus was compiled by members of the English Department at the University of Murcia from late 2001 to mid 2002. The design of the corpus in terms of distribution per register, text types, etc., follows a similar scheme to the one planned for the *Cumbre Corpus* of Spanish. The design of the latter corpus is explained in detail in Sánchez et al. (1995) for the early 8-million version. The same design with more data has been kept in later enlargements. Currently, a version of 40 million words can be purchased at SGEL publishers.

[4] This solution is supported by previous findings in the literature. Some studies have concluded that "the types of relationships among senses are more or less random and unpredictable," and that "rule sets for the online derivation of different senses of a given word cannot be determined in any systematic way" (Ide and Wilks 2006: 61).

usage whose area of influence gradually shades into the meaning of other collocations of the same word. A graphic representation of collocations is shown in Figure 1.

Table 1. Correspondences between senses and collocations on different levels of granularity. With reference to three usages of the noun *break*, the table illustrates a stepwise decomposition of meaning-context correlations.

		Granularity level (constellational hierarchies)				
		Broader granularity: hyper-domain (1st level sense discrimination)		Finer granularity: sub-domain (2nd level sense discrimination)		
		Semantic features	Contextual features (collocation)	Semantic features		Contextual features (collocation)
S e n s e c l a s s s e s	1.	'opportunity'	*get the break* ...			
	2.	'period of time' 'stop to have a rest'	*short break* ...	2.1	'pause'	*minutes hours* ...
				2.2	'holiday'	*accommodation hotel* ...
	...	...	...	...	...	...

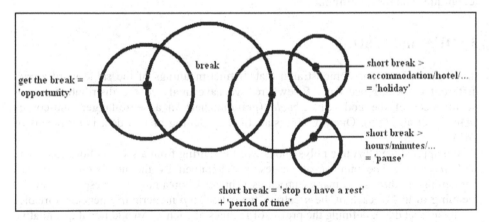

Fig. 1. Sample structure of lexical constellations around the node *break*. The chart provides a graphical display of the same sense-meaning correlations shown in Table 1.

The Model of Lexical Constellations demands a method to decompose meanings stepwise into the senses of more specific collocations. This can be achieved by means of reiterated discriminant function analysis (DFA hereafter). In a first stage, DFA is applied to a corpus that has been *coarsely* sense-tagged. The input of this manual semantic annotation is a lexical entry which contains information about remote meanings. In the next step, each of the coarser (first-level) senses opens up a more specific *lexical sub-entry* which contains information about the semantic variants of each first-level sense. Each of these variants corresponds to a finer-grained (second-level) sense. The sub-corpus with the contexts of each coarse meaning is in turn sense-tagged, and this time the input is the specific lexical sub-entry of each first-level sense. After this step, DFA is applied individually to each of the coarse-grained senses in order to obtain the specific context features of each of their finer-grained semantic variations. Each successive application of the algorithm descends one level in the hierarchy of lexical constellations, thus discovering more and more specific sense differentiation information. Thus far, the algorithm has only been applied to the first level of sense differentiation. Reiterations of the algorithm at successive levels are planned for forthcoming research.

In contrast to other statistical methods used in WSD, we shall not rely on probabilistic methods, such as Bayes' statistics (Duda et al. 2001, Gale et al. 1992, Leacock et al. 1993, Pedersen and Bruce 1997, etc.), which base their analysis on conditional or joint probability distributions of categories and contexts. Our interest is rather looking at the pattern of relationships between several variables simultaneously, which is precisely one of the tenets of lexical constellations: the simultaneous relationship between several collocates. To fulfil this goal, we need to resort to multivariate statistics, in particular to that multivariate technique that allows us to develop taxonomies or systems of classification, such as DFA. In addition, multivariate statistics can also help us to summarize data and reduce the number of variables necessary to describe it.

In the following sections, we shall describe with more detail the probabilistic techniques and the algorithm.

3   DFA and WSD

Previous research has demonstrated that distinct meanings of the same word attract different co-occurrence data. Elsewhere, we have analysed the distribution of co-occurrences of the node Sp. *abuela* (grandmother) in a sense-tagged sub-corpus (Almela et al. 2006). One possible statistical modelling of this data is by means of DFA.

We applied the DFA to a polysemous word w starting from a set of collocational data with n entries. The number of entries is determined by the number of sentences containing w, that is, as many entries as sentences containing w, irrespective of the meaning of w. For each of the n entries, we extracted p numeric independent variables (collocational data), defining the profile of features of each n. An additional quantitative dependent variable is considered with as many categories as word senses w has. This variable is used to assign group membership (meaning) and to define the group to which each sentence (or item) belongs to. The resulting table is of size table $n*(p+1)$, where each case appears with its profile and a group membership assignment.

The discriminant mathematical model will be obtained out of the table $n*(p+1)$ and might allow us to examine the profile of new items (sentences containing w) and assign them to the most likely group (meaning).

When the classification of the items is just between two groups of k classifying variables, a single discriminant function is required. In general, when the classification of the items is among G groups $(G>2)$, the number of discriminant axes is given by $min(G-1, p)$. Therefore, we can get up to $G-1$ discriminant axes, if the number of explanatory variables p is greater or just as $G-1$. Each one of the discriminant functions D_i results into a linear function of the p explanatory variable X, that is to say:

$$D_i = u_{i1} X_1 + u_{i2} X_2 + \cdots + u_{ik} X_k, \; con \; i=1, 2, ..., G-1 . \tag{1}$$

The $G-1$ discriminant axes are defined by the vectors $u_1, u_2,..., u_{G-1}$ respectively:

$$u_1 = \begin{bmatrix} u_{11} \\ u_{12} \\ \vdots \\ u_{1k} \end{bmatrix} \quad u_2 = \begin{bmatrix} u_{21} \\ u_{22} \\ \vdots \\ u_{2k} \end{bmatrix} \quad \cdots \quad u_{G-1} = \begin{bmatrix} u_{(G-1)1} \\ u_{(G-1)2} \\ \vdots \\ u_{(G-1)k} \end{bmatrix} . \tag{2}$$

We can conclude that the discriminant axes are the components of the normalized vectors related to the values of matrix $W^{-1}F$, ordered in decreasing order (the greater the own value, the better the discriminant axis).

As for the contrasts of significance, DFA for multiple groups, that is, when more than one discriminant function is estimated (for example, when there are three groups), calculates specific contrasts to determine whether each one of the values λ_i, obtained from the resolution of the equation $W^{-1}Fu = \lambda u$, is statistically significant or not. That is, DFA determines which variable(s) are the best predictors for the meaning assignment of word w in sentence n. This is done by means of Wilks' Λ, in conjunction with Bartlett's V:

$$-V = -\left\{ n-1-\frac{k+G}{2} \right\} Ln(\Lambda) \to \chi^2_{k(G-1)} \qquad \Lambda = \frac{|W|}{|T|} . \tag{3}$$

The null hypothesis of this resistance is H_0: $\mu_1 = \mu_2 =... = \mu_G$, and has to be rejected, as this would indicate that variables used lack of the discrimination power.

We shall start by defining the classifying variables used. Each of these variables refers to the word-collocate with respect to position or distance to the word we want to disambiguate. For example, the qualifying variable $pre5$ contains the collocate 5 word-positions to the left of the word we want to disambiguate.

Previous analysis and research on the optimal window span for disambiguation purposes revealed that the interval [-5, +5] is more than adequate[5], since it contributes enough information without overloading the volume of the data. This results into 10 classifying variables (5 words before and 5 after the word under investigation).

Due to the nominal nature of the data (words: strings of characters), we converted randomly the nominal variables into discrete ones.

For each polysemous word under investigation, we introduce the data in a matrix with the following features:

---

[5] Unpublished Research Memorandum of the project Ref.: HUM2004-00080/FILO. On request, the authors of this paper will be pleased to facilitate access to the aforementioned Memorandum.

Feature 1. Rows: the matrix will have as many rows as sentences containing the ambiguous word (with all its meanings): $n = n_1 + n_2 + ... + n_i$, where i is total number of meanings of the word.

Feature 2. Columns: the matrix will have 11 columns, corresponding to the 10 classifying variables, plus the discriminant variable, that is, the associated meaning of the word within each sentence.

Previous data preparation of the matrix:

1) Removing repeated items, since they just evidence duplicated sentences without contributing additional information, but increase the volume of the data and slow down the algorithm performance.
2) Normalizing the data of the classifying variables by means of a logarithmic transformation.
3) Computing the mean of all classifying variables; and in order to relate all means we computed the grand mean. In addition, the value of the grand mean will be negative signed in those instances where no collocate occurs (empty position). This is done as a centralization measure and to diminish the dispersion of the data.
4) Removing outliers from the data set; outliers can be a major source of skewness in the data set. Therefore, it is important to exclude outliers so that they do not introduce possible bias into our analysis.
5) Inputting the resulting matrix into the statistical package SPSS and computing DFA: the classifying variables are the collocational data [-5, +5], and the discriminant variable is the meaning, with *rank = number of meanings*. Regarding the prior probabilities, we defined all groups equal, since there are major size differences among the meaning sample sentences. We do also save the discriminant scores as well as the probabilities of group membership. Next, we examine and interpret the following output:
   a. Wilks' λ tests the null hypothesis: that is, among the sentences (population) the meanings (groups) do not differ from one another on mean for any of the discriminant functions. This Wilks' λ is evaluated with a chi-square approximation (values of λ close to 0 are statistically significant and indicate that the variables discriminate).
   b. Eigenvalues: the Eigenvalues reflect how much 'work' each function does in discriminating between groups (meanings), that is, the total among-groups variability. The higher its value, the more discrimination power the function has.
   c. Canonical correlations measure the deviations of the discriminant scores between groups with respect to the total deviations without distinguishing groups. If its value is high (close to 1), the dispersion is due to the differences between groups, and consequently the function is a powerful discriminator.
   d. Cross validation: this technique consists of leaving out an item (sentence) of the sample, re-compute the discriminant function and re-assign the left-out item to any of the existing groups. This reiterative process is performed with all items (sentences). Finally, the total percentage accuracy is calculated.

6) Refining of the discriminant analysis:
   a. Analysis of the scatter diagrams: allow a quick visual evaluation of the spatial distribution of each element, as well as of the centroids of each group (meanings). These diagrams might give us valuable information on possible ambiguities of the data or atypical cases.
   b. Median line box plot: allows us to refine group assignment by means of analysing the dispersion or concentration of the medians.
   c. Box plot of outliers: represents the distribution of the elements of a variable. It is a representative diagram of the dispersion of the elements, and allows us to detect atypical data.
   The elimination of elements is carried out in order to enhance the discrimination power of the groups, with minimal changes of the original data. Our aim is to delimit the set of items around its own centroids.
7) Re-computing a DFA with the same characteristics in order the improve Wilks' λ index and the cross validation. The process is repeated until the results are accurate and satisfactory, and no further refinement is possible.

4 The Algorithm in Action

In what follows we shall illustrate the algorithm performance on an example, the Spanish common noun: *abuela*. The five meanings analysed are:

1) *La madre del padre o de la madre de una persona* (The mother of one's father/mother)
2) *INFML (frec des) Mujer anciana o de avanzada edad* (Elderly lady)
3) *INFML Indica incredulidad o duda por parte del oyente* (Something that produces doubts or incredulity on the part of the listener)
4) *INFML Se dice irónicamente de una persona que se alaba a sí misma en exceso* (Used ironically of a person who praises her/himself in excess)
5) *VULG Indica, irónicamente, el aumento inoportuno de personas o cosas cuando ya hay muchas o demasiadas en un lugar* (Used ironically to express the inopportune increase of people or things when there are already many or too many in a place)

(From Sánchez 2001)

From the Cumbre Corpus (20 million version), we extracted all concordance sentences with the noun *abuela* and classified them according to the meanings above; the resulting sense distribution was the following:

Table 2. Sense distribution for *abuela*

Sense	Counts	%
1	893	94,10
2	32	3,37
3	4	0,42
4	14	1,48
5	6	0,63
	949	100,00

Next,

1) All repeated items were removed from the concordance sentences, leaving each disambiguated concordance to just a window span of [-5 +5];
2) The nominal variables (co-occurrences) were randomly converted into discrete ones;
3) The data of the classifying variables were normalized by means of a logarithmic transformation;
4) The means of all classifying variables and the grand mean were computed; the grand mean resulted into 5.418;
5) The grand mean, negatively signed, was instantiated in those positions where no collocate occurred (empty position);
6) Outliers were removed from the data set;
7) The resulting matrix was input into the statistical package SPSS and DFA was computed (the classifying variables are the collocational-data [-5, +5], and the discriminant variable is the meaning);
8) Evaluation and interpretation of the following output:
    a. Wilks' λ tests the null hypothesis, showing whether the variables used discriminate positively or not. *Table 3* indicates that all variables discriminate significantly (all *sig. values* are < *0,05*) that is, among the sentences (population) the meanings (groups) do not differ from one another on mean for any of the discriminant functions. This Wilks' λ is evaluated with a chi-square approximation (values of λ close to 0 are statistically significant and indicate that the variables discriminate).

Table 3. Wilks' λ. The *sig. values* are all statistically significant[6].

Test of function(s)	Wilks' Lambda	Chi-square	df	Sig.
1 through 4	,307	367,165	40	,000
2 through 4	,678	120,521	27	,000
3 through 4	,847	51,516	16	,000
4	,945	17,635	7	,014

    b. Eigenvalues, also called the *characteristic root* of each discriminant function, reflects the ratio of importance of the dimensions which classify cases of the dependent variable. The higher the values, the more discrimination power the function has. *Table 4* reflects that Function 1 has the most discrimination power (1,213), explaining 74,2 % of the whole variance.
    c. The canonical correlations show that all functions discriminate, being function 1 the most powerful discriminator of all, with a score of 0,74.
    d. The cross validation reveals a high accuracy percentage of the DFA model: 96,9 %.
9) One of the most positive and powerful contributions of DFA is that once the functions are known, we can construct a model that allows us prediction of membership (meaning). This is done by means of the resulting discriminant function coefficients (*Table 5*).

---

[6] *Tables 3-6* show SPSS outputs.

Table 4. Eigenvalues and canonical correlation

Function	Eigenvalue	% of Variance	Cumulative %	Canonical correlation
1	1,213	74,2	74,2	,740
2	,249	15,2	89,4	,446
3	,115	7,0	96,4	,322
4	,058	3,6	100,0	,235

Table 5. Discriminant function coefficients

	Function			
	1	2	3	4
pre5log	,033	,023	,040	-,077
pre4log	-,123	,113	,232	,064
pre3log	,028	,068	-,165	,043
pre2log	,036	-,226	-,004	-,137
pre1log	-,118	,258	-,038	,168
pos1log	,070	-,025	,169	,079
pos2log	,181	-,170	,000	,030
pos3log	,126	-,121	-,037	,192
pos4log	,139	,208	,108	,017
pos5log	,242	,131	-,082	-,212
(Constant)	-4,153	-1,114	-,535	-,666

10) Finally, we get centroids, that is, the mean discriminant scores for each of the dependent variable categories for each of the discriminant functions. We want the means to be well apart to show that the discriminant function is clearly discriminating. The closer the means, the more errors of classification there will likely be.

Table 6. Centroids

SIG	Function			
	1	2	3	4
1	,217	,028	-,025	-,016
2	-2,946	,931	1,169	1,118
3	-9,058	1,075	-1,788	-,464
4	-1,592	-5,075	-1,318	1,437
5	-3,697	-2,053	1,829	-1,089

5   Some Considerations and Conclusions

It is precisely the initial robustness of the different distribution of co-occurrence data (Almela et al. 2006) that has motivated the present study, on the assumption that distinct meanings of the same word attract different co-occurrence data.

Our first goal was to try to model this behaviour in a most economical way. That is, low computer cost and raw corpus data. The starting point was extracting full concordance sentences, all containing the same ambiguous word and hand-sense-tagged the sentences according to the meaning of that word, according to the sense definitions of a standard paper dictionary. This supervised method gave us valuable data on sense distributions and co-occurrence data around the sense distributions.

One of the revealing findings was the little overlapping of co-occurrences among senses, which is very much in favour for continuing experimenting with Lesk's based algorithms (Lesk 1986, Cowie et al. 1992, Stevenson and Wilks 2001, etc.), using real co-occurrence and/or collocational data extracted from a corpus (Cantos 1996), instead of sets of dictionary entries.

A distinctive characteristic of our project is the reiteration of the algorithm at successive levels of sense differentiation. This reiteration is intended to represent various degrees of sense granularity. Each of these levels is represented in terms of a hierarchy of lexical constellations. In the present paper, we have illustrated the application of the algorithm to obtaining sense classifying information for coarser senses. The next step in our research project is the application of the algorithm to obtaining more specific (refined/granular) levels of sense-meaning correlation. Currently, the lexical sub-entries of each first-level sense are in preparation.

All in all, the Model of Lexical Constellations combines some ideas of the generative lexicon with corpus-based techniques of collocational description. It is useful to develop actual senses from underspecified semantic representations. The dynamic behaviour of sense extension supersedes the well-known limitations of static enumerative sense inventories (Fellbaum et al. 2005). However, the extraction of collocational patterns from surface text facilitates a more realistic method than the formulation of abstract rule sets.

References

Agirre, E., Edmonds, P. (eds.): Word Sense Disambiguation. Algorithms and Applications. Springer, Dordrecht (2006)

Agirre, E., Edmonds, P.: Introduction. In: Agirre, E., Edmonds, P. (eds.) (2006) 1–28

Almela, M.: From Words to Lexical Units: A Corpus-Driven Account of Collocation and Idiomatic Patterning in English and English Spanish. Peter Lang, Frankfurt am Main Berlin Bern Bruxelles New York Oxford Wien (2006)

Almela, M., Sánchez, A., Cantos, P.: Lexico-Semantic Mapping of Meanings in English and Spanish: A Model of Analysis. In: Bravo, J.M. (ed.): *Aspects of Translation*. Universidad de Valladolid (2006) 11–43

Bruce, R., Wiebe, J.: Word-Sense Disambiguation Using Decomposable Models. In: Proceedings of the 32nd Annual Meeting of the Association for Computational Linguistics. Las Cruces, NM (1994) 139–146

Cantos, P.: Lexical Ambiguity, Dictionaries, Corpora. Servicio de Publicaciones de la Universidad de Murcia (1996)

Cantos, P., Sánchez, A.: Lexical Constellations: What Collocates Fail to Tell. International Journal of Corpus Linguistics, Vol. 6/2 (2001) 199–228

Cowie, J., Joe, Guthrie, A., Guthrie, L.: 992. Lexical Disambiguation Using Simulated Annealing. In: Proceedings of the 14th International Conference on Computational Linguistics (COLING), Nantes, France (1992) 359–365

Duda, R. O., Hart, P. E., Stork, D. G.: Pattern Classification. John Wiley & Sons, New York (2001)

Gale, W. A., Church, K. W., Yarowski, D.: Work on Statistical Methods for Word Sense Disambiguation. In: AAAI Fall Symposium Series: Probabilistic Approaches to Natural Language (Working Notes). Cambridge, MA (1992) 54–60

Ide, N., Véronis, J.: Word Sense Disambiguation: The State of the Art. Computational Linguistics, Vol. 24/1 (1998) 1–40

Ide, N., Wilks, Y.: Making Sense about Sense. In: Agirre, E., Edmonds, P. (eds.) (2006) 47–74

Kilgarriff, A.: Dictionary Word Sense Distinctions: An Enquiry into their Nature. Computers and the Humanities, Vol. 26 (1993) 365–387

Kilgarriff, A.: I Don't Believe in Word Senses. Computers in the Humanities, Vol. 31/2 (1997) 91–113

Kilgarriff, A.: Word Senses. In: Agirre, E., Edmonds, P. (eds.) (2006) 29–46

Leacock, C., Miller, G., Randee, T., Bunker, R.: A Semantic Concordance. In: Proceedings of the 3rd DARPA Workshop on Human Language Technology. Plainsboro, New Jersey (1993) 303–308

Lesk, M.: Automated Sense Disambiguation Using Machine-Readable Dictionaries: How to Tell a Pine Cone from an Ice Cream Cone. Proceedings of the 1986 ACM SIGDOC Conference, Toronto, Canada (1986) 24–26

Pedersen, T., Bruce, R.: A New Supervised Learning Algorithm for Word Sense Disambiguation. In: Proceedings of the Fourteenth National Conference on Artificial Intelligence. Providence, RI (1997) 604–609

Pustejovski, J., Boguraev, B.: Lexical Semantics: The Problem of Polysemy. Clarendon, Oxford (1996)

Sánchez, A., Sarmiento, R., Cantos, P., Simón, J. (eds.): CUMBRE. Corpus lingüístico del español contemporáneo. Fundamentos, metodología y aplicaciones. SGEL, Madrid (1995)

Sánchez, A. (Ed.): Gran Diccionario de Uso del Español Actual. SGEL, Madrid (2001)

Stevenson, M., Wilks, Y.: The Interaction of Knowledge Sources in Word Sense Disambiguation. Computational Linguistics, Vol. 27/3 (2001) 321–349

Rule-Based Protein Term Identification with Help from Automatic Species Tagging

Xinglong Wang

School of Informatics
University of Edinburgh
2 Buccleuch Place
Edinburgh EH8 9LW, Scotland
xwang@inf.ed.ac.uk

Abstract. In biomedical articles, terms often refer to different protein entities. For example, an arbitrary occurrence of term *p53* might denote thousands of proteins across a number of species. A human annotator is able to resolve this ambiguity relatively easily, by looking at its context and if necessary, by searching an appropriate protein database. However, this phenomenon may cause much trouble to a text mining system, which does not understand human languages and hence can not identify the correct protein that the term refers to. In this paper, we present a Term Identification system which automatically assigns unique identifiers, as found in a protein database, to ambiguous protein mentions in texts. Unlike other solutions described in literature, which only work on gene/protein mentions on a specific model organism, our system is able to tackle protein mentions across many species, by integrating a machine-learning based species tagger. We have compared the performance of our automatic system to that of human annotators, with very promising results.

1 Introduction

Biomedical literature provide a wealth of information on genes, proteins and their interactions. To make this vast quantity of data manageable to biologists and to utilise them in conjunction with bioinformatics methods, it is desirable to automatically organise the free text information into machine-readable, well-defined form. A growing body of work has been devoted to recognition of protein and gene names, and to extraction of their interactions. In this paper, we report our work on another fundamental task of identification of "ambiguous" mentions of biological entities in documents, which we believe has not been adequately addressed in the literature.

We call the task of grounding a biological term in text to a specific identifier in a referent database as *Term Identification* (TI) [1]. TI is crucial for the automated processing of the biomedical literature [2,3]. For example, a system that extracts protein-protein interactions would ideally collapse interactions involving the same proteins, which might appear in different word forms in articles. This

A. Gelbukh (Ed.): CICLing 2007, LNCS 4394, pp. 288–298, 2007.

paper describes our system for identification of protein entities.[1] We summarise the sources of ambiguity and the corresponding disambiguation tasks that need to be carried out as follows:[2]

1. **Term Normalisation** [4]. A protein term may appear in text in various forms, such as orthographic variants (e.g., *IL-5* and *IL5*), acronyms or abbreviations (e.g., *IL5* for *Interleukin-5*), etc. Term normalisation is to "normalise" such variants to their canonical form, as recorded in a protein database.
2. **Term Disambiguation** [1]. A protein term may refer to different protein entities across different model organisms (e.g., *IL5* can be *IL5 Homo sapiens* or *IL5 Rattus norvegicus*). Also, it may refer to different protein entities within the same model organism (e.g., *IL-5* for *interleukin 5* **precursor** or *interleukin 5* **receptor** of *Homo sapiens*). A term disambiguation module resolves the ambiguity and associates the term to a unique identifier.

Our TI system addresses both tasks. Specifically, the TI system approaches the first challenge by a rule-based fuzzy matching algorithm. For the second task, we studied several solutions and compared their performances. The best approach utilises a machine learning species-tagger, which was trained on human-annotated data and then automatically assigns a model organism to a protein mention. If the mention is still ambiguous, a heuristic rule is applied to resolve the remaining ambiguity. Experimental results show that our best term identification system achieved an F1 score that exceeded 85% of the inter-annotator agreement (IAA).

This paper is organised as follows: Section 2 provides an overview on related work on TI. Section 3 describes the data and the protein database that we have worked on. We also explain the evaluation metrics for measuring inner-annotator agreement and our system. Section 4 details our solutions to term identification where we tackle both term normalisation and term disambiguation. We emphasise one approach that integrates a species tagger to help resolve ambiguity, as it performed best in our evaluation. We finally draw conclusions and propose future research directions in Section 5.

2   Related Work

The identification of terminology in the biomedical literature is one of the most challenging research topics in the last few years both in Natural Language Processing and in biomedical research communities. Krauthammer and Nenadic [1] provides an excellent overview to the task and state-of-the-art solutions to it. They summarise three main steps to successful identification of terms from literature: term recognition, term classification and term mapping. As the names

---

[1] Our experiments focus on protein entities, but our techniques should be applicable to other biological entities such as genes or mRNAs.

[2] Our TI system is designed for term identification rather than term recognition. We used a separate Named Entity Recognition system to generate a list of protein mentions for our system to identify.

suggest, term recognition "picks up" single or several adjacent words that indicate the presence of domain concepts; term classification categorises the terms into biomedical classes, such as proteins, genes or mRNAs; and term mapping links terms to well-defined concepts in referent data sources, such as controlled vocabularies or databases. The first two steps are normally covered by Named Entity Recognition, which has been relatively better studied. The third step is essentially term identification, which is arguably more challenging because it involves resolving language ambiguity, where simple pattern matching and machine learning approaches are often not adequate.

Chen et al [5] collected gene information from 21 organisms and quantified naming ambiguities within species, across species, with English words and with medical terms. Their study shows that intra-species ambiguity in gene names was negligible at 0.02%, whereas across-species ambiguity was high at 14.2%. It suggests that resolving species ambiguity is an effective step towards gene name identification. Fang et al [6] reported their identification system based on automatically built synonym dictionaries and string matching techniques. However, their system restricts itself to identification of only human genes.

Recently, the BioCreAtIvE workshop [7] task 1B provided an excellent forum for research in term identification. Participating systems were required to produce lists of gene identifiers for occurrences of genes and gene products, in three model organisms (Yeast, Fly and Mouse), mentioned in sets of biomedical abstracts. Most systems [8,9,10,11,12,13,14] presented in the workshop followed a three-step procedure of term recognition, approximate search in lexicon and term disambiguation. However, they are different in details and a wide range of rule-based and machine learning techniques were applied.

Note that the BioCreAtIvE task and other previous work are different from ours in two ways. First, most of them identify gene names, whereas our task requires protein term identification, which is in general equally important for biomedical text mining applications. In specific applications such as extraction of protein-protein interactions, identification of protein names is even more important. In addition, protein name identification could be more challenging, as researchers observed that protein names tend to be more ambiguous [15] than genes, because protein names a) are inclined to contain multiple words than gene names and b) their naming convention is more diverse.

Second, in the BioCreative 1B task, the gene names to identify were species specific.[3] According to our experience and reports in previous work [5,8], this largely reduces their ambiguity and made the task easier. Our term identification system, on the other hand, tackles protein terms across multiple species, which is more likely to happen in real world text mining applications, where species of biological entities are often not explicitly expressed in biomedical articles.

---

[3] Some researchers did use results from species identification as a feature to help perform species-specific term normalisation (e.g., [8]), although systematical study on species identification has not been reported.

3 Data and Ontology

Our TI system is a hybrid of rule-based and machine learning techniques, some of which require a protein database and manually annotated data. We used a commercial protein ontology, the *Cognia Molecular* (CM), as our referent protein database. It is derived from an early version of *RefSeq*[4] and similar to *RefSeq*, it comprises of protein records covering many species. The TI system assigns unique CM identifiers to ambiguous terms in texts.

We then hired a group of biologists and asked them to manually assign CM IDs to mentions of proteins in a collection of 584 biomedical articles taken from *PubMed Central*.[5] The TI annotation[6] involves linking a protein mention in text to a unique CM ID, where the annotators were asked to resolve any lexical ambiguity that might exist, based on contextual information and CM. They were also advised to pay attention to the species that a protein mention belongs to during the manual identification.

When the annotation process finished, we split the annotated data into 3 folds: training data (64%), development test (devtest) data (16%) and blind test data (20%)[7]. We analysed the manually annotated training data as follows:

1. Correct normalisation (24.3%): Terms are linked to their unique identifiers in CM.
2. Unknown (1.63%): Identification of these protein mentions could not be determined, and therefore were not assigned CM identifiers.
3. Not available in the ontology (2.48%): The protein mentions and their species could be identified but they were not included in CM;
4. Species overriding (68.5%): The annotators recognised the protein names and found them in CM, but they could not find the correct species for them; in which case they were advised to assign CM IDs of the same proteins but in *Homo sapiens* to the mentions and then assign the correct species to it.
5. Experimental proteins but not real proteins (3%) were not normalised.
6. Protein complexes (0.05%) were not normalised.

In the experiments reported in this paper, we only made use of the portion of the data that were correctly normalised (ie., category (1)), because essentially, only protein mentions in this portion can be correctly identified with respect to CM ontology. We noticed that the majority of the data belong to the "species overriding" category, which might be due to incompleteness of CM.[8] It also reflects the fact that protein mentions in biomedical articles belong to a wide range

---

[4] See http://www.ncbi.nlm.nih.gov/RefSeq/

[5] See http://www.pubmedcentral.nih.gov/. The collection of papers used were a combination of abstracts and full-length papers.

[6] The annotation process was aiming to provide high-quality data not only for TI, but also for other text mining systems such as Named Entity Recognition and Relationship Extraction.

[7] Training data were used to train machine learning systems, which then tune their parameters on the devtest data. Evaluation was carried out on blind test data, which were unseen by the machine learn system, and therefore would reflect an unbiased performance.

[8] The CM ontology contains proteins across 22 species.

of species, which further confirms our observation that a species identifier would be very important for real world text mining systems.

We had 5% of the training data double-annotated for calculation of inter-annotator agreement (IAA).[9] In detail, we arbitrarily took one annotation as gold standard and the second as system output, and calculated F1 score for the second annotation.[10] The IAA on this task is 69.55%, which we think is reaonable, given the fact that the IAA on the task of English Word Sense Disambiguation is only about 67.0% [16], where native speaking annotators were asked to disambiguate the meaning of uses of common polysemous English words such as *interest*.[11] We measure the performance of TI in the same way with precision, recall and F1, which are then compared to IAA.

4   Hybrid Approachs to TI

The target of our TI system is to associate a CM ID to every mention of a protein in a document. In general, we approached the target following the two-step procedure of term normalisation and term disambiguation. We utilise a rule-based term normaliser which matches protein mentions in text to entries in CM. If there is a match, then the CM ID of the entry is assigned to the mention. Having multiple matches indicates that the protein mention in question is ambiguous, in which case the term disambiguation module is invoked. We have experimented with a few disambiguation methods and the best performing one takes advantage of a machine-learning-based species tagger and a heuristic rule.

More specifically, our final TI system repeats the following steps until all protein mentions are identified:

1. Associate candidate identifiers to a protein mention, by performing an approximate search in CM. If a single candidate is returned, then the protein mention is monosemous and assign this identifier to it; otherwise, go to Step (2).
2. Identify the species of the protein mention, using an automatic species tagger. Then compare the predicted species to the species associated with the candidate identifiers and filter out all identifiers whose species do not match the predicted one. If there is only one candidate left, assign it to the protein mention; otherwise, go to Step (3).
3. Apply a heuristic rule to rank the remaining candidate identifiers and assign the top-ranked one to the protein mention;

The first step (term normalisation) is described in Section 4.1. Steps 2 and 3 together perform term disambiguation and are detailed in Section 4.2. The same section also describes other disambiguation approaches that we tried but performed less well.

---

[9] Due to constraints on time and resources, we only had 5% data doubly annotated.

[10] F1 score is $\frac{2 \times precision \times recall}{precision + recall}$, where *precision* is the number of correctly identified terms divided by the total number of terms identified, and *recall* is the number of correctly identified terms divided by the total number of identified terms in the gold standard dataset.

[11] The word *interest* can be used for the "excitement of feeling" sense, or the "fee paid for use of money" sense, among others, according to context.

4.1   Assigning Potential CM Identifiers to Protein Mentions

The first step of TI is to assign one or many potential CM identifiers to a protein mention. It is achieved by looking up the CM ontology and matching the protein mention in text, to its potential "synonyms" in CM. The CM IDs of its synonyms are then assigned to the protein mention in question, as its candidate identifiers. Note that this is not a task of exact string matching, because, as we mentioned, names of proteins occur in articles in a variety of forms, including orthographic variants, abbreviations, acronyms, etc., which may not be the same as what they appear to be in CM.

We devised a set of rules for this matching process, based on our observations and previous work in literature [8]. Rules are divided into two sets. The first set were used to expand CM ontology: they were applied to every entry and the generated terms were added to CM. This resulted in an enriched CM with $186,863$ entries, in contrast to the original one with $153,997$ entries. The rules are:

1. Lowercase the item;
2. Remove/Add space between w and x, eg. "TEG 27" $\Rightarrow$ "TEG27";
3. Remove/Add hyphen between w and x, eg. "TEG-27" $\Rightarrow$ "TEG27";
4. Replace space between w and x with hyphen and vice versa, eg. "TEG 27" $\Rightarrow$ "TEG-27";

Where w denotes a token with multiple letters, and $x \in \mathcal{D} \cup \mathcal{L} \cup \mathcal{G}$, where $\mathcal{D}$ are tokens containing digits only, $\mathcal{L}$ are tokens containing a single letter only and $\mathcal{G}$ denote the set of English spelling equivalents to Greek letters (eg. alpha, beta, etc). We can see that this set of rules are employed to capture the orthographic variants of protein mentions.

The other set of rules are applied to the protein mentions on-the-fly during term identification. Each rule generates a variant of the mention and then it is used to query the enriched ontology. The matched entries are then retrieved. Repeat this process until all the rules are attempted. Note that these rules are ordered: if there are more-than-one matches, the matches are ranked according to the order of the rules that generated them. In detail, search the enriched CM using the following queries:

1. The original term as in text.
2. Lowercased form of the term.
3. The abbreviation/definition form of the term, acquired by searching a list of pairs of definition and abbreviation/acronym extracted from the document being processed, using an algorithm developed by Schwartz and Hearst [17].
4. If a word starts with a lower-case letter, followed by an upper-case letter, remove the preceding lower-case letter (eg. "hTAK1" $\Rightarrow$ "TAK1").

The rationale of the last rule is that the preceding small letter might be added by the authors to denote species of a protein mention, whereas the ontology may only contain the original form of the protein without the species indicating prefix.

At the end of this step, for each protein mention appearing in the text, one or many CM identifiers are retrieved from the expanded CM ontology. If a mention has only one match, the matching ID is assigned to it. Otherwise, proceed to the next step where term disambiguation is carried out.

4.2   Term Disambiguation

For every protein mention, the term disambiguation module selects a unique identifier from the pool of candidates generated for this mention in the previous step. We experimented with four disambiguation systems. We first describe the approach that performed best in our evaluation and then the alternatives.

Disambiguation with Help from Species Tagging. As mentioned, knowing the host species of a protein mention can largely reduce its ambiguity. Therefore, we split the disambiguation task into two stages: we first predict its species to reduce the "cross-species" ambiguity. If a mention still maps to multiple identifiers, we resolve the "intra-species" ambiguity using a heuristic rule.

Species tagging can be treated as a text classification problem: a species tagger attempts to classify the piece of context surrounding a protein mention to the predefined categories of species, where a context is often represented by a set of features [18]. Following this idea, we developed two species taggers. The first one is rule-based. We first compile a list of 'species' words, which indicate specific species. For example, *mouse* is a 'species' word indicating *mus_musculus*, and *Escherichia coli* is a 'species' term for *escherichia_coli*. Intuitively, if a 'species' word appears in nearby context, a protein mention can be assumed to belong to the species that this 'species' word indicates[12].

The second species tagger uses the Support Vector Machines (SVM) classifier,[13] whose idea is to map the set of training data into a higher dimensional feature space $\mathcal{F}$ via a mapping function ϕ and then construct a separating hyperplane with maximum margin. Recall that the protein mentions in our manually annotated data are linked to their CM IDs, which are species specific. Therefore, they can be used as training data for our SVM based species tagger. The features we used are contextual word lemmas within a window size of 50 around the target protein entity, where the lemmas are TFIDF weighted. Table 1 shows 10-fold cross-validation performances of our machine learning and rule-based species taggers, respectively. The machine learning approach outperformed rule-based approach by 6.6% on average, and therefore we adopted the SVM based species tagger in our final system.

It is possible that protein names are still ambiguous within the same species, in which case we use a heuristic rule to resolve the remaining ambiguity. After species tagging, if a protein mention (p) still maps to multiple candidate identifiers, we use an algorithm to score every occurrence of a candidate identifier and then the scores for the same identifiers are accumulated. The identifier bearing the highest accumulated score is then assigned to the protein mention.

More formally, suppose our approximate matching algorithm retrieved n synonyms for a protein mention p, from CM. Let's denote the set of synonyms as

---

[12] This rarely happens but, when two 'species' words appear in equal distance at the left-hand side and the right-hand side, we assign the protein mention the species indicated by the 'species' word on the left.

[13] We use the Weka implementation of this machine-learning algorithm. See: http://www.cs.waikato.ac.nz/~ml/weka/

Table 1. Comparison of performance on species-tagging, with machine learning (ML) or Rule-based (R) species taggers (ST). All figures are in percentage (%).

Experiments	1	2	3	4	5	6	7	8	9	10	avg
ML-ST	41.0	69.5	66.4	53.9	47.8	36.8	48.6	68.8	71.9	55.0	**56.0**
R-ST	50.2	40.6	64.2	67.4	52.1	22.0	44.8	49.3	35.6	67.5	**49.4**

$S = \{s_1, s_2, ..., s_i, ...s_n\}$, where each synonym s_i maps to a set of CM identifiers: $ID_{s_i} = \{id_{s_{i1}}, id_{s_{i2}}, ..., id_{s_{ij}}, ...id_{s_{im}}\}$. m is the number of identifiers that a synonym s_i has. Therefore, $\mathcal{ID} = \bigcup_{i=1}^{i=n} ID_{s_i}$ is the set of candidate identifiers that p may link to. Note an identifier in $\mathcal{ID}$ may occur in multiple ID_{s_i} sets. An occurrence of id_i ($i \in [1, |\mathcal{ID}|]$) in ID_{s_i} is scored in a way that, if it is the lowest numbered identifier in ID_{s_i}, we assign it a score 3; otherwise we assign it a score 1. This weighting rewards the lowest numbered identifier in an arbitrary set ID_{s_i}. Then scores for all occurrences of id_i are accumulated. Repeat this procedure for every id_i in $\mathcal{ID}$, where $i \in [1, |\mathcal{ID}|]$, and the identifier id_i that bears the highest accumulated score is assigned to the protein mention p.

The heuristic behind the weight assignment (ie., weight 3 to the lowest numbered ID and 1 to others) is that CM IDs are formed with an uppercase P and digits (e.g., *P00678045*). We observed that the lower numbered IDs tend to occur more often than the higher numbered ones, and therefore the lower numbered IDs are more likely to become the correct identifiers for a protein mention. The next section describes another disambiguation method which empirically proved this observation.

Other Disambiguation Methods. We also implemented three other disambiguation methods. First, as a baseline approach, we assign to a protein mention an arbitrary identifier taken from the pool of candidate identifiers associated to it. The second method is also straightforward. As we mentioned, we observed that the CM IDs are formed with an uppercase P and digits (e.g., *P00678045*). We sort the candidate IDs in numerical order with respect to the numerical part in the IDs and then assign the lowest numbered ID to the protein mention. If this system outperforms the first one, it means that the ordering of CM IDs are not arbitrary and lower numbered IDs are more likely to be the correct identifiers.

We applied a Vector Space Model (VSM) in the third system. In detail, in order to disambiguate a protein mention (p), we represent the textual context that p appears in as a vector of N word features, which we call a 'context' vector, where each feature has an 1 or 0 value to indicate occurrence or absence of a non-functional word. Similarly , we build n 'definition' vectors for all of the candidate identifiers, where 'definition' means description (ie., synonyms, species, etc) of a candidate identifier in CM. The 'context' vector is then compared to the 'definition' vectors using the cosine similarity measure.[14] The identifier

---

[14] Cosine similarity: $corr(v, w) = \dfrac{\sum_{i=1}^{N} v_i w_i}{\sqrt{\sum_{i=1}^{N} v_i^2 \sum_{i=1}^{N} w_i^2}}$, where v and w are vectors and N is the dimension of the vector space.

Table 2. Performance (%) of the four disambiguation systems in TI as evaluated on devtest data, ranked by F1

System	Precision	Recall	F1
Species tagging+Heuristic ranking	64.1	55.5	59.5
Lowest id	52.1	46.4	49.1
VSM	48.9	43.5	46.0
Random id	47.3	41.1	44.1

with a 'definition' vector that is most similar to the 'context' vector is assigned to the protein mention.

The performance of the 4 systems are compared as shown in Table 2. The first system with a species-tagger is in lead for a large margin. Interestingly, the second system that selects the lowest CM ID significantly outperformed the one that assigns random ID. This indicates that the lowest numbered ID in a mention's candidate ID set has more chances to be its identification. This heuristic is used in the first system and empirically worked. The third system that compares 'context' vectors and 'description' vectors did not perform as well as we expected. One of the reasons might be that the glosses of identifiers in CM are too short, which causes the 'definition' vectors too sparse to be representative. There are two possible solutions that we could try in the future: one is to use a better ontology that have more extensive descriptions for its protein entries, and the other is to use smoothing techniques to alleviate the data sparseness problem.

4.3   Results

The best result of TI was achieved by combining machine-learning based species tagging and rule-based disambiguation. Table 3 shows the precision, recall and F1 of our system, as evaluated on devtest data and blind test data,[15] together with

Table 3. TI performance on Devtest data. ST denotes 'species tagging'. All figures are in percentage (%).

Dataset	IAA	ST Accuracy	Precision	Recall	F1	% to IAA
devtest	69.55	75.60	64.14	55.51	**59.51**	85.56
test	69.55	-	65.10	56.42	**60.44**	86.90

IAA. Recall that IAA indicates the performance by human experts on the same task. Our TI system has achieved a very promising performance that exceeded 85% of IAA. Also note that the machine-learning species tagger achieved an

---

[15] Evaluation on blind test data was carried out independently by a third-party organisation who only evaluated the TI system as a whole. This explains why the performance of species tagging on the blind test data is unknown.

accuracy of 75.60% on the development test data, which is much higher than its performance of 10-fold cross-validation on the training data.[16]

5   Conclusions

Our TI system automatically links mentions of proteins in biomedical texts to IDs in a referent protein database. It achieves this in two steps of term normalisation and term disambiguation. The first step involves collection of all potential IDs that can be associated to the mention in question, using fuzzy-matching rules. This approximate searching process found corresponding entries to protein mentions in our devtest data 86.53% of the time. It is highly possible that multiple CM IDS are retrieved for a single protein mention (over 73% cases, as estimated on devtest data). Our disambiguation module resolves the ambiguity by using machine-learning species tagging and a heuristic rule.

One of the distinctive features of our system is that it integrates assignment of the species as an indispensable part, which makes it capable of tackling identification of protein mentions across a number of species. Experimental results have shown our TI system achieved promising results. Note that our species tagger can also be used independently in text mining systems that require identification of model organism,

We carried out our work using a commercial protein database and manually annotated data. In the future, we will investigate the possibility of using publicly available protein databases, such as *RefSeq*. We will also study the feasibility of training the species tagger using automatically acquired training data, hence to make a completely unsupervised system.

References

1. Krauthammer, M., Nenadic, G.: Term identification in the biomedical literature. Journal of Biomedical Informatics (Special Issue on Named Entity Recogntion in Biomedicine) **37(6)** (2004) 512–526
2. Hirschman, L., Morgan, A.A., Yeh, A.S.: Rutabaga by any other name: extracting biological names. J Biomed Inform **35(4)** (2002) 247–259
3. Tuason, O., Chen, L., Liu, H., Blake, J.A., Friedman, C.: Biological nomenclature: A source of lexical knowledge and ambiguity. In: Proceedings of Pac Symp Biocomput. (2004) 238–249
4. Nenadic, G., Ananiadou, S., McNaught, J.: Enhancing automatic term recognition through term variation. In: Proceedings of 20th Int. Conference on Computational Linguistics (Coling 2004), Geneva, Switzerland (2004)
5. Chen, L., Liu, H., Friedman, C.: Gene name ambiguity of eukaryotic nomenclatures. Bioinformatics (2005) 248–256

---

[16] The evaluation was performed by an independent third party. Therefore the test data was unaccessable to us and we could only give the overall score of the TI system but not evaluate the species-tagger, which is a subsystem to TI.

6. Fang, H., Murphy, K., Jin, Y., Kim, J.S., White, P.S.: Human gene name normal-ization using text matching with automatically extracted synonym dictionaries. In: Proceedings of BioNLP'06, New York, USA (2006)

7. Hirschman, L., Colosimo, M., Morgan, A., Columbe, J., Yeh, A.: Task 1B: Gene list task BioCreAtIve workshop. In: BioCreative: Critical Assessment for Information Extraction in Biology. (2004)

8. Hanisch, D., Fundel, K., Mevissen, H.T., Zimmer, R., Fluck, J.:   ProMiner: Organism-specific protein name detection using approximate string matching. BMC Bioinformatics **6(Suppl 1):S14** (2005)

9. Crim, J., McDonald, R., Pereira, F.: Automatically annotating documents with normalized gene lists. BMC Bioinformatics **6(Suppl 1):S13** (2005)

10. Fundel, K., Güttler, D., Zimmer, R., Apostolakis, J.: A simple approach for protein name identification: prospects and limits. BMC Bioinformatics **6(Suppl 1):S15** (2005)

11. Tamames, J.: Text detective: A rule-based system for gene annotation. BMC Bioinformatics **6(Suppl 1):S10** (2005)

12. Hackey, B., Nguyen, H., Nissim, M., Alex, B., Grover, C.: Grounding gene mentions with respect to gene database idntifiers. In: BioCreAtIvE Workshop Handouts. (2004) Granada, Spain.

13. Liu, H.: BioTagger: A biological entity tagging system. In: BioCreAtIvE Workshop Handouts. (2004) Granada, Spain.

14. Morgan, A., Hirschman, L., Colosimo, M., Yeh, A., Colombe, J.: Gene name identification and normalization using a model organism database. J Biomedical Informatics **37** (2004) 396–410

15. Hanisch, D., Fluck, J., Mevissen, H., Zimmer, R.: Playing biology's name game: identifying protein names in scientific text. Pac Symp Biocomput **403-14** (2003)

16. Mihalcea, R., Chklovski, T., Killgariff, A.: The Senseval-3 English lexical sample task. In: Proceedings of the Third International Workshop on the Evaluation of Systems for the Semantic Analysis of Text (Senseval-3). (2004)

17. Schwartz, A., Hearst, M.: A simople algorithm for identifying abbreviation defini-tions in biomedical texts. In: Proceedings of the Pacific Symposium on Biocom-puting. (2003)

18. Ghanem, M., Guo, Y., Lodhi, H., Zhang, Y.: Automatic scientific text classification using local patterns: KDD Cup 2002. In: ACM SIGKDD Explorations Newsletter. Volume 4(2). (2003) 95–96

Unsupervised Discrimination of Person Names in Web Contexts

Ted Pedersen[1] and Anagha Kulkarni[2]

[1] University of Minnesota, Duluth, MN 55812, USA
[2] Carnegie Mellon University, Pittsburgh, PA 15213, USA

Abstract. Ambiguous person names are a problem in many forms of written text, including that which is found on the Web. In this paper we explore the use of unsupervised clustering techniques to discriminate among entities named in Web pages. We examine three main issues via an extensive experimental study. First, the effect of using a held–out set of training data for feature selection versus using the data in which the ambiguous names occur. Second, the impact of using different measures of association for identifying lexical features. Third, the success of different cluster stopping measures that automatically determine the number of clusters in the data.

1 Introduction

As the Web increases in coverage, there is a growing problem of ambiguity, since different people or organizations can share the same name. In this paper we evaluate the effectiveness of unsupervised methodologies that cluster short contexts based on their similarity. We apply these techniques to the problem of discriminating among named entities as found in Web pages.

These techniques are based on the Distributional Hypothesis (e.g., [3], [6]) which holds that words that occur in similar contexts will tend to have similar meanings. Our approach is to cluster Web contexts that contain an ambiguous name such that each resulting cluster represents a particular entity. These contexts are approximately 100 word–long passages of text taken from Web pages, where an ambiguous name is located in the middle of the context.

These methods have previously been applied to discriminating among the meanings of ambiguous names and words, or grouping short contexts based on their topic. Specific examples where these methods have been applied include word sense discrimination (e.g., [11], [12]), email clustering (e.g., [4]), and named entity discrimination (e.g., [10]).

The techniques we will describe are language independent (c.f., [9]) and as such only rely on lexical features that can be identified in raw corpora or Web pages. They do not incorporate any syntactic or linguistic information, nor do they utilize any manually created or maintained knowledge sources. As such they are ideal for Web contexts, which are often not well formed and include many strings that are not typically a part of knowledge bases or dictionaries. While our

A. Gelbukh (Ed.): CICLing 2007, LNCS 4394, pp. 299–310, 2007.
© Springer-Verlag Berlin Heidelberg 2007

evaluation is done with English language texts, these methods can be applied to Web contexts in any other language.

This paper reviews our methods of feature selection, paying particular attention to several different measures of association we evaluate. It then outlines the cluster stopping methods we use to predict the number of clusters automatically, and then describes how these clusters can be evaluated. We then discuss our experimental data and the results we obtained.

2   Lexical Features

A corpus of feature selection data is used to identify the bigram features that will represent the Web contexts to be clustered (i.e., the evaluation or test data). The feature selection data may be the evaluation data itself, or a separate corpus of held out training data that will not be clustered.

Bigrams are ordered pairs of words that occur next to each other. These are selected by identifying which of these pairs occur together more often than we would expect by chance. We compare Fisher's Exact Test[7], the Log-Likelihood Ratio[1], the Odds Ratio, and Pointwise Mutual Information (PMI).

All of these measures are based on word and bigram counts obtained from the feature selection data. Figure 1 summarizes the notation that we use to represent the bigram counts, which are stored in a 2×2 contingency table. Each bigram

	cat	$\neg$cat	totals
big	$n_{11}= 10$	$n_{12}= 20$	$n_{1+}= 30$
$\neg$big	$n_{21}= 40$	$n_{22}= 930$	$n_{2+}= 970$
totals	$n_{+1}=50$	$n_{+2}=950$	$n_{++}=1000$

Fig. 1. Representation of Bigram Counts

observed in the feature selection data is considered a candidate bigram and has a table associated with it. In Figure 1 the candidate bigram is *big cat*. The value of n_{11} shows how many times *big cat* occurs in the corpus. The value of n_{12} shows how often bigrams occur where *big* is the first word and *cat* is not the second. Likewise, n_{21} indicates how many bigrams occur where *big* is not the first word but *cat* is the second Finally, n_{22} is the count of bigrams where neither the first word is *big* nor is the second word *cat*. The counts in n_{1+} and n_{+1} indicate how often *big* and *cat* occur as the first and second words of any bigram in the corpus. The total number of bigrams in the corpus is represented by n_{++}, which is the sum of all the interior cell counts.

We make use of a stop–list to exclude bigrams made up of non-content words. We create our stop list automatically by computing the Inverse Document Frequency (IDF) for each word that occurs in the feature selection data. This is equal to the number of Web contexts in the feature selection data divided by the number of Web contexts in which the given word occurs. Any word with an IDF greater than or equal to 10 is considered a stop word since this means that the word occurs in 10% or more of the contexts, and may be of limited value in discrimination since it occurs so widely. Any bigram consisting of one or two stop words or that does not exceed a given frequency cutoff is not used as a feature. Below we describe each of the measures that we used for identifying lexical features.

Pointwise Mutual Information is defined as shown in Equation 1.

$$PMI = \log \frac{n_{11}}{m_{11}} = \log \frac{n_{11} * n_{++}}{n_{1+} * n_{+1}} \tag{1}$$

PMI is simply the ratio of the observed number of times the candidate bigram occurs (n_{11}), divided by the number of times this bigram would be expected to occur if the words in the bigram were truly independent (m_{11}). The expected value is calculated by taking the the product of the marginal totals n_{1+} and n_{+1} and dividing by the sample size n_{++}.

If the observed value is much greater than the expected value, this means that the bigram has occurred more often than would be expected by chance, and the pair of words is strongly associated and should be selected as a feature. A bigram is used as a feature if it has a PMI score of 5 or above, which means intuitively that the bigram has occurred at a rate 5 times expected by chance.

PMI suffers from a well known bias towards bigrams that are made up of words that only occur with each other, and in fact gives the highest score to any bigram that only occurs 1 time, and where the words that make up the bigram only occur in that bigram. While this is not desirable behavior in general, when identifying significant bigrams this can actually be a positive characteristic. In many cases the distribution of identities in ambiguous Web names is very skewed, and the features associated with one name may dominate to the point where the features of the other name can not even be recognized. However, if there is very distinct bigram that occurs with a low frequency name, it can still be identified by PMI since it will rise to the top even with relatively low frequency.

The Log–Likelihood Ratio (G^2) is defined as shown in Equation 2.

$$G^2 = 2 * \sum_{i,j} n_{ij} * \log * \frac{n_{ij}}{m_{ij}} \tag{2}$$

where n_{ij} is the observed count of bigrams, where i and j are 1 or 2 and are defined as shown in Figure 1. The value of G^2 indicates the degree to which the occurrence of that bigram deviates from what would be expected by chance. Thus, the larger the G^2 value the more likely that the words in the bigram are not independent. Any bigram with a G^2 value greater than or equal to 3.84 is considered a feature. This is the value associated with a 95% probability that the words in the bigram are not independent. This value comes from the Chi–squared distribution, which approximates the distribution of the Log–Likelihood Ratio and can therefore be used as a source of critical values.

Note that PMI is in fact one term in the G^2 equation (when i and j are both equal to 1). However, rather than focusing on just the count and expected value of the candidate bigram, G^2 considers the counts of the other bigrams in the sample as well. This allows for a formal test of statistical significance, which answers the question of how likely it would be for the candidate bigram to be drawn from the given sample, if the words in the candidate bigram are truly independent.

Fisher's Exact Test([2], [7]) computes the probability that an observed bigram is statistically significant by exhaustively computing the probability of every possible contingency table that would lead to the marginal totals that are in the observed table.

When performing Fisher's Exact Test on a 2×2 contingency table the marginal totals n_{1+} and n_{+1} and the sample size n_{++} must be fixed at their observed values. Given this, the value of n_{11} determines the value of n_{12}, n_{21} and n_{22}. All of the possible 2×2 tables that adhere to the fixed marginal totals are generated and the probability of each table is computed using the hyper-geometric distribution as is shown in Equation 3.

$$P = \frac{1}{n_{11}!n_{12}!n_{21}!n_{22}!} * \frac{n_{1+}!n_{2+}!n_{+1}!n_{+2}!}{n_{++}!} \tag{3}$$

A left sided test will tell how likely it is for a bigram to occur less frequently than the one we have observed with the given marginal totals. Thus, a high value of P means that the bigram is statistical significant, since it is much more likely that bigrams would occur less frequently that we observed if they were independent. We can calculate P by adding the probabilities of all the possible 2×2 contingency tables where n_{11} is less than the observed value. Any candidate bigram with a total probability greater than or equal to 0.95 is considered a feature, which is equivalent to the threshold used in the log–likelihood ratio.

The Odds Ratio is defined as shown in Equation 4.

$$odds = \frac{\frac{n_{11}}{n_{21}}}{\frac{n_{12}}{n_{22}}} = \frac{n_{11} * n_{22}}{n_{21} * n_{12}} \tag{4}$$

The numerator is the odds of *big cat* occurring versus X *cat*, where X can be any word other than *big*. The denominator is the odds of *big* Y occurring, where Y can be any word other than *cat*, versus any bigram that does not include *big* as the first word and *cat* as the second word. This ratio can also be expressed as the cross product of the counts in the contingency table, as shown in Equation 4. The higher this ratio, the greater the odds that the candidate bigram is significant. We use a value of 1,000 as our threshold for the odds ratio.

3   Second Order Context Representation

We represent the Web contexts to be clustered using a second order representation that follows from [12] and is based directly on [11].

We create a matrix from the bigrams identified as features, where the rows represent the first word in a bigram, and the columns represent the second. The cell values are the scores found for the bigrams by whichever of the measures above were used. Each row of this matrix forms a vector that represents the words that follow that particular word in the bigrams identified as features.

Each context to be clustered is represented such that each word in the context for which a row vector exists is replaced by that vector. Recall that in our feature selection process we removed any bigrams that contained one or two stop words, so the words in the contexts that will be represented are content words. After the vectors are substituted for the words, any words for which there are no corresponding vectors are removed, and the vectors are averaged together to represent the context. Each context is represented by such a vector, and these become the input to the clustering algorithm.

4   Cluster Stopping

We use the method of Repeated Bisections for clustering. This is a hybrid method that repeatedly bisects the contexts so as to maximize a given criterion function. We have used the I2 internal criterion function, which is a measure of within–cluster (intra) similarity. This measures the distance of all the contexts in that cluster to the centroid, and the goal is to find clusters where that distance is minimized.

While there are existing approaches that carry out word sense discrimination (e.g., [5], [11], [12]), these have required that the user specify in advance the number of clusters to be discovered. This is a significant limitation, since in general a user will not know this number, and in fact discovering it might be a goal of the experiment in the first place.

Instead, we rely on three cluster stopping measures introduced in [8] to determine the number of clusters automatically. These include the Adapted Gap Statistic [13], the PK2 measure, and the PK3 measure. As such we do not need to specify ahead of time the number of clusters that we expect to find, this is determined automatically. We find a solution with 1 cluster, then 2 clusters, and so forth, up to a number of clusters where there is no further improvement in the quality of the solution. Then, we examine the trend of criterion function scores (I2) for these successive solutions, and identify the point at which adding to the number of clusters does not significantly improve upon the quality of the solution.

The PK2 measure compares the value of the criterion function for successive pairs of clusters k and $k - 1$. When this ratio approaches 1, then the creation of additional clusters is not improving the quality of the solution, and should be stopped. The PK3 measure takes the ratio of the criterion function value at k with the sum of the criterion functions at $k - 1$ and $k + 1$. PK3 will be close to 1 if these three values form a line, meaning that the criterion function is still improving, since the line will break at the point where a plateau exists and the scores no longer improve. When using PK2 or PK3, we select the value of k that is closest to but still greater than one standard deviation in the value of the PK2 or PK3 score.

The Gap Statistic compares the observed and expected values of the criterion function. The expected values are estimated from a randomly generated data set that maintins the same marginal totals as the observed data. Thus, this data represents the same population as that of the observed data, except that it is made up of noise. When random data is clustered the criterion function should exhibit a relatively consistent score as k increases, which will quantify the amount of noise present in the data. Selecting the number of clusters reduces to finding the point where the difference between criterion function score of the observed and expected values is greatest. This is the point at which the observed data is least like noise, and the point where the optimal number of clusters exists.

5   Experimental Data

We have manually disambiguated Web contexts obtained from the Google Search Engine API to create gold standard data for five different ambiguous names:

> Richard Alston, Sarah Connor, George Miller, Ted Pedersen, Michael Collins

Web contexts for each of these names was collected in May 2006 using the Google API, as supported by the CPAN module WebService-GoogleHack-0.15. The top 50 html (or htm) pages found when searching for each of these names were retrieved, and any links from those pages to pages in the same domain were followed and those pages retrieved. However, the links on the second level pages were not traversed.

All the pages retrieved were formatted and cleaned as follows. First, all HTML tags were stripped away using the CPAN module HTML-Format-2.04. This data was divided into contexts using the freely available NameConflate program (version 0.16)[1]. Each context contains a single ambiguous name. Note that contexts may contain variants of the names listed above, such as *M. Collins* or *Ted A. Pedersen*.

Each Web context consists of approximately 100 total words, where the ambiguous name is located in the center of the context. Table 1 shows the number of contexts associated with each name, and the distribution of identities associated with the contexts:

---

[1] http://www.umn.edu/home/tpederse/tools.html

Table 1. Name Data

Name: Identity	Count	%	Name: Identity	Count	%
Richard Alston:	247		Michael Collins:	359	
Choreographer	176	71.3	Irish Leader	269	74.9
Senator (Australia)	71	28.7	MIT Professor	41	11.4
Sarah Connor:	150		Wisconsin Professor	32	8.9
German Singer	109	72.7	NASA Astronaut	17	4.7
Terminator Character	41	27.3	Ted Pedersen:	333	
George Miller:	286		Minnesota Professor	255	76.6
Congressman (USA)	217	75.9	Children's Author	43	12.9
Film Director (Australia)	57	19.9	Son of Sea Captain	25	7.5
Princeton Professor	12	4.2	TV Writer	10	3.00

6 Evaluation

After the clusters have been discovered, they are aligned with the gold standard data such that the agreement between the two is maximized. Each discovered cluster is aligned to a single gold standard cluster, and it is possible that the number of discovered clusters will be more or less than the gold standard amount.

The quality of the clustering is scored using the F–measure, which is the harmonic mean of precision and recall. We define precision to be the number of contexts that are assigned to their correct class, divided by the number of contexts that are assigned a class. Recall is defined as the number of contexts assigned to their correct class, divided by the total number of contexts. Precision and recall differ because the clustering algorithm may decide not to cluster a context, and if the clustering algorithm creates more clusters than there are in the human gold standard, the extra clusters that remain after alignment with the human gold standard are discarded.

Thus, the F-measure provides an indication of how well the clustering is being carried out both in terms of discovering the number of clusters, and then in terms of the quality of the resulting clusters.

Note that in clustering if all of the Web contexts for a given name are assigned to the same cluster, the F–Measure will be equal to the percentage of the majority identity in the data. Thus, this serves as a baseline measure to which we can compare.

7 Experimental Results

For each of the five names in the evaluation data, we carried out a number of experimental variations. The feature selection data was either the contexts to be clustered themselves, or contexts (articles) from the New York Times portion of the English GigaWord Corpus. We used the first 25,000 and 75,000 contexts as our two sets of feature selection data. We also experimented with four different measures of association for feature selection, and three different methods of cluster stopping.

Table 2. ALSTON results : 2 identities, majority 71.26

	nyt-25 5	nyt-75 5	nyt-25 10	nyt-75 10	nyt-25 20	nyt-75 20	test 2	test 5
Fisher								
gap	3 68.32	2 **88.66**	3 77.64	3 73.33	3 80.19	3 72.68	1 71.26	1 70.99
pk2	3 68.32	2 **88.66**	3 77.64	3 73.33	3 80.19	3 72.68	41 16.36	25 17.58
pk3	3 68.32	2 **88.66**	3 77.64	3 73.33	3 80.19	3 72.68	21 27.27	10 35.18
man	2 90.28	2 **88.66**	2 **99.19**	2 88.66	2 **99.10**	2 88.66	2 81.38	2 60.45
ll								
gap	4 73.60	3 91.97	4 71.83	3 85.71	4 70.83	5 67.18	1 71.26	1 70.99
pk2	3 90.83	5 72.02	4 71.83	5 67.72	4 70.83	5 67.18	8 60.06	5 47.59
pk3	4 73.60	3 91.97	4 71.83	2 **95.14**	4 70.83	2 93.12	4 71.17	7 47.59
man	2 92.31	2 88.26	2 92.71	2 **95.14**	2 91.90	2 93.12	2 79.76	2 53.55
odds								
gap	1 71.26	1 71.26	1 71.26	1 71.26	1 71.26	1 71.26	6 58.33	1 **72.08**
pk2	5 60.10	5 59.38	5 58.45	4 70.16	5 57.67	4 66.15	5 55.64	5 44.25
pk3	3 50.66	3 65.48	5 58.45	4 70.16	6 55.43	4 66.15	6 58.33	7 46.30
man	2 58.70	2 60.32	2 **90.28**	2 83.00	2 68.42	2 85.02	2 72.06	2 58.33
pmi								
gap	3 72.49	3 69.47	3 77.83	3 72.16	3 78.73	3 71.35	1 71.26	1 70.99
pk2	3 72.49	3 69.47	3 77.83	3 72.16	3 78.73	3 71.35	48 13.58	32 18.91
pk3	3 72.49	3 69.47	3 77.83	2 **89.47**	3 78.73	2 **89.47**	5 64.48	31 8.91
man	2 91.90	2 89.07	2 **99.19**	2 89.47	2 **99.19**	2 89.47	2 88.66	2 83.98

Table 3. CONNOR results : 2 identities, majority 72.67

	nyt-25 5	nyt-75 5	nyt-25 10	nyt-75 10	nyt-25 20	nyt-75 20	test 2	test 5
Fisher								
gap	1 72.67	2 57.33	2 66.00	2 62.00	1 72.67	3 72.22	3 58.91	1 69.57
pk2	3 **79.20**	2 57.33	4 75.21	4 70.16	4 76.73	3 72.22	4 58.91	4 43.97
pk3	3 **79.20**	2 57.33	4 75.21	4 70.16	4 76.73	2 62.00	6 55.90	4 43.97
man	2 **66.00**	2 57.33	2 **66.00**	2 62.00	2 64.00	2 62.00	2 52.38	2 49.28
ll								
gap	2 50.00	2 50.00	28 40.43	7 52.94	13 48.48	2 50.00	1 **70.07**	1 69.57
pk2	3 52.55	2 50.00	3 52.01	2 50.00	3 66.92	2 50.00	4 61.72	4 37.07
pk3	2 50.00	2 50.00	2 50.00	2 50.00	2 50.00	2 50.00	9 50.73	2 49.28
man	2 50.00	2 50.00	2 50.00	2 50.00	2 50.00	2 50.00	2 **51.02**	2 49.28
odds								
gap	1 72.67	1 72.67	1 72.67	1 72.67	1 72.67	6 80.74	1 70.07	1 69.82
pk2	4 56.59	9 54.98	4 48.63	9 73.56	4 53.28	14 73.23	4 61.72	4 37.07
pk3	2 63.33	2 67.33	5 59.65	3 77.24	3 47.79	2 **90.00**	3 61.72	2 48.73
man	2 63.33	2 67.33	2 67.33	2 78.67	2 61.33	2 **90.00**	2 51.02	2 48.73
pmi								
gap	1 72.67	1 72.67	4 66.11	1 72.67	2 68.67	1 72.67	2 63.95	1 69.82
pk2	3 **80.16**	2 65.33	4 66.11	2 65.33	4 62.98	3 78.71	4 66.39	4 45.30
pk3	2 59.33	2 65.33	4 66.11	2 65.33	4 62.98	3 78.71	4 66.39	4 45.30
man	2 59.33	2 65.33	2 66.67	2 65.33	2 **68.67**	2 65.33	2 63.95	2 50.91

Table 4. MILLER results : 3 identities, majority 75.87

	nyt-25 5	nyt-75 5	nyt-25 10	nyt-75 10	nyt-25 20	nyt-75 20	test 2	test 5
Fisher								
gap	2 63.99	1 **75.87**	2 72.88	1 **75.87**	2 60.49	1 **75.87**	6 46.25	2 60.84
pk2	4 61.79	26 27.41	4 49.90	4 49.62	5 54.12	5 47.71	6 46.25	5 43.51
pk3	5 53.23	3 62.94	3 56.99	2 59.09	2 60.49	2 57.34	6 46.25	3 60.14
man	3 **67.83**	3 62.94	3 56.99	3 61.54	3 62.24	3 59.79	3 62.59	3 60.14
ll								
gap	3 43.36	3 43.01	2 51.05	3 41.96	2 55.94	3 46.50	6 52.44	6 38.03
pk2	4 51.17	4 42.03	4 46.63	4 38.72	5 42.54	4 40.15	6 **57.37**	6 38.03
pk3	3 43.36	3 43.01	3 50.35	6 38.31	3 39.86	6 39.45	4 54.34	4 44.07
man	3 43.36	3 43.01	3 50.35	3 41.96	3 39.86	3 46.50	3 **65.03**	3 55.24
odds								
gap	1 **75.87**	10 38.71	1 **75.87**	1 **75.87**	1 **75.87**	1 **75.87**	7 42.57	1 **75.87**
pk2	6 44.30	5 37.69	5 48.18	6 40.92	4 50.39	5 49.61	5 43.12	4 41.78
pk3	4 45.60	7 38.57	3 44.41	6 40.92	4 50.39	5 49.61	7 42.57	4 41.78
man	3 **48.60**	3 46.85	3 44.41	3 44.06	3 44.41	3 45.80	3 39.51	3 43.01
pmi								
gap	2 58.74	2 58.04	1 **75.87**	2 62.24	2 63.99	1 **75.87**	7 50.44	1 **75.87**
pk2	4 50.58	5 48.57	5 52.71	7 51.76	5 54.47	5 49.04	6 50.44	5 50.51
pk3	10 36.36	2 58.04	2 63.29	7 51.76	6 55.62	6 49.48	7 50.44	4 48.58
man	3 62.59	3 60.84	3 **66.43**	3 47.55	3 **66.43**	3 61.54	3 46.50	3 59.09

Table 5. COLLINS results : 4 identities, majority 74.93

	nyt-25 5	nyt-75 5	nyt-25 10	nyt-75 10	nyt-25 20	nyt-75 20	test 2	test 5
Fisher								
gap	5 48.40	2 73.54	5 41.82	2 71.59	3 80.19	2 72.42	1 74.93	1 74.93
pk2	4 61.28	3 44.85	5 41.82	4 64.62	3 80.19	5 60.45	3 **90.25**	5 71.02
pk3	2 62.40	2 73.54	2 59.05	2 71.59	3 80.19	2 72.42	3 **90.25**	5 71.02
man	4 61.28	4 52.92	4 54.60	4 64.62	4 42.90	4 55.99	4 **65.18**	4 62.12
ll								
gap	6 47.86	9 46.61	5 57.96	6 48.59	5 41.92	7 48.58	7 54.10	1 74.93
pk2	5 46.94	6 46.25	5 57.96	5 49.77	5 41.92	5 51.07	6 51.24	6 63.53
pk3	6 47.86	3 52.09	7 48.21	6 48.59	4 52.92	5 51.07	2 **69.92**	4 46.24
man	4 48.19	4 40.95	4 49.58	4 37.88	4 **52.92**	4 39.28	4 52.09	4 46.24
odds								
gap	1 **74.93**	1 **74.93**	32 27.90	1 **74.93**	1 **74.93**	1 **74.93**	6 49.21	1 **74.93**
pk2	5 45.20	6 57.92	6 45.16	6 47.78	6 40.87	5 47.27	6 49.21	5 55.89
pk3	4 55.99	8 52.01	4 42.62	4 44.29	9 43.69	6 35.16	6 49.21	5 55.89
man	4 **55.99**	4 45.40	4 42.62	4 44.29	4 49.30	4 44.57	4 36.49	4 51.53
pmi								
gap	3 71.03	3 45.13	3 64.35	3 43.73	5 50.38	4 52.92	1 74.93	1 74.93
pk2	5 42.94	5 53.89	5 50.84	5 57.01	5 50.38	4 52.92	5 55.95	5 59.41
pk3	3 71.03	5 53.89	5 50.84	5 57.01	5 50.38	9 57.20	4 **75.21**	4 55.99
man	4 57.38	4 52.09	4 64.35	4 50.70	4 45.96	4 52.92	4 **75.21**	4 55.99

Table 6. PEDERSEN results : 4 identities, majority 76.58

	nyt-25 5	nyt-75 5	nyt-25 10	nyt-75 10	nyt-25 20	nyt-75 20	test 2	test 5
Fisher								
gap	3 47.75	2 47.15	2 63.66	2 55.56	3 60.96	3 42.94	1 **76.58**	1 **76.58**
pk2	5 43.69	3 42.34	5 48.15	4 35.74	3 60.96	4 35.74	5 56.12	7 53.83
pk3	5 43.69	2 47.15	2 63.66	2 55.56	3 60.96	3 42.94	3 43.84	9 51.05
man	4 40.54	4 41.44	4 **45.05**	4 35.74	4 38.74	4 35.74	4 43.24	4 37.84
ll								
gap	2 69.97	8 41.78	2 54.65	3 45.95	2 49.25	3 51.05	1 **76.58**	1 **76.58**
pk2	5 45.98	6 35.19	5 52.97	6 46.45	5 48.61	6 42.88	5 50.99	6 46.84
pk3	2 69.97	6 35.19	2 54.65	6 46.45	2 49.25	3 51.05	7 62.97	8 47.45
man	4 52.85	4 42.04	4 **60.66**	4 40.24	4 55.86	4 51.05	4 46.55	4 49.25
odds								
gap	1 **76.58**	1 **76.58**	1 **76.58**	1 **76.58**	1 **76.58**	1 **76.58**	1 **76.58**	1 **76.58**
pk2	5 32.01	5 50.00	5 32.00	5 40.20	5 40.89	5 32.41	5 45.44	5 48.40
pk3	4 43.54	5 50.00	3 58.26	3 39.94	5 40.89	5 32.41	7 45.44	5 48.40
man	4 43.54	4 **44.74**	4 42.34	4 39.94	4 38.44	4 41.74	4 42.64	4 42.34
pmi								
gap	3 46.55	3 45.05	2 46.85	2 45.35	2 63.36	2 45.95	1 **76.58**	1 **76.58**
pk2	4 42.04	4 40.84	4 49.55	4 41.14	4 38.14	3 43.54	6 62.41	6 47.54
pk3	3 46.55	2 45.05	3 49.55	4 41.14	2 63.36	4 42.94	2 64.86	5 46.05
man	4 42.04	4 40.84	4 49.55	4 41.14	4 38.14	4 42.94	4 45.05	4 **55.26**

The results of our experiments are shown in Tables 2, 3, 4, 5, and 6. Each table is organized as follows. The feature selection data is indicated in the columns: nyt-25 and nyt-75 refer to the 25,000 and 75,000 context collections from the New York Times, and *test* refers to the use of the evaluation data as feature selection data. The numbers below the feature selection data are the frequency cutoffs used. Remember that these indicate that the words that make up a bigram feature must have occurred at least that many times in the feature selection data.

The measures of association and the cluster stopping techniques are shown in the rows. Note that *man* refers to when we set the number of clusters manually to the value that we know to be correct. The integer values in the table are the number of clusters predicted by the cluster stopping method, and the F-Measure obtained with the given combination of settings.

8   Discussion and Conclusions

For each measure of association in our tables of results, we indicate the highest F–Measure attained by the cluster stopping measures (gap, pk2, pk3) and the manually set number of clusters (man). These values are shown in bold face. It would seem that the manual setting of the same number of clusters as is found in the gold standard data should be the best case scenario. However, we can see a number of cases where the discovered number of clusters results in a better

F–Measure even if the number of clusters discovered does not agree with the evaluation data. This can occur because the evaluation data is rather skewed and some of the very small classes are difficult to discover and overall results may improve simply by ignoring those classes.

Across all of the names, we observe that the results based on using the held–out set of training data tend to be somewhat better than those based on using the evaluation data for feature selection. It may be that the evaluation data is simply not large enough to provide a reasonable set of features to perform discrimination.

We can see that for the Alston, Connor, and Collins results there are combinations of settings that result in F–Measures significantly higher than the majority class. However, for the Miller and Pedersen results no combination of settings exceeds that majority class. This initially surprised us since both of these names have fairly distinct senses. However, upon examining the features we found that the contexts for the majority classes were extremely rich in text, while the minority sense were somewhat impoverished. Thus, no matter what kind of feature identification techniques were employed, it was simply not possible to identify features for any of the minority classes.

In general there is not a clearly superior measure of association for all five of the names. In the Alston data the log–likelihood ratio achieved the highest results, in the Connor data it was Pointwise Mutual Information, and in the Collins data it was Fisher's Exact Test. For the Miller and Pedersen data none of the measures of association fared particularly well.

Among the cluster stopping methods, the Adapted Gap Statistic did somewhat better with the more difficult Pedersen and Miller data since it often predicted just one cluster, which results in an F–Measure equal to the majority class. In the case of a hard discrimination decision, this is actually not a bad option, since in effect the cluster stopping algorithm is saying it is unable to make any distinctions so it leaves all the contexts in the same cluster. With the Alston, Connor, and Miller data in general PK2 and PK3 performed slightly better than the Adapted Gap Statistic.

Acknowledgments

This work was supported by a National Science Foundation Faculty Early CAREER Development Award (#0092784).

All of the experiments in this paper were carried out with version 0.95 of the SenseClusters package, freely available from http://senseclusters.sourceforge.net.

References

1. T. Dunning. Accurate methods for the statistics of surprise and coincidence. *Computational Linguistics*, 19(1):61–74, 1993.
2. R. Fisher. *The Design of Experiments*. Oliver and Boyd, London, 1935.
3. Z. Harris. *Mathematical Structures of Language*. Wiley, New York, 1968.

4. A. Kulkarni and T. Pedersen. Name discrimination and email clustering using unsupervised clustering and labeling of similar contexts. In *Proceedings of the Second Indian International Conference on Artificial Intelligence*, pages 703–722, Pune, India, December 2005.

5. E. Levin, M. Sharifi, and J. Ball. Evaluation of utility of LSA for word sense discrimination. In *Proceedings of the Human Language Technology Conference of the NAACL, Companion Volume: Short Papers*, pages 77–80, New York City, June 2006.

6. G.A. Miller and W.G. Charles. Contextual correlates of semantic similarity. *Language and Cognitive Processes*, 6(1):1–28, 1991.

7. T. Pedersen. Fishing for exactness. In *Proceedings of the South Central SAS User's Group (SCSUG-96) Conference*, pages 188–200, Austin, TX, October 1996.

8. T. Pedersen and A. Kulkarni. Selecting the right number of senses based on clustering criterion functions. In *Proceedings of the Posters and Demo Program of the Eleventh Conference of the European Chapter of the Association for Computational Linguistics*, pages 111–114, Trento, Italy, April 2006.

9. T. Pedersen, A. Kulkarni, R. Angheluta, Z. Kozareva, and T. Solorio. An unsupervised language independent method of name discrimination using second order co-occurrence features. In *Proceedings of the Seventh International Conference on Intelligent Text Processing and Computational Linguistics*, pages 208–222, Mexico City, February 2006.

10. T. Pedersen, A. Purandare, and A. Kulkarni. Name discrimination by clustering similar contexts. In *Proceedings of the Sixth International Conference on Intelligent Text Processing and Computational Linguistics*, pages 220–231, Mexico City, February 2005.

11. A. Purandare and T. Pedersen. Word sense discrimination by clustering contexts in vector and similarity spaces. In *Proceedings of the Conference on Computational Natural Language Learning*, pages 41–48, Boston, MA, 2004.

12. H. Schütze. Automatic word sense discrimination. *Computational Linguistics*, 24(1):97–123, 1998.

13. R. Tibshirani, G. Walther, and T. Hastie. Estimating the number of clusters in a dataset via the Gap statistic. *Journal of the Royal Statistics Society (Series B)*, pages 411–423, 2001.

Learning for Semantic Parsing

Raymond J. Mooney

Department of Computer Sciences, University of Texas at Austin
1 University Station C0500, Austin, TX 78712-0233, USA
mooney@cs.utexas.edu

Abstract. Semantic parsing is the task of mapping a natural language
sentence into a complete, formal meaning representation. Over the past
decade, we have developed a number of machine learning methods for inducing semantic parsers by training on a corpus of sentences paired with
their meaning representations in a specified formal language. We have
demonstrated these methods on the automated construction of natural-
language interfaces to databases and robot command languages. This
paper reviews our prior work on this topic and discusses directions for
future research.

1 Introduction

Semantic parsing is the task of mapping a natural language (NL) sentence into
a complete, formal *meaning representation* (MR) or logical form. A *meaning
representation language* (MRL) is a formal unambiguous language that allows
for automated inference and processing, such as first-order predicate logic. In
particular, our research has focused on applications in which the MRL is "executable" and can be directly used by another program to perform some task
such as answering questions from a database or controlling the actions of a real
or simulated robot. This distinguishes the task from related tasks such as semantic role labeling [8] and other forms of "shallow" semantic parsing which do
not generate complete, formal representations.

Over the past decade, we have developed a number of systems for learning
parsers that map NL sentences to a pre-specified MRL [44,35,37,24,17,39,23].
Given a training corpus of sentences annotated with their correct semantic interpretation in a given MRL, the goal of these systems is to induce an efficient
and accurate semantic parser that can map novel sentences into this MRL. Some
of the systems require extra training input in addition to (NL, MR) pairs, such
as syntactic parse trees or semantically annotated parse trees.

In this paper, we first describe the applications we have explored and their
corresponding MRLs, and then review the parsing and learning systems that we
have already developed for these applications, along with experimental results
on their performance. We then discuss important areas for future research in
learning for semantic parsing.

A. Gelbukh (Ed.): CICLing 2007, LNCS 4394, pp. 311–324, 2007.
© Springer-Verlag Berlin Heidelberg 2007

2   Sample Applications and Their MRLs

We have previously considered two MRLs for performing useful, complex tasks. The first is a database query language, primarily using a sample database on U.S. geography. The second MRL is a coaching language for robotic soccer developed for the RoboCup Coach Competition, in which AI researchers compete to provide effective instructions to a coachable team of agents in a simulated soccer domain [9].

When exploring NL interfaces for databases, the MRL we have primarily used is a logical query language based on Prolog. We have primarily focused on queries to a small database on U.S. geography. This domain, GEOQUERY, was originally chosen to test corpus-based semantic parsing due to the availability of a hand-built natural-language interface, GEOBASE, supplied with Turbo Prolog 2.0 [3]. The language consists of Prolog queries augmented with several meta-predicates [44]. Below is a sample query with its English gloss:

`answer(A,count(B,(state(B),const(C,riverid(mississippi)),traverse(C,B)),A))`

"How many states does the Mississippi run through?"

The same query language has also been used to build NLI's for databases of restaurants and CS-job openings, including a component that translates our logical queries to standard SQL database queries [36,35]. The resulting formal queries can be executed to generate answers to the corresponding questions.

RoboCup (`www.robocup.org`) is an international AI research initiative using robotic soccer as its primary domain. In the Coach Competition, teams of agents compete on a simulated soccer field and receive advice from a team coach in a formal language called CLANG. In CLANG, tactics and behaviors are expressed in terms of if-then rules. As described in [9], its grammar consists of 37 non-terminal symbols and 133 productions. Below is a sample rule with its English gloss:

`((bpos (penalty-area our))  (do (player-except our {4}) (pos (half our))))`

"If the ball is in our penalty area, all our players except player 4 should stay in our half."

The robots in the simulator can interpret the CLANG instructions which then strongly affect their behavior while playing the game. The semantic parsers we have developed for this MRL were part of a larger research project on advice-taking reinforcement learners that can accept advice stated in natural language [25].

3   Systems for Learning Semantic Parsers

Our earliest system for learning semantic parsers called CHILL [44,35] uses Inductive Logic Programming (ILP) [26] to learn a deterministic parser written in Prolog. In our more recent work, we have developed three different approaches

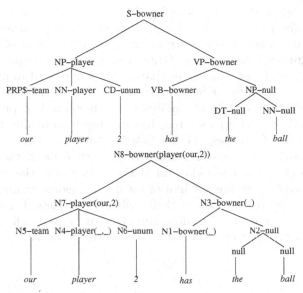

Fig. 1. The SAPT and its Compositional MR Construction for a CLANG Sentence

to learning statistical semantic parsers that are more robust and scale more effectively to larger training sets. Each exploits a different advanced technology in statistical natural language processing. SCISSOR [17,18] adds detailed semantics to a state-of-the-art statistical syntactic parser (i.e. the Collins parser [12]), WASP [39] adapts statistical machine translation methods to map from NL to MRL, and KRISP [23] uses Support Vector Machines (SVM's) [13] with a subsequence kernel specialized for text learning [27]. We briefly review each of these systems below. A version of our GEOQUERY data has also been used to evaluate a system for learning semantic parsers using probabilistic Combinatorial Categorial Grammars (CCG) [45].

3.1 SCISSOR

SCISSOR (Semantic Composition that Integrates Syntax and Semantics to get Optimal Representations) [17,18] learns a statistical parser that generates a *semantically augmented parse tree* (SAPT), in which each internal node is given both a syntactic and a semantic label. We augment Collins' head-driven model 2 [12] to incorporate a semantic label on each internal node. By integrating syntactic and semantic interpretation into a single statistical model and finding the globally most probable parse, an accurate combined analysis can be obtained. Once an SAPT is generated, an additional step is required to translate it into a final MR.

In an SAPT, each internal node in the parse tree is annotated with a semantic label from the MRL. The left half of Fig. 1 shows the SAPT for a simple sentence in the CLANG domain. The semantic labels (shown after the dashes) are *concepts* in the MRL. Some *type concepts* do not take arguments, like *team* and *unum* (uniform number). Some concepts, referred to as *predicates*, take an ordered list of arguments, like *player* and *bowner* (ball owner). Each predicate has a set of known semantic constraints on its arguments, specified in terms of concepts that can fill each argument, such as *player(team, unum)* and *bowner(player)*. A special semantic label *null* is used for nodes that do not correspond to any concept in the domain. Training data for SCISSOR consists of (NL, SAPT, MR) triples.

First, an enhanced version of Collin's parser is trained to produce SAPTs instead of purely syntactic parse trees by adapting it to predict two labels for each node instead of one (see [17] for details). Next, a recursive procedure is used to compositionally construct the MR for each node in the SAPT given the MRs of its children. The right half of Fig. 1 illustrates the construction of the MR for the SAPT in the left half of the figure (nodes are numbered in the order in which the construction of their MRs are completed). In this process, semantic constraints are used to determine how to properly fill the arguments of a predicate for a node with the MRs of the node's children.

3.2 WASP

WASP (Word Alignment-based Semantic Parsing) [39] uses state-of-the-art Statistical Machine Translation (SMT) techniques [4,5,41,10] to learn semantic parsers. SMT methods learn effective machine translation systems by training on *parallel corpora* consisting of human translations of documents into one or more alternative natural languages. The resulting translators are typically significantly more effective than manually developed systems and SMT has become the dominant approach to machine translation. We have adapted such methods to learn to translate from NL to MRL rather than from one NL to another.

WASP requires no prior knowledge of the NL syntax, although it assumes that an unambiguous, context-free grammar (CFG) of the target MRL is available. Since MRLs are formal computer-interpretable languages, such a grammar is usually easily available. First, an SMT word alignment system, GIZA++ [28,5], is used to acquire a bilingual lexicon consisting of NL substrings coupled with their translations in the target MRL. As formal languages, MRLs frequently contain many purely syntactic tokens such as parentheses or brackets, which are difficult to align with words in NL. Consequently, we found it was much more effective to align words in the NL with productions of the MRL grammar used in the parse of the corresponding MR. Therefore, GIZA++ is used to produce an N to 1 alignment between the words in the NL sentence and a sequence of MRL productions corresponding to a top-down left-most derivation of the corresponding MR. A sample partial alignment is shown in Fig. 2.

Complete MRs are then formed by combining these NL substrings and their translations under a parsing framework called a synchronous CFG (SCFG) [1], which forms the basis of most existing statistical syntax-based translation models [41,10]. In an SCFG, the right hand side of each production rule contains two strings, in our case one in NL and the other in MR. Derivations of the SCFG simultaneously produce NL sentences and their corresponding MRs. The bilingual lexicon acquired from word alignments on the training data is used to construct

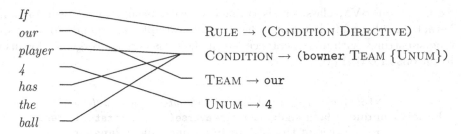

Fig. 2. Partial word alignment for the CLANG statement and its English gloss

a set of SCFG production rules. A probabilistic parser is then produced by training a maximum-entropy model using expectation maximization (EM) to learn
parameters for each of these SCFG productions, similar to the methods used in
[30,45]. To translate a novel NL sentence into its MR, a probabilistic chart parser
[34] is used find the most probable synchronous derivation that generates the
given NL, and the corresponding MR generated by this derivation is returned.

3.3 KRISP

KRISP (Kernel-based Robust Interpretation for Semantic Parsing) [23] uses
SVMs with string kernels to build semantic parsers that are more robust in
the presence of noisy training data. SVMs are state-of-the-art machine learning
methods that learn maximum-margin separators to prevent over-fitting in very
high-dimensional data such as natural language text [22]. They can be extended
to non-linear separators and non-vector data by exploiting *kernels* that implicitly create an even higher dimensional space in which complex data is (nearly)
linearly separable [32]. Recently, kernels over strings and trees have been effectively applied to a variety of problems in text learning and NLP [27,43,11,6,7]. In
particular, KRISP uses the string kernel introduced in [27] to classify substrings
in an NL sentence.

First, KRISP learns classifiers that recognize when a word or phrase in an
NL sentence indicates that a particular concept in the MRL should be introduced into its MR. Like WASP, it uses production rules in the MRL grammar
to represent semantic concepts, and it learns classifiers for each production that
classify NL substrings as indicative of that production or not. When semantically
parsing a sentence, each classifier estimates the probability of each production
covering different substrings of the sentence. This information is then used to
compositionally build a complete MR for the sentence.

KRISP learns a semantic parser iteratively, each iteration improving upon the
parser learned in the last iteration. In each iteration, for every production π
in the MRL grammar, KRISP collects positive and negative examples. In the
first iteration, the set of positive examples for production π contains all sentences whose MR parse tree uses the production π. The set of negative examples
includes all of the other training sentences. Using these positive and negative

examples, an SVM classifier[1] is trained for each production π using a string kernel. In subsequent iterations, the training examples are refined to more specific substrings within the sentences until the classifiers converge, analogous to iterations in EM [14].

NL: *"Which rivers run through the states bordering Texas?"*
Functional query language: answer(traverse(next_to(stateid('texas'))))
Parse tree of the MR in functional query language:

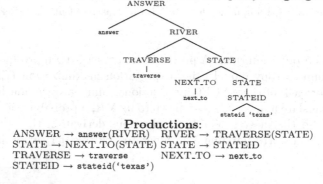

Productions:
ANSWER → answer(RIVER)   RIVER → TRAVERSE(STATE)
STATE → NEXT_TO(STATE) STATE → STATEID
TRAVERSE → traverse   NEXT_TO → next_to
STATEID → stateid('texas')

Fig. 3. An example of an NL query and its MR and its parse tree

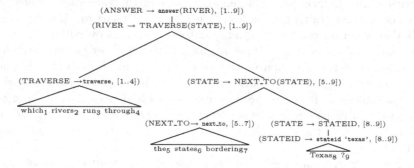

Fig. 4. Semantic derivation of the example in Fig. 3

During semantic parsing, KRISP uses these classifiers to find the most probable *semantic derivation* of a sentence. A *semantic derivation* of an NL sentence is a parse tree of an MR such that each node in the tree covers a substring of the sentence. The substrings covered by the children of a node are not allowed to overlap, and the substring covered by the parent must be the concatenation of the substrings covered by its children. Figure 4 shows a semantic derivation of the geography query and its MR parse shown in Fig. 3. The MRL used is a functional version of the formal database query language. The probability that

---

[1] We use the LIBSVM package available at: http://www.csie.ntu.edu.tw/~cjlin/libsvm/

a given production covers its corresponding substring is estimated using the SVM classifier for that production. Assuming independence, the probability of a semantic derivation is computed as the product of the probabilities for each of its productions. An adaptation of Earley's context-free parsing algorithm [15] is used to efficiently compute the most probable semantic derivation for a novel sentence, and this derivation directly determines its output MR.

4   Experimental Evaluation

Two corpora of NL sentences paired with MRs were used to evaluate our approaches. For CLANG, 300 pieces of coaching advice were randomly selected from the log files of the 2003 RoboCup Coach Competition. Each formal instruction was translated into English by one of four annotators [24]. The average length of an NL sentence in this corpus is 22.52 words. For GEOQUERY, 250 questions were collected by asking undergraduate students to generate English queries for the given database. Queries were then manually translated into logical form [44]. The average length of an NL sentence in this corpus is 6.87 words. The queries in this corpus are more complex than those in the ATIS database-query corpus used in the speech community [46] which makes the GEOQUERY problem harder, as also shown by the results in [29].

Semantic-parser learning was evaluated using standard 10-fold cross validation. A given system may be unable to parse a particular sentence and therefore fail to produce an output MR. For each system, we measured the number of novel test sentences that resulted in complete MRs, and the number of these MRs that were correct. For CLANG, an MR is correct iff it exactly matches the correct representation, up to reordering of the arguments of commutative operators like **and**. For GEOQUERY, an MR is correct iff the resulting query retrieved the same answer as the gold-standard MR when submitted to the database. The performance of each parser was then measured in terms of *precision* (the percentage of completed MRs that were correct) and *recall* (the percentage of all sentences with correctly generated MRs).

We used the version of CHILL presented in [35], which uses the improved COCKTAIL ILP system and produces more accurate parsers than the original version presented in [44]. In the GEOQUERY domain, we also compare to the original hand-built semantic parser GEOBASE.

Figure 5 shows the precision and recall learning curves for GEOQUERY, and Fig. 6 shows similar results for CLANG. Since CHILL is very memory intensive, it could not be run with larger training sets from the more complex CLANG corpus, where overall it does quite poorly. Although the precision of the commercial manually-developed system GEOBASE is fairly high, its recall is very low, illustrating the advantages of a learning approach. Overall, the three new learning systems do very well in both domains, learning quite accurate parsers after seeing a modest amount of training data. In general, SCISSOR gives the best results, but it also requires more detailed supervision in the form of SAPTs in addition to MRs. SCISSOR does particularly well on longer sentences where

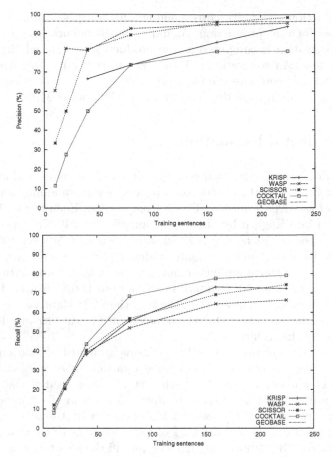

Fig. 5. Precision and Recall Learning Curves for GEOQUERY

having a detailed traditional syntactic analysis helps in composing the correct MR. CHILL, which performs quite well in the GEOQUERY domain, does quite poorly on the longer, more complex sentences in the CLANG domain, where its local, deterministic decisions are less accurate.

The GEOQUERY corpus has also been translated into Spanish, Turkish, and Japanese. CHILL, KRISP, and WASP have also learned semantic parsers for these languages [37,23,39] and the accuracy results are similar to those shown above for English, demonstrating the generality of these approaches. SCISSOR has not been tested on this data since it requires additional supervision in the form of SAPTs, which are currently unavailable for these languages. Since KRISP relies on probabilistic string classifiers and does not require sentences to be parsable by a symbolic grammar, it is more robust to noisy input than the other systems. Experiments on artificially adding noise to sentences by simulating speech-recognition errors have demonstrated that KRISP's accuracy degrades less rapidly as more noise is added to the corpus [23].

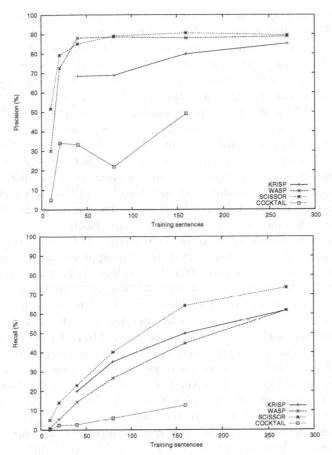

Fig. 6. Precision and Recall Learning Curves for Robocup CLANG

5   Future Research

Although overall SCISSOR is somewhat more accurate in our current experimental results, this is not surprising since it requires additional human annotation in the form of SAPTs. Recent results have shown that WASP and KRISP can also be adapted to benefit from the information in SAPTs; however, they still do not quite match the accuracy of SCISSOR. Therefore, we are currently exploring how, during training, the construction of SAPTs might be automated given only (NL MR) pairs and a general syntactic parser for the given natural language.

Currently, our evaluation of semantic parsers has been restricted to limited domains. This is largely due to the difficulty of developing an open-domain MRL and constructing a large annotated corpus of (NL MR) pairs for domain general text. As more general large corpora are developed that are annotated with deeper semantic representations, such as the OntoNotes corpus currently being assembled [21], we plan to test our systems on them. Given appropriately annotated large corpora, we are reasonably hopeful that our methods will scale to more general domains. A related direction of research is adapting our systems to learn "shallower" semantic parsers that produce incompletely formalized semantic representations such as those used in the FrameNet project [16].

However, we also believe there are many practical applications of domain-specific semantic parsers. Although the first NL database interfaces were developed in the 1970's [40,38,20], the technology was never successfully commercialized because of the significant manual software-engineering effort required to develop specialized systems for individual databases. We believe that by using learning techniques to automatically construct systems from annotated corpora, NL database interfaces could finally become a commercial technology. By asking existing database administrators to simply keep logs of the NL queries they receive and the formal (e.g. SQL) queries they construct in response, the requisite corpus of annotated data could be assembled quite easily.

Another way to obtain the requisite supervision is to allow ordinary users themselves to provide the necessary feedback. One approach to allowing a system to learn from its user community after it is deployed is to ask users to confirm a correct interpretation when the system finds a query to be ambiguous. If a system (or an ensemble of several different systems) finds a query ambiguous and produces multiple alternative formal interpretations, the competing queries can be paraphrased back into NL and the user asked to pick the correct one. The chosen interpretation can then be used as a new training example to improve the system. We have recently produced a generation system that produces natural language from formal queries by inverting our WASP system to translate in the opposite direction. Such an NL generation system could be used paraphrase alternative formal interpretations for the user.

Nevertheless, developing training corpora in which each sentence is manually annotated with a detailed formal MR is typically a very difficult and time-consuming process. Ideally, a system would be able to learn language like a human child, by being exposed to utterances in a rich perceptual context. By inferring the meaning of a sentence from the context in which it was uttered, a sentence-meaning pair could be automatically constructed. Methods for inducing semantic parsers from sentences annotated with MRs could then be applied to the resulting data. Although in general it is not possible to infer a unique meaning for a sentence from context, in the vast majority of cases, the context greatly restricts its range of possible meanings. There has been some work on inferring the meanings of individual words given a corpus of sentences each paired with an ambiguous set of multiple possible MRs [33]; however, unlike our work on semantic parsing, this work does not address the issues of learning to disambiguate words and phrases and compose their meanings into semantic representations of complete sentences.

The general problem of *symbol grounding*, how the meaning of abstract symbols is grounded in an agent's perceptual environment and experience, has been argued to be a critical issue in developing truly intelligent artificial systems [19]. Clearly, a deep understanding of most natural language requires capturing the connection between the abstract concepts underlying words and phrases and their embodiment in the physical world. There has been some recent work on inferring a grounded meaning of individual words or short referring expressions from visual perceptual context [31,2,42]. However, the syntactic complexity of the natural language used in this work is very restrictive, many of the systems use existing knowledge of the language, and most of them use static images to learn language describing objects and cannot use dynamic video to learn language describing actions. None of this existing work makes use of modern statistical-NLP parsing techniques or learns to build detailed symbolic meaning representations of complete, complex sentences. Developing robust systems that can learn to semantically interpret complex natural language given only exposure to utterances in a perceptual context is a very challenging and important problem for future research. Addressing this problem will require tightly integrating a variety of techniques from computational linguistics, machine learning, knowledge representation, computer vision, and robotics.

6   Conclusions

Semantic parsing is an important task that has a variety of interesting applications. This paper has reviewed several systems that we have developed for learning semantic parsers from corpora annotated with formal meaning representations. Results on automatically acquiring NL interfaces to databases and simulated robotic systems were used to demonstrate the capabilities of our existing systems. There are a number of challenging problems for future research and hopefully this paper will motivate more researchers to explore new methods for automatically acquiring parsers that can produce complete, formal semantic representations.

Acknowledgements

I would like to thank Ruifang Ge, Yuk Wah Wong, and Rohit Kate for developing and evaluating the systems discussed in this paper and John Zelle and Cynthia Thompson for important earlier contributions. This research was supported by the U.S. Defense Advanced Research Projects Agency under grant HR0011-04-1-0007 and a gift from Google Inc. All opinions expressed are solely those of the author.

References

1. Alfred V. Aho and Jeffrey D. Ullman. *The Theory of Parsing, Translation, and Compiling*. Prentice Hall, Englewood Cliffs, NJ, 1972.
2. David Bailey, Jerome Feldman, Srini Narayanan, and George Lakoff. Modeling embodied lexical development. In *Proceedings of the Nineteenth Annual Conference of the Cognitive Science Society*, 1997.

3. Borland International. *Turbo Prolog 2.0 Reference Guide*. Borland International, Scotts Valley, CA, 1988.
4. Peter F. Brown, John Cocke, Stephen A. Della Pietra, Vincent J. Della Pietra, Frederick Jelinek, John D. Lafferty, Robert L. Mercer, and Paul S. Roossin. A statistical approach to machine translation. *Computational Linguistics*, 16(2):79–85, 1990.
5. Peter F. Brown, Vincent J. Della Pietra, Stephen A. Della Pietra, and Robert L. Mercer. The mathematics of statistical machine translation: Parameter estimation. *Computational Linguistics*, 19(2):263–312, June 1993.
6. Razvan C. Bunescu and Raymond J. Mooney. A shortest path dependency kernel for relation extraction. In *Proceedings of the Human Language Technology Conference and Conference on Empirical Methods in Natural Language Processing*, pages 724–731, Vancouver, BC, 2005.
7. Razvan C. Bunescu and Raymond J. Mooney. Subsequence kernels for relation extraction. In Y. Weiss, B. Schölkopf, and J. Platt, editors, *Advances in Neural Information Processing Systems 18: Proceedings of the 2005 Conference*, 2006.
8. Xavier Carreras and Luis Marquez. Introduction to the CoNLL-2004 shared task: Semantic role labeling. In *Proceedings of the Eighth Conference on Computational Natural Language Learning (CoNLL-2004)*, Boston, MA, 2004.
9. Mao Chen, Ehsan Foroughi, Fredrik Heintz, Spiros Kapetanakis, Kostas Kostiadis, Johan Kummeneje, Itsuki Noda, Oliver Obst, Patrick Riley, Timo Steffens, Yi Wang, and Xiang Yin. Users manual: RoboCup soccer server manual for soccer server version 7.07 and later, 2003. Available at `http://sourceforge.net/projects/sserver/`.
10. David Chiang. A hierarchical phrase-based model for statistical machine translation. In *Proceedings of the 43nd Annual Meeting of the Association for Computational Linguistics (ACL-05)*, pages 263–270, Ann Arbor, MI, June 2005.
11. Michael Collins. New ranking algorithms for parsing and tagging: Kernels over discrete structures, and the voted perceptron. In *Proceedings of the 40th Annual Meeting of the Association for Computational Linguistics (ACL-2002)*, pages 263–270, Philadelphia, PA, July 2002.
12. Michael J. Collins. Three generative, lexicalised models for statistical parsing. In *Proceedings of the 35th Annual Meeting of the Association for Computational Linguistics (ACL-97)*, pages 16–23, 1997.
13. Nello Cristianini and John Shawe-Taylor. *An Introduction to Support Vector Machines and Other Kernel-based Learning Methods*. Cambridge University Press, 2000.
14. Arthur P. Dempster, Nan M. Laird, and Donald B. Rubin. Maximum likelihood from incomplete data via the EM algorithm. *Journal of the Royal Statistical Society B*, 39:1–38, 1977.
15. Jay Earley. An efficient context-free parsing algorithm. *Communications of the Association for Computing Machinery*, 6(8):451–455, 1970.
16. Charles J. Fillmore, Baker, Collin F., and Hiroaki Sato. The FrameNet database and software tools. In *Proceedings of the Third International Conference on Language Resources and Evaluation (LREC)*, pages 1157–1160, Las Palmas, 2002.
17. R. Ge and R. J. Mooney. A statistical semantic parser that integrates syntax and semantics. In *Proceedings of the Ninth Conference on Computational Natural Language Learning (CoNLL-2005)*, pages 9–16, Ann Arbor, MI, July 2005.

18. R. Ge and R. J. Mooney. Discriminative reranking for semantic parsing. In *Joint Conference of the International Committee on Computational Linguistics and the Association for Computational Linguistics (COLING-ACL-06)*, Sydney, Australia, July 2006.

19. S. Harnad. The symbol grounding problem. *Physica D*, 42:335–346, 2004.

20. G. G. Hendrix, E. Sacerdoti, D. Sagalowicz, and J. Slocum. Developing a natural language interface to complex data. *ACM Transactions on Database Systems*, 3(2):105–147, 1978.

21. E. H. Hovy, M. Marcus, M. Palmer, S. Pradhan, L. Ramshaw, and R. Weischedel. OntoNotes: The 90% solution. In *Proceedings of Human Language Technology Conference / North American Association for Computational Linguistics Annual Meeting (HLT-NAACL-06)*, New York, NY, 2006.

22. Thorsten Joachims. Text categorization with support vector machines: Learning with many relevant features. In *Proceedings of the Tenth European Conference on Machine Learning (ECML-98)*, pages 137–142, Berlin, 1998. Springer-Verlag.

23. R. Kate and R. J. Mooney. Using string-kernels for learning semantic parsers. In *Joint Conference of the International Committee on Computational Linguistics and the Association for Computational Linguistics (COLING-ACL-06)*, Sydney, Australia, July 2006.

24. R. J. Kate, Y. W. Wong, and R. J. Mooney. Learning to transform natural to formal languages. In *Proceedings of the Twentieth National Conference on Artificial Intelligence (AAAI-2005)*, pages 1062–1068, Pittsburgh, PA, July 2005.

25. G. Kuhlmann, P. Stone, R.J. Mooney, and J.W. Shavlik. Guiding a reinforcement learner with natural language advice: Initial results in RoboCup soccer. In *Proceedings of the AAAI-04 Workshop on Supervisory Control of Learning and Adaptive Systems*, San Jose, CA, July 2004.

26. Nada Lavrac and Saso Dzeroski. *Inductive Logic Programming: Techniques and Applications*. Ellis Horwood, 1994.

27. Huma Lodhi, Craig Saunders, John Shawe-Taylor, Nello Cristianini, and Chris Watkins. Text classification using string kernels. *Journal of Machine Learning Research*, 2:419–444, 2002.

28. Franz Josef Och and Hermann Ney. A systematic comparison of various statistical alignment models. *Computational Linguistics*, 29(1):19–51, 2003.

29. Ana-Maria Popescu, Alex Armanasu, Oren Etzioni, David Ko, and Alexander Yates. Modern natural language interfaces to databases: Composing statistical parsing with semantic tractability. In *Proceedings of the Twentieth International Conference on Computational Linguistics (COLING-04)*, Geneva, Switzerland, August 2004.

30. Stefan Riezler, Detlef Prescher, Jonas Kuhn, and Mark Johnson. Lexicalized stochastic modeling of constraint-based grammars using log-linear measures and EM training. In *Proceedings of the 38th Annual Meeting of the Association for Computational Linguistics (ACL-2000)*, pages 480–487, Hong Kong, 2000.

31. Deb Roy. Learning visually grounded words and syntax for a scene description task. *Computer Speech and Language*, 16(3):353–385, 2002.

32. John Shawe-Taylor and Nello Cristianini. *Kernel Methods for Pattern Analysis*. Cambridge University Press, 2004.

33. Jeffrey M. Siskind. A computational study of cross-situational techniques for learning word-to-meaning mappings. *Cognition*, 61(1):39–91, October 1996.

34. Andreas Stolcke. An efficient probabilistic context-free parsing algorithm that computes prefix probabilities. *Computational Linguistics*, 21(2):165–201, 1995.

35. L. R. Tang and R. J. Mooney. Using multiple clause constructors in inductive logic programming for semantic parsing. In *Proceedings of the 12th European Conference on Machine Learning*, pages 466–477, Freiburg, Germany, 2001.

36. Lappoon R. Tang and Raymond J. Mooney. Automated construction of database interfaces: Integrating statistical and relational learning for semantic parsing. In *Proceedings of the Joint SIGDAT Conference on Empirical Methods in Natural Language Processing and Very Large Corpora(EMNLP/VLC-2000)*, pages 133–141, Hong Kong, October 2000.

37. Cynthia A. Thompson and Raymond J. Mooney. Acquiring word-meaning mappings for natural language interfaces. *Journal of Artificial Intelligence Research*, 18:1–44, 2003.

38. David L. Waltz. An English language question answering system for a large relational database. *Communications of the Association for Computing Machinery*, 21(7):526–539, 1978.

39. Yuk Wah Wong and Raymond J. Mooney. Learning for semantic parsing with statistical machine translation. In *Proceedings of the 2006 Human Language Technology Conference - North American Chapter of the Association for Computational Linguistics Annual Meeting (HLT/NAACL-06)*, pages 439–446, New York City, NY, June 2006.

40. William A. Woods. Lunar rocks in natural English: Explorations in natural language question answering. In Antonio Zampoli, editor, *Linguistic Structures Processing*. Elsevier North-Holland, New York, 1977.

41. Kenji Yamada and Kevin Knight. A syntax-based statistical translation model. In *Proceedings of the 39th Annual Meeting of the Association for Computational Linguistics (ACL-2001)*, pages 523–530, Toulouse, France, 2001.

42. Chen Yu and Dana H. Ballard. On the integration of grounding language and learning objects. In *Proceedings of the Nineteenth National Conference on Artificial Intelligence (AAAI-2004)*, pages 488–493, 2004.

43. D. Zelenko, C. Aone, and A. Richardella. Kernel methods for relation extraction. *Journal of Machine Learning Research*, 3:1083–1106, 2003.

44. John M. Zelle and Raymond J. Mooney. Learning to parse database queries using inductive logic programming. In *Proceedings of the Thirteenth National Conference on Artificial Intelligence (AAAI-96)*, pages 1050–1055, Portland, OR, August 1996.

45. Luke S. Zettlemoyer and Michael Collins. Learning to map sentences to logical form: Structured classification with probabilistic categorial grammars. In *Proceedings of 21th Conference on Uncertainty in Artificial Intelligence (UAI-2005)*, Edinburgh, Scotland, July 2005.

46. Victor W. Zue and James R. Glass. Conversational interfaces: Advances and challenges. In *Proceedings of the IEEE*, volume 88(8), pages 1166–1180, 2000.

The Usefulness of Conceptual Representation for the Identification of Semantic Variability Expressions

Zornitsa Kozareva, Sonia Vázquez, and Andrés Montoyo

Departamento de Lenguajes y Sistemas Informáticos
Universidad de Alicante
{zkozareva,svazquez,montoyo}@dlsi.ua.es

Abstract. The need of the current Natural Language Processing applications to identify text segments that express the same meaning in different ways, evolved into the identification of semantic variability expressions. Most of the developed approaches focus on the text structure, such as the word overlaps, the distance between phrases or syntactic trees, word to word similarity, logic representation among others. However, current research did not identify how the global conceptual representation of a sentences can contribute to the resolution of this problem. In this paper, we present an approach where the meaning of a sentence is represented with the associated relevant domains. In order to determine the semantic relatedness among text segments, Latent Semantic Analysis is used. We demonstrate, evaluate and analyze the contribution of our conceptual representation approach in an evaluation with the paraphrase task.

1 Introduction

The identification of text snippets that express the same semantic meaning in different surface forms became an inseparable module for current NLP systems such as Question Answering, Text Summarization, Information Extraction among others. A major component for the semantic variability expressions are paraphrases. Given two text snippets, the paraphrase rules identify words such as the synonyms "car" and "vehicle", complex phrases "X married Y" and "Y is the husband of X", or even whole sentence, which can replace each other but still transmit the same meaning of the text.

Most of the developed approaches focus on the automatic collection of paraphrase rules [1], [11], [2]. Others identify whether two sentences are paraphrases of each other or not by measuring the ratio of the overlapping words [9], or the word-to-word semantic similarity [3]. [18] captured paraphrase rules by a probabilistic projection of the texts and information from the web. [2] aligned text segments to determine whether they are equivalent or not, [8] estimated the edit distance of the syntactic trees between two texts.

A. Gelbukh (Ed.): CICLing 2007, LNCS 4394, pp. 325–336, 2007.
© Springer-Verlag Berlin Heidelberg 2007

However, all these approaches suffer from global conceptual representation, and fail to understand the meaning of the text. In this paper, we present a hypothesis according to which the determination of relevant domain labels among the different word syntactic categories can provide a powerful way to establish the semantic relations among text segments. Since the domains are related to text coherence, this means that words occurring in coherent texts maximize the domain similarity of the texts. Imagine a text segment where the verb "eat" and the noun "cake" appear, both of them are conceptually related to food and the domain alimentation.

Previously, the usage of domain information was successfully applied to Word Sense Disambiguation [13], Information Extraction [17], Definite Description [14] and Information Retrieval [7]. For our approximation, we demonstrate how conceptual representation can function during the identification of semantically equivalent expressions. We have evaluated the performance of our approach with paraphrases corpus, but of course this approach can be applied with no restrain to the resolution of answer validation or textual entailment.

The paper is structured as follows. Section 2 presents the extraction of Relevant Domains [19] and Latent Semantic Analysis. Section 3 shows a walk-through example for paraphrases identification by global conceptual representation. Section 4 reports the obtained results with the Microsoft Paraphrase data and finally we conclude in Section 5.

2 Conceptual Representation Space with Latent Semantic Analysis

The Latent Semantic Analysis (LSA) [4] [10] corpus-based approach has been previously applied to various NLP tasks such as Information Retrieval, Information Extraction, Question Answering, Text Summarization among others. Although the systems can obtain good results in a specific domain, the problems arise when we want to acquire knowledge for a general domain. To surmount this obstacle, we present a conceptual representation approach with LSA. Instead of the traditional term-document matrix, we construct a term-conceptual matrix from two lexical resources: WordNet Domains and WordNet alignment with SUMO.

2.1 WordNet Domains

The semantic domains provide a natural way to establish the semantic relations among words. They can be used to describe texts and to assign a specific domain from previously established domain hierarchy.

Based on this idea, a new resource called WordNet Domains (WND) [12] has been developed. This resource uses information from WordNet [6] and labels each word sense with semantic domains from a set of 200 domain labels. These labels are obtained from the Dewey Decimal Classification and are hierarchically organized. This information is complementary to WordNet and is useful to obtain new relations among the words.

In order to obtain the WND resource, each word of WordNet is annotated with one or more domain labels. One of the most important characteristic of WND is that each domain label can be associated to different syntactic categories. This is an interesting feature because we can relate words of different syntactic categories with the same domain and obtain new relations that previously does not exist in WordNet.

For example, the domain 'Economy' is associated with the nouns (bank, money, account, banker, etc), the verbs (absorb, amortize, discount, pay, etc) and the adjectives (accumulated, additional, economic, etc). Moreover, these domain labels have been associated to different senses of the same word and thus we can distinguish the meaning of each word using the domains. The word "plant" has three different domain senses: 'Industry, Botany, Theatre' and in order to establish its word sense, we can use the domain information of other words that are seen in the context of "plant" ("it is an industrial plant to manufacture automobiles", "a plant is a living organism laking the power of locomotion").

Taking advantage of the properties of this resource, we formulate the following hypothesis: the conceptual representation of a text can be obtained when the contextual information provided by its words is used.

In WordNet, each word sense has a definition[1] like in a dictionary and the words in the gloss are used to obtain the specific context for the sense. Respectively, the word sense has a domain label which contains the global concept for this sense. Our assumption is that words that form part of the gloss are highly probable to be associated to the same concept of the word. For instance, "plant#1"[2] is associated to the domain 'Industry'. It gloss contains: 'buildings for carrying on industrial labor; "they built a large plant to manufacture automobiles"'. From the gloss, the words "building", "carry", "industrial", "labor", "plant", "manufacture" and "automobile" are semantically related to the domain 'Industry' and thus they can help us to understand the concept of the definition word.

Taking into account this principle, we extracted from WordNet a list with all words and their associated domains. Then, we used the information provided by the context to build the conceptual representation space of LSA.

2.2   WordNet Alignment with SUMO

The Suggested Upper Merged Ontology (SUMO) [15] is an ontology that is obtained from the merging of publicly available ontological content into a single, comprehensive, and cohesive structure with around 800 terms. In our approximation these terms are used as relevant domains. The SUMO ontology is aligned with the WordNet lexical database on the basis of the synonymy, hypernymy

---

[1] Gloss.

[2] Plant with sense one.

and instantiation relations. So each WordNet synset is associated to a SUMO concept.

The information added by the SUMO ontology into WordNet is useful to the WND resource, because we establish the global concept of the words using the concepts of SUMO. The final relevant domain resource is a list of words tagged with the concepts of SUMO. The main idea for the usage of the WND and SUMO resources is that we want to study the effect of the usage of two different types of ontologies: a coarse-grained (WND) and a fine-grained (SUMO). In our experimental work we determine the effect of the ontological specification over the final textual conceptual representation.

In order to see the differences between SUMO and WND we extract the SUMO concepts for the same three senses of "plant": "Stationary_Artifact", "Plant", "Social_Role". We observe the pairs WND-SUMO concepts: "Industry"–"Stationary_Artifact", "Plant"–"Botany", "Social_Role"–"Theatre" and we realize that the SUMO ontology is fine-grained in comparison with the WND.

Figure 1 shows a part of the SUMO and WordNet ontologies so that the different degree of specialization of the hierarchies can be seen.

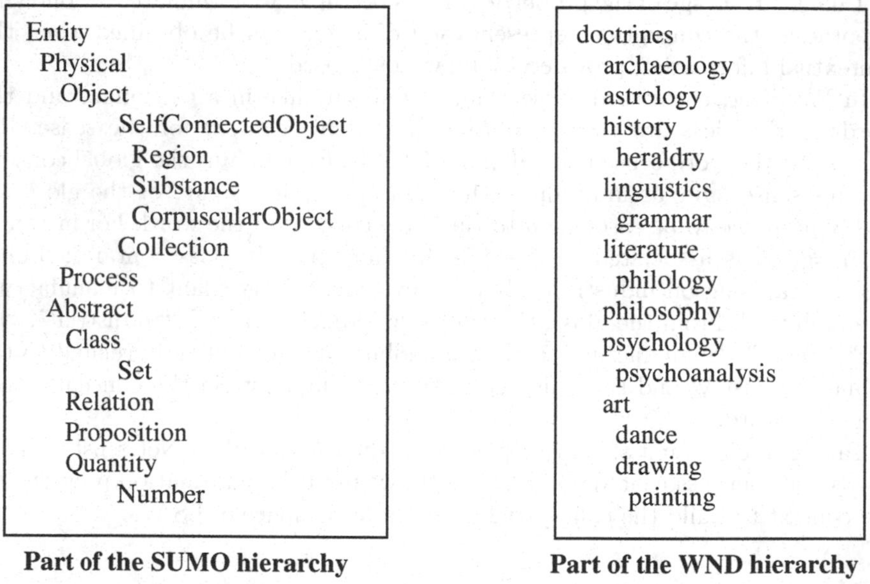

Entity	doctrines
Physical	archaeology
Object	astrology
SelfConnectedObject	history
Region	heraldry
Substance	linguistics
CorpuscularObject	grammar
Collection	literature
Process	philology
Abstract	philosophy
Class	psychology
Set	psychoanalysis
Relation	art
Proposition	dance
Quantity	drawing
Number	painting
Part of the SUMO hierarchy	**Part of the WND hierarchy**

Fig. 1. SUMO and WND hierarchies

2.3   Latent Semantic Analysis

The traditional usage of LSA is based on a text corpus represented as a $M \times N$ co-occurrence matrix, where the rows M are words and the columns N are documents, phrases, sentences or paragraphs. Each cell in this matrix contains the number of times that a word occurs in the context of a column.

Once the matrix is obtained, it is decomposed using Singular Value Decomposition (SVD). In this way the initial dimensions are reduced into a new distribution which is based on similar contexts. This reduction makes the similarity among the words and the contexts to become more apparent.

Our approach is based on the idea that semantically related words appear in the same contexts. However, the contexts we use are not a specific corpus divided in documents or paragraphs, but words related to a specific concept (e.g. domain) that belongs to a predefined hierarchy. In our case, the domains are derived from WND and SUMO and with this information we construct the conceptual matrix of LSA.

However, we want to rank the words not only on the basis of their meaning, but also on the basis of their co-occurrences with other words. Therefore, we applied the Mutual Information (MI) 1 and Association Ratio (AR) 2 measures which can relate the words with the domains.

$$MI(w_1, w_2) = log_2 \frac{P(w_1|w_2)}{P(w_1)P(w_2)} \tag{1}$$

$$AR(w, Dom) = Pr(w|Dom) \, log_2 \frac{Pr(w|Dom)}{Pr(w)} \tag{2}$$

MI provides information about the pairwise probability of two words w_1 and w_2 compared to their individual probabilities. When there is a real association between two words w_1 and w_2, their joint probability $P(w_1, w_2)$ is much larger than $P(w_1)P(w_2)$, and $MI(w_1, w_2) \gg 0$. For the cases where w_1 and w_2 are not related, $P(w_1, w_2) \approx P(w_1)P(w_2)$, therefore $MI(w_1, w_2) \approx 0$. When w_1 and w_2 are in complementary distribution, then $P(w_1, w_2)$ is less than $P(w_1)P(w_2)$, and $MI(w_1, w_2) \ll 0$.

Adapting this notion to our approach, we used w_1 in the aspect of a word we are observing and w_2 in the aspect of a domain D from the WND that corresponds to the word w_1. The values are normalized with the number of word–domain pairs N in the WND. Once the relation between the words and the domains is obtained, AR is applied and the conceptual space of LSA is constructed.

3   A Walk-Through Example

We illustrate the application of the relevant domains and LSA with a paraphrase example. Given two text segments, we want to obtain their conceptual spaces and then determine a score that reflects the semantic similarity relatedness of the texts. According to this text cohesion score and an empirically derived threshold, the segments are considered as paraphrases of each other or not.

First, the two texts segments as shown in Figure 2 are lemmatized with Tree-Tagger [16] part-of-speech tagger. This is done because the LSA conceptual matrix is build from the lemmatized words in WordNet. The relevant domains for these segments are obtained only for the nouns, the verbs, the adverbs and the adjectives of the two text segments. The underlined words in Figure 2 are those whose relevant domains are going to be considered during the generation of the text conceptual representation.

Text Segment 1: <u>Women</u> who <u>eat</u> potatoes and other <u>tuberous</u> vegetables during <u>pregnancy</u> may be at <u>risk</u> of <u>triggering</u> <u>type</u> 1 <u>diabetes</u> in their <u>children</u>, Melbourne <u>researchers</u> <u>believe</u>.

Text Segment 2: Australian <u>researchers</u> <u>believe</u> they have <u>found</u> a <u>trigger</u> of <u>type</u> 1 <u>diabetes</u> in <u>children</u> - their <u>mothers</u> eating potatoes and other <u>tuberous</u> vegetables during <u>pregnancy</u>.

Fig. 2. Text segments number 1634 from the paraphrase corpus

Starting with each of the two text segments and for each of the previously selected word categories, we determine the corresponding relevant domains from WordNet and SUMO. Figure 3 shows the set of WordNet relevant domains that correspond to each one of the words and their associated probabilities to the relevant domains according to the association ratio measure.

Once the words are associated to the domains, then the overlapping domains between the two text segments are determined. For this step, we use LSA, which returns a list of the most common relevant domains for Text Segment 1 and Text Segment 2. In the experiment, we consider the first twenty most relevant domains, but in our example in Table 1 we list only the first nine relevant domains.

Table 1. LSA list of the nine most relevant domains for the two text segments

LSA domains in segment 1		LSA domains in segment 2	
Domain	Similarity	Domain	Similarity
applied_science	0.770537	applied_science	0.793825
pharmacy	0.740445	pharmacy	0.777943
philology	0.717400	ecology	0.713885
publishing	0.716576	transport	0.709478
theology	0.714463	biology	0.705481
pedagogy	0.705165	botany	0.701570
telecommunication	0.700763	university	0.694129
university	0.698827	publishing	0.693940
psychoanalysis	0.697876	chemistry	0.693747

Finally, a ranking function calculates the average value of the coinciding domains and determines only one candidate domain according to which the

Text Segment 1:
woman={sexuality 0.236904, fashion 0.074808, person 0.072525, athletics 0.048517, jewellery 0.042176}
eat={gastronomy 0.168685, ecology 0.034430, folklore 0.026185, physiology 0.017776, anthropology 0.012501}
potato={agriculture 0.056402, gastronomy 0.009348, entomology 0.004056, racing 0.003743, medicine 0.002409}
tuberous={agriculture 0.000782, biology 0.000284, botany 0.003115, botany 0.003115, gastronomy 0.002218}
vegetable={gastronomy 0.040430, zootechnics 0.023290, agriculture 0.022609, earth 0.009891, body_care 0.009335}
pregnancy={surgery 0.027848, physiology 0.025092, medicine 0.005344, anatomy 0.002291, color 0.001075}
risk={insurance 0.049295, exchange 0.015876, enterprise 0.013756, industry 0.001393, commerce 0.001289}
trigger={commerce 0.002437, computer_science 0.001999, factotum 0.000088 }
type={zoology 0.052495, philology 0.048450, bowling 0.043687, publishing 0.023217, biology 0.018311}
diabetes={pharmacy 0.006108, medicine 0.005782, alimentation 0.000724, time_period 0.000290, factotum 0.000020...}
child={ethnology 0.008168, acoustics 0.006704, color 0.002306, body_care 0.001732, economy 0.001036}
researcher={person 0.000636, factotum 0.000010}
believe={doctrines 0.195175, theology 0.155574, pure_science 0.137293, folklore 0.079765, religion 0.067227}
Text Segment 2:
researcher={person 0.000636, factotum 0.000010}
believe={doctrines 0.195175, theology 0.155574, pure_science 0.137293, folklore 0.079765, religion 0.067227}
find={zoology 0.102364, chemistry 0.072100, statistics 0.045846, geology 0.043141, astrology 0.042836}
trigger={commerce 0.002437, computer_science 0.001999, factotum 0.000088 }
type={zoology 0.052495, philology 0.048450, bowling 0.043687, publishing 0.023217, biology 0.018311}
diabetes={pharmacy 0.006108, medicine 0.005782, alimentation 0.000724, time_period 0.000290, factotum 0.000020}
child={ethnology 0.008168, acoustics 0.006704, color 0.002306, body_care 0.001732, economy 0.001036}
mother={archaeology 0.014541, anthropology 0.003027, computer_science 0.000241, administration 0.000241, biology 0.000239}
eat={gastronomy 0.168685, ecology 0.034430, folklore 0.026185, physiology 0.017776, anthropology 0.012501}
potato={agriculture 0.056402, gastronomy 0.009348, entomology 0.004056, racing 0.003743, medicine 0.002409}
tuberous={agriculture 0.000782, biology 0.000284, botany 0.003115, botany 0.003115, gastronomy 0.002218}
vegetable={gastronomy 0.040430, zootechnics 0.023290, agriculture 0.022609, earth 0.009891, body_care 0.009335}
pregnancy={surgery 0.027848, physiology 0.025092, medicine 0.005344, anatomy 0.002291, color 0.001075}

Fig. 3. The first five relevant domains per word according to the association ratio measure

two texts are strongly or weakly semantically related. This candidate domain contains the global conceptual representation of the texts. To determine this domain, we compare each of the domains listed in Table 1 from Text Segment 1 to those of Text Segment 2. The most relevant domain for the two text segments is determined by the highest probability domain relevance value. The final result of the ranking function contains the global representation domain for the two text segments. For our example, the most relevant domain is applied_science. It includes the subdomains agriculture, alimentation, gastronomy.

4   Evaluation

In order to estimate the effectiveness of the developed conceptual representation approach, we carried out an experimental evaluation with a paraphrasing corpus[3]. The evaluation task consists in given two text segments, the system has to determine whether the text are paraphrases of each other or not.

4.1   Microsoft Paraphrase Corpus

The paraphrase corpus [5] we worked with has been automatically collected from the web. The number of train instances is 4076, and the number of test instances is 1725.

Each paraphrase pair consists of two text segments for which the semantic variability has to be determined. An example of a paraphrase pair is "Inhibited children tend to be timid with new people, objects, and situations, while uninhibited children spontaneously approach them." and " Simply put, shy individuals tend to be more timid with new people and situations."

4.2   Evaluation Measures

The performance of our conceptual representation model for the resolution of paraphrases is evaluated with the following measures.

$$Precision = \frac{number\, of\, correct\, answers\, found\, by\, the\, system}{number\, of\, answers\, given\, by\, the\, system} \qquad (3)$$

$$Recall = \frac{number\, of\, correct\, answers\, found\, by\, the\, system}{total\, number\, of\, correct\, answers\, in\, the\, corpus} \qquad (4)$$

$$F_{\beta=1} = \frac{2 \times Precision \times Recall}{Precision + Recall} \qquad (5)$$

$$Accuracy = \frac{number\, of\, answers\, given\, by\, the\, system}{total\, number\, of\, correct\, answers\, in\, the\, corpus} \qquad (6)$$

4.3   Results

We have conducted two types of experiments. In the first one, we study how to represent the concept of two texts using the WordNet and SUMO domains, while in the second experiment we examine whether the usage of a fine-grained

---

[3] http://research.microsoft.com/nlp/msr_paraphrase.htm

or coarse-grained ontology is better. This observations are made when Word-Net is annotated with the SUMO ontology. The results from the carried out experiments are shown in Table 2.

In this table we show the performance of the system during its development and test stage. We have examined several empirical thresholds, in order to determine the most significant one. A threshold value of 0.8 corresponds to a high assurance that two text are paraphrases of each other, because the probability of LSA domain determination is above 0.8. In the experiments we found out that all thresholds below 0.4 perform the same. This observation is made with the WordNet and SUMO domains. Therefore, we consider the 0.4 threshold as a robust one.

Table 2. Conceptual representation for paraphrase identification

	Data Set	Thresh	Acc	Prec	Rec	F
WordNet Domains	Train	0.8	80.29	72.97	70.83	71.89
		0.6	97.35	68.91	96.07	80.26
		0.4	**98.52**	68.36	97.82	**80.48**
	Test	0.8	80.34	72.08	70.44	71.25
		0.6	97.10	67.50	95.64	79.14
		0.4	**98.26**	66.84	97.38	**79.27**
WordNet Annotated with SUMO	Train	0.8	38.59	81.69	09.08	16.34
		0.6	94.28	69.44	91.53	78.97
		0.4	**96.27**	68.93	94.47	**79.71**
	Test	0.8	40.05	81.29	09.85	17.57
		0.6	93.50	68.67	90.23	77.99
		0.4	**95.18**	68.11	92.76	**78.55**
text similarity approach	Test	–	68.80	74.10	81.70	77.70

For the paraphrase resolution task, our approach transmits not only the meaning of the text but also the global concept. During the train and test phase, WordNet and SUMO performed alike however, the coarse-grained hierarchy of WordNet domains gave more precise results. The only differences among the two experiments are observed when we worked with high threshold values. WordNet domains had a variation of 10% across the thresholds, while SUMO's performance ranged from 16 to 79%. This is due to assurance score established from the relevant domains. While in WordNet the domain overlap is always with high probability, in SUMO the domains are more specialized and the probability to find an overlaps among them is lower. Of course this does not mean that fine-grained domains hamper the conceptual representation, it only indicated that a lower probability threshold is needed.

During the error analysis, we found out sentences which have no common domains at all and where determined as non-paraphrase. However, these texts had common sub-domains. One interesting approximation in the future is to study how the sub-domains affect the global conceptual representation and estimate the semantic variability.

In Table 2, we show a comparative study with the text similarity approach of [3], which is also evaluated with the same paraphrase data. It can be seen that our global conceptual representation approach performs better. Establishing word-to-word similarity or text-to-text similarity does not explain the meaning of the text, therefore our approach is better not only from the point of view of the coverage of the correctly established paraphrase examples, but also from the point of view that we measure similarity among different syntactic categories of words on behalf of the same concept. In this way we have a reasonable explanation how and to what extend the two text segments are semantically related.

4.4 Discussion

Some limitations for the development of the conceptual representation are due to the FACTOTUM domain. This domain groups words with no specific domain. Therefore, when a text segment has many words belonging to the FACTOTUM domain, we cannot obtain the global concept of the sentence.

The precision in our approach can be improved when we establish correctly the senses of the words in the gloss. Because in this approximation, the words in the gloss were not disambiguated and we were assuming that they belong to the domain of the defined word. To resolve this problem and to improve the performance, the ExtendedWordNet resource is going to be used. In this way, we will have a better mapping between the words in the gloss and their corresponding domains.

Regarding SUMO's experiments, we saw that considering only the first twenty relevant domains is not representative enough for the modelling of the conceptual space. This is due to SUMO's fine-grained ontology. In the future we will expand the number of SUMO's relevant domains.

In conclusion we can say that the identification of semantically variable expression with conceptual representation is possible and obtains better results than text-to-text similarity approaches. We used the paraphrase data to demonstrate the applicability and the usefulness of the conceptual representation approach. Of course, this approach can be used to identify semantic variability expressions for other task such as textual entailment, answer validation or to find similar sentences related to different semantic categories of Named Entities.

5   Conclusions

We have described an approach for global conceptual representation of text segments using relevant domains. Our hypothesis is that domains constitute a fundamental feature of text coherence, therefore words occurring in coherent portion of texts maximize the domain similarity.

To build the conceptual space of the text, LSA is employed. In this study we observe the effect of fine-grained and coarse-grained ontologies from which the relevant domain resources are extracted. To demonstrate the usefulness of our conceptual approach, we have evaluated it with the paraphrase resolution task.

The results show that the conceptual representation approach we propose is reliable and performs better than the already developed lexical overlap, or text-to-text similarity approaches. One advantage of this method is the ability to extract the global meaning of the texts and give reasonable explanation why two texts are considered semantically equivalent.

In the future, we will use this approximation to develop a repository of Named Entity context examples which are representatives of various semantic categories, such as Person_Politics, Person_Sport, Person_Musician among others.

Acknowledgements

This research has been funded by the Spanish Government under project CICyT number TIC2003-07158-C04-01 and PROFIT number FIT-340100-2004-14.

References

1. Regina Barzilay and Kathleen McKeown. Extracting paraphrases from a parallel corpus. In *ACL, 2001.*, pages 50–57.
2. Regina Barzilay and Kathleen McKeown. Learning to paraphrase: An unsupervised approach using multiple-sequence alignment. In *HTLT-NAACL, 2003.*, pages 16–23.
3. Courtney Corley and Rada Mihalcea. Measures of text semantic similarity. In *Proceedings of the ACL workshop on Empirical Modeling of Semantic Equivalence.*, 2005.
4. Scott Deerwester, Susan T. Dumais, George W. Furnas, Thomas K. Landauer, and Richard Harshman. Indexing by latent semantic indexing. In *Journal of the American Society for Information Science.*, volume 41, pages 321–407, 1990.
5. Bill Dolan, Chris Quirk, and Chris Brockett. Unsupervised construction of large paraphrase corpora: Exploiting massively parallel news sources. In *Proceedings of the 20th International Conference on Computational Linguistics, Geneva, Switzerland.*, 2004.
6. Christiane FellBaum. *WordNet, an electronic lexical database.* MIT Press, 1998.
7. Julio Gonzalo, Felisa Verdejo, Carol Peters, and Nicoletta Calzolari. Applying eurowordnet to cross-language text retrieval. pages 113–135, 1998.
8. Milen Kouylekov and Bernardo Magnini. Tree edit distance for recognizing textual entailment: Estimating the cost of insertion. In *Proceedings of the PASCAL Challenges Workshop on Recognising Textual Entailment, 2006.*, pages 17–20.
9. Zornitsa Kozareva and Andrés Montoyo. Paraphrase identification on the basis of supervised machine learning techniques. In *FinTAL*, pages 524–533, 2006.
10. Thomas Landauer and Susan Dumais. A solution to plato's problem: The latent semantic analysis theory of acquisition. In *Psychological Review*, pages 211–240, 1997.
11. Dekang Lin and Patrik Pantel. Discovery of inference rules for question answering. *Natural Language Engineering, 4(7)*, pages 343–360.

12. Bernardo Magnini and Gabriela Cavaglia. Integrating Subject Field Codes into WordNet. In M. Gavrilidou, G. Crayannis, S. Markantonatu, S. Piperidis, and G. Stainhaouer, editors, *Proceedings of LREC-2000, Second International Conference on Language Resources and Evaluation*, pages 1413–1418, Athens, Greece, 2000.

13. Bernardo Magnini, Carlo Strapparava, Giovanni Pezzulo, and Alfo Gliozzo. Using domain information for word sense disambiguation. In *SENSEVAL-2, 2001.*

14. Rafael Muñoz and Andrés Montoyo. Definite description resolution enrichment with wordnet domain labels. In *IBERAMIA*, pages 645–654, 2002.

15. I. Niles and A. Pease. Linking lexicons and ontologies: Mapping wordnet to the suggested upper merged ontology. *Proceedings of the 2003 International Conference on Information and Knowledge Engineering (IKE 03). Las Vegas, Nevada*, 2003.

16. Helmut Schmid. Probabilistic part-of-speech tagging using decision trees. In *International Conference on New Methods in Language Processing, Manchester, UK, 1994.*

17. Mark Stevenson and Mark A. Greenwood. Learning information extraction patterns using wordnet. In *Proceedings of the 3rd International Conference of the Global WordNet Association (GWA'06)*, 2006.

18. Idan Szpektor, Hristo Tanev, Ido Dagan, and Bonaventura Coppola. Scaling web-based acquisition of entailment relations. In *Proceedings of Empirical Methods in Natural Language Processing*, 2004.

19. Sonia Vázquez, Andrés Montoyo, and German Rigau. Using relevant domains resource for word sense disambiguation. In *IC-AI*, pages 784–789, 2004.

Characterizing Humour: An Exploration of Features in Humorous Texts

Rada Mihalcea[1,2] and Stephen Pulman[2]

[1] Computer Science Department, University of North Texas
rada@cs.unt.edu
[2] Computational Linguistics Group, Oxford University
sgp@clg.ox.ac.uk

Abstract. This paper investigates the problem of automatic humour recognition, and provides and in-depth analysis of two of the most frequently observed features of humorous text: human-centeredness and negative polarity. Through experiments performed on two collections of humorous texts, we show that these properties of verbal humour are consistent across different data sets.

1 Introduction

This paper addresses two research questions concerned with the characteristics of textual humour. First, are humorous and serious texts separable, and does this property hold for different datasets? To answer this question, we use two different data sets of verbal humour – a collection of short one-liners and a set of humorous news articles – and attempt to automatically separate them from their non-humorous counterparts.

Second, if humorous and serious texts are separable, what are the distinctive features of humour, and do they hold across datasets? In answer to this second question, we attempt to identify some of the most salient features of verbal humour, and analyse their occurrence in the two data sets.

While these are interesting issues in themselves, there is also a medium-term practical application for 'humour' recognition in the design of conversational agents of various types: detecting and responding appropriately to humour is a characteristic of natural human interaction that is conspicuously lacking in implemented systems. In the longer term, by gaining insight into the mechanisms underlying humour, we hope to increase our understanding of aspects of the creative use of language, i.e. uses of language which go beyond 'banal humorless prose' and display some reflective and self-aware properties. While these are pre-eminently displayed in creative works like novels or poetry, they are also present in more everyday phenomena like humour.

The paper is organized as follows. We first review related work in computational humour, and briefly cover some of the most recent methods for humour generation and recognition. We then describe the two data sets used in this paper, and briefly overview two machine learning techniques for text classification. Next, we address the first question, and present the results obtained in the automatic classification of humorous and non-humorous data sets. We then present some of the characteristics of verbal humour as observed in an analysis of humorous texts, and provide a detailed analysis of two

A. Gelbukh (Ed.): CICLing 2007, LNCS 4394, pp. 337–347, 2007.

of the most dominant features: human-centeredness and negative polarity. Finally, we conclude with a discussion.

1.1 Related Work

While humor is relatively well studied in scientific fields such as linguistics [1] and psychology [4,15], to date there is only a limited number of research contributions made toward the construction of computational humour prototypes. Most of the computational approaches to date on style classification have focused on the categorization of more traditional literature genres, such as fiction, scitech, legal, and others [7], and much less on creative writings such as humor.

One of the first attempts in computational humor is perhaps the work described in [2], where a formal model of semantic and syntactic regularities was devised, underlying some of the simplest types of puns (*punning riddles*). The model was then exploited in a system called JAPE that was able to automatically generate amusing puns.

Another humor-generation project was the HAHAcronym project [16], whose goal was to develop a system able to automatically generate humorous versions of existing acronyms, or to produce a new amusing acronym constrained to be a valid vocabulary word, starting with concepts provided by the user. The comic effect was achieved mainly by exploiting incongruity theories (e.g. finding a religious variation for a technical acronym).

Another related work, devoted this time to the problem of humor comprehension, is the study reported in [17], focused on a very restricted type of wordplays, namely the "Knock-Knock" jokes. The goal of the study was to evaluate to what extent wordplay can be automatically identified in "Knock-Knock" jokes, and if such jokes can be reliably recognized from other non-humorous text. In our own previous work, we have studied the problem of automatic humour recognition using content and stylistic features [9], and have evaluated the use of large collections of humorous texts for improving widely used computer applications such as email [11].

2 Datasets for Computational Humour

There have been only a relatively small number of previous attempts targeting the computational modeling of humour. Among these, most of the studies have relied on small datasets, e.g. 195 jokes used for the recognition of knock-knock jokes [18], or 200 humorous headlines analysed in [3], and such small collections may not suffice for the robust learning of features of humorous text.

More recently, we proposed a Web-based bootstrapping method that automatically collects humorous sentences starting with a handful of manually selected seeds, which allowed us to collect a large dataset of 16,000 one-liners [9]. In this paper, we use the corpus of one-liners, as well as a new dataset that we introduce in this paper consisting of humorous news articles. By considering two different datasets, we hope to be able to derive more definite and robust conclusions about the characteristic features of humorous texts.

2.1 One-Liners

A one-liner is a short sentence with comic effects and an interesting linguistic structure: simple syntax, deliberate use of rhetoric devices (e.g. alliteration, rhyme), and frequent use of creative language constructions meant to attract the readers' attention. While longer jokes can have a relatively complex narrative structure, a one-liner must produce the humorous effect "in one shot", with very few words. These characteristics make this type of humor particularly suitable for use in an automatic learning setting, as the humor-producing features are guaranteed to be present in the first (and only) sentence.

Starting with a short *seed* set consisting of a few one-liners manually identified, the algorithm proposed in [9] automatically identifies a list of webpages that include at least one of the seed one-liners, via a simple search performed with a Web search engine. Next, the webpages found in this way are HTML parsed, and additional one-liners are automatically identified and added to the seed set. The process is repeated several times, until enough one-liners are collected.

Take my advice; I don't use it anyway.
I get enough exercise just pushing my luck.
I took an IQ test and the results were negative.
A clean desk is a sign of a cluttered desk drawer.
Beauty is in the eye of the beer holder.

Fig. 1. Sample examples of one-liners

Two iterations of the bootstrapping process, started with a small seed set of ten one-liners, resulted in a large set of about 24,000 one-liners. After removing the duplicates using a measure of string similarity based on the longest common subsequence, the resulting dataset contains 16,000 one-liners, which are used in the experiments reported in this paper. The one-liners humor style is illustrated in Figure 1, which shows five examples of such one-sentence jokes.

2.2 Humorous News Articles

The second dataset we consider consists of daily stories from the newspaper "The Onion" – a satiric weekly publication with ironic articles about current news, targeting in particular stories from the United States. It is known as "the best satire magazine in the U.S."[1] and "the best source of humour out there"[2].

We collected all the articles published during August 2005 – March 2006, which resulted in a dataset of approximately 2,500 news articles. We cleaned all the HTML tags, eliminated the header containing information specific to the newspaper, and finally removed all the news articles that felt outside the 1000–10,000 character length range. This process left us with a final dataset of 1,125 news stories with humorous content. Figure 2 shows a sample article from this dataset.

---

[1] Andrew Hammel, German Joys, http://andrewhammel.typepad.com
[2] Jeff Grienfield, CNN senior analyst, http://www.ojr.org/

Canadian Prime Minister Jean Chrétien and Indian President Abdul Kalam held a subdued press conference in the Canadian Capitol building Monday to announce that the two nations have peacefully and sheepishly resolved a dispute over their common border. Embarrassed Chrétien and Kalam restore diplomatic relations. "We are – well, I guess proud isn't the word – relieved, I suppose, to restore friendly relations with India after the regrettable dispute over the exact coordinates of our shared border," said Chrétien, who refused to meet reporters' eyes as he nervously crumpled his prepared statement. "The border that, er... Well, I guess it turns out that we don't share a border after all." Cheétien then officially withdrew his country's demand that India hand over a 20-mile-wide stretch of land that was to have served as a demilitarized buffer zone between the two nations." Really, I think the best thing for us to do is forget about the whole thing as quickly as possible," Cheétien added.

Fig. 2. Sample news article from "The Onion"

3   Automatic Humour Recognition

The first question we are concerned with is whether the humorous texts represent a distinct genre that can be easily and reliably distinguished from other non-humorous datasets. To answer this question, similar to our previous work [9], we formulate the humor-recognition problem as a traditional classification task, and feed positive (humorous) and negative (non-humorous) examples to an automatic classifier.

In particular, in this study we are concerned with the *semantic* characteristics of humour, and therefore we focus our attention on content classification, as opposed to stylistic features as used in previous work [9]. The content of humorous texts is thus "compared" against the content of serious texts using standard text classification techniques.

To perform the classification task, in addition to positive (humorous) examples, we also need a set of negative (serious) texts. For each humorous dataset, a collection of negative examples was constructed, identified as texts that are non-humorous, but similar in structure and composition to the humorous examples. We do not want the automatic classifiers to learn to distinguish between humorous and non-humorous examples based simply on text length or obvious vocabulary differences. Instead, we seek to enforce the classifiers to identify humor-specific features, by supplying them with negative examples similar in most of their aspects to the positive examples, but different in their comic effect.

3.1   Negative Datasets

For each humorous dataset, we collected an equal number of non-humorous examples, by mixing texts from three or four different sources. The purpose of seeking different sources for the construction of the negative non-humorous dataset is to avoid the bias that could be introduced by a specific source or genre.

For the one-liners, we created a negative dataset consisting of a mix of sentences following the same length restrictions (10–15 words). We combined: (1) *Reuters* titles, extracted from news articles published in the Reuters newswire over a period of one year (8/20/1996 – 8/19/1997); (2) *Proverbs* extracted from an online proverb collection; (3) *British National Corpus (BNC)* sentences; and (4) sentences from the *Open Mind Common Sense* collection of commonsense statements.

For the news articles, the negative examples were collected from three different sources: (1) articles drawn from *Los Angeles Times*; (2) newstories from the *Foreign Broadcast Information Service*; and finally (3) texts extracted from the *British National Corpus*. All the non-humorous examples were constrained to have a similar structure to "The Onion" articles – stories with a length of 1,000–10,000 characters.

3.2 Text Classification

We ran classification experiments using two frequently used text classifiers, Naïve Bayes and Support Vector Machines, selected based on their performance in previously reported work, and for their diversity of learning methodologies.

Naïve Bayes. The main idea in a Naïve Bayes text classifier is to estimate the probability of a category given a document using joint probabilities of words and documents. Naïve Bayes classifiers assume word independence, but despite this simplification, they perform well on text classification. While there are several versions of Naïve Bayes classifiers (variations of multinomial and multivariate Bernoulli), we use the multinomial model, previously shown to be more effective [8].

Support Vector Machines. Support Vector Machines (SVM) are binary classifiers that seek to find the hyperplane that best separates a set of positive examples from a set of negative examples, with maximum margin. Applications of SVM classifiers to text categorization led to some of the best results reported in the literature [6].

3.3 Classification Results

For each humorous dataset, we ran classification experiments with respect to their "negative" non-humorous counterpart. The documents were tokenized and stemmed prior to classification; no other pre-processing was applied.

All the evaluations are performed using stratified ten-fold cross validations, for accurate estimates. The baseline for all the experiments is 50%, which represents the classification accuracy obtained if a label of "humorous" (or "non-humorous") would be assigned by default to all the examples in the data set. Table 1 shows the classification accuracies obtained with each of the classifiers.

Table 1. Classification accuracy for the two humorous datasets

Classifier	One-liners	News articles
Naive Bayes	79.69%	88.00%
SVM	79.23%	96.80%

The results indicate that humorous and non-humorous data are clearly separable, using exclusively linguistic features. Not surprisingly, the classification accuracy for the news articles is higher than for the one-liners, most likely due to the larger size of the documents in the newstories' collection. The different gap between the SVM and the Naive Bayes classification accuracies can be probably attributed to the same reason, with the SVM classifier leading to results close to 100% in the case of the newstories, but to results slightly worse than those obtained with the Naive Bayes classifier in the case of the one-liners.

Perhaps even more importantly than the classification results are the features that can be learned from the classifiers' output, which can help us characterize the linguistic properties of humour. In the following, we describe the features identified in a previous examination of linguistic properties of verbal humour, and provide an in-depth, larger-scale evaluation of the two main characteristics of humour: human-centeredness and negative polarity.

4   Characteristics of Verbal Humour

In a previous analysis of the features of verbal humour [10], we tried to identify and classify the content-based humor-specific features characteristic to the one-liner data set. By examining by hand the most discriminative content-based features learned during the text classification process, we tried to classify them into semantic classes. The following frequently occurring word classes emerged:

Human-centric vocabulary. Jokes seem to constantly make reference to human-related scenarios, through the frequent use of words such as *you, I, man, woman, guy*, etc. For instance, the word *you* alone occurs in more than 25% of the one-liners (*"You can always find what you are not looking for"*), while the word *I* occurs in about 15% of the one-liners (*"Of all the things I lost, I miss my mind the most"*). This supports earlier suggestions made by Freud [5], and later on by Minsky [12], that laughter is often provoked by feelings of frustration caused by our own, sometime awkward, behaviour.

Negation. Humorous texts seem to often include negative word forms, such as *doesn't, isn't, don't*. A large number of the jokes in our collection contain some form of negation, e.g. *"Money can't buy you friends, but you do get a better class of enemy"*, or *"If at first you don't succeed, skydiving is not for you."*

Negative orientation. In addition to negative verb forms, jokes seem to also contain a large number of words with a negative polarity, such as adjectives with negative connotations like *bad, illegal, wrong* (*"When everything comes your way, you are in the wrong lane"*), or nouns with a negative load, e.g. *error, mistake, failure* (*"User error: replace user and press any key to continue"*). Both the negative verb forms and the words with negative orientations are potential reflections of the incongruity-based theories of humor.

Professional communities. Many jokes seem to target professional communities that are often associated with amusing situations, such as lawyers, programmers, policemen. For instance, about 100 one-liners in our collection fall under this category, e.g. *"It was so cold last winter that I saw a lawyer with his hands in his own pockets."*

Human "weakness". Finally, the last significantly large semantic category that we identified refers to events or entities that are often associated with "weak" human moments, including nouns such as *ignorance, stupidity, trouble* (*"Only adults have trouble with child-proof bottles"*), *beer, alcohol* (*"Everybody should believe in something, I believe I'll have another beer"*), or verbs such as *quit, steal, lie, drink* (*"If you can't drink and drive, then why do bars have parking lots?"*). As mentioned before, this kind of vocabulary seems to relate to theories of humor that explain laughter as an effect of frustration or awkward feelings, when we end up laughing "at ourselves" [12].

On a higher level, these characteristics can be classified into two main classes. First, *human-centric vocabulary, professional communities*, and *human "weakness"* can be grouped into the larger category of **human centeredness**. Second, *negation, negative orientation*, and *human "weakness"* all have to do with the broader category of **polarity orientation**. In the following, we analyse each of these categories in turn, and bring evidence of a high correlation between humorous text and each of these two features.

5 Human Centeredness

For a more robust evaluation of the human-centeredness property of the humorous texts, we implemented a system that measures the weight of the most discriminatory features learned from the text classification process with respect to given semantic classes considered relevant for human-centeredness.

Specifically, we begin by creating a list of salient features for the humorous dataset. Starting with the features identified as important by the Naive Bayes classifier (a threshold of 0.3 was used in the feature selection process), we select all those features that have a total weight exceeding a given threshold T, where a feature weight is calculated for each category (humorous/non-humorous) and is determined as the probability of seeing the feature in a given category. We then calculate the *humorous score* of a feature as the ratio between the weight in the humorous corpus and the total weight in the entire mixed corpus. This results in a score within the [0–1] interval, with a value closer to 1 indicating a feature representative for the humorous texts, and a value close to 0 corresponding to high saliency features for the non-humorous dataset. In the evaluations reported below, we use a threshold T of 100, which allows us to extract the top 1,500 most discriminatory features for each dataset.

Next, given a certain semantic class, we measure the *weight* of that semantic class with respect to the most discriminatory features by adding up the corresponding weights, and normalizing with respect to the size of the semantic class. For instance, assuming a semantic class that includes the words *I, me, myself,* with the *humorous scores* of 0.88, 0.65, and 0.55 respectively measured on the humorous dataset, the weight of the given semantic class is then measured as $(0.88 + 0.65 + 0.55)/3 = 0.69$[3].

By using semantic classes, we can generalize over the individual word features learned from the classifiers' output, and derive *categories* of words representative for the humorous data. Note that a semantic class that has no correlation with the humorous

---

[3] Correspondingly, the weight of the semantic class in the non-humorous texts is measured as $1 - 0.69 = 0.31$.

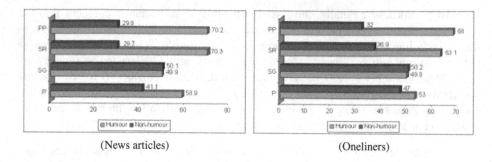

(News articles)   (Oneliners)

Fig. 3. Semantic classes reflecting human-centeredness within humorous texts. PP = personal pronouns; SG = social groups; SR = social relationships; P = persons.

features of a text will result in an approximately equal weight (0.50) measured on the humorous and non-humorous texts.

To measure the human-centeredness characteristic of humorous texts, for each dataset we extracted the top 1,500 most discriminatory features, and subsequently measured the weight of four semantic classes that we considered relevant for the property of human-centeredness: *persons, social groups, social relations*, and *personal pronouns*. The first three categories are derived automatically from WordNet, by listing all the nouns found in the synsets subsumed by the node {*person, individual, someone, somebody, mortal, human, soul* (20,676 nouns are extracted), {*relative, relation*} and {*relationship, human relationship*} (351 nouns), and {*social group*} (2,393 nouns). The fourth category is constructed by listing exhaustively all the personal pronouns in the English language.

Figure 3 shows the weight of each semantic class with respect to humorous and non-humorous data, for each of the two datasets (one-liners and news articles). Our hypothesis concerning the human-centeredness of humour seems to be confirmed, with a much higher weight measured for the semantic classes of *persons, social relationships*, and *personal pronouns* in humorous texts. In particular, social relationships (e.g. *wife, husband, son*) and personal pronouns (e.g. *I, you*) seem to have high prevalence in humorous data. Rather surprisingly, social groups do not correlate with humorous texts, having an equal weight distribution between humorous and non-humorous data. Although we initially thought that this WordNet class would help us uncover the category of *professional communities*, on closer inspection it turns out that the nouns relevant for such communities (e.g. *programmer, lawyer*) are represented under the semantic class of *person*. Instead, the *social group* category includes more organization-related nouns such as *church, university*, or *council*, which are not necessarily representative for humorous text.

6   Polarity Orientation

The second humour characteristic we are investigating is concerned with the polarity orientation of humour. In a previous manual analysis of humorous features (Section 4),

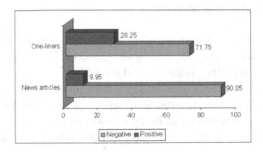

Fig. 4. Polarity orientation of humorous data

we observed a frequent use of negative verbal forms in humorous texts, as well as other words with negative orientation (e.g. negative adjectives), or denoting human "weakness." In order to take this analysis to the next step, and investigate on a larger scale the polarity orientation of humour, we have implemented a tool for automatic sentiment analysis, and used this tool to annotate the two humorous datasets used in the current study.

Starting with a dataset annotated for "positive" and "negative" orientation, we implemented a classification system that has the ability to automatically indicate the semantic orientation of a text. Specifically, we are using the dataset of 10,662 short text fragments introduced in [13], and feed the 5,331 "positive" and the 5,331 "negative" fragments into a Naive Bayes classifier. In a ten-fold cross validation experiment, the accuracy of the system was determined as 78.15%, which compares favorably with previous results reported on the same dataset [13].

Using this sentiment analysis tool, we automatically annotate the two humorous datasets, with results shown in Figure 4. These results seem to confirm our hypothesis that humour tends to have a strong negative orientation, with 71.74% of the one-liners being labeled as negative, and as many as 90.04% of the news articles from "The Onion" having a negative annotation. Interestingly, regular text also tends to have a slight tendency toward the negative, with 56.26% of the mix of "serious" sentences being determined as having a negative orientation. General "serious" news articles are even more negative, with 67.60% labeled as negative, perhaps reflecting the general negative trend of the stories typically reported in the news.

Interestingly, by analyzing the annotations, several of the examples labeled as positive seem to include words with a negative orientation, whose strength was perhaps not high enough to be selected as negative by the automatic classifier. For instance, "CURSOR: What you become when your system crashes." is labeled as an example with positive orientation, despite the word "crashes" that seems to indicate a negative outcome. Conversely, "I love deadlines, especially the whooshing sound as they fly by." is labeled as negative, perhaps because of a frequent occurrence of "deadline" in negative contexts, despite the fact that this one-liner does not have a clear negative connotation. A larger training dataset with polarity annotations, perhaps integrating manual annotations of jokes, is likely to improve the accuracy of the annotations.

7 Discussion and Conclusions

The questions with which we began were: (1) Are humorous and serious texts separable, and does this property hold for different datasets? and (2) If so, what are the distinctive features of humour, and do they hold across datasets?

In answer to the first of these questions, we have shown that humorous and serious texts can be separated at the linguistic level, and also that this holds for at least two different datasets: short one-liners, and longer news articles. Of course, there are many other types of humorous and non-humorous prose and it may be that some of these are more difficult to separate.

In trying to address the second question, by analysis of the linguistic features that emerged as important for the classifiers, we hypothesized two main characteristics of humour: human-centeredness and negative orientation, which were validated through larger scale experiments of annotations on the two datasets. In a sense, one might have predicted the human centeredness *a priori*, given that humour seems to be a specifically human property, but the negative orientation we found is less obvious: indeed, from the generally positive effects associated with humour, one might have expected the opposite.

As Ritchie [14] suggests, it is probably misguided to look for **the** defining property of humour, but we may make some speculations on the basis of our findings as to one of its possible functions. It does not seem completely implausible that some varieties of humour act as a kind of "natural therapy" whereby tensions related to **negative** scenarios concerning **humans** (us) are relieved, by emphasizing them in a context which leads to them being exorcised through laughter.

References

1. ATTARDO, S. *Linguistic Theory of Humor.* Mouton de Gruyter, Berlin, 1994.
2. BINSTED, K., AND RITCHIE, G. Computational rules for punning riddles. *Humor 10*, 1 (1997).
3. BUCARIA, C. Lexical and syntactic ambiguity as a source of humor. *Humor 17*, 3 (2004).
4. FREUD, S. *Der Witz und Seine Beziehung zum Unbewussten.* Deutike, Vienna, 1905.
5. FREUD, S. *Der Witz und Seine Beziehung zum Unbewussten.* Deutike, Vienna, 1905.
6. JOACHIMS, T. Text categorization with Support Vector Machines: learning with mny relevant features. In *Proceedings of the European Conference on Machine Learning* (1998), pp. 137–142.
7. KESSLER, B., NUNBERG, G., AND SCHUETZE, H. Automatic detection of text genre. In *Proceedings of the 35th Annual Meeting of the Association for Computational Linguistics (ACL97)* (Madrid, July 1997).
8. MCCALLUM, A., AND NIGAM, K. A comparison of event models for Naive Bayes text classification. In *Proceedings of AAAI-98 Workshop on Learning for Text Categorization* (1998).
9. MIHALCEA, R., AND STRAPPARAVA, C. Making computers laugh: Investigations in automatic humor recognition. In *Proceedings of the Human Language Technology / Empirical Methods in Natural Language Processing conference* (Vancouver, 2005).
10. MIHALCEA, R., AND STRAPPARAVA, C. Learning to laugh (automatically): Computational models for humor recognition. *Computational Intelligence 22*, 2 (2006), 126–142.

11. MIHALCEA, R., AND STRAPPARAVA, C. Technologies that make you smile: Adding humor to text-based applications. *IEEE Intelligent Systems 21*, 5 (2006).
12. MINSKY, M. Jokes and the logic of the cognitive unconscious. Tech. rep., MIT Artificial Intelligence Laboratory, 1980.
13. PANG, B., AND LEE, L. A sentimental education: Sentiment analysis using subjectivity summarization based on minimum cuts. In *Proceedings of the 42nd Meeting of the Association for Computational Linguistics* (Barcelona, Spain, July 2004).
14. RITCHIE, G. *The Linguistic Analysis of Jokes*. Routledge, London.
15. RUCH, W. Computers with a personality? lessons to be learned from studies of the psychology of humor. In *Proceedings of the The April Fools Day Workshop on Computational Humour* (2002).
16. STOCK, O., AND STRAPPARAVA, C. Getting serious about the development of computational humour. In *Proceedings of the 8th International Joint Conference on Artificial Intelligence (IJCAI-03)* (Acapulco, Mexico, August 2003).
17. TAYLOR, J., AND MAZLACK, L. Computationally recognizing wordplay in jokes. In *Proceedings of CogSci 2004* (Chicago, August 2004).
18. TAYLOR, J., AND MAZLACK, L. Computationally recognizing wordplay in jokes. In *Proceedings of CogSci 2004* (Chicago, August 2004).

Representing Emotions with Linguistic Acuity

Hye-Jin Min and Jong C. Park

Computer Science Division EECS Department, KAIST
373-1 Guseong-dong, Yuseong-gu Daejeon 305-701 South Korea
{hjmin,park}@nlp.kaist.ac.kr

Abstract. For a robot to make effective and friendly interaction with human users, it is important to keep track of emotional changes in utterance properly. Emotions have traditionally been characterized by intuitive but atomic categories or as points in evaluation-activity dimensions. However, this characterization falls short of capturing subtle emotional changes either in narration or in text, where the vast majority of information is presented with a host of linguistic constructions that convey emotional information. We propose a novel representation scheme for emotions, so that such important features as duration, target and intensity can also be treated as first-class citizens and systematically accounted for. We argue that it is with this new mode of representation that the subtlety of the emotional flow in utterance can be properly addressed. We use this representation to encode the emotional states and intentions of characters in the drama scripts for soap opera and describe how it is utilized in conjunction with parsing for lexicalized grammars.

Keywords: Emotion Representation, Lexicalized Grammar, Human Computer Interaction.

1 Introduction

There is currently much attention to building intelligent and believable robots (or embodied conversational agents - ECAs) that react properly at the right moment in the course of a dialog. For them to achieve acceptable performance, it is necessary to keep track of emotional changes, as well as intentional changes, of a human user or users during conversation and interaction. Emotions have thus been widely studied for robots and ECAs, but the present focus in the field is not much on uncovering subtle emotional changes from the linguistic context but on speech, facial expressions and motion-related aspects in multimodal databases. When emotional changes are modeled, the representation scheme utilizes categories and abstract dimensions.

Emotion-related information in text is much more expressive than can be captured by these representational devices, and it is essential to identify such information properly. For example, complex (or mixed) emotions can be delivered by coordinate structures and adverbs that indicate various grades of strength, along with many other characteristic syntactic structures. In particular, it is through these syntactic structures that we can identify the target of a particular

A. Gelbukh (Ed.): CICLing 2007, LNCS 4394, pp. 348–360, 2007.

emotion, the time when such an emotion is experienced, and the strength of the emotion.

In this paper, we propose a novel representation scheme with emotion labels that encode three distinct features, i.e., target, duration, and intensity, and use it to annotate drama scripts for soap opera with explicit emotional cues by extracting those features from the scripts during or after syntactic parsing in a lexicalized grammar framework.

The rest of the paper is organized as follows. Section 2 reviews the related work. Section 3 examines emotions in soap opera in some detail. Section 4 proposes an annotation scheme for drama scripts with emotion information. Section 5 shows our linguistic analysis. Section 6 describes how the emotion information is utilized in conjunction with parsing for lexicalized grammars. Section 7 concludes with discussion and further work.

2   Related Work

Representation schemes for emotions that have been proposed in the literature are mostly based on psychology theories. Among them, categorical representations are the most simple and widely used, with an emotion word such as anger or happiness indicate the corresponding emotional state. Many psychologists have proposed basic and atomic categories, where the representative category set by Ekman [1] consists of 6 basic categories that are based on marked facial expressions. Dimensional representations are used to characterize emotional states with valence (negative/positive) and arousal (active/passive) from Osgood's three semantic dimensions, or, evaluation, potency, and activity [2]. Dimensional representations are continuous so that the emotional states that can not be described as discrete categories can also be modeled. However, an additional dimension is necessary to distinguish emotions with the same valence and arousal such as fear and anger. Appraisal representations capture emotional states in terms of eliciting conditions, such as their familiarity, intrinsic pleasantness, or relevance to one's goals [3]. Such details can be used to identify the cause of the emotions from the context, or to predict them in AI systems.

To help recognize the emotions of a human user and synthesize the emotions of an artificial agent, several multimodal emotional databases have been annotated with emotion information. EmoTV corpus [4], a collection of TV interviews with a wide range of body postures and monologues in French, was annotated by ANVIL [5], an annotation tool that uses both categorical and dimensional labels. Two annotators labeled the emotions in each segment and the results were classified into 14 categories. The inter-coder agreement was rather low, due mostly to the blended emotions or complex emotions. Another real-life corpus at a medical emergency call center was annotated with multi-level granularity, from valence-level to fine-grained categorical level, to capture blended emotions [6]. However, only non blended emotions were used by the detection algorithm. The intensity and meta-data annotations are not tried.

Belfast database [7] incorporates chat shows, religious programs, and discussions from TV in English. FEELTRACE tool [8] is used to annotate recognized emotional state in terms of two continuous dimensions, activation and evaluation. The results show that extreme activation is present in all modalities, and information of prosody is a good source for labeling. However, positive data tend to be rated as neutral so a finer classification is called for.

Practical applications such as conversation programs via email or chat [9, 10, 11], an opinion-based question answering system [12], and a dialog-based tutor system [13] utilized sentiment or emotion detection for more effective and friendly interaction. Conversation programs represent emotions as basic categories based on facial expressions or an appraisal theory [3]. They also use intensity as a numerical value from common-sense knowledge. For opinion mining or a tutor system, emotions are represented with activation values (positive, negative, neutral with rough intensity). Both representations are consistent with annotation schemes of multimodal databases. However, they fall short of capturing the subtle changes of emotion either in narration or in text, which is a distinct contribution of the textual data.

Multimodal databases are good sources of identifying diverse shades of emotions and annotating them with contributing modalities such as prosody, facial expression, or body postures. However, textual information has not been studied yet, which conveys subtle emotional changes with a number of linguistic constructions. We discuss what characteristics of emotions need to be detected from the text and how they are represented in the next section.

3 Emotions in Soap Opera

The main reason for detecting emotions during conversation between a human user and a robot would be to make the robot react properly according to the user's emotional cues. We are currently working on enhancing the functions of service robots for elderly people with emotion recognition, generation and expression. We have analyzed drama scripts for soap opera written in Korean whose main episodes are on family affairs with the elderly in order to identify the available types of emotional cues in the daily lives of the elderly. The text scripts contain about 1500 sentences, in three 30 minute episodes. We have selected 41 scenes that contain explicitly expressed emotions for a deeper linguistic analysis as collected initially by simple keyword patterns.

The text scripts display rather explicit emotional changes overall and thus can work as a good model for a robot to follow, for several reasons. First, they contain diverse situations of the daily lives of the ordinary (including the elderly), and thus the identified emotions are not biased to any specific valence or category. Second, it is easy to follow emotional changes of a character by taking the character's individual differences in the context into account. Third, there is a balanced amount of multimodal information such as facial expressions, speeches, and behaviors, as well as descriptions of situations in scenes, so it is possible to take into consideration complex interactions among various types of information such as textual and other multimodal information.

We have focused mainly on the utterances in which the characters express their emotions verbally. It is assumed that directly expressed emotions are more tightly related to the character's intention, so that the robot would be able to pay more attention to such utterances for a proper response.

3.1 Types of Emotional Cues

We have classified four types of emotional cues in the soap opera. The criteria for this classification are the types of the expected reactions of the listener and the temporal ranges of the expected effects of the expressed emotion. The expected reactions include immediate actions or speeches according to the emotion, acknowledgement of recognizing the expressed emotion, and accepting the emotion as topical information. Their temporal ranges are dependent on their identities and the start and end points of the corresponding emotion. Some of the representative examples are shown below.[1]

1. (a) Scene 5. Garden
   Young [Why can't you answer to me? Can't you hear what I say?]
   Eun (Halfway staring at her...)
   Young [Eun!]
   Eun (Keep staring at her)
   Young [Hey, look at this tiny one] (Pushing her at forehead)
   (b) Scene 57. Street at night
   Eun [..I am so thankful today]
   KeyJung [You need to take a taxi]
   Eun [I think so. Thank you, and good bye]
   (c) Scene 8. Cafe
   Song [Did you bring Eun?]
   Mrs. Bae [Yeah, but I am so sick of her]
   Song [Why?]
   Mrs. Bae [She is spoiled by her grandmother. It's so unbearable. And I can't imagine why she should be so sly] (Stirring her coffee with a teaspoon, tasting it, and adding another spoonful of sugar)
   (d) Scene 49. Room
   Keum and Eun, lying down side by side
   Keum [..We are so poor. I can't think of any time when we were well off]
   Eun [We were a little well off when we lived near the bridge]
   Keum [Yeah, that's true, when Mom was working..]
   Eun [I was most depressed when we lived in Hakye-dong]
   Keum [Yeah..]

---

[1] In the examples, sentences in Korean are translated into corresponding ones in English. However, subtle emotional details that are culturally-based may not show up exactly as they are in the original sentences.

Instructive Utterance with Emotion. When the speaker wants the listener to do something, she tends to express her immediate emotion directly toward the listener to convey the urgency and importance, as well as the specification, of the request. For the listener's effective decision making on what and how he should do next, an ability to detect the speaker's emotion properly would be quite useful. In this case, the expected reaction may be immediate actions or speeches according to the corresponding emotion and its temporal range is very short. For example, a girl may become angry at her younger brother because he did not follow her request, so she may demand him again to say yes. Here, if he wants her sister to ease the anger, he would have to answer right away (cf. (1a)).

Emotion Conveyance. The speaker often notifies the listener of her mind with a verbally explicit emotional expression to let him know of her current emotion. In this case, the speaker expects the listener to acknowledge that he recognized the emotion, where the temporal range is short but continuous. For example, when the listener helps the speaker, the speaker may say 'Thank you' to express her current emotion (cf. (1b)).

Emotion Sharing. The speaker sometimes talks about her emotional experiences with someone to the listener, who is a third party, so the main purpose of expressing emotions in this case is to share them with the listener. In this case, no matter how strong the intensity of the emotion is, the actual intensity of the emotion the listener should notice may not be so strong. The acknowledgement from the listener does not have to be so strong as in the case of emotion conveyance, but the temporal range is longer than that of emotion conveyance. For example, if a mother grumbles at her friend about her daughter, her friend would normally listen to her and nod in sympathy (cf. (1c)).

Emotion as Topic of Conversation. The speaker talks about her emotions in the past, but her current emotion may have nothing to do with those in the past. In this case, they are regarded just as a kind of topic information that she brings up for conversation. It is important for the listener to see whether the expressed emotion is still in effect or not. For example, two sisters may talk about their poor childhood together in the past, but the expressed negative emotion should not be confused as still in effect (cf. (1d)).

These classified cues based on the expected reactions of the listener and the temporal ranges of the effects of the emotion are represented as the directionality towards the character the speaker expresses her emotion (Target), the time difference between the moment the emotion actually takes place and the moment the speaker expresses it (Duration), and the actual intensity the listener or the listeners should notice, which is affected by the target of the expressed emotion and the time difference (Intensity). Table 1 shows the values of these features in each cue.

Table 1. Characteristics of emotional cues

	Duration	Target	Intensity
instructive utterance with emotion	current immediate	listener	same as expressed
emotion conveyance	current or past continuous but short	listener	same as expressed
emotion sharing	current or past continuous	others or none	lower than expressed
emotion as topic of conversation	past not in effect anymore	others or none	not affected

Figure 1 shows the ratio of the frequency of emotional cues. Emotion conveyance is the major emotional cue, but other minor cues should also be recognized correctly for appropriate responses. These types of cues are also applicable to other domains such as conversational agents or dialogue-based tutor systems. However, the priority of such types may be dependent on the goal of each domain. For example, the acknowledgement of recognizing the expressed emotion would be the most important in tutor systems, where the level of understanding is strongly tied to the expressed emotions of a student.

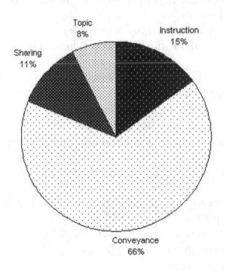

Fig. 1. Ratio of the frequency of emotional cues

4   Annotating Text with Emotions

The main conventions for annotating a corpus with emotions are to label well-known emotion words or phrases with emotion labels or values in the evalution-activity dimensions, along with those in the dimensions of duration, target and intensity, as proposed in Section 3. There are several emotional cues with annotation in Example 2.

2. Scene 14. Living Room
   Mr. Park [Oh]
   Seems to have remembered something, stands up to open the closet to take out a medicine bottle inside, and then sits down again.
   Mrs. Park (Wondering what it is..)
   Mr. Park [Please take these three times a day. They are calcium supplements](Holding the plastic medicine bottle)
   Mrs. Park [Why calcium supplements?]
   Mr. Park [I hear bones get weaker when women experience
   the menopause. I don't like to see you become a shortie
   like others.]
   (Worry),(starts(c1, ts)),(l:wife,t:wife),
   (surface@none@middle, real@none@same)
   Mrs. Park [My bones are strong.]
   (...)
   Mr. Park [Do you want to give these gold earrings to Bonghee, or to donate to the national campaign for gold collection?]
   Mrs. Park [We can't donate such a small amount. Let's just give them to Key. If he doesn't like to use them, he may just as well return them to the original owner.]
   Mr. Park [What if he actually wears them?]
   Mrs. Park [Even if he does, it won't last long. People like to disobey others anyway.]
   Mr. Park (Sighes)[I don't know whom he takes after..
   I really don't like it.
   (Hatred), (during(c1, ts)), (l:wife,t:son),
   (surface@very@high, real@very@lower)
   I have not much to say if someone asks me about the job of the second-born son.]
   Mrs. Park [Please don't be so ashamed of his job.]
   (...)
   Mr. Park (Opening)[..I am most happy when I pick your ears with your head on my lap like this.]
   (Happiness), (starts(c1, ts)), (l:wife,t:wife),
   (surface@most@high, real@most@same)
   Mrs. Park (Faint smile)

The first expressed emotion is 'emotion conveyance' with mild (Intensity) worry about the listener (Target) for a short time (Duration) because of the un-realized event. The second expressed emotion is related to 'emotion sharing' with a current mild and continuous hatred or disgust (Intensity, Duration) towards not his wife but his son (Target). The emotional cue of the last one is 'emotion conveyance', represented as current happiness towards the listener (Target) for a short time (Duration) with the same amount of intensity as the verbally expressed one (Intensity). Therefore the main emotional flow of the husband at this point is towards his wife with 'worry' and 'happiness', but 'hatred' is not so evident as those. Table 2 shows more details of the representation conventions.[2]

The proposed representation is different from the existing ones in several ways. It focuses on relative information rather than absolute values. For instance, we describe a temporal range when the emotion is in effect for Duration, and the real intensity as compared to the surface intensity for Intensity, so that we will be able to assign absolute values after combining emotion information from other modalities. In addition, it distinguishes targets from the listener or listeners, so that the strength of an emotion dependent on the target's existence in the speaker's sight could be described. Emotional tendency to a specific person can also be characterized likewise.

Table 2. Conventions for emotion annotation

Convention	Description
Emotion Label	([well-known emotion words or evaluation-activity values])
Duration	(current, immediate: equal(c1, ts) or current, continuous but short: starts(c1, ts) or past, continuous but short: starts(p1, ts) or current, continuous: during(c1, ts) or past, not in effect anymore: finishes(p1, ts))
Target	(l:[listener], t:[target])
Intensity	(surface@[meaning]@[as expressed in utterance], real@[meaning]@[actual intensity noticeable])

5   Linguistic Analysis

To identify emotion labels and features from text scripts, we need to disambiguate arguments and expressions, reassess the emotional weight of a given expression by taking other constituents into consideration, and strengthen vague expressions into marked ones with the help of specific constituents at several linguistic levels.

---

[2] We utilized an emotion-explicit vocabulary in Korean for well-known emotion words [14], and temporal interval relations for the convention of duration [15].

5.1 Words with Explicit Emotional Senses

The words containing explicit emotional senses, namely, emotion labels, duration and intensity, are in part good starting points for identifying emotional cues within an emotion carrying utterance unit. Table 3 shows the types of words and the descriptions. We discuss how to identify these cues by the proposed linguistic analysis in rest of the subsections.

Table 3. Words with explicit emotional senses

Convention	Type	Examples
Emotion Label	emotion words with directionality	Anger, Sorry-for, ...
	emotion words with desirability	Joy, Depression, ...
	evaluative words	Goodness, Badness, ...
Duration	temporal adverbs	today, now, these days, ...
	temporal conjunctions	when, if, ...
Intensity	adverbs	very, little, ...
	exclamation	wow, oh, oops, ...

5.2 Disambiguating Arguments and Expressions

To identify targets of an emotion correctly, we need to distinguish the speaker from the targets, and the listener from others as well. Nominative, accusative, and dative case markers are helpful for the former. For the latter, when the target is the listener, it is usually omitted, because the speaker doesn't have to call him out loud, who is in the same place. Thus we assume that the omitted target is the listener.

We also need to disambiguate the emotion words that take diverse types of targets such as people, objects or events. For example, the target of 'frighten' could be a person or an event that the speaker has experienced. Case markers are helpful to identify if the word belongs to emotion words with directionality. And if it places a noun clause in the position of a target as the thematic role, it may belong to emotion words with desirability. Also, if it modifies a noun phrase, which is an object or a person, we should regard it as a characteristic expression rather than an emotional one.

5.3 Reassessing the Emotional Weight of a Given Expression

The speaker's current emotion is not usually expressed with a temporal adverbial clause or a conditional clause, because the moment in these clauses is not identical to the moment when the speaker expresses her emotion verbally. For instance, a man may say to his wife "I hate it whenever our son comes home late". His current emotion is close to 'Neutral' rather than immediate 'Hatred'. In addition, when an emotion word or an evaluative word appears in an interrogative sentence, it is not the expressed emotion of the speaker. It can not be taken to indicate the expressed emotion of the speaker, since it might have been used by the speaker to ask about the listener's emotion as in "Are you happy?".

Nevertheless, some cases should not be just ignored but analyzed more rigorously with additional cue words. For example, if a demonstrative adjective or adverb such as 'like this' is placed in the temporal or conditional clause, it is the clue that the moment of the clause is current. The third emotion in Example 2 is the case in point. In addition, the emotions with those clauses sometimes indicate other emotions such as worry in Example 3. The younger brother expresses worry about his elder brother by assuming that his elder brother would regret in a certain condition. Example 4 also shows the case with a rigorous analysis for interrogative sentences. The speaker sometimes emphasizes her emotion ironically in the interrogative form (4a) or asks about the listener's emotion with her expectation as shown in (4b).

3. Key [Brother, if you get married now, you will surely regret it. You can't live the life of a bachelor twice, you know? This is the best time of your life...]

4. (a) Mr. Park [Do I look like a person who likes to get a rich daughter-in-law?]

   (b) KeyJung [On my way to a bookstore, I saw a beggar's play.]
       Key [Well..Isn't it fun to watch?]

5.4 Strengthening Vague Expressions into Marked Ones

People often express their emotions by an exclamation such as 'Wow' or a sigh. However, such exclamations alone may not represent any emotion, because there are many different emotions in sentences with the same exclamation as in Example 5. The emotion in (5a) is close to 'Joy' or 'Positive', and that in (5b) is close to 'Anger' or 'Negative'. Without the exclamation, both cases would have vague emotions. In addition, some evaluative words that are commonly used in only 'positive' or 'negative' sense may have an inverted sense in the sentence with exclamation words as in Example 6.

5. (a) Oh my god it is so nice. Oh my god.
   (b) Oh my god. Look at you, you are so spoiled by good luck.

6. You are doing so well, darn it.

$$\begin{array}{ccc}
\text{onul} & \text{cengmal} & \text{kamsahaysseyo} \\
\text{today} & \text{so} & \text{thankful}
\end{array}$$

$$
\begin{array}{ccc}
s : [EMO@TENSE, & s : [EMO@TENSE, & s : [gratitude@past, \\
EXPR, TAR, & EXPR, TAR, & EXPR, TAR, \\
today, INTENSITY] & TIME, (surface@so@high)] & TIME, INTENSITY] \\
/s : [EMO@TENSE, & /s : [EMO@TENSE, & \\
EXPR, TAR, & EXPR, TAR, & \\
TIME, INTENSITY] & TIME, INTENSITY] &
\end{array}
$$

$$\xrightarrow{\quad\quad} s : [gratitude@past, EXPR, TAR,$$
$$TIME, (surface@so@high)]$$

$$\xrightarrow{\quad\quad} s : [gratitude@past, EXPR, TAR, today, (surface@so@high)]$$

Fig. 2. CCG derivation

6   Encoding Emotions with Parsing

We show how to annotate text with emotion information during (or after) syntactic parsing with a lexicalized grammar. We use Combinatory Categorial Grammar (CCG, [16]) to extract the necessary information from natural language sentences as discussed in Sections 4 and 5. CCGs make it possible to use a single derivation for the analyses of syntactic, semantic and discourse information in a sentence, by utilizing the relevant information as 'categories' encoded in each lexical item. Each category consists of syntactic and semantic information separated by ':'. Syntactic information is either *np* or *s* with an additional feature having values 'case' or words for emotion labels. The semantic information describes the necessary information for the purpose of estimating the correct valence or emotion label with features such as duration, target, and intensity. Table 4 shows the details of each argument. Figure 2 shows an example CCG derivation of the Korean sentence, whose meaning is "I am so thankful today."

Table 4. Semantic information

Argument	Description
EMO@TENSE	[Well-known emotion words or
	evaluation-activity values]@[Tense]
EXPR	[The experiencer]
TAR	[Possible targets (either listener or other persons)]
TIME	[Temporal information for duration]
INTENSITY	[Surface intensity for actual intensity]

After getting the necessary information for emotion representation, we convert the derived information to the proposed representation. Figure 3 shows the relation between derived information and the values of conventions.

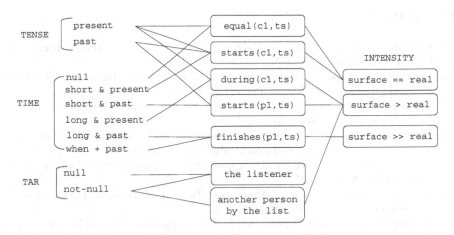

Fig. 3. Relations between derived information and conventions

7 Discussion and Conclusion

We have discussed in this paper the distinct features of emotions from text to identify subtle emotional cues of a human user and represented them with emotion labels, duration, target, and intensity. To acquire more accurate and unambiguous information for the representation, we need to consider additional linguistic constructions such as coordination structures for blended emotions, anaphoric expressions for target, and discourse structures for disambiguating cues. The use of a CCG framework achieves some of these goals, thanks to its flexible notion of syntactic constituents, but much more study is called for. In addition, an analysis for repetitive phrasal patterns affecting intensity or epithets conveying some strong negative emotions in a given context would also be effective.

Combining information from diverse modalities is considered as a hard problem. We believe that we should take the characteristic of each modality into account to handle the conflict among different modalities in a corpus. The HU-MAINE research group has proposed EARL (Emotion and Annotation Representation Language) to allow users to annotate emotions with combinations of categories, abstract dimension, and an appraisal theory [17]. We expect that the proposed representation in text could compensate for the lack of information from other modalities by adding informative tags into such a language.

Acknowledgments. This research was performed for the Intelligent Robotics Development Program, one of the 21st Century Frontier R&D Programs, and Brain Science Research Center, funded by the Ministry of Commerce, Industry and Energy of Korea.

References

1. Ekman, P.: Basic emotions, In Dalgleish T. and J.M. Power (Eds.), Handbook of Cognition & Emotion, New York (1999) 301–320
2. Osgood, C.E., May, W.H., Miron, M.S.: Cross-cultural Universals of Affective Meaning, University of Illinois Press, Urbana (1975)
3. Ortony, A., Clore, G.L., Collins, A.: The Cognitive Structure of Emotions, Cambridge University Press (1988)
4. Abrilian, S., Devillers, L., Buisine, S., Martin, J.C.: EmoTV1: Annotation of Real-life Emotions for the Specification of Multimodal Affective Interfaces, In Proceedings of 11th International Conference on Human-Computer Interaction (HCI International) (2005) 22–27
5. Kipp, M.: Anvil - A Generic Annotation Tool for Multimodal Dialogue, In Proceedings of Eurospeech'01 (2001) 1367–1370
6. Vidarascu, L., Devillers, L.: Real-life Emotion Representaion and Detection in Call Centers Data, ASCII 2005, Lecture Notes in Computer Science, Vol.3784. Springer-Verlag, Berlin Heidelberg (2005) 739–746
7. Douglas-Cowie, E., Devillers, L., Martin, J., Cowie, R., Savvidou, S., Abrilian, S., Cox, C.: Multimodal Databases of Everyday Emotion: Facing up to Complexity, In Proceedings of INTERSPEECH 2005, Lisbon, Portugal, September (2005) 813–816
8. Cowie, R., Douglas-Cowie, E., Savvidou, S., McMahon, E., Sawey, S., and Schroder, M.: "FEELTRACE": An Instrument for Recording Perceived Emotion in Real Time, ISCA Workshop on Speech & Emotion (2000) 19–24
9. Liu, H., Liberman, L., Selker, T.: A Model of Textual Affect Sensing using Real-World Knowledge, In Proceedings of International conference on User Interface, Miami, Florida, USA, January (2003) 125–132
10. Zhe, X., Boucouvalas, A.: Text-to-Emotion Engine for Real Time Internet Communication, In Proceedings of the International Symposium on Communication Systems, Networks and DSPs, Staffordshire University, UK, July (2002) 164–168
11. Fitrianie, S., Wiggers, P., Rothkarantz, L.J.M.: A Multi-modal Eliza Using Natural Language Processing and Emotion Recognition, In Proceedings of Text, Speech, and Dialogue (TSD) 2003, LNAI 2807 (2003) 394–399
12. Wilson, T., Wiebe, J., Hoffman, P.: Recognizing contextual polarity in phrase-level sentiment analysis, In Proceedings of HLT/EMNLP, Vancouver, October (2005) 347–354
13. Litman, D.J., Forbes-Riley, K.: Predicting Student Emotions in Computer-Human Tutoring Dialogue, In Proceedings of the 42nd Annual Meeting of the Association for Computational Linguistics, Barcelona, Spain, July (2004) 352–359
14. Ahn, S., Lee, S., Kwon, O.: Activation Dimension: A Mirage in the Affective Space, Korean J. of Social Psychology, 7(1), (1993) 107–123
15. Gabbay, D.M., Kurucz, A., Wolter, F., Zakharyaschev, M.: Many-Dimensional Modal Logics: Theory and Applications, Elsevier Science B.V. (2003)
16. Steedman, M.: The Syntactic Process, The MIT Press (2000)
17. The Humaine Research Group: the Emotion Annotation and Representation Language specification, http://emotion-research.net/earl/index_html (2006)

An Evaluation of UNL Usability
for High Quality Multilingualization
and Projections for a Future UNL++ Language

Christian Boitet[1], Igor M. Boguslavskij[2], and Jesus Cardeñosa[3]

[1] GETA, CLIPS, IMAG, BP53, 385 rue de la Bibliothèque
38041 Grenoble cedex 9, France
Christian.Boitet@imag.fr
[2] IPPI PAN GSP-4, Bol'shoj Karetnyj per. 19,
Moscow 101447, Russia
bogus@iitp.ru
[3] VAI, AI Department, UPM Campus de Montegancedo
28660 Boadilla del Monte
Madrid (Spain)
carde@fi.upm.es

Abstract. In a recent experiment on translating a web site into 4 languages, we have confirmed that using MT results in "translator's mode" can reduce the human work to produce good translations of complex sentences (25 w) at a rate of 25 mn/p with all-purpose commercial MT and at 20 mn/p with lab quality MT. A subexperiment has shown that using deconversions from quality-checked interlingual representations (UNL graphs) reduced the time spent down to 10 mn/p. Reducing the considerable time now needed for producing and checking UNL graphs is possible, which leads to very good usability prospects in situations involving many target languages and allowing for interactive disambiguation of source text or correction of interlingua. An analysis of improvable aspects in both interlingua design and resource building leads to a "roadmap" towards "UNL++" in the framework of the U++C consortium, including strong mutualization (collaborative volunteer work) and open-source aspects.

1 Introduction

The need for crosslingual communication as well as the number of languages involved is dramatically increasing. Europe has 21 official languages (from 9 in 1982) and soon to become 23, India 18, etc. Commercial software is typically translated (localized) into 25—40 languages, Open Source software like Mozilla into 70. Needs increase for the 4 main "translational situations", which are, in increasing order of difficulty of automation:

1. production of high-quality (HQ) translation by bilinguals (dissemination by bilinguals),
2. understanding text or speech in an unknown language (assimilation),
3. production of HQ translation from an unknown language (HQ assimilation by monolinguals),

A. Gelbukh (Ed.): CICLing 2007, LNCS 4394, pp. 361–373, 2007.

4. production of HQ translation into unknown languages (HQ dissemination by monolinguals).

The first is the easiest to automate, because bilingual experts basically only need good lexical support to produce quality results. It is very important to emphasize here that HQ translation by bilingual professional translators is usually ONLY into their native language(s), and not from their native language into the near-native language. This is different from other professions like bilingual secretaries who are not trained translators, and who are usually expected to translate in both directions. Therefore, HQ translation by professional translators is only in the direction of Dissemination (Outbound/Outward) translation.

For complex sentences with an average of 25.6 words, there are 2 steps corresponding to the workflow of a traditional human translation cycle. The first step is a first draft with a "proposed" HQ draft translation, and the second step is the editing/proofreading stage of the first draft. The first draft is produced in about 60 mn/page[1], in "translator's mode" (the source text is first read and understood) and the second step produces a HQ final result in 20 mn/p, in "revisor's mode" (the first draft is read and corrected, and the source text is consulted only if necessary), a total of 80 mn/page. For less complex sentences, these times go down to 45+15=60 mn/page[2]. In general, (Allen 2006) reports that using outputs of commercial MT systems as "pre-translations" can divide the total time by 3, to 25 or 20 mn/page[3].

The second task (assimilation by a monolingual) is more difficult: MT outputs which can be used quite efficiently in the previous situation can be almost ununderstandable by somebody not knowing the source language. Example: "he is a big shot and bronzed" instead of "he has a long and bronzed arm"[4]. Everybody has the experience of getting a web page translated by a "web translator": in most cases, the general topic can at least be roughly understood, but the exact details about what is said and meant cannot be understood. In other words, it is easier to simply detect a potentially interesting passage than to measure the full comprehension of such a passage.

Automating the third task can be done by building "expert" MT systems specialized to the typology and domain at hand. That has been achieved by hand-crafted heuristic symbolic MT systems (such as METEO or ALT/Flash), by dynamic adaptation of symbolic systems augmented with weights, by pure or hybrid example-based (EBMT) and by statistical MT systems (SMT).

Automating the last task seems to be impossible without integrating translation into an authoring environment and thus making it possible to get the "intended meaning" of the author through interactive disambiguation, and/or by imposing a controlled language.

---

[1] A standard page is about 250 words long in English.

[2] At EACL-05, Comprendium mentioned 60 mn using only dictionaries, 30 mn with translation memory, and 5 mn using a tailored MT system making the best of the parallelism between Spanish, Catalan and Galician.

[3] At AMTA-2004, J. Allen reported an experiment where the pre-translation and in-translation processing steps (candidate identification for dictionary building + coding + testing the terms in translation mode, plus verification and retranslation) took 6.5—7 hours for 8000 words, and final post-editing stage 30-45 minutes, or 26+4 = 30 mn/page, a division by 3.

[4] Real example from a "longest match" MT system on "Il a le bras long et bronzé" — "avoir le bras long" means "to be a big shot".

Next to the problem of producing translations "good enough" for the task at hand, there is the problem of producing them for many language pairs. Translating through "pivot" (interface) natural languages is possible if an excellent first translation is produced. It is not an option with unrevised MT of general texts, even with the best systems, because the intermediate text often if not always contains ungrammaticalities, ambiguities, and unknown source words. Building N(N-1) direct systems is also not an option in most situations[5].

A possible solution is to "compose" transfer-based MT systems through intermediate descriptors of the "pivot language", getting a "linguistic pivot" architecture. But understanding and hence directly editing a complex structure that fully represents a NL utterance is next to impossible for most people.

The last solution is to use a "pivot" architecture based on an abstract interlingua. Semantico-pragmatic pivots have been used successfully for restricted situations[6], but it seems impossible to extend them to handle general language. By contrast, semantico-linguistic pivots have been used successfully, in particular in the MT systems ATLAS-II (Fujitsu), PIVOT (NEC), CICC (ODA), and KANT/CATALYST (CMU/Caterpillar).

UNL (Universal Networking Language) has been introduced in 1996 by H. Uchida, the main designer of ATLAS-II, as an "open" successor of the CICC interlingua, itself a successor of the ATLAS-II proprietary pivot. A UNL (hyper)graph represents a disambiguated abstract structure of an English utterance equivalent to the utterance (in any language) to be represented, and its symbols (relations, attributes, and lexemes, called UW) are English words, acronyms or structured strings built from English words or acronyms. Understanding UNL graphs is quite easy for anybody having a high school level English (GRE and GMAT exams, say), hence for the vast majority of developers in today's world. See www.undl.org for more details.

In this paper, we try to evaluate the usability of UNL in a real setting, and propose ways to improve it to a point where 10 complex pages could be obtained (in a mutualizing — work sharing — setting) after 1 day in 20 or more languages, and require less than 1 hour of human work for each version (each target language).

In the first section, we describe a recent experiment on translating the Unesco B@bel web site into 4 languages, which confirmed that the use of MT "pre-translations" to get good translations can divide the human work time by 3 or more, and that the use of "deconversions" from quality-checked UNL graphs can divide it by up to 8, not counting the time needed for producing and checking UNL graphs. The second section presents an analysis of improvable aspects in both interlingua design and resource building, and the third a "roadmap" towards a "U++" framework, including strong mutualization and open-source aspects.

---

[5] Although Ph. Koehn has recently built SMT systems for the 110 language pairs of the EuroParl corpus, the minimum size of the parallel corpus seems to lie between 50 and 200M words (200K to 800K pages). Adding a new language may need 10 years of human translation (at a rate of 20K pages of debates a year). Porting to many typologies requires to find large enough parallel corpora.

[6] The very first was the TITUS system at the Institut Textile de France (Ducrot 1976). Task-oriented Speech Translation systems such as MASTOR-1 (IBM) also use that technique — and are built by statistical means.

2 Embedding a Comparative Task-Related Evaluation of UNL in a Real Translation Task

The main goal of the experiment was to study how to automate and "mutualize" the multilinguization of web sites and other documents of Unesco and other international cultural bodies in the future. The 3 partner labs working on the project:

- translated the textual material (in English) of the B@bel UNESCO web site, equivalent to 173 standard pages (43200 words), into French, Spanish, Russian and Chinese, with an "operational" output quality;
- evaluated the gain obtained by using MT systems to produce "pre-transations" of the whole material (SYSTRAN v5.0 Premium for French, Spanish and Chinese[7], and ETAP-3 of the IPPI lab for Russian);
- evaluated the gain obtainable by using UNL: we produced 906 "good" UNL graphs for the most complex part of the corpus ($\approx$23200 words), a time-consuming task[8], automatically deconverted[9] them in French, Spanish and Russian, and post-edited sample results in various settings;
- created a web site for distributed development, and put all results on it.

2.1 Steps of the Experiment

We used an SQL dump of the Unesco/B@bel data base to build our own database of "polyphrases" (sets of versions of a sentence in the source and target languages as well as in UNL), thereby segmenting B@bel "text containers" into sentences, and factorizing identical source sentences in the same polyphrase. A web site for translation and UNL-ization was implemented as an extension of an existing UNL deconversion web service. We produced the final translation into French, Russian, Spanish, and Chinese, using a simple Excel format (see Annex) to work in "translator's mode" and to measure times.

In parallel, we produced UNL graphs, created missing UWs (UNL lexemes), and linked them to associated dictionary entries in English, French, Russian and Spanish. A semi-automatic analyzer and editor of UNL graphs was used to help enconversion for about half the graphs while the other half was created manually. Some time (not directly measured) was spent on unifying the UNL-ization process itself (how to "encode" various phenomena).

Existing deconverters were improved to cope with this corpus, and were run on the 906 graphs. A sample of 50 of the obtained deconversions (about 5 standard pages of 250 words) was then used as pre-translations and post-edited.

---

[7] Chinese was translated but could not be evaluated.

[8] Even if their construction is automated, they must be revised to ensure a high quality, so that deconversions are the best possible.

[9] We use "analysis" and generation" if staying in the same "lexical space", "enconversion" and deconversion" if there is a change of lexical space (a lexical transfer).

2.2 Measured Results

Here are the main results.

- Using MT outputs as pre-translations, and working in translator's mode (reading the source text, then looking at the pre-translation and making the best of it), divides the total human translation time (80 mn/p[10]) by more than 3 (25 mn/p) using SYSTRAN v5.0 and by 4 (20 mn/p) using ETAP-3.
- Deconversion outputs were post-edited under various ergonomic conditions, in time sessions ranging from 10 to 25 mn/p (with or without seing the UNL graph).
- Producing UNL graphs manually and semi-automatically took 4.5 h/p to 3.2 h/p, including the time ot add missing dictionary entries.
- Producing a new UW and linking it to Spanish took 100 s and 123 s (~2 mn).

2.3 Potential Actual and Future Gains

Results and projections (for 10 & 20 target languages) are summarized in the following table, where lines UNL-sa1 and UNL-sa2 are projections for mid-term and long-term speed-ups in graph creation.

Table 1. Measures and projections[11]

Text type	Simple (12 w/s)				Complex (25 w/s)			
10 target languages	1st draft	Bil. Rev	UNL Rev	Tot	1st draft	Bil. Rev	UNL Rev	Tot
H only	45	15	—	60	60	20	—	80
H+TM	20	5	—	25	30	10	—	40
MT-gen	0	15	—	15	0	25	—	25
MT-spec	0	5	—	5	0	15	—	15
UNL-man	120	—	10	22	240	—	10	34
UNL-sa1	*20*	—	*8*	*10*	*30*	—	*8*	*11*
UNL-sa2	*10*	—	*5*	*6*	*15*	—	*5*	*6.5*
20 target languages (UNL-man time is spread over them)								
UNL-man	120	—	10	16	240	—	10	22
UNL-sa1	*20*	—	*8*	*9*	*30*	—	*8*	*9.5*
UNL-sa2	*10*	—	*5*	*5.5*	*15*	—	*5*	*5.7*

Hence, using MT is a viable option, immediately usable for the existing commercial "language pairs[12]", and using an architecture based on UNL or a UNL-like "pivot" will probably be more time-saving and applicable to many more target languages in the future. Even with manual production of the UNL graphs, if 20

---

[10] mn/p = minute per page, h/p = hour per page, w/s = word per sentence.

[11] TL = target language, H = human, TM = translation memory, MT-gen = general purpose MT, MT-spec = specialized MT, UNL-man = manual creation of UNL graphs, UNL-sa1, 2 = semi-automatic creation of same, UNL-Rev = revision of deconverted text.

[12] A "pair" is taken here to be *ordered,* as in mathematics: there are 2 language pairs for any set of 2 different languages.

target languages are considered, using UNL to translate general texts with complex sentences should be more efficient than using classical MT general-purpose systems... which anyway don't exist[13] and cannot be built for hundreds of language pairs (380 now in Europe only).

3 Aspects to Improve in the UNL Way

Improvements to be introduced concern the development process, the specification of the language, and tools.

3.1 Common Development Web Platform

Although the experiment web site offers a very useful possibility, namely to instantly produce a drawing of any correct UNL graph, and to edit the dictionary and the translations, it is not yet sophisticated enough to be used as a "web translator workstation", nor as a "UNL graph factory". What is needed is:

- a common lexical database available on the web for day to day cooperative work;
- web-enabled editing facilities usable on the database of texts and graphs;
- a web-oriented meta-EDL [14] communicating with the EDLs of developers (different tools are used for different languages).

3.2 UNL Specification and UW Construction

The UNL project (UNLP) was launched as an international academic cooperation project led by the IAS/UNU[15], mostly funded by the Japanese ASCII company. Funding dwindled in 1998 when the Japanese "bubble" exploded, and there was no opportunity to discuss and adopt necessary improvements.

The most important problems concerning the specifications are:

- Absence of arguments on UWs and arcs in UNL graphs.(1) Semantic relations cannot be reliably assigned to arguments of predicates, so that ambiguities arise (e.g. "John$_{agt}$ gives a book$_{obj}$ to Dan$_{ben}$ for Mary$_{ben}$" and "John$_{agt}$ gives a book$_{obj}$ for Dan$_{ben}$ to Mary$_{ben}$"[16]). (2) The same relation may connect both an argument and an adjunct to the same predicate (e.g *borrow* and *dur*(ation): *He borrowed money for three years* (argument) – *He has been borrowing money all his life* (non-argument). Because of this, we need to have an argument label on relations in the graph.

- Unsatisfactory UW creation process: the SMTP-based "UW gate" was never usable in real time, and the absence of comments prevented common understanding and coherent development of the UW lexicon;

---

[13] See http://www.translatorscafe.com/cafe/MegaBBS/
thread-view.asp?threadid=4693&messageid=62125#62125 (12/12/06).
[14] EDL = Environment for Developing Lingware.
[15] Institute of Advanced Studies of the United Nations University, Tokyo.
[16] Using 2 relations, *ben* and *gol*, does not help unless they are associated in advance to some arguments in the dictionary.

- Impossibility of consensus-based evolution of the specifications within the UNLP organization, something unacceptable in an academic and cooperative endeavour;
- UNL multilingual document format based on HTML: special tags such as [S], [/S], {org}, {/org}, {unl}, {/unl} and a notation for attributes were introduced before XML existed, in a quite clever way. A standard and as simple XML format is needed to take advantage of XML-associated tools.

3.3 Need for Open Source and More Tools

The UNLP distributes some tools (UNL-html viewer, UNL verifier, Dictionary Builder, and the rule-based languages EnCo and DeCo), which is remarkable considering the small size of the Tokyo-based team. But they run only under Windows, are access-restricted and not Open Source, and bugs are rarely fixed. The following Open Source tools are needed:

- UNL-graph editors: there are some, but not robust enough, and not usable on the web.
- Debugged & open versions of EnCo, DeCo, the Specialized Languages for Linguistic Programming (SLLPs) rule-based programming languages distributed by the UNLP.
- XML-based tools: format converters, XML-based viewer complementing the UNLP HTML-viewer, editors of full documents containing UNL and multilingual versions.
- New, more powerful NLP tools: DeCo and EnCo have no variables, no facility for structured programming, and cannot produce multiple solutions, although they offer backtracking. Useful tools include:
  - FST-based tools for morphology (with EnCo and DeCo, more than 15K rules had to be written for Russian);
  - Tools for multiple scored analysis: dependency, constituent or mixed;
  - Tree↔graph converters;
  - Tree-transformation tools[17]
- Corpus-based learning tools: although the UNL design is simple enough to teach newcomers quite quickly and get results in new languages in a few months, scaling up is a very time-intensive task.
  - To port to new languages, aligners between text and UNL trees (unfolded UNL graphs) would make it possible to "infer" deconverters and enconverters from parallel corpora containing UNL.
  - To speed up development, tools should be developed to produce UWs from existing lexical resources.

4 A New Impetus: The U++ Consortium

We describe now the "roadmap" on which the new "U++ consortium" (U++C) is working.

---

[17] From "learnable" Thatcher & Wright Tree-FST to systems like TELESI (Chauché, LIRMM), ROBRA (Ariane system, Grenoble), GRADE (MU-system, Kyoto) or GWS (ISS, Singapore), etc.

4.1 Goals

This non profit, open-source oriented organization was created by some UNL language centers and external partners just before the CICLING-05 conference, in the presence of Pr. T. Della Senta, president of the UNDL foundation. Its goals are to promote the development of UNL-related standards, and to offer related open-source resources and tools contributed *à la Linux* and *à la W3C*. The U++C complements the UNDL in various ways. In particular, it will participate as such in project proposals in answering EU calls, which UNDL is not considering due to its statute (a Swiss foundation under Unitar/UN). Another point is that it tries to set clear, measurable performance goals for concrete applications corresponding to urgent needs, while UNDL is promoting more futuristic research, for instance on "UNL encyclopedia", "semantic computing", and "knowledge management". As the "UNL" name and logo are reserved by UNDL and UNLP, we have introduced a new name, U++C, to show at the same time the relation and the difference.

Here are the concrete goals the U++C proposes to reach in 3-4 years.

- Translation and maintenance times:

Table 2. Time objectives of U++C

Text type	Simple (12 w/s)				Complex (25 w/s)			
20 TL	U++ creat.	Bil. Rv	U++ Rv	Tot /TL	U++ creat.	Bil. Rev	U++ Rev	Tot /TL
UNL-m	120	—	10	16	240	—	10	22
U++	5	—	2	2.25	10	—	4	4.5
	0.5 UW/p	NL dict.	NL proc.	Tot /TL	1 UW/p	NL dict.	NL proc.	Tot /TL
Ling. devt	2	1	1	2.1	2	4	1	5.1
Total	7	1	2.5	4.35	12	4	5	9.6

- Operational integration: integrate UNL in at least 2 types of applications, such as multilingual public web site (as B@bel), cause-oriented document translation, Open Source software localization, specific operation of multilingual document production/assimilation.
- Delay for contribution quality enhancement: 10 complex pages should be obtainable (in a mutualized setting) after 1 day, in 20 or more languages, and require less than 1 hour (6 mn/p) of human work for each version (each target language).

4.2 Roadmap

In this paper, we call UNL++ the variant on UNL on which the U++C is working.

4.2.1 U++C Lexicon

4.2.1.1 Evolution from UWs to XUWs. We propose the term "eXtended UW" or XUW for the U++C variant of UWs. Since the XUW dictionary is a collection of meanings coming from different languages, XUWs should be:

- complex and flexible enough to express all meanings of all natural languages.
- simple enough to be understood by people from different languages and cultures.
- built with reference to widely used theories & resources, to get very large potential cooperation and contributions.
- accompanied by structured comments in English.

A UW[18] is made of an English "headword" and a list of restrictions. The evolution towards XUW will include the following (described in more detail in a still internal document written by the 2nd author).

- Use of WordNet (WN) to get a 1st degree intuitive & open disambiguation "tag":
  - if a headword X is the first element of a synset, and Y is its most immediate hypernym in a given sense, the UW is built from: `X(icl>Y)`. Example:

```
pen(icl>writing implement)
pen(icl>enclosure)
```

  - if X is not the first element of the synset, then the UW has the form: `X(icl>Y, equ>Z)`, where Y is the most immediate hypernym and Z is the first term of the synset. Example:

```
pen(icl>enclosure, equ>playpen)
pen(icl>correctional institution, equ>penitentiary)
```

- Indication of arguments with their semantic restrictions: Examples:

```
give(icl>do, agt.@A>thing, obj.@B>thing, gol.@C>thing)
borrow(icl>do, agt.@A>thing, obj.@B>thing, src.@C>volitional
    thing, dur.@D>time)
```

There are abbreviation rules: the preceding XUW (meaning "borrow something for some time) is the same as `borrow(icl>do, src.@C> volitional thing, dur.@D>time)` because all transitive verbal XUWs of type `do` have the 2 default arguments `(agt.@A>thing, obj.@B>thing)`.

If there is a restriction on a default, it must be expressed: `wash(icl>do, obj>cloth)` for *stirat'* in Russian (as opposed to *myt'*, used for dishes, hands, etc.). Note that the UNL knowledge-base (KB), if it contains the considered meaning, is useful to get the argument structure, while WN is not (until now).

- Other semantic restrictions are further indicated. Example: to land (*prizemljat'sja* vs. *vysazhivat'sja* in Russian) gives

```
land(icl>do, plf>sky)   //for a plane
land(icl>do, plf>water) //for a ship
```

- Special headwords
  - Allowing quoted headwords: even in English, some dictionary entries use accented characters illegal in UWs.

---

[18] UW = Universal Word: a UW denotes 1 (ideally) or more "lexical meanings" of at least one natural language.

- Special XUWs for mathematical expressions & relations, figures and icons, anchors, hyperlinks, references (to bibliography, footnotes…), punctuations (e.g. bulleted or numbered lists).

They cannot simply be put inside double quotes, as now. In particular, formulas can behave as predicates (a<b) or as nouns (a+b), and contain many special symbols not currently allowed. This has to be further elaborated.

- Direct and scope notations for complex English headwords which cannot all possibly be in the dictionaries.
  - Direct notation is simple but ambiguous, and requires to include part of an English parser in each deconverter:

```
national_radio_center(icl>place)
```

- Scope notation is more precise. If the XUW is not in a U++C-NL dictionary, the content of its headword is unfolded as a scope and compositional deconversion can be attempted. Example:

```
'(mod:01(center.@entry, radio) (mod(center.@entry, national'
(icl>place)
```

We thus know that "national" modifies "radio center" and can deconvert accordingly.

4.2.1.2 Practical Process. Development is planned in "batches":

- start from an available set corresponding to a real application (probably B@bel)
- then complete with most frequent English vocabulary with all meanings & refine if necessary for some NL.
- then augment according to applications.

Transformation steps for each "batch" of XUWs are the following: (1) use WN to get 1st degree intuitive & open disambiguation "tag"; (2) link with languages whenever possible; (3) build structured comments semi-automatically and complete them; (4) add arguments and semantic restrictions; (5) add other semantic restrictions.

4.2.2 Multilingual Lexical Database

It will contain the XUWs and their equivalent lemma in all languages considered in various versions, and should function in wiki mode. The source codes of the distant deconverters and enconverters do not have to be in the database, but enough to generate them should be there, as well as appropriate comments in the corresponding NL.

The structure of this database will extend that of the gohan.imag.fr/unldeco/ web server. It is inspired from the Papillon multilingual lexical database (3-tiers architecture) and is being built on the same Jibiki generic platform.

Logically, it is a large XML tree with a first level for XUWs (id, synonymous notations, comment, and metadata), then a level for the NL, then (under each language) the equivalent lemmas, in their different versions.

Physically, we use an SQL Database Management System such as PostGres with usual structured metadata and simple representation (id, XML string [, XML binary tree]) for the content. This way, the logical structure may change while the physical structure remains the same.

4.2.3 Multilingual Parallel Corpora

Again, this will be developed as an extension of the web sites built by the U++C partners since a few years. The current, incomplete version has been built with Enhydra so that it generates dynamic web pages corresponding to a subset of the corpus. It is already possible to edit the texts in natural languages and the textual form of the UNL graphs, but the challenge is to make it possible to interact graphically with the graphs through the web, and to make the "coedition" idea (Boitet & Tsai 2002) operational.

4.3 Spreading UNL Usage

The third but not least goal of the U++C is to promote the use of UNL in various contexts. There are 2 main directions:

- Embedding UNL in various applications and scenarios, such as Cross-Lingual Information Retrieval, Text and speech translation and Semantic web (UNL annotations)
- Extending UNL to many languages, by cloning from "near" languages and learning from parallel corpora.

5 Conclusion

Using deconversions from quality-checked interlingual (IL) representations such as UNL graphs is potentially a better approach to the production of HQ translations of general texts in dozens of languages than to try to build a quadratic number of classical binary MT systems. Even if the cost to produce HQ graphs is now high (3 to 4 h/p for complex text), it is quite low when spread over many target languages, and the overall cost is lower and is a better return on investment than the classical approach.

Going through a semantico-linguistic IL such as UNL also permits direct edition or indirect coedition of the IL, and hence, for the first time in history, sharing post-editing across the target languages. Nevertheless, IL creation should and can be sped up considerably, to 5-20 mn/p according to text complexity. We have described improvements in the engineering context as well as in the UNL specification and a "roadmap" to go from UNL to UNL++.

In concrete terms, the goals of the recently created U++ consortium are to lower the human time spent on producing HQ translations to less than 5 mn/p (respectively 3 mn/p) for complex (resp. simple) sentences, and less than 10 mn/p (resp. 5 mn/p) if counting the total human effort (adding work on lingware, whatever kind it is).

Thanks to a wiki-like organization, and to incremental improvement of the most important parts of the documents, the delay to get 10 pages translated in 20 languages or more could be less than 1 day (1h of wiki post-edition).

Acknowledgments

This work has been partially funded by Unesco contract number 4500020224. The authors would also like to thank deeply Jean-Philippe Guilbaud, Étienne Blanc, Gilles

Sérasset, Carolina Gallardo Pérez, and Leonid Iomdin, who contributed in an essential way to the work reported here. Thanks should also go to Jeff Allen and to the reviewers, for constructive and interesting improvements.

References

1. J. Allen (2006) *Documents and references on post-editing MT*. web site. http://www. geocities.com/mtpost-editing/
2. E. Blanc (2001) *From graph to tree : Processing UNL graph using an existing MT system.* Proc. First UNL Open Conference - Building Global Knowledge with UNL, Suzhou, China, 18-20 Nov. 2001, UNDL (Geneva), 6 p.
3. Boguslavsky, N. Frid, L. Iomdin, L. Kreidlin, I. Sagalova & V. Sizov (2000) *Creating a Universal Networking Language Module within an Advanced NLP System.* Proc. COLING-2000, Saarbrücken, 31/7—3/8/2000, ACL & Morgan Kaufmann, vol. 1/2, 83-89.
4. C. Boitet (2002a) *Advantages of the UNL language and format for web-oriented crosslingual applications.* Proc. Seminar on linguistic meaning representation and their applications over the World Wide Web, Penang, 20-22/8/2002, USM, 4 p.
5. C. Boitet (2002b) *A rationale for using UNL as an interlingua and more in various domains.* Proc. LREC-02 First International Workshop on UNL, other Interlinguas, and their Applications, Las Palmas, 26-31/5/2002, ELRA/ELDA, 23—26.
6. C. Boitet & W.-J. Tsai (2002) *Coedition to share text revision across languages.* Proc. COLING-02 WS on MT, Taipeh, 1/9/2002, 8 p.
7. J. Coch & K. Chevreau (2001) *Interactive Multilingual Generation.* Proc. CICLing-2001 (Computational Linguistics and Intelligent Text Processing), Mexico, February 2001, Springer, 239-250.
8. J.-M. Ducrot (1982) *TITUS IV*. In "Information research in Europe. Proc. of the EURIM 5 conf. (Versailles)", P. J. Taylor, ed., ASLIB, London.
9. J. Hutchins, W. Hartman & E. Hito (2005) *Compendium of Translation Software (directory of machine translation systems and computer-aided translation support tools.* EAMT (on behalf of IAMT), TIM/ISSCO, Geneva, 127 p. (Earlier editions of the Compendium, which list older systems and older versions of current systems, are available as PDF files from: http://ourworld.compuserve.com/homepages/WJHutchins/compendium. htm)
10. G. Sérasset & C. Boitet (1999) *UNL-French deconversion as transfer & generation from an interlingua with possible quality enhancement through offline human interaction.* Proc. MT Summit VII, Singapore, 13-17 September 1999, Asia Pacific Ass. for MT, 220—228.
11. G. Sérasset & C. Boitet (2000) On UNL as the future "html of the linguistic content" & the reuse of existing NLP components in UNL-related applications with the example of a UNL-French deconverter. Proc. COLING-2000, Saarbrücken, 31/7—3/8/2000, ACL & Morgan Kaufmann, vol. 2/2, 768—774.
12. X. Shi & Y. Chen (2001) *A UNL Deconverter for Chinese.* Proc. UNL-2001, Suzhou, April 2001, IPM, 6 p.
13. H. Uchida (1989) *ATLAS*. Proc. MTS-II (MT Summit), Munich, 16-18 août 1989, 152-157.
14. H. Uchida (2004) *The Universal Networking Language (UNL) Specifications Version 3 Edition 3*. UNL Center, UNDL Foundation, December 2004, 43 p. http://www.undl.org/ unlsys/unl/UNLSpecs33.pdf

Annex: Examples

ID (n° en cours)	nb_car	nb_car_val	nb_tot_mots	nb_pages	h_debut	duree_incr	duree_fin	duree_tot	nb_p_page		original (anglais)	traduction finale (français)	tr-SYSTRAN-5 (en_fr)
189	290	1196	35	8321	1,74				36	20.7	l. 1723 (11195/3779): 1196 car, 143 mots		
16601_name_en_1	25	28	3	3	0,01	0	0	0	0	0.0	Multilingual Web Browser.	Navigateur Web multilingue.	Web browser multilingue.
16601_scshort_en_3	223	223	24	27	0,10	0	0	0	0	0.0	This project was carried out within Initiative B@bel in cooperation with SIL International to support efforts aimed at developing software/tools promoting multilingualism in cyberspace.	Ce projet a été mené au sein de l'initiative B@bel en coopération avec SIL International pour soutenir des efforts visant à développer les logiciels/outils favorisant le multilinguisme dans le Cyberspace.	Ce projet a été mis à exécution dans l'initiative B@bel en coopération avec SIL international pour soutenir les efforts visés développant le logiciel/outils favorisant le multilinguisme dans Cyberspace.
16601_sclong_en_5	207	207	26	53	0,10	0	0	0	0	0.0	SIL International has developed Graphite engine which supports the display of complex and non-Roman scripts and is available for free download on the SIL International's website.	SIL International a développé le moteur Graphite qui supporte l'affichage des scripts complexes et non romains et est disponible en téléchargement libre sur le site Web de SIL International.	SIL International a développé le moteur de graphite qui soutient l'affichage des manuscrits complexes et non-Romains et est disponible pour le téléchargement libre sur le site Web international de SIL.
16601_sclong_en_6	239	239	28	81	0,11	0	0	0	0	0.0	The project will involve the incorporation of graphite's unique functionalities in other software applications, thereby contributing to the creation and dissemination of content in many currently lesser-used languages.	Le projet comportera l'incorporation des fonctionnalités uniques de Graphite dans d'autres applications logicielles, contribuant de ce fait à la création et à la diffusion du contenu dans beaucoup de langues actuellement moins utilisées.	Le projet comportera l'incorporation des fonctionnalités uniques du graphite dans d'autres applications de logiciel, contribuant de ce fait à la création et à la diffusion du contenu dans beaucoup de langues actuellement peu-utilisées.
16601_sclong_en_7	177	178	21	102	0,08	0	0	0	0	0.0	These products will also be freely disseminated with basic documentation facilitating the incorporation of Graphite by software developers in other products.	Ces produits seront également librement disséminés avec la documentation de base facilitant l'incorporation de Graphite par des réalisateurs de logiciel dans d'autres produits.	Ces produits également librement disséminés avec la documentation de base facilitant l'incorporation du graphite par des réalisateurs de logiciel dans d'autres produits.
16601_sclong_en_8	25	28	3	105	0,01	0	0	0	0	0.0	Multilingual web browser.	Navigateur Web multilingue.	Web browser multilingue.
16601_sclong_en_9	140	131	17	122	0,07	0	0	0	0	0.0	Web-page/site creation is one of the most common form of web publishing and information dissemination in cyberspace.	La création de page/sites Web est une des formes les plus communes d'édition sur le Web et de diffusion de l'information dans le cyberspace.	Le page Web/création d'emplacement est un de la forme la plus commune d'édition de Web et de diffusion de l'information dans le cyberspace.
16601_sclong_en_10	197	197	30	152	0,12	0	0	0	0	0.0	By developing a beta version of a web browser that supports creation and viewing of web pages in Burmese the ability to create and disseminate multilingual information will be promoted.	En développant une version bêta d'un navigateur Web qui supporta la création et la visualisation des pages Web en Birman, la capacité de créer et diffuser l'information multilingue sera favorisée.	En développant une bêta version d'un web browser qui soutient la création et la visualisation des pages Web dans le Birman la capacité de créer et diffuser l'information multilingue sera favorisé.
16601_sclong_en_11	79	79	10	162	0,04	0	0	0	0	0.0	The open-source Mozilla browser has been used for this development.	Le navigateur Mozilla à source ouvert a été employé pour ce développement.	Le navigateur de Mozilla d'ouvrir-source a été employé pour ce développement.

Here is a UNL graph with some corrections, for the English sentence:

It [Attawik.net] provides a content management system that allows native speakers to write, manage documents and offer online payments in the Inuit language

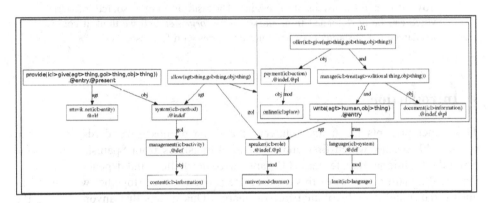

```
agt(provide(icl>give(agt>thing,gol>thing,obj>thing)).@entry.@present,
    attavik.net(icl>entity).@eld)
obj(provide(icl>give(agt>thing, gol>thing,obj>thing)).@entry.@present,
    system(icl>method).@indef)
gol(system(icl>method).@indef,management(icl>activity).@def)
obj(management(icl>activity).@def,content(icl>information))
agt(allow(agt>thing,obj>thing,gol>thing),system(icl>method).@indef)
gol(allow(agt>thing,obj>thing, gol>thing), speaker(icl>role).@indef.@pl)
obj(allow(agt>thing,obj>thing, gol>thing), :01)
obj:01(offer(icl>give(agt>thing,gol>thing,obj>thing)), payment(icl>action).@indef.@pl)
and:01(offer(icl>give(agt>thing,gol>thing,obj>thing)), manage(icl>treat(agt>volitional
    thing,obj>thing)))
obj:01(manage(icl>treat(agt>volitional thing,obj>thing)), document(icl>information).@indef.@pl)
and:01(manage(icl>treat(agt>volitional thing,obj>thing)), write(agt>human,obj>thing).@entry)
agt(:01, speaker(icl>role).@indef.@pl)
man(:01, language(icl>system).@def)
mod(speaker(icl>role).@indef.@pl,native(mod<human))
mod:01(payment(icl>action).@indef.@pl,online(icl>place))
mod(language(icl>system).@def,Inuit(icl>language))
```

Transfer-Based MT from Spanish into Basque: Reusability, Standardization and Open Source

Iñaki Alegria, Arantza Diaz de Ilarraza, Gorka Labaka, Mikel Lersundi,
Aingeru Mayor, and Kepa Sarasola

IXA Taldea, Informatika Fakultatea.University of the Basque Country,
649 PK. 20080 Donostia. Basque Country
i.alegria@ehu.es
http://ixa.si.ehu.es

Abstract. We present an open architecture we have designed in a project for machine translation from Spanish into Basque based on rules. The main objective has been the construction of an open, reusable and interoperable framework which can be improved in the next future combining it with the statistical model. The MT architecture reuses several open tools and it is based on an unique XML format for the flow between the different modules, which makes easer the interaction among different developers of tools and resources. Being Basque a resource-poor language this is a key feature in our aim for future improvements and extensions of the engine. The result is an open source software which can be downloaded from *matxin.sourceforge.net,* and we think it could be adapted to translating between other languages with few resources.

1 Introduction

This paper presents the main architecture and the proposed standards of an open source MT engine, which first implementation translates from Spanish into Basque using the traditional transfer model [9] and based on shallow and dependency parsing. One of the main novelties of this architecture is open-source (together with pilot linguistic data) and it is distributed free of charge. This means that anyone having the necessary computational and linguistic skills will be able to adapt or enhance it to produce a new MT system, even for other pairs of related languages or other NLP applications.

The design and the programs are independent from the languages, so the software can be used for other projects in MT especially when lesser-used languages are used. Depending on the languages included in the adaptation it will be necessary to add, reorder and change some modules, but it will not be difficult because an unique XML format is used for the communication among all the modules.

The project has been integrated in the *OpenTrad* initiative (*www.opentrad.com*), a government-funded project shared among different universities and small companies [6], which will also include MT engines for translation among the main languages in

A. Gelbukh (Ed.): CICLing 2007, LNCS 4394, pp. 374–384, 2007.

Spain. The main objective of this initiative is the construction of an open, reusable and interoperable framework.

In the *OpenTrad* project two different but coordinated designs have been carried out:

- A shallow-transfer machine translation engine for similar languages (Spanish, Catalan and Galician by the moment). The MT architecture uses finite-state transducers for lexical processing, hidden Markov models for part-of-speech tagging, and finite-state based chunking for structural transfer. It is named *Apertium* and it can be downloaded from *apertium.sourceforge.net*.
- A deeper-transfer engine for the Spanish-Basque pair, which will be described in this paper. It is named *Matxin* and it is stored in *matxin.sourceforge.net* and it is a continuation of previous work in our group [7].

Some of the components (modules, data formats and compilers) from the first architecture are used in the second. Indeed, an important additional goal of this work is testing which modules from the first architecture can be integrated in deeper-transfer architectures for more difficult language pairs.

The following sections give an overview of the architecture (sec. 2), the formats defined for the interoperation among the different modules (sec. 3), the encoding of linguistic data (sec. 4), the programs (sec. 5) and the evaluation (sec. 6). Finally, we give some concluding remarks (sec. 7).

2 General Architecture

The engine is a classical transfer system consisting of 3 main components: analysis of source language, transfer from the source to the target language and generation of the output. The main features are interoperability with other linguistic resources and convergence with other engines in the *OpenTrad* project through the use of an unique XML structure.

The main modules are five: de-formatter, analyser, transfer, generation and reformatter.

The analyzer, transfer and generation are based on three objects:

- nodes corresponding to lexical units (lexical form, lemma, POS tag and inflection information)
- chunks corresponding to syntactic units (type and dependencies among the nodes in the chunk)
- sentences (type and dependencies among the chunks in the sentence).

Because it is a general purpose engine no semantic disambiguation is applied (it is very difficult to improve the most probable sense), but a large number of multi-word units representing collocations, named-entities and complex terms are included in the bilingual dictionary in order to reduce the influence of this limitation. In the near future we will try solving semantic ambiguity inside a concrete domain. There is an exception: in the case of prepositions we try to desambiguate using the information about the argument structure of the verb.

2.1 The De-formatter

It separates the text to be translated from the format information (RTF, HTML, etc.). Two files are generated from the input: one with the format information and other with the source text for the translation process. In the first file links to the source texts are included. After the analysis phase, *ord* (order of the words in the chunk and of the chunks in the sentence) and *alloc* (position in the analysed text) (see section 3) attributes are added to the output in order to be able to link the translated text from the format file.

2.2 The Analyzer

The analyzer of the source language has to be a dependence grammar based engine. So, a module including tokenization, part-of-speech tagging, shallow parsing and dependence analysis will be necessary.

In order to reusing resources in our system the analysis is not included in *Matxin* and another open source engine, *FreeLing,* is used and its output is converted to the proposed interchange format.

FreeLing [5], basically a shallow-parser for Spanish and English, has been augmented with a dependency parser for Spanish during the *Opentrad* project [10]. This module links the dependencies among tokens in the chunk, and among chunks in the sentence. The output is an XML structure where the main elements are the chunks in the sentence, and the nodes (words) in the chunks.

The result from the analysis and the information managed in the next modules includes information about the three main objects: nodes, chunks and sentences.

2.3 The Transfer Module

The transfer module is also based on the three main objects in the translation process: words or nodes, chunks or phrases and sentences.

First, lexical transfer is carried out using a bilingual dictionary compiled into a finite-state transducer. We use the XML specification of *Apertium* engine..

Then, structural transfer at the sentence level is applied, and some information is transferred from some chunks to others and some chunks may disappear. Grammars based on regular expressions are used to specify these changes.

For example, in the Spanish-Basque transfer, the person and number information of the object and the type of subordination are imported from other chunks to the chunk corresponding to the verb chain.

Finally the structural transfer at the chunk level is carried out. This process can be quite simple (i.e. noun chains between Spanish and Basque) or more complex (i.e. verb chains in the same case).

2.4 The Generation

The XML file coming from the transfer module is passed on the generation module.

In the first step syntactic generation is performed in order to decide the order of the chunks in the sentence and the words in the chunks. Several grammars are used for this purpose (section 4.2).

Morphological generation which decides the target surface forms based on the lemmas and morphological information is carried out in the last step. In the generation of Basque the main inflection is added to the last word in the chunk (in Basque: the declension case, the number and other features are assigned to the whole noun phrase at the end of the last word), but in verb chains additional words need morphological generation. Bearing in mind reusability, standardization and open source, a previous morphological analyzer/generator for Basque [3] has been adapted and transformed to the format used in *Apertium*.(see 4.1 section).

2.5 The Re-formatter

Finally, the *re-formatter* links the translated text (result of the previous modules), and the format file (saved in the first module), rebuilding a formatted text from the links.

In this process some inconsistencies can be found and the presentation of some documents can include light changes.

```
<!ELEMENT  SENTENCE       (CHUNK+)>
<!ATTLIST  SENTENCE
       ord          CDATA          #REQUIRED
       ref          CDATA          #REQUIRED
>
<!ELEMENT  CHUNK  (NODE, CHUNK*)>
<!ATTLIST  CHUNK
       ord  CDATA                  #IMPLIED
       type (sn|grup-sp|grup-verb|conj-subord|F|.) #REQUIRED
       si   (subj|obj|...)         #IMPLIED
       ref  CDATA                  #IMPLIED
>
<!ELEMENT  NODE   (NODE*)>
<!ATTLIST  NODE
       ord          CDATA          #IMPLIED
       form         CDATA          #IMPLIED
       lem          CDATA          #REQUIRED
       pos          CDATA          #IMPLIED
       mi           CDATA          #REQUIRED
       ref          CDATA          #IMPLIED
       alloc        CDATA          #REQUIRED
```

Fig. 1. DTD for the output format of the analysis module

3 Formats for Interaction

A unique DTD specification (a simplified version is shown in fig. 1) has been designed to communicate the analysis, transfer and generation modules using XML tags.

```
<SENTENCE ord='1'>
<CHUNK ord='2' type='grup-verb' si='top'>
  <NODE ord='4' alloc='19' form='sacude' lem='sacudir'
                                          mi='VMIP3S0'/>
  <CHUNK ord='1' type='sn' si='subj'>
     <NODE ord='3' alloc='10' form='atentado' lem='atentado'
                                          mi='NCMS000'>
        <NODE ord='1' alloc='0' form='Un' lem='uno' mi='DI0MS0'/>
        <NODE ord='2' alloc='3' form='triple' lem='triple'
                                          mi='AQ0CS0'/>
     </NODE>
  </CHUNK>
  <CHUNK ord='3' type='sn' si='obj'>
     <NODE ord='5' alloc='26' form='Bagdad' lem='Bagdad'
                                          mi='NP00000'/>
  </CHUNK>
  <CHUNK ord='4' type='F-term' si='modnomatch'>
     <NODE ord='6' alloc='32' form='.' lem='.' mi='Fp'/>
  </CHUNK>
</CHUNK>
</SENTENCE>
```

Fig. 2. Output from the analysis module in the example

The main aim is to guarantee the interoperability among the modules, so that different developers can build or change one or several modules. Although post-editing is not included in the project, the format is able to save enough information for it.

Communication among submodules in each module uses the same format. An XSLT stylesheet is ready in order to help the analysis of the data among the different modules. Figure 2 shows the format for the analysis (*Un triple atentado sacude Bagdad – A triple explosion shook Bagdad*). It can be observed that a hierarchy system (it is clearer in fig. 3 when the XSLT stylesheet is applied) is used in order to explain the dependencies among chunks and among nodes in the chunk. It is a simple but powerful format. The attributes *alloc* and *ref* are managed in order to recovery the format in the input text, *mi* is for morphological information and *si* for the syntactical one. The attribute *ord* is used for ordering the elements in the sentence. The same DTD used for the output of the analysis is also used for the output of the transfer and generation steps, but optional *ref* attribute appears in order to remember the order in the original sentence.

After the transfer (Fig. 4) although slight changes in the structure the main changes are produced in the values of the attributes which will be correspond to Basque lemma and morphological or syntactical information instead of the corresponding Spanish information. The *ord* attribute disappears, because a new order will be calculated in the next step. The *form* attribute disappears too, waiting to the morphological generation.

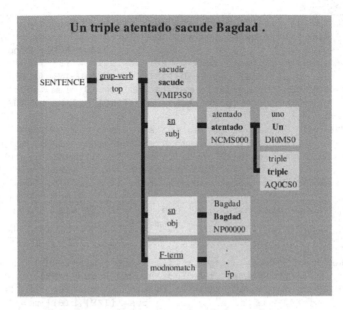

Fig. 3. Output after applying the XSLT stylesheet

```
<CHUNK ref='2' type='adi-kat' si='top' headpos='[ADI][SIN]'
       headlem='_astindu_' trans='DU' objMi='[NUMS]' cas='[ABS]'
                                                      length='2'>
   <NODE ref='4' alloc='19' lem='astindu' pos='[NAG]'
       mi='[ADI][SIN]+[AMM][ADOIN]+[ASP][EZBU]'>
     <NODE ref='4' alloc='19' lem='edun' pos='[ADL]'
                                         mi='[ADL][A1][NR_HU]'/>
   </NODE>
   <CHUNK ref='1' type='is' si='subj' mi='[NUMS]' headpos=
         '[IZE][ARR]' headlem='atentatu' cas='[ERG]' length='3'>
     <NODE ref='3' alloc='10' lem='atentatu' pos='[IZE][ARR]'
                                             mi='[NUMS]'>
         <NODE ref='1' alloc='0' lem='bat' pos='[DET][DZH]'/>
         <NODE ref='2' alloc='3' lem='hirukoitz' pos='[IZE][ARR]'/>
     </NODE>
   </CHUNK>
   <CHUNK ref='3' type='is' si='obj' mi='[NUMS]' headpos=
         '[IZE][LIB]' headlem='Bagdad' cas='[ABS]' length='1'>
     <NODE ref='5' alloc='26' lem='Bagdad' pos='[IZE][LIB]'
                                           mi='[NUMS]'/>
   </CHUNK>
   <CHUNK ref='4' type='p-buka' si='modnomatch' headpos='Fp'
                       headlem='.' cas='[ZERO]' length='1'>
     <NODE ref='6' alloc='32' lem='.' pos='Fp'/>
   </CHUNK>
</CHUNK>
```

Fig. 4. Output of the transfer module in the example

```
<CHUNK ord='2' ref='2' type='adi-kat' si='top' headpos=
     '[ADI][SIN]' headlem='_astindu_' trans='DU' objMi='[NUMS]'
                                    cas='[ABS]' length='2'>
   <NODE form='astintzen' ord='0' ref='4' alloc='19' lem='astindu'
          pos='[NAG]' mi='[ADI][SIN]+[AMM][ADOIN]+[ASP][EZBU]'>
      <NODE form='du' ord='1' ref='4' alloc='19' lem='edun'
                    pos='[ADL]' mi='[ADL][A1][NR_HU][NK_HU]'/>
   </NODE>
   <CHUNK ord='0' ref='1' type='is' si='subj' mi='[NUMS]' headpos=
           '[IZE][ARR]' headlem='atentatu' cas='[ERG]' length='3'>
      <NODE form='atentatu' ord='0' ref='3' alloc='10' lem=
                    'atentatu' pos='[IZE][ARR]' mi='[NUMS]'>
         <NODE form='batek' ord='2' ref='1' alloc='0' lem='bat'
                              pos='[DET][DZH]'/>
         <NODE form='hirukoitz' ord='1' ref='2' alloc='3'
                          lem='hirukoitz' pos='[IZE][ARR]'/>
      </NODE>
   </CHUNK>
   <CHUNK ord='1' ref='3' type='is' si='obj' mi='[NUMS]' headpos=
              '[IZE][LIB]' headlem='Bagdad' cas='[ABS]' length='1'>
      <NODE form='Bagdad' ord='0' ref='5' alloc='26' lem='Bagdad'
                          pos='[IZE][LIB]' mi='[NUMS]'/>
   </CHUNK>
   <CHUNK ord='3' ref='4' type='p-buka' si='modnomatch'
              headpos='Fp' headlem='.' cas='[ZERO]' length='1'>
      <NODE form='.' ord='0' ref='6' alloc='32' lem='.' pos='Fp'/>
   </CHUNK>
</CHUNK>
```

Fig. 5. Output of the generation module in the example

After the generation (Fig. 5) new information about order and word-form is added using the same XML structure..

4   Linguistic Data

An adequate documentation of the code and auxiliary files is crucial for the success of open source software.

In the case of a MT system, this implies carefully defining a systematic format for each source of linguistic data used by the system. At structural or syntax level the most of the grammars are based on regular expressions. At lexical level, morphological and bilingual dictionaries are used following the XML based proposal for the *Apertium* technology for dictionaries.

4.1   Dictionaries

Several dictionaries have been designed: morphological generation, lexical transfer, preposition transfer and verb subcategorization.

Morphological dictionaries. They establish the correspondences between surface forms and lexical forms for Basque and contain the following items:

- a definition of the alphabet (used by the tokenizer).
- a section defining the grammatical symbols used in a particular application to specify lexical forms (symbols representing concepts such as *noun, verb, plural, present,* etc.),
- a section defining paradigms (describing reusable groups of correspondences between parts of surface forms and parts of lexical forms).
- one or more labelled dictionary sections containing lists of "surface form — lexical form" correspondences for whole lexical units (including contiguous multi-word units).

Paradigms may be used directly in the dictionary sections or to build larger paradigms.

A finite-state transducer based library imported from the *Apertium* project manages the transfer and generation procedures using these dictionaries. More details about these formats and technology are shown in [4].

Bilingual dictionaries. They have a very similar structure and establish correspondences between source language lexical forms and target language lexical forms, but they seldom use paradigms.

A Spanish-Basque bilingual dictionary for lexical transfer and a Basque morphological dictionary for morphological generation, both in the proposed format, are included in the *Matxin* repository.

The "preposition-postposition" transfer process is carried out using a different dictionary where disambiguation is expressed using selection conditions. In the selection conditions chunk level attributes are used doing reference to the actual or the parent chunk.

The forth main dictionary manages the verb subcategorization during the generation process. For each verb a sorted list of elements including transitivity and postposition is specified. The first case which matches will be selected during the generation.

Finally, in order to separate programs and linguistic information and to manage resources from different origins, additional small dictionaries are included for several functions: conversion of syntax tags, semantic information for generation (in Basque different postpositions are used for living beings), mapping of features (for disagreements between bilingual and morphological dictionaries).

4.2 Grammars

Four main grammars are necessary for structural changes: transfer at chunk level (*intrachunk*), transfer at sentence level (*interchunk*), generation at chunk level and generation at sentence level.

Transfer at sentence level is specified in order to move syntactical attributes between chunks. The rules are expressed using 3 fields: attributes of the parent element (chunk), attributes of the child element (node or chunk) and type of movement (up or down).

The transference at chunk level is more complex. The rules of the grammar are declaratives and use complex regular expressions which, in order to simplify the program, are compiled into simpler regular expressions. The following three types of rules are used: (a) identification and markup rules; (b) attribute replacement rules; (c) cleaning rules. A grammar for the complex transfer process of verb chains from Basque to Spanish has been written using this specification and good results are obtained. More information about the format and the implementation can be obtained in [2].

The generation grammar at chunk level (*intrachunk*) specifies the final order of the elements in the chunk. For each chunk type a regular expression based on the syntactical information specifies the order of the elements in the chunk. After matching the root element of the chunk, the additional elements will be matched in function of its syntactical information.

The generation grammar at sentence level (*interchunk*) is based on rewriting rules where for two connected chunks (parent and children) the order is specified. The program carries out recursive process (it examines the analysis tree in postorder) to get the last result.

An additional grammar is used in order to reorder the morphological elements in the word before the morphological generation, due to the fix order necessary in this last process.

5 The Programs

The result of the project is composed by two components:

- an open-source library programmed in C++, which manages the text flow in the specified XML format and looks up in dictionaries and grammars.
- dictionaries and grammars for the transfer and generation in the pair Spanish-Basque.

This information is stored in a CVS repository publicly available at the website *matxin.sourceforge.net*. The library is quite powerful but not too complex, so this open source could be easily adapted to new languages.

6 Evaluation

At he moment we are tuning the lexical resources and evaluating the results for the Spanish/Basque system using *FreeLing* and *Matxin*. The quantitative evaluation uses the open source evaluation tool IQMT and figures are given using BLEU and NIST measures [8]. The evaluation corpus is composed by 50 phrases among 8 and 20 words taken randomly from some newspapers.

The first results can be observed in Table 1. Four different results are given; the first using two handmade translations as reference. This is the most habitual method. A second evaluation has been carried out adding a third reference, which is obtained editing the automatic translation in order to obtain a closer correct translation. This is

Table 1. Results of evaluation in the four cases:

Case	BLEU-3	BLEU-4	NIST-3
2 references	0.113	0.056	0.349
3 references	0.268	0.159	0.519
2 references and stemming	0.224	0.146	0.457
3 references and stemming	0.383	0.296	0.620

not useful for comparing with other systems, but it is an important information about the performance of the engine.

As Basque is an agglutinative language fewer and longer words than in the source text are obtained, so results are lower for the same quality of translation. Figures in the third and fourth rows are equivalents to first and second ones, but after applying a stemmer which divides some words in two, lemma and declension.

7 Conclusions

This paper has shown the design and development of an open transfer based MT architecture, which has been tested for the Spanish-Basque pair. The data are independent from the programs and have a clear specification, especially for the dictionaries which are XML based. All the communication among modules are carried out using an unique XML format.

Following the reusing philosophy inherent to the free software development some of the components (modules, data formats and compilers) are inherited from previous open-source projects (*FreeLing* and *Apertium*). It could be adapted to translating between other languages with few resources to be in the market of MT engines. We will try firstly for translating from English into Basque.

A deeper formalization and standardization in the grammars is necessary. In addition to this, in a near future we want to face to the principal remaining problem: resolving semantic ambiguity, where we are considering applying word-sense disambiguation based on the experience in our group [1].

Finally we want to combine the transfer based paradigm with statistical and example based paradigms in an open-source environment.

Acknowledgements. Work partially funded by the Spanish Ministry of Industry, Commerce and Tourism through project *EurOpenTrad* (FIT-350401-2006-5).

References

1. Agirre E., Martinez D. The Basque Country University system: English and Basque tasks. Proceedings of the 3rd ACL workshop on the Evaluation of Systems for the Semantic Analysis of Text (SENSEVAL).(2004)
2. Alegria I., A. Diaz de Ilarraza, G. Labaka, M. Lersundi. A. Mayor, K. Sarasola, A FST grammar for verb chain transfer in a Spanish-Basque MT System. Proc. of the Finite State Methods in Natural Language Processing workshop. (2005)

3. Alegria I., Artola Zubillaga X., Sarasola K. Automatic morphological analysis of Basque. Literary & Linguistic Computing Vol. 11, No. 4, 193-203. Oxford University Press. Oxford. (1996).
4. Armentano-Oller C, A. Corbí-Bellot, M. L. Forcada, M. Ginestí-Rosell, B. Bonev, S. Ortiz-Rojas, J. A. Pérez-Ortiz, G. Ramírez-Sánchez, F. Sánchez-Martínez, An open-source shallow-transfer machine translation toolbox: consequences of its release and availability. Proceedings of OSMaTran: Open-Source Machine Translation workshop, MT Summit X. (2005)
5. Carreras, X., I. Chao, L. Padró and M. Padró . FreeLing: An open source Suite of Language Analyzers, in Proceedings of the 4th International Conference on Language Resources and Evaluation (LREC'04). (2004)
6. Corbí-Bellot M., M. L. Forcada, S. Ortiz-Rojas, J. A. Perez-Ortiz, G. Ramirez-Sanchez, F. Sanchez-Martinez, I. Alegria, A. Mayor, K. Sarasola. An open source Shallow-Transfer Machine Translation Engine for the Romance Languages of Spain. Proceedings of the EAMT2005. (2005)
7. Díaz de Ilarraza A., Mayor A., Sarasola K. Reusability of Wide-Coverage Linguistic Resources in the Construction of a Multilingual Machine Translation System. Proc of MT 2000. University of Exeter.(2000)
8. Giménez J., E. Amigó, C. Hori. Machine Translation Evaluation Inside QARLA. In Proceedings of the International Workshop on Spoken Language Technology (IWSLT'05) (2005)
9. Hutchins, W. and Somers, H. An Introduction to Machine Translation. Academic Press. (1992).
10. Mayor A., J. Atserias , E. Comelles TXALA un analizador libre de dependencias para el castellano. In Proc. of the XXI SEPLN (2005)

Dependency-Based Chinese-English Statistical Machine Translation

Xiaodong Shi, Yidong Chen, and Jianfeng Jia

Department of Computer Science, Xiamen University
Xiamen 361005, Fujian, China
{mandel,ydchen}@xmu.edu.cn

Abstract. We present a Chinese-English Statistical Machine Translation (SMT) system based on dependency tree mappings. We use a state-of-the-art dependency parser to parse the English translation of the Penn Chinese Treebank to make it bilingual and then learn a tree-to-tree dependency mapping model. We also train a phrase-based translation model and collect a bilingual phrase lexicon to bootstrap a treelet translation model. For decoding, we use the same dependency parser on Chinese, using a log-linear framework to integrate the learned translation model with a variety of dependency tree based probability models, and then find the best English dependency tree by dynamic programming. Finally the English tree is flattened to produce the translation. We evaluate our system on the 863 and NIST 2005 Chinese-English MT test data and find that the dependency-based model significantly outperforms Caravan, our phrase-based SMT system which participated in NIST 2006 and IWSLT 2006.

1 Introduction

Recent advances in Statistical Machine Translation [Brown et al1993] have shown that syntax based model [Wu 1997, Yamada and Knight 2001] offers clear advantages to the still main-stream phrase based approaches [Koehn 2003]. There are a number of syntax-based approaches, among which finite state transducer based [Casacuberta 2004], constituent tree based [Yamada and Knight 2001], and dependency tree-based [Ding 2005, Fox 2005] are the main ones. Compared with the constituent tree used in the phrase structure grammar, the dependency tree model offers a number of advantages. For example, it is noted that different phrase structure grammar is often arbitrary in assigning complex phrase categories such as the noun phrases because there are so many types of them. Either each grammarian can have his/her own say in choosing a particular number of phrasal categories, or choose a theoretically appealing but practically inadequate linguistic theory (like X-bar theory), or revert to rather impoverished phrase type as found in Penn Treebank [Marcus 1993]. Because dependencies usually only exist between words, this problem is avoided. The dependency relation in a typical dependency model is more convenient in determining deeper semantic relations such as predicate-argument structure, whereas constituent-based Treebanks have to be augmented with functional tags, which, however, is often dropped in statistical parsing to alleviate data sparseness [Collins 1999]. Dependency

A. Gelbukh (Ed.): CICLing 2007, LNCS 4394, pp. 385–396, 2007.
© Springer-Verlag Berlin Heidelberg 2007

model is naturally lexicalized, and lexicalization is often the key to the success in recent advances in NLP tasks such as part-of-speech tagging [Lee 2000] and statistical parsing [Collins 1997]. Because dependency tree is more cross-lingual than constituent tree [Fox 2002], syntax-based machine translation based on dependency grammar is a promising avenue to explore.

A number of people have explored Dependency-based Statistical Machine Translation (henceforth DPSMT) approaches. Among others, the following works are especially representative:

1. [Alshawi et al 2000] encoded translation of two dependency structures through the synchronized hierarchical alignment of two strings. A collection of finite state head transducers were learned from a bitext and a Viterbi-like search of an optimal derivation over a transduction graph was performed to extract the best translation. No language model was employed.

2. [Cmejrek et al 2003] presented a simple DPSMT model in which source and target dependency trees were largely isomorphic and only simple lexical transfer was employed. Though there was some reordering of dependents, no language model was employed.

3. [Fox 2005] described a DPSMT model based on the noisy channel model, where the translation model encoded lexical translation probability, part-of-speech tag conversion probability, a head position probability, and a structural mutation probability. A constituent syntax based language model [Charniak 2003] was used to aid the decoding process.

4. [Ding 2005] introduced probabilistic synchronous model in which each source dependency tree was decomposed into a series of Elementary Tree (ET) non-deterministically and each ET was then transduced into a target ET. The target ETs were finally combined to generate the target sentence. A (probably bigram) language model was employed. This work was done on Chinese-English.

5. [Quirk 2005] described a Dependency Treelet Translation system which used dependency tree with a tree-based ordering model in combination with conventional phrased SMT models to produce state-of-the-art translations. They used a log-linear framework [Knoke 1980] to integrate a variety of feature model including a trigram language model.

In this paper we presents a more sophisticated DPSMT model which features a bottom-up decoding using learned treelet mapping, and a dependency-based language model, in a log-linear framework. It differs from [Quirk 2005] in 3 aspects: First, we use bilingual dependency parsing whereas in [Quirk 2005] only source language is parsed. Second, we use a phrased based SMT model to bootstrap the treelet mapping learning phase to get a more accurate mapping model. Third, we also use a dependency-based language model in decoding.

The rest of the paper is organized as follows. Section 2 describes our dependency-based translation model in detail, and Section 3 outlines the training process, including some particular problems on Chinese-English dependency mapping. Section 4 briefly describes the decoding process. Section 5 presents the experiments and the evaluation result. Section 6 concludes with directions for future research.

2 The Dependency Based Translation Model

In [Brown et al 1993] the fundamental equation of SMT is introduced:

$$\widehat{e} = \arg\max_{e} P(e)P(f \mid e) \tag{1}$$

where a language model and a translation model are combined with equal weight. This can be thought of as a special case of a log-linear model:

$$\widehat{e} = \arg\max_{e} \log \prod_{i} P_i^{\lambda_i}(e, f) = \arg\max_{e} \sum_{i} \lambda_i P_i(e, f) \tag{2}$$

when $i = 2, P_1(e, f) = P(e), P_2(e, f) = P(f \mid e), \lambda_1 = \lambda_2 = 1$. We will call these probability functions feature functions (not necessarily joint probability distributions though we write them as functions of e, f). The real-valued weights λ_i of feature functions in a log-linear model show the relative importance of the feature, and can be trained empirically using well known optimization techniques (e.g. [Och 2003]) if training data is available. We will adopt such a framework in our DPSMT model.

As most of the other works in DPSMT, our method also relies on the parsing of the source language (in our case it is Chinese) and we assume an optimal source dependency tree D_s is produced from the source sentence $\mathbf{s}$. The dependency relations in D_s are labeled by functional categories representing subject, object, time, location, etc. The source tree is then transformed into the target by *treelet* mapping, where a treelet is a connected subgraph of the dependency tree, as in [Quick 2005]. The decoder tries to find a complete cover of the tree by an optimal set of treelets, which is then mapped to a target tree D_t. Most of our feature functions therefore are functions based on the source and target dependency tree D_s and D_t. For the time being eight features are used in our model and we will now describe these sub-models one by one:

1. **Treelet translation probability** $p(\widehat{f} \mid \widehat{e})$. Treelets are connected subgraphs of the dependency tree, thus the smallest such tree is a node. However, when talk about treelet translation, we exclude treelet pairs both of which are complete subtrees, which are accounted for by the phrase translation model.

Definition 1. A treelet is a connected subset of a dependency tree (V, E) where V is the set of vertices (nodes) and E is the set of edge (dependency relations). However, we allow the nodes in a treelet to be a *variable* where the lexical word is not specified.

We may regard the treelet as a *phrasal form* (like a sentential form in the formal language theory [Aho & Ullman 1972]), and the ground case where only words are involved is not considered a treelet pair. Consider the following Chinese-English translation pair:

Chinese:	他	把	书	给	我
Pinyin:	ta	ba	shu	gei	wo
gloss:	He		book	give	me
English:	He gave the book to me				

The dependency trees are shown in Figure 1.

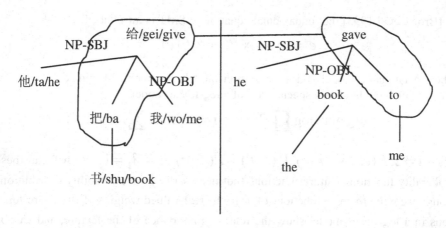

Fig. 1. Bilingual dependency trees and word translations, and a treelet mapping. Encircled edges and nodes are treelets.

In the figure a treelet pair is linked. This kind of treelet mapping is similar to the alignment template [Och 2004], however the graphical representation has more information encoded:

$$(X) 把(Y) 给(Z) <=> (X) \text{ gave } (Y) \text{ to } (Z) \tag{3}$$

Where relations include <X,NP-SBJ,给>, <Z,NP-OBJ,给>,… …

In Och's alignment, the *variables* in the template are usually word classes, and a template is a sequence of consecutive words. Here an entire subtree can be represented as a variable, and words need not to be continuous ([Quirk 2005] allowed discontinued phrases such as "ne … pas" in dependency SMT.). It's precisely because of this that treelets are more powerful to encode translation patterns. Notice that when two treelets are paired, the dependency relationship between the head and the dependents may not hold. If the mapping is non-isomorphic, a head in the source may become a dependent in the target. And there are situations involving more complex structural and lexical changes (cf the example in [Gildea 2004]). The treelet translation paradigm is flexible enough to accommodate such complexities. The approach we take here is that we just align: no mutation on the source side is performed to enable better alignment with the target tree (cf. [Fox 2005], [Dorr 2002], because non-isomorphism is not a problem. In fact, it is a feature of cross-language syntactic variations. The aim of treelet mapping is to learn such correspondences, isomorphic or not.

The probability is estimated using Maximum Likelihood Estimation (MLE) when treelet mapping is identified in the annotated bilingual dependency treebank.

2. **Treelet reordering model** $O(\widehat{f} \mid \widehat{e})$. It should be noted that the position of the arguments of the predicate (be it a verb, an adjective, or a nominalization like "*the*

arrest of X by Z') is often already modeled in the treelet mapping. So we need only model optional arguments and freely occurring adjuncts of the head. As in [Quirk 2005], we model each such dependent independently. We have at our disposal a list of conditioning variables in deciding the relative order of the dependents: in addition to source and target words, part-of-speech, head-relative position of the dependent, we include the important source and target dependency relations in our conditioning variables:

$$p(\Delta_t \mid < d_i, h_i, POS(d_i), POS(h_i), dep\_rel(d_i, h_i) >_t,$$
$$< d_i, h_i, POS(d_i), POS(h_i), dep\_rel(d_i, h_i), \Delta >_s) \tag{4}$$

Where Δ is the relative order (-2, -1, 1, 2,...). This model is smoothed using back-off techniques and linear interpolation (deleted interpolation).

3. **Phrase translation probability** $p(\tilde{f} \mid \tilde{e})$. This is the probability as in the phrase based SMT system.

$$p(\tilde{f} \mid \tilde{e}) = \frac{N(\tilde{f}, \tilde{e})}{\sum_{\tilde{f}'} N(\tilde{f}', \tilde{e})} \tag{5}$$

4. **Word-for-word translation probability** $lex(f_j \mid e_i)$. Like the classical IBM model, we take the Viterbi alignment of each sentence:

$$lex(f_1^J \mid e_1^I) \approx lex(f_1^J \mid e_1^I, a) = \prod_{j=1}^{J} \frac{1}{|\{i \mid (j,i) \in a\}|} \sum_{\forall (j,i) \in a} p(f_j \mid e_i) \tag{6}$$

Actually we just use the probabilistic lexicon produced by Giza++[1].

5. **Target ngram language model** $ngram\_lm(e)$. We use a standard trigram language model.

$$ngram\_lm(e) = \prod_{i=1}^{n} p(w_i \mid w_{i-2}, w_{i-1}) \tag{7}$$

6. **Target dependency language model** $dep\_lm(e)$. [Chelba et al1997] showed the usefulness of a dependency based language in speech recognition. It captures of long-distance information normally not captured by an n-gram model. Our formula is

$$dep\_lm(e) = \prod_{i=1}^{n} p(d_i, rel \mid h_i) \tag{8}$$

7. **Source target sentence length correlation probability** $p(\mid f \mid \mid e \mid)$. Most system uses the simple feature such as the length of the target sentence to avoid preference for shorter sentence. We think normally longer sentences are translated longer so we use $p(\mid f \mid \mid e \mid)$ instead.

8. **Treelets count bonus/penalty** J. The more treelets are mapped, the more reliable the translation is. So we prefer the translation in which treelets span more words (useful when the source sentence has many parses, which is usually the case).

---

[1] http://www.fjoch.com/GIZA++.html

3 The Training of Treelet Mapping

3.1 Data Preparation

We use the Penn Chinese Treebank [Xue 2005] and its English translation to train the treelet mapping. First we have to make a bilingual corpus. Several problems must be addressed in the corpus conversion.

We convert the Penn Treebank (both English and Chinese) into the dependency tree using the tools provided by Nivre[2]. Then the data is used to train the Ryan McDonald's MSTParser[3]. The trained English dependency parser is used to parse the 325 files of the English translation of the Penn Chinese Treebank. Now we got a Bilingual Dependency Treebank (BDT).

At the same time, we use Giza++ to train a word alignment model using the sentences in BDT. We run Giza++ in both directions to get one-to-many alignments and then grow these alignments up to 6 words long to extract all the bilingual phrases ([Chen 2006]) and store them in a phrase lexicon. In this way we get all the phrase translation pairs (including word-to-word translations). The following table shows a few phrases extracted:

Table 1. Sample phrases

Chinese ($\tilde{f}$)	English ($\tilde{e}$)	$p(\tilde{f} \mid \tilde{e})$
结构 的	of the structure	0.5
结构 的	structure of	0.16666667
结构 的	of the structure of	0.5
结构 的	the structure of	0.25

We will use these phrases to bootstrap a treelet translation model. [Koehn 2003] has shown that using only phrases which are constituents will degrade a phrase-based SMT system. So simply filtering each bilingual phrase through the dependency parser to get a dependency translation model will probably not do any good (Koehn did not do syntax decoding anyway, this may be another reason). The next section will describe our approach.

3.2 Training of Treelet Translation Probability

Standard state-of-the-art phrase based translation model is deficient in at least two important aspects: (1) a poor reordering model which does not use syntactic information, and (2) a phrase table which cannot encode translation patterns. The dependency treelet translation model, in our opinion, will remedy these problems.

After using the phrase lexicon to induce the initial treelet mapping, we try to use the Expectation Maximization to train a hopefully better treelet alignment model. We approximate the probability by a set of n-best alignments as follows:

---

[2] Downloaded from http://w3.msi.vxu.se/~nivre/research/Penn2Malt.html
[3] Downloaded from http://www.cis.upenn.edu/~ryantm/software/MSTParser/

$$p(f_1^J \mid e_1^I) = \sum_A p(f_1^J, A \mid e_0^I) \qquad (9)$$

For simplicity, in our experiment we only consider a single Viterbi alignment $\widehat{A}$, which is calculated by the following formula:

$$\widehat{A} = \arg\max_A p(f_1^J, A \mid e_0^I)$$

$$= \arg\max_A dep\_lm(e) \prod_{i=1}^{L} p_A(\widehat{f}_i \mid \widehat{e}_i) O(\widehat{f} \mid \widehat{e}) lex(f_i \mid e_i) \qquad (10)$$

Where L (for *link*) is the number of paired treelets, and $p_A(\widehat{f}_i \mid \widehat{e}_i)$ is the treelet translation probability, which is trained by the EM algorithm. In the first place, treelets are generalized from the phrase mappings by substituting *variables* for sub phrases (forming a subtree). We will also try to generate new treelets to get better coverage. This is done by the following algorithm outline:

Algorithm 1: Treelet Translation Probability Estimation.

1.1   Project the *good* phrase pairs from the phrase lexicon unto the dependency trees to get the initial treelets, using the phrase probability as the initial treelet probability.

$$p(\widehat{f} \mid \widehat{e}) = p(\widetilde{f} \mid \widetilde{e})$$

1.2   Do the following for N iterations

1.2.1   For each treelet pair, set the counts to 0: $C(\widehat{f}, \widehat{e}) = 0$

1.2.2   For each dependency tree pair

1.2.2.1   Find the Viterbi Alignment $\widehat{A}$. Calculate a subset of alignments $\{A\}$ whose probability are within a threshold of the probability of the Viterbi alignment $\widehat{A}$. For each treelet pair $(\widehat{f}, \widehat{e})$ in the Viterbi alignment, generate new treelet pairs by using three operations (*generalize, expand and shrink*) and re-align the trees.

1.2.2.2   For all the treelet pairs in these alignments:

$$C(\widehat{f}, \widehat{e}) + = p_{prev}(\widehat{f}, \widehat{e})$$

1.2.3   Re-estimate   treelet   translation   probability   using

$$\text{MLE: } p(\widehat{f} \mid \widehat{e}) = \frac{C(\widehat{f}, \widehat{e})}{\sum_{\widehat{f}} C(\widehat{f}, \widehat{e})}$$

In algorithm 1, the treelet operations are used to generate better or wider-coverage alignments. For example, to generate the treelet pair (3), we have to turn the object of the proposition 把 /ba into a variable, thus covering more phrases headed by 给/gei/give. The generated treelets usually has a clear syntactic structure, and can span multi-level of nodes, which are hard to be captured by a phrase based model if they are not complete subtrees.

Some syntax-based approaches (especially CFG based) are assuming a synchronous approach [Wu 1997, Melamed 2004]. We think synchrony is best captured on the sentence level. The treelet mapping in our model does not need to be isomorphic, although nodes deleted or added are still to be modeled (similar to NULL word alignment of the IBM models).

3.3 Chinese-English Specific Treatment

Words are not used equal. The so-called functional words play a more important part in ensuring the grammaticality of the sentence. In choosing the best alignments in the training data, we considered closed-class functional words and some specific words such as light verbs. These words are candidates to exclude when generating new treelets and are not generalized to word classes when transforming the treelets.

Some content words must be translated, e.g., numerical words, personal names, location names. The phrase table has lots of such alignment errors. We use language specific processing to eliminate such phrases. Punctuations and numerical word standardization are also performed. On the other hand, Proper names are good to generalize in treelets.

This language specific approach can be carried to the extreme, e.g. writing specific treelet mapping rules manually. However, we do not go such far.

4 The Decoder

We use a bottom-up *head-driven* decoding scheme. All the treelet pairs generated in the training stage are indexed by the head of the treelet, which is normally the node nearest to the root of the sentence.

After the optimal dependency tree is generated by the parser, bottom-up dynamic programming is used to store partial target dependency subtrees at each *head* of the dependency subtree. We use a log-linear framework to integrate a variety of features described in Section 2. A beam search is used to rank the partial trees. The target tree with the highest probability at the head of the whole sentence is used to generate the final translation.

This approach is basically the same as that of [Quirk 2005].

5 Experiments and Results

5.1 Training and Test Data

The training and test data is summarized in Table 2.

The Penn CTB is used to train the phrase model and the dependency treelet model. Only 4172 sentences of 325 files are used (CTB 1.0). Not all CTB 5.0 sentences have English translations. However, the whole English and Chinese Treebanks are used to train the parser. We test the result on the NIST 2005 MT evaluation data and China "863" 2005 MT evaluation data. Both test data are news-related.

Table 2. Data

	English	Chinese	Comment
Training sentences	49208	18772	For Parser training
LDC2003E07	4172	4172	598864 phrases extracted
LDC2005T06	10317	10317	2458049 phrases extracted[4]
Test Set1 sentences		1082	NIST 2005
Test Set2 sentences		489	"863" 2005

5.2 Experiments

We evaluate our dependency based decoder against two phrase-based decoders. One is the freely downloadable decoder, Pharaoh, by Philip Koehn. The other is Caravan, which is written by us and takes part in the NIST 2006 and IWSLT 2006 MT evaluations[5]. We test a number of combinations. The first case is unfair against the phrase-based decoders. For the phrase based system, we only use 4172 sentences in Table 2 to train the phrase table, while the dependency model has additional training data of the parser. For our DPSMT, we trained 10 iterations of the EM algorithm. We used a common trigram language model when decoding. The results were shown in Table 3.

Table 3. Experiment 1 for 4172 sentences

	Pharaoh	Caravan	DPSMT
NIST 2005 BLEU	0.0753	0.1008	0.1558
"863" 2005 BLEU	0.0548	0.0926	0.1346

In the second case, we added more bilingual training data to the phrase based models. We added a bilingual news corpus with about 10,000 sentences from LDC. Then the result became:

Table 4. Experiment 2 for 14489 sentences

	Pharaoh	Caravan	DPSMT
NIST 2005 BLEU	0.1421	0.1908	0.1925
"863" 2005 BLEU	0.0768	0.1349	0.1672

The experiments showed that DPSMT can achieve comparable results with our phrase based SMT system. However, if we look at official NIST evaluation results[6], we can see we are still behind most of the (phrase based) systems. A close look at the

---

[4] Combined with LDC2003E07.

[5] Caravan is now open sourced. It is announced in the 2nd China SMT workshop held in Beijing Oct 17-18, 2006, as a part of the SilkRoad SMT package. For more information see http://mtgroup.ict.ac.cn/ssmt2006/jy.htm

[6] http://www.nist.gov/speech/tests/mt/mt05eval_official_results_release_20050801_v3.html

Penn Treebank dependency relations used by the Nivre conversion tool revealed that there were only 12 dependency relations:

ROOT, AMOD, DEP, NMOD, OBJ, P, PMOD, PRD, SBAR, SUB, VC, VMOD

These relations are too coarse to discern important syntactico-semantic distinctions. For example, all relations with a noun head are marked with a **NMOD,** which loses important distinctions between different types of modifiers.

In the 3rd experiment we make a finer distinction among these relations. Specifically, we differentiated **NMOD**, reversed the direction of the dependency relationship between the auxiliary and the verb (which obscures important lexical co-occurrence information: Penn Treebank is correct in saying that syntactically auxiliary is the head of the verb, but semantically it is just the opposite), and marked several important relationships between an adverbial and a verb (such as *time* and *location*). After re-training our parsers, we got the following results:

Table 5. Experiment 2 for 14489 sentences

	DPSMT
NIST 2005 BLEU	0.2353
"863" 2005 BLEU	0.2031

The experiment shows that for syntax based model to work, important syntax distinctions must be captured. We think further experiments are necessary to make further progress in this respect.

5.3 Discussions

With an extra of two monolingual dependency treebanks to train a dependency parser, we obtained a DPSMT model that performs significant better than the phrase-based model. The strength of DPSMT lies in the fact that it can incorporate lexical and cross-lingual syntactic transformations naturally. Though there is still much work to be done, our work shows that DPSMT is a promising avenue to explore.

DPSMT is simpler than CFG based SMT, so we have less serious data sparseness problem. And because our model has syntactic variables in the treelets, it can also capture informal translation patterns in a formal way. In a sense, Example Based Machine Translation can also be modeled by the treelet mapping. However, our model is more powerful because syntactical structures are at our disposal.

In recent years we see more linguistically-rich models in SMT. This trend is just the opposite of the notorious Jelinek saying: "Every time I fire a linguist, the performance of our speech recognition system goes up!"

6   Conclusions and Future Work

We presented a DPSMT model that is promising in generating better quality machine translations. Its novel features include a richer syntax-based translation model and a dependency language model.

The log-linear framework can allow for more features. We could easily add reverse feature functions of the features 1, 2, 3, 4 to our model ($p(\hat{e} \mid \hat{f})$, $O(\hat{e} \mid \hat{f})$, $p(\tilde{e} \mid \tilde{f})$, $lex(e_i \mid f_j)$) in the decoding process. Also, we can add more syntax constraints in the target tree. We plan to investigate these possibilities in the future.

The quality of the bilingual Treebank arguably can play a very important role. Our training data is still lacking in that we don't have a manually aligned bilingual dependency Treebank. Because our dependency Treebank is converted from a CFG Treebank, some information loss is inevitable. We plan to experiment on more dependency treebanks such as the HIT Chinese dependency Treebank [Liu 2006].

Acknowledgements

This work is supported by the National Natural Science Foundation of China (Grant No. 60573189 and Grant No, 60373080), National 863 High-tech Program (Grant No 2004AA117010-06) and the Fujian Provincial Key Scientific Research Project (Grant No 2006H0038). We thank the students Hui Zhang and Yu Chen who carried out most of the experiments and the reviewers for making this paper better.

References

1. Aho A. V., Ullman J. D.: *The Theory of Parsing, Translation, and Compiling, Volume I: Parsing*, Prentice-Hall, Inc., Englewood Cliffs, NJ, 1972.
2. Alshawi, H., Bangalore S., Douglas S.: Learning dependency transduction models as collections of finite state head transducers. *Computational Linguistics*, 2000, 26(1): 45-64.
3. Brown P., DellaPietra S., DellaPietra V., Mercer R.: The mathematics of machine translation: Parameter estimation. *Computational Linguistics*. 1993,19(2): 263-312
4. Casacuberta F., Vidal E.: Machine translation with inferred stochastic finite-state transducers, *Computational Linguistics*, 2004, 30(2), 205-225.
5. Chelba C., Engle D., Jelinek F., Jimenze V., Khudanpur S., Mangu L., Printz H., Ristad E., Rosenfeld R., Stolcke A., Wu D.: Structure and performance of a dependency language model. *EUROSPEECH'97*. Rhodes, Greece. 1997.
6. Charniak, E., Knight, K., Yamada, K. Syntax-based Language Models for Statistical Machine Translation. In *Proceedings of the 9th Machine Translation Summit*, 2003.
7. Chen Y.D. Shi X. D.: The XMU Phrase-Based Statistical Machine Translation System for IWSLT 2006. In Proceedings of IWSLT. Kyoto Japan. 2006, pp. 153-157.
8. Cmejrek M., Curin J., Havelka J.: Czech-English Dependency-based Machine Translation. In *Proceedings of EACL 2003*, pp. 83–90, April 12–17, 2003.
9. Collins M.: Three generative, lexicalized models for statistical parsing. In *Proc. of ACL-97*.
10. Collins M.: *Head-Driven Statistical Models for Natural Language Parsing*, PhD-thesis, University of Pennsylvania, PA. P. Desain and H. Honing, 1999
11. Dorr B. J., Pearl L., Hwa R., Habash N.: DUSTer: A Method for Unraveling Cross-Language Divergences for Statistical Word-Level Alignment. In *Proceedings of the Fifth Conference of the Association for Machine Translation in the Americas*, 2002.

12. Fox H. J.: Phrasal Cohesion and Statistical Machine Translation, In *Proceedings of the 2002 Conference on Empirical Methods in Natural Language Processing (EMNLP 2002)*, pp. 304-311.
13. Fox H. J.: Dependency-based Statistical Machine Translation, In *Proceedings of the 2005 ACL Student Workshop*.
14. Gildea D.: Dependencies vs. constituents for tree-based alignment. In *Proceedings of the EMNLP*, 2004. pp. 214–221
15. Koehn P., Och F. J., Marcu D.: Statistical Phrase-Based Translation. In *Proceedings of NAACL/HLT*, 2003.
16. Knoke, D. and P.J. Burke 1980. Log-Linear Models. Sage Publications, Inc. Newberry Park, California, USA.
17. Lee S. Z., Tsujii J., and Rim H. C.: Lexicalized Hidden Markov Models for Part-of-Speech Tagging. In *Proceedings of 18th International Conference on Computational Linguistics*, Saarbrucken, Germany, August 2000
18. Liu T., Ma J. S., Li S.: Building a Dependency Treebank for Improving Chinese Parse. *Journal of Chinese Language and Computing*, 2006, 16 (4): 207-224
19. Marcus M., Santorini B., Marcinkiewicz M.: Building a large annotated corpus of English: The Penn treebank. *Computational Linguistics*, 1993, 19(2).
20. Melamed I. D.: Statistical machine translation by parsing. In *Proceedings of the 42nd Annual Meeting of the Association for Computational Linguistics: ACL 2004*, pp. 653-660.
21. Och F.J., Minimum error rate training in statistical. machine translation, in *Proceedings of the ACL*, Sapporo, Japan, 2003, pp. 160–167
22. Och F. J., Ney H.: The alignment template approach to statistical machine translation. *Computational Linguistics*, 2004. 30(4).
23. Quirk C., Menezes A., Cherry C.: Dependency Treelet Translation: Syntactically Informed Phrasal SMT, In *Proceedings of the 43rd Annual Meeting of the Association for Computational Linguistics*, Ann Arbor, Michigan, USA. July 2005.
24. Wu D.: Stochastic inversion transduction grammars and bilingual parsing of parallel corpora. *Computational Linguistics,* 1997, 23(3):377-404.
25. Xue N., Xia F., Chiou F. D., Palmer M.: Building a Large Annotated Chinese Corpus: the Penn Chinese Treebank, *Journal of Natural Language Engineering*, 11(2): 207-238, 2005
26. Yamada, K. Knight, K.: A Syntax-based Statistical Translation Model. In *Proceedings of the Conference of the Association for Computational Linguistics*: ACL 2001.

Asymmetric Hybrid Machine Translation for Languages with Scarce Resources

Algirdas Laukaitis and Olegas Vasilecas

Vilnius Gediminas Technical University, Saulėtekio al. 11,
LT-10223 Vilnius-40, Lithuania
{algirdas.laukaitis, olegas}@fm.vtu.lt

Abstract. Half of the world speaks languages that are out of the machine translation and natural language processing technologics mainstream. Then the choice of natural language technology for a given language pair is greatly impacted by technology and resources available. In this paper we describe a hybrid architecture and technology for rapid dcvclopment of the machine translation system from English to low-density languages. We use state of the art English language processing technologies and resources to transform (compress) the language into the more abstract form. The abstraction level of the transformation is adapted to our knowledge of the low-density (foreign) language. Then statistical machine translation is used to induce translation rules. All tests and implementations have been done on the English – Lithuanian language pair. Some of the findings of the research can be useful for all, novel and old machine translation language pairs.

Keywords: Hybrid machine translation, natural language processing, ontology, rapid development, low-density languages.

1 Introduction

There are only several languages (German, Spanish, French, Italian, Portuguese, Arabic, Japanese, Korean, Chinese, Dutch, Greek, Russian) that are covered by the most popular machine translation engines (SYSTRAN, GOOGLE, PROMPT, etc.) and major research projects [9], [16]. Almost in all cases English is the *"other side"* language of the translation. In this paper we discuss our findings about how to build English and the low-density, scarce resources language pair hybrid machine translation engine from scratch. The scarce resources we understood as the availability of digital text materials and ready to use state of the art natural language processing technologies for that particular language. The main idea of the paper is an employment of existing stable and reliable English language processing resources (morphology, syntax and lexical semantics) in the machine translation preprocessing stage.

English - Lithuanian language pair, not used in any other machine translation research project before, is the subject of our investigation. The Lithuanian language [22] is included in the Baltic group of Indo-European languages and represents the

A. Gelbukh (Ed.): CICLing 2007, LNCS 4394, pp. 397–408, 2007.

West Baltic subgroup. It has a very rich morphology for all open word classes and it shows evident relation with Slavic morphology. The nouns in Lithuanian have 7 cases, 3 numbers and 2 genders. Verbs have a lot of forms: 4 tenses, 3 types of conjugation, 3 moods and a great plenty of verbal forms like participles, semi-participles, infinitives and supine. But we don't have 100 men years of resources for the developers to fully grasp the peculiarities of the English-Lithuanian translation. Anyhow, we don't have the 100 megabytes (MB) of pre-aligned text for the brute force statistical machine translation. What we do have is about 1MB of parallel English – Lithuanian corpus, short description of Lithuanian morphology and several small dictionaries on the Web. Our goal in this project was to build the machine translation system that learns from new data and is calibrated by the English language linguistic resources.

In this paper we take a very mechanical approach of the Lithuanian language (in the rest of the paper we often call it a foreign language) and that is the language: 1) where each word can have several cases (for Lithuanian it is up to 18), 2) morphology is observed and discovered by a web-crawling agent, 3) the syntax and lexical semantics are discovered by software agent who is aware of the English language syntax and lexical semantics and who has a small amount of the bilingual corpus.

The rest of the paper is organized as follows. In section 2 we describe the state of the art English language processing resources that can be found on the Internet for free download. The results and findings of the section have value on its own: i.e. we spend almost one year just for searching and evaluating the English natural language processing resources and in the section we report our final findings. In section 3 the generation of the generalized syntax and lexical semantics templates with different abstraction levels are presented. Asymmetric hybrid machine translation (AHMT) architecture is discussed in section 4. Evaluation of received results is the subject of section 5.

2   Natural Language Processing Resources

A subject of current interest in the machine translation world is the rapid development of systems for novel language pairs when often on of the languages is English [13], [6]. Often, the other language in question can be unknown to system developers and they must either acquire the necessary knowledge and technology or devise methods that will automatically acquire necessary resources. For many of the candidate languages there exists relatively little of suitable training material, thus restricting the scope of purely statistical approach. Therefore, one need to resort to other sources and first step in that direction is to look at the present state of the art in the natural language processing technologies. Figure 1 shows the final structure of the resources we identified in the preliminary stage of the project. The resources are divided into three categories: 1) English language resources are used to drive the whole learning and knowledge gathering process, 2) some bilingual translation resources are mandatory if we are dealing with the translation between high-density and low-density language pair, 3) for the same reasons, we admit the existence of the "*small amount*" low-density language resources. Next, the issue of the resources is addressed in more details.

English language package contains five modules:

WordNet Ontology. WordNet [14] is the words ontology base that contains words semantic relationships in the synset form, a set of synonyms representing a distinct concept. Additionally it describes words hypernym-hyponym relationships that can help us to measure words semantic distances. Our work exploits both properties of the ontology. It helps to resolve the natural language disambiguation problem by groping words in the synsets forms. With the WordNet ontology we can extend the size of the bilingual dictionary e.g. the translation of *"chalet, cabin, hacienda, manse, etc,"* can be replaced, if not found in the bilingual dictionary, by the translation of the word *"house"* if such exist in the bilingual dictionary. All mentioned words are hyponyms of the word *"house".* Even more reliable and efficient than bilingual dictionary extension is the use of the ontology in the generation of generalized translation templates.

GATE NLP - Natural Language Processing Engine. GATE - General Architecture for Text Engineering - is a well-established infrastructure for customisation and development of natural language processing (NLP) components [2], [3]. It is a robust and scalable infrastructure for NLP and allows users to use various modules of NLP as the plugging. All modules within the GATE produced annotations - pairs of nodes pointing to positions inside the document content, and a set of attribute-values, encoding linguistic information. Finite state transducer within the GATE generates several forms of English grammar by annotating words and phrases in the sentence. Additionally, the named entities identification is carried out with the help of the *Gazetteer lookup* module.

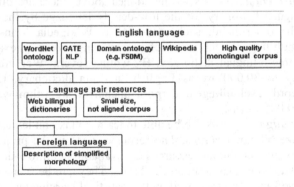

Fig. 1. Stage 1. Identified asymmetry of resources: English – foreign language pair.

Domain ontology (e.g. FSDM). The Domain Ontology defines declaratively the set of the domain and application specific concepts and their relationships. When translating specific domain concepts and named entities from source to the target languages the general words ontology is not able to resolve senses disambiguation problem. The IBM's Information Framework Financial Services Data Model (FSDM) [8] has been used for the present research to tests translations in the financial services domain. The model is divided into a number of levels with a different level of abstraction: the 'A' level with nine data concepts that define the scope of the enterprise model (*involved party, products, arrangement, event, location, resource items, condition, classification, business*), the 'B' level with business concepts hierarchies (more than 3000 concepts), the 'A/B' level with business solutions (integrates business solutions with more than 6000 concepts) and 'C' level – entity relationship ER diagram with about 6000 entities, relationships and attributes.

Wikipedia. Wikipedia is an international project that uses Wiki software to collaboratively create a general knowledge encyclopaedia [24]. To our surprise, we found that no project in the area of the machine translation utilise the potential of multilingual knowledge base presented at the Wikipedia portal. First of all, we build the Wikipedia format aware agent that extracts words and named entities form the URL links of related articles. In that way extended dictionary has more potential than any bilingual dictionary build by small group of experts. Another important area of Wikipedia employment in the machine translation and in computational linguistics areas is the ability to disambiguate the words and phrases based on their occurrence in the semantically related articles.

High quality monolingual corpus. The archives like project Gutenberg [18] present high quality collections of digital materials. Only the high-density languages can supply enough materials for fully automated statistical machine translation. Nevertheless, we used such archives to query and process the English language materials. The software agent equipped with our technology is able to process about 1 MB of textual information per week (almost like a human reader). The most of the processing time is spend on queering Internet search engines like Google or Yahoo to get number of phrases counts and then to build language models.

Language pair resources package contains two modules:

Web bilingual dictionaries. As we mentioned above, there are difficulties in the assembling bilingual dictionary for the low-density language by the pure statistical approach. On the other hand, such resources as Wikipedia (translations can be extracted from multilingual URL cross-references) can serve as an example for "*easy way*" to build some bilingual dictionary. By writing several Web crawlers we were able to build up to 30.000 words English-Lithuania dictionary. Using WordNet ontology and word level bilingual corpora alignment algorithm we were able to extend it up to 60.000 words.

Small size not aligned corpus. To be able to learn syntax and lexical rules we need to have small size bilingual corpus. The resources used in the project are given in Table 1. We are sure that similar resources are available in all low-density languages especially, translations of classic literature books. They can be scanned with modern text recognition software and then used by the statistical learning techniques. We used commercially available software to scan several books and it showed remarkably good performance.

Table 1. The bilingual resources used in the experiment

Name	Text size in MB
Texts from classic literature	0.6 Mb
Local law documents	0.2 MB
International law documents	0.1 MB
Web pages	0.1 MB

Foreign language package contains one module:

Description of simplified morphology. Morphological analysis is the process of separating grammatical information and stems from the corpora words. The foreign language words in our system can have up to 18 cases for such languages like Lithuanian. We used very simplified morphology description form [23] and coded the knowledge from it into the set of 62 rules that described the relationship between stem and ending for the nouns, verbs and adjectives. With such rules and with heuristics to handle exceptions we build Lithuanian words dictionary where each word can have up to 18 cases. The dictionary was build by crawling the Web and filtering out the words with low occurrences. The final product of the analysis was the table of about 50.000 records with the key column representing the lemma of the word and 18 columns - the cases of the words. Transformation of the Defoe example (see belov) with such morphological table will look like: *"I Case15 that the Case1 Case3 of Case2 and Case2 Case11 much more than I Case4 in a Case6"* (in our examples, we are not using Lithuanian words in the assumption that the readers of the paper will be unfamiliar with the Lithuanian language).

Our purpose in the research was to induce all complexity of language pair translation by mapping on the one-side English language templates produced from sophisticated syntax and lexical analysis and on the other side, the low-density language *"mechanical"* analysis product i.e. one table that describes the morphology knowledge of the low-density language.

3 Monolingual Natural Language Processing

In this section, the description of an initiation mechanism, which generalizes translation templates from a corpus, is presented. At the first stage of the initiation, all words and some phrases are annotated with their complete set of grammatical information. After the grammatical analysis is completed, the semantic analysis processes annotates the corpus. No new examples are generated from the foreign language corpora; only examples from English language corpora are inserted into the database. Figure 1 shows the processing steps employed in preparation of the translation templates. In the rest of the section, each process is described in more details.

To be more explicit in the explaining these processes we use the following example. Two sentences are extracted from the corpora. One is from *"Robinson Crusoe"* a novel by Daniel Defoe and the second one is from *"Smoke Bellew"* a novel by Jack London.

Defoe: *"I found that the forty bushels of barley and rice were much more than I could consume in a year."*

London: *"And he found that the upper stake of the latter was lower than the lower stake of the former."*

The sentences were selected from the linguistic database using the following criteria: "The set of the most similar abstracted sentences from novels of Daniel Defoe and Jack London". We received several pairs of the sentences and picked the ones shown above. The identical parts from the abstracted sentences are marked in

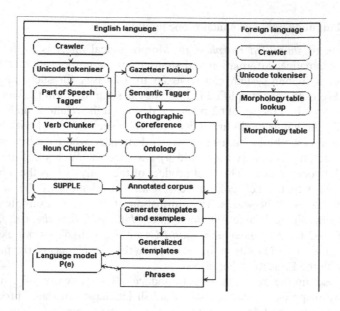

Fig. 2. Processing steps for generation of generalized templates and examples

bold. They are identical on the abstraction level we call *(B+2)*, which is explained below. Now, we present in details, the steps of the natural language processing.

English language. *Unicode tokeniser.* The Unicode tokeniser splits the text into simple tokens and is used for the following steps of the language processing.

Part of Speech Tagger. The tagger is a modified version of the Brill tagger, which produces a part-of-speech tag as an annotation on each word or symbol. The list of tags can be found in [7]. For example, the part of the sentence above: "*I found that the forty bushels*" will be transformed into the following representation: "PRP VBD IN DT NN NNS", where PRP - probably possessive pronoun, VBD - verb past tense, IN-preposition or subordinating conjunction, DT – determiner, NN – noun, NNS - noun (plural).

Verb Chunker. The rule-based verb chunker is based on a number of grammars. The GATE has 68 rules for the identification of verb groups. The finite state transducer within the system produced annotations for the first sentence in our example in the following form:

Defoe: "*I {tense=SimPas, type=FVG, voice=active} that the forty bushels of barley and rice {tense=SimPas, type=FVG, voice=active} much more than I {tense=none, type=MODAL, voice=none} in a year.*"

Noun Chunker. The Noun phrase chunker module is an implementation of the Ramshaw and Marcus chunker [19] within the GATE system. After the noun phrase chunker process we get the following form in our example:

Defoe: "*NounChunk found that NounChunk of NounChunk were NounChunk than NounChunk could consume in NounChunk.*"

London: "*And NounChunk found that NounChunk of NounChunk was NounChunk than NounChunk of NounChunk.*"

From those steps, in the grammatical analysis, we can create the whole variety of the language grammatical representations. As a consequence, we chose the one that had enough information to induce translation rules for the foreign language. We call such choice the level B representation. It can be found iteratively starting from the more abstract representation (i.e. noun, verb, determiner, etc.), then adding grammar resolution details. The section 5 presents experimental results of such procedure.

Gazetteer lookup. The gazetteer uses the lists of named entities and annotates text with class labels such as cities, organisations, days of the week, etc. One of the generalized representations is prepared by replacing each named entity with the class label of that entity.

Semantic Tagger. Semantic tagger provides finite state transduction over annotations based on regular expressions. It produced additional set of named entities and we replace each named entity with the class label.

Orthographic Coreference. The module adds identity relations between named entities found by the semantic tagger. Named entities class labels replace such tokens.

SUPPLE The Sheffield University Prolog Parser for Language Engineering. It is a bottom-up parser that constructs syntax trees and logical forms for English sentences. The divisions of the sentence are the starting sets of phrases for the linguistic database.

Ontology. The ontology process used WordNet ontology and   IBM's (FSDM) to produce more abstract representations of the documents by replacing words with the hypernym of the word (WordNet) or with the name of the more abstract class ((FSDM) and documents from financial domain).

4   Towards Asymmetric Hybrid Translation Machine

In the 70s and the 80s the area of machine translation was dominated by the rule-based approach (RBMT). The performance of these systems depended on the number and quality of rules. Few commercial RBMT systems have been successful. At the 90s, when more digital materials became available, corpus-based machine translation (CBMT) systems started to gain attention. From CBMT paradigm appeared a number of MT versions: example-based machine translation (EBMT), translation memories (TM) and statistics-based machine translation (SMT) are the most popular attempts to gain from corpora based approach.

At the beginning the hybridization of MT primarily concentrated on the technical aspects and the experience accumulated by the hybridization attempts has been done primary in the pairs of high-density languages. Nevertheless, there was many attempts to use hybridization and the interest for such approach is growing continuously. The use of monolingual and parallel corpora to support RBMT systems has been investigated in [20]. Authors of the paper demonstrated that the linkage of different MT paradigms improves the quality of translation. Extraction of new translation units out of bilingual text and their compilation into (RBMT) systems has been attempted in the [21]. Combination of   EBMT with RBMT paradigms has been attempted in [23]. Our approach differs from many mentioned and unmentioned approaches in the way that the system is preprocessing English language at the firs stage and only then calibration of the bilingual translation is started. Additionally, our contribution is primary orientated towards new languages where the major concern is the practical working system and monolingual language processing is a keystone in the methodology.

Figure 3 shows the hybrid machine translation architecture that is based on the state of the art, freely available technologies for English language processing. The central element of the architecture is an integration of the language processing framework GATE and WordNet ontology into the machine translation process. The rule they play in the translation process has been explained in the section above. Next, the discussion will focus for the rest of modules.

Sentences and documents. In the system they represents the storage of a text items and are used for further processing.

Bilingual corpus. It contains the collection of textual documents in English and foreign languages.

Web search. The component is used to verify the soundness of the phrases structure by querying web search engines.

Direct Examples. From bilingual corpora extracted phrases. They are labelled with label *"abstraction level 0"* to mark the fact that no abstractions are made on them.

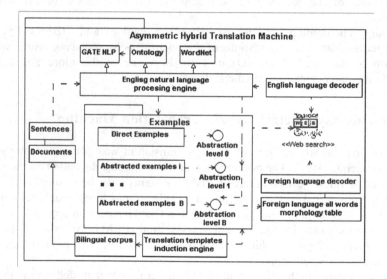

Fig. 3. Asymmetric hybrid machine translation architecture induced by the asymmetry of linguistic resources

Translation templates induction engine is based on the statistical machine translation paradigm [1]. The main idea of the statistical machine translation is founded on the noisy channel model. We translate the source sentences $\{f_1, f_2 \ldots f_J\}$ into a target language sentences $\{e_1, e_2 \ldots e_I\}$ using stochastic models and maximization of the log-likelihood for parameters estimation. Given the source language sentences f, we have to choose the target language sentences e that maximises the probability $P(e \mid f)$:

$$\hat{e} = \arg\max_{e} P(e \mid f) = \arg\max_{e} P(e) \cdot P(f \mid e). \tag{1}$$

This probability can be represented as a product of the language model probability $P(e)$ and the translation model probability $P(f \mid e)$. Those two probabilities can be modelled independently of each other. The translation model describes the correspondence between the words in the source sentence and the words in the target sentence whereas the language model describes how well sentence is represented in the context of the language. To introduce the alignments between a pair of strings the translation model (1) can be rewritten in the following way:

$$\hat{e} = \arg\max_{e} P(e) \cdot \sum_{a} P(f, a \mid e), \tag{2}$$

where a are called alignments and represent a mapping of words positions. Alignments are introduced into model as the hidden variable and there are many ways in which $P(f, a \mid e)$ can be written as the product of a series of conditional probabilities. For more detailed description see [1].

In the case of a pure statistical machine translation we have three parts: 1) a language model, 2) a translation model and 3) a decoder. The language model and the translation model we presented above the only difference in our case is that the source and target sentences are abstracted by the technique presented in the previous section. For the decoder, instead of using statistical methods like [5], [12], we use the bilingual dictionary, induced translation templates and a web search engine to validate the soundness of the translated phrase.

Table 2. The idea of the sentence incremental abstraction

Level	Representation
0	Later, in the Bohemian crowd of San Francisco, he was called Kit Bellew.
1	Later, in the Bohemian [gathering] of San Francisco...
2	Later, in the Bohemian [social group] of San Francisco...
...	
i	Later, in the <Unknown> [social group] of <Location>, he was [labelled] <Person>.
...	
B-1	Later, in the <Unknown> NC of <Location>, he SimPas2 <Person>.
B	Later, in NC of NC, he SimPas2 NC.
B+1	Later, in NC of NC, NC SimPas2 NC.
B+2	Later, IN NC IN NC, NC SimPas2 NC.
...	

In order to get more intuitive insight into the concept of language abstraction, we present table 2 where several abstraction forms are given. The label NC means *noun chunk*, SimPas2 – on of the forms of English verbs, IN - preposition or subordinating conjunction. At the beginning of the abstraction we use WordNet ontology to replace some words by hypernym of the word. In the example the word *crowd* has direct hypernym gathering and the word *gathering* has direct hypernym *social group*. At some abstraction level (i) *we* can use additional anthologies or finite state transducers for named entities identification. In the example "*San Francisco*" has been replaced by <Location> and "*Kit Bellew*" by <Person> labels. The language on the abstraction level B is the representation which we use to induce translation templates. By using some metric of the translation quality we can adjust the level B representation to our knowledge of the foreign language structure. Table 3 in the final section of the paper presents experimental results for the Lithuanian language.

English language decoder. Let's say that in the translation from the foreign language to English we found the abstract template: "*Later in NC…* ". By using a bilingual dictionary we can generate testable hypotheses: {*Later in crowd, Later in throng, Later in the crowd, Later in the throng,* …}. After examining the set of hypotheses on the Web search engine, decoder produces the set of frequencies for these phrases. In our example the set was given looks like: {2 ,0 ,96 ,4 , , }. Then the phrase with the highest score is chosen.

Foreign language decoder functionality is the same as English language decoder functionality.

5 Evaluation Results

BLEU (BiLingual Evaluation Understudy) [11] was the metric used in our experiment. The standard BLEU measures the similarity between machine translations and translations made by humans. In this paper the 3-gram approach as the BLUE metric parameter was chosen. For the reference we used the 7-language MULTEXT-East corpus [4], [15]. Additionally 20 documents from European Union law corpora [17] was selected. Error rates for the translation from English to Lithuanian are shown in Tables 3 and 4.

Table 3. English – Lithuanian and Lithuanian – English translation BLEU error rate and its dependence from language abstraction level (size of corpus ~ 0.5 MB)

	0	B-1	B	B+1	B+2
EN-LT	0.04	0.17	0.25	0.15	0.09
LT-EN	0.03	0.13	0.21	0.16	0.11

Table 4. English – Lithuanian and Lithuanian – English translation BLEU error rate and dependency form translation templates abstraction level (size of corpus ~ 1 MB)

	0	B-1	B	B+1	B+2
EN-LT	0.04	0.18	0.29	0.25	0.20
LT-EN	0.03	0.16	0.23	0.19	0.18

We can see that there is a decrease in the error rate when we reached abstraction level B and when we reached the maximum size of parallel corpus for training.

6 Conclusions

In this work, we presented the new architecture and methodology for the hybrid approach in the field of machine translation. The novelty of proposed solution is in the use of pre-processed English language resources and only then translation rules are induced from small bilingual corpus. The method can be useful for the new languages as the pre-processed English language resources can be replicated to each new project and then tuned for final processing. English-Lithuanian language pair translations demonstrated that that obtained translation results are comparable with those for the other language pairs if we able to found balance between resources available and representation abstraction level. We believe that the results can be further improved by the use of more intelligent Web crawlers for obtaining more bilingual information and by integrating such crawlers within translation system for the online translation. Some induced rules that are found to be redundant can be removed with the similar technique as in [10]. We hope to investigate this possibility in future publications.

References

1. Brown, P. F., Della Pietra V. J., Della Pietra, S. A., Mercer, R. L.: The Mathematics of Statistical Machine Translation: Parameter Estimation. Computational Linguistics, 19(2), (1993) 263-311.
2. Cunningham, H.: GATE, a General Architecture for Text Engineering. Computers and the Humanities, 36, (2002) 223–254.
3. Cunningham H., Maynard D., Bontcheva K., Tablan V., GATE: A Framework and Graphical Development Environment for Robust NLP Tools and Applications. In proc. of the 40th Anniversary Meeting of the Association for Computational Linguistics, (2002), 168-175.
4. Erjavec, T.: MULTEXT-East Version 3: Multilingual Morphosyntactic Specifications, Lexicons and Corpora. Fourth International Conference on Language Resources and Evaluation, (2004), 1535-1538.
5. Germann, U., Jahr, M., Knight, K., Marcu, D., and Yamada, K.: Fast decoding and optimal decoding for machine translation. In: Proceedings of the 39th ACL. Toulouse, France, (2001), 228–235.
6. Foster, G., Gandrabur, S., Langlais, P., Macklovitch, E., Plamondon, P., Russell, G., and Simard, M.: Statistical machine translation: Rapid development with limited resources. In Machine Translation Summit IX, New Orleans, USA, (2003), 110–117.
7. Gaizauskas, R., Rodgers, P., Cunningham, H., and Humphreys, K.,: GATE User Guide." Department of Computer Science, University ofSheeld, Department of Computer Science, University of Sheeld, (1996).
8. IBM. IBM Banking Data Warehouse General Information Manual. Available from on the IBM corporate site http://www.ibm.com.
9. Jurafsky, D., Martin, J.,H.: Speech and Language Processing. Prentice Hall, Englewood Cliffs, NJ, (2000).
10. Kenji I., Sumita E., and Matsumoto Y.: Feedback cleaning of machine translation rules using automatic evaluation. In Proceedings of the 41st Annual Meeting of the Association for Computational Linguistics, (2003), 447–454.

11. Kishore P., Roukos, S., Ward, T., Zhu, W. J.: BLEU: a method for automatic evaluation of machine translation. In Proceedings of the 40th Annual Meeting of the ACL, (2002) 311–318.
12. Knight, K.: Decoding complexity in wordreplacement translation models. Computational Linguistics, 25(4) (1999) 607–615.
13. Lavie, A., Probst, K., Peterson, E., Vogel, S., Levin, L., Font-Llitjos, A., Carbonell, J. A Trainable Transfer-based Machine Translation Approach for Languages with Limited Resources. In Proceedings of Workshop of the European Association for Machine Translation, Valletta, Malta (2004).
14. Miller, G.A.: WordNet: A Dictionary Browser, Proc. 1st Int'l Conf. Information in Data, (1985) 25–28.
15. Multext-East Home Page MULTEXT-East: Multilingual Text Tools and Corpora for Central and Eastern European Languages. http://nl.ijs.si/ME/ .
16. Nirenberg, S., : Machine Translation – Theoretical and Methodological Issues, Cambridge University Press, Cambridge, (1987).
17. Official Journal of the European Union. http://eur-lex.europa.eu .
18. Project Gutenberg . http://www.gutenberg.org/wiki/Main_Page .
19. Ramshaw, L., Marcus., M.: Text Chunking Using Transformation-Based Learning. In Proceedings of the Third ACL Workshop on Very Large Corpora, (1995).
20. Streiter, O., Leonid I., Munpyo H., Ute H.: Learning, Forgetting and Remembering: Statistical Support for Rule-Based MT. In: Hybrid Approaches to MT. Streiter, Oliver, Michael Carl and Johann Haller (eds.). (2000).
21. Streiter, O.,Leonid I.: Learning Lessons from Bilingual Corpora: Benefits for Machine Translation. Journal of Corpus Linguistics (2000).
22. The Historical Grammar of Lithuanian language. The Indo-European Database (TIED). http://indoeuro.bizland.com/atree.html.
23. Turcato, D., Paul Mc. F.,, Popowich, F., Toole, J.: A unified examplebased and lexicalist approach to Machine Translation. In: Hybrid Approaches to MT. Streiter, Oliver, Michael Carl and Johann Haller (eds.). (2000).
24. Wikipedia. http://en.wikipedia.org/wiki/Main_Page .

CL-Guided Korean-English MT System
for Scientific Papers

YoungKil Kim, Munpyo Hong, and Sang-Kyu Park

ETRI, NLP Team
161 Gajeong-dong, Yuseong-gu, 305-350 Daejeon, Korea
{kimyk,munpyo,parksk}@etri.re.kr

Abstract. This paper addresses a Korean-English machine translation system for scientific papers. The MT system is supported by CL (Controlled Language)-guided source language rewriting. After analyzing the translation errors of the system, we defined Korean rewriting rules to avoid the linguistic obstacles that may affect the translation accuracy. To support this, a Korean CL-checker was implemented. We showed that this CL-guided MT system can improve the translation accuracy by about 13% by adopting CL rewriting rules. However, this improvement is still not enough for various purposes, because most of the users of the MT system may want to submit the translated texts to a conference or an academic journal. As the MT output contains erroneous expressions, a language model module was added to the pattern-based MT engine. The system automatically detects expressions with low frequency and asks the authors to examine the translation. By adopting CL rewriting rules and language model module to the existing MT engine, almost "professional" translations can be obtained.

1 Introduction

Writing a scientific paper or technical documents in English is a hard and pain-taking job for many Koreans who are not fluent in English writing and speaking. From this reason, many Korean engineers and scientists tend to summarize and express their ideas in Korean and then to translate the Korean sentences into English. In translating the original Korean sentences into English, they resort to their knowledge about English grammar and vocabulary. In many cases, they have to submit their academic papers without major corrections of English by native speakers or whatsoever. As they rely only on their knowledge of English, they tend to make the same errors repeatedly as they have made before.

Recently in Korea, MT has attracted renewed attention from both industry and government since the successful launching of Korean-English patent machine translation service at KIPO (Korean Intellectual Property Office) [1]. The skeptical views on Korean related MT has subsided since the development of Korean-English patent MT system. One of the major factors that contributed to the success of Korean-English patent MT is a well-organized customization process. After the thorough linguistic

A. Gelbukh (Ed.): CICLing 2007, LNCS 4394, pp. 409–419, 2007.
© Springer-Verlag Berlin Heidelberg 2007

studies about Korean patent documents, the lexical goals were set. Also, the analysis modules were correspondingly customized to deal with the peculiarities of Korean patent document.

In this paper we will present our current effort to develop a paper translation system which aims at the translation of academic papers written in Korean into English. The main purpose of the translation of Korean into English is to help researchers or students to submit their papers to a conference or an academic journal. A major difference between Korean-English patent MT and paper MT lies in the purpose of the translation. In the case of patent MT, the main purpose of MT is to help the foreign patent examiners to find out which patents are relevant to his or her goals, i.e. it is for cross-lingual information retrieval and extraction. On the contrary, the purpose of the MT for scientific papers is to submit a paper to a conference or a journal. That is, in this case the quality of the translation must be almost professional.

To our knowledge, there is no MT system that can generate a "professional" English translation for a given Korean input in a single shot. One of the major obstacles to "professional" translation of Korean sentences is a long sentence. Typically, a long sentence makes the correct analysis of the input difficult. Although, the length of a sentence does not always reflect the complexity of the sentence, it can be treated as a relatively reliable criterion to measure the complexity [2].

To overcome the obstacles for "professional" translations, we designed a controlled language checker for Korean. The "controlled" Korean is given to the MT engine as an input. There have been few research activities on controlled Korean, if any. In this work we present our attempts to design a "controlled Korean" and the controlled Korean checker. In the experiments we will show that a "controlled" input can lead to about 10~15 % improvement of translation quality. However, this improvement is still not enough to be ready for a submission.

As our MT engine employs a pattern-based approach, the translation results may sometimes look unnatural due to wrong pattern matchings. To deal with this problem, we added a language model module to the end of the main translation engine. The language model has been widely used as a post-processing step to enhance the generation performance in MT systems [3]. Our system detects an unnatural expression through the assessment of the probability of a given translated word sequence appearing in English scientific papers, and the system asks the users to examine the translation. In this way, a user can finish his or her translation job much faster and more conveniently.

In section 2 we will survey some major works on controlled language. Section 3 deals with the customization of Korean-English MT system for scientific papers. Section 4 describes the CL-guided source language rewriting and example expression based target language rewriting. In section 5, we show experiment results. Finally, conclusions and future work are presented in Section 6.

2   Related Works

Designing a controlled language can be driven from two perspectives: Firstly, a controlled language can be designed to enhance the understandability and readability. Secondly, a controlled language can be designed so that it can improve the machine translation quality. There is no clear-cut definition as to what a controlled language should be like. Usually, a controlled language consists of a controlled vocabulary and syntax. Most of the works on controlled language focus on how to design a grammar rules and lexicon for a given language. cf. [3,4,5,6]. To make a decision whether the major "controlling" should take place in the lexicon or in the syntax is very critical. In the "AECMA"-approach [7], the emphasis was put rather on the lexicon. In contrast, in designing a controlled German, Lehrndorfer et al. [2] put the emphasis on the syntax, allowing rather a less restricted vocabulary.

In our current setting, the controlling should take place on the syntactic level, because we are dealing with users from various academic backgrounds. It is difficult to design a controlled vocabulary for each academic domain from practical reasons. In order to design a fragment of "controlled Korean", we analyzed a corpus of Korean and its English MT results. From this, we extracted about 10 Korean syntactic construction types that the current MT system sometimes fails to analyze correctly. Our experiments will show that only by introducing this kind of rewriting rules, we can achieve about 10~15 % improvement. In a similar case, Shirai et al. [8] reported that when applying rewriting rules to Japanese to English translation, the translation quality is improved by 20 %.

3 Customizing Korean-English MT System for Scientific Papers

Under the auspices of Ministry of Information and Communication we developed a Korean-English MT system for patent documents from 2004 to 2005. This year, the MT system was customized for scientific papers. The customization process includes a construction of translation resources, such as terms with high-frequency and translation patterns that were extracted from the papers, and the modification of engine modules after linguistic studies of academic papers. Furthermore a CL-guided Korean rewriting functions was implemented to improve the translation quality.

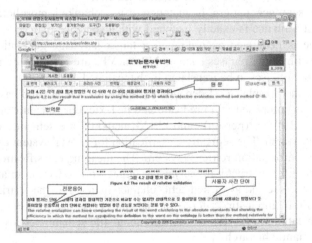

Fig. 1. Korean-English CL-guided MT system for scientific papers

3.1 Korean POS Tagger and Syntactic Analyzer

In this paper MT system, the Korean POS tagger and syntactic analyzer of Korean-English Patent MT System were employed. The morphological and syntactic characteristics of patent documents are almost similar to those of paper texts, because they all belong to the same kind of technical documents. As was in the patent documents, the sentences in the scientific papers show some peculiar morphological and syntactic characteristics, including the frequent use of derived words and the biased POS tagging tendency of ambiguous words, locality of the syntactic dependency, and etc.

The proper treatment of a prefix and suffix is especially important in the morphological processing of papers, as many technical terms are derived nouns. To filter out irrelevant POS candidates during the POS tagging, we designed a rule table which shows the connectivity between the morphemes in an Eojeol[1]. The Korean syntactic analyzer analyzes the predicate-argument-adjunct structure for each predicate using the so-called verb patterns and lexical co-ocurrences and the structure between predicates employing predicate-predicate structure patterns. To customize the syntactic analyzer, we constructed verb patterns with high frequency and predicate-predicate dependency patterns that were extracted from the paper sentences.

3.2 Pattern-Based Generation

In the viewpoint of target language generation, this MT system can be classified as a pattern-based MT system. For the English generation, three types of patterns including sentence patterns, verbal patterns and noun patterns are employed, as in Type1~3. After the morphological and syntactic analysis, the morphological results and dependency structure of Korean input sentence are generated and the English generator uses the translation patterns to generate the English sentence.

Firstly, the sentence pattern is matched using chunked morphological results. When the input sentence is exactly matched with a sentence pattern as in type 1, the target language is generated according to a target language generation part of the pattern. At this time, the phrases such as NPs or VPs are recursively translated until there are no more phrases to be translated in the matched pattern.

Secondly, each verb phrase of dependency structure is generated based on the verbal pattern that is composed of a predicate and its lexical or semantic arguments as in Type2. In Type 2, "사람(person)" and "방법(method)" are semantic codes that are used in the MT system. The semantic classification for an MT system can be different from that for an information retrieval system. The meaning classification of a noun is usually employed for a structural analysis or target word selection in an MT system. From this reason, such kind of syntactic characteristics and the sharing of a target word can be useful linguistic criteria for semantic classification. Based on this, we classified the meaning of Korean nouns with about 400 semantic codes allowing for 9 levels in the semantic hierarchy [9].

---

[1] An Eojeol is a spacing unit. It corresponds to a bunsetsu in Japanese.

Thirdly, if the argument of the matched verb pattern is a noun phrase, the noun phrase is translated based on the noun pattern that is composed of its lexical or semantic arguments as in Type3.

Type1: Sentence Patterns
 e.g)   본논문(*this   paper*)+에서   NP1+를   설계하(*design*)+고
구현하(*implement*)+다 > In this paper, we have designed and developed NP1

Type2: Verbal Patterns
 e.g) A=사람(*person*)!가 B=방법(*method*)!를 설계하(*design*)!다 > A design:v B

Type3: Noun and Adverbal Patterns
 e.g) A=사건(*event*)!의 일례 > an example of A

3.3 Long Sentence Processing

In machine translation, the quality and the efficiency of translation of long sentences is very low. It is because as the length of a sentence goes up, the syntactic ambiguity of sentence increases rapidly [10]. Also, in the machine translation using the sentence pattern, a high translation quality can be obtained, but as the length of input sentence increases, a critical coverage problem is encountered [11]. For these problems, a long sentence should be partitioned into smaller fragments and translated with smaller units.

We collected 150 Korean papers including 19,996 sentences and analyzed the characteristics of the paper sentences. The analysis shows that a sentence is composed of 18.71 Eojeols on the average, compared with 12.3 Eojeols in general Korean newspaper articles. The sentences in a paper are relatively long and complex, and the Korean long sentence usually consists of several simple sentences connected with a verbal connective ending.

Such long sentences are one of the biggest obstacles that affect the translation accuracy, because a parser generally has difficulties in parsing such long sentences, which makes the readability of the translated sentences quite low.

To solve the long sentence problem, we use a syntactic clue, verbal ending morphemes followed by "," to partition a long sentence into several "proper sized" sentences that can be parsed easily.

Segmentation Clue : verbal ending morphemes followed by "," such as:
 -   "verb stem + 고 (and) + comma"
 -   "verb stem + ㄴ 후 (after) + comma"
 -   "verb stem + ㄴ 경우에 (in case that) + comma"

We collected the sentences that are composed of over 20 Eojeols, including verbal ending morphemes followed by ",". And we analyzed the segmentation accuracy of those morphemes followed by ",", compared with the predicate pattern based method of our MT system. As shown in Table 1, the predicate-predicate dependency accuracy of predicate pattern based method is 71%. But, when we use verbal ending morpheme clues followed by ",", the accuracy of predicate-predicate dependency improves to 89%. Therefore, in translating a long sentence in the paper, we can use the clue to segment an input sentence into several "proper sized" sentences. By doing this we can not only improve the accuracy of the structural analysis, but also generate the English sentences that are easier to read and understand.

Table 1. Predicate-Predicate Dependency Accuracy

Method	Using Predicate Patterns	Using verbal ending morpheme clues followed by ","
Predicate-Predicate Dependency Accuracy	71%	89%

However, this verbal ending morpheme clues often don't appear in many of the long sentences. We analyzed the 20,388 paper sentences and calculated the number of sentences including the verbal ending morpheme clue. Because a sentence of over 3 predicates has an ambiguity in determining the dependency of the predicate-predicate, we need the dependency clue in Korean sentences to improve the performance of the MT System for scientific papers. However, unfortunately, 70.64% of the sentences that include more than 3 predicates don't have the verbal ending morpheme clue, as shown in Table 2. If we could restrict authors simply to commas where it is necessary as is guided by Korean CL checker, we could improve the translation quality of long sentences significantly.

Table 2. Occurrence frequency of the verbal ending morpheme clue

The frequency of verbal ending morphemes in a sentence	The number of sentences	The number of sentences including the verbal ending morpheme clue
0	291	0
1	2,481	0
2	4,545	286(6.17%)
3	4,252	712(16.75%)
4	3,138	781(24.89%)
5	2,243	572(25.50%)
6	1,456	701(48.15%)
7	804	317(39.43%)
8	597	290(48.58%)
9	320	252(78.75%)
Over 10	261	212(81.23%)
Total of over 3	13,071	3,837(29.36%)

4 CL-Guided Machine Translation

To overcome the obstacles for "professional" translations, we defined CL rewriting rules to avoid the linguistic obstacles and designed a controlled language checker for Korean. And we added a language model module to present the candidates of unnatural expression to a paper author, so that he or she examines the translation, referring to example expressions. In this way, the author can finish his or her translation job much faster and more conveniently.

4.1 CL Rules for Source Language Rewriting

Firstly, we analyzed the most frequent and fatal translation errors of our MT system for scientific papers and defined CL rules for Korean rewriting to avoid the linguistic constructions that affect the translation accuracy. We could find many CL rules for Korean rewriting, but there are only a handful of rules to be used for implementing the CL-guided functions. Some important rewriting rules are as follows:

Rule 1. Avoid writing a long sentence and use proper symbols such as comma and colon:

In dealing with long sentences, we used a syntactic clue, i.e. verbal ending morphemes followed by "," to partition a long sentence into several "proper sized" sentences that can be parsed and generated easily. However, if there are no such clues in an input sentence that has 4 verbal phrases as in Figure 2, the system analyzes the

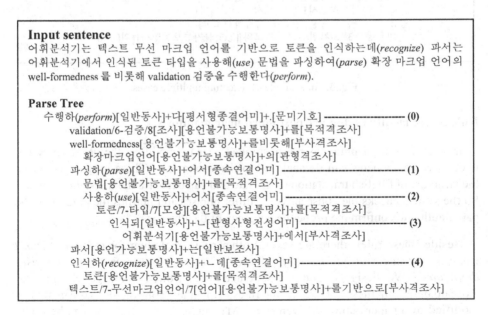

Fig. 2. Segment candidates based on a parse tree

input sentence to get the parse tree. After the system extracts the parse tree, it can recommend (1) and (4) position in parallel with a main verb "수행하(*perform*)" as the candidates to segment the input sentence. If a paper author selects the proper segment positions for the MT system, the system uses the confirmed segment clue to translate a long sentence more accurately and naturally.

Rule 2. Don't use multiple cases or expressions within a verb phrase:

When a Korean paper author writes a paper in Korean, multiple cases or identical expressions are sometimes repeated in a verb phrase. These expressions make English translations unnatural and can decrease the translation quality. The following sample sentence has two object cases within a verbal phrase as in Figure 3. After the system gets the parse tree of an input sentence, it can check multiple cases or multiple expressions within a phrase and notify the multiple morphemes to the paper author.

Input sentence
LOD 는 대용량 3 차원 모델의 형상을(*obj*) 단순한 단계까지 여러 형상을(*obj*)
생성하는(*generate*) 기술이다(*be*).

Parse Tree
이(*be*)[긍정지정사]+다[평서형종결어미]+.[문미기호]
　　기술[용언불가능보통명사]+이[보격조사]
　　　생성하(*generate*)[일반동사]+는[관형사형전성어미]
　　　　여러/18-형상/8[모양][용언불가능보통명사]+를(*obj*)[목적격조사]
　　　　단계[용언불가능보통명사]+까지[일반보조사]
　　　　　단순하[성상형용사]+ㄴ[관형사형전성어미]
　　　　　형상[용언가능보통명사]+를(*obj*)[목적격조사]
　　　　　　대용량/7-3/15-차원/7-모델/7[모양][용언불가능보통명사]+의[관형격조사]
　　LOD[외국어]+는[보격조사]

Fig. 3. An example of detecting multiple cases

Rule 3. Use modifiers that are positioned near modifiees:

In case a modifier phrase is not positioned near its modifiee, the dependency between two components can be analyzed in the wrong way. These expressions make the structure of English translation inaccurate and can decrease the translation quality. So the system checks the consecutive modifier phrases and notifies the phrases to the paper author to confirm the proper dependency of the phrases.

Besides these rules, there are several other rules, including for example *"Don't write a sentence that has no subject case", "Register unknown terms in a user dictionary"* We designed and implemented a controlled language checker for Korean based on these CL rewriting rules. And the "controlled" Korean that is modified by a paper author is given to the MT engine as an input and can be translated more accurately.

4.2 Target Language Rewriting Using Example Expressions

The "controlled" input can lead to an improvement of translation quality. However, this improvement is still not enough to be ready for a submission. As our MT engine employs a pattern-based approach, the translation results may sometimes look unnatural due to wrong pattern matchings. To deal with this problem, we offered the example expression search tool as in Figure 4. For automatically detecting and suggesting unnatural expression in a translated sentence, we added the n-gram language model module to the search tool.

Fig. 4. Example expression search tool

We collected over 100,000 scientific papers and extracted about 8.5 million sentences. For supporting quick searches of example expressions, we indexed the sentences using inverted index files and built n-gram(n=2,3,4,5 ...) phrase frequency DB to show the occurrence frequency of the translated phrases. So, the system can offer the occurrence frequency of translated expressions to a paper author. And then the author can search the similar expressions about the translated expressions that are considered to be unnatural due to low occurrence frequencies, and modify the wrong expressions, referring to example expressions that were used in the previous papers.

5 Evaluation

We estimated the translation accuracy with 100 test sentences randomly extracted from papers. The average length of a sentence was 18.7 words. The scoring criteria were described in Table 3 [1]. The translation accuracy (TA) is calculated by the formula, $TA = [(S_1 + S_2 + ... S_n)/n]*(100/4)$ (%) where S_1 is the evaluated score of the first sentence and "n" is the number of evaluated sentences.

Table 3. Scoring criteria for evaluating the translation accuracy

Score	Criterion
4	The meaning of a sentence is perfectly conveyed
3.5	The meaning of a sentence is almost perfectly conveyed except for some minor errors (e.g. wrong article, stylistic errors)
3	The meaning of a sentence is almost conveyed (e.g. some errors in target word selection)
2.5	A simple sentence in a complex sentence is correctly translated
2	A sentence is translated phrase-wise
1	Only some words are translated
0	No translation

3 professional translators were hired for the evaluation and the estimated scores were summed and the average was calculated. The accuracy of 2 methods was shown in Table 4.

Table 4. Translation accuracy of translation methods

Translation Method	Translation Accuracy
ETRI Machine Translation (ETRIMT)	70.5% (282/400)
CL-guided Korean Rewriting + ETRIMT	83.8% (335/400)

The initial translation accuracy of the machine translation is 70.5%. The original translation is understandable, but the translation quality cannot reach the level enough to submit to an international conference or an academic journal. In contrast, the MT result combined with our fragment of Korean CL improved by about 13%. We are still working to find out the positive and negative effects of n-gram based language model that automatically detects possible unnatural translations and suggests the authors to revise the detected mis-translations.

6   Conclusion

In this paper, the Korean-English paper machine translation system was supported by a fragment of Korean CL. We showed that the MT translations accuracy can be improved by about 13% by introducing the controlled Korean and CL checker. Further, we introduced the idea of adding language model to help the non-native English authors to find the parts that they need to possibly revise or proof-read. In the future, it is necessary to improve the translation performance of the machine translation system so that the paper author can obtain the translations of the higher quality within shorter time. And the accuracy of the segmentation candidate guessed by the structural analysis has to be improved to make an author's rewriting work easier. The various functions supporting CL-guided machine translation will be added.

Acknowledgement

This work was funded by the Ministry of Information and Communication of Korean government.

References

1. Hong, M., Kim, Y., Kim, C., Yang, S., Seo, Y., Ryu, C., Park, S.: Customizing a Korean-English MT System for Patent Translation, MT-Summit (2005)
2. Anne Lehrndorfer : Kontrolliertes Deutsch, Gunter Narr Verlag, Tuebingen (1996)
3. Fu-Hua Liu, Liang Gu, Yuqing Gao and Michael Picheny : Use of Statistical N-gram Models in Natural Language Generation for Machine Translation, ICASSP (2003)
4. Teruko Mitamura, Controlled language for multilingual MT, MT-Summit (1999)
5. G. Adriaens and D. Schreuers : From COGRAM to ALCOGRAM: Toward a controlled English grammar checker, in COLING [COL92], (1992) 595-601.
6. N. E. Fuchs, U. Schwertel, R. Schwitter : Attempto Controlled English (ACE) Language Manual, Version 3.0, Technical Report, Department of Computer Science, University of Zurich (1999).
7. AECMA : A Guide for the Preparation of Aircraft Maintenance Documentation in the International Aerosace Maintenance Language, AECMA Simplified English (1995).
8. Shirai, S., Ikekaha, S., Yokoo, A. and Ooyama, Y : Automatic Rewriting Method for Internal Expressions in Japanese to English MT and Its Effects, In proceedings of the Second International Workshop on Controlled Language Applications(CLAW-98) (1998).
9. Kim, Y, Hong, M, Kim, C, Park, S : Word Sense Disambiguation Using Lexical and Semantic Information within Local Syntactic Relations, The 30th Annual Conference of the IEEE Industrial Electronics Society (2004)
10. Roh, Y, Seo Y, Lee, K, Choi, S : Long Sentence Partitioning using Structure Analysis for Machine Translation, NLPRS (2001).
11. Seo Y, R, Y, Lee, K, Park, S : CaptionEye/EK: English-to-Korean Caption Translation System using the Sentence Pattern, MT-Summit (2001).

Comparing and Integrating
Alignment Template and Standard Phrase-Based
Statistical Machine Translation

Lin Xu[1,*], Xiaoguang Cao[1], Bufeng Zhang[2], and Mu Li[3]

[1] Lab of Pattern Recognition and Intelligent System,
Image Processing Center, BeiHang University, China
lin_lin_xu@sa.buaa.edu.cn, xgcao@buaa.edu.cn
[2] AI Lab, Computer Science and Technology, Tianjing University, China
bufengzhang@tju.edu.cn
[3] Microsoft Research Asia
muli@microsoft.com

Abstract. In statistical machine translation (SMT) research, phrase-based methods have been receiving more interest in recent years. In this paper, we first give a brief survey of phrase-based SMT framework, and then make detailed comparisons of two typical implementations: alignment template approach and standard phrase-based approach. At last, we propose an improved model to integrate alignment template into standard phrase-based SMT as a new feature in a log-linear model. Experimental results show that our method outperforms the baseline method.

1 Introduction

Phrase-based model uses the phrase as the basic unit of machine translation (MT). It considers the contextual information of words and simplifies the translation complexity. Two typical phrase-based statistical machine translation (SMT) systems are alignment template (AT) approach and standard phrase-based (SP) model. In NIST2002 MT evaluation, Och's alignment template SMT (AT-SMT) system came in first place. In the NAACL2006 workshop on European language SMT, Koehn's standard phrase-based system (SP-SMT) outperformed the other 13 participating groups. These results indicate that AT-SMT and SP-SMT are state-of-the-art SMT models.

In 2003, Tomás made a basic introduction to both systems, proposed a lineal combination of them [1]. But he did not make further comparisons on their different components, he just combined the two systems in a simple lineal way using Translation Word Error Rate (TWER) as a metric.

In this paper, we describe our research on phrase-based SMT, provide a brief survey of phrase-based SMT first, including the related works and framework of phrase-based SMT, then we compare SP-SMT and AT-SMT systems concretely

---

* The work on this paper was conducted when the first author was visiting Microsoft Research Asia.

A. Gelbukh (Ed.): CICLing 2007, LNCS 4394, pp. 420–431, 2007.

in different aspects. Moreover, we analyze their advantages and disadvantages through implementing both systems separately and doing a series of experiments measured by BLEU score [14]. After that, we give an improved model by integrating AT and SP-SMT. The idea is to make alignment template's generality effective on SP-SMT, that is to say, to combine advantages of both systems.

The organization of the paper is as follows. In section 2, we give a brief survey. In section 3, we make concrete comparisons of both systems. We introduce the integrated model in section 4. We present the experiments and discuss the result in section 5 and conclude in section 6.

2   Survey of Phrase-Based SMT

MT is challenging because of the highly complex, irregular and diverse nature of natural language. It is impossible to accurately model all the linguistic rules and relationships that are involved in the translation process, and therefore MT has to arrive at decisions based on incomplete data. A principled approach to this problem is to apply statistical methodologies to provide machines with optional decisions given the incomplete data.

Original SMT systems by Brown et al. [2] assumed a word-to-word alignment between the source and target languages. A shortcoming of a single-word based model is that it does not take into account contextual information for translation decisions. Phrase-based model is more robust because the alignment is performed on a bigger granularity, i.e. substrings. Och's AT approach [3] can be reframed as a phrase translation system; Yamada and Knight [4] used phrase translation in a syntax-based translation system; Marcu and Wong [5] introduced a joint-probability model for phrase translation; Zens [6] presented a phrase-based model based on bilingual phrase pairs; Koehn et al. [7] provided a SP system, suggesting that data sparseness took over when faced with lengthy phrases.

In recent years, improvements on these phrase-based systems have been demonstrated. Och used maximum entropy models to combine features into a log-linear model and improve the AT approach in [8] [9]. Koehn et al. enhanced their SP-SMT by trying new features and optimizing heuristic functions in [10]. Kumar et al.'s weighted finite state transducer which was inspired by the AT translation model [11]. Alexandra provided a scalable phrase-based joint probability model that used SP models to restrict and guide the training of a joint probability model [12]. Chiang presented a Hierarchical phrase-based model that was formally a synchronous context-free grammar model but was learned from a bi-text without any syntactic information [13]. Yaser Al-Onaizan [21] and Xiong [20] proposed reordering models for phrase-based SMT, which significantly improved the system's performance.

The flow of a common phrase-based SMT is described in Figure 1 and illustrated as follows: Phrase-based SMT is based on the noisy channel model. It uses Bayes rule to formulate the translation probability for translating a foreign sentence f into English e as:

$$\operatorname*{argmax}_{e} p(e|f) = \operatorname*{argmax}_{e} p(f|e)p(e) \qquad (1)$$

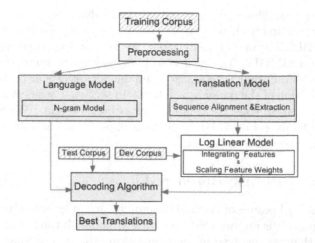

Fig. 1. SMT Implementation Flow

$p(e)$ is N-gram language model. We focus our attention on the translation model $p(f|e)$. This probability displays the relationship between the words of the source and target sentences, which can be explained by means of the hidden variable a:

$$p(f|e) = \sum_a p(a, f|e) = \sum_a p(a|e)p(f|a, e) \tag{2}$$

$$= \alpha(e) \sum_a p(f|a, e) = \alpha(e) \sum_{\tilde{e}:\tilde{e}\epsilon e} \sum_{\substack{\tilde{f}:\tilde{f}\epsilon f; \\ |\tilde{e}|=|\tilde{f}|}} p(\tilde{f}|\tilde{e}) \tag{3}$$

In Equation (2), a denotes the alignment of the target sentence e and source sentence f. In equation (3), we assume that all alignment have the same probability $\alpha(e)$. This parameter is not relevant for translation and will be omitted. $\tilde{e}$, $\tilde{f}$ is the sequence in e and f separately. Equation (3) is an alternative expression of equation (2), where the monotone alignment is explicitly indicated.

Phrase-based SMT is based on a set of bilingual sequences that must be previously obtained in order to perform the translation. In this paper, we obtain bilingual sequences from word-based alignment using GIZA++ toolkit [15]. In SP-SMT, the sequence is called "phrase" (continuous words); In AT-SMT, the sequence is called "alignment template" (continuous word classes). The heuristics we use in sequence alignment and extraction are described in [16].

The decoder selects the most likely translation by maximizing the sum of probabilities over a set of feature functions $h_m(e, f)$ scaled by weights λ_m:

$$\hat{e} = \operatorname*{argmax}_e p(e|f) = \operatorname*{argmax}_e \sum_{m=1}^{M} \lambda_m h_m(e, f) \tag{4}$$

The log linear model [8] provides a natural framework to integrate many components and to weigh them based on their performance by maximizing the likelihood on a parallel training corpus f_1^S, e_1^S.

$$\lambda_m = \operatorname*{argmax}_{\lambda_m} \left\{ \sum_{s=1}^{S} logp_{\lambda_m}(e_s|f_s) \right\} \tag{5}$$

The weights used to scale the feature functions are found via Minimum Error Rate Training (MERT) [17]. These weights are tuned using a small held-out development set, and using the BLEU score of the system as the optimization metric.

3   Comparisons of SP-SMT and AT-SMT

3.1   Sequence Alignment Model

SP-SMT. The SP-SMT alignment model is induced from equation (3). In equation (3), if we assume that the phrase $\tilde{f}_i$ is produced only by $\tilde{e}_i$, we can write:

$$p(\tilde{f}|\tilde{e}) = \prod_{i=1}^{|\tilde{f}|} p(\tilde{f}_i|\tilde{e}_i) \tag{6}$$

where $\tilde{f}_i$, $\tilde{e}_i$ is phrase. That is to say, the aligned phrase is induced by aligned words. So SP-SMT is a phrase level translation. The phrase inducing process is as follows: From word-alignment bilingual pairs produced by Giza++ toolkit, we get word alignment matrix using symmetric heuristics similar to [5]. The aligned phrases are then extracted from the alignment matrix and their translation probabilities are calculated according to the lexical probabilities (the heuristics of phrase extraction and lexical weight calculation are similar to [16]).

The key to good translation performance is having an effective phrase translation table which is the final outcome of phrase alignment. Some entries of this are in Figure 2. The probability attached at the end of each phrase pair is the relative frequency probability of the phrase $\tilde{f}_i$ to phrase $\tilde{e}_i$. Any phrase pair ap-

he said ||| 他 说 ||| 0.09677419
he says ||| 他 说 ||| 0.09677419
as he said ||| 他 说 ||| 0.0322580
he describes||| 他 说 ||| 0.0322580

Fig. 2. Entry examples in phrase translation table

pearing in phrase translation table provides a candidate translation pair between a source language model and a target language segment. But for phrases that do not appear in phrase translation table, SP-SMT does not work and considers them as the unknown words.

AT-SMT. One obvious drawback of SP-SMT is that it does not have a generalization capability in word reordering. If we try to translate the Chinese phrase " 他笑" to English, but it does not appear in the training corpus, the SP-SMT model cannot output the correct sequence - "he smiles".

But AT-SMT can solve this problem successfully by adding an alignment template z in the phrase translation of equation (3):

$$p(\tilde{f}|\tilde{e}) = \sum_z p(z|\tilde{e})p(\tilde{f}|z,\tilde{e}) \qquad (7)$$

AT-SMT adds generalization capability to the bilingual phrase lexicon by replacing the words with word classes and also by storing the alignment information for each sequence pair. These generalized and alignment-annotated sequence pairs are called alignment templates [7]. Formally, the alignment template z is a triplet $(F_i^{J'}, E_i^{J'}, \tilde{A})$ that describe the alignment $\tilde{A}$ between a source class sequence $F_i^{J'}$ and a target class sequence $E_i^{J'}$. This triplet is obtained by grouping words into equivalent classes, which is a standard method in statistical language modeling. Och used an exchange algorithm to obtain an optimization criterion for bilingual word classes by applying a maximum-likelihood approach to the joint probability of a parallel corpus [8].

The alignment template generation process (shown in Figure 3) is as follows: We apply the GIZA++ toolkit to first find word alignment from the bilingual pairs. Then we replace all the words in the word alignment matrix by their class number, so we get the aligned word class sequences. Finally we extract the alignment template using the heuristics similar to the phrase extraction in SP-SMT. The probability of using AT to translate a specific source language is also estimated by means of relative frequency.

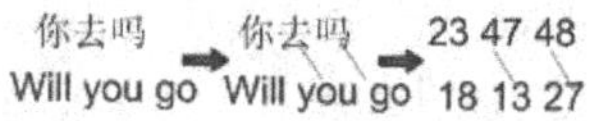

你去吗 ➡ 你去吗 ➡ 23 47 48
Will you go Will you go 18 13 27

Fig. 3. Generalization process in AT-SMT

The aligned alignment template is the key to good translation performance in AT-SMT. Unlike the phrase translation table of SP-SMT, it cannot show the alignment of true phrase pairs directly. So it increases the debugging difficulty in the building of SMT system.

3.2   Feature Functions

The probability that is assigned to a translation entry is the product of the probabilities of features as described in section 2. Therefore, the selection of features and feature weights are critical to the process. Features are combined in a log-linear model. Each feature is assigned an initial weight randomly, and then it is optimized directly against the BLEU evaluation metric on the held-out data through MERT.

Each of the features contributes information over one aspect of the characteristics of a good translation. The following are the features used in the experiments and Table 1 specifies the features used by each of the two systems.

- The *Distortion Model* allows reordering of the input sentence, but at a cost: The more reordering, the more expensive the translation.
- The *Language Model* ensures that the output is a fluent target sentence (e.g. English sentence).
- The *Phrase translation* (both directions) table ensures that the source phrase and the target phrase are effective translations of each other.
- The *Lexical translation probability* (both directions) table ensures that the source word and the target word are effective translations of each other.
- The *Phrase Penalty* ensures that the number of phrases in the target sentence does not get too big or too small.
- The *Word Penalty* ensures that the number of words in the target sentence does not get too big or too small.
- *Alignment Template Selection* ensures that the source template and the target template are good translation pairs of each other.
- *Conventional Lexicon* is used to count how many entries of a conventional lexicon co-occur in the given sentence pair. The belief is that the conventional dictionary is more reliable than the automatically trained lexicon.

Table 1. Basic Features used in SP-SMT and AT-SMT

	SP-SMT	AT-SMT
Different Features	Phrase translation table Phrase Penalty	Alignment Template Selection Conventional Lexicon Phrase Alignment
Common Features	Distortion Model, Language Model, Word Penalty, Lexical Translation Probability	

3.3 Decoding Process

The decoding process is a process to search for the most optimal translation of the sentence. It should be possible to translate a sentence of reasonable length within a few seconds of computing time. We accomplish such an efficient algorithm by searching in a breadth-first manner with pruning: beam search [18]. Both systems employ this method, but they are different in their detailed implementation because of the difference of sequence alignment models.

SP-SMT. The decoder starts with an initial hypothesis. A new hypothesis is expanded from an existing hypothesis by the translation of a phrase as follows: A sequence of untranslated foreign words and a possible English phrase translation for them are selected. A final hypothesis with the highest probability and no untranslated foreign words is the output of the search. This process is illustrated in Figure 4.

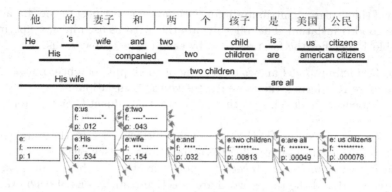

Fig. 4. Decoding process of SP-SMT

The hypotheses are stored in stacks and we prune out weak hypotheses based on the probability costs. The probability assigned to a translation is a product of feature probability costs as described in [18]. For each stack, we only keep a beam of the best n hypotheses.

AT-SMT. The new expanded hypothesis in AT-SMT contains all the information required to efficiently perform computations needed in the search, such as the final target word produced, the state of language model, and the alignment template instantiation, etc. for details see [9].

AT-SMT's decoding process is more complex than SP-SMT because of the application of bilingual word classes [19]. Because AT must generalize the segmented source sentence first (all words are replaced by word classes) before starting with an empty hypothesis. However, their processes are similar in the beam search process.

Comparing with SP-SMT, the template is applied between real words, so word class is the entity during the decoding. For example, in Figure 5, $C_2C_3C_4$ is aligned to $l_{11}l_{12}$ which is the most probable alignment template instantiation indicated in the alignment template table. But we cannot judge whether this alignment relation is correct until the alignment templates are filled in by real words. On the contrary, in SP-SMT, e.g. if "孩子" is aligned to "children", we

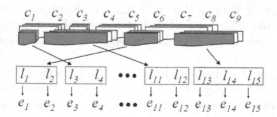

Fig. 5. Decoding process of AT-SMT

can clearly judge this alignment relation is proper. So on one hand, AT increases the generality of SMT system and overcomes the limitations of the corpus, on the other hand, it complicates the decoding process.

4   Integration AT into SP-SMT

As we mentioned, AT has the generality, SP has detailed and concrete information, and the two models are complementary. The essential of Tomás's combing model [1] is a lineal combination (equation (8)) of both systems (equation (6) and (7)). The relevance factor α is an experimental value, the tuning of which is necessary to get the most optimal translation. This combining method is easy slip to a bad trap, because the tuning of the parameter is not automatic.

$$pr(\tilde{f}|\tilde{e}) = (1 - \alpha) \prod_{i=1}^{|\tilde{f}|} p(\tilde{f}_i|\tilde{e}_i) + \alpha \sum_z p(z|\tilde{e})p(\tilde{f}|z, \tilde{e}) \qquad (8)$$

In this paper, our improved model is easier and automatic. The basic idea is to use SP system as the baseline system and AT as the $(M + 1)th$ improving feature for SP. Since decoding adopts log-linear model to integrated features, we get our improved model just by integrating equation (7) to equation (4):

$$\hat{e} = \operatorname*{argmax}_e p(e|f) = \operatorname*{argmax}_e \sum_{m=1}^{M} \lambda_m h_m(e, f) + \lambda_{M+1} p(z|e)p(f|z, e) \qquad (9)$$

In the decoding process, when phrase $\tilde{f}$ is choosing its translation $\tilde{e}$, it just needs to consider their relative AT translation probability. And a log-linear model that integrates SP system is easy to implement for decoder as shown in equation (9).

5   Experiments

We use LDC NIST2002 corpus to carry out the experiments in the multi-domain task of Chinese-English translation. The training corpus contains more than 10 million words, 600K parallel sentences, covering news, legal and political proceedings. Both the development corpus and test corpus have four references which are not included in training corpus.

In this paper, we measure SP-SMT and AT-SMT systems using BLEU as the metric from the following dimensions firstly:

- *corpus*: different sizes of in-domain or out-of-domain corpora.
- *language*: different language pairs, e.g. Chinese-English, French-English.
- *feature*: combination of additional features and their contributions.

Then we do experiments to check the integration of both models. All results presented in our experiments are just relative values and not the systems' best results. The combinations of the feature parameters are not the optimal ones because what we are interested in is the comparison and integration of the SP and AT models. The script to calculate BLEU score we adopted in our experiment is standard LDC NIST script.

5.1   Corpus

For in-domain test corpus, we test both systems in different training corpus pairs raging from 50K to 600K. For out-of-domain test corpus (out-of-domain means the test corpus's theme or sentence expression style is different from training corpus or most phrases do not appear in training corpus), we experiment on the largest size of training corpus. We select the trigram model trained by the SRILM toolkit [1] for the language model.

Table 2. BLEU on different size training corpus

System	Parallel Pairs in Training Corpus (BLEU)			
	50K	300K	600K	600K (Out-of-domain)
SP-SMT	18.36	21.16	22.05	8.7
AT-SMT	18.68	20.53	21.46	15.31

From the results shown in table 2, for in-domain data, when the training corpus is smaller, AT-SMT outperforms the SP-SMT. However, as the size of the training corpus increases, the number of phrase pairs in SP-SMT increases rapidly, and SP-SMT's results get better than AT-SMT. For the out-of-domain data, AT-SMT's performance exceeds SP-SMT depending on its generality made by bilingual word classes which can handle the data sparseness to some extent. The phrase translation table is the most important part in SP-SMT whose translation quality directly depends on phrase pairs. So, the more phrase pairs that appear, the better the translation becomes.

5.2   Feature

The nature of log-linear model makes it easy to integrate disparate features into the decoder. And best feature values can be obtained through MERT. We choose their common features and carry out the experiments on the baseline system to test the usability and feature sensitivity of both systems.

New features in Table 3 are added to the baseline system in turn such that the contribution of each feature can be seen. The results indicate that 4-gram language model or larger and a distortion model helps immeasurably. Named Entity (NE) in preprocessing is a challenge in natural language processing, especially in Chinese, but good NE can improve the translation quality. However, the sequence extraction length (phrase length in SP-SMT, template length in

Table 3. BLEU on new feature effect (baseline's setting: 600K training corpus, in-domain test corpus, trigram Language Model)

New features	SP-SMT	AT-SMT
Baseline	22.05	21.46
NE in preprocessing	22.26	21.67
Sequence extraction length=5	22.41	21.63
Large Language Model, ngram=4	23.78	22.70
Distortion Model limit=4	23.61	22.82
Combination of all above features	25.44	23.78

AT-SMT)-the impact is not as strong as described in [7]. The combination results of these features are also listed. In fact, obtaining the best combination of various feature parameters is not a trivial issue. The Edinburgh System has described the effect of combined features in their system description in [10] [22]. These are consistent with our findings.

5.3 Language

SMT has the advantage of being rule-free and language independent. So we test the systems' language applicability using French-English pairs (NAACL 2006[2]). Table 4 shows both systems work well on European language translation[3]. But

Table 4. BLEU on French-English translation (trigram, Max. distortion limit length=6, Max sequence extraction length=5)

system	French-English (688k pairs)	
	In domain	Out Domain
SP-SMT	29.59	26.38
AT-SMT	26.93	26.02

AT-SMT still underperforms SP-SMT. The reason for this is that AT-SMT's word class provides the generality but not enough precision, so on a large training corpus like the one provided by NAACL2006, when the translation probability table of SP-SMT covers most phrase in test corpus, SP-SMT will certainly achieve a higher BLEU score.

5.4 Integration Method

The Integration method makes AT a feature in SP-SMT. So we just check its performance based on SP-SMT. Moreover, in the above experiments, SP-SMT performs better on large training corpus both for French-English and Chinese-English.

---

[1] Http://www.speech.sri.com/projects/srilm/

[2] Http://www.statmt.org/wmt06/

[3] Best result for French-English translation is 30.42 ± 0.86 on NAACL2006.

Table 5. Bleu score of SP-SMT and integration method

system	Chinese-English	French-English
SP-SMT	22.05	29.59
Integration	22.89	30.00

It is proved that Alignment template is helpful in choosing phrase pair n-best lists as shown in table 5. By integrating the two models, the advantages of both SP-SMT and AT-SMT are made use of.

6   Conclusions

In this paper, we outlined two phrase-based SMT systems: SP-SMT and AT-SMT. We gave a brief survey on phrase-based SMT first and then contrasted AT-SMT and SP-SMT in many aspects. Additionally, we completed a series of experiments to compare the quality of the two systems. The following are the findings from the current study:

1. Both systems are sub-branches of phrase-based system. However, SP-SMT is much easier to implement than AT-SMT, requires less time in the entire training, parameters tuning and decoding processes. But in terms of the dependency on the training corpus, AT approach is less dependent and can get better results in out-of-domain test corpus.
2. Towards combing the advantages of both systems for a better translation solution, integrating AT-SMT into SP-SMT as a new feature is an easy and effective way to improve SP-SMT translation quality. Moreover, optimal parameters can be automatically gotten through MERT.

In the future, we are interested in experimenting with more sophisticated translation models to get better translation quality either by improving upon the adaptivity of each model or by pursuing a better integration of the two systems.

References

1. Jesús Tomás and Francisico Casacuberta. Combining Phrase-based and Template-Based alignment models in Statistical Translation. IbPRIA, 2003.
2. Peter F. Brown et al. The methematics of statistical machine translation:Parameter estimation. Computational Linguistics, 1999.
3. Franz J. Och. Improved Alignment Models for Statistical Machine Translation. Proc. of the Joint Conf. of Empirical Methods in Natural Language Processing and Very Large Corpora. June, 1999.
4. Kenji Yamada and Kevie Knight. A syntax-based statistical translation model. In proc. Of the 39th Annual Meeting of ACL, Toulouse, France, July, 2001.
5. Daniel Marcu and William Wong. A phrase-based, joint probability model for statistical machine translation. In proceeding of EMNLP, 2002.

6. Richard Zens, Franz Josef Och, Hermann Ney. Phrase-based Statistical Machine Translation. In M. Jarke, J. Koehler, and G. Lakemeyer, editors, 25th German Conf. on Artificial Intelligence (KI2002).
7. Philipp Koehn et al. Statistical Phrase-Based Translation. HLT/NAACL, 2003.
8. Franz J. Och and Hermann Ney. Discriminative Training and Maximum Entropy Models for Statistical Machine Translation, ACL, 2002.
9. Franz Josef Och and Hermann Ney. The alignment template approach to statistical machine translation. Accepted for publication in Computational Linguistics, 2004.
10. Philipp Koehn et al. Edinburgh System Description for 2005 IWSLT Speech Translation Evaluation, 2005.
11. Shankar Kumar et al. A weighted finite state transducer translation template model for statistical machine translation. Natural Language Engineering 1 (1): 1-41, 2004.
12. Alexandra Claire Birch Mayne. Scalable Phrase-Based, Joint Probability Model for Statistical Machine Translation. Master of Science Cognitive Science and Natural Language Processing School of Informatics University of Edinburgh, 2005.
13. David Chiang. A hierarchical Phrase-Based Model for Statistical Machine Translation. Proc. Of the 43rd Annual Meeting of the ACL, June, 2005.
14. Kishore Papineni. BLEU: a Method for Automatic Evaluation of Machine Translation, Proc. Of the 40th ACL, July, 2002.
15. Franz J. Och. GIZA++: Training of statistical translation models. Http://www-i6.informatik.rwth-aachen.de/õch/softeware/GIZA++.html. 2000.
16. Philipp Koehn. Pharaoh:Training Manual, 2004.
17. Franz J. Och. Minimum Error Rate Training in Statistical Machine Translation, ACL, 2003.
18. Philip Koehn. Pharaoh: a Beam Search Decoder for Phrased-based Statsistical Machine Translation Models, User Mannual and Description for version 1.2, Technical report, USC Information Science Institute, August, 2004.
19. Franz J. Och, An Efficient Method for Determining Bilingual Word Classes. Proceedings of EACL, 1999.
20. Deyi Xiong, Qun Liu, Shouxun Lin. Maximum Entropy Based Phrase Reordering Model for Statistical Machine Translation, ACL, 2006.
21. Yaser Al-Onaizan, Kishore Papineni. Distortion Models for Statistical Machine Translation. ACL, 2006.
22. Abhishek Arun et al. Edinburgh System Description for the 2006 TC-STAR Spoken LanguageTranslation Evaluation, 2006.

Dependency Analysis and CBR to Bridge the Generation Gap in Template-Based NLG

Virginia Francisco, Raquel Hervás, and Pablo Gervás

Departamento de Ingeniería del Software e Inteligencia Artificial
Universidad Complutense de Madrid, Spain
{virginia,raquelhb}@fdi.ucm.es, pgervas@sip.ucm.es

Abstract. The present paper describes how dependency analysis can be used to automatically extract from a corpus a set of cases - and an accompanying vocabulary - which enable a template-based generator to achieve reasonable coverage over conceptual messages beyond the explicit scope of the templates defined in it. Details are provided on the actual process of partial automation that has been applied to obtain the case base, together with the various ingredients of the template-based generator, which applies case-based reasoning techniques. This module resorts to the taxonomy of concepts in WordNet to compute similarity between concepts involved in the texts. A case retrieval net is used as a memory model. The set of data to be converted into text acts as a query to the system. The process of solving a given query may involve several retrieval processes - to obtain a set of cases that together constitute a good solution for transcribing the data in the query as text messages - and a process of knowledge-intensive adaptation which resorts to a knowledge base to identify appropriate substitutions and completions for the concepts that appear in the cases, using the query as a source. We describe this case-based solution for selecting an appropriate set of templates to render a given set of data as text, we present numeric results of system performance in the domain of press articles, and we discuss its advantages and shortcomings.

1 Introduction

A classic problem in natural language generation is the "generation gap" described by Meteer [1], a discrepancy between what can be expressed in the text plan and what the particular realization solution can actually convert into text. This is particularly apparent in template-based generators, which have recently achieved widespread acceptance. Template-based solutions for natural language generation rely on reusing fragments of text extracted from typical texts in a given domain, having applied to them a process which identifies the part of them which is common to all uses, and leaving certain gaps to be filled with details corresponding to a new use. For instance, when conveying the information that *Alice married Christopher in Birmingham*, a template such as _ *married* _ *in* _ may be used, filling in the gap with appropriate strings for Alice, Christopher and Birmingham.

A. Gelbukh (Ed.): CICLing 2007, LNCS 4394, pp. 432–443, 2007.

In terms of templates, the "generation gap" occurs when the input calls for messages not explicitly contemplated in the set of templates in use. Whereas more complex natural language generation systems based on the use of grammars can have rich stages devoted to selecting fresh combinations of words to convey the same meaning, template-based systems are faced with an additional difficulty. Meanings not explicitly contemplated may be conveyed by a combination of templates whose meanings overlap to cover the full meaning required. However, the fact that templates are made up of words that are not accessible to the system makes the system blind to the possible ways of combining them. Annotating the templates with tags that indicate the circumstances under which it is appropriate to use the template would solve the problem, but it eliminates some of the advantages of the template solution over more knowledge-rich approaches.

Case-based reasoning (CBR) is a well established problem solving technique that searches for solutions to new problems in terms of how similar problems have been solved in the past. This is very close to template-based generation, which can be basically understood as reusing fragments of text extracted from typical texts in a given domain, having applied to them a process which identifies the part of them which is common to all users, and leaving certain gaps to be filled with details corresponding to a new use. Applying specifically a case-based solution to template-selection presents the advantage that the information needed to solve the problem can be obtained from the original examples of appropriate use that gave rise to the templates. By associating a case with each template, with case attributes consisting of conceptual descriptions of the arguments that were used for the template in the original instance, a case-based reasoning solution can be employed to select the best template for realizing a particular message.

The present paper describes a case-based solution for the task of selecting adequate templates for realizing messages describing actions in a given domain. The goal is to achieve coverage of a broad range of messages by combining instances of a restricted set of templates, and providing automated means for dealing with overlaps between the information conveyed by the templates found.

2   Case Based Reasoning Techniques and Dependency Analysis

This section provides a brief outline of the basic CBR techniques employed in the paper, the lexical database used to provide the reference taxonomy of concepts, and the dependency analysis tool employed for the automatic construction of the case base.

2.1   Case Based Reasoning Techniques and Technologies

Case-based Reasoning (CBR) [2] is a problem solving paradigm that uses the specific knowledge of previously experienced problem situations. Each problem is considered as a domain case, and a new problem is solved by retrieving the most similar case or cases, reusing the information and knowledge in these cases to solve the problem, revising the proposed solution, and retaining the parts of this experience likely to be useful for future problem solving. General knowledge about the domain under consideration usually plays a part in this cycle by supporting the CBR processes.

Case based reasoning solutions must rely on efficient storage and retrieval of the cases. A good solution for this problem is to store cases in a Case Retrieval Net (CRN) [3]. Case Retrieval Nets are a memory model developed to improve the efficiency of the retrieval tasks of the CBR cycle. They are based on the idea that humans are able to solve problems without performing an intensive search process, but they often start from the given description, consider the neighbourhood, and extend the scope of considered objects if required. CRNs organize the case base as a net of Information Entities (IEs) which represent any basic knowledge item in the form of an attribute-value pair. A case then consist of a set of such IEs, and the case base is a net with nodes for the entities observed in the domain and additional nodes denoting the particular cases. IE nodes may be connected by similarity arcs, and a case node is reachable from its constituting IE nodes via relevance arcs. Different degrees of similarity and relevance are expressed by varying arcs weights. Given this structure, case retrieval is carried out by activating the IEs given in the query case, propagating this activation according to similarity through the net of IE nodes, and collecting the achieved activation in the associated case nodes.

Case-based reasoning techniques have been applied in the past [4,5] to the problem of selecting specific verb templates as lexical realizations for actions described conceptually in the input. The system described in that work operated over manually built resources (vocabulary, case-base, and taxonomy used as reference). This restricted greatly the coverage that it could achieve. The solution presented in this paper involves a similar application of CBR methodology, but relies on state-of-the-art techniques of linguistic analysis to automate the necessary processes of building vocabulary and case base from domain corpora, as well as resorting to an existing lexical database to provide the taxonomy.

2.2   The Role of Taxonomies in Computing Similarity

A crucial operation in any CBR system is establishing similarities between query and cases, which can usually be reduced to searching for similarities between particular domain items that make up the query and the corresponding items in the cases. A popular solution is to rely on a taxonomy of concepts to deal with this task. Similarity between concepts is computed in terms of the distance traversed over the taxonomical structure to reach one from the other.

Currently, a number of efforts in the area of language engineering are aimed to the development of systems of basic semantic categories (often called "upper-level ontologies"), to be used as main organizational *backbones*, suitable to impose a structure on large lexical repositories. Examples of such systems are the PENMAN Upper Model [6], the Mikrokosmos ontology [7], and the WordNet

[8] upper structure. Machine learning techniques have been used to build *mapping dictionaries*, lexicons of elementary semantic expressions and corresponding natural language realizations [9].

WordNet is by far the richest and largest database among all resources that are indexed by concepts. For this reason, WordNet has been chosen as initial lexical resource for the development of the module presented in this paper. WordNet is an on-line lexical reference system organized into synonyms sets - or *synsets* -, each of them representing one underlying lexical concept, linked by semantic relations like synonymy or hyponymy. This organization makes it possible to use WordNet as a knowledge source. The hypernymy/hyponymy relation can be considered equivalent to the "isa"/"r-isa" relation, and it induces a taxonomical hierarchy over the set of available concepts.

WordNet is not organized according to individual *words*, it is organized according to *concepts*. Due to linguistic phenomena such as polysemy and synonymy, there is potentially a many-to-many mapping between concepts and words. This raises the important problem of Word Sense Disambiguation [10] (WSD), which has by itself deserved the attention of many researchers. At this point, WordNet provides some help: the *tag count* field for synsets. This field allows us to order, within a synset, which of the nouns is more *usual* in a generic corpus (in this case, the Brown Corpus [11]).

```
O(
EO  ()          fin         C      *
1   President   ~           N      2   s        (gov accuse)
2   accused     accuse      V      EO  i        (gov fin)
E2  ()          president   N      2   subj     (gov accuse)
3   Georgia     ~           N      2   obj      (gov accuse)
4   of          ~           Prep   2   mod      (gov accuse)
5   terrorism   ~           N      4   pcomp-n  (gov of)
)
```

Fig. 1. Example of dependency tree for the sentence *President accused Georgia of terrorism*

2.3 Dependency Analysis

The basic idea of the dependency analysis is that the syntactic structure of a sentence is described in terms of dependency relations between pairs of words (a parent and its child). These relations compose a tree (the dependency tree). Dependency analysis has been used succesfully for several applications: multilingual machine translation [12], recognising textual entailment [13], and automatic evaluation of question-answer systems [14].

MINIPAR [15] analyses English texts with high accuracy and efficiency in terms of time. An example of the dependency tree generated by MINIPAR for the sentence *President accused Georgia of terrorism* is given in Figures 1 and 2.

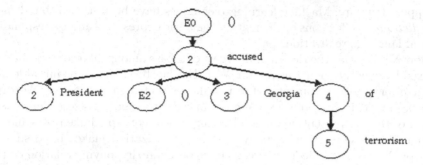

Fig. 2. Example of the graphical representation of the dependency tree for the sentence *President accused Georgia of terrorism*

3 Using Dependency Analysis to Build a Case-Base for Template Selection

A template-based generator selects a set of string fragments - which are deemed suitable to describe the concepts to be transmitted - and then composes them in a particular way to produce a final string corresponding to a sentence. The string fragments may correspond to atoms - strings that corresponds to words or phrases which will appear in the final text as they are - or templates - strings with place holders at positions where other string are to be inserted. This is an acceptable method when operating in restricted domains, but results can be poor if complex concepts or actions have to be expressed. Such complex structures may require the introduction of lexical chains that are employed exclusively for a specific referent or verb in some context. This introduces an unwanted rigidity in the system, because it makes the task of extending the vocabulary an arduous one.

To facilitate this task, we have defined an automated process of jointly building the vocabulary and the case-base for a case-based template-selection module. This module relies on subsequent processing of its output by an accompanying surface realization module. This module is in charge of putting together the selected terms and templates. Additionally, it carries out a basic orthographic transformation of the resulting sentences. Templates are converted into strings formatted in accordance to the orthographic rules of English - sentence initial letters are capitalized, and a period is added at the end.

3.1 Basic Operation of the Case-Based Template-Selection Module

The case-based reasoning module implements two of the four basic stages of a classic CBR cycle: retrieval and reuse of cases from the case base. No automated solution to the revision and retainment stages is contemplated so far, due to the fact that a very complex set of linguistic, cognitive and pragmatic constraints must be taken into account when validating any natural language solutions generated in this manner. The contribution of an expert in the domain is required to revise the results achieved by the module.

The retrieval task starts with a partial or complete problem description - a partial description of the action -, and ends when a matching previous case has been found. In our module, the retrieval of cases is directly handled by the Case Retrieval Net and its method of similarity propagation. Starting from a partial description of the action we need to lexicalise, the retrieval of the more similar cases is done by calculating an activation value for each case in the case base. The ones with higher activation are the more similar ones to the given query. This calculation is performed in three steps: (1) the IE nodes that correspond to the query are activated, (2) the activation is propagated according to the similarity values of the arcs, and (3) the achieved activations in the previous step are collected in the associated case nodes. Once we have the final activation in the cases, the one with the higher value is returned by the net. It would be possible to take not only the most similar one, but a set with the most similar cases to the query.

Each retrieved case has an associated template from the vocabulary for the verb or action it represents. In the process of reusing the case we have obtained from the net, we have to substitute the attribute values of the past case with the query values.

3.2   The Resources Required: Case Base and Vocabulary

The vocabulary contains all the lexical information essential to write the final text. A lexical tag made up of one or more words is assigned to each concept in the domain. This is used for lexicalising individual concepts, with little choice given. The vocabulary for actions or verbs becomes more complex: it is stored in the form of cases, where each case stores not only the corresponding template - solution of the case -, but also additional information concerning the elements involved in the action and the role that those elements play in the action - description of the case. A case is not an abstract instance of a verb or action, but rather a concrete instance in which specific actors, locations and objects appear.

Examples of cases are given below. The associated templates are shown below for each case:

```
LEX:       ACTOR:    OBJECT:  OF:
accuse_of  president Georgia  terrorism
```

_ accused _ of _


```
LEX:          ACTOR:   LIKE:
behave_like   leaders  Stalinists
```

_ behave like _

It is important to take into account that the structure of the cases is not rigid. They will not always have the same elements, nor in the same order. A clear example is provided by the verbs 'leave' and 'go', both involving some kind of movement. The first one has an attribute From to indicate where the actor is coming from, whereas the second one has an attribute To that indicates his destination.

Cases are stored in a Case Retrieval Net. This model is appropriate for the problem under consideration, because on one hand our cases consist of attribute-value pairs that are related with one another, and on the other hand the queries posed to the module will not always be complete. To find a lexical tag for a given action, the CRN is queried with the class of elements involved in the action.

The vocabulary of the module is built from the case base. For each attribute-value pair in the cases an information entity is created. For each case, a node is created which holds references to the information entities that are contained. When introducing an IE, if that entity has already appeared in another case it is not duplicated. Instead, another association is created between the new case and the existing information entity.

As IEs are inserted to form the net, it is necessary to establish a measure of similarity between them. The hyponymy/hypernymy relation of WordNet can be seen as a "isa" relation. WordNet can therefore be used as a taxonomy over which to automatically calculate the similarity between the concepts appearing in the cases. This requires some additional measures when creating the case base, to ensure that all elements appearing as arguments anywhere in the case base are adequately covered by WordNet. A preliminary filter is applied to the automatically generated cases, so that if one of the elements of a case is not found in WordNet, the case is discarded. From our initial corpus 297 cases were generated, and 179 of them were discarded using WordNet, being our final case base formed by a total of 118 cases.

The similarity between two entities is calculated by taking into account the distance between them and using Formula 1.

$$sim(c1, c2) = 1 - (distance(c1, c2)/20) \qquad (1)$$

The distance between two concepts is calculated by finding their first shared ancestor or hypernym, and adding up the distance between this ancestor and each of the concepts. It is also necessary to have a similarity value for each entity with itself. This value is always the maximum possible, because the distance between the entity and itself is 0.

Each of the IEs is related to the cases to which it belongs with a certain value of relevance. In the implemented module we have chosen that all the elements in a case has relevance 0.5.

3.3 Constructing the Case Base from the Dependency Trees for the Corpus

In order to obtain the case base automatically we have developed a method based on MINIPAR, which gives a dependency tree for every sentence, and based on this tree we select every verb and the words related to it. This section explains the process followed to obtain the different cases involved in a text and their templates. Firstly MINIPAR processes the texts and generates a dependency tree for each of the sentences. Each tree is analysed in order to obtain the following elements:

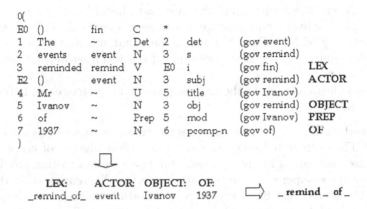

Fig. 3. Dependency tree, template and related case for *The events reminded Mr Ivanov of 1937*

- The verbs involved in each sentence. The process looks for every node in the tree marked as a verb during lexical analysis. Each of the verbs found in the sentence will give rise to a new case. The stems of the verbs as identified by MINIPAR are stored in the LEX attribute field of the case.
- The nodes which depend on each of the verbs. Once we have the children of every verb we process them in search for the rest of the elements required to build the cases and templates:
    - Subject of the verb. MINIPAR identifies for each verb a special node that is marked as subject of that verb during lexical analysis. The stem of the subject node is stored in the ACTOR attribute field of the case.
    - Objects of the verb. In a similar way, MINIPAR identifies objects of the verb. The stem of the object node is stored in the OBJECT attribute field of the case.
    - Prepositions. MINIPAR identifies with a special label the prepositions that appear in the sentence. Each preposition found in the sentence gives rise to a new field in the case. This new field is labelled with the preposition itself as name of the attribute.
    - Words related to prepositions. MINIPAR indicates dependency relations for every word. The nouns that act as head of the nodes related to the prepositions identified in the previous step are used as values for the preposition attributes discovered in the previous step.

An example of dependency tree and the case and template generated for the sentence *The events reminded Mr Ivanov of 1937* is given in Figure 3.

4   Evaluation and Discussion

In order to evaluate the feasibility of our proposal we carried out some preliminary tests over a set of news items in four different domains: politics, sport, science, and health. These news items contain 96 sentences in total which generate 297 cases. To evaluate the automated generation of cases we have generated the cases for every news item and then we have checked the correctness of each of the cases. The average percentage of success is over 50%. This is not related to the acurracy of MINIPAR but to the fact that our first approximation to the problem only uses the basic elements of the resulting dependency tree, as described above.

Analysing instances where the process produced incorrect cases indicated five main reasons for failure:

- **Nested cases.** There are some cases that have as object or as actor another case. The current representation does not allow nesting of cases, so these subcases are not being recognized. Our first solution to this problem is to represent the super-case and the sub-case as two different cases. In the super-case the nested case has a special representation which is considered during the retrieval as "every word", having maximum similarity with any other concept. An example is the sentence "Russian President accuses Georgia of acting like Stalinists". Here, we have two cases: one for the sentence "Russian President accuses Georgia of" where the value of the attribute *of* is "NC" (which represent the nested case) and another case for the sentence "acting like Stalinists".
- **Actor mistakenly identified.** In some cases the actor is not identified or the word MINIPAR points as subject is not the correct one. An example is the sentence "Foetuses as early as 12 weeks appearing to "walk" in the womb", where MINIPAR has decided that the subject for the verb "appear" is the word "weeks", although the correct choice is "foetuses".
- **Object mistakenly identified.** In some cases the object is not identified as object in the lexical analysis. An example is the sentence "foetuses become viable and potentially self-aware", where MINIPAR has not taken as object of the verb "become" any word. The correct choice would have been "viable" and "self-aware".
- **Verb mistakenly identified.** In some sentences the verb is not well identified by MINIPAR. An example is the sentence "This testing and spectacular track built a lead of more than 20 seconds over Schumacher", where "track" has been identified as a verb.
- **Prepositions mistakenly identified.** In some sentences the preposition is not well identified because MINIPAR considers that the preposition is not related to the verb. An example is the sentence "Mr Saakashvili has accused the Kremlin of hysteria", where "of" is not considered a preposition related to "accused" but is related to "Kremlin".

Figure 4 shows the relative contribution to the total error of each source of failure in terms of percentages of the total number of processed cases.

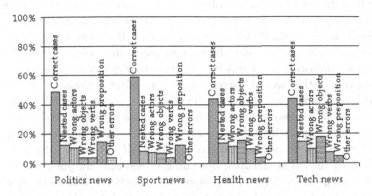

Fig. 4. Percentage of wrong cases group by reasons

5 Conclusions and Future Work

Dependency analysis provides a good first approximation for extracting automatically the information needed for case-based template selection. Full coverage of the initial corpus is not a priority since texts to be generated need not match those in the corpus precisely. Even with the current restrictions imposed by the internal representation, the success rate for that stage of the process is close to 50%. This indicates that a portion of the corpus can be converted into cases from the point of view of the information appearing in the sentences. The proposed solution is therefore easily scalable to larger corpora.

Even when the incorrect cases are not representing the exact information extracted from the corpus, they can be valid cases for the CBR module, not disturbing its functionality. Some of them would be discarded by WordNet's filter, and most of the remainder will have low similarities with the queries whenever they have resulted in nonsensical information.

The use of WordNet as a taxonomical knowledge base provides acceptable means for validating input lexical items. However, if used as the only validation mechanism, it lowers effective system coverage, largely because WordNet does not include proper nouns. This leads to the elimination of more than half of the cases extracted from the documents in the initial sample because the elements appearing in them were not covered by WordNet. A possible addition to the system would be a knowledge base for proper nouns as well as general concepts.

An issue that needs to be addressed is whether dependency analysis is the most adequate tool for the particular needs of the extraction process required. Similar processes to those presented in this paper must be tested using constituent analysis as means for accessing the linguistic structure of sentences in the corpus, and the results compared with those presented here. Further work will consider alternative language analysis tools and lexical resources.

One of the points to take into account in the future versions is the resolution of pronominal references. In the current version the pronouns are taken as value of the different fields (actor, object, ...). A method for anaphora resolution must be developed in future versions in order to solve this problem.

The resulting texts would improve significantly if a more complex set of templates were considered. Template-based generators have obtained results comparable to more elaborate solutions by resorting to recursive use of templates [16]. In our approach, this would correspond to allowing actions to be represented as nested cases, where a case would be constructed not only of attribute-value pairs, but also attribute-case pairs, where the value for some attribute may itself be a complete case - with an associated template. Recursive nesting of cases would allow recursive use of templates. MINIPAR provides sufficient information to identify nested structures, but the retrieval and adaptation stages would have to be adapted to deal with this recursive nature. This issue is related to the scalability of the solution in the sense that scalating the solution to more complex linguistic constructs would need to address the problem of improving the complexity of the cases.

The similarity being employed in the current version establishes a normalising upper limit independent of the depth of WordNet as a taxonomy. This should be corrected in subsequent versions.

The automatic process of acquiring the cases leads to situations where the sentences *"someone has something"* and *"someone says something"* give rise to cases with only two elements: an actor and an object. For the system these two cases are in principle equivalent. However, the CBR process ensures their correct use by resorting to the contextual information available in the original sentences from which the cases were extracted: both of them will probably have had a person as subject, but the kind of element that is had will be conceptually different from the kind of element that can be said. This allows the system to perform reasonably well in spite of the apparent sparsity of explicit knowledge employed.

Acknowledgements

Partially supported by the Spanish Ministry of Education and Science project TIN2006-14433-C02-01, and research group grant UCM-CAM-910494, jointly funded by Universidad Complutense de Madrid and the Comunidad Autónoma de Madrid (D.General de Universidades e Investigación).

References

1. Meteer, M.W.: The generation gap: the problem of expressibility in text planning. PhD thesis, Amherst, MA, USA (1990)
2. Aamodt, A., Plaza, E.: Case-based reasoning : Foundational issues, methodological variations, and system approaches (1994)
3. Lenz, M., Burkhard, H.D.: Case Retrieval Nets: Basic Ideas and Extensions. In: KI - Kunstliche Intelligenz. (1996) 227–239

4. Hervás, R., Gervás, P.: Case Retrieval Nets for Heuristic Lexicalization in Natural Language Generation. In Cardoso, A., Bento, C., Dias, G., eds.: Progress in Artificial Intelligence (EPIA 05). Number LNAI 1036, Covilha, Portugal, Springer-Verlag (2005)
5. Hervás, R., Gervás, P.: Case-based reasoning for knowledge-intensive template selection during text generation. In: Proc. of the 8th European Conference on Case-Based Reasoning, Springer-Verlag (2006)
6. Bateman, J.A., Kasper, R.T., Moore, J.D., Whitney, R.A.: A General Organization of Knowledge for Natural Language Processing: the PENMAN upper model (1990)
7. Mahesh, K.: Ontology development for machine translation: Ideology and methodology. Technical Report MCCS-96-292 (1996)
8. Miller, G.A.: Wordnet: a lexical database for English. Commun. ACM **38** (1995) 39–41
9. Barzilay, R., Lee, L.: Bootstrapping lexical choice via multiple-sequence alignment. In: Proc. of the EMNLP'02. (2002) 164–171
10. Ide, N., Veroni, J.: Word Sense Disambiguation: The State of the Art. Computational Linguistics (1998) 1–40
11. Nelson Francis, W., Kucera, H.: Computing Analysis of Present-day American English. Brown University Press, Providence, RI (1967)
12. Maxwell, D., Schubert, K.: Metataxis in Practice: Dependency Syntax for Multilingual Machine Translation. Foris Publications (1989)
13. Kouylekov, M., Magnini, B.: Tree edit distance for recognizing textual entailment: Estimating the cost of insertion. In: Proceedings of the Second PASCAL Challenges Workshop on Recognising Textual Entailment, Venezia, Italia. (2006)
14. Herrera, J., Peñas, A., Rodrigo, A., Verdejo, F.: UNED at PASCAL RTE-2 Challenge. In: Proceedings of the Second PASCAL Challenges Workshop on Recognising Textual Entailment, Venezia, Italia. (2006)
15. Lin, D.: Dependency-based evaluation of MINIPAR. In: Proc. of Workshop on the Evaluation of Parsing Systems, Granada, Spain (May 1998)
16. McRoy, S., Channarukul, S., Ali, S.: A Natural Language Generation Component for Dialog Systems. In Cox, M., ed.: Working Notes of the AAAI Workshop on Mixed-Initiative Intelligence (AAAI99). (1999)

Experiments on Generating Questions About Facts

Vasile Rus[1], Zhiqiang Cai[2], and Arthur C. Graesser[2]

[1] Department of Computer Science
[2] Department of Psychology
Institute for Intelligent Systems
The University of Memphis
373 Dunn Hall
Memphis, TN 38152
USA
{vrus, zcai, a-graesser}@memphis.edu

Abstract. This paper presents an approach to the problem of factual Question Generation. Factual questions are questions whose answers are specific facts: who?, what?, where?, when?. We enhanced a simple attribute-value (XML) language and its interpretation engine with context-sensitive primitives and added a linguistic layer deep enough for the overall system to score well on user satisfiability and the 'linguistically well-founded' criteria used to measure up language generation systems. Experiments with open-domain question generation on TREC-like data validate our claims and approach.

1 Introduction

A natural human capacity, present in early childhood as a primary form of discovery, has been barely studied by the Computational Linguistics community. There is so much attention paid lately to Question Answering (QA) [22] that its complementary task is almost missed. In general, language generation is a more difficult task to address but we don't believe that is the major reason why Question Generation (QG), the topic of this work, should be neglected. Asking questions is so natural to us that we don't think of it as an issue worth being discussed or investigated as part of a systematic scientific effort. Yet, psycholinguistics studies [25] have shown that asking questions, especially deep questions, can significantly increase learning gains of college students. It is based on this evidence that this paper comes forward with an approach to address the task of Question Generation. The task can be viewed as a subtask of the larger natural language generation (NLG) area with possible significant impact on a series of applications such as Question Answering [22] and Intelligent Tutoring Systems (ITS) [8]. We ran experiments on open-domain TREC-like QA[1] data to inform us about the performance of our approach to Question Generation.

---

[1] TREC stands for Text Retrieval Conference. More information on TREC can be found at http://trec.nist.gov

A. Gelbukh (Ed.): CICLing 2007, LNCS 4394, pp. 444–455, 2007.

2   Why Question Generation?

A good question at the right moment can save the day. A drawback of current QA evaluations with regard to the human-system interaction is the assumption that the user's question is asked at the intended or optimal level of specification. Whenever a user is given a QA system and a task to perform (with the aid of a QA system), there is the unrealistic assumption that the user will know exactly what questions to ask and in what order. The truth is that the process of asking questions is a very complex mechanism. Studies confirm that low-knowledge adults ask low quality shallow questions [6]. In [7], it is reported that the average college student asks only 0.17 questions per hour in the classroom; this is 6 hours for a typical college student to ask 1 question. They also reported that the quality of the student's questions is disappointing. Students in tutoring sessions on research methods in college asked only about 6 deep-reasoning questions per hour in a tutoring session that encouraged them to ask questions. Deep reasoning questions are about explanations and invite lengthier answers (such as why, why-not, how, and what-if). Given that most learners need guidance on what sort of questions to ask, it would be great to develop a Question Generator that is capable of helping and training users to generate good questions when engaged in an information-seeking task with a QA system or learning with the aid of an ITS [8,5].

The rest of the paper focuses mainly on the Question Generation approach and its evaluation. We conducted one experiment and present quantitative results on open domain question generation on TREC-like data and discuss the possible integration of a Question Generator component in a QA system.

3   AutoTutor

We have started our work on question generation from a previous effort on authoring tools for AutoTutor [8]. It is therefore worthwhile to briefly describe AutoTutor and the AutoTutor Script Authoring Tool (ASAT) to better understand the roots of the question generation research effort.

AutoTutor [5] is a dialog-based tutoring system that has been used by colleges to teach conceptual physics and computer literacy. AutoTutor improves learning by approximately one letter grade (e.g. from B to C) compared with a pretest or student reading the textbook on similar content [4,21]. AutoTutor presents a problem that taps into deep knowledge, holds a dialogue with students, and helps them solve the problem by using sophisticated tutoring techniques. Recently, ASAT (AutoTutor Script Authoring Tool) has been developed to guide script writers to create curriculum scripts for AutoTutor [17]. With ASAT, new curriculum scripts can be easily created and be implemented into AutoTutor. AutoTutor's curriculum scripts consist of a problem, ideal answers, misconceptions and dialogue moves such as hints and prompts. Ideal answers are broken into smaller sentential units called expectations. The following example shows an expectation and the associated hints and prompts associated in the curriculum script of a Physics tutor:

Expectation: There are no horizontal forces on the packet after release.
Hint 1: What can you say about the horizontal forces on the packet?
Hint 2: After release, in which direction is there zero force on the packet?
Prompt 1: After release, the packet is not affected by any force that is _____?
Prompt 2: After release, there are zero horizontal forces on the _____?
Prompt 3: There are zero horizontal forces on the packet after _____?
Prompt 4: After release, the horizontal force on the packet is _____?

As you can see from this example, the hints and prompts can be easily derived from the expectation by designing simple rules which transform the expectation onto hints and prompts. Rules specify when they are applicable and what is the format of the output question. For example, we can form a template question from Hint 1 "What can you say about X?", which should be applied for any noun phrase X from the source sentence (see *Rule* below). For the above expectation and template question, we can output the 3 questions below labeled *Output 1, 2*, and *3*, one for each of the three noun phrases in the expectation: "horizontal forces", "the packet", and "horizontal forces on the packet":

Rule: If "X" is a noun phrase in the source sentence, then ask "What can you say about X?"
Input: There are no horizontal forces on the packet after release.
Output 1: What can you say about horizontal forces?
Output 2: What can you say about the packet?
Output 3: What can you say about the horizontal forces on the packet?

Instead of human handcrafting of these hints and prompts, a question generator to automatically generate them is needed. One solution is to develop a platform consisting of a mark-up language that allows easy authoring of manipulation rules and an interpretation engine that can apply the rules to new data. A rule is a pair composed of a *pattern* and *template*. The *template* is a lexical, syntactic, and semantic structure that generates a question when its unspecified elements are instantiated. The templates are triggered only when certain conditions are met. Those conditions are encoded in what we call a *pattern*. The pattern and template form a *category*, the core structure of our question generation framework.

The bottom line is instead of experts authoring specific questions for each topic we ask them to author general patterns for question generation that are generally applicable to any topic and any subject.

4   Related Work

In order to better position our effort in the landscape of previous work we briefly define the three categories of question manipulation.

After extensive search we could not find major work directly attempting to explore question generation in its most intuitive sense: any mechanism whose input is a sentence (not another question as in question reformulation - see below) and whose output is one or more questions in natural language related to the input sentence. Based on this understanding, previous efforts can be classified in the following three categories: *query/question reformulation, pseudo question generation,* and *limited question generation.*

The first category, *query/question reformulation,* is a weak form of the question generation task as defined in this paper. As already stated, in question generation the input is a sentence (typically a non-question sentence) whereas the output is a set of questions related to the input sentence. In contrast, query and question reformulation take as input a question and produce a question or query as output. Further, question generation is an open-domain task as opposed to the domain-specific (database access) orientation of query reformulation. Query/question reformulation helps non-expert users to access and improve their process of querying databases. While query reformulation involves reformulating queries in formal languages in order to improve the query process, question reformulation involves reformulating a question in natural language posed by the user as a substitute to a query in a formal language (such as SQL, a relational database query language). A representative system in this category is the CO-OP system [12], which implements question reformulation through paraphrasing in the context of database access. A related system is TextMap [9]. TextMap is a QA system that has a question and query reformulation component aimed at improving the overall performance of the QA process.

Question Generation per se has been coined by different researchers with interpretations different from the straightforward and natural interpretation that we use here. In a recent work, [10] use the term question generation to refer to sentences with gaps used in multiple choice language tests in which the students is asked to choose from a list of options the word that best fills the gap in a given sentence so that the most appropriate sentence is formed. Since the generated output is not a question we consider this work as not being true question generation. We call this *pseudo question generation.*

The only work we are aware of that addresses the question generation problem close to how we define it here is presented in [14]. Mitkov and Ha developed a computer-aided procedure for generating multiple-choice questions given a set of documents on a topic. The procedure first identifies candidate concepts and corresponding sentences in which they appear. Given the sentence, it uses a shallow parser, transformational rules and WordNet [13] to map it into its interrogative form. The system can handle sentences whose structure is SVO or SV (S-Subject; V-Verb; O-Object). For instance a SVO sentence is transformed into the question "Which HVO?" where H is the hypernym of the S term. The few structures that can be handled led us to call it limited question generation. Mitkov and Ha provide quantitative results for the cost-efficiency and quality of their procedure by way of user satisfiability studies similar to the ones we present later in this paper. Due to the limited number of sentence structures they can handle their work is a small scale attempt to question generation. Since our approach has an authoring component the number of sentence structures that can be handled is open, thus, allowing us to believe this is the first serious attempt to question generation.

5   Our Approach to Question Generation

Language generation is one of the grand challenges of natural language processing and artificial intelligence [27,3,15]. It is beyond the scope of this project to solve all of the complexities of a full-fledged language generator.

Our approach to question generation was inspired by studies on sentence generation by humans. In particular, we rely on [26] who explored verbal fluency in humans and discovered that people use pattern matching and mapping rules as a strategy when they generate sentences. Pattern matching and mapping rules are at the core of our question generation framework.

Our goal is to build a robust and flexible question generator that could handle a variety of questions in any domain. To achieve this goal, we envisioned a pattern-based framework of two major components: an expressive language for authoring the patterns and an interpreter of the language that executes the actual generation. The authoring language and its associated editor allows the description of patterns and templates, i.e. of categories. The generation engine interprets the categories and applies them to an input sentence. Categories are specified as a collection/database.

The advantages of this architecture, which decouples the authoring from the actual generation, are manifold. First, it abstracts away the generation engine from the authoring process. Moving to a new domain or new language does not require modifications of the generation engine. Second, different policies can be embedded in the engine without affecting the authoring part, for instance we can have a policy of giving higher priority to a pattern to trigger when more than one may trigger. Third, it allows variables to be included in the patterns and semantic features to be parameterized components of patterns. This leads to a reduced number of patterns to cover a variety of linguistic contexts. Patterns are context-sensitive in that variables are dynamically assigned based on surrounded context at instantiation. Lastly, our decoupled architecture makes the whole system more manageable.

Let us see where our approach fits when compared to similar systems. First, our approach is a good example of a method that uses rich templates and generation mechanism that bring it closer to standard natural language generation (NLG) systems. In a recent squib [19], they debate over the perceived inferior performance of template-based approaches to the generation of language as opposed to standard NLG systems. They claim that the distinction between the two categories of systems "is becoming increasingly blurred" and our system is yet another proof of that. While the primary element of our system is the template, the generation mechanism is performed in several stages and various levels of linguistic information are used along the way including lexical-semantics (WordNet [13]), gender and number manipulations, subject-verb agreement, and semantic categories from a named entity recognizer. Secondly, from a black-box point of view, we can label our system a text-to-text (T2T) generation system since it takes as input a textual sentence and generates as output a textual questions. Nevertheless, our system is more than a T2T system as defined in [16] because it goes well beyond word/phrases manipulations with abstract, non-linguistic operators as employed by [16]. Our question generator does have abstract string manipulators similar to the ones in [16] as a legacy from AIML (Artificial Intelligence Mark-up Language).

6   The Question Generation Mark-Up Language

QG-ML was inspired by the performance of AIML (Artificial Intelligence Mark-up Language). AIML enables people to define stimulus-response transformations for chatterbots [11,23]. While AIML is quite successful for common chat, it is limited in casual dialogs and simple question answering categories. AutoTutor functions more directly as a question asking system: given the expectations associated with an answer stored in the curriculum, AutoTutor needs to generate adequate questions as hints and prompts to help the learner to learn. This requires the identification of syntactic and semantic properties of phrases in a given text. Our markup language is designed to perform such complex tasks. Although it was designed for question generation, it can actually be used to generate any other type of sentences. We give our language the name "QG-ML", standing for "Question Generation Markup Language".

QG-ML is a new, more expressive, language that extends AIML with variables, function calls, and deeper structural and semantic features that allow a natural way to capture the semantics of the original sentence. The core of the language is the *pattern-template* pair, called a *category*. Both a pattern and template are syntactic structures extended with lexical and semantic features, variables and function calls. The role of the pattern is to match against a parsed input sentence while the role of the template is to generate question by manipulating elements of the pattern. More formally we define an enhanced syntactic structure as a $\pi = (T, C, V, P)$ where T is a syntactic tree, C a set of constraints (lexical and semantic), V a set of variables or function calls that can dynamically take different values, and P a set of policies that is used to specify mechanisms such as *give higher priorities for certain patterns and templates*. T's leaf nodes may contain a lexical item (word) or a variable name which in a pattern will take as its value the whole subtree of the input sentence starting at that node or will be replaced by its value in a template. Leaves may also contain a function call which will be replaced by the returned value. Function calls are present in templates (not patterns) to handle context dependent generation steps such as morphological aspects of lexicalization. Variables and functions play the role of gaps in the D2S method [20] and its implementation in GoalGetter[18], a system that generates soccer reports in Dutch. Patterns can contain wildcards (*) indicating any input. The most general pattern is "*" which will match any input. A pattern such as "The president of the United States *" will match any input sentence starting with "The president of the United States". Internal nodes of Ts usually contain non-terminals with semantic or lexical constraints: <VP head_lemma="be"> means a VP subtree with the head being verb 'be' while <NP Person="true"> means a NP subtree with the head word denoting a person.

Let us now look at AIML and then at our extension of it which we call Natural Language Generation Mark-Up Language (QG-ML) in order to see how the above schema is implemented.

6.1   AIML

AIML (http://www.alicebot.org/) stands for Artificial Intelligence Mark-Up Language. AIML is XML-compliant and its main purpose is to allow you to create conversational patterns for a chat-bot, similar or better than the famous ELIZA [24]. AIML helped creating the first Alicebot, A.L.I.C.E., the Artificial Linguistic Internet Computer Entity. According to its creators, AIML is a reincarnation of a previous non-XML grammar called AIML.

AIML allows to create AIML objects composed of topics and categories.

The most important units of AIML are:

- <aiml>: the tag that begins and ends an AIML document
- <category>: the tag that marks a "unit of knowledge" in an Alicebot's knowledge base
- <pattern>: used to contain a simple pattern that matches what a user may say or type to an Alicebot
- <template>: contains the response to a user input

There are also 20+ additional tags often found in AIML files, and it's possible to create your own "custom predicates". Among the most powerful tags are <srai> that implements recursion by allowing templates to contain other templates. The <srai> tag facilitates features such as symbolic reduction, word/ phrase order manipulations, synonymy, spelling and grammar corrections, detecting keywords anywhere in the input, and conditional. AIML also contains limited context facilities through the use of the tag <that> which refers to the previous sentence/utterance and human-supervised self-learning through a process called targeting.

AIML allows the creation of knowledge for chat-bots based on the A.L.I.C.E. free software technology. AIML is simple and can be easily extended, as any XML language. There are a variety of free AIML interpreters or engines, most notably Program D, that are available for use.

6.2   Question Generation Mark-Up Language (QG-ML)

The Question Generation Mark-up Language (QG-ML) was developed on top of AIML.

The major difference between QG-ML and AIML is in the pattern language. While AIML pattern language consists of words and two wildcard symbols (_

and *) the QG-ML pattern and template language incorporates a linguistic layer including lexico-syntactic structures, variables, and function calls.

The template language in AIML, as in QG-ML, is expressive. It supports variables, conditional responses, recursive calls to other categories, and data saving. We incorporate in those elements lexico-syntactic structures and shallow semantic elements.

6.3   Example of a Category

Let us take a look at the QG-ML script for the example rule in the previous section:

<category>
<pattern>
<NP>_np_</NP>
</pattern>
<template>
What can you say about _np_?
</template>
</category>

The category-pattern-template structure is, once again, borrowed from AIML. A pattern indicates a specific sub-tree that needs to be checked against the input sentence, whereas a template is the transformation rule to be applied to the input sentence to create a question. A category consists of a combination of patterns and templates which can be used to generate questions. The tag <NP> refers to "Noun Phrase". It is one of the tags from the Penn Treebank tag set(http://www.cis.upenn.edu/ treebank/). The expression _np_ is used as a variable to save the words in the noun phrase. The difficult part of writing a category is to form a pattern, which needs help from a syntactic parser. A pattern is considered as a simplified syntax tree, following the rules below:

- A pattern is formed from any sub-tree of a syntactic tree
- All sub-trees of a tree node can be removed, with a variable to denote text content of the sub-trees
- The tag <star> is used to ignore some of the sub-trees of a tree node without remembering the content text
- A variable is a string of symbols starting and ending with an '_'

6.4   Interpreter of the Mark-Up Language

An interpreter of the mark-up language needs to integrate a syntactic parser and some other computational linguistic modules, such as named entity identifier, time-location expression labeler, etc. We created a web tool (http://HIDDEN/) that can be used to create categories and generate questions. The syntax parser for this tool is Charniak parser [1][2] and the major lexico-semantics component is WordNet [13].

7   Evaluation and Experimental Results

We tested our question generation framework on a set of questions and their associated answers from TREC's Question Answering track. Given the answer we developed categories that would generate the question. We used some of the pairs to develop a collection of categories and the others to evaluate the performance of the system.

We used precision as our metric to report performance. Precision is the proportion of good questions out of all generated questions. Recall is harder to grasp since given a sentence the number of questions that one can generate is theoretically endless. A generated question is a 'good' question if two annotators agreed on that. The Kappa-statistic for inter-annotator agreement was high (0.92).

7.1   Factual Question Generation

We used the set of 200 factual questions and sentences with the correct answer from the first TREC-8 QA track (see *http://trec.nist.gov*). The TREC-like questions are called factual questions because they ask about specific facts, i.e. the answer is a short, factual answer. For instance, *What is the capital of Italy?* whose answer is *Rome*. Table 1 shows factual question types and examples.

Table 1. Examples of factual questions from TREC QA track

Type	Question
WHO	Who is the voice of Miss Piggy?
WHAT	What does the Peugeot company manufacture?
WHERE	Where is Microsoft's corporate headquarters located?
WHEN	When did Nixon die?
HOW	How many people live in the Falklands?
OTHER	Name the first private citizen to fly in space.

In a first trial, we developed categories for questions 1 to 100. The categories were developed based on the answer sentence for each given question. The goal was to develop a category which would generate the question from the answer sentence. We then tested the 100 categories on the following 100 questions. We broke the test set on two equal sets: from 101 to 150 and from 151 to 200. We wanted to see if there are any major differences in performance that may be influenced by different distributions of questions. Table 2 summarizes the results.

In our next trial we try to see how much improvement in performance is determined by an increase in the set of categories. We developed 50 more categories based on the answer sentences for questions 101-150. We keep the test set the same and we measure the performance using the 1-100 categories and then 1-150 categories. The results are summarized in Table 3.

Table 2. Results using the first 100 categories

Test Set	Good Question	Bad Questions	Average Good Questions	Precision
101-150	72	67	1.5	0.52
151-200	83	68	1.66	0.54

Table 3. Results for the test set 151-200 with two sets of categories

Categories Set	Good Question	Bad Questions	Average Good Questions	Precision
1-100	83	68	1.66	0.54
1-150	131	81	2.62	0.62

8 Future Work

QG-ML is a new, more expressive, language that extends AIML with variables, function calls, and deeper structural and semantic features that allow a natural way to capture the semantics of the original sentence. The semantic features are limited so far but the XML-like language is easily extendable. The plan is to enrich it in the near future with a paraphrasing facility and a powerful named-entity recognizer that will allow us to detect particular semantic categories (such as persons) and to use this new information to trigger the right pattern to generate the question. For example, person names in the input sentence would recommend a who question (Who discovered ...?) or its what variants (What researcher discovered ?). We do have as of now a weak Named Entity Recognizer that can recognize person names and places based on WordNet and which limits the applicability of our current systems to TREC-QA-like factual questions (Who-What-When-Where). In addition, there are two other features we want to include in the proposed research: an indicator of the appropriateness of a particular language pattern for a particular user category (i.e., low-vs high-knowledge users) and use machine learning algorithms to automatically learn question generation patterns.

9 Conclusions

We presented in this paper a framework for the task of Question Generation. A framework based on the notion of pattern-template pair was presented and applied to generating factual questions from TREC-like data on question answering. The results obtained are promising. A major advantage of the proposed approach is its general applicability as opposed to previous attempts on particular domains or particular sentence structures.

Acknowledgements

This research was supported by the National Science Foundation (REC 0106965 and ITR 0325428), the Institute of Education Sciences (R305H050169), and the DoD Multidisciplinary University Research Initiative administered by ONR under grant N00014-00-1-0600. Any opinions, findings and conclusions or recommendations expressed in this paper are those of the authors and do not necessarily reflect the views of NSF, IES, DOD or ONR.

References

1. Charniak,E. 2001. Immediate-head parsing for language models. In Proceedings of the 39th Annual Meeting of the Association for Computational Linguistics, pages 116-123, Toulouse, France, July. Association for Computational Linguistics.
2. Charniak,E., Johnson,M. 2005. Coarse-to-fine n-best parsing and maxent discriminative reranking. In Proceedings of the 43rd Annual Meeting of the Association for Computational Linguistics (ACL'05), pages 173-180, Ann Arbor, Michigan, June. Association for Computational Linguistics.
3. Dale, R., Scott,D., di Eugenio,B. 1998. Special issue on natural language generation. Computational Linguistics, 24(3):346-353, September.
4. Graesser,A.C., McNamara,D.S., Louwerse,M.M., and Cai,Z. 2004a. Coh-metrix: Analysis of text on cohesion and language. Behavior Research Methods, Instruments, and Computers, 36-2:193-202.
5. Graesser,A.C., Lu,S., Jackson,G.T., Mitchell,H., Ventura,M., Olney, A., Louwerse,M.M. 2004b. Autotutor: A tutor with dialogue in natural language. Behavioral Research Methods, Instruments, and Computers, pages 180-193.
6. Graesser,A.C., Olde,B. 2003. How does one know whether a person understands a device? the quality of the questions the person asks when the device breaks down. Journal of Educational Psychology, 95:524-536.
7. Graesser,A.C., Person,N. 1994. Question asking during tutoring. American Educational Research Journal, 31:104-137.
8. Graesser,A.C., VanLehn,K., Rose,C.P., Jordan,P.W., Harter,D. 2001. Intelligent tutoring systems with conversational dialogue. AI Magazine, 22(4):39-52.
9. Hermjakob,U., Echihabi,A., Marcu,D. 2002. Natural language based reformulation resource and web exploitation for question answering.
10. Hoshino,A., Hiroshi,N. 2005. A real-time multiple-choice question generation for language testing: A preliminary study. In Jill Burstein and Claudia Leacock, editors, Proceedings of the Second Workshop on Building Educational Applications Using NLP, pages 17-21. The Association for Computational Linguistics, The Association for Computational Linguistics, June.
11. Mauldin,M.L. 1994. Chatterbots, tinymuds, and the turing test: entering the loebner prize competition. In Proceedings of the twelfth national conference on Artificial intelligence, volume 1, pages 16-21, Seattle, Washington, United States. AAAI, AAAI Press.
12. McKeown,K.R. 1983. Paraphrasing questions using given and new information. American Journal of Computational Linguistics, 9(1):1-9.
13. Miller,G. 1995. Wordnet: A lexical database. Communications of the ACM, 38(11):39-41, November.
14. Mitkov,R., Ha,L.A. 2003. Computer-aided generation of multiple-choice tests. In Jill Burstein and Claudia Leacock, editors, In Proceedings of the HLT-NAACL 2003 Workshop on Building Educational Applications Using Natural Language Processing, pages 17-22, Edmonton, Canada, May. The Association for Computational Linguistics, The Association for Computational Linguistics.

15. Reiter,E., Dale,R. 2000. Building Natural Language Generation Systems. Cambridge University Press, Cambridge.
16. Soricut,R., Marcu,D. 2005. Towards developing generation algorithms for text-to-text applications. In Proceedings of the Association for Computational Linguistics Conference (ACL-2005), Ann Arbor, MI., June 25-30.
17. Susarla, S., Adcock,A., Van Eck,R., Moreno,K., Graesser, A.C. 2003. Development and evaluation of a lesson authoring tool for autotutor. In V. Aleven et al. editors, AIED 2003 Supplemental Proceedings (pp. 378-387). Sydney, Australia: University of Sydney School of Information Technologies., pages 378-387, Sydney, Australia. University of Sydney School of Information Technologies.
18. Theune,M., Klabbers,E., de Pijper, J-R., Krahmer, E., Odijk, J. 2001. From data to speech: A general approach. Natural Language Engineering, 7(1):47-86.
19. van Deemter,K., Krahmer,E., Theune,M. 2005. Real versus template-based natural language generation: A false opposition? Computational Linguistics, 31(1):15-23.
20. van Deemter,K., Odijk,J. 2005. Context modelling and the generation of spoken discourse. Speech Communication, 21(1/2):101-121.
21. VanLehn, K., Graesser,A.C., Jackson,G.T., Jordan,P., Olney,A., Rose,C.P. 2005. When is reading just as effective as one-on-one interactive tutoring? In B. Bara, editor, Proceedings of the 27th Annual Meetings of the Cognitive Science Society, Mahwah, NJ. Erlbaum.
22. Voorhees, E.M. 2001. Overview of TREC 2001. In Text REtrieval Conference.
23. Wallace, R. 2004. Be Your Own Botmaster. ALICE A. I. Foundation. Weizenbaum, Joseph. 1966. Eliza - a computer program for the study of natural language communication between man and machine. Communications of the ACM., 9(1):36-45, January.
24. Weizenbaum, J. 1966. Communications of the ACM Volume 9, Number 1 (January 1966): 36-35.
25. Wisher, R.A., Graesser,A.C. (2005). Question asking in advanced distributed learning environments. In S.M. Fiore and E. Salas (Eds.), Toward a science of distributed learning and training. Washington, D.C.: American Psychological Association.
26. Zock, M., 1997. Recent Advances in Natural Language Processing, chapter Sentence generation by pattern matching: the problem of syntactic choice, pages 317-352. Current Issues in Linguistic Theory. Benjamins, Amsterdam. 17
27. Jurafsky,D., Martin,J., 2000. Speech and Language Processing, Prentice-Hall, 2000, ISBN: 0-13-095069-6

Expert vs. Non-expert Tutoring: Dialogue Moves, Interaction Patterns and Multi-utterance Turns

Xin Lu[1], Barbara Di Eugenio[1], Trina C. Kershaw[2],
Stellan Ohlsson[1], and Andrew Corrigan-Halpern[1]

[1] University of Illinois at Chicago, Chicago IL, USA
{xlu4,bdieugen,stellan,ahalpe1}@uic.edu
[2] University of Massachusetts Dartmouth, North Dartmouth MA, USA
tkershaw@umassd.edu

Abstract. Studies of one-on-one tutoring have found that expert tutoring is more effective than non-expert tutoring, but the reasons for its effectiveness are relatively unexplored. Since tutoring involves deep natural language interactions between tutor and student, we explore the differences between an expert and non-expert tutors through the analysis of individual dialogue moves, tutorial interaction patterns and multi-utterance turns. Our results are a first step showing what behaviors constitute expertise and provide a basis for modeling effective tutorial language in intelligent tutoring systems.

1 Introduction

It has been widely reported that natural language is important to learning. Fox[1] observed that one-on-one tutoring involves a collaborative construction of meaning, a process that arises from a natural language interaction or dialogue between individuals. To enhance interactive learning in Intelligent Tutoring Systems (ITSs), natural language interfaces are used to deliver instructional feedback. With such an interface, researchers try to make the ITSs act like real human tutors, especially like expert tutors.

Tutors with different levels of expertise may behave differently and have different effects on learning. Some recent research[2][3] shows that expert tutors engender better learning outcomes than non-expert tutors. This means that a computational model of expert tutoring will improve the effectiveness of ITSs. But it is not yet well understood what makes expert tutoring more effective and which features of tutoring dialogues should be included in interfaces to ITSs. There are two possible reasons why those issues are still under investigation: there are no comprehensive comparisons between expert and non-expert tutors; expert tutors tend to use more complex strategies and language[4]. Our research aims at exploring the difference between expert tutors and non-expert tutors from the natural language point of view.

A. Gelbukh (Ed.): CICLing 2007, LNCS 4394, pp. 456–467, 2007.

Our tutoring domain concerns extrapolating complex letter patterns[5], which is a well known task for analyzing human information processing in cognitive science. Given a sequence of letters that follows a particular pattern, the student is asked to find the pattern and create a new sequence from a new starting letter. For example, the pattern of the sequence "ABMCDM" is: "M" as a chunk marker separates the whole sequence into two chunks of letters progressing according to the alphabet. Then with a starting letter "E", to maintain this pattern, the student needs to finish the sequence as "EFMGHM". Only knowledge of the alphabet is required in this domain. We collected dialogues in this domain. During the training session, each student goes through a curriculum of 13 problems of increasing complexity. The training will improve the student's ability in solving letter pattern problems. To test the performance, each student also needs to solve two post-test problems, each 15 letters long, via a computer interface.

We collected tutoring dialogues with three tutors, one expert, one novice, and one lecturer who is experienced in teaching, but not in one-on-one tutoring. Comparison of the student's performance showed that the expert tutor was significantly more effective than the other two tutors. We analyzed the individual tutor and student moves independently[3] and found that some behaviors of our tutors do not support the predictions from literatures[6]. Tutoring is an interaction between tutor and student so tutor moves and student moves are not independent. And also tutors are likely to use more than one utterance in a single turn. Our next step was to compare the expert tutor to the non-expert tutors in interaction patterns and multi-utterance turns.

In this paper we first introduce our previous work in study of human tutors including data collection and annotation, and our analysis of dialogue moves. Then we study the interaction patterns and multi-utterance turns by comparing expert and non-expert tutors. At last we conclude and discuss future work.

2   Our Previous Work

To investigate the effectiveness of expert tutors, we ran experiments in the letter pattern domain with three different tutors: the expert tutor with years of experience in one-on-one tutoring; the lecturer with years of experience in lecturing but little experience in one-on-one tutoring; the novice tutor with no experience in teaching or tutoring. We also have a control group of students with no tutoring at all. There are 11 students in each group, who are all psychology majored freshmen and native speakers in English. Comparing the post-test performance of the four groups of student shows that the expert tutor is significantly more effective than the other two tutors and control (no tutoring) on both post-test problems[3]. The post-test performance is the average number of letters correct out of a total of 90 letters (in 6 trials, each trial starts from a new letter) for each problem per subject.

The dialogues on two specific problems in the curriculum were transcribed and annotated from the videotapes which recorded the tutors' interaction with the subjects. For each tutor, six subjects' dialogues were transcribed and annotated with the tutor and student moves by utterance. The annotation scheme is based on the literature[6][7]. The tutor moves include four high level categories, reaction, initiative, support, conversation. Tutor reaction and initiative are also subcategorized.

- Reaction: the tutor reacts to something the student says or does, which is subcategorized as follows:
  Answering: answering a direct question from the student
  Evaluating: giving feedback about what the student is doing
  Summarizing: summarizing what has been done so far
- Initiative is subcategorized as follows:
  Prompting: prompting the student into some kind of activity, further subcategorized as:
  - **General:** laying out what to do next – *Why not try this problem*
  - **Specific:** trying to get a specific response from the student – *What would the next letter be?*

  Diagnosing: trying to determine what the student is doing – *Why did you put a D there?*
  Instructing: providing the student with information about the problem. Further subcategorized as:
  - **Declarative:** providing facts about the problem – *Notice the two Cs here? They are separating different parts of the problem*
  - **Procedural:** giving hints or tricks about how to solve problem – *Start by counting the number of letters in each period*

  Demonstrating: showing the student how to solve the problem. – *Watch this. First I count the number of letters between the G and J here.*
- **Support:** the tutor encourages the student in his/her work without referring to particular elements of the problem
- **Conversation:** acknowledgments, continuers, and small talk

Corresponding to the tutor moves, there are six categories in our student moves:

- **Explanation:** explaining what the student said or did, reasoning, or thinking aloud – *and see I put them like together.*
- **Questioning:** asking the tutor a question
- **Reflecting:** evaluating one's own understanding – *I don't really understand about the whole c thing.*
- **Reaction:** reacting to something the tutor says, further subcategorized:
  - **Answering:** directly answering a tutor's question
  - **Action Response:** performing some action (e.g., writing down a letter) in response to the tutor's question or prompt
- **Completion:** completing a tutor's utterance
- **Conversation:** acknowledgments, continuers, and small talk

Two independent groups, each group with two annotators, coded the tutor moves and the student moves on all the dialogues. The Kappa coefficient is used to evaluate agreement[8][9]. After several rounds of annotation, the intercoder agreement on most of the categories reached an acceptable level (perfect

Table 1. Kappa Values and Percentages of Student and Tutor Moves by Tutor

Student Move	Kappa	Novice	Lecturer	Expert	Tutor Move	Novice	Lecturer	Expert
Explanation	0.64	7.5	26.3	19.8	Answering	10.1	5.4	1.4
Questioning	0.89	18.3	8.4	6.8	Evaluating	16.4	12.9	7.8
Reflecting	0.65	14.2	16.5	13.9	Summarizing	6.9	16.7	16.6
					General-Prompting	4.4	3.3	4.1
Answering	0.80	25	27.1	35.4				
Action-Response	0.97	12.5	10.4	9.7	Specific-Prompting	17.6	27.7	13.9
Completion	0.43	0	0.8	0.8	Diagnosing	2.5	3.3	3.3
					Declarative-Instructing	22.6	6.2	4.0
Conversation	0.71	9.4	16.9	10.5	Procedural-Instructing	0.6	4.4	17.2
					Demonstrating	6.3	0.0	11.1
					Support	0.6	0.6	5.4
					Conversation	9.4	16.9	10.5

agreement 0.8<Kappa≤1, or substantial agreement 0.6<Kappa≤0.8). Table 1 reports the Kappa values for each category of student move. Only the category "completion" is not very reliable because there are only a few cases. The detail Kappa values for tutor moves can be found in[3]. Table 1 reports the percentages of student and tutor moves by tutor. After analyzing both the tutor and student moves independently, we found that some behavior of our tutors supports the predictions on effective tutoring from the literatures[6][10]:

– the expert tutor and the lecturer summarize more than the novice;
– subjects with the expert tutor and the lecturer do more explanations than the subjects with the novice tutor.

However, some behaviors of the expert tutor are different from the predictions. Compared to the lecturer, the expert tutor does less specific prompting and his students explain less. This contradicts the claim that students learn best when they construct knowledge by themselves, and that as a consequence, the tutor should prompt and scaffold students, and leave most of the talking to them [6]. This led us to look for other aspects that make the expert tutor more effective. Interestingly, we found that the expert tutor does much more procedural instructing, demonstrating and supporting than the non-expert tutors. Consistently, the novice tutor does much more declarative instructing. So these moves will be the most interesting features which we are going to look into deeply.

3   Study of Tutorial Interaction Patterns

In order to distinguish the expert tutor from the non-expert tutors, our study of interaction patterns focuses on the following two issues:

Table 2. A Transcript Fragment from the Expert's Tutoring

Line	Utterances	Annotation
38	**Tutor:** how'd you actually get the n in the first place?	Diagnosing
39	**Student:** from here I count from c to g and then just from n to r.	Answering
40	**Tutor:** okay so do the c to g.	Specific Prompting
41	**Tutor:** do it out loud so I can hear you do it.	Specific Prompting
42	**Student:** $c\ d\ e\ f$.	Explanation
43	**Student:** so it's three spaces.	Answering
44	**Tutor:** okay so it's three spaces in between.	Summarizing
45	**Student:** $n\ o\ p\ q$ and r.	Explanation
46	**Tutor:** okay.	Evaluating
47	**Tutor:** you obviously made a mistake the first time.	Evaluating
48	**Tutor:** one of the more obvious methods would be like just count backwards and double-check everything.	Procedural Instructing

Tutor-Student Interaction Patterns: What's the difference between each group of students' behaviors after each type of tutor move?

Student-Tutor Interaction Patterns: How do the expert tutor and the non-expert tutors respond differently to each type of student move?

Table 2 presents a fragment from a transcript of the expert's tutoring. A pair of moves which appear in sequence is an interaction pattern. For example, after the tutor's diagnosing in line 38, the student gives an answer in line 39. This forms a tutor-student interaction pattern — "T–diagnosing + S–answering". Then the tutor does a specific prompting, so line 39 and line 40 form a student-tutor interaction pattern — "S–answering + T–specific prompting". The student's explanations in line 42 and line 45 show that he is explaining his answer in line 39. Totally there are 72 possible types of tutor-student pattern and 72 possible types of student-tutor pattern, which are the combinations of 12 categories of tutor move and 6 categories of student move (For the moment, we left out "Conversation"s in tutor move and student move, since some of them are not so related to expert tutoring.)

3.1 Tutor-Student Interaction Patterns

We ran Chi-square on the frequencies of all tutor-student interaction patterns. Across all patterns, there are significant differences in student's reactions to tutor moves between the novice tutor and the other two tutors ($p < 0.01$). In each type of pattern that started with a specific tutor move, each group of students reacts significantly differently ($p < 0.05$) to each type of tutor move with the exception of specific prompting. More specifically, we found:

- **Answering:** the novice tutor's answer is followed by student's questioning, not for the other two tutors;

- **Evaluating:** the lecturer's evaluating leads to much more student's explanation but much less reflecting than the expert and novice tutor;
- **Summarizing:** with the novice tutor students almost never react to summarizing; the lecturer's summarizing leads to more student's reflecting; on the contrary, the expert tutor's leads to more student's explanation (e.g. in Table 2, the expert tutor summarizes in line 44 and then in line 45 the student does explanation);
- **General Prompting:** the students with the expert tutor never have questions after his general prompting, but they do with the non-expert tutors;
- **Specific Prompting:** the specific prompts from the expert tutor and the lecturer lead the students to explain much more than for the novice tutor (e.g. in Table 2, the expert tutor does specific prompting in line 41 and then in line 42 the student does explanation); to the tutor's specific prompting, the students with the novice tutor respond with many more questions than with the other tutors;
- **Procedural Instructing:** the lecturer's procedural instructing leads to more reflecting (i.e. assessing one's own understanding); the expert tutor's leads to more explanation;
- **Demonstrating:** with the novice tutor and the lecturer, students hardly react to demonstrating; on the contrary, the expert tutor's demonstrating leads to any kind of student move.
- **Support:** with the novice tutor and the lecturer, students hardly react to support; on the contrary, the expert tutor's support leads to any kind of student move.

Comparing the expert tutor with the lecturer, although he does specific prompting significantly less than the lecturer and his students do less explanation than the lecturer's students, he tends to use more varied strategies to have the students self-explain, instead of just specific prompting. Comparing the expert with the other two tutors, the expert's answering, general and specific prompting must be clearer to the students, since the students have no questions. Also demonstrating and support are the most interesting strategies that make the expert tutor different from the other tutors. The left part of Table 3 summarizes the tutor-student interaction patterns in which the expert tutor is different from the non-expert tutors.

3.2 Student-Tutor Interaction Patterns

From the ITS point of view, how the tutor reacts to a student move is more helpful for building a tutorial model. There are significant differences ($p < 0.02$) in tutor's reactions to student moves between all the tutors. Further we analyze the student-tutor interaction patterns in the following two directions:

1. how the tutors react differently to each type of student move;
2. using each type of tutor move, which student moves the tutors react to.

In the first direction we found:

Table 3. Interaction Patterns of the Expert Tutor

Tutor-Student		Student-Tutor	
Tutor Move	Student Move	Student Move	Tutor Move
Summarizing	Explanation	Explanation	Diagnosing
Procedural Instructing	Explanation	Summarizing	Diagnosing
Demonstrating	Explanation	Reflecting	General Prompting
Demonstrating	Reflecting	Reflecting	Declarative Instructing
Support	Answering	Reflecting	Procedural Instructing
		Reflecting	Demonstrating
		Action Response	Summarizing
		Action Response	Procedural Instructing

- **Explanation:** the novice tutor summarizes much less than the expert tutor and the lecturer; in response to a student's explanation, the lecturer uses specific prompting much more than the other moves and the other tutors;
- **Questioning:** the expert tutor does not answer immediately or directly, but the non-expert tutors do;
- **Reflecting:** the expert tutor uses much more procedural instructing, demonstrating and general prompting;
- **Answering:** the novice uses many fewer specific prompts but much more evaluating and declarative instructing — she immediately delivers the knowledge or the solution;
- **Action Response:** the expert tutor uses much more summarizing and procedural instructing — actions involve procedures, so summarizing and procedural instructing may be more appropriate.

In the second direction (using each type of tutor move, which student moves the tutors react to), we found:

- **Evaluating:** the expert tutor and the lecturer evaluate the student's explanation more than the student's answer and reflecting (e.g. in Table 2, after the student's explanation in line 45 the expert tutor evaluates it in line 46);
- **Summarizing:** the expert tutor and the lecturer summarize more after a student's explanation, reflecting and action response — those involve more information to be summarized;
- **Specific Prompting:** the lecturer does specific prompting after any kind of student move instead of just in response to answering like what the novice and expert tutor do;
- **Diagnosing:** the expert tutor diagnoses after any kind of student move, not just the student's reaction moves (answering and action response);
- **Declarative Instructing:** the expert tutor mostly does declarative instructing after the student's reflecting — only does it when the student directly expresses lack of some concepts;
- **Procedural Instructing:** the expert tutor and the lecturer do more procedural instructing after the student's reflecting;

– **Demonstrating:** the expert tutor does more demonstrating after the student's reflecting, the lecturer never does demonstrating — in this particular domain, demonstration is more useful.

The right part of Table 3 summarizes the student-tutor interaction patterns in which the expert tutor is different from the non-expert tutors.

4   Study of Multi-utterance Turns

While we were studying the interaction patterns, we observed that not all of tutor's specific prompting are immediately followed by any student move: 35.6% of the expert tutor's specific prompting is not immediately followed by any student move, which is much higher than that of the lecturer's (21.5%) and the novice's (25%). For example, in Table 2, the expert tutor does specific prompting in line 40 but this specific prompting is followed by another specific prompting, instead of a student turn. This may be because most of the time the expert tutor does specific prompting in multi-utterances. This phenomenon also appears for other tutor moves, like from line 46 to line 48: in this single turn, the expert tutor uses three utterances, two categories of move.

Multi-utterances usually mean that in a single turn the tutor or the student make a sequence of moves (more than one) successively without being interrupted. The number of utterances in a single turn is called the "length" of the multi-utterance turn. The utterances are segmented based on the CHILDES transcription manual[11], which the transcribers used. So the first question is: what is the difference between the expert tutor and the non-expert tutors in lengths and frequencies of tutor multi-utterance turns and student multi-utterance turns? To answer this question, we counted the lengths and frequencies of tutor multi-utterance turns and student multi-utterance turns in each tutoring transcripts (for both problem 2 and problem 9 in the curriculum, three tutors, there are a total of 36 transcripts). Then we ran ANOVA on the counts to see whether there are significant differences between each two of tutors and between the two problems. (One-way ANOVA — analysis of variance, is a statistical procedure for testing the null hypothesis that several univariate data sets have the same mean. When significant, ANOVAs are followed by Games-Howell tests to determine which condition is significantly different from the others.)

Figure 1(a) shows the average lengths of multi-utterance tutor and student turns per problem. There is a significant difference in the average length of multi-utterance student turns between problem 2 and problem 9 ($p < 0.03$). Problem 9 is much more complex than problem 2 so the students use more utterances in a single turn.

Figure 1(b) shows the average lengths of multi-utterance tutor and student turns per tutor. The average length of the expert tutor's multi-utterance turn is significantly greater than the non-expert tutors' ($p < 0.005$). This means that the expert tutor talks more in each turn. The length of the expert tutor's multi-utterance turn varies from 1 to 22, but the maximum length of the Lecturer's is 9 and only two turns of the novice tutor have a length greater than 7. We

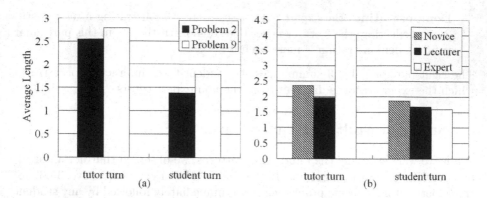

Fig. 1. Average Length of Multi-Utterance Tutor and Student Turns, per Problem(a) and per Tutor(b)

Table 4. Percentages of Each Category of Tutor Move Followed by Another Tutor Move, per Tutor

Tutor Moves	Novice(%)	Lecturer(%)	Expert(%)
Answering	5	7.212	0.743
Evaluating	13.75	**22.6**	9.653
Summarizing	**11.25**	30.77	22.77
General Prompting	5	3.365	4.455
Specific Prompting	8.75	14.9	7.673
Diagnosing	3.75	0.962	2.723
Declarative Instructing	**40**	10.58	5.198
Procedural Instructing	1.25	7.212	**23.02**
Demonstrating	11.25	**0**	15.59
Support	0	0.481	**6.188**

ran Chi-square on the length distributions of the three tutors' turns and there are significant differences between tutors in length 1, length 3 and length 4 ($p < 0.05$). The expert tutor's turns with only one utterance are significantly fewer than the non-expert tutors, but his 3-utterance and 4-utterance turns are significantly more than the novice tutor. It supports that the expert tutor tends to talk more in each single turn. The next question is how differently the expert tutor organizes his turn from the non-expert tutors. We analyzed the multi-utterance patterns of tutor turns with regards to how the tutors follow up differently each particular tutor move. First we looked at the differences between tutor as concerns which categories of tutor move are more likely followed by another tutor move. We ran Chi-square on the data in Table 4 (Numbers in boldface refer to significant differences). We found:

– the novice tutor has significantly fewer summarizing, but many more declarative instructing followed by another move than the expert tutor and the lecturer ($p < 0.003$ in both cases);

- the expert tutor has significantly more procedural instructing and support followed by another move than the non-expert tutors ($p < 0.004$ in both cases);
- the lecturer has much more evaluating but no demonstrating followed by another move than the novice and expert tutors ($p < 0.03$ in both cases);

Procedural instructing teaches the student how to solve a problem procedurally so it can seldom be completed by one single utterance. So we speculate that the expert tutor likes to use completed procedural instructing to help students. Before continuing the tutoring, the expert tutor also likes to encourage his student by support which would push students to move forward.

Like for interaction patterns, it is more meaningful to find out that after each category of tutor move, how the expert tutor differs in the following move from the non-expert tutors. We ran Chi-square on the frequencies of all the multi-utterance patterns of the tutors. Across all patterns, there are significant differences in the following moves to each category of tutor move between all the tutors ($p \approx 0$). More specifically, we found:

- **Answering:** the expert tutor does specific prompting much more than the non-expert tutors after answering — this shows our expert tutor does often prompt and scaffold students but normally after his answering to students' question;
- **Evaluating:** the expert tutor and the lecturer do specific prompting much more than the novice tutor after evaluating; the expert tutor does procedural instructing much more than the non-expert tutors;
- **Summarizing:** the expert tutor does summarizing in multiple utterances much more than the non-expert tutors;
- **General Prompting:** the expert tutor does much fewer specific prompting than the non-expert tutors after general prompting;
- **Specific Prompting:**
  - the expert tutor and the lecturer do procedural instructing much more than the novice tutor after specific prompting;
  - all the three tutors do specific prompting in multiple utterances;
- **Diagnosing:** the expert tutor does much more procedural instructing and support than the non-expert tutors after diagnosing;
- **Declarative instructing:** the expert tutor does much more procedural instructing and demonstrating, but much fewer specific prompting than the non-expert tutors, after declarative instructing;
- **Procedural Instructing:** the expert tutor does procedural instructing in multiple utterances much more than the non-expert tutors; he also does much more demonstrating, but much fewer specific prompting than the non-expert tutors, after procedural instructing;
- **Demonstrating:** the lecturer never does demonstrating but the novice and expert tutors do demonstrating in multiple utterances;
- **Support:** the expert tutor does almost any kind of tutor move after support.

Comparing the novice tutor with the expert tutor and the lecturer, she does declarative instructing after almost any kind of tutor move much more than

Table 5. Patterns of Multi-Utterance Turns of the Expert Tutor

Tutor Move	Tutor Move
Answering	Specific Prompting
Evaluating	Procedural Instructing
Summarizing	Summarizing
Diagnosing	Procedural Instructing
Diagnosing	Support
Declarative Instructing	Procedural Instructing
Declarative Instructing	Demonstrating
Procedural Instructing	Procedural Instructing
Procedural Instructing	Demonstrating
Support	Summarizing
Support	Procedural Instructing
Support	Support

the other two tutors. This supports our finding that the novice tutor tends to give out the information or tell the solution directly. These findings above hint at why the expert tutor is much more effective than the non-expert tutors even though he prompts less, talks more and leaves less talking to students comparing to the lecturer: the expert tutor summarizes more completely, does procedural instructing and demonstrating more effectively and encourages students by support before moving on. Table 5 summarizes the patterns of multi-utterance turns in which the expert tutor is different from the non-expert tutors.

5   Conclusions and Future Work

Our analysis of tutorial dialogue moves, interaction patterns and multi-utterance turns provides plenty of information to distinguish expert from non-expert tutors. The expert tutor is much more effective than the non-expert tutors because of the following behaviors and natural language features:

1. Instead of delivering information directly, demonstrates or models the process for solving the problem (demonstrating, procedural instructing);
2. Before moving on, finds success, and reinforces effort, in even minor accomplishment (support)— although there are not so many supports in the tutoring dialogues, the expert tutor does it in various situations and much more frequently than the non-expert tutors;
3. Summarizes and reviews (summarizing);
4. Assesses the situation not only after a student's answer or action (diagnosing);
5. Uses questions to enhance problem solving (prompting).

After highlighting what makes the tutoring expertise, we will be able to model the expert tutoring. With all the dialogues, we will then use machine learning techniques to learn tutorial rules for generating effective natural language feedback in ITSs. We have already developed a baseline ITS to solve the letter pattern problems and did some experiments on the baseline system with different kinds of simple feedback messages[3]. The baseline ITS engendered better learning outcomes than the control (no tutoring) but its performance is still far below the expert tutor. So we will embody the tutorial rules in the final version of the letter pattern ITS which is able to deliver more effective feedback.

Finally, our findings on the effectiveness of the expert tutor and features of his tutoring are based on a small dataset, and on one single tutor. They clearly need to be repeated in a larger dataset, or with different tutors and / or in different domains. We are transcribing more dialogues in this letter pattern extrapolating domain and also collecting tutoring dialogues in another domain — basic data structure and algorithms. For this introductory computer science domain, we will again compare expert and non-expert tutoring so that we will have a very comprehensive study of expert tutoring. This study will contribute to computationally modelling expert tutoring in ITSs.

Acknowledgements

This work is supported by grant N00014-00-1-0640 from the Office of Naval Research.

References

1. Fox, B.: The human tutorial dialogue project. Lawrence Erlbaum Associates (1993)
2. Chae, H. M., Kim, J. H., and Glass, M.: Effective behaviors in a comparison between novice and expert algebra tutors. Proceedings of Sixteenth Midwest AI and Cognitive Science Conference (2005) 25–30
3. Di Eugenio, B., Kershaw, T. C., Lu, X., Corrigan-Halpern, A., and Ohlsson, S. : Toward a computational model of expert tutoring: a first report. 19th International conference of Florida Artificial Intelligence Research Society (2006) 28–55
4. Glass, M., Kim, J. H., Evens, M. W., Michael, J. A., and Rovick, A. A.: Novice vs. expert tutors: a comparison of style. Proceedings of Tenth Midwest Artificial Intelligence and Cognitive Science Conference (1999)
5. Kotovsky, K. and Simon, H.: Empirical tests of a theory of human acquisition of information-processing analysis. British Journal of Psychology, **61** (1973) 243–257
6. Chi, M. T., Siler, S. A., Jeong, H., Yamauchi, T., and Hausmann, R. G.: Learning from human tutoring. Cognitive Science, **25** (2001) 471–533
7. Litman, D. J., Rose, C. P., Forbes-Riley, K., Vanlehn, K., Bhembe, D., and Silliman., S.: Spoken versus typed human and computer dialogue tutoring. Proceedings of 7th International Conference on Intelligent Tutoring Systems (2004)
8. Carletta, J.: Assessing agreement on classification tasks: The kappa statistic. Computational linguistics, **22** (1996) 249–254
9. Di Eugenio, B. and Glass, M.: The kappa statistic: a second look. Computational linguistics, **30** (2004) 95–101
10. Landsberger, J.: Feedback to improve Study Guides (2005)
11. MacWhinney, B.: The CHILDES project.Tools for analyzing talk: Transcription Format and Programs, volume 1, 3rd edition. Lawrence Erlbaum (2000)

A Competitive Term Selection
Method for Information Retrieval*

Franco Rojas López[1], Héctor Jiménez-Salazar[1], and David Pinto[1,2]

[1] Faculty of Computer Science,
BUAP, Puebla, 72570
Ciudad Universitaria, Mexico
{frl99, hgimenezs}@gmail.com
[2] Department of Information Systems and Computation,
UPV, Valencia 46022,
Camino de Vera s/n, Spain
davideduardopinto@gmail.com

Abstract. Term selection process is a very necessary component for most natural language processing tasks. Although different unsupervised techniques have been proposed, the best results are obtained with a high computational cost, for instance, those based on the use of entropy. The aim of this paper is to propose an unsupervised term selection technique based on the use of a bigram-enriched version of the transition point. Our approach reduces the corpus vocabulary size by using the transition point technique and, thereafter, it expands the reduced corpus with bigrams obtained from the same corpus, i.e., without external knowledge sources. This approach provides a considerable dimensionality reduction of the TREC-5 collection and, also has shown to improve precision for some entropy-based methods.

1 Introduction

Vector Space Model (VSM) was proposed by Salton [15] in the 1970's. This model states a simple way to represent documents of a collection by using vectors with weights according to the terms appearing in each document. Even though several other approaches have been tried, such as representative pairs [10] or documents tokens, terms vector representation remains a topic of interest. Main attraction stills on VSM because it provides a framework for several applications of Natural Language Processing (NLP) such as text categorization, clustering, summarization and so on. Particularly, in Information Retrieval (IR), several experiments have shown a sucessful use of VSM. In this model, each document is represented as a vector whose entries are weights of terms of the vocabulary obtained from a text collection. Specifically, given a text collection $\{D_1, \ldots, D_M\}$ with vocabulary $V = \{w_1, \ldots, w_n\}$, the vector $\overrightarrow{D_i}$ of dimension n, corresponding

---

* This work has been partially supported by the BUAP-701 PROMEP/103.5/05/1536 grant and FCC-VIEP-BUAP.

A. Gelbukh (Ed.): CICLing 2007, LNCS 4394, pp. 468–475, 2007.

to the document D_i, has entries d_{ij} representing the weight of the term w_j in D_i:

$$d_{ij} = tf_{ij} \cdot idf_j, \tag{1}$$

where tf_{ij} is the frequency of term w_j in document D_i, $idf_j = \log_2(\frac{2M}{df_j})$, and df_j is the number of documents in which w_j appears. In collections of hundreds of documents, the dimension of the vector space can be of tens of thousands. Therefore, a key element in text representation consists basically of the adequate selection of important terms, i.e., those that do not affect the retrieval, clustering, or categorization process, implicit in the application. Besides, a reduction of the vocabulary dimensionality without affecting the effectiveness is expected. It is important, from the reason just explained, to explore new mechanisms to represent texts, with the minimal number of terms and, the maximum tradeoff of precision and recall.

In [17] , for instance, R. Urbizagástegui used the *Transition Point* (TP) to show its usefulness in text indexing. TP is a frequency value that splits the vocabulary of a text into two sets of terms (low and high frequency). This technique is based on the Zipf Law of Word Ocurrences [19] and also on the refined studies of Booth [2]. These studies are meant to demonstrate that mid-frequency terms are closely related to the conceptual content of a document. Therefore, it is possible to hypothesize that terms closer to TP can be used as index terms of a document. A typical formula used to obtain this value is: $TP = \frac{-1+\sqrt{8*I_1+1}}{2}$, where I_1 represents the number of words with frequency equal to 1 (see [17]). Alternatively, TP can be found as the first frequency that is not repeated from a non-increasing frequency-sorted vocabulary; since a feature of low frequencies is that they tend to repeat [2]. Particularly, in the experiments we have carried out, we used this approach. Additionaly, the Transition Point technique has shown a good performance in term selection for text categorization [9] and clustering [12].

TP is derived from items underlying in the signifier form, because of its intrinsic property of statistical regularity in the texts. By using ontologies, dictionaries and other lexical resources, it is possible to affect the signifier substance [4]. Thus, TP can be used to affect form and substance by using terms related to it. However, the use of some lexical resources, such as WordNet, would not be factible because of its wide domain, carrying out to discard several terms belonging to the specific application domain. Regarding the usefulness of the later remark, the set of terms selected by TP may be increased with related terms, namely TP enriched approach [14].

On the other hand, M. A. Montemurro [6] did a statistical analysis of some set of words without knowledge of the grammatical structure of the documents analized. He used the entropy concept for sorting sets of words, based on the role that these words play in a set of documents from the literature domain. Entropy measures the amount of information contained in a system [3]. So, given a system S with $s_1, \ldots, s_n$ states, the entropy of S is $H(S) = -\sum_i p_i \log(p_i)$, being $p_i = \Pr(s_i)$. This means that a deterministic system lacks of information if $H(S) = 0$, since $p_i = 1$ (the same argument is valid if $p_i = 0$). On the other hand, a system whose states have the same probability $(p_i = 1/n)$ will have the maximum of information $H(S) = \log n$. We must not confuse the information that a system has with the information that can be extracted from it; in other words, the less information we have from a system, the bigger amount of information the system will have; the information of a system is a measurement of our ignorance. In a text collection we can consider a) the words, w, that have high probability to appear in all the documents $(\Pr(w) \approx 1)$; b) words that are not uniformly distributed in the collection of texts, i.e., those which are concentrated in some document; and, c) those words that are uniformly distributed in a corpus. The last one has a high value of significance in terms of information, compared with the two former and may be used to represent the text.

This work explores an alternative to the classic representation based on the VSM for IR. Entropy was used in [5] for IR processes on a small text collection, but results were not conclusive. TP has been also used in this context [13], obtaining good results: reducing dimensionality and outperforming classical representation. In [14] an enrichment of the term selected by TP for cross-lingual information retrieval was presented, but results were not indicative of better performance due to the noisy terms in multilingual collections. Our contribution here consists in clarify the uselfulness of each of these methods by using the TREC-5 standard collection as a common reference. Besides, we have tried to enhance the obtained results by providing a combination of such approaches.

Following sections present the term selection and weighting schemata, experiments done by using the TREC-5 collection, results, and a discussion with conclusions.

2   Term Selection and Weighting

In this section we describe in detail each dimensionality reduction method explored in our experiments. The description of the method is presented first and, thereafter, an explanation of the representation schema is given.

2.1   Entropy

Determination of a set of words that characterize a set of documents given, is the focus of our work. Given a set of documents $D = \{D_1, D_2, ..., D_M\}$, and N_i the number of words in the document D_i, the relative frequency of the word w_j in D_i is defined as follows:

$$f_{ij} = \frac{tf_{ij}}{N_i^{tf_{ij}}}, \tag{2}$$

and

$$p_{ij} = \frac{f_{ij}}{\sum_{j=1}^{m} f_{ij}} \tag{3}$$

is the probability of the word w_j be in D_i. Thus, entropy of w_j can be calculated as:

$$H(w_j) = -\sum_{i=1}^{M} p_{ij} \log p_{ij}. \tag{4}$$

The representation of a document D_i is given by the VSM, whenever terms have high entropy. Let H_{max} be the maximum value of entropy on all the terms, $H_{max} = \max_j H(w_j)$, the representation based on entropy of D_i is

$$H_i = [w_j \in D_i | H(w_j) > H_{max} \cdot u], \tag{5}$$

where u is a threshold which defines the level of high entropy. In our experiments we have set $u = 0.5$.

2.2   Transition Point

Given a document D_i and its vocabulary $V_i = \{(w_j, tf_i(w_j))|w_j \in D_i\}$, where $tf_i(w_j) = tf_{ij}$, let TP_i be the transition point of D_i. A set of important terms which will represent the document D_i may be calculated as follows:

$$R_i = \{w_j|((w_j, tf_{ij}) \in V_i), (TP_i \cdot (1-u) \le tf_{ij} \le TP_i \cdot (1+u))\}, \tag{6}$$

where u is a value in $[0, 1]$. Some experiments presented in [13] have shown that $u = 0.4$ is a good value for this threshold.

For the representation schema, we consider that the important terms are those whose frequencies are closer to the TP. Therefore, a term with frequency very "close" to TP will get a high weight, and those "far" to TP will get a weight close to zero. For each term $w_j \in R_i$, its weight, given by Equation (1), is modified according to the distance between its frequency and the transition point, obtaining a new value for its "term frequency" (see Equation (7)).

$$tf'_{ij} = \|R_i\| - |TP_i - tf_{ij}| \tag{7}$$

2.3   Term Enrichment

Although TP certainly reduces space dimensionality by increasing precision, it obtains a low recall. Due to this fact we are proposing to enrich the terms selected by this method with those which have similar characteristics, by using a co-occurrence bigrams-based formula. Formally, given a document D_i made up of only those terms selected by using the TP approach (R_i), the new important terms for D_i will be obtained as follows:

$$R'_i = R_i \cup \{w'|(w_j \in R_i), (v = w'w_j \text{ or } v = w_jw'), (v \in D_i), (tf_i(v) > 1)\}. \tag{8}$$

That is, we only used a window of size one around each term of R_i, and a minimum frequency of two for each bigram was required as condition to include new terms.

As R_i, weighting for enriched terms follows Equations (1) and (7). Terms $\{w'|w' \in R'_i \wedge w' \notin R_i\}$ will use directly the Equation (1).

2.4 Union of Entropy and TP

This representation takes advantage of the benefit of both approaches, TP and entropy. TP represents text independently, whereas entropy obtains better discriminant terms, therefore, we have selected those terms that satisfy either of these two conditions. The representation of a document D_i is then given by:

$$H_i' = H_i \cup R_i \tag{9}$$

In this approach two weighting criteria were adopted for the representation schema. Terms provided by H_i (Equation (5)) and R_i (Equation (6)) are weighted by Equations (1) and (7), respectively. The procedure for determining H_i' was to add, to the set R_i, all the terms that satisfy H_i. Thereafter, terms $w_j \in H_i \cap R_i$ are weighted by Equation (7).

3 Experiments

Three experiments were performed in this work, first we determined the performance of the entropy schema, H; then we used an enrichment of TP, TP'; finally the union of the both TP and H was done. The dataset and the results obtained are described in the following subsections.

3.1 Data Description

We have used the TREC Spanish Corpora, produced by the Linguistic Data Consortium (LDC)[1], for our experiments. Particularly, one corpus of the TREC-5 collection which consists of 50 topics (queries) and 57,868 documents in Spanish language from the "El Norte" mexican newspaper was selected. The average size of vocabulary of each document is 191.94 terms. Each of the topics has associated its set of relevant documents. On average, the number of relevant documents per topic is 139.36. The documents, queries and relevance judgements (qrels) used in the experiments were all taken from TREC-5.

3.2 Results

Figure 1 shows an interpolation of the average precision at different standard recall levels [1]. Two of these curves were previously presented: the classical VSM and TP [13]; therefore, we are using them as a reference for our own results. The three remained curves were obtained by using the representation schemas presented at section 2: H, terms obtained by using entropy; TP', enriched terms by bigrams; and H+TP, the union of H and TP.

The TP-based method shows a better performance than the classical VSM by using low computational resources. On the other hand, the entropy-based method has a very good performance but with a higher computational cost. The

---

[1] http://www.ldc.upenn.edu/Catalog/CatalogEntry.jsp?catalogId=LDC2000T51

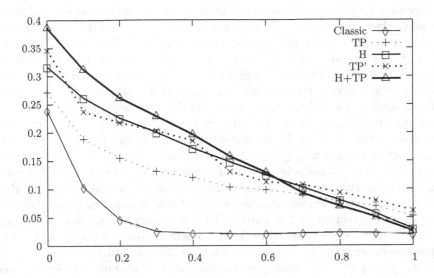

Fig. 1. Performance of term selection using entropy (H) and transition point (TP)

TP approach, enriched with bigrams, obtained a similar performance than the entropy. Finally, the union of entropy and TP curve may indicate that weighting procedure (by using both Equation (1) and (7)) did not give an adequated importance to terms, since precision diminished after of 0.6 recall level.

The vocabulary size for each method is shown in Table 1. Entropy did the highest reduction (it just uses 3.3% from original term space). TP enrichment obtained the highest vocabulary size, except for VSM, but its results are competitive with the entropy method and, with so much light computation consumption than entropy does.

Table 1. Term reduction methods and the vocabulary size obtained for TREC-5

Method name	Vocabulary size	Percentage of reduction
VSM	235,808	0.00
TP	28,111	88.08
H	7,870	96.70
TP'	36,442	84.55
H+TP	29,117	87.66

4   Discussion

Text representation, by using the VSM, implies the problem of selecting the minimal set of index terms and, thereafter, the calculation of their weights. Despite the fact that VSM and the classical weighting have several decades of existence, nowadays they are in essence being used in a diversity of NLP tasks; e.g., text categorization, text clustering, and summarization. It is well known the empirical fact that by using all terms of a text commonly produces a noisy effect in the representation [16]. Besides, the high dimensionality of the term space has led to an index term analysis. For instance, Salton et al. [15] proposed a measurement of discrimination for index terms, i.e., terms defining vectors in the space that better discerned what documents answer a particular query. They concluded that, given a collection of M documents, the "more discriminant" terms have a frequency in the range $[\frac{M}{100}, \frac{M}{10}]$. A similar experiment was carried out in [8], showing that term frequencies around TP overlap the above range. This result suggested to analyze the discriminant value of terms in a neighborhood of TP [7]. TP have a good performance due to the use of mid-frequencies terms, however, many important terms in a document have a frequency far from TP. In this work, such terms were included in the document representation through a very simple procedure (bigrams), outperforming the TP method.

Entropy property of reaching maximum value with equiprobable outcomes says that the terms are used, among texts, with a relative constant frequency. This is an indicator supported by intertextual frequency on a text collection. Therefore, it would not be possible to apply the method on isolated texts or heterogeneous texts collections. We have seen, that the H method had very good performance, but the computation of the entropy for each term of the collection has a very high computational cost.

Conjecture, formuled in [5], established that *terms with balanced use through the texts collection is a characteristic related with the Zipf's Law [19]: minimum effort to write a text entails a moderate use on some words, which is revealed by entropy.* When dealing with many texts, it may be interpreted as *preserving the regularity of occurrence of such words, as if they were relevant because of their role in the texts as pivots.* In fact, from the experiments carried out in this work, it was shown that TP enrichment performed in similar manner as the entropy method. Besides, in the experiment which joins entropy and TP, the most of the terms selected by entropy were also selected by TP (87.21%). Furthermore, just the 0.78% of the H-terms do not belong to the set provided by TP'. This fact is confirmed by comparing the TP' precision-recall curve with the H curve (Fig. 1). However, there is a high amount of TP'-terms (6,711) that do not belong to neither, the TP-term nor the H-term set. This set of terms introduces an unstable behaviour at TP' curve: good terms and noisy terms distribute relevant and non relevant texts throughout of all retrieved results.

Up to now, we have tested the methods proposed in only one collection, but further investigations should consider other datasets in order to see if the given conclusions carry out in those as well.

A clear advantage of the methods presented in this paper are their unsupervised nature and language independence which makes them suitable for their use in a wide variety of NLP tasks.

References

1. Baeza-Yates, R. & Ribeiro, N.: *Modern Information Retrieval*, Addison Wesley, 1999.
2. Booth A.: A law of occurrence of words of low frequency, *Information and Control*, 10 (4), pp. 383–396, 1967.
3. C. E. Shannon, *The Bell System Technical Journal* 27, 379 (1948).
4. Gelbukh, A.; Sidorov, G. & Guzman-Arenas, A.: Use of a weighted topic hierarchy for text retrieval and classification, *LNCS 1692*, pp 130-135, 1999.
5. Jiménez-Salazar, H.; Castro, M.; Rojas, F.; Miñón, E.; Pinto, D. & F. Carcedo: Unsupervised Term Selection using Entropy, *Research on Computing Science* 14, ISSN 1665-9899, pp. 163–172, México, 2005.
6. Montemurro, M.A. & Zanette D. H.: Entropic Analysis of the role of the words in literaty texts, CoRR, arXiv:cond-mat/0109218, v1 12, sep 2001.
7. Moyotl, E.: *DPT: un método de selección de términos para categorización de textos*, Master in Computer Science Thesis, FCC-BUAP, 2005 (*In spanish*).
8. E. Moyotl & H. Jiménez: An Analysis on Frequency of Terms for Text Categorization, *Procesamiento del Lenguaje Natural*, ISSN 1135-9948, pp 141-146, España.
9. Moyotl, E. & Jiménez, H.: Enhancement of DPT Feature Selection Method for Text Categorization, LNCS 3406, pp. 706–709, 2005.
10. Pérez-Carballo, J. & Strzalkowski, T.: Natural Language Information Retrieval: progress report, *Information Processing and Management* v.36(1), Elsevier, pp. 155–178, 2000.
11. Pinto, D.; Jiménez-Salazar, H.; Rosso P. & Sanchis, E.: BUAP-UPV TPIRS: A System for Document Indexing Reduction at WebCLEF. Accessing Multilingual Information Repositories, CLEF 2005, *LNCS 4022*, 2006.
12. Pinto D.; Jiménez-Salazar, H. & Paolo Rosso: Clustering Abstracts of Scientific Texts using the Transition Point Technique, *LNCS 3878*, pp. 536–546, 2006.
13. Rojas, F.; Jiménez, H.; Pinto, D. & Aurelio López: Dimensionality reduction for Information Retrieval, *Research on Computing Science*, Vol 20, pp 107–112 2006.
14. Rojas, F.; Jiménez, H. & Pinto, D.: Text Reduction-Enrichment at WebCLEF, In *Proceedings of CLEF 2006*, pp. 53, 2006.
15. Salton, G., Wong, A. & Yang, C.: A Vector Space Model for Automatic Indexing, *Communications of the ACM*, 18(11) pp. 613–620, 1975.
16. Sebastiani, F.: Machine Learning in Automated Text Categorization, *ACM Computing Surveys*, 34(1), pp. 1–47, 2002.
17. Urbizagástegui, A.R.: Las Posibilidades de la Ley de Zipf en la Indización Automática, http://www.geocities.com/ResearchTriangle /2851/RUBEN2.htm, 1999 (*In spanish*).
18. Yang, Y., Pedersen, P.: A Comparative Study on Feature Selection in Text Categorization, *Proc. of ICML-97, 14th Int. Conf. on Machine Learning*, pp. 412–420, 1997.
19. Zipf, G.K.: *Human Behaviour and the Principle of Least Effort*, Addison-Wesley, 1949.

Incorporating Passage Feature Within Language Model Framework for Information Retrieval

Ke Dang, Tiejun Zhao, Haoliang Qi, and Dequan Zheng

MOE-MS Key Laboratory of Natural Language Processing and Speech, Harbin Institute of
Technology, Harbin, China 150001
{kedang,tjzhao,qhl,dqzheng}@mtlab.hit.edu.cn

Abstract. Passage feature has been proved very useful in document retrieval.
In this paper, we successfully incorporate the passage feature into language
model framework by extending the Jelinek-Mercer smoothing. This scheme not
only increases the precision of document language model but also can let the
passage feature act well in the documents that are not very long. We compare
our schemes with 4 baselines: the unigram language model and the passage
language model with Jelinek-Mercer and Dirichlet smoothing. Experimental results on the TREC collections indicate that our method significantly outperforms the unigram language model and gets better performance than passage
language model in collections whose documents are not very long.

1 Introduction

Many features have been utilized in the information retrieval models. The most popular features may be the *tf* and *idf*, which are used in many models. We Also know that
the principle of relevance judgement between a query and a document relies on the
relevance probability of a portion of the document, not necessarily every portion of
the document, and the query. It is easy to understand: if a person want to find information about "information retrieval" from some documents, then a document with
just a passage concerning "information retrieval" should be checked. Because of this
principle, the passage-level evidence has been proved to be very useful of improving
the retrieval accuracy especially for long documents with complex internal structural
[1;2;3;4;5;]. The underling assumption is that: a relevant document may have several
subtopics and only a subtopic is very relevant to the query, and the passages regarding
other subtopics may act as noise passages, which may reduce the possibility of view-
ing this document as a relevant document. The common method of these studies utilizing the passage information is first to divide every document into passages and then
to compute the relevant possibility of each passage to the query, and then rank the
documents according to their most relevant passages. In other words, these methods
rank the passages and use a passage, the one most relevant to the query, to represent
the whole document. The main advantage of these methods is that they reduce the risk
of the "noise passages", which may be very much in the long documents so that these

A. Gelbukh (Ed.): CICLing 2007, LNCS 4394, pp. 476–484, 2007.

methods get higher accuracy in the collections with many long documents. Nevertheless, the disadvantage is that a long document with several highly relevant passages would be underestimated, so the Hearst and Plaunt [6] had used the sum of several passages to represent the document, indicating that this method is more effective than the single passage. This result demonstrates that the information in the passages other than the most similar one should also be considered in the ad hoc retrieval. Also, in a document that is not very long and the topic of the whole document is concentrated, using just a part of a document to represent the whole document would inevitably lose the useful information such as the main topic of the document. So we'd better utilize the advantage of passage information and, at the same time, do not ignore whole-document level information. This is one motivation of this paper.

Our other motivations come from the language model framework. Ponte and Croft [7] have first applied this approach to the information retrieval area. From that time, many studies had extensively been done under this framework [8;4;9;10;11;12;13]. One direction of these studies is to directly concentrate on the smoothing techniques, whose most important effect is to assign some weights to the unseen words and address the data sparseness. But we can also view the smoothing techniques as being incorporating some beneficial features-the collection information, for example. One of the most effective smoothing methods is that of Jelinek-Mercer. The form of this smoothing method is convenient to incorporate other useful information such as the cluster information of the similar documents [12], and this method is proved to be effective. This is another motivation of our work.

As discussed above, we incorporate the passage information in a document language model framework by extending the Jelinek-Mercer smoothing methods. Utilizing passage information in a language model framework is actually not new [4]. But there are many differences between our work and theirs: in our work we just use the passage information only as feature to further smooth the document language model instead of directly using the passage to rank the document, and we have not used the relevance model [11]. Their work is one of the baselines of our work.

In the rest of this paper: Section 2 reviews previous research regarding the language model and passage retrieval. Section 3 presents our methods of incorporating the passage information into language model framework. Section 4 presents our experimental methods and results on TREC collections. Conclusions are presented in section 5.

2 Previous Work

2.1 Passage Retrieval

A passage means a sequence of words in a document. The most common methods of passage retrieval are to use the highest-possibility one passage or several passages of a document to represent the document and then use the rank of these passages to rank the document.

At least 3 kinds of passages had been proposed and tested in order to achieve higher passage retrieval accuracy. The first one depends on the original segmentation of the documents by the authors including the sentences, paragraphs, and sections.

These methods believe that the natural blocks of the documents may imply the sub-topics of the documents. The second one divides the document into semantic passages according to the subtopics of a document [6;14;5;15;16]. The algorithms of finding semantic passages include locating passage boundaries based on lexical cohesion [16], decompositing the text into segments and themes [14], the texttiling algorithm [15] and etc. This kind of passage can be beneficial when the authors have not explic-itly segment the document by subtopics. The third one names windows which are sequences of fixed-length words. Windows may start at the beginning of the docu-ment [1] or at any place of a document [2;3]. Experiments show that this kind of pas-sages can yield effective results.

2.2 Language Model in Information Retrieval

The main idea of this language model method is to view every document d_i in collec-tion C as a document language model D_i (i=1...k, k is the number of documents in C) and assume that the query $Q=q_1q_2..q_m$ (m is the number of terms in Q) generated from this document language model. The probabilities that their document language model generate the query is $P(Q/D_i)$ [7]. In order to rank the documents, the posterior prob-ability $P(D_i/Q)$ is needed. According to the Bayesian formulation:

$$P(D_i \mid Q) = \frac{P(Q \mid D_i) * P(D_i)}{P(Q)}$$

Given a Query Q, $P(Q)$ for all $P(D_i/Q)$ is the same number, which can not affect the ranking. All the $P(D_i)$ can be assumed to be equal. So the following formulation can be got:

$$P(D_i \mid Q) \infty P(Q \mid D_i) = P(q_1q_2..q_m \mid D_i)$$

If we view the query as a sequence of terms and treat every term as a independent event, then:

$$P(Q \mid D_i) = \prod_{j=1}^{m} P(q_j \mid D_i)$$

eventually we can rank the documents by computing the probability $P(q_j/D_i)$. Intui-tively this possibility can be got by the Maximum Likelihood Estimation (MLE) method:

$$P_{ML}(q_j \mid D_i) = \frac{c(q_j, d_i)}{\sum_{w \in d_i} c(w, d_i)}$$

Here, $c(q_j,d_i)$ is the number of occurrences of the term q_j in document d_i. Obviously, since the document may not contain every term in query and the $c(q_j,d_i)$ may be zero, $P(Q/D_i)$ would be zero, which is called data sparseness problem. To solve this prob-lem, smoothing techniques are used, which assigns a possibility larger than zero to the term that does not appear in the document. Many smoothing methods have been pro-posed in the information retrieval area and two methods have been approved to be effective [13]. They are the Jelinek-Mercer(JM) and Dirchlet (Dir) smoothing tech-niques. We call them LM+JM and LM+Dir model in the rest of the paper:

$$P_{JM}(q_j \mid D_i) = \lambda P_{ML}(q_j \mid D_i) + (1-\lambda)P(q_j \mid C) \tag{1}$$

$$P_{Dir}(q_j \mid D_i) = \frac{c(q_j, d_i) + \mu P(q_j \mid C)}{\sum\limits_{w \in d_i} c(w, d_i) + \mu} \tag{2}$$

Where λ is the parameter of the Jelinek-Mercer method. Its value is between 0 and 1. C is the document collection. μ is the parameter of Dirchlet Method. Its ordinary value is between 0 and 10000. From the formulations, the smoothing methods can be viewed as incorporating the collection information into the maximum likelihood estimation of the term q_j. The forms of the formulations are convenient to incorporate the other useful information to improve the accuracy.

Liu and Croft [12] had made use of the cluster feature by extending the Jelinek-Mercer smoothing technique:

$$P_{Cluster}(q_j \mid D_i) = \lambda P_{ML}(q_j \mid D_i) + (1-\lambda)[\beta P_{ML}(q_j \mid Cluster_{d_i}) + (1-\beta)P(q_j \mid C)]$$

Where $Cluster_{di}$ is the cluster that includes d_i. This approach had been tested to be effective and it was approved that incorporating cluster information into document language model by linear interpolation is generally more effective approach to cluster-based retrieval than directly ranking clusters[12]. This is an important motivation that let us think out the way of incorporating the passage information in language model framework.

Liu and Croft [4] had used the passage information in the language model framework. The first experiment they did is from the passage retrieval perspective. Step 1 : Divided the documents into passages. Step 2: Ranked all the passages from the same or different documents. Step 3: Ranked the documents according to their best passage. Their 2,3,4 experiments used the relevance model [11]. However, there are many differences between our work and theirs: their first experiment comes from the passage retrieval perspective-using just a part of a document to represent the whole document, thus not explicitly considered the whole-document information. Our method considers the passages just as a feature which is incorporated in the document language model and we keep both the passage information and whole-document information, because we think the whole-document information would be very useful in document retrieval especially for the documents which are not very long. Their second, third and fourth experiments had used the relevance model. The experiments show that the 2,3,4 experiments perform well in the collections that have many long documents, but because the relevance model inherently integrates the relevant documents' information, it is difficult to tell what the contribution of the passage information is. But our methods are more simple and we show explicitly the effect of the passage information.

3   Incorporating Passage Information into the Language Model Framework

Because we want to utilize the passage feature in a document and at the same time keep the whole document information, which would be useful in the not-very-long document, we incorporate the passage information in a document language model framework by extending the Jelinek-Mercer smoothing methods. We first divide every document into passages and rank the passages. Then for each document d_i, we can get the best passage p_i. We will use the p_i to further smooth the document language model D_i. We can get the PJM model:

$$P_{PJM}(q_j \mid D_i) = \lambda_1 P_{ML}(q_j \mid p_i) + \lambda_2 P_{ML}(q_j \mid D_i) + (1 - \lambda_1 - \lambda_2)P(q_j \mid C) \tag{3}$$

From the equations, we can see that we emphasize the terms that occur in the best passage p_i, by which we incorporate the passage level information. We have also tested other forms of smoothing: we first smooth passage p_i with document model D_i by Dirichlet smoothing method, then the smoothed passage and document model is further interpolated with the collection C. Moreover, we first smooth document model D_i with collection C by Dirichlet smoothing method, then the smoothed document and collection model is further interpolated with passage p_i. But the PJM model perform better than them empirically. We use PJM model to compare with the classical document language model using Jelinek-Mercer and Dirichlet smoothing techniques and the passage language model used in [4], because we can view the document language model and the passage language model in [4] to be the extreme case of PJM model where λ_1 or λ_2 is zero.

4   Experiments and Results

4.1   Experiment Design

We use three different collections of TREC for evaluation: WSJ, FR and WSJ+FR. Some statistics are shown in Table 1. We choose WSJ collection as the representation of collections mainly including the short documents, and the FR collection as the representation of collections mainly including the very long documents. The FR+WSJ collection are selected as the heterogeneous collection where the documents' length vary very much. All documents have been processed in standard manner: stop words were removed and terms were stemmed. The queries are TREC topics 51-100 (title field only). The document sets come from TREC disk 1 and 2.

Table 1. Statistics of Data Set

Coll.	Description	Size(MB)	# Doc.	Mean # Terms/Doc
WSJ	Wall Street Journal(1990-92) disk 2	242	74520	466
FR	Federal Register(1988-89) disk 1, 2	469	45820	1504
WSJ & FR	Wall Street Journal(1990-92) & Federal Register(1988-89) disk 1, 2	711	120340	861

Our new model can be viewed as extending LM+JM model described in section 2.2, so it is our baseline model. Also, passage language model described in [4] is another baseline model. The formulations can be summarized below:
Passage Language Model + Jelinek-Mercer (PLM+JM model):

$$P_{JM}(q_j \mid D_i) = \lambda P_{ML}(q_j \mid P_i) + (1-\lambda)P(q_j \mid C) \tag{4}$$

Passage Language Model + Dirchlet (PLM+Dir model):

$$P_{Dir}(q_j \mid D_i) = \frac{c(q_j, P_i) + \mu P(q_j \mid C)}{\sum_{w \in p_i} c(w, p_i) + \mu} \tag{5}$$

The passage we use in this paper is half-overlapped windows similar to the one in [1] and the same as that of [4]. All passages have the same fixed-length. The first passage starts at the first term of the document, and the next passage starts from the middle position of the previous passage. We choose this kind of passage because it can get effective results in previous passage retrieval experiments [1;4]. In our experiments, we set passage length to 200.

There are also many other free parameters, for example, the λ in the LM+JM model. We empirically set the λ from 0.3 to 0.8, we find λ=0.5 can get the best average precision in WSJ collection on query 51-100. So we set λ=0.5 when using LM+JM and PLM+JM model, $\lambda_1 + \lambda_2$=0.5($\lambda_1 = \lambda_2$=0.25) when using PJM model. Using the same way, we set μ=1000 when using LM+Dir, PLM+Dir model. Moreover, in all the models, we get the best passage p_i using the LM+Dir model with μ=1000.

The models' performances are measured by the non-interpolated average precision (AvgP) and 11-point recall/precision. We use Lemur 4.2[17] to carry out all the experiments.

4.2 Experimental Results

Table 2 and 3 present our experimental results, where we compare our PJM model with unigram language model and passage language model.

Table 2. Overall Comparison over TREC collections, query 51-100

Coll		LM	PLM	PJM		
		AvgP	AvgP	AvgP	%chg over LM	%chg over PLM
WSJ	JM	0.2322	0.2359	0.2469	+6.33%	+4.66%
	Dir	0.2369	0.235		+4.22%	+5.06%
FR	JM	0.2208	0.323	0.2885	+30.66%	-10.7%
	Dir	0.2529	0.3154		+14.07%	-8.53%
WSJ+FR	JM	0.2193	0.2218	0.2346	+6.98%	+5.77%
	Dir	0.2173	0.2229		+7.96%	+5.25%

Table 3. Comparison between Unigram language model with Jelinek-Mercer smoothing and PJM model, query51-100

	WSJ			FR		
	LM +JM	PJM	% chg	LM +JM	PJM	% chg
Rel	2172			502		
Rel.Retr	1544	1584	+2.59	255	296	16.08
0.0	0.5594	0.5580	-0.35	0.4238	0.4376	+3.26
0.1	0.4097	0.4475	+9.23	0.3121	0.3993	+27.94
0.2	0.3710	0.3825	+3.10	0.2716	0.3885	+43.04
0.3	0.3017	0.3168	+5.00	0.2663	0.3569	+34.02
0.4	0.2567	0.2716	+5.80	0.2572	0.3046	+18.42
0.5	0.2340	0.2487	+6.28	0.2526	0.2993	+18.49
0.6	0.1934	0.2167	+12.05	0.1914	0.2574	+34.48
0.7	0.1490	0.1665	+11.74	0.1789	0.2418	+35.16
0.8	0.1149	0.1349	+17.41	0.1551	0.2170	+39.91
0.9	0.0734	0.0894	+21.80	0.1442	0.2029	+40.71
1.0	0.0289	0.0318	+10.03	0.1059	0.1722	+62.61
Avg	0.2322	0.2469	+6.33	0.2208	0.2885	+30.66

	WSJ+FR		
	LM +JM	PJM	% chg
Rel	2674		
Rel.Retr	1667	1709	+2.52
0.0	0.5427	0.5806	+6.98
0.1	0.3943	0.4369	+10.80
0.2	0.3538	0.3647	+3.08
0.3	0.2934	0.3015	+2.76
0.4	0.2396	0.2608	+8.85
0.5	0.2160	0.2339	+8.29
0.6	0.1828	0.2045	+11.87
0.7	0.1380	0.1503	+8.91
0.8	0.1015	0.1169	+15.17
0.9	0.0695	0.0759	+9.21
1.0	0.0188	0.0244	+29.79
Avg	0.2193	0.2346	+6.98

LM refers to unigram language model. It is the basic baseline of our models. the difference between the LM and PJM is that PJM further emphasizes the importance of the terms occurring in the best passage, by which PJM model incorporating the passage feature in the unigram language model. The comparison between the LM and PJM would demonstrate the effect of the passage feature in the language model framework. Moreover, it would also indicate the role of the way of incorporating the passage feature by linear interpolation. Table 3 presents the comparison between the LM+JM and PJM. Almost in all the recall level, PJM outperforms the LM+JM. Specifically, over the WSJ and WSJ+FR collection, our PJM model performs better than LM+JM and LM+Dir. This indicates that passage feature can be useful even in the not very long documents and heterogeneous collections. Over the FR collection, PJM outperform LM+JM significantly by 30.66% and 14.07%. This demonstrates that the passage feature perform very well in the long documents after being incorporated in the unigram language model

PLM refers to the Passage Language model, the difference between the PLM and PJM is that PJM has kept the whole-document's information. We observe that the PJM achieve better results than PLM in the WSJ and WSJ+FR collection. This indicates that the whole-document information is helpful in the documents that are not very long. But the PLM gets a high precision in the FR collection. The reason may be that the documents in FR are very long and the advantage of the passage information is so strong that it exceeds the advantage of the whole-document information.

In summary, some conclusions can be drawn from the experiments:

1. Our way of using the linear interpolation to incorporate the passage feature acts well.
2. Our motivation of keeping both the passage information and whole-document information also can achieve improvement over just keeping one of them. PJM achieve better performance than LM. PJM also can get better performance than PLM in collections whose documents are not very long.

5 Conclusion

We have proposed a new model that incorporating the passage information into the language model framework. Our model utilizes three kinds of information to ad hoc retrieval: the passage level information, the document level information and the collection level information. The passage level information can be seen as the passage that is the most similar to the query. And we use the language model framework and linear interpolation to combine them together effectively. Our approach can be seen as the extension of the unigram language model with Jelinek-Mercer smoothing or passage language model. We did experiments on the TREC collections and compared our approach to the two baseline models. The empirical results indicate that our approach can achieve better performance over the unigram language model, especially in the long documents. And our approach can get better performance than passage language model in collections whose documents are not very long.

References

1. Callan, J.P.: Passage-level evidence in document retrieval. In B.W. Croft & C.J. van Rijsbergen (Eds.), Proceedings of the 17th annual international ACM-SIGIR conference on research and developments in information retrieval, Dublin, Ireland, July (1994) 302-310

2. Kaszkiel, M. and Zobel, J.: Passage retrieval revisited. In N. J. Belkin, D. Narasimhalu, & P. Willett (Eds.), Proceedings of the 20th annual international ACM-SIGIR conference on research and development in information retrieval, Philadelphia, PA (1997) 178-185

3. Kaszkiel, M. and Zobel, J.: Effective ranking with arbitrary passages. Journal of the American Society For Information Science and Technology, 52(4): (2001) 344-364.

4. J. Xu and B. Croft.: Passage retrieval based on language models The 11th International Conference on Information and Knowledge Management , McLean , (2002)

5. Ponte, J., and Croft, W.B.: Text segmentation by topic.In Proceedings of the 1st European conference on research and advanced technology for digital libraries, (1997)113-125

6. Hearst, M.A., and Plaunt, C.: Subtopic structuring for full-length document access. In R. Korfhage, E. Rasmussen, & P. Willet (Eds.), Proceedings of the 16th annual international ACM-SIGIR conference on research and development in information retrieval, Pittsburgh, PA, (1993) 59-68

7. Ponte, J., and Croft, W.B.: A language modelling approach to information retrieval. In Proceedings of the 21st annual international ACM-SIGIR conference on research and development in information retrieval, New York: ACM. (1998) 275-281

8. Berger, A. and Lafferty, J.: Information retrieval as statistical translation. Proceedings of the 22nd annual international ACM-SIGIR conference on research and development in information retrieval. (1999) 222-229

9. F. Song and W. B. Croft.: A general language model for information retrieval. Proceedings of the 22nd annual international ACM-SIGIR conference on research and development in information retrieval, ,Berkeley, CA., (1999) 279-280

10. Miller, D. H., Leek, T., and Schwartz, R.: A hidden Markov model information retrieval system. In Proceedings of the 1999 ACM SIGIR Conference on Research and Development in Information Retrieval, (1999)214-221

11. Lavrenko, V. and Croft, B.: Relevance-based language models. In Proceedings of the 2001 ACM SIGIR Conference on Research and Development in Information Retrieval. (2001)120-127

12. Xiaoyong Liu, W. Bruce Croft: Cluster-Based Retrieval Using Language Models. Proceedings of the 27th annual international ACM-SIGIR conference on research and development in information retrieval. (2004)

13. C. Zhai and J. Lafferty.: A study of smoothing methods for language models applied to ad hoc information retrieval. In Proceedings of the 2001 ACM SIGIR Conference on Research and Development in Information Retrieval, (2001)334-342

14. Salton, G., Allan, J. and Singhal, A.K.: Automatic text decomposition and structuring. Information Processing and Management, 32(2), (1996)127-138

15. Hearst, M. A.: TextTiling, a quantitative approach to discourse segmentation. Technical Report 93/24 Sequoia 2000 Technical Report, University of California, Berkeley. (1993)

16. J. C. Reynar.: An automatic method of finding topic boundaries. In Proceedings of the 32nd Annual Meeting of the Association for Computational Linguistics(student session), Las Cruces, New Mexico, USA, July 1994

17. Ogilvie, P. and Callan, J.: Experiments using the lemur toolkit. In Proceedings of the Tenth Text Retrieval Conference (TREC-10), (2001)103-108

Enhancing Cross-Language Question Answering by Combining Multiple Question Translations

Rita M. Aceves-Pérez, Manuel Montes-y-Gómez, and Luis Villaseñor-Pineda

Laboratorio de Tecnologías del Lenguaje,
Instituto Nacional de Astrofísica, Óptica y Electrónica, México
{rmaceves, mmontesg, villasen}@inaoep.mx

Abstract. One major problem of state-of-the-art Cross Language Question Answering systems is the translation of user questions. This paper proposes combining the potential of multiple translation machines in order to improve the final answering precision. In particular, it presents three different methods for this purpose. The first one focuses on selecting the most fluent translation from a given set; the second one combines the passages recovered by several question translations; finally, the third one constructs a new question reformulation by merging word sequences from different translations. Experimental results demonstrated that the proposed approaches allow reducing the error rates in relation to a monolingual question answering exercise.

1 Introduction

Question Answering (QA) has become a promising research field whose aim is to provide more natural access to the information than traditional document retrieval techniques. In essence, a QA system is a kind of search engine that allows users to pose questions using natural language instead of an artificial query language, and that returns exact answers to the questions instead of a list of entire documents.

QA is a complex task that combines techniques from information retrieval, natural language processing and machine learning. Recent results from the Cross Language Evaluation Forum[1] [6] made evident this complexity showing accuracies from 68.95% (for monolingual French) to 11.5% (for monolingual Portuguese).

On the other hand, Cross Language Question Answering (CLQA) addresses the situation where the questions are formulated in a language different from that of the document collection. In this case, a user can use one language to search information from documents written in other languages. This is useful, because it would be tiresome to write the question over and over again in many languages, and also because many users have a good passive knowledge of several languages, but their active knowledge is more restricted [3].

Evidently, CLQA has many advantages over standard QA. In particular, it allows users to access much more information in an easier and faster way. However, it introduces additional challenges caused by the language barrier.

---

[1] http://clef-qa.itc.it/

A. Gelbukh (Ed.): CICLing 2007, LNCS 4394, pp. 485–493, 2007.

Most current CLQA systems deal with the language barrier problem by translating the questions to the document's language [4, 9, 10, 12, 13]. This solution is very intuitive and seems effective, but it is too sensitive to the translation errors. This effect was noticeable in the QA report from the last CLEF edition [6]. There, the results corresponding to the best system were 67.89% of accuracy for the French monolingual task and 45.26% for the English-French bilingual exercise [6]. These results indicate that the translation errors caused a relative drop in accuracy of about 33%.

Given the great impact of the translation errors in the final answer accuracy, recent CLQA systems apply various techniques in order to reduce the error rates of the translation module. For instance, [5] performs a triangulated translation using English as a pivot language, and [13] translates the question keywords using a bilingual dictionary as well as EuroWordNet. Some other works combine the capacities of several translation machines[2]. In particular, [12] generates a term-by-term translation combining two different translation machines and a dictionary, and [9] constructs an expanded "bag of words" query gathering terms from several question translations as well as their synonyms extracted from EuroWordNet.

In this paper, we propose some new methods to tackle the language barrier problem in CLQA. Similar to previous approaches, these methods also center around the idea of combining the capacities of several translation machines. However, they consider not only the construction of a new query reformulation by gathering terms from several translations, but also the selection of the best translation from a given set and the combination of passages recovered by different question translations. Furthermore, the proposed methods have a great potential to be used in many CLQA scenarios since they do not make use of additional language-dependent resources such dictionaries or ontologies.

The rest of the paper is organized as follows. Section 2 describes the three proposed methods for tackling the language barrier problem in a CLQA application. Section 3 presents the evaluation results. Finally, section 4 gives our conclusions and describes some future work.

2   Proposed Methods

As we mentioned, one major problem in current CLQA systems is the translation of the user questions. In order to reduce the drop in accuracy caused by the translation mistakes, we propose to combine the capacities of multiple translation machines. This idea is mainly supported in the following assumptions:

1. Given that machine translation is a complex task, there is still not available a perfect translation machine.
2. Different translation machines tend to produce –slightly– different and –partially–correct question translations.
3. The more frequent a term is in the set of translations, the more chances that the original word has been translated correctly.

---

[2] Similar ideas have been proved in other fields. For instance, [11] proposes a method that combines several WSD systems by selecting the one best for each specific word.

Based on these assumptions we designed three different methods (or architectures) for CLQA. The first method selects the most fluent translation from a given set, and then delivers it to a monolingual QA system. The second method combines the passages recovered by several question translations in one single set, and then uses these passages to extract the answer to the given question. Finally, the third method constructs a new question reformulation by merging word sequences from different translations, and then sends this new query to a monolingual QA system.

The following subsections describe in detail the proposed methods.

2.1 Method 1: "Selecting the Best Translation"

Figure 1 shows the general scheme of this method. It consists of three basic steps. First, the question is translated to the target language (i.e., the language of the document collection) using a number of translation machines. Second, all translations are evaluated and the best one is selected. Finally, the selected translation is given to a monolingual QA system in order to obtain the desired answer.

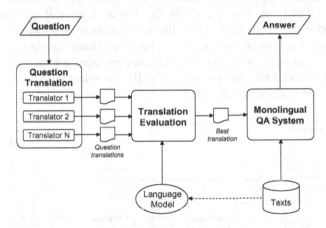

Fig. 1. CLQA Method considering the selection of the best translation

An accepted criterion to evaluate the quality of translations indicates that the most fluent output text corresponds to the best translation. A known mechanism to determine the fluency of a given translation is to measure it pertinence to a predefined language model [1]. The language model judges the probability that a test data –in this case a translation– fits to that language. In our particular case, we propose to measure the pertinence of the translations with respect to the target document collection.

2.1.1 Translation Evaluation

The pertinence of a translation to the target document collection is based on how much it fits in the collection n-gram model. In order to quantify this attribute we apply a general n-gram test on the translation. An n-gram test computes the entropy (or perplexity) of some test data –the question translation– given an *n*-gram model. It is an assessment on how probable is to generate the test data from the *n*-gram model[3]. The entropy is calculated as follows:

$$H = -\frac{1}{Q} \sum_{i=1}^{Q} \log P(w_i | w_{i-1}, w_{i-2}, ..., w_{i-N+1})$$

where w_i is a word in the *n*-gram sequence, $P(w_i/ w_{i-1}, w_{i-2}, ..., w_{i-N+1})$ indicates the probability of observing w_i right after the occurrence of the *n*-gram $w_{i-1}, w_{i-2}, ..., w_{i-N+1}$, Q is the number of words of the test data, and N is the order of the *n*-gram model.

The final score for a translation is expressed by its perplexity, defined as $B = 2^H$. In this case, the lowest perplexity value indicates the most probable expression on the target collection, and therefore, the most pertinent translation.

2.2   Method 2: "Combining Passages from Several Translations"

In order to take advantage of all translations we consider the combination of passages recovered by all of them. Figure 2 shows the general scheme of this method. It considers the following procedures. First, the user question is translated to the target language by several translation machines. Then, each translation is used to retrieve a set of relevant passages. After that, the retrieved passages are combined in order to form one single set of relevant passages. Finally, the selected passages are analyzed and a final question answer is extracted.

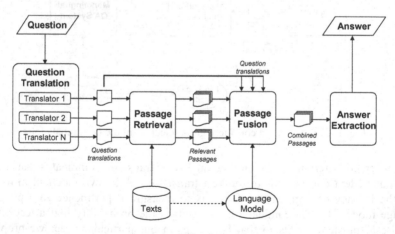

Fig. 2. CLQA Method considering the combination of passages

The main step of this method is the combination of the passages. This combination is based on the pertinence of the translations to the target document collection. This pertinence, as in the previous method, expresses how a given translation fits in the *n*-gram model calculated on the target document collection. The idea is to combine the passages favoring those retrieved by the more pertinent translations.

---

[3] The *n*-gram model was constructed using the method described in [15].

2.2.1 Passage Combination

This module combines the retrieved passages from each translation in one single set. Its purpose is to favor passages recovered by the more pertinent translations. The following formula is used to calculate the number of passages from a given translation that will be included in the combined passage set.

$$E_x = \frac{k}{\displaystyle\sum_{i=1}^{n} \frac{1}{B_i} \times B_x}$$

In this formula E_x indicates the number of selected passages from the translator x, that is, the extension of x in the combined set. B_x is the perplexity of the translator x (refer to section 2.1.1), n is the number of translation machines used in the experiment, and k indicates the number of passages retrieved by each translator as well as the total extension of the combined set[4].

2.3 Method 3: "Constructing a Question Reformulation"

After analyzing several question translations we could notice that (*i*) correct word sequences tend to occur in more than one translation, i.e, they are repeated, and that (*ii*) slightly different translations may contain different correct translations for the same word, i.e, they tend to use some synonyms. Based on these observations we propose to combine several question translations in one single question reformulation. This reformulation contains all words occurring in more than one question translation.

Figure 3 shows the general scheme of this method. It considers three basic steps. First, the user question is translated to the target language by several translation machines. Then, all translations are combined to form a new single question reformulation. Finally, this question reformulation is given to a monolingual QA system in order to obtain the desired answer. The following subsection describes the procedure to combine a set of question translations.

2.3.1 Combining Translations

The combination of translations aims to capture the common words among the different translations and to maintain in some way the relative order of the words in the question reformulation. This idea is different than other previous methods [8, 12] in that it goes beyond the bag-of-words approach, since it considers word sequences as well as it frequency of occurrence.

The procedure to combine the translations is as follows: Given a set of question translations T:

1. *Extract the set of maximal frequent word sequences from T.* A maximal frequent word sequence is a sequence of words that occurs more than a predefined threshold and that is not a subsequence of another frequent sequence.
2. *Select the more frequent sequence as the initial query reformulation.*
3. *Add to the initial query reformulation the content words from other sequences.* These words must not be contained in the initial query reformulation.

---

[4] In the experiments we set $k = 20$, which corresponds to the best performance rate of our monolingual QA system [7].

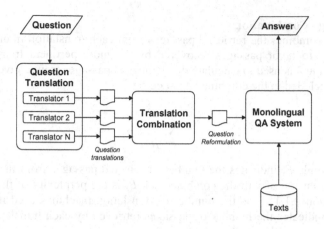

Fig. 3. CLQA Method using a question reformulation

3   Experimental Results

3.1   Experimental Setup

For the experimental evaluation we used a set of 286 factoid questions extracted from the CLEF Multi-Eight corpus as well as the CLEF Spanish document collection consisting of 454,045 news documents.

The evaluation considered three bilingual experiments: English-Spanish, French-Spanish and Italian-Spanish. For translating the questions to Spanish we used three different translation machines[5]: Systran, Worldlingo, Fretranslation.

For the experiments we used the passage retrieval and answer extraction components of the TOVA question answering system [7]. We selected this system because it was one of the best in the Spanish QA task at the 2005 edition of the CLEF. We also used the data-mining tool described in [2] in order to compute the maximal frequent word sequences required by one of the methods. In this case, we established a threshold $\sigma = 2$, which indicated that a word sequence was frequent if it was contained in at least two different translations.

3.2   Results

As we previously mentioned, one major problem of state-of-the-art Cross Language Question Answering systems is the translation of user questions. Several QA reports [6, 14] indicate that the translation errors cause an important drop in accuracy for cross-language tasks with respect to the monolingual exercises. Based on this fact, we evaluated the impact of our methods by measuring the fall of accuracy[6] in the answer extraction caused by the question translation in relation to the Spanish monolingual QA task.

---

[5] www.systranbox.com, www.worldlingo.com, www.freetranslation.com
[6] The accuracy indicates the percentage of correctly answered questions. It is calculated as the radio between the number of found answers and the number of questions.

Table 1 shows the fall of accuracy, indicated as an error rate, corresponding to the three bilingual experiments. In this table, the first three columns indicate some baselines, which correspond to the error rates generated by each translation machine when they were used independently. On the other hand, the last three columns show the error rates obtained when we applied each one of the proposed methods.

Table 1. Error rates with respect to the Spanish monolingual task

	Baselines (a single translation machine)			Our Methods		
	TM1	TM2	TM3	Best Translation	Passages Combination	Query Reformulation
English-Spanish	25%	28%	27%	14%	12%	10%
French- Spanish	28%	30%	28%	17%	16%	15%
Italian- Spanish	30%	45%	41%	41%	24%	13%

The results indicate that our three methods reduced –in the majority of the cases– the fall in accuracy, and produced lower error rates than using one single translation machine. For instance, for the English-Spanish exercise we could reduce the error rate from 25% (corresponding to the best single translation machine) to just 10% using the query reformulation method. For the French-Spanish task, the error rate moved from 28% to 15%, while for the Italian-Spanish we reduced it from 30% to 13%.

It also is important to notice that the worst results correspond to the Italian-Spanish exercise. We believe these results were consequence of the bad quality of the used translators (with error rates from 30-45%). In particular, this situation greatly affects the performance of the best translation method, since no translation fit well to the language model.

Finally, it is also important to point out that the best methods were those that combine the capacities of all translations. Specifically, the query reformulation method produced the best results. We consider this performance is due because it simulates a kind of query expansion, retaining just the most confident words of all translations.

4   Conclusions and Future Work

In this paper we presented three different methods to tackle the language barrier problem in CLQA. These methods consider the selection of the most fluent translation form a given set, the combination of the passages recovered by different question translations, and the construction of a question reformulation by merging word sequences from several translations.

The experiments indicated that the three proposed methods allowed reducing the fall in accuracy, and produced lower error rates than using any translation machine independently. They also gave some evidence about that the best methods were those that combine the capacities of all question translations, namely, the passage combination method and the query reformulation approach. These results confirmed our hypothesis that all translations are partially correct and that using information from all of them allows identifying answers that could not be find using one single question translation. Nevertheless, it is important to emphasize that our conclusions are not completely general, since our results are in some extent dependent to the used QA system, especially to the passage retrieval system, as well as to the target language and the document collection.

As future work we plan to do some additional experiments in order to determine some parameters of the methods. In particular, we plan to: (*i*) use more translation machines in order to determine the number and the quality of the selected translators; (*ii*) experiment with other target languages; and (*iii*) evaluate the performance of the proposed methods when using some other QA systems.

Acknowledgements. This work was done under partial support of CONACYT (Project Grant 43990). We also like to thanks to the CLEF organizing committee as well as to the EFE agency for the resources provided.

References

1. Callison-Burch C., and Flournoy R. A Program for Automatically Selecting the Best Output from Multiple Machine Translation Engines. In Proceedings of the Machine Translation Summit VIII, Santiago de Compostela, Spain, 2001.
2. García-Hernández Rene A., Martínez Trinidad José Francisco, Carrasco-Ochoa Jesús Ariel: A Fast Algorithm to Find All the Maximal Frequent Sequences in a Text. CIARP 2004: 478-486.
3. Gonzalo J. Scenarios for interactive cross-language retrieval systems. Proceedings of the Workshop of Cross-Language Information Retrieval: A Research Roadmap Workshop held at the 25th Annual International ACM SIGIR Conference. Tampere, Finland, 2002.
4. Jijkoun Valentin, Mishne Gilad, Rijke Maarten de, Schlobach Stfan, Ahn David, Muller Karin. The University of Amsterdam at QA@CLEF 2004. In CLEF, editor, Proceedings CLEF-2004 Lecture Notes in Computer Science, pp. 321-324, 2004.
5. Laurent Dominique, Séguela Patrick, and Nègre Sophie. Cross lingual question answering using QRISTAL for CLEF 2005. In Working Notes, CLEF Cross-Language Evaluation Forum, Vienna, Austria. 2005.
6. Magnini B., Giampiccolo Danilo, Forner Pamela, Ayache Christelle, Osenova Petya, Peñas Anselmo, Jijkoun Valentin, Sacaleanu Bogdan, Rocha Paulo, Sutcliffe Richard. Overview of the CLEF 2005 Multilingual Question Answering Track. CLEF 2006, Alicante, España, 2006.
7. Montes-y-Gómez, M., Villaseñor-Pineda, L., Pérez-Coutiño, M., Gómez-Soriano, J. M., Sanchis-Arnal, E. & Rosso, P. INAOE-UPV Joint Participation in CLEF 2005: Experiments in Monolingual Question Answering. CLEF 2005, Vienna, Austria, 2005.
8. Neumann Günter and Sacaleanu Bogdan. DFKI's LT-lab at the CLEF 2005 multiple language question answering track. In Working Notes, CLEF Cross-Language Evaluation Forum, Vienna, Austria. 2005.
9. Pablo-Sánchez César de, González-Ledesma Ana, Martínez-Fernández José Luis, Guirao José Maria, Martinez Paloma, and Moreno Antonio. MIRACLE's 2005 approach to crosslingual question answering. In Working Notes, CLEF Cross- Language Evaluation Forum, Vienna, Austria. 2005.
10. Perret L., "Question answering system for the French language", In CLEF, editor, Proceedings CLEF-2004 Lecture Notes in Computer Science, pp. 295-303.

11. Saarikoski H., Legrand S., Gelbukh A. Defining Classifier Regions for WSD Ensembles Using Word Space Features. MICAI-2006. Lecture Notes in Artificial Intelligence, N 4139, Springer, 2006.
12. Sutcliffe Richard F. E., Mulcahy Michael, Gabbay Igal, O'Gorman Aoife, White Kieran, Slatter Darina: "Cross-Language French-English Question Answering using the DLT System at CLEF 2005" In: Working Notes of the 6th Workshop of the Cross-Language Evaluation Forum, CLEF 2005. Sept. 2005, Wien.
13. Tanev Hristo, Negri Matteo, Magnini Bernardo, and Kouylekov Milen. The DIOGENE question answering system at CLEF-2004. In Working Notes, CLEF Cross-Language Evaluation Forum, pages 325–333, Bath UK. 2004.
14. Vallin A., Giampiccolo D., Aunimo L., Ayache C., Osenova P., Peñas A., de Rijke M., Sacaleanu B., Santos D. & Sutcliffe R. Overview of the CLEF 2005 Multilingual Question Answering Track. CLEF 2005, Vienna, Austria, 2005.
15. Villaseñor-Pineda L., Montes-y-Gómez M., Pérez-Coutiño M. and Vaufreydaz D.. A Corpus Balancing Method for Language Model Construction. Conference on Intelligent Text Processing and Computational Linguistics CICLing-2003, D.F., Mexico, February, 2003. Lecture Notes in Computer Science, vol. 2588, Springer, 2003.

The Negative Effect of Machine Translation on Cross–Lingual Question Answering*

Sergio Ferrández and Antonio Ferrández

Natural Language Processing and Information Systems Group
Department of Software and Computing Systems
University of Alicante, Spain
{sferrandez,antonio}@dlsi.ua.es

Abstract. This paper presents a study of the negative effect of Machine Translation (MT) on the precision of Cross–Lingual Question Answering (CL–QA). For this research, a English–Spanish Question Answering (QA) system is used. Also, the sets of 200 official questions from CLEF 2004 and 2006 are used. The CL experimental evaluation using MT reveals that the precision of the system drops around 30% with regard to the monolingual Spanish task. Our main contribution consists on a taxonomy of the identified errors caused by using MT and how the errors can be overcome by using our proposals. An experimental evaluation proves that our approach performs better than MT tools, at the same time contributing to this CL–QA system being ranked first at English–Spanish QA CLEF 2006.

1   Introduction

At present, the volume of on-line text in natural language in different languages that can be accessed by the users is growing continuously. This fact implies the need for a great number of tools of Information Retrieval (IR) that permit us to carry out multilingual information searches.

Multilingual tasks such as IR and Question Answering (QA) have been recognized as an important issue in the on-line information access, as it was revealed in the the Cross-Language Evaluation Forum (CLEF) 2006 [6].

IR is the science that studies the search for information in documents written in natural language. QA is a more difficult task than IR task. The main aim of a QA system is to localize the correct answer to a question written in natural language in a non-structured collection of documents.

In the Cross-Lingual (CL) environments, the question is formulated in a different language from the one of the documents, which increases the difficulty. The multilingual QA tasks were introduced in the CLEF 2003 [7] for the first time. Since them, most of the CL–QA system uses MT systems to translate the

---

* This research has been partially funded by the Spanish Government under project CICyT number TIC2003-07158-C04-01 and by the European Commission under FP6 project QALL-ME number 033860.

A. Gelbukh (Ed.): CICLing 2007, LNCS 4394, pp. 494–505, 2007.
© Springer-Verlag Berlin Heidelberg 2007

queries into the language of the documents. But, this technique implies a drop around 30% in the precision with regard to the monolingual task.

In this paper, a study of the negative effect of Machine Translation (MT) on the precision of Cross–Lingual Question Answering (CL–QA) is presented, designing a taxonomy of the identified errors caused by MT. Besides, a proposal to overcome these errors is presented which reduces the negative effects of the question translation on the overall accuracy of CL–QA systems.

The rest of the paper is organized as follows: section 2 describes the state of CL-QA systems. Afterwards, an empirical study of the errors of MT is described. And the analysis of the influence of MT errors on CL–QA is shown in section 3. Section 4 presentes our approach for CL-QA that minimices the use of MT. Besides, section 5 presents and discusses the results obtained using all official English questions of QA CLEF 2004 [8] and 2006 [6]. Finally, section 6 details our conclusions and future work.

2   State of the Art

Nowadays, most of the implementations of current CL-QA systems are based on the use of on-line translation services. This fact has been confirmed in the last edition of CLEF 2006 [6].

The precision of CL-QA systems is directly affected by its ability to correctly analyze and translate the question that is received as input. An imperfect or fuzzy translation of the question causes a negative impact on the overall accuracy of the systems. As Moldovan [9] stated, Question Analysis phase is responsible for 36.4% of the total of number of errors in open-domain QA.

Next, we are focusing on the bilingual English–Spanish QA task, because the CL–QA system used for the evaluation works in these languages. Nowadays, at CLEF 2006 [6], three different approaches are used by CL-QA systems in order to solve the bilingual task. The first one [10] uses an automatic MT tool to translate the question into the language in which the documents are written. This strategy is the simplest technique available. In this case, when compared to the Spanish monolingual task, the system loses about 55% of this precision in the CL task.

On the other hand, the system [1] translates entire documents into the language in which the question is formulated. This system uses a statistical MT system that has been trained using the European Parliament Proceedings Parallel Corpus 1996–2003 (EUROPARL).

Finally, the system BRUJA [5] translated the question using different on-line machine translators and some heuristics. This technique consults several web services in order to obtain an acceptable translation.

The previously described strategies are based on the use of MT in order to carry out the bilingual English–Spanish task, and all of them try to correct the translation errors through different heuristics. The low quality of MT provides a load of errors inside all the steps of the localization of the answer. These facts cause an important negative impact on the precision of the systems. And it can be checked on the last edition of CLEF 2006 where the cross lingual system obtains less than 50% of correct answer compared to the monolingual task.

In the next section, a taxonomy of the identified errors caused by MT in CL–QA is shown, and how the errors are overcome using our proposals.

3   Taxonomy of the MT Errors for CL–QA

In this section, our classification of different errors caused by the use of MT is described. The taxonomy is designed using the CLEF 2004 [8] set of 200 English questions, this year the bilingual English–Spanish task was introduced for the first time.

The set of 200 English questions are translated into Spanish using on-line MT services[1]. The errors noticed during the translation process are the following: wrong word–by–word translation, wrong translated sense, wrong syntactic structure, wrong interrogative particle, wrong lexical-syntactic category, unknown words and wrong proper name.

Table 1 shows the seven different types of error that compose our taxonomy, as well as the percentages of appearance in the English questions of CLEF 2004. Next, each type is described in detail as well as the problems that the wrong translations cause in the CL–QA process.

Table 1. Types of translation errors and percentage of appearance on CLEF 2004 set of question

Type of translation error	Percentage
Wrong Word–by–Word Translation	24%
Wrong Translated Sense	21%
Wrong Syntactic Structure	34%
Wrong Interrogative Particle	26%
Wrong Lexical-Syntactic Category	6%
Unknown Words	2.5%
Wrong Proper Name	12.5%

3.1   Wrong Word–by–Word Translation

This kind of error causes a lot of problems during the search of the correct answers in the CL–QA process, since it inserts words in the translation that should not be inserted.

In this type, the MT replaces words in the source language with their equivalent translation into Spanish, when there is not one–to–one correspondence between English language and Spanish language. Table 2 shows an example of this type of wrong translation in the question 002 at CLEF 2004.

---

[1] MT1: http://www.freetranslation.com, MT2: http://www.systransoft.com and MT3: http://babelfish.altavista.com

Table 2. Wrong Word–by–Word Translation

English Question	How much **does** the world population increase each year?
Right Spanish Question	¿Cuánto aumenta la población mundial cada año?
Translation into Spanish	¿Cuánto **hace** el aumento de población de mundo cada año?

In the previous example, the MT system inserts the verb "*hace*" which is not useful to the CL-QA process, this fact introduces a negative effect that does not permit the QA system to find out the answer.

The MT services produces this error in a 24% of the questions.

3.2 Wrong Translated Sense

Some wrong translations are produced when a single word has different senses according to the context in which the word is written. The MT service translates the 21% of the question with at least one wrong word sense. Table 3 shows an example, the question 065 at CLEF 2004 where the word "*sport*" is translated erroneously into the Spanish word "*luce*" (to show off).

Table 3. Wrong Translated sense

English Question	What **sports** building was inaugurated in Buenos Aires in December of 1993?
Right Spanish Question	¿Qué edificio **deportivo** fue inaugurado en Buenos Aires en diciembre de 1993?
Translation into Spanish	¿Qué **luce** edificio se inauguró en Buenos Aires en diciembre de 1993?

Sometimes these errors are able to modify completely the sense of the question and cause a great negative effect in the precision of the CL–QA system.

3.3 Wrong Syntactic Structure

In this case, the wrong translation produces changes in the syntactic structure of the question. This type of our taxonomy causes a lot of errors in the phase of question analysis within the QA process, since this phase is usually based on syntactic analysis. Table 4 shows an example, the question 048 at CLEF 2004 where the structure of the question has been strongly modified.

This kind of translation error is the most common error encountered during translation (34%).

When the CL–QA system is fundamentally based on syntactic analysis of the question and the documents, the changes in the syntactic structure of the

Table 4. Wrong Syntactic Structure

English Question	How many people died in Holland and in Germany during the 1995 floods?
Right Spanish Question	¿Cuántas personas murieron en las inundaciones de Holanda y Alemania en 1995?
Translation into Spanish	¿**Murieron** cuántas personas en Holanda y en Alemania durante las 1995 **inundaciones**?

question influence negatively producing errors that do not permit the system to localice the answers.

In the previous example, a syntactic analysis of the wrong translated question returns an erroneous noun phrase, "*[1995 inundaciones]*", in which the year "*1995*" is tagged as a determinant. The right translation has to obtain two independent noun phrases : "*[1995]*" and "*[inundaciones]*" (floods).

3.4   Wrong Interrogative Particle

A QA system develops two main tasks in the phase of question analysis: 1) the detection of the expected answer type; and 2) the identification of the main syntactic blocks (SB) of the question.

Table 5. Wrong Particle Interrogative

English Question	What is the official German airline called?
Right Spanish Question	¿**Cómo** se llama la aerolínea oficial alemana?
Translation into Spanish	¿**Qué** se llama la linea aérea alemana oficial?

The wrong translation of the particle interrogative of the question causes a wrong detection of the expected answer type. This fact does not allow the QA system to carry out a correct run. The MT tool carries out this type of error in the 26% of the questions. In all these question, the detection of the expected answer type is, in most cases, erroneous.

In table 5, the question 025 at CLEF 2004 is shown, where the MT services makes a mistake in the particle interrogative.

3.5   Wrong Lexical-Syntactic Category

This kind of problem causes wrong translations, such as nouns that are translated into verbs. In this type of situations, the extraction of the correct answer is impossible to carry out. Table 6 describes an example, the question 092 at CLEF 2004 where the noun "*war*" is translated into the verb "*Guerreó*" (to fight).

Table 6. Wrong lexical-syntactic category

English Question	When did the Chaco War occur?
Right Spanish Question	¿Cuándo fue la **Guerra** del Chaco?
Translation into Spanish	¿Cuándo **Guerreó** el Chaco ocurre?

3.6 Unknown Words

In these cases, the MT service does not know the translation of some words. These words, because they are not translated, are not useful for CL–QA purposes. As it is shown in table 7, in the question 059 at CLEF 2004 the word "*odourless*" is unknown by the MT service.

Table 7. Unknown Words

English Question	Name an **odourless** and tasteless liquid.
Right Spanish Question	Cite un **líquido** inodoro e insípido.
Translation into Spanish	Denomine un **odourless** y líquido insípido.

3.7 Wrong Proper Name

This kind of wrong translations is the a typical error that encountered during translation using the MT service.

These problems do not allow the QA system to be able to find out the correct solution. For example, in the question 112 at CLEF 2004 (see table 8), the proper name "*Bill*" is translated into the common noun "*Cuenta*" (bill). This fact does not permit to know who is *Bill Clinton*.

Table 8. Wrong Proper Name

English Question	Who is Bill Clinton?
Right Spanish Question	¿Quién es **Bill** Clinton?
Translation into Spanish	¿Quién es **Cuenta** Clinton?

4 Our Approach to CL–QA

In this section, our approach to open domain CL-QA system called BRILI [2] is detailed. BRILI (Spanish acronym for "Question Answering using Inter Lingual

Index module") introduces two improvements that alleviate the negative effect produced by MT:

- Unlike the current bilingual English–Spanish QA systems, the question analysis is developed in the original language without any translation. The system develops two main tasks in the phase of question analysis:

  1) the detection of the expected answer type, the system detects the type of information that the answer has to satisfy to be a candidate of an answer (proper name, quantity, date, ...).

  2) the identification of the main SB of the question. The system extracts the SB that are necessary to find the answers.

- The system considers more than only one translation per word by means of using the different synsets of each word in the Inter Lingual Index (ILI) Module of EuroWordNet (EWN).

Next, using the previous examples of wrong translations, the application of our approach to overcome the problems is described.

4.1   Solution to Wrong Word–by–Word Translation

In this problem, the MT service inserts words in the translation that should not be inserted. Our method resolves this mistake by making an analysis of the question in the original language. Afterwards, the system choose the SB that must be translated and that are useful to the extraction of the answer. In our case, these SB are referenced using the ILI.

- **English Question:** *How much **does** the world population increase each year?*
- **Wrong Translation:** *¿Cuánto **hace** el aumento de población de mundo cada año?*
- **SBs:**

```
[world population]
[to increase]
[each year]
```

- **Keywords to be referenced using ILI:** world population increase each year

In the previous example, the words "*How much does*" are discarded to the extraction of the answer phase in the QA process.

4.2   Solution to Wrong Translated Sense

This kind of error is produced when a single word has different senses according to the context in which the word is written. Our approach solves this handicap considering more than only one translation per word by means of using the different synsets of each word in the ILI module of EWN.

- **English Question:** *What **sports** building was inaugurated in Buenos Aires in December of 1993?*
- **Wrong Translation:** *¿Qué **luce** edificio se inauguró en Buenos Aires en diciembre de 1993?*
- **References of the word "sport" using ILI:** *deporte deporte* coña socarronería mucación mutante deportista

In the previous example, the method finds more than one Spanish equivalents for the word *"sport"*. Each ILI synsets is appropriately weighted by Word Sense Disambiguation (WSD) mechanisms [4]. In this case, the most valuated Spanish word would be *"deporte"*.

4.3 Solution to Wrong Syntactic Structure

In this case, the MT tool produces changes in the syntactic structure of the question that cause errors within the question analysis phase. This mistake is solved by our method by making an analysis of the question in the original language without any translation. This behavior is shown in the next example:

- **English Question:** *How many people died in Holland and in Germany during the 1995 floods?*
- **Wrong Translation:** *¿**Murieron** cuántas personas en Holanda y en Alemania durante las 1995 **inundaciones**?*
- **SBs:**

> [people]
> [to die]
> [in Holland and in Germany during the 1995 floods]

- **Keywords to be referenced using ILI:** people die Holland Germany floods

4.4 Solution to Wrong Interrogative Particle

The wrong translation of the particle interrogative of the question causes a wrong detection of the expected answer type. Our approach resolves this problem applying the syntactic patterns that determine the expected answer type to the question in the original language without any translation.

- **English Question:** *What is the official German airline called?*
- **Wrong Translation:** *¿**Qué** se llama la línea aérea alemana oficial?*
- **English Pattern:**

> [WHAT] [TO BE] [AIRLINE]

- **Expected answer type:** group

4.5 Solution to Wrong Lexical-Syntactic Category

This kind of error causes wrong translations when, for example nouns are translated into verbs. Our method uses ILI to reference nouns and verbs independently, this strategy is shown in the next example.

- **English Question:** *When did the Chaco War occur?*
- **Wrong Translation:** *¿Cuándo Guerreó el Chaco ocurre?*
- **References of the noun "war" using ILI:** *guerra*
- **References of the verb "to occur" using ILI:** acaecer tener-lugar suceder pasar ocurrir

4.6   Solution to Unknown Words

In these cases, the MT service does not know the translation of some words. Our technique minimices this handicap by using the ILI module.

On the other hand, the words that are not in EWN are translated using an on-line Spanish Dictionary[2]. Furthermore, our method uses gazetteers of organizations and places in order to translate words that are not linked using the ILI module.

In the next question, it is shown an example of this solution:

- **English Question:** *Name an odourless and tasteless liquid.*
- **Wrong Translation:** *Denomine un odourless y líquido insípido.*
- **References of the word "odourless" using ILI:** -
- **Translated word using an on-line Spanish Dictionary:** inodoro

4.7   Solution to Wrong Proper Name

These wrong translations do not allow the QA system to be able to find out correct solutions. Our method, in order to decrease the effect of incorrect translation of the proper names, the achieved matches using these words in the search of the answer are realized using the translated word and the original word of the question. The found matches using the original English word are valuated a 20% less.

This strategy is shown in the next example:

- **English Question:** *Who is Bill Clinton?*
- **Wrong Translation:** *¿Quién es Cuenta Clinton?*
- **References of the words "Bill Clinton" using ILI:** cartel Clinton
- **SBs used to the extraction of the answer:**

```
[cartel Clinton]
[Bill Clinton]
```

5   Evaluation

In this section, the experiments that prove the improvement of our method are shown. The evaluation has been carried out using a CL–QA system that is based on our approach and it has been compared with the QA system using the MT[3] service.

---

[2] http://www.wordreference.com
[3] http://www.freetranslation.com/

The main aim of this section is to value our CL–QA strategy. In order to make this, the CLEF 2004 and 2006 sets of 200 English question and the EFE 1994–1995 Spanish corpora are used.

Table 9 shows the achieved experiments, where the column 4 details the improvement in relation to the using of MT and in the case of the others participants at CLEF 2006, the column 4 shows the decrement in relation to our method. Besides, the obtained precision[4] for each dataset is shown in the column 3.

Also, in table 9, we show the precision of the monolingual Spanish task of the used QA system (see rows 1 and 4) and the precision of the currents participants at CLEF 2006 (see rows 7, 8 and 9).

Table 9. Evaluation

	Approach	Dataset	Precission (%)	Improvement (%)
		CLEF 2004		
1	Spanish QA system	200 Spanish questions	38.5	+28.44
2	Our method + QA system	200 English questions	34	+19.12
3	MT + QA system	200 English questions	27.5	−
		CLEF 2006		
4	Spanish QA system	200 Spanish questions	36	+52.7
5	Our method + QA system	200 English questions	20.50	+17.07
6	MT + QA system	200 English questions	17	−
	Others participants at	**CLEF 2006**[6]		Decrement (%)
7	QA system [10]	200 English questions	6	−70.73
8	QA system [1]	200 English questions	19	−7.31
9	QA system [5]	200 English questions	19.5	−4.87

The experimental evaluation shows up the negative effect of the MT services on CL–QA. In the tests using the MT tool, the errors produced by the question translation (see rows 3 and 6) generate worse results than using our method (see rows 2 and 5: +19.12% at CLEF 2004 and +17.07% at CLEF 2006). Besides, our approach obtains better results than other participants at CLEF 2006 (see the decrement in relation to our method in rows 7, 8 and 9).

These experiments prove that our approach obtains better results than using MT (where the lost of precision in the CL task is around 29% at CLEF 2004 and 50% ant CLEF 2006) and other current bilingual English–Spanish QA systems. Furthermore, this affirmation is corroborated checking the official results on the last edition of CLEF 2006 [6] where our method [3] has being ranked first at the bilingual English–Spanish QA task.

---

[4] Correct answers return on the first place.

6   Conclusion and Future Work

This paper presents a taxonomy of the seven identified errors caused using MT services and how the errors can be overcome using our proposals in order to solve QA task in cross lingual environments.

Our method carries out two tasks reducing the negative effect that is inserted by the MT services. Our approach to CL–QA tasks carries out the question analysis in the original language of the question without any translation. Besides, more than one translation per word is considered by means of using the different synsets of each word in the ILI module of EuroWordNet.

The tests on the official CLEF set of English questions prove that our approach generates better results than using MT (+19.12% at CLEF 2004 and +17.07% at CLEF 2006) and than other current bilingual QA systems [6].

Further work will study the possibility to take into account a Name Entity Recognition to detect proper names that will not be translated in the question. For instance, using the question 059 at CLEF 2006, *What is Deep Blue?*, the words "Deep Blue" should not be translated.

Furthermore, the gazetteers of organizations and places will be extended using multilingual knowledge of extracted from Wikipedia[5] that is a Web-based free-content multilingual encyclopedia project.

References

1. M. Bowden, M. Olteanu, P. Suriyentrakorn, J. Clark, and D. Moldovan. LCC's PowerAnswer at QA@CLEF 2006. *In Workshop of Cross-Language Evaluation Forum (CLEF)*, September 2006.
2. S. Ferrández, A. Ferrández, S. Roger, P. López-Moreno, and J. Peral. BRILI, an English-Spanish Question Answering System. *Proceedings of the International Multiconference on Computer Science and Information Technology. ISSN 1896-7094*, 1:23–29, November 2006.
3. S. Ferrández, P.López-Moreno, S. Roger, A. Ferrández, J. Peral, X. Alavarado, E. Noguera, and F. Llopis. AliQAn and BRILI QA System at CLEF-2006. *In Workshop of Cross-Language Evaluation Forum (CLEF)*, 2006.
4. S. Ferrández, S. Roger, A. Ferrández, A. Aguilar, and P. López-Moreno. A new proposal of Word Sense Disambiguation for nouns on a Question Answering System. *Advances in Natural Language Processing. Research in Computing Science. ISSN: 1665-9899*, 18:83–92, February 2006.
5. M.A. García-Cumbreres, L.A. Ureña-López, F. Martínez-Santiago, and J.M. Perea-Ortega. BRUJA System. The University of Jaén at the Spanish task of CLEFQA 2006. *In Workshop of Cross-Language Evaluation Forum (CLEF)*, September 2006.
6. B. Magnini, D. Giampiccolo, P. Forner, C. Ayache, V. Jijkoun, P. Osevona, A. Peñas, , P. Rocha, B. Sacaleanu, and R. Sutcliffe. Overview of the CLEF 2006 Multilingual Question Answering Track. *In Workshop of Cross-Language Evaluation Forum (CLEF)*, September 2006.

---

[5] http://www.wikipedia.org/

7. B. Magnini, S. Romagnoli, A. Vallin, J. Herrera, A. Peñas, V. Peinado, F. Verdejo, and M. Rijke. The Multiple Language Question Answering Track at CLEF 2003. *Comparative Evaluation of Multilingual Information Access Systems: 4th Workshop of the Cross-Language Evaluation Forum, CLEF, Trondheim, Norway, August 21-22, 2003, Revised Selected Papers. Lecture Notes in Computer Science*, 2003.
8. B. Magnini, A. Vallin, C. Ayache ang G. Erbach, A. Peñas, M. Rijke, P. Rocha, K. Simov, and R. Sutcliffe. Overview of the CLEF 2004 Multilingual Question Answering Track. *Comparative Evaluation of Multilingual Information Access Systems: 5th Workshop of the Cross-Language Evaluation Forum, CLEF, Trondheim, Norway, August 21-22, 2003, Revised Selected Papers. Lecture Notes in Computer Science*, 2004.
9. D.I. Moldovan, M. Pasca, S.M. Harabagiu, and M. Surdeanu. Performance issues and error analysis in an open-domain question answering system. *ACM Trans. Inf. Syst*, 21:133–154, 2003.
10. E.W.D. Whittaker, J.R. Novak, P. Chatain, P.R. Dixon, M.H. Heie, and S. Furui. CLEF2005 Question Answering Experiments at Tokyo Institute of Technology. *In Workshop of Cross-Language Evaluation Forum (CLEF)*, September 2006.

Using Clustering Approaches to Open-Domain Question Answering

Youzheng Wu[1,2], Hideki Kashioka[1], and Jun Zhao[2]

[1] NiCT-ATR 2-2-2 Hikaridai "Keihanna Science City" Kyoto 619-0288 Japan
{youzheng.wu, hideki.kashioka}@atr.jp
[2] NLPR CASIA No.95 Zhongguancun East Road Beijing 100080 China
jzhao@nlpr.ia.ac.cn

Abstract. This paper presents two novel clustering approaches and their application to open-domain question answering. The *One-Sentence-Multi-Topic* clustering approach is first presented, which clusters sentences to improve the language model for retrieving sentences. Second, regarding each cluster in the results for *One-Sentence-Multi-Topic* clustering as aligned sentences, we present a pattern-similarity-based clustering approach that automatically learns syntactic answer patterns to answer selection through *vertical* and *horizontal clustering*. Our experiments on Chinese question answering demonstrates that *One-Sentence-Multi-Topic* clustering is much better than K-Means and is comparable to PLSI when used in sentence clustering of question answering. Similarly, the pattern-similarity-based clustering also proved to be efficient in learning syntactic answer patterns, the absolute improvement in syntactic pattern-based answer extraction over retrieval-based answer extraction is about 9%.

1 Introduction

Open-domain question answering (QA) returns the exact answer to a natural language question, which is identified from a large collection of documents. The typical pipeline architecture consists of a question analyzer, a relevant passages/sentences retriever, an answer candidate extractor and an exact answer selector. Each of these components plays a very important role in open-domain QA. Most of the recent QA approaches have adopted semantic taggers, WordNet, parsers, ontologies and hand-tagged corpora to pinpoint answers [1, 2, 3, 4].

Compared with conventional document retrieval, question answering has various unique characteristics. For instance, it is difficult for traditional document retrieval to identify the user's exact intentions, while intention analysis is practical for open-domain question answering. Given the query {发明/invent, 电话/telephone}, the search engine cannot identify what the required information is that the user wants to know. However, when given the question {谁发明了电话? /who invented telephone?}, it is easy for QA to identify that the user is searching for the person who invented telephone, but not other information about the question. In fact, most of the components of QA can benefit from such distinct characteristics. This paper mainly focuses on the researches conducted on

A. Gelbukh (Ed.): CICLing 2007, LNCS 4394, pp. 506–517, 2007.
© Springer-Verlag Berlin Heidelberg 2007

mining these characteristics to improve the overall performance of sentence retrieval and the answer selector in question answering.

For sentence retriever, a novel sentence-clustering approach called the *One-Sentence-Multi-Topic* is presented, which only utilizes the results obtained from the question analyzer. The basic idea is to identify the topics of sentences according to *candidate answers*, and then organize the sentences into corresponding clusters according to these candidates. *In other words, a particular type of entity is expected for each question, and every special entity of that type found in a retrieved sentence is regarded as a cluster/topic.* It's to note that cluster and topic have the same meaning in this paper and can be interchanged. Obviously, *One-Sentence-Multi-Topic* clustering is more adaptive for various questions. Based on sentence clustering, we adopted a cluster-based language model to retrieve sentences in open-domain question answering, which involved incorporating the topics of sentences into the language model to improve it for retrieving sentences.

For answer selector, a novel pattern-similarity-based clustering approach is presented to learn the syntactic answer patterns of all types of questions from the Web. Our approach is a kind of unsupervised machine learning because no <question, answer> seeds are needed as the seeds for learning. The main idea can be summarized as follows. Given two or more questions for each type of question, the approach can automatically learn the corresponding answer patterns from the Web through *web retrieval, sentence clustering, pattern extraction, vertical clustering* and *horizontal clustering*. In order to evaluate the learned syntactic answer patterns, we apply them to the answer extraction module of open-domain question answering.

2 Sentence Clustering for Cluster-Based Language Model

Many approaches to retrieving sentences in open-domain question answering have recently been presented. For example, Ittycheriah and Roukos [4] presented the vector space model. Emmanuel et al. [5] presented the language model, and Murdock and Croft [6] presented the translation model. However, the translation model is limited because it is difficult to obtain a training corpus. Compared to the vector space model, the language model is theoretically attractive and a potentially very effective probabilistic framework for researching information retrieval problems [7].

However, the language model for information retrieval is not yet mature and suffers from numerous complicated problems that remain unsolved. One of the main problems with the language model is that each document model (estimated from each document) is interpolated with the same collection model (estimated from the whole collection) through a unified parameter. Therefore, it does not make any one particular document more probable than any other, on the condition that no document originally contains the query term. In other words, if a document is relevant, but does not contain the query term, it is still no more probable, even though it may be topically related. This paper presents a cluster-based language model for sentence retrieval in question answering to overcome the disadvantages of the language model.

2.1 Main Idea

The main idea behind the cluster-based language model for sentence retrieval is to group the retrieved sentences into several clusters (called sentence clustering), integrate the topics of sentences into the language model through the aspect model, and combine sentence model $p_{ML}(w \mid S)$, cluster model $p_{ML}(w \mid T)$, and collection model $p_{ML}(w \mid C)$ into a mixed model. The idea can be formulated as Eq. (1).

$$p(w \mid S) = a \times p_{ML}(w \mid S) + (1-a) \times \big(\beta \times p_{ML}(w \mid T) + (1-\beta) \times p_{ML}(w \mid C)\big), \quad (1)$$

where $p_{ML}(w \mid S)$ and $p_{ML}(w \mid C)$ can be estimated by maximum likelihood. $p_{ML}(w \mid T)$ is in the form of the term distribution over the topic, associated with the distribution of topics over the sentence, which can be expressed by Eq. (2).

$$p_{ML}(w \mid T) = \sum_{t \in T} p(w \mid t) p(t \mid S), \quad (2)$$

where T is the set of clusters/topics and $p(t \mid S)$ is the topic sentence distribution, which means the distribution of the topic over the sentence. $p(w \mid t)$ is the term topic distribution, which means the term distribution over the topics.

The topic-related sentences to build the cluster model $p_{ML}(w \mid T)$ should be grouped into corresponding clusters to estimate the probabilities of $p(t \mid S)$ and $p(w \mid t)$. However, conventional clustering approaches like K-Means are not suitable for clustering sentences because the sentences are too short and they have too few features to cluster them. This paper presents a novel sentence-clustering approach called the *One-Sentence-Multi-Topic* to resolve this problem,.

2.2 *One-Sentence-Multi-Topic*

The principle of *One-Sentence-Multi-Topic* clustering can be explained using the following example. The retrieved sentences and the candidate answers for question Q1 {谁发明了电话？/who invented telephone?} are listed in Table 1.

Table 1. Sentences and Corresponding Candidate Answers

ID	Sentences	Candidate Answers
S1	1876年3月10日贝尔发明电话。/Bell invented telephone on Oct. 3rd, 1876.	贝尔/Bell
S2	西门子发明了电机，贝尔发明电话，爱迪生发明电灯。/ Bell, Siemens, and Edison invented telephone, electromotor and electric light respectively.	西门子/ Siemens 贝尔/Bell 爱迪生/ Edison
S3	最近，移动电话之父库珀再次成为公众焦点。/The public has recently paid a great deal of attention to Cooper who is the father of the cell phone.	库珀/Cooper
S4	1876年，贝尔发明了电话。/In 1876, Bell invented telephone.	贝尔/Bell
S5	接着，1876年，美国科学家贝尔发明了电话；1879年美国科学家爱迪生发明了电灯。/Subsequently, American scientist Bell invented phone in 1876; Edison invented electric light in 1879.	贝尔/Bell 爱迪生/Edison
S6	1876年3月7日，贝尔成为电话发明的专利人。/On March 7th, 1876, Bell became the patentee of telephone.	贝尔/Bell
S7	贝尔不仅发明了电话，还成功地建立了自己的公司推广电话。/Bell not only invented telephone, but also established his own company to spread his invention.	贝尔/Bell

Table 1. (*continued*)

S8	在首只移动电话投入使用30年以后，其发明人库珀仍梦想着未来电话技术实现之日到来。/Thirty years after the invention of the first mobile phone, Cooper still anticipated when the future phone's technology would be implemented.	库珀/Cooper
S9	库珀表示，消费者采纳移动电话的速度之快令他意外，但移动电话的普及率还没有达到无所不在，这让他有些失望。/Cooper said, he was surprised at the speed that the consumers had switched to mobile phones; but the popularity of mobile phone is not ubiquitous, which disappointed him a little.	库珀/Cooper
S10	英国发明家斯蒂芬将移动电话的所有电子元件设计在一张纸一样厚薄的芯片上。/English inventor Stephen designed the paper-clicked CMOS chip, which included all electronic components.	斯蒂芬/Stephen

One-Sentence-Multi-Topic clustering will organize the above sentences into their corresponding clusters according to the candidate answers, which are, {贝尔/Bell, 西门子/Siemens, 爱迪生/Edison, 库珀/Cooper, and 斯蒂芬/Stephen}. Here, the candidate answers can also be regarded as the names of the clusters. The principle of *One-Sentence-Multi-Topic* can be summarized as follows.

1. *If a sentence includes M different candidate answers, then the sentence consists of M different topics.* For example, sentence S5 in Table 1 includes two topics, the names of the topics are 贝尔/Bell and 爱迪生/Edison.
2. *Different sentences have the same topic if their candidate answers are the same.* For example, sentences S4 and S5 in Table 1 have the same topic name of 贝尔/Bell.

The sentence clustering results in Table 1 based on *One-Sentence-Multi-Topic* clustering are listed in Table 2.

Table 2. Results of Sentence Clustering

Names of Topics	Sentence IDs	Names of Topics	Sentence IDs
贝尔/Bell	S1 S2 S4 S5 S6 S7 S8	库珀/Cooper	S3 S8 S9
西门子/Siemens	S2	斯蒂芬/Stephen	S10
爱迪生/Edison	S2 S5		

After sentence clustering, $p(w|t)$ and $p(t|S)$ can be estimated with Eq. (3) and (4).

$$p(w|t) = \frac{n(w,t)}{\sum_{w'} n(w',t)} \text{ and} \tag{3}$$

$$p(t|S) = \frac{1/kl_{st}}{\sum_{i=1}^{k}(1/kl_{st})} \qquad kl_{st} = KL(s||t) = \sum_{w} p_{ML}(w|s) \times log \frac{p_{ML}(w|s)}{p_{ML}(w|t)}, \tag{4}$$

where kl_{st} is the Kullback-Leibler divergence between a sentence with a cluster/topic, and k denotes the number of clusters/topics.

2.3 Experiments with Sentence Retrieval

Research on Chinese open-domain question answering, however, is still at an early stage. And there has also been no public platform for evaluating Chinese open-domain question answering. In this paper, we use the evaluation environment presented by Wu et al. [12] which is similar to the TREC question answering track [8]. The documents collection is about 1.8 Gb, which was downloaded from the Web, and 7050 Chinese testing questions were collected via four different approaches. The style of the questions is almost the same as the TREC QA-style, except all questions are written in Chinese.

We randomly select 807 testing questions for this experiment that are fact-based, short-answer questions. Moreover, the answers to all testing questions are named entities identified by Wu et al. [13]. Table 3 shows the details. Note that, LOC, ORG, PER, NUM, and TIM denote the questions whose answer types are location, organization, person, number and time respectively. SUM means all question types.

The sentence retrieval system returns a ranked list of the sentences for each testing question, and is strictly evaluated using the mean reciprocal rank (MRR) [8].

Table 3. Distribution of Testing Questions

PER	LOC	ORG	TIM	NUM	SUM
165	311	28	168	135	807

2.3.1 Cluster-Based Language Model for Sentence Retrieval

The experimental results for the cluster-based language model based on the *One-Sentence-Multi-Topic* are shown in Table 4 and the relative improvements over the baseline system are listed in the brackets. Here, the baseline system means the standard language model for sentence retrieval.

Table 4. Cluster-based Language Model Based on *One-Sentence-Multi-Topic*

	PER	LOC	ORG	TIM	NUM	SUM
MRR1	60.61%	49.20%	53.57	53.57	45.19	51.92
	(+5.24%)	(+7.75%)	(+36.4%)	(+4.65%)	(+0.00%)	(+5.81%)
MRR5	67.45%	57.70%	59.76%	61.68%	55.51%	59.54%
	(+2.68%)	(+5.79%)	(+17.2%)	(+0.31%)	(+4.22%)	(+2.78%)
MRR20	68.58%	59.44%	59.87%	62.07%	54.33%	61.02%
	(+2.91%)	(+5.54%)	(+16.2%)	(-0.43%)	(-0.51%)	(+2.92%)

From Table 4, we can find that integrating the clusters/topics of the sentence into the language model can improve the performance of sentence retrieval. For example, the relative improvements in *MRR1*, *MRR5* and *MRR20* for all types of questions are 5.81%, 2.78% and 2.92%, respectively. The experiment reveals that the cluster-based language model based on the *One-Sentence-Multi-Topic* effectively retrieves sentences in Chinese open-domain question answering.

2.3.2 Comparison with PLSI and K-Means

As we know, PLSI and K-Means clustering approaches can also be used in sentence clustering. Therefore, in this section, the comparative experiments will be conducted to compare the cluster-based language model based on PLSI and K-Means with that based on the proposed approach, i.e., the *One-Sentence-Multi-Topic*. Table 5 gives the performance of the cluster-based language model based on PLSI and K-Means.

Table 5. Cluster-based Language Model Based on PLSI and K-Means

		PER	LOC	ORG	TIM	NUM	SUM
PLSI	*MRR1*	60.61%	47.91%	39.29%	50.00%	47.01%	*50.62%*
	MRR5	67.30%	56.16%	51.01%	60.42%	54.34%	*59.00%*
	MRR20	68.32%	57.98%	52.05%	61.55%	55.64%	*60.35%*
K-Means	*MRR1*	55.15%	42.44%	39.29%	47.62%	42.93%	*46.03%*
	MRR5	63.12%	51.60%	49.88%	58.01%	51.75%	*55.20%*
	MRR20	64.25%	53.68%	50.33%	59.02%	52.76%	*56.63%*

Comparing Table 5 with Table 4, we can find that the differences between the *One-Sentence-Multi-Topic* and PLSI are not significant. However, the *One-Sentence-Multi-Topic* is much better than the K-Means, the relative improvements in *MRR1*, *MRR5* and *MRR20* over K-Means are 12.8%, 7.86%, and 8.23% respectively.

3 Pattern-Similarity-Based Clustering to Learn Answer Patterns

As the same meaning in natural language, can often be expressed in various ways, mismatches between question and answer-bearing sentences are very common. Open-domain question answering should be able to deal with this flexibility and diversity in natural language.

One solution is to parse the question and the answer-bearing sentences into semantic representations, and semantically match them to find the answer. However, many techniques for natural language processing are still in their early stages. It is challenging to conduct deep linguistic processing and deal with the flexibility and the diversity in natural language. In fact, producing presentations of the question semantics and answer-bearing sentence semantics, and conducting semantically matching is not the only alternative. Surface text analysis like pattern-based approach can also be used to solve the problems and many English question answering systems [9, 10, 11] have obtained the surprising performances in TREC using the pattern-based approach. We also apply a pattern-based approach to tackle the obstacles in Chinese open-domain question answering.

The focus of the pattern-based techniques is to obtain the answer patterns for various types of questions and numerous supervised machine learning approaches have been presented [3, 9, 10, 11], which are heavily dependent on <question, answer> training seeds. In order to improve the recall of the supervised approaches, all forms of the answer to the question should be supplied. However, this is difficult because of the diversity in answer. For instance, the answer to the question "where was Mao Zedong born?" could be 湖南/Hunan, "湖南省/Hunan Province", 韶山/Shaoshan, "韶山冲/Shaoshan Chong", "韶山市上屋场/Shangwu Chang, Shaoshan City", etc. In this case, if only one of the <question, answer> seeds is provided to the approaches, the answer patterns that only appear in the other <question answer> seeds will be lost, and thus the recall of the supervised approaches will be adversely influenced. To overcome the disadvantages of the supervised approaches, we present a novel pattern-similarity-based clustering to automatically learn answer patterns.

3.1   Architecture for Answer Pattern Learning

The architecture for the proposed approach consists of nine steps, *query term extraction and classification, query expansion, web retrieval, sentence splitting and retrieval, sentence clustering, pattern extraction, vertical clustering, horizontal clustering,* and *pattern evaluation*. Specifically, the *query term extraction and classification module* segments the question, extracts query terms, and classifies the terms into two types, *q_focus* and *q_i*. Here, *q_focus* means the key phrase or word representing the object the question is asking about, and *q_i* means the other terms in the question. The *query expansion module*, the *web retrieval module*, and the *sentence splitter and retrieval module* are similar to the approaches by Ravichandran et al. [3] and Du et al. [11]. The *sentence clustering module, pattern extraction module, vertical clustering module, horizontal clustering modules* are the kernel modules in our approach and will be explained in detail in sections 3.2~3.4 respectively. The *pattern evaluation module* is also the same as the approach in Ravichandran et al. [3].

3.2   Sentence Clustering and Pattern Extraction

Collecting aligned sentences is the first step in learning answer patterns to the questions. Most current approaches have built aligned sentences from retrieved sentences according to <question, answer> training seeds. In this paper, aligned sentences are collected with the *One-Sentence-Multi-Topic* mentioned in section 2.2. In other words, each cluster in the results for *One-Sentence-Multi-Topic* sentence clustering is regarded as aligned sentences.

When aligned sentences are available, the patterns can be extracted by finding the shortest path between the anchors in the sentences. Here, *q_focus* terms and candidate answers serve as anchors, and dependency syntactic patterns are extracted. To extract dependency syntactic patterns, sentences are parsed using a dependency parser [14] which was reported to achieve about 80% precision.

The process of extracting syntactic patterns is similar to those in [3] and [11]. Fig.1 gives an example of extracting dependency syntactic pattern. In Fig.1, the *q_focus* term "悲惨世界/Les Miserables" and the candidate answer 雨果/Hugo serve as anchors, the shortest dependency structure between the anchors such as "悲惨世界 /Les Miserables ← 是/is → 代表作/representative work → 雨果/Hugo" is finally converted into the syntactic pattern "*q_focus* ← 是/is → 代表作/representative work → *answer*" where *q_focus* and *answer* are slots to fill in. After *sentence clustering* and *pattern extraction*, the pattern clusters are obtained for each question.

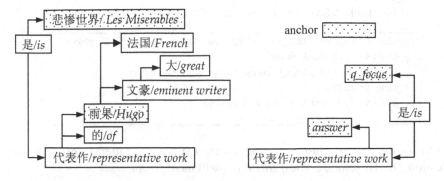

Fig. 1. Example of Syntactic Pattern Extraction

3.3 Vertical Clustering

Because the answers to the question may be multiform, some of the pattern clusters are answer patterns corresponding to the question and should be merged into a cluster to improve the recall of the learning approach. In supervised learning approaches, a user should provide as many forms of answer as possible to resolve diversity in the answer. However, there is no need to provide the answer to the question with the unsupervised learning approach. *Vertical clustering* is used to identify various forms of the answers. Because clustering is conducted within the pattern clusters of a question, we call it *vertical clustering*.

[*Vertical clustering*]: *If some pattern clusters correspond to answer patterns, then their similarities are comparatively high. If the similarities are higher than threshold V1, they should be grouped. Similarities with vertical clustering can be estimated with Eq. (5).*

$$sim\left(C_i, C_j\right) = \sum sim\left(C_{im}, C_{jn}\right) \qquad sim\left(C_{im}, C_{jn}\right) = \begin{cases} 1 & if \quad C_{im} = C_{jn}, \\ 0 & else \end{cases} \qquad (5)$$

where C_i represents the *i-th* pattern cluster, C_j represents the *j-th* pattern-cluster. C_{im} represents the *m-th* pattern in the *i-th* cluster, and C_{jn} represents the *n-th* pattern in the *j-th* cluster.

For instance, Tables 6 and 7 list some patterns in pattern clusters C_i and C_j of question Q2 { 《悲惨世界》的作者是谁？/who is the author of Les Miserables?}.

Table 6. Some Patterns in Pattern Cluster C_i from Question Q2

< PatternClusterNo> 雨果/Hugo </ PatternClusterNo>

q_focus ← *answer*

q_focus ← 是/is → 代表作/representative work → *answer*

q_focus ← 有/has → 作品/work → *answer*

q_focus ← 改编/adapted → 由/from → 名著/masterpiece → *answer*

q_focus ← 是/is → 作品/work → *answer*

q_focus ← 作品/work → *answer*

......

Table 7. Some Patterns in Pattern Cluster C_j from Question $Q2$

<PatternClusterNo > 维克多·雨果/Victor Hugo</ PatternClusterNo>
q_focus ← 完成/finish → *answer*
q_focus ← 是/is → 代表作/representative work → *answer*
q_focus ← *answer*
q_focus ← 有/has → 作品/work → *answer*
......

Obviously, pattern clusters C_i and C_j are the answer patterns corresponding to question $Q2$. Therefore, *vertical clustering* will merge them.

3.4 Horizontal Clustering

Because the answer patterns corresponding to the question type is still in the dark after *vertical clustering*, *horizontal clustering* is done to identify the answer pattern cluster of the question type. *Horizontal clustering* is conducted between the pattern clusters of different questions.

[*Horizontal clustering*]: *If the similarities between a pattern cluster of question A and a pattern cluster of question B are higher than threshold H1, we should also group them. After vertical and horizontal clustering, the pattern cluster that is composed of the most original pattern clusters (before vertical and horizontal clustering) is the answer pattern corresponding to the question type. Similarities with horizontal clustering can be estimated with Eq. (6).*

$$sim(C_k, C_l) = \sum sim(C_{km}, C_{ln}) \quad sim(C_{km}, C_{ln}) = \begin{cases} 1 & if \ C_{km} = C_{ln} \\ 0 & else \end{cases}, \quad (6)$$

where C_k is the *k-th* pattern cluster of question A, and C_l is the *l-th* pattern cluster of question B. C_{km} is the *m-th* pattern in the *k-th* cluster and C_{ln} is the *n-th* pattern in the *l-th* cluster.

For example, Table 8 lists some patterns for pattern cluster C_k from question $Q2$ {《悲惨世界》的作者是谁? /who is the author of Les Miserables?}. Table 9 lists some patterns for pattern cluster C_l from question $Q3$ {《便衣警察》是谁的作品? /who wrote Plainclothes Police?}. $Q2$ and 3 belong to the same question type. Clearly, as cluster C_k in Table 8 and cluster C_l in Table 9 are answer patterns corresponding to questions $Q2$ and $Q3$, C_k and C_l should be merged into a cluster.

Table 8. Some Patterns in Pattern Cluster C_k from Question $Q2$

<PatternClusterNo> 维克多·雨果/Victor Hugo </PatternClusterNo>
q_focus ← *answer*
q_focus ← 是/is → 代表作/masterpiece → *answer*
q_focus ← 有/has → 作品/work → *answer*
q_focus ← 改编/adapted → 由/from → 名著/masterpiece → *answer*
q_focus ← 是/is → 作品/work → *answer*
q_focus ← 作品/work → *answer*
......

Table 9. Some Patterns in Pattern Cluster C_l from Question $Q3$

< PatternClusterNo > 海岩/Haiyan </ PatternClusterNo >
q_focus ← 作品/work → *answer*
q_focus ← 小说/fiction → *answer*
q_focus ← 是/is → 处女作/maiden work → *answer*
q_focus ← 作者/author → *answer*
q_focus ← 创作/write → *answer*
......

3.5 Experiments with Unsupervised Answer Pattern Learning

Using the approach described in the previous sections, we are able to learn the syntactic answer patterns for the following question types. In order to validate the learned syntactic answer patterns, we apply them in the answer extraction module of Chinese open-domain question answering. In this experiment, 72 training questions and 178 testing questions are selected from Wu et al. [12] which are plotted in Fig.2.

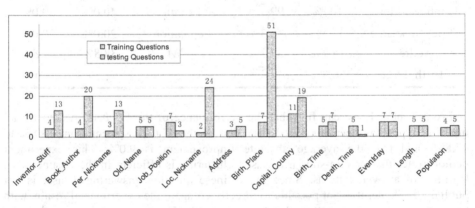

Fig. 2. Distribution of Question Types

The numbers of the learned syntactic answer patterns corresponding to each question type are shown in Table 10, which are obtained using the proposed unsupervised learning approach.

Table 10. Statistics for the Learned Syntactic Answer Patterns

Question Type	No.	Question Type	No.	Question Type	No.
Inventor_Stuff	137	Loc_Nickname	31	Death_Time	13
Book_Author	132	Address	191	Event_Day	176
Per_Nickname	153	Birth_Place	83	Length	144
Old_Name	94	Capital_Country	322	Population	45
Job_Position	237	Birth_Time	22	*SUM*	*1780*

This section will discuss syntactic pattern-based answer extraction (*SP_bAE*) in Chinese open-domain question answering, which is evaluated using the metric of precision [8] to validate the performance of the unsupervised answer patterns learning approach. Retrieval-based answer extraction (*R_bAE*) is implemented as the baseline for comparison, which is based on the cluster-based language model for sentence retrieval. The performances of the baseline and syntactic pattern-based answer extraction are shown in Table 11.

Table 11. Comparison of *R_bAE* and *SP_bAE*

Question Type	R_bAE	SP_bAE	Question Type	R_bAE	SP_bAE
Inventor_Stuff	38.5%	38.5%	Capital_Country	100%	100%
Book_Author	50.0%	75.0%	Birth_Time	57.1%	71.4%
Per_Nickname	76.9%	100%	Death_Time	100%	100%
Old_Name	60.0%	40.0%	Event_Day	28.6%	42.9%
Job_Position	100%	66.7%	Length	40.0%	60.0%
Loc_Nickname	33.3%	33.3%	Population	20.0%	20.0%
Address	15.7%	37.3%	*SUM*	*38.8%*	*47.8%*
Birth_Place	36.8%	10.5%			

From Table 11, we can find that the performance of the *SP_bAE* system for all question types has been improved over that of the *R_bAE* system from 38.8% to 47.8%, and that the average absolute improvement is 9.0%. This experiment demonstrates that pattern-similarity-based clustering is efficient in the unsupervised learning of answer patterns. Since the Chinese question answering dataset is not publicly available, it is not possible to directly compare the experimental results with the supervised answer pattern learning approach. However, we believe that the performance of our approach is comparable to that of the conventional techniques, even though it does not depend on <question, answer> training seeds.

4   Conclusion and Future Work

The input of a question answering system is natural language question which contains richer information than the query in traditional document retrieval. This paper mainly focuses on mining richer information to improve sentence retrieval and unsupervised syntactic answer pattern learning in open-domain question answering.

We first present a *One-Sentence-Multi-Topic* sentence clustering approach to the cluster-based language model to improve sentence retrieval for answering question. Our experiments on Chinese open-domain question answering reveal that *One-Sentence-Multi-Topic* clustering is much better than K-Means and is comparable to PLSI when used in sentence clustering for answering question.

Second, to resolve the disadvantages with the supervised learning approaches that heavily depend on <question, answer> training seeds, a novel pattern-similarity-based clustering approach is presented to automatically learn syntactic answer patterns for answer selector. The basic ideas behind the approach lay in: each cluster in the results for *One-Sentence-Multi-Topic* clustering is regarded as aligned sentences; *vertical clustering* is to identity the multi-forms of the answer to the question, and *horizontal clustering* is to identity the answer pattern for the question type. Our experiments reveal that the improvement in syntactic pattern-based answer extraction over retrieval-based answer extraction is about 9%.

Because sentence clustering is supported by a semantic tagger that is presently a named entity identifier, we only conduct experiments on those questions whose answers are named entities [13]. Other questions will be studied in future work. Moreover, although the current similarities in patterns for *vertical* and *horizontal clustering* are simple, they will be expanded in the future. As our approach is not language specific, we intend to apply it to other language question answering system to compare the proposed techniques with state-of-the-art factual open-domain question answering systems.

References

1. D. Moldovan, S. Harabagio, R. Girju, P. Morarescu and F. Lacatsu, A. Novischi. LCC Tools for Question Answering. In Proc. of TREC 2002.
2. E. H. Hovy, U. Hermjakob and C. Y. Lin: The Use of External Knowledge of Factoid QA. In Proc. of TREC 2001.
3. D. Ravichandran and E. Hovy. Learning Surface Text Patterns for a Question Answering. In Proc. of ACL Conference. 2002.
4. A. Ittycheriah and S. Roukos. IBM's Statistical Question Answering System-TREC 11. In Proc. of TREC, Gaithersburg, Maryland, November, 2002.
5. A. C. Emmanuel and W. B. Croft. V. Murdock. Answer Passage Retrieval for Question Answering. In Proc. of SIGIR2004, pp.516-517, 2004.
6. V. Murdock and W. B. Croft. Simple Translation Models for Sentence Retrieval in Factoid Question Answering. In Proc. of SIGIR2004 Workshop on IR4QA, pp.31-35.
7. J. Y. Nie. Integrating Term Relationships into Language Models for Information Retrieval. Report at ICT-CAS.
8. E. M. Voorhees. Overview of the TREC 2004 Question Answering Track. In Proc. of TREC 2004.
9. M. M. Soubbotin and S. M. Soubbotin. Use of Patterns for Detection of Likely Answer Strings: A Systematic Approach. In Proc. of TREC 2002, Maryland, November, 2002.
10. S. Dumais, M. Banko, E. Brill, J. Lin and Andrew Ng. Web Question Answering: Is More Always Better? In Proc. of SIGIR2002, Tampere, Finland, 2002.
11. Y. P. Du, X. J. Huang, X. Li and L.D. Wu. A Novel Pattern Learning Method for Open Domain Question Answering. In Proc. of IJCNLP2004, Sanya, China.
12. Y. Z. Wu, J. Zhao, X. Y. Duan and B, Xu. Building an Evaluation Platform for Chinese Question Answering Systems. In Proc. of First NCIRCS2004. Shanghai.
13. Y. Z. Wu, J. Zhao and B. Xu. Chinese Named Entity Recognition Model Based on Multiple Features. In Proc. of HLT/EMNLP 2005, Vancouver, Canada, pp.427-434,.
14. X. Y. Duan, J. Zhao and B. Xu. Building Chinese Dependency Parser Using SVM. Term Report, 2003.

A Little Known Fact Is ...
Answering *Other* Questions Using
Interest-Markers

Majid Razmara and Leila Kosseim

CLaC laboratory
Department of Computer Science and Software Engineering
1400 de Maisonneuve Blvd. West
Montreal, Quebec, Canada H3G 1M8
m_razma@cse.concordia.ca, kosseim@cse.concordia.ca

Abstract. In this paper, we present an approach to answering "Other" questions using the notion of *interest marking terms*. "Other" questions have been introduced in the TREC-QA track to retrieve *other interesting facts* about a topic. To answer these types of questions, our system extracts from Wikipedia articles a list of *interest-marking* terms related to the topic and uses them to extract and score sentences from the document collection where the answer should be found. Sentences are then re-ranked using universal interest-markers that are not specific to the topic. The top sentences are then returned as possible answers. When using the 2004 TREC data for development and 2005 data for testing, the approach achieved an F-score of 0.265, placing it among the top systems.

1 Introduction

In this paper, we describe a method for answering a new type of questions: "Other". Since 2004, the TREC Question Answering Track has introduced a new type of challenge: answering "Other" questions [1]. The test set consists of a series of questions relating to a particular target (or topic). Each question series consists of factoid questions, list questions and ends with exactly one "Other" question. For example, question series # 69 of TREC-2005 is:

69		Target: France wins World Cup in soccer
69.1	FACTOID	When did France win the World Cup?
69.2	FACTOID	Who did France beat for the World Cup?
69.3	FACTOID	What was the final score?
69.4	FACTOID	What was the nickname for the French team?
69.5	FACTOID	At what stadium was the game played?
69.6	FACTOID	Who was the coach of the French team?
69.7	LIST	Name players on the French team.
69.8	OTHER	Other

A. Gelbukh (Ed.): CICLing 2007, LNCS 4394, pp. 518–529, 2007.
© Springer-Verlag Berlin Heidelberg 2007

The answer to the "Other" question is meant to be interesting information about the target that is not covered by the preceding questions in the series, and should consist of a snippet of text, called a nugget, extracted from the AQUAINT document collection. To evaluate the answers, for each "Other" question, NIST assessors create a list of acceptable information nuggets about the target. Some of the nuggets are deemed *vital*, some are *okay* and others are *uninteresting*. Systems are then evaluated based on precision and recall of the nuggets, and ultimately the F-measure with $\beta = 3$[1]. *Vital* and *okay* nuggets are evaluated differently: the number of *vital* nuggets are used to compute both recall and precision; while *okay* nuggets are used for precision only.

Answering "Other" questions is a difficult task because we don't really know what we are looking for. There is no exact definition of what constitutes a *vital* and an *okay* answer and humans themselves may have different opinions about how interesting a nugget is. In fact, at TREC-2005, the University of Maryland submitted a manual run for the "Other" questions [2] where a human had identified manually what he considered to be interesting nuggets for each questions. This manual run was then submitted for judging along with automatic runs and received an $F(\beta = 3)$ score of 0.299. This low score seems to show that humans do not agree easily on what constitutes an interesting (*vital* or *okay*) piece of information.

The remainder of the paper is organized as follows. In Section 2 we discuss our approach in detail. Section 3 presents the results of the generated sentences with the 2004 and 2005 TREC data. Section 4 then presents related work, and finally in Section 5, we present future directions.

2   Answering "Other" Questions

Fundamentally, our approach to answering *Other* questions is based on the hypothesis that interesting sentences can be identified by:

1. target-specific interest marking terms (e.g. *Titanic* ⇒ *White Star Line*, *assassination of J.F. Kennedy* ⇒ *Lee Harvey Osward*, *November 22*), and
2. universal interest marking terms (e.g. *first man on the moon*, *150 people died*)

To identify these interest marking terms, we did not use the AQUAINT document collection, where the answer should be found. The AQUAINT collection consists of newspaper articles that do not necessarily present the highlights of a target. An article presents detailed facts regarding the target but not an overview. A rich resource to find interesting facts related to many targets is an encyclopedia. Many target types are described and the content of each article is a short summary that highlights the most interesting facts – precisely what we are looking for. To find target-specific interest markers, we therefore used the Wikipedia online encyclopedia[2]. Wikipedia contains more than 1 million

---

[1] Which means that recall is three times more important than precision.
[2] http://en.wikipedia.org

encyclopedic entries for various topics ranging from famous persons, to current events, to scientific information. The chances of finding an article on the topic of an *Other* question is therefore high, and we can extract potentially interesting terms from these entries without much noise. These terms are then searched in the AQUAINT document collection to extract interesting sentences that are then re-ranked using universal interest marking terms. Sentences with the highest scores are finally presented as interesting nuggets.

2.1   Finding the Wikipedia Article

The first stage to answering an *Other* question is to find the proper Wikipedia article. This process is shown in Figure 1. First, we generate a Google query using the target of the question. The target is first parsed, stop words are removed, and consecutive capitalized words are quoted together as a single term. Because verbs in the targets are usually in the present tense (e.g. "Russian submarine Kursk sinks", "France wins World Cup in soccer") while in the Wiki article, verbs are usually in the past tense (e.g. "It *sank* in the Barents Sea", "The tournament was *won* by France"), they are not included in the query. The remaining words and quoted terms are then ANDed and sent to the Google API to search the Wikipedia sub-domain.

If several Wikipedia articles satisfy the query, the first one is taken. However, if no Wikipage satisfies the query, then we try to loosen the query. Considering that quoted terms often have a non-compositional meaning, we keep them as is but OR single words. If this is not sufficient, then we gradually remove the last single word from the end. Finally, if still no Wikipedia article is found, then we simply drop Wikipedia and take the top N documents[3] of the AQUAINT collection using the original query.

2.2   Extracting Target-Specific Interest Markers

After the Wikipage or top N AQUAINT documents are retrieved, interest-marking terms are extracted from the page (or pages). Because the Wikipedia entries consist of rather short documents (with an average of 400 words per article[4]), we only consider named entities as interesting terms. These are extracted with the GATE NE tagger[5]. If the number of terms of a specific semantic type (Date, Location, Person and Organization) is abnormally high (20 terms for each semantic type), then we assume that the page does not present a balanced overview of the highlights, but presents a specific point-of-view about the target and will therefore be biased towards that point-of-view. For example, if a Wikipedia article on an event (e.g. the *1998 World Cup*) contains a large number of person names, then we assume that the article is biased towards describing the people involved (e.g. the soccer players) as opposed to *Other* interesting information. To avoid

---

[3] Between 3 to 10 depending on whether the number of keywords is large enough.
[4] http://en.wikipedia.org/wiki/Wikipedia:Words_per_article
[5] http://gate.ac.uk

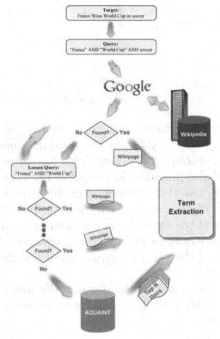

Fig. 1. Finding a Wikipedia article for the target "France wins World Cup in soccer"

this, we set a threshold on the number of terms for each semantic category that we keep. After removing terms occurring only once, the N most frequent terms are kept (in our case, 20).

We approximate co-reference resolution, by using word overlap. For example in answering the target "Port Arthur Massacre" we may find in the Wiki article the terms "Port Arthur" and "Port Arthur Massacre". To consider both terms as a single concepts, we separate longer terms that overlap with shorter ones into sub-term (e.g. "Port Arthur" and "Massacre").

2.3   Finding Interesting Sentences

Once we have a set of interesting terms for each target, we search for the N most relevant documents in AQUAINT. These documents are retrieved by the Lucene search engine[6] using the same query generated for the target as in the Wikipage search (see section 2.1). If the appropriate Wikipage has been found then we also use a secondary query from the title of the Wikipage in order to get more documents related to the target. This secondary query is ORed to the Google query. For example, for the target "France wins World Cup in soccer" we have:

---

[6] http://lucene.apache.org

Google Query =   "France" AND "World Cup" AND soccer
Wikipage Title = 1998 FIFA Word Cup

and we generate:

Lucene Query = (1998 AND "FIFA World Cup") OR
               ("France" AND "World Cup" AND soccer)

If too many documents are returned through the Lucene search with this new query, then we add content words from the previous questions of that target (i.e. factoid and list question) to the query with less priority in order to focus the search. Since NIST also provides the output of the PRISE search engine with the target as query, we take the intersection of the top 25 documents returned by Lucene and the top 25 documents returned by PRISE. The idea is that if the two IR systems retrieved the same document using two different queries, then we should be more confident of its pertinence. Experimentally, we observed that taking the intersection of the two IR outputs increased the final F-measure by 0.02 with our testing set.

Within the documents chosen as the domain, the frequency of each interest marking term is then computed. For each term, we compute a weight as the logarithm of its frequency.

$$Weight(T_i) = Log(Frequency(T_i))$$

This weight represents how interesting a term is as a function of its frequency in the related documents. The less frequent a term, the less interesting it is considered.

2.4   Ranking Interesting Sentences

All sentences from the domain documents are then scored according to how interesting it is. This is computed as the sum of the weight of the interesting terms it contains.

$$Score(S_i) = \sum_{j=1}^{n} Weight(T_j) \quad | \ T_j \in S_i \ \ \forall 1 \le j \le n$$

In order to increase the precision, we try to remove any extra characters on both ends of the sentence which do not contain much interesting material. Two kinds of information are removed: the source of the news at the beginning of sentences (e.g. *WASHINGTON (AP) –* ...) and markers of reported speech at the end of sentences (e.g. ..., *local newspaper Daily Telegraph reported*).

After scoring the sentences and throwing away those with a score of zero (i.e. no interesting term in the sentence), we try to remove paraphrases. In order not to remove false paraphrases, we play it conservatively, and only remove lexically similar sentences. Either the sentences are almost equivalent to each other at the string level or they share similar words but not the same syntax. To compare sentences, we have used the *SecondString* package[7], an open-source Java-based package of approximate string-matching techniques [3]. For removing the first kind of similarity, the Jaccard algorithm was used and for the second kind, the Jensen-Shannon was used. Both algorithms compute similarity based on token distance.

2.5   Universal Interest Markers

Once the sentences are ranked based on the target-specific interesting terms, we boost the score of sentences that contain terms that generally mark interesting information regardless of the topic. Such markers were determined empirically by analyzing the previous TREC data.

Superlatives: We hypothesized that an interesting sentence would typically contain superlative adjectives and adverbs. People are interested in knowing about the *best*, the *first*, the *most wonderful*, and find normal or average facts uninteresting.

To verify this hypothesis, we computed the percentage of superlatives in *vital*, *okay* and *uninteresting* sentences from the 2004 data. For *vital* and *okay* sentences, we used the nuggets submitted by the 2004 participants and judged by the TREC assessors. For *uninteresting* sentences, we extracted sentences from the top 50 AQUAINT documents from the domain documents (see section 2.3) which do not contain *vital* or *okay* nuggets. The results, shown in Table 1, clearly show an increase in the use of superlatives in *vital* compared to *okay* and *uninteresting* sentences. When re-ranking nuggets, the score of a sentence that contains superlatives is therefore given a bonus. Experimentally, we set this bonus to be 20% of the original sentence score per superlative it contains.

Numerals: We also hypothesized that sentences containing numbers probably contain interesting information also. For example, "Bollywood produces 800 to 900 films a year" or "Akira Kurosawa died at age 88". To verify this, we also compared the percentage of numerals in *vital*, *okay* and *uninteresting* sentences on the same corpora. The results, shown in Table 1, again indicate that numerals are used more often in *vital* and *okay* sentences as opposed to *uninteresting* sentences. To account for this, the score of sentences containing numerals gets boosted by 20% for each numeral it contains. However, numerals that are part of a date expression such as *Sep 27, 2000* are excluded because we already considered them interesting terms from the Wikipedia entry.

Interest Marking Keywords: In addition to superlative and numerals, we also wondered if for specific target types, different terms are typically regarded as interesting. For example, information on someone's birth or death, the founders

---

[7] http://secondstring.sourceforge.net

Table 1. Ratio of superlatives and numerals in each type of sentence

Sentence Type	Corpus Size	Superlatives	Numerals
Vital	49,102 words	0.52 %	2.46 %
Okay	56,729 words	0.44 %	2.26 %
Uninteresting	2,002,525 words	0.26 %	1.68 %

of an organization, the establishment of an entity ...would all be considered interesting. These terms do not fit any specific grammatical category, but just happen to be more frequent in interesting nuggets. This is similar to the work of [4] (see section 4). To identify these terms, we analyzed the data of the 2004 *Other* questions. The data set consisted of:

1. The factoid and list questions of each target, because they mostly ask for interesting information.
2. The *vital* and *okay* answers to *Other* questions given by the TREC assessors[8].
3. The actual answers to *Other* questions given by participants and judged *vital* and *okay* by NIST.

All these were stop-word removed and stemmed, then the frequency of each word was computed. The score of a keyword was computed as:

$$Score(K_i) = Freq(K_i) \times Distrib(K_i)^2$$

where $Freq(K_i)$ is the frequency of a keyword and $Distrib(K_i)$ is the number of targets whose sources contain the keyword. The intuition behind this scoring function is to favor keywords that are referred to in a high number of targets as opposed keyword that appears frequently, but only for a few targets. Hence a keyword K_i that occurs in a high number of targets is considered more important than a keyword K_j occurring more often (i.e. $Freq(K_j) > Freq(K_i)$) but in a smaller number of targets (i.e. $Distrib(K_j) < Distrib(K_i)$).

To identify terms that appear more often in interesting sentences as opposed to *uninteresting* sentences, we also built such a list of terms from the *uninteresting* answers submitted by the participants to the 2004 TREC QA (i.e. answers not considered as either *vital* or *okay*). Then, we computed the ratio of their scores as:

$$ScoreRatio(K_i) = \frac{Score_{int}(K_i)}{Score_{uni}(K_i)}$$

Where $Score_{int}(K_i)$ refers to the score of K_i in the *vital* and *okay* sentences and $Score_{uni}(K_i)$ refers to the score of K_i in the *uninteresting* sentences.

Table 2 shows the 15 top-ranking keywords that were extracted from all target types combined. As the table shows, the ranking of *most* and *first* verifies the importance of boosting superlatives.

In order to make a specific list of interesting keywords for each target type, we did the same work for each category of questions (person, organization and

---

[8] Available at http://trec.nist.gov/data/qa/2004_qadata/04.other_answers.txt

Table 2. Interest-marking keywords in all target types and for each type of target

Rank	All Target Types	Thing	Person	Organization
1	found	kind	born	chang
2	die	fall	servic	publish
3	associ	public	serv	establish
4	life	found	become	first
5	begin	countri	film	leader
6	publish	offici	general	associ
7	first	field	old	larg
8	public	program	movi	found
9	servic	develop	chairman	releas
10	group	director	place	project
11	death	begin	receiv	group
12	see	discov	begin	lead
13	countri	particl	win	organ
14	old	power	life	begin
15	most	figur	intern	provid

thing). Table 2 also shows the list of frequent keywords per target type. Initially, we planned to consult a specific sublist according to the type of our target. For example, if the target is a person, then we only consult the person sublist. However, because we did not have much confidence in our target type tagger; we preferred to play it safe and we re-constructed a global list from the concatenation of the top 15 keywords of each sublist. This has two advantages to using the initial all-target type list. First, it allows us to make sure that each target type is equally represented in the global list. Although, the 2004 question set is not composed of thing, person and organizations targets in equal proportion, the 2005 question series contains equal number of questions for those target types. In addition, a re-constructed global list prevents us from considering terms that do not have a particularly high score in any one sublist, but occurs in every sublist with an average score; therefore having a high overall score, but not a high score in any one sublist (e.g. "see" and "most"). Sentences containing terms from the final re-constructed list are given a bonus of 20% per term, except if the term also appears in the previous questions of the target.

3   Results and Analysis

Once sentences have been extracted and sorted by their scores, they are evaluated. Since there exists no automatic standard scoring system for this task, we compared our sentences automatically to the assessor answers given by NIST and the actual answers submitted by all participants. If our sentence is identical to a *vital* or *okay* answer, we mark it as such. If our sentence is not identical but is a substring of a longer *vital* or *okay* nugget, then to determine whether it contains the required information, we compare it to the assessor answers of that target (marked as *vital* or *okay*) using the token-based Jensen-Shannon similarity function[9]. If our sentence is closer to the assessor answer than the longer nugget is, then we consider our sentence as a correct one and mark it the same way the long answer is marked (*vital* or *okay*). Having a list of sentences marked as *vital*, *okay* or *uninteresting*, we can then evaluate the score of the question using the same F-measure (with $\beta = 3$) as used at TREC.

Since the TREC-"Other" task has only been introduced in 2004, we only have 140 such questions to develop and test the approach (65 questions for 2004 and 75 questions for 2005[10]). We therefore used the 2004 *Other* questions as the training set and the 2005 questions for testing. The results of the overall approach are shown in Table 3 along with the contribution of each type of universal marker. The figure marked *All* refers to the final score of the system when using all markers; while *All - X* refers to all markers except for X. *Best* and *Median* refer to the best and median score of all systems submitted to TREC-2005.

Table 3. Test results with the 2005 *Other* questions

Markers Used	F-measure
All	0.265
All - Superlative Markers	0.255
All - Numeral Markers	0.257
All - Other Markers	0.266
Best	0.248
Median	0.156

As the table shows, numeral and superlative markers increase the results somewhat; while, surprisingly, the keyword markers do not. We suspect that this is due to two main reasons:

1. To extract the interest marking keywords, a small corpus was used. We only had sentences related to 65 targets of 2004, which were composed of approximately 132,000 words; 44,000 words, for each of the three targets.
2. The TREC 2004 question series do not include the *event* target type; while this type of target accounts for 24% of the questions in 2005. Since we identified the keyword markers from the 2004 data, we have no specific markers for event types of target. In fact, if we compare the results of the approach per target type (i.e. Person, Event, Organization and Thing) we can clearly see that the F-score is lower for the *event* target type compared to the other target types (see Table 4).

---

[9] http://secondstring.sourceforge.net

[10] At the time the experiments were made, the TREC-2006 assessor judgments had not been released. The TREC-2006 evaluations became available later, and relieved that our approach achieved a score of 0.199 (median of 12.5), the 3rd highest score at TREC-2006.

Table 4. Test results with the 2005 questions per target type

Target Type	Nb of Targets	F-measure
Person	19	0.300
Thing	19	0.277
Organization	19	0.268
Event	18	0.210

4 Related Work

Previous approaches to answering *Other* questions have mainly been addressed within the TREC confines, and only since 2004 [5, 6]. The most widely used approaches are based on patterns, keywords and question generation techniques.

In the pattern-based approach, a set of predefined patterns that seem to present interesting information are extracted from the answers of the previous years' *Other* questions. Then the target is applied to the patterns to generate a potentially interesting string that is searched in the document collection. [7], for example, use a variety of strategies including the use of definition-patterns. For example, the pattern TARGET, which... is used to identify nuggets that define the target, and hence is deemed to contain interesting information. [8] also use patterns for extracting useful information and some semantic features to score sentences. These semantic features include comparative adjectives, digits, topic related verbs and topic phrases. [9] also use patterns and a summarizer based on lexical chains to extract a sentence as a summary of a passage.

On the other hand, keywords are also used to find the answers to *Other* questions. [10], for example, use syntactic information to identify interesting nuggets in the ACQUAINT collection. They identify sentences where the target appears in the subject or object position, then use a list of interest-marking keywords (similarly to our approach) to rank these sentences. [10] also uses the Wikipedia online encyclopedia to re-rank the sentences. However, they do not analyze the article per se to find interesting terms, but rather the corresponding XML file to look for the meta-data on the target and identify the categories the article belongs to. These categories are then used as keywords to re-rank the nuggets. As opposed to their work, we further re-rank the nuggets by using the universal interest markers. [11] identifies sentences that contain more than 50% of the words in the targets as candidate sentences. In ranking those sentences, those having more overlap with the target are given higher scores. Finally, [12] use statistics about word triplet co-occurrences from the documents related to each target then, extract snippets corresponding to the most frequent word triplets.

The third main approach used can be qualified as question generation that attempts to answer *Other* questions using *Factoid* or *List* question answering approaches. [7], for example, first classifies the targets according to their type, then creates a list of potential questions for each type of target. For example, if the target is of type *musician-person*, a set of questions such as *What is the name of the band of TARGET* or *What kind of singer is TARGET* are generated.

Using their factoid module, they then find answers for these typically interesting questions.

Some question answering systems use both pattern-based and keyword-based approaches. In [13], a web knowledge acquisition module determines which kind of knowledge base should be searched based on the target type. Then, the basic score of a candidate sentence is assigned either by searching the definitions about the target from online knowledge bases or by keywords and their frequencies. Finally, based on the target type, a set of structured patterns is used to re-rank the candidate sentences. [14] use a list of terms related to each target extracted from Web pages, Wikipedia and Britannica pages. Then Two types of patterns were used: lexical patterns (e.g. "X which is", "like X") and part-of-speech and named entity patterns (e.g. "TARGET, WD VBD").

Other less popular approaches have also been proposed. For example, in [15], three strategies are exploited: a nugget can be extracted either by searching a database of definitional contexts, searching the corpus for a nugget including many keywords from the Websters Dictionary definition, or extracting all sentences from the top documents and using Wikipedia synonyms of the target. [7] also tries to locate specific named entities in the nuggets corresponding to the target types. For example, if the target is a person, then nuggets containing dates, quantities and locations are deemed more interesting.

5   Summary and Future Work

This paper proposed a keyword-based approach to extracting interesting sentences to answer *Other* questions. The method is based on the identification of target-specific and universal interest markers. Target-specific markers are identified by named entities found in the Wikipedia online encyclopedia. The frequency of these named entities in the AQUAINT documents are then used as a measure of how interesting they really are. Target-independent markers of interest are defined as the most frequent terms in the TREC-2005 *vital* and *okay* nuggets and include superlatives, numerals and specific keywords. Using these markers, we extract and rank sentences from the AQUAINT collection and return the top-scoring ones as the answer. When using the 2004 TREC data for development, the approach achieved an F-score of 0.265 with the 2005 TREC questions, placing it above the best scoring TREC-2005 system. We participated in TREC-2006, but the results have not been issued yet.

Currently, the system is highly dependent on the Wikipages; changing the term extraction source to something more robust (e.g. the top N web pages or top N AQUAINT documents) seems promising. In addition, we need to perform proper co-reference resolution on the Wikipedia terms; this would allow to better rank and identify the interesting terms. Also, computing lexical chains (as in [9]) may improve results as better target-specific markers can be identified; this needs to be investigated. Currently, to represent interesting facts, we only consider individual terms. A more precise method would ultimately be to expand the approach to extracting entire predicate structures; with roles and arguments.

Although the use of the universal keyword markers did not seem to improve results, we still believe it is an interesting venue. Since we have very little training data to identify these keywords, we plan to try to expand the ones we have with lexical semantics. Finally, since the result of event targets is rather weak, we need to focus more on this kind of targets.

Acknowledgement. This research was financially supported by a grant from NSERC and Bell University Laboratories. The authors would like to thank the anonymous reviewers for their comments on an earlier version of the paper.

References

[1] Voorhees, E.M.: Overview of the TREC 2004 Question Answering Track. [5]
[2] Voorhees, E.M., Dang, H.T.: Overview of the TREC 2005 Question Answering Track. [6]
[3] Cohen, W.W., Ravikumar, P., Fienberg, S.E.: A Comparison of String Distance Metrics for Name-Matching Tasks. In: Proceedings of the IJCAI Workshop on Information Integration on the Web (IIWeb), pages 73-78, Acapulco, Mexico (2003)
[4] Ahn, K., Bos, J., Curran, J.R., Kor, D., Nissim, M., Webber, B.: Question Answering with QED at TREC-2005. [6]
[5] Voorhees, E.M., Buckland, L.P., eds.: Proceedings of the Thirteenth Text REtreival Conference, Gaithersburg, Maryland, National Institute of Standards and Technology (NIST) (2004)
[6] Voorhees, E.M., Buckland, L.P., eds.: Proceedings of the Fourteenth Text REtreival Conference, Gaithersburg, Maryland, National Institute of Standards and Technology (NIST) (2005)
[7] Harabagiu, S., Moldovan, D., Clark, C., Bowden, M., Hickl, A., Wang, P.: Employing Two Question Answering Systems in TREC-2005. [6]
[8] Wu, M., Duan, M., Shaikh, S., Small, S., Strzalkowski, T.: ILQUA An IE-Driven Question Answering System. [6]
[9] Ferres, D., Kanaan, S., Dominguez-Sal, D., Gonzalez, E., Ageno, A., Fuentes, M., Rodriguez, H., Surdeanu, M., Turmo, J.: TALP-UPC at TREC 2005: Experiments Using a Voting Scheme Among Three Heterogeneous QA Systems. [6]
[10] Ahn, D., Fissaha, S., Jijkoun, V., Muller, K., Rijke, M., Sang, E.: Towards a Multi-Stream Question Answering-As-XML-Retrieval Strategy. [6]
[11] Chen, J., Yu, P., Ge, H.: UNT 2005 TREC QA Participation: Using Lemur as IR Search Engine . [6]
[12] Roussinov, D., Chau, M., Filatova, E., Robles-Flores, J.: Building on Redundancy: Factoid Question Answering, Robust Retrieval and the Other. [6]
[13] Wu, L., Huang, X., Zhou, Y., Zhang, Z., Lin, F.: FDUQA on TREC2005 QA Track. [6]
[14] Gaizauskas, R., Greenwood, M., Harkema, H., Hepple, M., Saggion, H., Sanka, A.: The University of Sheffield's TREC 2005 Q&A Experiments. [6]
[15] Katz, B., Marton, G., Borchardt, G., Brownell, A., Felshin, S., Loreto, D., Louis-Rosenberg, J., Lu, B., Mora, F., Stiller, S., Uzuner, O., Wilcox, A.: External Knowledge Sources for Question Answering. [6]

Adapting the JIRS Passage Retrieval System to the Arabic Language

Yassine Benajiba, Paolo Rosso, and José Manuel Gómez Soriano

Dpto. Sistemas Informáticos y Computación (DSIC),
Universidad Politécnica de Valencia, Spain
{ybenajiba, prosso, jogomez}@dsic.upv.es

Abstract. The need of having a Passage Retrieval (PR) system for Arabic texts is due essentially to our aim to build an Arabic Question Answering (QA) system in our research team. We have chosen working on the PR system to be our first step to pursue our aim because being the core component and its quality will affect directly the performance of the QA system. JAVA Information Retrieval System (JIRS) is a PR QA-oriented system, multi-platform, open source and free to use. JIRS uses an n-gram model and it is language-independent. It separates language configuration files to make easier its adaptation to any language. In this paper, we report the different challenges when adapting the JIRS to the Arabic language.In order to evaluate JIRS on Arabic, we had to develop an Arabic test-bed using the multilingual CLEF QA one as guideline. We also report the results obtained in our experiments where we retrieved Arabic passages with JIRS first without any text prepro-cessing and second performing a prior light-stemming on the documents of the test-bed. The preliminary results show that it is possible to obtain a first Arabic passage retrieval system adapting JIRS on pre-processed text with a light-stemmer.

1 Introduction

Information Retrieval (IR) systems allow users to find the relevant web sites and/or documents by only providing a query to the system. These systems had great success merely because the Internet is growing fast and a manual detection of a needed document is practically impossible for a simple user. However, the new trend in the field is a new type of systems for users who are not willing to navigate on the Internet and only need a concise answer to a specific question. The QA systems were defined as systems allowing to a user to introduce a question written in natural language to the system, and then answering to this question with a natural language sentence.

Most of the QA systems search the answer in open-domain non-structured documents. Therefore, a QA system is mainly composed of three modules: (i) Question Analysis; (ii) Passage Retrieval; and (iii) Answer Extraction. In the first module, the question is processed to obtain some useful information such as the type of answer we are looking for. A search engine is generally used to search for

A. Gelbukh (Ed.): CICLing 2007, LNCS 4394, pp. 530–541, 2007.
© Springer-Verlag Berlin Heidelberg 2007

the documents which may contain the answer. Furthermore, a processing of these documents is needed to obtain the passages with high probability of containing the answer. This step is performed by a Passage Retrieval (PR) module. Finally, the third module extracts the answer from the passages returned by the PR module with the help of the information obtained in the Question Analysis step. The PR module proved to be a core module because the quality of the retrieved passage affects highly the quality of the global QA system [22]. In fact, it would be impossible to extract the answer if the passages do not contain it.

The QA task is a complex and challenging task both for building a QA system and for evaluating it [5]. TREC[1](Text REtrieval Conference) and CLEF[2](Cross Language Evaluation Forum) are two international competitions allowing to the researchers in this area to compare their systems. Both Monolingual and Cross-Lingual QA tasks were organised in these competitions. However, in this paper we will be concerned mainly by the monolingual task. The best accuracy in the monolingual task in CLEF 2006 was 68.95% achieved by [18] for the French language using intensive Natural Language Processing (NLP) techniques both in the indexing step and in the answer extraction module. In the second position [25] with 52.63% for the Spanish language using mainly lexical pattern matching and statistical approaches which makes their system more independent of the language than the previous one. Whereas in the third position was for [11] for the French language adopting as well a statistical approach. It is also reported that in order to answer factoid questions their QA system relies mainly on the information provided by the Named Entities Recognition (NER) module. In the TREC competition the systems adopted by the participants were more complex than the ones seen in CLEF. The questions are harder to analyze because they are related to a common, given target [28], i.e. a good anaphora resulotion is needed. The proceedings of the TREC 2006 have not been published yet. For this reason, in this paper we only report systems that gave good results in the TREC 2005. [15] obtained the best score in the TREC 2005 with 53.4%. They used a syntactical parser and a NER system as tools accessible to improve the performance of the system. Whereas for answer selection they used statistical methods. This system has the peculiarity of using a module named "logical prover" which uses semantic information to proof the correctness of the answer. [26] obtained the second position in the TREC 2005, with an accuracy of 46.4%. The authors report that the good results obtained with this system are due to the dependency relation matching technique used in the answer extraction module. Finally, [8] obtained the third position with 24.6%. This other system adopt a multi-agent structure, with each agent relying on a different QA approach and then, at the end, a combination technique is used to combine all the answers and produce one final answer of the system.

In the CLEF and TREC conferences, the participating QA systems were systems performing on many languages (English, French, Spanish, Italian, Dutch, ...) but unfortunately, the Arabic QA task did not figure among the defined QA

---

[1] http://trec.nist.gov/
[2] www.clef-campaign.org/

tasks. However, some efforts were conducted to build QA systems oriented to the Arabic language. In [23], a knowledge-based QA system is described; unfortunately, in the paper no results are shown and the system has a quite special architecture since answers are extracted from a knowledge-base (structured data). Moreover, in [14] a QA system based on the 3-module generic architecture (question analysis, passage retrieval and answer extraction) which is adopted by most of the QA systems is illustrated. For the test, four native Arabic speakers with university education presented 113 questions to the system and judged *themselves* whether the answer of the system was correct or not. The author reports a precision and a recall reaching 97.3%. However, as we mentioned above, there are no Arabic QA tasks which provide a test-bed allowing a general test for any Arabic QA system, so the reliability of the reported results keep on being very low since such precision and recall were not achieved in any other language.

In this paper, we present the first step of building an Arabic QA system obeying to the general norms reported in the CLEF conference. Studying the best performing QA systems and considering the experience of our research team in the QA task we estimated that the best way to proceed in building a QA system is to start by building an efficient and reliable PR module. The idea behind the work we present in this paper, is to use a language-independent PR system for the Arabic language. However, any language-independent system needs language-dependent techniques to tune it for a better performance on the target language. Therefore, the main task in this work is to study the JIRS and the Arabic language and find out through reliable (CLEF based) experiments the needed techniques for adapting JIRS to the Arabic language and improve its performance. Moreover, we built three necessary corpora to test the system: (i) a corpus of documents; (ii) a corpus of questions and (iii) a corpus containing the correct answers of each question. The last corpus is needed as a reference to the system in order to compute the accuracy.

As a possible PR system for our Arabic QA system, we decided to investigate the possibilty of adapting the language-independent Java Information Retrieval System (JIRS). Many are the systems participating in different tasks of CLEF 2005 [24], [12] and 2006 [6] [25], [10] are JIRS-based. This shows that JIRS can be also employed in other NLP tasks than just QA [1]. JIRS proved to be efficient for the Spanish, Italian, French and English languages. The peculiarity of the Arabic language of being highly inflectional and, therefore, very different with respect to the above languages, made the study of the possibility of using JIRS very interesting and its adaptation very challenging.

The rest of this paper is structured as follows. In the Second section of this paper we will describe some important peculiarities of the Arabic language. Moreover, details about successful techniques for Arabic IR will be also presented. Section Three will illustrate with more details the main characteristics of the JIRS passage retrieval system. Finally, in the forth section we present the results of our preliminary experiments, and finally we draw some conclusions and discuss the further works to be done.

2   Retrieving Passages in Arabic

The Arabic language has many peculiarities which make even more challenging many of the NLP tasks, following we introduce some of the characteristics of Arabic:

(i) it is an alphabet-based language of 28 alphabets , 25 consonants and 3 vowels (long vowels), plus the short vowels, which are not considered as part of the alphabet because they are diacritics that may be added above or below characters. The short vowels are not used anymore in newspaper and this makes the text very ambiguous (because the same word with different short vowels could give different meanings, see the first example of Figure 1);

(ii) some of its characters might be combined to form one character (e.g. *Alif* and *Hamza*, *Alif* and *Madda*, *Waw* and *Hamza*, etc.). In newspapers some of these combinations are not used anymore. This makes these characters combinations another source of ambiguity (see below the second example of Figure 1);

(iii) the root of any of its words is a trial (three consonants) or quadriple (four consonants) verb. Any other form of the verb can be inflected from this root. There's a pattern to obtain any of these inflections, however there is not only one pattern for all the verbs. Moreover, irregular plurals are very common in the Arabic language. These peculiarities classify the Arabic language among the languages with very complex morphology;

(iv) Arabic is a highly inflectional language because the general form of a word is: *Prefix(es)* + *"stem"* + *Suffix(es)*. Therfore, a part of a sentence (e.g. *"in their house"*) may be expressed in Arabic with only one word (e.g. is *"bimanzilihim"*, see the third example of Figure 1). This peculiarity of the language causes a high data sparseness. In order to tackle this problem, [21] proposes a n-gram model based algorithm to segment the text in order to overcome data sparseness in Arabic texts. However, it is not very easy to implement the algorithm since a large manually segmented corpus is necessary for training. In our work, we will only use a light stemmer as described in the fourth section.

Nowadays, there are no available PR systems oriented to the Arabic language. This makes imposible a comparative study for determining the best approach for the Arabic PR task. Due to the fact that the PR task may be considered as a more specific subtask of IR, we investigated first the characteristics of some of the Arabic IR systems. The proceedings of Arabic/English Cross Lingual Retrieval (CLIR) task in TREC 2001[3] and 2002[4] were a valuable source of information because including an Arabic monolingual retrieval task as well.

In the study of the state of art of Arabic IR, we made a special emphasis on the characteristics of the best systems [27], [19] and [7]. We found out that in order to build a good IR system for Arabic texts it is very important to take in considerations some crucial aspects:

---

[3] http://trec.nist.gov/pubs/trec10/
[4] http://trec.nist.gov/pubs/trec11/

1ˢᵗ Example: (same word with different diacritics):
The word: جِد means : Seriousness
The word: جَد means : Grandfather

2ⁿᵈ Example: (character combinations):
Example of characters combinations: آ=ء+ا

If we omit this combination in the word رأيتنا (which means "you

have seen us"), will become رايتنا (which means "our flag")

3ʳᵈ Example: (example of Arabic word composition):
English part of a sentence: "in their house" Arabic translation:

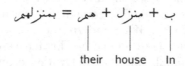

their   house   In

Fig. 1. Examples of some Arabic language characteristics

(i) *Text normalization:* There is no unique definition to text normalization in Arabic, but generally it consists of reducing all the variants of characters such as *"Alif"*, *"Waw"* or *"Alif maksoura"* in one form;

(ii) *Stop words:* Many researches used the stop words list that was published by Yaser Al-Onaizan in his web site[5]; (unfortunately, this URL is not available anymore;)

(iii) *Query expansion:* All the participants, used a blind feedback expansion. Lately, [29] carried out a study which showed that using a thesaurus for query expansion gives better results than the blind feedback expansion. The authors argue that this technique performed better because synonyms are widely used in Arabic texts and variety in expression is appreciated as a good writing style. However, even if this technique gave good results it is important to emphasize that it does not seem like a simple solution since an Arabic thesaurus is necessary. In this same work an automatic algorithm inferring a thesaurus from a parallel corpus is proposed. In the experiments, they used the UN parallel corpus;

(iv) *Light stemming:* This last technique consists of omitting affixes to overcome the data sparseness problem we described before. Some participants built their own light stemmers [7] whereas others used a light stemmer published by Kareem Darwish in his website[6]. Furthermore, among the participations of the SIGIR 2002[7] conference, in [19] a comparison between the different available light stemmers was carried out. In the paper the author also reports the list of prefixes and suffixes which give the best results for the IR task.

---

[5] http://www.isi.edu/~yaser/
[6] http://www.glue.umd.edu/~kareem/research/
[7] http://www.informatik.uni-trier.de/~ley/db/conf/sigir/sigir2002.html

3 The Arabic-JIRS Passage Retrieval System

As we have already mentioned, the PR module is a core component of a QA system. Thus, it was estimated worth to investigate PR modules oriented specifically to QA systems. Those PR modules are more focused on the texts which possibly contain the answer to the user's question than the documents related to the user's query. Many techniques have been investigated in this area. The most successful techniques were the ones based on density [17], [20], [3](JIRS is based on density, see Figure 2 and the JIRS architecture description below) and the ones based on terms overlap [4], [9]. However, there are other works which investigated the efficiency of the PR module when the order of the question terms is respected [2] and the possibility of using semantic information to obtain the relevant passages [16].

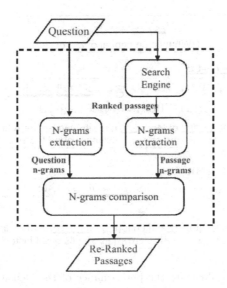

Fig. 2. The JIRS architecture

JIRS is a QA-oriented PR system and it can be freely downloaded from its main web page[8]. As illustrated in Figure 2 in order to index the documents the JIRS relies on an n-gram model. To retrieve the relevant passages it performs in two main steps [13]. In the first step it searches the relevant passages and assigns a weight to each of them. The weight of a passage depends mainly on the relevant question terms appearing in the passage. Thus, the weight of a passage can be expressed as:

$$w_k = 1 - \frac{log(n_k)}{1 + log(N)} \tag{1}$$

---

[8] http://jirs.dsic.upv.es

Where n_k is the number of passages in which the associated term to the weight w_k appears and N is the number of the system passages.

The second step performs only on the top "m" passages of the relevant passages returned by the first step (generally $m=1000$). In this step, JIRS extracts the necessary n-grams from each passage. Finally, using the question and the passage n-grams it compares them using the *Density Distance* model. The idea of this model is to give more weight to the passages where the most relevant question structures appear nearer to each other. For example, let us suppose the question and the two passages shown on Figure 3. The correct answer to the question is "Rabat". The Density Distance model would give more weight to the first passage because the distance between the words *capital* and *Morocco* is smaller than the distance between these same words in the second passage.

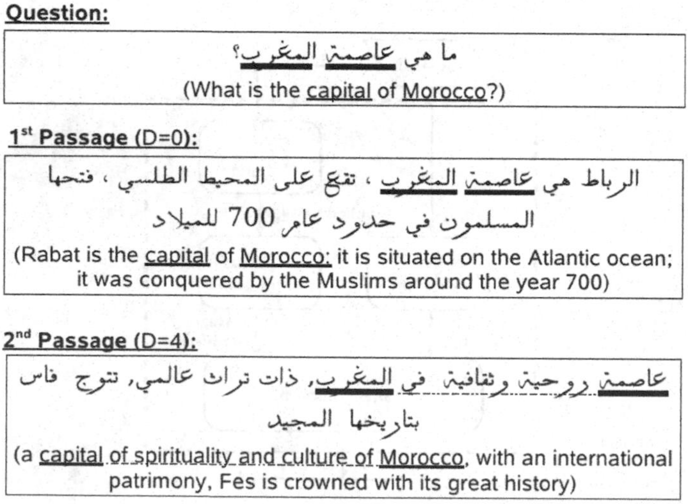

Question:

ما هي عاصمة المغرب؟

(What is the capital of Morocco?)

1st Passage (D=0):

الرباط هي عاصمة المغرب ، تقع على المحيط الطلسي ، فتحها
المسلمون في حدود عام 700 للميلاد

(Rabat is the capital of Morocco; it is situated on the Atlantic ocean;
it was conquered by the Muslims around the year 700)

2nd Passage (D=4):

عاصمة روحية وثقافية في المغرب, ذات تراث عالمي, تتوج فاس
بتاريخها المجيد

(a capital of spirituality and culture of Morocco, with an international
patrimony, Fes is crowned with its great history)

Fig. 3. An example to illustrate the performance of the Density Distance model (an English translation is given in between parenthesis)

In order to obtain a bigger weight for the passages that have a smaller distance between question structures, the Distance Density model of a passage p and a question q employs the following equation:

$$Sim(p,q) = \frac{1}{\sum_i w_i} \cdot \sum_x h(x) \frac{1}{d(x, x_{max})} \qquad (2)$$

Where x is an n-gram of p formed by q terms, w_i are the weights defined by (1), $h(x)$ can be defined as:

$$h(x) = \sum_k w_k \qquad (3)$$

and $d(x, x_{max})$ is the factor which expresses the distance berween the n-gram x and the n-gram with the maximum weight x_{max}, the formula expressing this factor is:

$$d(x, x_{max}) = 1 + k.ln(1 + D) \qquad (4)$$

Where D is the number of terms between x and x_{max} (the example given in Figure 3 shows an example where D=0 and another where D=4). The last version of the JIRS was reported to perform better than last year in all of the Spanish, French and Italian languages [6]. It was also reported in [6] that the JIRS showed better performance than the Lucene PR system[9] for the Spanish and French languages, whereas the same performance was reported for both systems for the Italian language.

The Arabic-JIRS version of the passage retrieval system relied on the same architecture of Figure 2. The main modifications were made on the Arabic language-related files (text encoding, stop-words, list of characters for text normalization, Arabic special characters, question words, etc.). The Arabic-JIRS is also available at the main web page[10].

4 Experiments and Results

4.1 Test-Bed for Arabic Question Answering[11]

In order to test the JIRS on Arabic in the same conditions in which were tested the QA systems which participated in the CLEF 2006 competition we had to develop a test-bed in Arabic with the same characteristics. The test-bed consists of:

(i) *The documents*: we have used a snapshot of the articles of the Arabic Wikipedia[12]. This makes a collection of 11,638 documents. A conversion from the XML to the SGML format was necessary to preprocess the corpus for JIRS;

(ii) *The questions*: we have manually built a set of 200 questions considering the different classes that were reported in the CLEF 2006 competition with the same proportion of each class [12]. These proportions are shown in Table 1;

(iii) *The correct-answers*: in order to obtain the *Coverage* (ratio of the number of the correct retrieved passages to the number of the correct passages) and *Redundancy* (average of the number of passages returned for a question) measures automatically from the JIRS, it is necessary to provide, for each of the 200 questions, a list containing all the possible answers. It is also very important to verify that each of these answers is supported by a passage in the collection. We have built the list of the correct-answers and manually verified the existence of each answer in at least one passage of the collection.

---

[9] http://lucene.apache.org/java/docs/
[10] http://jirs.dsic.upv.es
[11] http://www.dsic.upv.es/~ybenajiba
[12] http://ar.wikipedia.org

Table 1. CLEF 2006 classes Ratio

Class	Number of Questions
NAME	6
NAME.ACRONYM	1
NAME.PERSON	22
NAME.TITLE	1
NAME.LOCATION	6
NAME.LOCATION.COUNTRY	14
NAME.LOCATION.CITY	2
DEFINITION.ORGANIZATION	24
DEFINITION.PERSON	25
DATE	11
DATE.DAY	4
DATE.YEAR	2
QUANTITY	16
QUANTITY.MONEY	3
QUANTITY.DIMENSION	2
QUANTITY.AGE	2
GENERAL	59

4.2 Preliminary Results

Two experiments have been carried out to estimate the performance of the JIRS on Arabic text. The first expriment consisted of using the test-bed described above. Whereas in the second experiment we performed a light stemming on all the components of the test-bed before we started the retrieval test. The light stemmer we have used for our experiment is the one provided by Kareem Darwish. Figure 4 shows the coverage (a) and the redundancy (b) measures for both experiments.

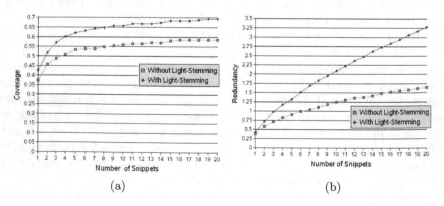

(a)   (b)

Fig. 4. Comparison of Coverage and Redundancy of JIRS over both light-stemmed and non-stemmed Arabic corpora

The results presented in Figure 4 show that JIRS can retrieve relevant passages also in Arabic, reaching a coverage up to 59% and a redundancy of 1.65 without performing any text preprocessing. However, we carried out a second experiment where we performed a light-stemming to overcome the high data sparesness problem due to the nature of the Arabic language. The light-stemming helped to raise the coverage up to 69% and the redundancy up to 3.28. The values obtained for redundancy show that we cannot reach a higher coverage if we do not use a bigger set of documents.

5   Conclusions and Further Work

In this paper we investigated how to develop a first efficient and reliable passage retrieval system for Arabic. The language-independent JIRS passage retrieval system was adopted in order to retrieve texts in Arabic. To evaluate the Arabic-JIRS PR system we had to manually build a test-bed in Arabic which is now freely available for the research community. We carried out experiments on both raw and light-stemmed Arabic texts because the Arabic language is highly inflectional and light-stemming helps significantly to tackle this problem. These experiments showed that with light-stemming the coverage measure raises up to 69% and the redundancy measure up to 3.28.

In the next future, we plan to test JIRS with a corpus of the same size as the corpora used in CLEF 2006 (around 454,000 documents). We would like also to investigate the use of various light-stemmers instead of just one.

Acknowledgments

The research work of the first author was partially supported by MAEC - AECI. We would like to thank the research project MCyT TIN2006-15265-C06-04 for partially funding this work.

References

1. Aceves-Pérez, R. M., Villaseñor-Pineda, L., Montes-y-Gómez, M.: Using N-gram Models to Combine Query Translations in Cross-Language Question Answering. *International Conference on Intelligent Text Processing and Computational Linguistics CICLing-2006*. Lecture Notes in Computer Science, vol. 3878, Springer, 2006.
2. Adriani, M., Rinawati: Finding Answers to Indonesian Questions from English Documents. In *Accessing Multilingual Information Repositories: 6th Workshop of the Cross-Language Evaluation Forum, CLEF 2005, Revised Selected Paper*. Vol. 4022 of *Lecture Notes in Computer Science*, pp. 510-516. Springer, 2006.
3. Amaral, C., Figueira, H., Martins, A., Mendes, A., Mendes, P., Pinto, C.: Priberams Question Answering System for Poteguese. In *Working Notes for the CLEF 2005 Workshop*. In *Accessing Multilingual Information Repositories: 6th Workshop of the Cross-Language Evaluation Forum, CLEF 2005, Revised Selected Paper*. Vol. 4022 of *Lecture Notes in Computer Science*, pp. 410-419. Springer, 2006.

4. Bouma, G., Mur, J., Van Noord, G., Van Der Plas, L., Tiedemann, J.: Question Answering for Dutch Using Dependency Relations. *Accessing Multilingual Information Repositories. 6th Workshop of the Cross-Language Evaluation Forum, CLEF 2005, Revised Selected Papers. Lecture Notes in Computer Science*, Vol. 4022, Springer, 2006.
5. Burger, J., Cardie, C., Chaudhri, V., Gaizauskas, R., Harabagiu, S., Israel, D., Jacquemin, C., Lin, C., Maiorano, S., Miller, G., Moldovan11, D., Ogden, B., Prager, J., Riloff, E., Singhal, A., Shrihari, R., Strzalkowski1, T., Voorhees, E., Weishedel, R.: Issues, Tasks and Program Structures to Roadmap Research in Question & Answering (Q&A). *Technical report, National Institute of Standards and Technology.*
6. Buscaldi, D., Gómez, J. M., Rosso, P., Sanchis, E.: The UPV at QA@CLEF 2006. In *Working Notes for the CLEF 2006 Workshop.*
7. Chen, A. and Fredric C. Gey: Building an Arabic Stemmer for Information Retrieval. In the *Proceedings of the TREC 2002.* Page 631.
8. Chu-Carroll, J., Czuba, K., Duboue, P., Prager, J.: IBM's PIQUANT II in TREC2005. in *the Proceedings of the Fourteenth Text REtrieval Conference*, 2005.
9. Ferrés, D., Kanaan, S., González, E., Ageno, A., Rodríguez, H., Turmo, J.: The TALP-QA System for Spanish at CLEF 2005. In *Accessing Multilingual Information Repositories: 6th Workshop of the Cross-Language Evaluation Forum, CLEF 2005, Revised Selected Paper.* Vol. 4022 of *Lecture Notes in Computer Science*, pp. 400-409. Springer, 2006.
10. Ferrés, D., Rodríguez, H.: TALP at GeoCLEF-2006: Experiments Using JIRS and Lucene with the ADL Feature Type Thesaurus. In *Working Notes for the CLEF 2006 Workshop.*
11. Gillard, L., Sitbon, L., Blaudez, E., Bellot, P., El-Béze, M.: The LIA at QA@CLEF-2006. *Working Notes for the CLEF 2006 Workshop.*
12. Gómez, J. M., Buscaldi, D., Bisbal-Asensi, E., Rosso, P., Sanchis, E.: QUASAR, The Question Answering System of the Universidad Politecnica de Valencia. In *Accessing Multilingual Information Repositories: 6th Workshop of the Cross-Language Evaluation Forum, CLEF 2005, Revised Selected Paper.* Vol. 4022 of *Lecture Notes in Computer Science*, pp. 439-448. Springer, 2006.
13. Gómez, J. M., Montes-y-Gómez, M., Sanchis, E., Rosso, P.: A Passage Retrieval System for Multilingual Question Answering. *a8th International Conference of Text, Speech and Dialogue 2005 (TSD'05). Lecture Notes in Artificial Intelligence (LNCS/LNAI 3658).* pp. 443-450. Karlovy Vary, Czech Republic. 2005.
14. Hammou, B., Abu-salem, H., Lytinen, S., Evens. M.: QARAB: A question answering system to support the Arabic language. In *the Proceedings of the workshop on computational approaches to Semitic languages, ACL* , pages 55-65, Philadelphia, 2002.
15. Harabagiu, S., Moldovan, D., Clark, C., Bowden, M., Hickl, A., Wang, P.: Employing Two Question Answering Systems in TREC-2005. in *the Proceedings of the Fourteenth Text REtrieval Conference*, 2005.
16. Hartrumpf, S.: Extending Knowledge and Deepening Linguistic Processing for the Question Answering System InSicht. In *Accessing Multilingual Information Repositories: 6th Workshop of the Cross-Language Evaluation Forum, CLEF 2005, Revised Selected Paper.* Vol. 4022 of *Lecture Notes in Computer Science*, pp. 361-369. Springer, 2006.
17. Ittycheriah, A., Franz, M., Zhu, W.-J., Ratnaparkhi, A.: IBM's Statistical Question Answering System. In *Proceedings of the Ninth Text Retrieval Conference (TREC-2002).* pp. 229-234.

18. Laurent, D., Séguéla, P., Négre, S.: Cross Lingual Question Answer ing using QRISTAL for CLEF 2006. *Working Notes for the CLEF 2006 Workshop.*
19. Leah S. Larkey, Allan, J., Margaret E. Connell, Bolivar, A., Wade, C.: UMass at TREC 2002: Cross Language and Novelty Tracks. In *the Proceedings of the TREC 2002.* Page 721.
20. Lee, G. G., Seo, J., Lee, S., Jung, II., Cho, B.-H., Lee, C., Kwak, B.-K., Cha, J., Kim, D., An, J., Kim, H., Kim, K.: SiteQ: Engineering high performance QA system using lexico-semantic pattern matching and shallow NLP. In *Proceedings of the Tenth Text Retrieval Conference (TREC-2002).* pp. 422-451.
21. Lee, Y., Papineni, K., Roukos, S., Emam, O., Hassan, H.: Language Model based Arabic Word Segmentation. In the *Proceedings of the 41st Annual Meeting on Association for Computational Linguistics.*
22. Llopis, F., Vicedo, J.L. , Ferrandez, A.: Passage Selection to Improve Question Answering. In *Proceedings of the COLING 2002 Workshop on Multilingual Summarization and Question Answering,* 2002.
23. Mohammed, F.A., Nasser, K., Harb, H.M.: A knowledge based Arabic question answering system (AQAS). *ACM SIGART Bulletin,* pp. 21-33, 1993.
24. Montes-y-Gómez, M., Villaseñor-Pineda, L., Pérez-Coutiño, M., Gómez-Soriano, J. M., Sanchis, E., Rosso, P.: A Full Data-Driven System for Multiple Language Question Answering. *Accessing Multilingual Information Repositories. 6th Workshop of the Cross-Language Evaluation Forum, CLEF 2005, Revised Selected Papers. Lecture Notes in Computer Science,* Vol. 4022, Springer, 2006.
25. Pérez-Coutiño, M., Montes-y-Gómez, M., López-López, A., Villaseñor-Pineda, L., Pancardo-Rodríguez, A.: A Shallow Approach for Answer Selection based on Dependency Trees and Term Density. *Working Notes for the CLEF 2006 Workshop.*
26. Sun, R., Jiang, J., Fan Tan, Y., Cui, H., Chua, T., Kan, M.: Using Syntactic and Semantic Relation Analysis in Question Answering. in *the Proceedings of the Fourteenth Text REtrieval Conference,* 2005.
27. Tomlinson, S.: Experiments in Named Page Finding and Arabic Retrieval with Hummingbird SearchServerTM at TREC 2002. In *the Proceedings of the TREC 2002.* Page 248.
28. Voorhees, E.: Over TREC 2005. In *the Proceeding of TREC 2005.*
29. Xu, J., Fraser, A., Weischedel, R.: Empirical Studies in Strategies for Arabic Retrieval. In *thr Proceedings of the 25th Annual Conference on Research and Development in Information Retrieval (ACM SIGIR).* 2002.

Using Question-Answer Pairs in Extractive Summarization of Email Conversations

Kathleen McKeown, Lokesh Shrestha, and Owen Rambow

Department of Computer Science
Columbia University
New York, NY, USA
{kathy, lokesh, rambow}@cs.columbia.edu

Abstract. While sentence extraction as an approach to summarization has been shown to work in documents of certain genres, because of the conversational nature of email communication, sentence extraction may not result in a coherent summary. In this paper, we present our work on augmenting extractive summaries of threads of email conversations with automatically detected question-answer pairs. We compare various approaches to integrating question-answer pairs in the extractive summaries, and show that their use improves the quality of email summaries.

1 Introduction

Email conversations are a natural means of getting answers to one's questions. And the asynchronous nature of email conversation makes it possible for one to pursue several questions in parallel. As a consequence, question-answer exchanges figure as one of the dominant uses of email conversations. In fact, in our corpus of email exchanges, we found that about 20% of all email threads focus primarily on a question-answer exchange, while about 40% of all email threads involve question-answer exchange of some form. For these types of email threads, a summary that can highlight the main question(s) asked and the response(s) given would be useful.

The most common technique for summarization is the use of sentence extraction using variants of lexical frequency [1,2,3]. In [4] we show that sentence extraction can also be successfully applied to summarize email threads if augmented with email-specific features and presented using the dialogic structure of email communication. However, these kinds of approaches ignore the key characteristics of question-answer exchange threads; an extractive summary may not include the answer to a question included in the summary. Consider an example summary of a thread of email conversation shown in Figure 1 which was produced by the sentence extraction based email thread summarization system described in [4]. While this summary does include an answer to the first question, it does not include answers to the two questions posed subsequently even though the answers are present in the thread. Further, in [5] we show that features derived from the structure of the thread of email conversations can be used to detect question-answer pairs in email conversations.

A. Gelbukh (Ed.): CICLing 2007, LNCS 4394, pp. 542–550, 2007.
© Springer-Verlag Berlin Heidelberg 2007

In this paper, we present a summarization system that builds on our previous research to establish novel approaches that integrate question-answer pairs in extractive summaries of email conversations, and show that such an integrative approach improves the quality of summarization for question-answer exchange threads.

Regarding "acm home/bjarney", on Apr 9, 2001, Muriel Danslop wrote:
Two things: Can someone be responsible for the press releases for Stroustrup?
Responding to this on Apr 10, 2001, Theresa Feng wrote:
I think Phil, who is probably a better writer than most of us, is writing up something for dang and Dave to send out to various ACM chapters. Phil, we can just use that as our "press release", right?
In another subthread, on Apr 12, 2001, Kevin Danquoit wrote:
Are you sending out upcoming events for this week?

Fig. 1. Sample summary obtained with sentence extraction

2   Previous and Related Work

While there has been no work on using automatically detected question and answer pairs in summarizing threads of email conversations, there has been some work on summarizing meetings that bears some relation to ours. [6], for example, presents a meeting summarization system which uses the MMR algorithm to find sentences that are most salient while minimizing the redundancy in the summary. The similarity weights in the MMR algorithm are modified using three features, including whether a sentence belongs to a question-answer pair. The use of question-answer pair detection is an interesting proposal that is also applicable to our work.

There has also been some work on individual email as well as archived discussion lists summarization. [7] describe work on summarizing individual email messages using machine learning approaches to learn rules for salient noun phrase extraction. [8] present work on email summarization by exploiting the thread structure of email conversation and common features such as named entities and dates. [9] also address the problem of summarizing archived discussion lists. They cluster messages into topic groups, and then extract summaries for each cluster. Also, [10] describe FASIL, an email summarization system for use in a voice-based Virtual Personal Assistant developed at University of Sheffield.

[11] present work on generating extractive summaries of threads in archived discussions. Sentences from the root message and from each response to the root extracted using *ad-hoc* algorithms crafted by hand. This approach works best when the subject of the root email best describes the "issue" of the thread, and when the root email does not discuss more than one issue. In our work, we do not make any assumptions about the nature of the email, and learn sentence extraction strategies using machine learning.

The work we present here attempts to establish novel approaches to the integration of automatically detected question-answer pairs in extractive summaries of threads of email conversations.

3   The Data

Our corpus consists of about 300 threads of emails sent during one academic year among the members of the board of a student organization at Columbia University. The emails deal mainly with planning events of various types, though other issues were also addressed. On average, each thread contains 3.25 email messages.

Two annotators were asked to perform two tasks: write summaries of the email threads in our corpus, and highlight and link question-answer (QA) pairs in the email threads. We did not provide instructions about how to choose content for the summaries, but we did instruct the annotators on the format of the summary; specifically, we requested them to use the past tense, and to use speech-act verbs and embedded clauses (for example, *Dolores reported she'd gotten 7 people to sign up* instead of *Dolores got 7 people to sign up*). We requested the length to be about 5% to 20% of the original text length, but not longer than 100 lines.

For question detection, the annotators were asked to highlight only those questions that seek information, independently of whether the question was posed in an interrogative form with a question mark, or was posed in a declarative form (e.g., "I was wondering if ..."). We asked annotators to ignore rhetorical questions (questions used for purposes other than to obtain the information the question asked). The annotators also marked the answers to the questions (if they were present in the same thread), explicitly linking an answer to the question it answers.

For the results we report in this paper, we used the subset of the threads in our corpus which have QA pairs identified by both the annotators, 44 email threads in total. We call this subset the SEQA threadset. Since we are interested in performance improvement of extractive summarization with the use of question-answer pairs in email threads, we confine our experiments to those email threads in our corpus that have at least one question-answer pair as annotated by the both annotators. The SEQA threadset has 157 messages and 629 individual sentences.

4   Extractive Summarization

To create the training data for our machine learning approach to extractive summarization, we represent each sentence of the email threads in the SEQA threadset with a feature vector along with its binary classification, which represents whether or not the sentence should be in a summary. Some of the features used include the standard set of features such as length, position in the document, TF*IDF scores of the terms in the sentences as well as other features derived from the nature of email conversation and the structure of the email thread. The binary classifications of the thread sentences are derived from the human written summaries. Since our annotators were not asked to categorize thread sentences according to whether the sentence should be a summary sentence or not, but rather asked to write the manual summaries (a more natural task), the task of categorizing the sentences for training data had to be done automatically. We used the sentence-similarity finder SimFinder [12] in order to rate the similarity of each sentence in a thread to each sentence in the corresponding manual summary. For each sentence in the thread, excluding sentences that are being quoted, signatures and the like, we retained the highest similarity score with the sentences corresponding manual summary. In other words, the SimFinder similarity for each thread sentence is measured for all the sentences in the manual summary; however the highest of these scores are retained as the score of the thread sentence. Using these highest scores, we ranked the thread sentences, and categorized a certain proportion of the top ranked thread sentences as summary sentences. We call this proportion the summary size.

While [4] assumes a summary size of 20%, for this paper, we investigated what summary size would best match the compression rates used by the human summarizers. Also, we investigated whether the use of SimFinder [12] in identifying summary sentences was a reasonable approach. To do this, we first randomly chose about 10% of the ACM threads, which we call gold standard threads, and manually classified the sentences in these threads, which we call gold standard sentences, according to whether these sentences' content was reflected in one of the human written summaries. Those gold standard sentences whose content were reflected in the corresponding human summary were given a classification of "Y", implying that the sentence is a summary sentence, and the rest were given a classification of "N", implying that the sentence is not a summary sentence, giving us the gold standard classification.[1] In doing this we found out that of the 109 total gold standard sentences from the selected threads, 59 were selected as being reflected in the human written summaries while 50 were disregarded. This implies a compression rate of less than 50% (50/109) for the selected threads while we had instructed the annotators to use a compression rate of about 80%. After obtaining the gold standard classifications, we used SimFinder to generate the automated classification. This was done by using SimFinder to score the gold standard sentences against their respective summary sentences. These scores were then used to automatically classify the gold standard sentences at different compression rates. For example, at a compression rate of 80%, the sentences with top 20% scores in a thread were classified as summary sentences. We then compared these SimFinder induced automated classification with the manual gold standard classification. The results are shown in Table 1.

Table 1. Results for comparing SimFinder induced sentence classification using various summary sizes with that of manual sentence classification

Summary size	20%	30%	40%	45%	50%	55%	60%
Recall	0.268	0.500	0.625	0.768	0.803	0.821	0.857
Precision	0.750	0.824	0.833	0.827	0.803	0.780	0.750
F-measure	0.394	0.622	0.714	0.796	0.803	0.80	0.80

Recall measures the proportion of the positive gold standard sentences that are correctly categorized using the SimFinder scores. Precision measures the proportion of the positively categorized sentences that are positive gold standard sentences. F-measure is

---

[1] While this process selects those sentences in an email thread whose content are reflected in the manual summaries, our use of SimFinder attempts to automate and approximate this manual process.

the harmonic mean of recall and precision. While F-measure score is the highest at a compression rate of 50%, precision at this rate is lower than that at a compression rate of 45%. Further, we are interested in minimizing the summary size also. These observations suggest that the best compression to use would be 55% (a summary size of 45%). Also, it is interesting to note that the precision score does not go below 75% for all the compression rates we investigated. This implies that SimFinder performs sufficiently well in the task of selecting thread sentences whose content are reflected in the human written summaries, and that our use of SimFinder in constituting the training and test sets for our machine learning experiments is justified.

We obtained two datasets using the SEQA threadset. Dataset A using the sentence classifications derived from the thread sentences' similarity with Annotator A's human summaries (using SimFinder), and Dataset B using those of Annotator B (also using SimFinder). The kappa statistic for the agreement between the classifications derived from the summaries of the two annotators is 0.45, while the f-measure is 0.68.

For the experiments we discuss here, we used Ripper [13] as our machine learning tool to learn classifiers for sentence extraction. The results we present are based on Rouge evaluation of machine generated extractive summaries with human model summaries. We use the results of extractive summarization as a baseline for comparison against our various approaches to integration of questions and answers. We call this baseline approach SE. Using this SE approach and the datasets A and B, we obtained results shown in the first two rows of Table 2.

5   Question-Answer Pair Detection

In the task to highlight QA pairs in our corpus, Annotator A had identified 80 threads with QA pairs among the 200 threads that she had worked on. Annotator B had identified 61 threads with QA pairs among 138 threads he had worked on. The kappa statistic [14] for identifying question segments is 0.68, and for linking question and answer segments given a question segment is 0.81, indicating that identification of question and answer segments is a more objective task than writing a summary.

In order to include questions and answers in email summaries, we first need to be able to detect them in the input email threads. In [5] we present work on the detection of question and answer pairs in email threads, and show that various features based on the structure of email threads can be used in conjunction with lexical similarity of discourse segments for question-answer pairing. Using the human annotations on the SEQA threadset and a classification approach based on thread structure and lexical similarity similar to [5], we trained classifiers for QA pair detection on our corpus, resulting in a precision score of 0.728, recall score of 0.732 and F-Measure score of 0.730. These classifiers were then used to identify the question-answer segment pairs in the SEQA threadset.

6   Integrating Question-Answer Pairs with Extractive Sentences

We have identified three approaches to integrating automatically detected question-answer pairs in threads of email conversations with their extractive summaries. The first approach is to use the fact that a sentence figures as an answer to a question asked earlier in the thread as an additional feature in our machine learning-based extractive summarization approach. We call this approach SE+A. The second approach, called SE+QA, is to add automatically detected answers to questions that appear in the extractive summaries, and questions whose answers appear in the extractive summaries but are not in the extractive summary. Effectively, the second approach tries to improve the coherence of extractive summaries by adding questions to extracted answers and answers to extracted questions so that the summary reader has a better context for understanding the summary. In the third approach, called QA+SE, we start with automatically detected question-answer pair sentences which are then augmented with extractive sentences that do not appear already in the question-answer pair sentences.

Table 2 shows the results of these various approaches to integrating QA pairs sentences with extractive sentences. The first column declares the integration approach, the second column the dataset. The first three score columns show ROUGE-1, ROUGE-2, and ROUGE-L recall scores for the machine summaries with the two model summaries. The model summaries we use here are human summaries written by our two annotators. The second three score columns show the average ROUGE-1, ROUGE-2, and ROUGE-L recall scores of one model summary against the other, for showing agreement between the two model summaries and for comparing against the Rouge scores of our approaches. The final column shows the size of machine generated summary.

It can be seen from Table 2 that all of our machine generated summaries stay within the range of summary size employed by our human summarizers on the average, 45%. All of our three approaches to integration of QA pairs in extractive summaries show an improvement over SE, plain extractive summarization, with respect to both f-measure score and the Rouge-1 score. Among our three approaches, SE+QA performs a little better than the other two approaches for the dataset based on annotator A, while QA+SE performs marginally better with the dataset based on annotator B. We have no explanation for this difference at the present time, but point out that A's dataset is 33% larger than B's. Further, if we compare the Rouge-1 scores of machine summaries, column 6 in Table 2, with the Rouge-1 scores of the model summaries, column 9 in Table 2, we can estimate the performance of our machine summaries with that of human performance. For example, using approach SE, for dataset A, we get 52% (0.255/0.487) of human performance. With dataset A's best performing approach, SE+QA, we get 60% (0.293/0.487) of human performance. Similarly, with dataset B, we have 47% of human performance with approach SE, while with approach QA+SE, we get 55% of human performance. This represents an improvement of about 17%.

7 Postprocessing Extracted Sentences

Extracted sentences are sent to a module that wraps these sentences with the names of the senders, the dates at which they were sent, and a speech act verb. The speech act verb is chosen as a function of the structure of the email thread in order to make this structure more apparent to the reader. Furthermore, for readability, the sentences are sorted by the order in which they appear in the email thread.

Table 2. Summary of Results

		Rouge evaluation of machine summaries with two model summaries			Rouge evaluation of model summaries (human performance)			machine summary size
Approach	Dataset	R-1	R-2	R-L	R-1	R-2	R-L	%
SE	A	0.255	0.110	0.244	0.487	0.245	0.458	39%
SE	B	0.231	0.105	0.220	0.489	0.246	0.460	36%
SE+A	A	0.284	0.125	0.268	0.487	0.245	0.458	40%
SE+A	B	0.235	0.102	0.223	0.489	0.246	0.460	35%
SE+QA	A	0.293	0.129	0.279	0.487	0.245	0.458	46%
SE+QA	B	0.262	0.117	0.251	0.489	0.246	0.460	44%
QA+SE	A	0.280	0.121	0.266	0.487	0.245	0.458	43%
QA+SE	B	0.269	0.121	0.254	0.489	0.246	0.460	40%

8 Email Summarization Interface

We have developed a system for on-the-fly email categorization and summarization of email conversations that can be seamlessly integrated into a user's existing email client such as Microsoft Outlook. Our implementation of the email summarization interface employs a client-server architecture; the client portion of the model resides in a user's email client while the multi-user capable server can be run anywhere, and most possibly in a dedicated host in the network. The server accepts connections from the email client of any user, and upon authentication starts a session of client-server communication. During the duration of the session, the client and server each communicate with the other through XML formatted text messages. These messages tell the server which commands to invoke, and the client what the outcome of its requests are.

The client can make various requests such as categorization of individual email, categorization of an email thread, summarization of individual email, summarization of an email thread, and submission of an email for preprocessing. When new email arrives in a person's mailbox, these emails will be sent to the server for preprocessing. Preprocessing involves processing of the content and the headers of the email for future use in on-the-fly summarization and categorization. Currently, preprocessing involves extraction of email headers and content, removal of signatures, quoted material and greetings from the content of the email body, sentence boundary detection of the email body, part of speech tagging of the content of the email body, lemmatization of the content of the email body, creation of the email thread using the references to previous emails, and the categorization of individual emails. Preprocessing is especially a necessity for the summarization and categorization of email threads. Because an email thread might increase in size in time as new email messages arrive, with preprocessed data readily available, on-the-fly summarization of threads requires far less time than otherwise. A sample session is shown in Figure 2.

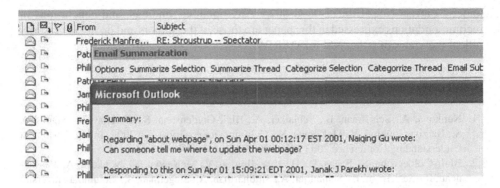

Fig. 2. The interface to our email summarizer in Microsoft Outlook, showing the new taskbar and a summarization window

9 Conclusion and Future Work

It has been shown that sentence extraction can also be successfully applied to summarize email threads if augmented with email-specific features. However, the dialogic nature of email communication means that extractive summaries may not include segments of conversations which would otherwise make the summaries more coherent, namely question and answer pairs. In this paper we presented work that attempts to overcome this shortcoming of extractive summaries. We presented various approaches to integrating automatically detected QA pairs of threads of email conversations with their extractive summaries. A comparison of the Rouge scores for our machine summaries with that for human summaries shows that all of our approaches to integration of QA result in an improvement over extractive summarization only. We received improvements of at least 14% in comparison with human performance for both the datasets using approach SE+QA. With dataset B, using approach SE+QA, we improve from 47% of human performance to as much as 55%, an improvement of about 17%.

In future work, we intend to perform an evaluation of the approaches we have identified here based on human feedback. While the approaches we have identified attempt to learn the process by which our annotators wrote their summaries, a difficult task as evident from our performance scores, we think that our use of extractive sentences for summarization can be further refined by learning extractive approaches that identify sub-sentence level content for summarization to obtain better results. Furthermore, use of abstraction in summarization is also an interesting area of research to us. In cases where multiple answers were offered to an opinion question, for example, the detection of agreement and disagreement in these answers can be used to generate an abstract summary of such question-answer exchanges.

Acknowledgements

This work was supported in part by the National Science Foundation under the KDD program and in part by the Defense Advanced Research Projects Agency (DARPA)

under Contract No. HR0011-06-C-0023. Any opinions, findings, and conclusions or recommendations expressed in this paper are those of the authors and do not necessarily reflect the views of either NSF or DARPA.

References

1. Nenkova, A., Schiffman, B., Schlaiker, A., Blair-Goldensohn, S., Barzilay, R., Sigelman, S., Hatzivassiloglou, V., McKeown, K.: Columbia university at duc 2003. In: 3rd Document Understanding Conference 2003 (DUC 2003). (2003)
2. Blair-Goldensohn, S., Evans, D., Hatzivassiloglou, V., McKeown, K., Nenkova, A., Passonneau, R., Schiffman, B., Schlaikjer, A., Siddharthan, A., Siegelman, S.: Columbia university at duc 2004. In: 4th Document Understanding Conference 2004 (DUC 2004). (2004)
3. Kupiec, J., Pedersen, J., Chen, F.: A trainable document summarizer. In: Proceedings of the 18th Annual International ACM SIGIR Conference on Research and Development in Information Retrieval, SIGIR'95, Seattle, WA (1995)
4. Rambow, O., Shrestha, L., Chen, J., Lauridsen, C.: Summarizing email threads. In: Proceedings of HLT-NAACL 2004 Short, Boston, USA (2004)
5. Shrestha, L., McKeown, K.: Detection of question-answer pairs in email conversations. In: Proceedings of the 20th International Conference on Computational Linguistics (COLING 2004), Geneva, Switzerland (2004)
6. Zechner, K.: Automatic summarization of open-domain multiparty dialogues in diverse genres. Computational Linguistics **28** (2002) 447–485
7. Muresan, S., Tzoukermann, E., Klavans, J.: Combining Linguistic and Machine Learning Techniques for Email Summarization. In: Proceedings of the CoNLL 2001 Workshop at the ACL/EACL 2001 Conference. (2001)
8. Lam, D., Rohall, S.L., Schmandt, C., Stern, M.K.: Exploiting e-mail structure to improve summarization. In: ACM 2002 Conference on Computer Supported Cooperative Work (CSCW2002), Interactive Posters, New Orleans, LA (2002)
9. Newman, P., Blitzer, J.: Summarizing archived discussions: a beginning. In: Proceedings of Intelligent User Interfaces. (2003)
10. Dalli, A., Xia, Y., Wilks, Y.: Fasil email summarisation system. In: Proceedings of the 20th International Conference on Computational Linguistics (COLING 2004), Geneva, Switzerland (2004)
11. Nenkova, A., Bagga, A.: Facilitating email thread access by extractive summary generation. In: Proceedings of RANLP, Bulgaria (2003)
12. Hatzivassiloglou, V., Klavans, J., Holcombe, M., Barzilay, R., Kan, M.Y., McKeown, K.: SimFinder: A flexible clustering tool for summarization. In: Proceedings of the NAACL Workshop on Automatic Summarization, Pittsburgh, PA (2001)
13. Cohen, W.: Learning trees and rules with set-valued features. In: Fourteenth Conference of the American Association of Artificial Intelligence, AAAI (1996)
14. Carletta, J.: Assessing agreement on classification tasks: The kappa statistic. Computational Linguistics **22** (1996) 249–254

NEO-CORTEX: A Performant User-Oriented Multi-Document Summarization System

Florian Boudin and Juan Manuel Torres Moreno

Laboratoire Informatique d'Avignon
BP 1228 F-84911 Avignon Cedex 9 France
{florian.boudin,juan-manuel.torres}@univ-avignon.fr
http://www.lia.univ-avignon.fr

Abstract. This paper discusses an approach to topic-oriented multi-document summarization. It investigates the effectiveness of using additional information about the document set as a whole, as well as individual documents. We present NEO-CORTEX, a multi-document summarization system based on the existing CORTEX system. Results are reported for experiments with a document base formed by the NIST DUC-2005 and DUC-2006 data. Our experiments have shown that NEO-CORTEX is an effective system and achieves good performance on topic-oriented multi-document summarization task.

Keywords: Automatic summarization, Statistical methods, Text mining, Query guided summaries.

1 Introduction

The Big companies, civil services and laboratories are confronted with a challenge: manage the mass of unstructured electronic textual documents. How to quickly find relevant information? How to display the information in a simple and fast way? The notion of automatic text summarization becomes one of the big subjects of Natural Language Processing (NLP). Rather than to diffuse whole documents, is it not preferable to diffuse only summaries containing the relevant information? Indeed, it is easier to read some lines than to read a huge number of pages to find out if the information wanted is there. In this paper, we present NEO-CORTEX, a system for summarizing multiple documents concerning a given topic. NEO-CORTEX was one of the five sentence selection systems used by the LIA-THALES system at the NIST Document Understanding Conference (DUC) 2006. This paper is organized as follows: Section 3 presents the overall system, Section 4 describes the adaptations made for the DUC 2006 task. In Section 5, we analyze the results of NEO-CORTEX system and Section 6 concludes and shows future work.

2 Background and Related Works

This paper describes an approach to topic-oriented multi-document summarization (MDS). Builds on previous work in single-document summarization (SDS),

A. Gelbukh (Ed.): CICLing 2007, LNCS 4394, pp. 551–562, 2007.
© Springer-Verlag Berlin Heidelberg 2007

this approach uses additional information about the document set as a whole, as well as individual documents. Generating an effective summary requires the summarizer to select, evaluate, order and aggregate items of information according to their relevance to a particular subject or purpose [1,2]. Introduced by Luhn [3] at the end of the fifties with the text-span deletion summarization system, automatic summarization is a process to transform source texts into a reduced target text in which the relevant information is preserved. Most of the works in sentence extraction applied statistical techniques (frequency analysis, overlap, etc.) to linguistic units such as terms, sentences, etc. Other approaches are based on the structure of the document (cue words, structural indicators) [4,5], the combination of information extraction and language generation, machine learning [6,7] to find patterns in text, lexical chains [8,9] or Rhetorical Structure Theory (RST) [10]. Previous works showed that researchers have extended various aspects of SDS approaches to apply to MDS. Our approach is based on the same principle but differs from these in several ways. It attempts to use a topic-independent SDS based mainly on statistical processing and to generate a query-relevant summary.

3   System Overview

The *COndensation et Résumés de TEXtes* [11] (CORTEX) is a performant and language independent SDS system [11,12,13]. The challenge was it's adaptation to a user-oriented MDS by introducing new features. The idea of CORTEX is to represent the text in an appropriate space and apply numeric treatments. In order to reduce the complexity, some reductions and filtering preprocessing are applied. Deletion of stop-words, words in high and very low frequency, text in brackets, figures and symbols. Each word is replaced by the stemming form of it's lemma to maximize coverage of relevant terms. The stemming algorithm used was the Porter stemmer [14]. The choice of combining lemmatization and stemming (see table 1) was done to overcome the problem of an incomplete lemma database (i.e. not containing all inflected and derived forms of words).

Table 1. Examples of lemmatization and stemming preprocessing. The third example shows the possible problem of incomplete lemma database (the word "natural" considered as non present in the lemma database).

Word	Lemma	Stem	Lemma + Stem
being	*be*	*be*	**be**
was	*be*	*wa*	**be**
natural	*·*	*natur*	**natur**

The system uses an optimal decision algorithm that combines several metrics (up to $\Gamma = 13$ metrics [12]) resulting from processing statistical and informational algorithms to the document vector space representation (represented as a term/sentence matrix γ and a presence matrix ξ (1), only terms of frequency greater than two appears). The value $\gamma_{y,x}$ means 0 if the word x is in the sentence y and a positive value otherwise (can be boolean or frequency). N is the word set cardinality of the document and M is the sentence number.

$$\gamma = \begin{pmatrix} \gamma_{1,1} & \gamma_{1,2} & \cdots & \gamma_{1,N} \\ \gamma_{2,1} & \gamma_{2,2} & \cdots & \gamma_{2,N} \\ \vdots & \vdots & \ddots & \vdots \\ \gamma_{M,1} & \gamma_{M,2} & \cdots & \gamma_{M,N} \end{pmatrix} ; \quad \xi_{j,m} = \left\{ \begin{array}{ll} 1 & \text{if } \gamma_{j,m} \text{ exists} \\ 0 & \text{elsewhere} \end{array} \right\} \tag{1}$$

The decision algorithm relies on all the normalized metrics (between $[0,1]$) combined in a sophisticated way and calculates the score ($Score_s^{cortex}$) for each sentence s. Two averages are calculated: the positive tendency, that is $\lambda_s > 0.5$, and the negative tendency, for $\lambda_s < 0.5$ (the case $\lambda_s = 0.5$ is ignored [1]). To calculate this average, we always divide by the total number of metrics Γ and not by the number of "positive" or "negative" elements (real average of the tendencies). So, by dividing by Γ, we have developed an algorithm more decisive than the simple average and even more realistic than the real average of the tendencies. Here is the decision algorithm that allows to include the vote of each metrics:

$$\sum^s \alpha = \sum_{v=1}^{\Gamma}(||\lambda_s^v|| - 0.5); \quad ||\lambda_s^v|| > 0.5 \tag{2}$$

$$\sum^s \beta = \sum_{v=1}^{\Gamma}(0.5 - ||\lambda_s^v||); \quad ||\lambda_s^v|| < 0.5 \tag{3}$$

v is the index of the metrics, $\sum_s^{\Gamma}$ is the sum of the absolute differences between $||\lambda||$ and 0.5, $\sum^s \alpha$ are the "positive" normalized metrics, $\sum^s \beta$ the negative normalized metrics and Γ the number of metrics used. The value attributed to every sentence is calculated in the following way:

if $(\sum^s \alpha > \sum^s \beta)$

$$\tag{4}$$

then $Score_s^{cortex} = 0.5 + \sum^s \alpha/\Gamma$: retain the sentence s
else $Score_s^{cortex} = 0.5 - \sum^s \beta/\Gamma$: not retain the sentence s

Λ^s is the value used for the final decision whether or not to retain the sentence s. In the end, N_P sentences are sorted according to this value $\Lambda^s; s = 1, \cdots, N_P$.

In order to summarize multiple documents, we have introduced two new parameters. A global parameter, the similarity between a document and the topic and a local parameter, the word overlap between a sentence and the topic.

---

[1] Simple average may be ambiguous if the value is close to 0.5, but the decision algorithm eliminates the sentences that their score is 0.5.

3.1   Similarity

The CORTEX scores of each sentences are calculated for a single document, the score scale must be normalized to take into account the relevance degree of each document to the topic. Indeed, a relevant sentence of a document can have a lower score than a non relevant sentence of another document. This is due to the inter-document independency of the scores calculated by CORTEX. The similarity parameter (5) is a cosine similarity [15] and allows us to compute the similarity of two vectors, which are in our case the whole document $\nu_d = (\nu^1, \nu^2, \cdots, \nu^n)$, $d = 1 \cdots Nb_{doc}$; Nb_{doc} is the total number of document and the topic $\omega_t = (\omega^1, \omega^2, \cdots, \omega^n)$, $t = 1 \cdots \tau$; τ is the total number of topics. The dimension n is the number of different terms contained in the document and the topic. Similarity is then calculated as:

$$Sim(\nu_d, \omega_t) = \frac{\sum \nu_d . \omega_t}{\sqrt{\sum \nu_d{}^2 + \sum \omega_t{}^2}} \qquad (5)$$

We use the $tf.idf$ [16] measure (term frequency, inverse document frequency) to obtain the weight of a term. This weight is a statistical measure used to evaluate how important a term is to a document. The importance increases proportionally to the number of times a term appears in the document but is offset by how common the term is in all of the documents in the collection. The idf measure was computed on the whole DUC document collection[2].

$$tf.idf_{\nu_d,j} = tf_{\nu_d,j} \times \log\left(\frac{Nb_{doc}}{n_j}\right) \qquad (6)$$

$tf_{\nu_d,j}$ is the frequency of the term j in the document ν_d, n_j is the number of documents in which the term j is present. Similarity values are normalized in $[0, 1]$.

3.2   Overlap

We have introduced this measure believing that the selected sentences have to share the same information as the topic. In order to quantify the shared information, we have chosen the number of common words between the topic and a sentence s. The Overlap, calculated for each sentence, is the normalized cardinality of the intersection between the sentence word set S and the topic word set T. This measure forces high ranking for sentences containing topic words and overcome the problem of high ranked sentence not containing any word of the topic.

$$Overlap(s, \omega_t) = \frac{card\{S \bigcap T\}}{card\{T\}} \qquad (7)$$

$card\{\bullet\}$ represents the cardinality of the set $\{\bullet\}$. $s = 1 \cdots N_L$, N_L is the total number of sentences. The Overlap values are normalized in $[0, 1]$.

---

[2] See section 4 for more informations about the DUC Conference.

3.3 Final Sentence Ranking

Similarity and Overlap parameters are used to refine the CORTEX scores. The final *Score* of a sentence s of a document ν_d and a topic ω_t is the linear combination:

$$Score = \alpha_0 \cdot CORTEX(s, \nu_d) + \alpha_1 \cdot Overlap(s, \omega_t) + \alpha_2 \cdot Sim(\nu_d, \omega_t) \; ; \quad (8)$$

$$\sum_i \alpha_i = 1$$

The α_i values are empirical weights associated with the intermediate scores [3] of a sentence. The summary is generated with the Λ sentences of high score. Λ is fixed by the user, it can be a ratio of the initial size of all documents or a fixed number of sentences.

The NEO-CORTEX system (see figure 1) is resulting from the application of Similarity and Overlap parameters over the CORTEX system.

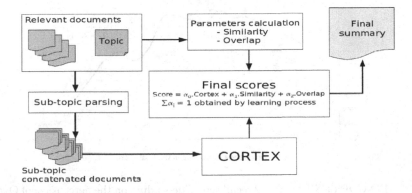

Fig. 1. General architecture of the NEO-CORTEX system, the process is applied for each couple of topic and relevant collection of documents

3.4 Evaluating Summary Quality

The evaluation of the summaries is a difficult task, it can be achieved by evaluating independently the summary (intrinsic way) or by evaluating the summary in a specific task such as Question Answering (extrinsic way). The summaries are evaluated as either manually or semi-automatically. The first approach requires high human time cost (each summary has to be read, evaluated and appreciated) and is very subjective (divergence between judges can be considerable). The second approach is more standardized and has the ability to be exactly repeatable but requires human-produced reference documents. Several different approaches

---

[3] We called intermediate $CORTEX(s, \nu_d)$ the score calculated in formula (4), $Sim(.)$ the score calculated by (5) and $Overlap(.)$ the score calculated by (7).

for semi-automatic evaluation exist such as Pyramid [17] or Basic Elements (BE) [18]. The Recall-Oriented Understudy for Gisting Evaluation (ROUGE) [19] semi-automatic approach was used for our experiments. Two ROUGE Recall measures was computed for our evaluations, ROUGE-2 (bigram co-occurrence), ROUGE-SU4 (skip bigram with unigram and maximum gap length of 4) an Basic Elements BE. They are officially used and adopted for the DUC task. All the ROUGE results of this paper are obtained with light post processing and hard cut at 250 words.

3.5   Tuning the Parameters for the DUC Task

We have tuned the α_i parameters of NEO-CORTEX using the DUC 2005 data-set. In order to find the optimal repartition of Overlap in the final sentence score, we have settled the Similarity parameter to 0 and realized a precise scanning (in step of 0.05) by increasing the Overlap until we obtained the optimal repartition. The optimal ROUGE-2 score is obtained with $\alpha_1 \approx 0.4$ (see figure 2).

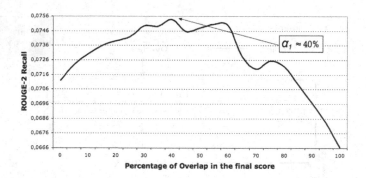

Fig. 2. NEO-CORTEX ROUGE-2 recall scores depending on the percentage of Overlap α_1 on the DUC 2005 dataset. The Similarity factor $\alpha_2 = 0$ and the $CORTEX$ factor $\alpha_0 = 1 - \alpha_1$ (Overlap). The optimal score is obtained with $\alpha_1 \approx 40\%$.

The optimal Similarity parameter α_2 is obtained by a similar way. The Overlap α_1 and the $CORTEX$ α_0 are settled to the previous optimal repartition ($\alpha_0 = 0.6$ and $\alpha_1 = 0.4$). The figure 3 shows two peaks (optimal values for α_2 parameter). As the DUC 2005 data-set is not enough important and in order to avoid errors due to the particularity of one corpus, we have empirically chosen the first peak, $\alpha_2 = 0.11$ (see figure 3) of the total repartition.

Previous experiments showed that the Overlap is more important than the Similarity. This is why we have firstly tuned the Overlap parameter. We have normalized the α_i values and found the optimal repartition of the parameters for the DUC 2005 data-set: $\alpha_0(CORTEX) = 0.54$ ($0.6 \rightarrow 0.54$) , α_1 (Overlap) $= 0.36$ ($0.4 \rightarrow 0.36$) and α_2 (Similarity) $= 0.10$ ($0.11 \rightarrow 0.10$). Further experiments confirmed that the parameters found are optimal.

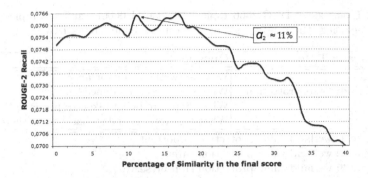

Fig. 3. NEO-CORTEX ROUGE-2 recall scores depending on the percentage of similarity α_2 on the DUC 2005 data-set. The Similarity factor $\alpha_2 = 1 - (\alpha_0(CORTEX) + \alpha_1(Overlap))$. The optimal score is obtained with $\alpha_2 \approx 11\%$.

4   Adaptations for DUC 2006 Task

The system task for DUC 2006 [4] is to model real-world complex Question Answering, in which a question cannot be answered by simply stating a name, date, quantity, etc. Given a topic and a set of 25 relevant documents [5], the task is to synthesize a fluent, well-organized 250-word summary of the documents that answers the question(s) in the topic statement.

4.1   Managing the Topics

A topic is composed by two parts, the title and the narrative part (containing the questions). In the same way as a human would make, we have parsed the topic to create sub-topics (see table 2). Indeed, each question of the narrative part needs to be answered, so we have chosen to create sub-topics that are the concatenation of the title and one of the topic's question of the narrative part. For each relevant document of the topic set, ζ document to be handle by CORTEX are created, ζ is the number of sub-topics.

4.2   Finding the Best Metrics for DUC 2006

The CORTEX system can use up to 13 metrics [12] to evaluate the sentence's pertinence, we have tested empirically a wide range of combinations and finally choose three metrics:

- Angle between a title and a sentence (A): Cosinus of the normalized scalar vector product between the sentence and the topic vector.

---

[4] http://www-nlpir.nist.gov/projects/duc/index.html
[5] Documents source: AQUAINT corpus. Articles from the Associated Press and New York Times (1998-2000) and Xinhua News Agency (1996-2000).

Table 2. Examples of DUC 2006 topics (D0603C, D0606F) and sub-topics resulting from their parsing (the sub-topics have been filtered and lemmatized)

Number and Title	Question(s)
D0603C Wetlands value and protection	Why are wetlands important? Where are they threatened? What steps are being taken to preserve them? What frustrations and setbacks have there been?
Sub-topic 1: wetland value protection important **Sub-topic 2:** wetland value protection threat **Sub-topic 3:** wetland value protection step preserve **Sub-topic 4:** wetland value protection frustration setback	
D0606F Impacts of global climate change	What are the most significant impacts said to result from global climate change?
Sub-topic 1: impact global climate change significant	

These two other metrics use a Hamming matrix H, a square matrix $N_L \times N_L$, in which every value $H[i,j]$ represents the number of sentences in which exactly one of the terms i or j is present.

$$H_{m,n} = \sum_{j=1}^{N_P} \left\{ \begin{array}{ll} 1 & \text{if } \xi_{j,m} \neq \xi_{j,n} \\ 0 & \text{elsewhere} \end{array} \right\} \quad \text{for } \begin{array}{l} m \in [2, N_L] \\ n \in [1, m] \end{array} \tag{9}$$

The Hamming matrix is a lower triangular matrix where index m represents the line and index n the column, corresponding to the index of words $(m > n)$. The main idea is that if two important words (may be synonyms) are in the same sentence, this sentence must certainly be important. The importance of every pair of words directly corresponds to the value in the Hamming matrix H.

- Hamming weight heavy (L): Among the sentences containing the same set of important words, how do we know which one is the best? i.e. wich one of these sentences is the more informative? The solution is to choose the one that contains the biggest part of the lexicon. Π = Sum of Hamming weight of words per segment × the number of different words in a sentence.
- Sum of Hamming weights of words by frequency (O): The sum of the Hamming weights of the words by frequencies uses the frequencies as factor instead of the presence. The sentences containing the most important words several times will be favored. O = The sum of the Hamming weights of the words × word frequencies.

We have tested a lot of metrics combinations as well as single metrics by trying to maximize the ROUGE measures (see figure 4). The other metrics [11] used in CORTEX system are: H for Perplexity; X for Sentence shape; B for partial $tf.idf$ (uses terms of frequency greater than one); F for Term Frequency (tf); P for Hamming weights of segments; D for Sum of probability frequencies;

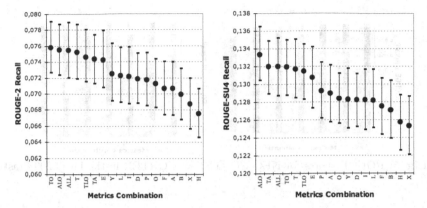

Fig. 4. NEO-CORTEX ROUGE scores in the DUC 2005 task depending on the metrics combination used. The ALL combination means all metrics of CORTEX.

Y for Hamming distances; E for Entropy; T for Sum of Hamming weights of words per segments; I for Interactivity of segments.

4.3   Managing the Sentence Length

The summary word limit, for the DUC 2005 and 2006 tasks, is 250 words. The NEO-CORTEX system was not able to choose between two sentences of same score but with different lengths. Is a n or $10n$ words sentence important for short summary ? We have introduced a smoothing of the CORTEX scores depending of the sentence length by dynamically calculate, for each document, a gaussian. Further experiments showed that using a sigmoid based smoothing instead of the gaussian would improve significantly the ROUGE scores.

5   Results

In this section we will compare the ROUGE scores of NEO-CORTEX and COR-TEX systems. We have compared the overall performances of NEO-CORTEX and CORTEX with the seven best ROUGE score metrics combinations on the DUC 2005 data-set. The ROUGE scores of all metrics combinations (see figure 5) are improved.

The NEO-CORTEX system was also compared to the other participants of the DUC 2005 evaluation (see figure 6). Our system achieves very good performance (best system for all ROUGE scores). The fact is that the training data-set used for tuning NEO-CORTEX was the DUC 2005 data-set. NEO-CORTEX is optimally tuned for the DUC 2005 evaluation, this explain why it is very performant.

In order to quantify the real perfomance of our system, we have also compared it to the participants of the DUC 2006 evaluation. The evaluation criteria in DUC 2006 remained same as DUC 2005, our summarization system performed well in the automatic evaluation (see figure 7).

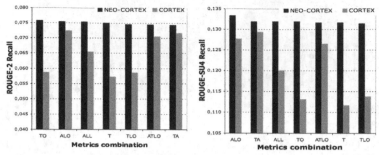

Fig. 5. ROUGE scores for NEO-CORTEX vs CORTEX in the DUC 2005 task

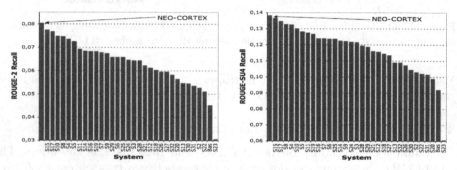

Fig. 6. ROUGE-2 recall (left) and ROUGE-SU4 recall (right) scores of NEO-CORTEX vs all participating systems in the DUC 2005 task

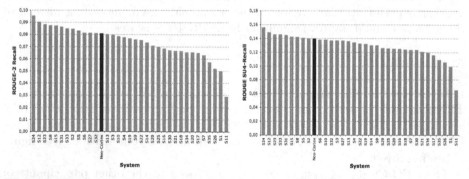

Fig. 7. ROUGE-2 recall (left) and ROUGE-SU4 recall (right) scores of NEO-CORTEX vs all participating systems in the DUC 2006 task. Neo-Cortex is ranked 13th in ROUGE-2 and 10th in ROUGE-SU4 over 35 systems.

6   Conclusion and Future Work

We have presented NEO-CORTEX, a multi-document summarization system based on the CORTEX system, and the participation in DUC 2006 task. Our experiments have shown that NEO-CORTEX is an effective system and achieves good performance on topic-oriented multi-document summarization task. NEO-CORTEX is however sensitive to the sentence segmentation, ROUGE scores have increased throughout our research time according to the segmentation quality enhancement. The ability of the system to be language independent is key point. Our participation in DUC 2006 was an excellent opportunity to evaluate the flexibility of the CORTEX system on a new and different task. In DUC 2006 the LIA-Thales fusion of five summarization systems among NEO-CORTEX, obtained very good results in the automatic evaluations (ranked 5th in ROUGE-SU4, 6th in ROUGE-2, 6th in BE and 6th in Pyramid) and achieved good performance in human evaluations (ranked 8th in the Resp-Overall) [20] . As always, there is a room for improvement and future work. In NEO-CORTEX, we would like to focus on improving our performance in metrics combinations, which we believe would enhance summaries quality. To that end, we are currently experimenting an incremental process, which in each step tries to find a different metrics combination. We would also like to use machine-learning to dynamically find the optimal α_i parameters of the sentence scoring and automatically adapt the system.

References

1. Mani, I., Maybury, M.T.: Advances in Automatic Text Summarization. The MIT Press (1999)
2. Mani, I.: Automatic Summarization. John Benjamins Publishing company (2001)
3. Luhn, P.: Automatic creation of literature abstracts. IBM Journal of Research and Development (1958) 155–164
4. Edmundson, H.: New Methods in Automatic Extracting. Journal of the ACM (JACM) 16(2) (1969) 264–285
5. Paice, C.D.: Constructing literature abstracts by computer: techniques and prospects. Inf. Process. Manage. 26(1) (1990) 171–186
6. Mani, I., Bloedorn, E.: Machine Learning of Generic and User-Focused Summarization. Arxiv preprint cs (CL/9811006) (1998)
7. Kupiec, J., Pedersen, J., Chen, F.: A trainable document summarizer. Proceedings of the 18th annual international ACM SIGIR conference on Research and development in information retrieval (1995) 68–73
8. Barzilay, R., Elhadad, M.: Using lexical chains for text summarization. Proceedings of the ACL Workshop on Intelligent Scalable Text Summarization (1997) 10–17
9. Stairmand, M.: A Computational Analysis of Lexical Cohesion with Applications in Information Retrieval. Unpublished PhD Thesis. UMIST Computational Linguistics Laboratory (1996)
10. Mann, W., Thompson, S.: Rhetorical Structure Theory: A Theory of Text Organization. University of Southern California, Information Sciences Institute (1987)
11. Torres-Moreno, J.M., Velázquez-Morales, P., Meunier, J.: Cortex: un algorithme pour la condensation automatique de textes. ARCo 2 (2001) 365
12. Torres-Moreno, J.M., Velázquez-Morales, P., Meunier, J.: Condensés de textes par des méthodes numériques. JADT 2 (2002) 723–734
13. Abdillahi, N., Nocera, P., Torres-Moreno, J.M.: Boîtes à outils TAL pour les langues peu informatisées: Le cas du somali. JADT (2006) 697 – 705

14. Porter, M.: An algorithm for suffix stripping. Program **14**(3) (1980) 130–137
15. Salton, G. In: Automatic text processing. Addison-Wesley Publishing Co. (1989)
16. Salton, G., McGill, M.: Introduction to modern information retrieval. Computer Science Series McGraw Hill Publishing Company (1983)
17. Passonneau, R., Nenkova, A., McKeown, K., Sigleman, S.: Applying the Pyramid Method in DUC 2005. Proc. of DUC 2005 at the Human Language Technology Conf./Conf. on Empirical Methods in Natural Language Processing (HLT/EMNLP) (2005)
18. Hovy, E., Lin, C., Zhou, L.: Evaluating DUC 2005 using Basic Elements. Proc. of DUC 2005 at the Human Language Technology Conf./Conf. on Empirical Methods in Natural Language Processing (HLT/EMNLP) (2005)
19. Lin, C.Y.: Rouge: A package for automatic evaluation of summaries. Technical report, Information Sciences Institute (2002)
20. Favre, B., Béchet, F., Bellot, P., Boudin, F., El-Bèze, M., Gillard, L., Lapalme, G., Torres-Moreno, J.M.: The LIA-Thales summarization system at DUC-2006. http://www-nlpir.nist.gov/projects/duc/index.html (2006)

Event-Based Summarization Using Time Features

Mingli Wu[1], Wenjie Li[1], Qin Lu[1], and Kam-Fai Wong[2]

[1] Department of Computing
The Hong Kong Polytechnic University
Kowloon, Hong Kong
{csmlwu, cswjli, csluqin}@comp.polyu.edu.hk
[2] Department of Systems Engineering and Engineering Management
The Chinese University of Hong Kong
Shatin, N.T., Hong Kong
kfwong@se.cuhk.edu.hk

Abstract. We investigate whether time features help to improve event-based summarization. In this paper, events are defined as event terms and the associated event elements. While event terms represent the actions themselves, event elements denote action arguments. After anchoring events on the time line, two different statistical measures are employed to identify importance of events on each day. Experiments show that the combination of $tf*idf$ weighting scheme and time features can improve the quality of summaries significantly. The improvement can be attributed to its capability to represent the trend of news topics depending on event temporal distributions.

1 Introduction

Available text information grows fast with the expansion of Internet. Automatic summarization technologies can help users identify main topics with bearable time cost. However, the quality of machine generated summaries can not match that of manual ones. Therefore, it is necessary to improve the performance of automatic summarization. The key problems are how to represent documents and how to identify important contents. Event is a natural unit to represent documents, especially for news reports. Encouraging summarization performance is reported in previous work [8, 19].

An event can be described as "who did what to whom when and where". Similar to the definition in [19], event is defined as event terms and the associated event elements at sentence level in this paper. Event terms represent the actions themselves, including verbs and action nouns. Event elements denote actions' arguments, such as participants, organizations, locations and times. For example, given the sentence "Yasser Arafat on Tuesday accused the United States of threatening to kill PLO officials", "accused" and "kill" are identified as an event terms, while "Yasser Arafat", "United States", "PLO" and "yesterday" are event elements.

News topics may shift over time. Among 30 document clusters of DUC 2001 dataset, about 10 clusters' model summaries consist of descriptions of some happenings at

A. Gelbukh (Ed.): CICLing 2007, LNCS 4394, pp. 563–574, 2007.

different times, which are presented clearly in the original texts. For example, the theme of cluster d41 is "the fires in California" and the model summary consists of descriptions about the fires in 1926, 1977, 1985, 1987 and 1990. This observation motivates us to investigate whether time features can help improve the quality of summaries for these clusters, in the context of event-based summarization.

Once events are anchored on the time line, their importance can be evaluated from local and global points of views. We employ two different statistical measures, i.e. $tf*idf$ and x^2. The weight of each sentence is the sum of weights of the event terms and event elements contained in it. Two kinds of sentence selection strategies are designed, sequential and robin selection. The combination of $tf*idf$ and sequential sentence selection based on sentence weight performs best. Compared with event-based summarization without time features, it improves the Rouge-1 score by 18.8% and Rouge-L score by 18.7% on two clusters of documents. In the further evaluation on ten clusters of documents, this approach achieved significant improvement when evaluated by human.

The remainder of the paper is organized as follows. Section 2 reviews the related work. Section 3 introduces the document representation on the time line. Section 4 then describes event weighting schemes and sentence selection strategies. Section 5 presents the experiments and discusses the results. Finally, Section 6 concludes the paper and suggests the future work.

2 Related Work

Document summarization technologies can be classified into two categories, extractive summarization and abstractive summarization. Extractive summarization is more effective at present. It can be dated back to [12] and [7]. With this approach, one can extract the most important sentences according to word frequency and word type, etc. Sentences with higher scores are then included in summary. $tf*idf$ weighting scheme is widely used to discriminate importance of words [4, 14]. In addition, surface features are also exploited such as position and length of sentence [14, 17]. To make the extraction model more adaptive with different document styles, machine learning method is employed in [10]. Similar to the algorithm in literature, one of our event weighting strategies is $tf*idf$, but it is adapted in a temporal context.

Recently, event-based summarization approaches has been investigated. In [8], event is defined as actions and named entities. Frequency of events is used to identify important sentences. Meanwhile, Vanderwende et al. [18] define event as dependency triples. Triple elements are connected by semantic relationships. Yoshioka et al. [20] employ similar approach to build document map. However they regard sentences as nodes in the map. Based on event map, both Vanderwende [18] and Yoshioka [20] employ PageRank algorithm to select important sentences. Encouraging results are reported, but time features are not considered.

Temporal information processing receives more attention nowadays, such as at TERN 2004 and ACE 2005. Two crucial problems in this field are identifying and normalizing temporal expressions from real texts. Among the reported research work, rule-based system achieves good performance [13, 15]. To focus on summarization techniques, temporal expressions are normalized manually and assigned to corresponding events manually in the work presented in this paper.

The application of temporal information in summarization has been considered in the past, but mostly based on publication dates. Given a sequence of news reports on certain topic, Alan et al. [2] extract sentences with usefulness and novelty to monitor changes. Usefulness is captured by considering whether a sentence can be generated by a language model created from the sentences seen to date. Novelty is captured by comparing a sentence to prior sentences. The evaluated performance need to be improved further. Afantenos et al. [1] discuss the techniques to summarize events happened in predictable time synchronously, such as football matches reported from at same times from different sources. Relations between events (messages) are defined on the axes of time and information source. These relations are determined by comparing different messages with heuristic rules. However, they do not report the evaluations on summaries.

Other researchers exploit distribution of events on time line by statistical measures. Swan and Allan [16] aimed at extracting and grouping important terms to generate "topics" defined by TDT. They employ x^2 statistics to measure the strength that a term is associated with a specific date. The subject evaluation shows the results are promising. Lim et al. [11] anchor documents on time line by the publication dates. Time slots (dates) are used to extract high frequency words in each slot, and then identify a topic sentence in the slot. Each sentence weight is adjusted by local and global high frequency words. They evaluate the system on Korean documents and report that time feature is helpful to improve the precision measure. Jatowt and Ishizuka [9] investigate the approaches to monitor the trends of dynamic web documents, which are different versions of documents on the time line. Based on distributions, terms are scored in order to identify whether they are popular and active. They employ a simple regression analysis about word frequency and time. A term's slop, intercept and variance are used to evaluate its importance. Unfortunately, they did not report quantitative evaluation results.

3   Event Representation on Time Line

Our event is defined at sentence level. Event terms and event elements are identified by a POS tagger and a named entity finder. Participants, organizations, locations and times are event elements. Verbs and action nouns between two event elements or near an event element within a limited distance are event terms. Action nouns are nouns that express meanings of action, e.g. "election" and "extension" etc. Hyponyms of "event" and "action" from WordNet are extracted as action nouns. The POS tagger and named entity finder we employed is GATE [6]. After tagging event terms and event elements, each sentence is represented by a collection of their instances.

Event can be instantaneous or durative. As Allen [3] proposed, interval can be used to represent a time point or duration. Points can be regarded as intervals with 'meeting places'. Thus on the time line, any instantaneous event can be represented by an interval with the same boundaries, i.e., a dot. A durative event is then represented as an interval with two boundaries or just one boundary if the other one is unknown. Time granularities mentioned with most news events are "day" or a coarser unit. So we use the "day" to measure the time line. Given this temporal unit, events are anchored on certain days.

In temporal logics, the meanings are different when one says an event happens at a day or in a day. If an event happens at a day, it happens at any time in a day. However, if it happens in a day, it actually happens at a particular time within a day. To simulate an event occurring on certain day, we simply represent it by a dot on the day, and let the weight of the dot to be 1. See the upper part of Fig. 1.

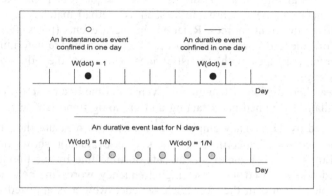

Fig. 1. Representation for events with two time ends

For other events with temporal granularities coarser than "day", such as "week", "month", "year" or "century", if the boundaries of time intervals can be identified, events will be represented by a set of dots, i.e. one dot per day in the mentioned intervals, see the lower part of Fig. 1 For example, "Peter arrived at Hong Kong in June, 2005." A set of dots will be used to denote the event, one dot per day in June 2005. As we assume each mention of an event is of same importance, thus the weight of each dot is equal to 1/30.

Some events may have no time period mentioned in a sentence. For example "Smith says the rebels have been dispersed", "Tom will leave U.S. after next Tuesday." Although an event of this type can not be located on the time line accurately, people always infer a time interval for it near the reference time. If the reference time is not mentioned clearly, the publication date is used instead. For these events, we simulate them with a series of discrete dots on the time line near the reference time.

It is observed that temporal granularity of most events is "day", and events in news report commonly occurred near reference time within a week. Therefore, in order to represent possible times of an event, we approximately employ 7 dots and place them into 7 temporal slots beside the reference time with same granularity, each dot per slot. If the reference time is given in "year" or "week" or "day", then the unit of time slots is also "year" "week" and "day".

For an event before or after the reference time, 7 dots will be placed on 7 time slots which are immediately before or after the reference time. For the event which occurs around the reference time, 3 dots are inserted before the reference day and 3 dots after the reference day. 1 dot is inserted on the reference day. Note that sum of weight scores of 7 dots equals to 1. They are shown in Fig. 2.

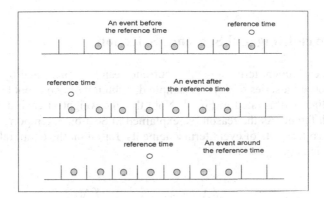

Fig. 2. Representation for events with one/no time end

We assume the normal distribution of weight for the event that occurs around the reference time.

$$f(x) = \frac{1}{\sqrt{2\pi}\sigma} e^{-\frac{(x-\mu)^2}{2\sigma^2}}$$

In the above equation, μ is the reference time, 3σ is equal to 7. It is assumed that the events are more likely to occur at the time slots closer to the reference time. By adding the right part of the symmetrical distribution function to the left part, we get the distribution function for the events occurred before the reference time (Fig. 3, "before"). Similarly, we can get the distribution for the events occurred after the reference time (Fig. 3, "after"). The weight of each dot $W(D, x)$ in Fig. 2 is equal to the area in Fig. 3 which is under the corresponding distribution function within the corresponding time slot.

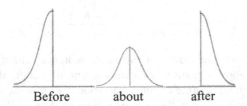

Before   about   after

Fig. 3. Distribution functions for weight of dots in Fig. 2

After the weight $W(D, x)$ of each dot on certain time slot x is calculated, if the temporal unit is coarser than "day" (1 unit = y days), then the weight of the event term/element on each day is computed as $W(D, x)/y$. If the temporal unit is finer than "day" (1 day = y units), then the weight of the event term/element on each day is computed as

$$t = x + (y / 2)$$
$$\sum W (D, t)$$
$$t = x - (y / 2)$$

4   Event Weighting and Sentence Selection

In Section 3, each event term/element occurrence can be represented by a dot on certain day or dots on a series of days. A sample distribution of two event terms/elements on the time line is illustrated in Fig. 4. Note that the weight of each dot on the time line can be different. As the reason we explained in Section 3, temporal unit "day" is employed to collect dots of event terms/elements. Based on the temporal distribution, events are weighted.

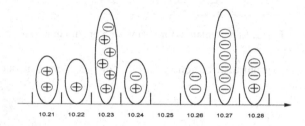

Fig. 4. Two event terms/elements on the time line ($\oplus$: an event term/element. $\ominus$: another event term/element)

Two different weighting schemes, $tf*idf$ and x^2, are used to estimate the importance of event term/elements on a particular day. Here tf is the sum of weight of the event term/element on a day. Possibly, the weights of some dots are not equal to 1. idf is equal to 1 over the number of days on which the event term/element happened. The x^2 algorithm is similar to that in [16]. It is defined as:

$$\chi^2 = \frac{N (ad - bc)^2}{(a + b)(a + c)(b + c)(b + d)}$$

Since N is a constant and does not influence sentence ranking, we omit it in our computation. In the above equation, a means the sum of weight of dots during the day t_0, and these dots represent same event term/element E. b is the sum of weight of all other dots during the day t_0. c is the sum of weight of dots on the days which are not t_0, and these dots represent same event term/element E. d represent the sum of weight of dots on the days which are not t_0, and these dots represent event terms/elements which are not E.

Given the weights of event terms and event elements on each day, then each sentence in the original documents will be weighted. When building event representation for each sentence, we keep the corresponding sentence ID with every instance of event term/element. Therefore the weight of a sentence is achieved by summing up all the weight of event terms /elements in the sentence. One event term/element may be represented by multiple dots on the time line.

We then propose two different strategies for sentence selection. To focus on the function of time features, we do not design any special algorithm to reduce redundant sentences in this study, although we are aware that some algorithms have been demonstrated helpful, like MMR [5]. All sentences are reverse ranked according to their weights first. Then sequential selection selects sentences one by one in each loop, until the length limitation of the summary is reached. Robin selection selects sentences with highest score for each year/month/day in each loop until the length of the summary is over limitation. We named the three robin approaches as Robin_Year, Robin_Month, and Robin_Day, respectively.

5 Experiments and Discussion

5.1 Preliminary Evaluation on Two Clusters

The data set we employed is DUC 2001 document collection. It contains 30 clusters and total 308 English news reports. As the focus of this study is summarization, we just tag the temporal expressions and assign temporal values to the corresponding events manually. However, we plan to automatically implement this procedure in the future. Given a sentence, if there is temporal specification about the events in a clause, such as a calendar date or a weekday, we will normalize the temporal expression and assign the date to this clause. Otherwise, we assign the publication date to this sentence. There may be different temporal values for different clauses in the same sentence.

In the preliminary evaluation, we preprocess two clusters and total 21 documents manually. For each cluster, there is one model summary composed by NIST assessors with the length of 200 words. ROUGE, a typical summarization evaluation package, is used to evaluate the quality of summaries. It compares machine generated summaries with model summaries based on unigram overlap, bi-gram overlap and overlap with long distance.

We investigate two weighting schemes with temporal features, tf*idf and x^2. Sentences are selected sequentially according to the reverse weight order. The baseline in our experiments is event-based summarization without temporal features. The results are shown in Table 1. From Table 1, we can see that event-based summarization with *tf*idf* weighting scheme based on temporal features performs better than the baseline and x^2, when evaluated by Rouge-1 score. The improvement from *tf*idf* on Rouge-2 score is also significant. It demonstrates that temporal features in *tf*idf* scheme are helpful to improve the quality of summaries.

However, x^2 weighting scheme does not bring notable improvement in the experiments. The reason is that x^2 values of some event terms/elements are much higher than those of other event terms/elements. When summing up weight of each event term/element as the weight of a sentence, they dominate the weight of the whole sentence. These dominant events may not represent the topic adequately.

Table 1. Results on event-based summarization with tf*idf and x^2

	Baseline	tf*idf	x^2
Rouge-1	0.271	0.322 (+ 18.8%)	0.282 (+ 4.1%)
Rouge-2	0.029	0.081 (+179.3%)	0.024 (-17.2%)
Rouge-L	0.252	0.299 (+ 18.7%)	0.263 (+ 1.1%)

Base on the *tf*idf* weighting scheme, sequential selection and robin selection are compared in the phase of sentence selection. The results are shown in Table 2. From table 2, we can see the sequential selection approach performs better than the robin selection approaches.

Table 2. Results on event-based summarization with sequential and robin sentence selection

	Robin_Year	Robin_Month	Robin_Day	Sequetial
Rouge-1	0.268	0.290	0.314	0.322
Rouge-2	0.018	0.018	0.057	0.081
Rouge-L	0.242	0.264	0.292	0.299

5.2 Evaluation on Ten Clusters

To further evaluate summaries generated by temporal-based summarization, we conduct two kinds of experiments on ten clusters of documents. The event-based summarization (baseline) and temporal-based summarization with *tf*idf* weighting scheme are compared in these experiments. In the first set of experiments, we employ ROUGE to evaluate the overlaps between events, which are extracted from model summaries, event-based summaries and temporal-based summaries. In the second set of experiments, we employ a graduate to judge whether each sentence in system generated summaries is relevant to a sentence in model summaries.

5.2.1 ROUGE Evaluation

Event terms and event elements are extracted from model summaries, event-based and temporal-based summaries respectively in the same way used to extract events from original documents. It is assumed that the extracted events represented the content of summaries. Instances of the same event term/element are kept in this evaluation. Then ROUGE is employed to evaluate word overlaps between events from machine summaries and model summaries. Fig. 5 shows the Rouge-1 scores of event-based summaries and temporal-based summaries. The average Rouge-1 score of event-based summarization is 0.160 and the average Rouge-1 score of temporal-based summarization is 0.144.

We also conduct another evaluation with ROUGE. In this evaluation, events are extracted from machine summaries and model summaries, but instances of the same event term/element are reduced as one concept. Then ROUGE is used to evaluate the overlap between events from machine summaries and model summaries. The results are shown in Fig. 6. The average Rouge-1 score of event-based summarization is 0.157 and the average Rouge-1 score of temporal-based summarization is 0.145.

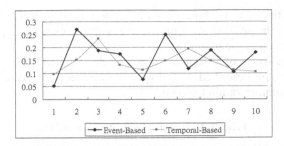

Fig. 5. Overlaps of event instances

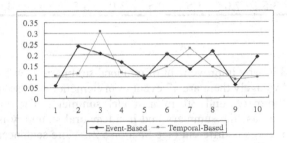

Fig. 6. Overlaps of event concepts

We can not see improvement brought by time features according to Fig. 5 and Fig. 6. The performance is improved on only five clusters, no matter we keep multiple instances of the same event or not. As ROUGE evaluate machine generated summaries based on N-gram overlap between model summaries and them, it is not sufficient to tell whether the meanings of these two kinds of summaries are same or relevant. Then we conduct another set of manual evaluations.

5.2.2 Subjective Evaluation
To judge the overlap between meanings of machine generated summaries and model summaries, we evaluate the relevance of each sentence in machine generated summaries with model sentences. The length limitations of the two kinds of summaries are both 200 words. There are 12.8 sentences in a model summary on average, while averagely there are 5.7 sentences in an event-based summary (baseline) and 6.6 sentences in a temporal-based summary.

The evaluation metrics are described as follows. First a subject is required to read all the documents and models summaries. The subject is required to judge whether each sentence of a machine generated summary is relevant to any sentence of the corresponding model summary. If meanings (participants, action, when, where, method, status) of a model sentence are same with the meanings of the machine generated sentence, or the subject can infer all of the meanings of the former from the meanings of the later, the machine generated sentence will receive the score "1"; If the subject can just infer part of the meanings of a model sentence from the machine generated sentence, then the machine generated sentence will receive the score "0.5". If the subject can not infer any meanings of any model sentence from a machine generated sentence, then the machine generated sentence will receive the score "0". If multiple rules can be applied for a machine generated sentence, then the final score will be the maximum of the multiple scores.

We sum up the scores of all sentences in a machine generated summary as its final score. The results are described as follows. We can see significant improvement of temporal-based summarization from table 3.

Table 3. Summaries Evaluated by a Subject

	C05	C08	C24	C28	C30	C32	C37	C41	C45	C50	Ave
Base	1.5	2.5	4.0	0	0	2.0	1.0	0	1.5	2.0	1.5
Temp	3.0	3.5	7.0	1.5	2.5	3.0	3.5	0	4.0	2.0	3.0

5.3 Discussion

We are interested in why improvement of temporal summaries can be seen in subjective evaluation. Averagely there are 47 event term/element in a base line summary, 48 in a temporal summary, and 30 in a model summary. The number of event terms/elements in a baseline summary and in a temporal summary is very close, but the number of sentences is different (see Section 5.2). More sentences are included in temporal summary. Therefore, more sentence candidates in temporal-based summaries can be judged.

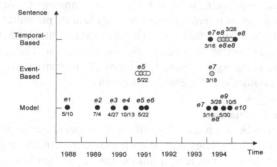

Fig. 7. The distribution of sentences in summaries on the time line

The model summaries of these ten clusters consist of a series of descriptions in different periods about certain topic, such as a film start, assassination, etc. We select sentences which burst on some days in temporal-based summarization. Events in these sentences are mentioned frequently on the bust days, while they are mentioned seldom on other days. The burst sentences are more likely the focus of certain period. Therefore, they are more likely to be relevant with sentences of model summaries.

While in event-based summaries without time features, we select sentences which contain event term/elements with higher centroid scores. The centroid scores are the average tf*idf weights over all documents. The events are "centroids" of clusters, but they may be not the focuses of different periods. Therefore, these sentences are less likely included in the model summaries, compared with the sentences in temporal-based summaries. The distribution of sentences in summaries on cluster d37 is presented in the Fig 7. A dark, gray and white dot denotes an event which is relevant, partially relevant and not relevant with an event in the model summary respectively. We can see that the temporal-based summary is better than the event-based summary in this figure, as it clearly denote the events in the model summary.

6 Conclusions and Future Work

We investigate whether time features help to improve performance of event-based summarization. $tf*idf$ and x^2 weighting scheme are employed to evaluate importance of event term/element on each day. Two kinds of sentence selection strategies are explored: sequential selection and robin selection. Experiments show that $tf*idf$ weighting scheme based on time features performs better than event-based summarization without time features. It can be concluded that time features are helpful to summarize the trend of news topics. We also find that robin selection does not improve the quality of summaries under the $tf*idf$ weighting scheme.

Temporal-based summarization ($tf*idf$ weighting scheme) improves Rouge-1 score of the base line by 18.8% and Rouge-L score by 18.7% in the preliminary experiments. To evaluate this approach further, we conduct the experiments on ten clusters. Significant improvement can be seen in the evaluation by subject. We attribute the improvement to the capability of temporal-based summarization to extract focus at different periods.

In the future, we plan to employ clustering technologies to select better representative sentence for different time periods and reduce redundancy between similar sentences. Then sentences in final summaries should cover different periods. We also plan to employ suitable time parser to extract and normalize temporal expressions, and then assign temporal value to corresponding event automatically.

Acknowledgement

The work presented in this paper is fully supported by a grant from the Research Grants Council of Hong Kong (project number: PolyU 5181/03E).

References

1. Afantenos, S.D., Karkaletsis V. and Stamatopoulos P.: Summarizing Reports on Evolving Events; Part I: Linear Evolution. Proceedings of Recent Advances in Natural Language Processing (2005)
2. Allan, J., Gupta, R., and Khandelwal, V.: Temporal Summaries of News Topics. Proceedings of the 24th Annual International ACM SIGIR Conference on Research and Development in Information Retrieval (2001), 10-18
3. Allen, J.F.: An Interval-based Representation of Temporal Knowledge. Proceedings of the 7th International Joint Conference on Artificial Intelligence (1981), 221-226

4. Brandow, R., Mitze, K., and Rau, L.F.: Automatic Condensation of Electronic Publications by Sentence Selection. Information Processing and Management (1995), 31(5):675-686

5. Carbonell, J. and Goldstein, J.: The use of MMR, diversity-based reranking for reordering documents and producing summaries. Proceedings of the 21th Annual International ACM SIGIR Conference on Research and Development in Information Retrieval (1998), 335–336

6. Cunningham, H., Maynard, D., Bontcheva, K., Tablan, V.: GATE: an Architecture for Development of Robust HLT Applications. Proceedings of the 40th Annual Meeting of the Association for Computational Linguistics (2002)

7. Edmundson H.P.: New Methods in Automatic Extracting. Journal of the Association for Computing Machinery (1969), 16(2):264-285

8. Filatova E. and Hatzivassiloglou, V.: Event-based extractive summarization. Proceedings of the 42th Annual Meeting of the Association for Computational Linguistics Workshop (2004), 104-111

9. Jatowt, A., Ishizuka, M.: Temporal Web Page Summarization. Proceedings of the 5th International Conference on Web Information Systems Engineering (2004), 303-312

10. Kupiec, J., Pedersen, J. and Chen, F.: A trainable document summarizer. In Proceedings of the 18th Annual International ACM SIGIR Conference on Research and Development in Information Retrieval (1995), 68-73

11. Lim, J.-M., Kang, I.-S., Bae J.-H., Lee J.-H.: Sentence Extraction Using Time Features in Multi-document Summarization. Information Retrieval Technology: Asia Information Retrieval Symposium (2004)

12. Luhn H.P.: The Automatic Creation of Literature Abstracts. IBM Journal of Research and Development (1958), 2:159-165

13. Mani, I. and Wilson, G.: Robust Temporal Processing of News. Proceedings of the 38th Annual Meeting of the Association for Computational Linguistics (2000)

14. Radev, D.R., Allison, T., et al.: MEAD - a Platform for Multidocument Multilingual Text Summarization. Proceedings of 4th International Conference on Language Resources and Evaluation (2004)

15. Schilder, F. and Habel, C.: From Temporal Expressions to Temporal Information: Semantic Tagging of News Messages. Proceedings of the 39th Annual Meeting of the Association for Computational Linguistics, Workshop on Temporal and Spatial Information Processing (2001), 65-72

16. Swan, R. and Allan, J.: Automatic Generation of Overview Timelines. Proceedings of the 23th Annual International ACM SIGIR Conference on Research and Development in Information Retrieval (2000), 49-56

17. Teufel, S. and Moens, M.: Argumentative Classification of Extracted Sentences as a First Step towards Flexible Abstracting. Advances in Automatic Text Summarization, Mani, I. and Maybury, M.T. (editors), 137-154. Cambridge, Massachusetts: MIT Press (1999).

18. Vanderwende, L., Banko, M. and Menezes, A.: Event-Centric Summary Generation. Available at http://duc.nist.gov/pubs.html (2004)

19. Wu, M.: Investigation on Event-Based Summarization. Proceedings of the COLING/ACL 2006 Student Research Workshop (2006)

20. Yoshioka, M. and Haraguchi, M.: Multiple News Articles Summarization Based on Event Reference Information. Working Notes of the 4th NTCIR Workshop Meeting. National Institute of Informatics (2004)

NLP-Based Curation of Bacterial Regulatory Networks

Carlos Rodríguez-Penagos, Heladia Salgado,
Irma Martínez-Flores, and Julio Collado-Vides

Programa de Genómica Computacional, Centro de Ciencias Genómicas.
Universidad Nacional Autónoma de México, Apdo. Postal 565-A, Avenida Universidad,
Cuernavaca, Morelos, 62100, Mexico
{crodriguezp,heladia,imartflo,collado}@ccg.unam.mx

Abstract. Manual curation of biological databases is an expensive and labor-intensive process in Genomics and Systems Biology. We report the implementation of a state-of-the-art, rule-based Natural Language Processing system that creates computer-readable networks of regulatory interactions directly from abstracts and full-text papers. We evaluate its output against a manually-curated standard database, and test the possibilities and limitations of automatic and semi-automatic curation of the so-called biobibliome. We also propose a novel Regulatory Interaction Mining Markup Language suited for representing this data, useful both for biologists and for text-mining specialists.

1 Introduction

Genomics and System Biology rely on vast amounts of data in order to profit from the sophisticated bioinformatics tools that model, analyze and interpret biological processes like gene regulation and metabolic pathways (Karp, 2001). These processes involve complex interactions between genes, transcriptions factors and other substances that can be visualized as networks of activation and repression triggering gene expression, controlling cell development and adaptability to environmental change. Most of the end result of biological research such as this materializes in textual publication in peer-reviewed journals, and has to be manually extracted (or *curated*, a very resource and labor-intensive task) in order to make this data amenable to computational analysis. Paralleling the sequenced genomes, the ever-expanding literature represented by the millions of papers in electronic repositories that have come to be known as the bibliome (Grivell, 2002) can literally overwhelm the ability of researchers to make sense of this flood of information.

The last ten years have seen a proliferation of Artificial Intelligence and Natural Language Processing (NLP) techniques to aid scientists. Good overviews of these recent approaches to data gathering and interpretation from textual sources (also referred to as Text-Mining) are Yandel & Majoros (2002), Krallinger et. al. (2005) and Scherf et. al. (2005). Although major challenges (like dealing with ambiguity and terminological variation) remain for full use of these applications in understanding and processing scientific documents, some of the techniques have reached a level of maturity that allow them to finally come out of the test bench and perform in the real

A. Gelbukh (Ed.): CICLing 2007, LNCS 4394, pp. 575–586, 2007.
© Springer-Verlag Berlin Heidelberg 2007

world. Information Extraction (IE) is one of the computational methods that have been used successfully in biological research. Compilation of the extremely complex networks of biochemical interactions that control developmental and functional processes in cells is a prime example of applications of these techniques to biology (see the BioCreative assays (Hirshman et. al. 2005), the PastaWeb (Demetriou et. al. 2002), GENIES (Friedman, et. al. 2001.) and BioRat (Corney et. al. 2004) systems, etc.).

In this work, we show how, and to what extent, a state-of-the-art NLP system can aid the manual curation process of transcriptional regulation in a bacterial organism, and how both approaches (manual vs. automatic curation) can complement each other. We will restrict our discussion as much as possible to NLP-related issues and introduce biological information only when needed to understand what and how our system is doing.

2   A Regulatory Network Extraction System

In order to test the capabilities of the extraction system reported here various corpora were gathered, involving either abstracts from Pubmed or full-text papers. We employed different strategies for the selection process, to be described later. Although we have experimented with machine-learning techniques to select documents relevant to *E. coli* K12 transcriptional regulation, in this work we used fairly standard search procedures, either gathering the lists of references from pre-curated databases (Ecocyc, RegulonDB), or doing various searches using the NIH Entrez facilities. Each selected corpus was first normalized and tokenized, separating all words and terms, dealing with abbreviations and punctuation and identifying sentential boundaries. For the overall architecture of the IE system, we adapted a rule-based pipeline as described in Saric et al. (2004). After preprocessing, we tagged the part-of-speech of each word using a customized version of Treetager (Schmid, 1994), and then ran a retagging module that substituted some of the POS tags for more semantically-oriented labels, such as *org* (organism), *nnpg* (protein/gene name), *actv* (activation verb), etc. For this Named-Entity Recognition task we used dictionaries and lists of biological entities created both inhouse and by other groups. We also implement a regular expression module for identifying genes and proteins that adhere to standard naming conventions. An accurate terminological inventory and a robust ontology can go far in ensuring a correct interpretation of the textual content.

The resulting output combined syntactic and semantic tags, and was fed into a SCOL parser (Abney 1996) that generated a tree-like structure by applying a grammar focused on the expression of biological concepts. This markup allowed for the recognition of biological entities and processes in relationships that can be inferred from the grammatical structure of the linguistic phrase. We adapted the core CASS grammars developed for the STRING-IE system (Saric et al. 2004) for transcriptional regulation. These rules constitute cascades of finite-state transducers that can identify semantic and syntactic features in tagged sentences. We implemented extensions of the rules to allow for corrections of minor errors and to handle verbal phrase (VP) coordination and simple anaphoric relationships which the original system didn't processed due to self-imposed restraints. Using these extensions, we were able to extract more than one relationship from a sentence such as [1] below.

After application of the CASS grammar rules, partially-parsed sentences were then converted into an intermediate xml format and processed by customized heuristic modules that a) identify the regulatory interactions that are to be extracted, b) identify, when possible, the kind of the interaction extracted (activation or repression) and c) create an xml output file with a regulatory network retrieved from the processed raw text. Figure 1 shows the processing pipeline of the extraction system we used for these experiments. For example, an "activation" relationship between CRP and acnB is one of the node of the regulatory network that can be inferred from a sentence such as [1].

[1] In contrast , acnB expression is activated by CRP and repressed by ArcA , FruR and Fis from PacnB .

We chose to use a Language-Engineering approach like the one used in the state-of-the-art STRING-IE system since in general we were concerned more with accuracy (precision) than with coverage (recall), and wanted to be fairly sure about the regulatory interactions we would be extracting. We also wanted to be able to modify the grammar rules to suit our purposes.

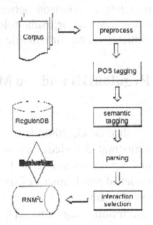

Fig. 1. Processing pipeline for Network Extraction system

3   A Markup Language for Mining Bacterial Regulatory Networks

The system's output is an xml file with a format we have called *Regulatory Network Mining Markup Language* (or RNM^{2}L), which allowed representation of the basic data relevant to Information Extraction of genetic regulation, both from the perspective of a biologist's interests (which genes/proteins were activated/repressed) and from the NLP specialist's needs (where was this information retrieved from, what linguistic rule was triggered for its retrieval, etc.). The following example shows some of the main features of a typical entry in RNM^{2}L from our experiments, depicting sentence [1] as a source. In the "interaction" node, the label *from* indicates the rule that allowed retrieval of that sentence, *source* refers to corpus where it was found, and *pmid* refers to the Medline identification number of the paper where this particular sentence was retrieved from:

```
<interaction ID="596" from="anaph+ev_act_expr_xr" ri_function="repressor"
    source="EcocycAbs">
<regulator GenProtID="ECK120011345" org="ecoli" type="nxpg"> ArcA </regulator>
<regulated GenProtID="ECK120002193" org="ecoli" type="nxpg"> acnB </regulated>
<evidence verb="repressed"/>
<sentence pmid="9421904"> In contrast , acnB expression is activated by CRP and repressed
    by ArcA , FruR and Fis from PacnB . </sentence>
</interaction>
```

Thus, we identify two entities, one the regulator and the other the regulated one, with unique ID numbers for each, and organism and semantic typing. Note that this entry represents only one of the four different one-to-one interactions that can be extracted from sentence [1]. We devised RNM^{2}L because: A) System Biology Markup Language (Hucka et. al. 2004), although very good at representing biochemical reactions (quantitatively and qualitatively) was too cumbersome for the more limited task of representing networks with discrete states, and B) because a more specialized tagging scheme would allow better comparison between networks extracted from different sources or with different systems or methodologies, while at the same time being useful both for NLP optimization and for biological interpretation.

4   Analyzed Corpora, RegulonDB and the Manual Curation Process

RegulonDB (Salgado, Gama-Castro, et. al, 2006) is the primary database of curation of original literature with experimental knowledge about the elements and interactions of the network of transcriptional regulation in *E. coli*, K-12 strain. RegulonDB can be considered a computational model of mechanisms of transcriptional regulation in this organism. The curation and annotation process starts by searching all articles that contain information about transcriptional regulation. The first step of this search is to gather abstracts from the PubMed database using a cascade of pertinent keywords. Then the abstracts of these papers are read by a team of 4 biologists-curators and further triage is done to select only the most relevant articles. Finally, the data extracted by reading those articles is added to the reference database. Although this curation process yields extremely high-quality data, it is a long-term and expensive proposition that can take years to complete.

For our evaluations of curation of *E. coli* regulatory networks, we collected different sets of abstracts and full-text papers that we assumed contained this information to varying degrees. Some were based on our manual curation efforts and others resulted from carefully crafted search strategies using the NCBI PubMed facilities.

The corpora used in our study is summarized in Table 1 below.

Table 1. Description of corpora used

ID	Name	# docs	type	description
RP	Regulon papers	2,475	full-text	Full text papers from the RegulonDB pmid references that were available online
RA	Regulon abstracts	3,075	abstracts	Abstracts from RegulonDB pmid references
EA	Ecocyc abstracts	13,334	abstracts	Abstracts from the Ecocyc database[1]
ST	STRING-IE	58,312	abstracts	Corpus generated by the STRING-IE team by searching in PubMed for "*E.coli*" (and synonyms), and two gene/protein names
RS	Search strategies	12,059	abstracts	Corpus generated by using the RegulonDB curator's search strategies
RN	Network references	724	full-text	Full-text papers from the RegulonDB database that curators have identified as referring specifically to the regulatory network

These triage strategies retrieved papers that represented different levels of coherence and of precision with regard to our domain of interest (transcriptional regulation). While searches ranging far and wide retrieved many references, a more focused search collected less documents, but more relevant ones. Thus, corpus RN, with curator-reviewed references to the regulatory network, constitutes the set of most relevant papers, while corpora ST and EA are more dispersed information sources. The different datasets analyzed reflect different purposes, and are clearly overlapping in many cases.

5   Evaluating the Network Extraction Task

To evaluate the regulatory networks extracted, a benchmarking tool was developed that checked each reported interaction against the RegulonDB database. We assumed this database to be a reliable golden standard of the final desired output, in contrast to the more customary evaluation methodologies that use a set of manually-annotated sentences from which a database of relevant information can be elicited. Since our database does not include the actual sentences from which the facts have been extracted[2] our automatic evaluation tool does not have available to it the linguistic expression of the accurate facts. This methodology involves, of course, some very strong assumptions about the completeness and exhaustiveness of the transcriptional regulation database, some of which this work was also meant to test. For example, we assumed that our network was accurately and completely curated, and that we had reviewed all papers relevant to this task. These assumptions (especially the second one) are questionable if we take them literally and at face value, but nonetheless can

---

[1] Ecocyc describes the genome and the biochemical machinery of *E. coli*.
[2] Although it does contain the PubMed identifiers of the papers curated.

be relied upon in this case (with the appropriate caveats), since *E. coli* K-12 is one of the best understood model organisms in the literature, and the Regulon database is carefully compiled and monitored.

Initially, all interactions that had a regulator gene/protein not included in the database (either by ID, name or synonym) were rejected. We didn't reject those interactions where the gene/protein was specified as a mutant or from another (mainly bacterial) organism, since valuable information was expressed using sentences such as the following: "In contrast, mutations in fadR significantly affected growth phase-dependent expression from the uspA promoter". Our main evaluation considered two cases, A) where the interaction is correctly identified with both the regulator and the regulated genes/proteins, and B) where, besides a correct identification of the involved entities, the nature of their relationship was also identified (as activation or repression). We calculated precision, recall and F-measure of the extracted networks by considering RegulonDB as the ultimate instance of a *E. coli* K-12 transcriptional regulation network.[3] Recall was estimated using the literature-attested 3,333 interactions in our reference database, considering dual activator-repressor pairs as one. This is not an orthodox measure of exhaustiveness, but since we were not using annotated corpora it was the closest we would get to knowing how many extractable phrases were extant in our RegulonDB corpora.

For precision we calculated two values: one (precision 1) where we used all the interactions retrieved (even if they were filtered out because the regulator gene/protein was not found in RegulonDB), and another one (precision 2) in which we only considered the subset of all interactions where the transcription-initial gene/protein was catalogued in the reference database. As with other aspects of these evaluations, we did this in order to understand what would happen in cases where we were dealing with other organisms for which we don't have all the information that we have available for *E. coli*, for instance, where we don't have an assumption of a completely curated network or not all transcription factors are known. Consequently, we created two different networks for each dataset: one where we multiplied interactions with previous knowledge about operons, two-component protein systems, heterodimers and other cases where multiple interactions are present or can be inferred, and another one where we assumed we didn't have any *ad hoc* information about those multi-entity objects.[4] In addition to the networks extracted from the different document collections described earlier, we also integrated a single network with all unique interactions retrieved from all the text-mining sources, in order to have a single text-mining sample that would be as exhaustive as possible, regardless of whether the initial search strategy was fine-grained (as in the RegulonDB sets) or coarse-grained as in the 195,000 Heidelberg abstract corpus. We present the resulting global text mining network of interactions attested from RegulonDB in Figure 2, alongside the actual RegulonDB network in Figure 3. Our final metrics for various dataset are shown in Table 2 below, and the data files and complementary material can be found at http://maya.ccg.unam.mx/ccg-ie/.

---

[3] We previously substracted from it all computational predictions, since they would conceivably not be present in experimental papers.

[4] Such networks, although less complete, would be more realistic with regard to the true capabilities of the extraction system, when applied to other less studied organisms.

Table 2. Final Network Extraction System Evaluation

Source	(1)	(2)	(3)	(4)	(5)	(6)	(7)	(8)	(9)	(10)
RegulonDB	3333	3843	-	3884	100.0%	100.0%	-	-	-	-
AS	3148	768	661	1429	45.0%	45.0%	0.45	0.77	0.45	0.57
RP	2650	711	605	1316	49.0%	42.0%	0.49	0.78	0.42	0.55
RN	1643	555	471	1026	62.0%	33.0%	0.62	0.85	0.33	0.47
AS*	2649	569	535	1104	41%	35%	0.41	0.72	0.35	0.47
RP*	2202	522	491	1013	46.0%	32.0%	0.46	0.74	0.32	0.45
RN*	1354	426	385	811	59.0%	26.0%	0.59	0.81	0.26	0.39
EA	627	262	140	402	64.0%	12.0%	0.64	0.95	0.12	0.22
RS	718	254	146	400	55.0%	12.0%	0.55	0.91	0.12	0.22
ST	691	199	143	342	49.0%	11.0%	0.49	0.90	0.11	0.19
RA	414	207	115	322	77.0%	10.0%	0.77	1.00	0.10	0.18

(Asterisk [*] indicates no multiple-unit objects added; **AS** .- From all sources, all interactions found)

1. Unique, non-repeated interactions found in file
2. Interactions that match RegulonDB
3. Interactions that match RegulonDB, and also match repressor/activator function
4. Overall matches (4+5)
5. % of total interactions in file which is correct (e.g. in RegulonDB)
6. % of RegulonDB represented by interactions in file
7. Precision 1: Number of overall matches (6) / unique interactions in file (2)
8. Precision 2: Number of overall matches (6) / interactions in file with RegulonDB regulator (3)
9. Recall: Number of overall matches / # of RegulonDB interactions
10. F-Measure: as per (Yang and Liu 1999)

   From a random sample of 96 interactions extracted, we established 81 of them as basically correct and 76 as completely correct,[5] for a 84% precision overall. The network that was gathered from all sources allowed us to obtain 45% of all the human-curated RegulonDB network, while the 700-plus selection of network-related papers (RN) accounted for 33% of that total. The artificial addition of multiple-entity objects like operons increased the size of the global network by 10% (324 interactions). In most datasets the increase was less significant, and as a whole the value of the information added with previous knowledge was not overly important.

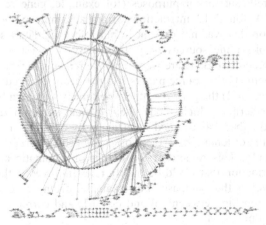

Fig. 2. From all text-mining sources, interactions retrieved that are in RegulonDB

---

[5] If the phrase was ambiguous with regard to function, it was marked as "unknown".

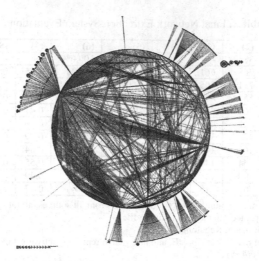

Fig. 3. All interactions in the RegulonDB Network

6 Evaluating Manual/Automatic Curation Strategies

We wanted to estimate how our triage and curation effort was holding up against all the potential information on the subject of transcriptional regulation on *E. coli* that was available in PubMed-based literature. Our curator-designed search strategies and subsequent filtering leave out almost 75% of all retrieved papers (although this ratio has changed with our evolving strategies and with the focus of research).

A biologist-curator reviewed a sample of the interactions which our system extracted, but that were not found in RegulonDB. This exercise allowed us to explore the information that, A) for whatever reason was not retrieved during the manual curation process but should have been, B) was processed incorrectly or C) although correct, was not relevant to our purposes (for example, gene regulation other than transcriptional). We found 19 interactions (from a sample of 96) that represented relevant information that was not present in our reference database, but that merited either a closer look at the sources or further analysis to establish if it should be incorporated into RegulonDB. There were multiple reasons for this information being missing, among them: 1) the source papers had not been retrieved for curation or had not been curated yet, or 2) the genes or other substances were mentioned with unusual synonyms, IDs or terms, which made their manual curation difficult, 3) or the evidence presented either was deemed insufficient by curators or was presented with high level of hedging or tentativity ("the molR gene probably regulates the expression of the chlD operon"). This review of the output of automatic annotation provided curators with information that could be highly relevant, even if they wouldn't add it immediately, as is, to the database. For example, from sentence [2] the system inferred the a relationship between rsd and bolAp1, and correctly annotated that we were dealing with a mutation:

> [2] As shown in Fig. 3A, the expression of bolAp1 in the rsd mutant strain was reduced to about 30% the level of wild-type strain.

Although such interactions shouldn't be automatically added to the database, they provide a context for, say, non-transcriptional regulation of sigma factors. Full processing of this data would require complex inference customized for biology. Other data that was not included in RegulonDB could nonetheless provide important context for biological interpretation associated with the annotation process. By doing a sweep of computer-generated curation, new or relevant information can be garnered that complements, expands or confirms human annotation.

Why didn't our IE system obtained a more complete network from these papers? First, there is the issue of the availability of full-text papers, which contain orders of magnitude more information than abstracts. From 3,110 RegulonDB pmids as of June 2006, we were able to retrieve full-papers only 2475, or 79.6% of total. We also had to deal with incorrect conversion from PDF, inconsistencies in term usage,[6] etc. Another problem is that not all the information we wanted was always presented in an explicit manner, or in a natural language format. Sometimes tables, graphics and illustrations allowed human curators to generate relevant information, for example by using some kind of inference. Another shortcoming of our extraction system is its inability to integrate information that was presented intersententially, that is, conceptually built-up in two or more neighboring sentences. This kind of discourse processing is, of course, trivial for human readers but challenging for NLP.

The sources used for the extraction were also decisive factors in how well the system performed. In order to compare the different triage techniques employed in RegulonDB, we estimated what could be termed the "informational density" of the different corpora. We correlated the total size of the network obtained from these sources, the number of distinct documents and the raw size of each one. Table 3 shows how one set of documents, even though might have a lower number of source documents, could have a bigger overall size and contain more of the desired interactions, and in this way we can compare more accurately the quality and quantity of the network information obtained with each of the datasets. One of the ratios we estimated was the percentage of all interactions obtained that were found in RegulonDB, another measured average size of each document in the corpus the ratio, while the last one how many RegulonDB interactions were obtained per document.

Table 3. Informational density of various corpora

Corpus	# docs	size (MB)	Regulon network	All network	% in Regulon	average doc size (kbs)	Interactions / docs
RN	724	24.9	1026	1643	62.4	65.9	1.41
RP	2475	99.0	1316	2650	49.6	40.0	0.53
RA	3075	3.3	322	414	77.7	1.07	0.1
EA	13334	14.4	402	627	64.1	1.08	0.03
RS	12059	12.3	400	718	55.7	1.02	0.03
ST	58312	10.7	342	691	49.5	0.18	0.005

The density of RegulonDB-related information shows that in a set of abstracts with less overall interactions than a full-text one with a similar number of documents, the relevant information would be more densely-packed although we can expect to

---

[6] Although this seems to be a lesser problem in *E. coli* than in other organisms where there are genes that use general language words such as "hedgehog".

retrieve a smaller quantity of information. Until the automatic triage issue is fully resolved, high-throughput Information Extraction techniques can help lessen the impact of this specific problem on total results, since the technology can go equally well through a lesser number of more informational papers than through many more less relevant papers, and still retrieve a significant, useful amount of interactions.

7 Discussion

How much valuable information was lost in those papers that were filtered out in the initial triage? Is a tightly-focused search-and-selection strategy better than casting a wider net? What is preferable when curating large-scale biological networks, exhaustiveness or precision in the data? Can automatic and manual annotation complement each other so we don't have to expect a trade-off? Similar previous work has focused on related, but somewhat different, issues: Rodriguez-Esteban et. al. (2006) evaluated the results of the GeneWays pathway Information Extraction system using Machine-Learning techniques to simulate the decision-making process of curators, when reviewing the results of such systems, thus framing the process as a classification problem ("correct/incorrect"). One conspicuous difference between their evaluation approach and ours is that we used RegulonDB as a (putatively perfect) golden standard, while they relied on manually-reviewed and training-testing data, albeit with measures of inter-annotator agreement to ensure objectivity. Karamanis et.al. (2007) have reported the use of NLP-based tools to assist curation of the fruit fly database, but their evaluations are grounded on the average time employed by curators to fill their forms and are thus not really comparable to our own methodologies for improving overall curation.

Unlike a system that would only present the final extracted databases to be corroborated by curators, our own system supplies (using RNM^2L markup) both the database information as well as the linguistic context from where it was extracted. It also provides a link to PubMed so users can go directly to the whole sources (abstract or papers). By going over automatically-curated information from a wider variety of sources, they would not only verify information already curated by more traditional means but will also encounter information that either escaped manual curation or could help contextualize previously captured information, like other regulatory non-transcriptional processes involving important genes in the reconstructed network, the role of sigmas and plasmids in the overall metabolic processes of the cell or even the conditions under which various biochemical reactions occur.

Many of the system's shortcomings have to do with mundane reasons, such as incomplete named-entity dictionaries, imperfect format conversion, word tokenization, reporter-gene occurrences, etc. Enhancement in these areas is time-consuming, but is also perfectly feasible and does not represent any technical hurdle, although adaptation of the system to other genomes and organisms can be tricky due to these same reasons. A more significant reason for some "errors" can be the inability of the system to do a fine-grained discrimination between different kinds of regulation, or of mutations or genes from other organisms.

Another source of possible errors is the handling of hedging and modal contexts such as those introduced by predicates expressing temptativeness and possibility ('it seems that'), trial ('we tested'), or possible future outcome ('might show that'), which are quite common in scientific publications (Saurí et. al., 2006). For example, from:

cstA expression in relA and relA spoT mutants was also examined .

We cannot infer with certainty that the interactions between cstA and relA or relA spoT were corroborated by experiments —although probably this was made clear in the following paragraphs.

Our experiences have shown that Natural Language Processing, although still far from being able to do full text interpretation or locate all the information that a trained human expert can gather from scientific papers, it can certainly be an extremely useful tool for curatorial efforts. Manual curation of the output of automatic processes can be a good way to complement more detailed reading of the literature, either for validating the results of what has already being curated or for discovering facts and information that might have been overlooked at the triage or annotation stages. By combining the exacting precision of human readers with the tireless abilities of Information Extraction systems to rapidly cover a lot of ground with reasonable accuracy, genomic data on other organisms less studied than *E. coli* or *S. cerevisia* (so-called *model organisms*) can be obtained for the high-throughput methods of the new Systems Biology of today.

References

Abney S (1996). Partial parsing via finite-state cascades. In Proceedings of the ESSLLI '96 Robust Parsing Workshop, pages 8–15, Prague, Czech Republic.

Corney, D. P. A., Buxton, B. F., Langdon W.B. and Jones, D. T. (2004) BioRAT: Extracting Biological Information from Full-length Papers, Bioinformatics (Nov 22 2004; vol. 20(17); pp. 3206-13).

Demetriou G, Gaizauskas R. (2002), Utilizing Text Mining Results: The PastaWeb System. In Proceedings of the Association for Computational Linguistics Workshop on Natural Language Processing in the Biomedical Domain, Philadelphia, July 11, pp. 77-84.

Friedman C, P. Kra, H. Yu, M. Krauthammer, and A. Rzhetsky. (2001). GENIES: a natural-language processing system for the extraction of molecular pathways from journal articles. Bioinformatics, 17 Suppl. 1:S74–S82.

Grivell L (2002) Mining the bibliome: searching for a needle in a haystack? New computing tools are needed to effectively scan the growing amount of scientific literature for useful information. EMBO Rep. 2002 Mar;3(3):200-3.

Hirschman L, Yeh A, Blaschke C, Valencia A.(2005) Overview of BioCreAtIvE: critical assessment of information extraction for biology. BMC Bioinformatics. 2005;6 Suppl 1:S1. Epub 2005 May 24.

Hucka M, Finney A, Bornstein BJ, Keating SM, Shapiro BE, Matthews J, Kovitz BL, Schilstra MJ, Funahashi A, Doyle JC, Kitano H. (2004) Evolving a lingua franca and associated software infrastructure for computational systems biology: the Systems Biology Markup Language (SBML) project. System Biology (Stevenage). 2004 Jun;1(1):41-53

Karamanis N, Lewin I., Sealy R., Drysdaley R., Briscoe E. (to appear) Integrating Natural Language Processing with Flybase Curation. Proceedings from Pacific Symposium on Biocomputing (2007)

Karp PD (2001) Pathway databases: a case study in computational symbolic theories. Science. 2001 Sep 14;293(5537):2040-4.

Krallinger M, Erhardt RA, Valencia A. (2005) Text-mining approaches in molecular biology and biomedicine. Drug Discov Today. 2005 Mar 15;10(6):439-45.

Rodriguez-Esteban R, Iossifov I, Rzhetsky A (2006) Imitating Manual Curation of Text-Mined Facts in Biomedicine. PLoS Comput Biol 2(9): e118

Salgado H, Gama-Castro S, Peralta-Gil M, Diaz-Peredo E, Sanchez-Solano F, Santos-Zavaleta A, Martinez-Flores I, Jimenez-Jacinto V, Bonavides-Martinez C, Segura-Salazar J, Martinez-Antonio A, Collado-Vides J. RegulonDB (version 5.0): Escherichia coli K-12 transcriptional regulatory network, operon organization, and growth conditions. Nucleic Acids Res. 2006 Jan 1;34(Database issue):D394-7.

Saric J., Jensen L., and Rojas I. (2004) Large-scale Extraction of Gene Regulation for Model Organisms in an ontological context *In Silico Biology*, **5**, 0004.

Saurí, R, Verhagen M. and Pustejovsky J. (2006). Annotating and Recognizing Event Modality in Text. In Proceedings of the 19th International FLAIRS Conference, FLAIRS 2006. Melbourne Beach, Florida. May 11-13, 2006.

Scherf M, Epple A, Werner T. (2005) The next generation of literature analysis: integration of genomic analysis into text mining. Brief Bioinform. 2005 Sep;6(3):287-97.

Schmid H. (1994) Probabilistic part-of-speech tagging using decision trees. In Proceedings of International Conference on New Methods in Language Processing, September 1994

Yandell MD, Majoros WH. (2002) Genomics and natural language processing. Nature Reviews Genetics. 2002 Aug; 3 (8):601-10.

Exploiting Category Information and Document Information to Improve Term Weighting for Text Categorization*

Jingyang Li and Maosong Sun

National Laboratory of Intelligent Technology and Systems,
Dept. of Computer Sci. & Tech., Tsinghua University, Beijing 100084, China
lijingyang@gmail.com, sms@tsinghua.edu.cn

Abstract. Traditional *tfidf*-like term weighting schemes have a rough statistic — *idf* as the term weighting factor, which does not exploit the category information (category labels on documents) and intra-document information (the relative importance of a given term to a given document that contains it) from the training data for a text categorization task. We present here a more elaborate nonparametric probabilistic model to make use of this sort of information in the term weighting phase. *idf* is theoretically proved to be a rough approximation of this new term weighting factor. This work is preliminary and mainly aiming at providing inspiration for further study on exploitation of this information, but it already provides a moderate performance boost on three popular document collections.

1 Introduction

Term weighting has always been a fundamental step in text information processing tasks, such as information retrieval (IR), text categorization, etc. This concept was first introduced in IR (see [1,2]), for which the *tfidf* term weighting scheme became a byword for Rocchio algorithm. Since text categorization is a task with many connections to IR (see [3]), they share many models, including the *tfidf* term weighting scheme. Hence it is not only used in the Rocchio algorithm but also as a pre-requisite phase for other text-applicable classifiers such as Support Vector Machines (see [4,5]). Some theoretical analysis of *tfidf* was carried out afterwards (see [6,7,8]) and to some extent made the implicit assumption of *tfidf* classifiers explicit.

Nevertheless, text categorization and IR are different tasks; roughly speaking, text categorization is a supervised learning task while IR is usually a unsupervised task. *tfidf* term weighting scheme comes from IR and does not involve the training information for text categorization, while the other phases of text categorization do, such as the *dimensionality reduction* and *classifier induction*.

* This research is supported by the National Natural Science Foundation of China under grant number 60573187 and 60321002, and the Tsinghua-ALVIS Project co-sponsored by the National Natural Science Foundation of China under grant number 60520130299 and EU FP6.

A. Gelbukh (Ed.): CICLing 2007, LNCS 4394, pp. 587–598, 2007.

1.1   Feature Selection and Term Weighting

Feature selection and term weighting are two common phases of text categorization. They are connected and seem similar at first glance, but they are designed for different purposes, which is not often clarified in literature.

Text categorization tasks. Term selection schemes generally take account of two criteria: *coverage* — the selected terms should not be too sparse in the corpus(see [9]); and *distinctness* — the occurrences of the selected terms in a document should be helpful to judge which category the document belongs to.

In term weighting phase, each term-document pair (x_i, d_j) is given a value w_{ij} which should exactly reflect the contribution of x_i to the significance of d_j's belongingness to some category (x_i's *supporting category*). For *tfidf* term weighting function, $tf(x_i, d_j)$ (as well as other variations, e.g. $\log(tf(x_i, d_j)+1)$ for smoothing) is a multiplier relying on the current document d_j. While the other multiplier — *term weighting factor* $\omega(x_i) = idf(x_i)$ is only related with term x_i itself. Hence $\omega(x_i)$ should only reflect x_i's distinctness but not the coverage.

Considering the possible general term weighting scheme $w_{ij} = tf(x_i, d_j) \cdot \omega(x_i)$ (referring to [8], here *tf* is the "possibility" part and ω is the "information" part which two together compose the *feature quantity*), a common approach to improve term weighting is to assign the term weighting factor $\omega(x_i)$ a better measure instead of $idf(x_i)$ which reflects the distinctness more precisely (such as [7]).

1.2   Category Information and Document Information

The *tfidf* weighting scheme does not make use of the category label information on the training documents (named "unsupervised term weighting" by [7]) as term selection does with *IG* or χ^2 statistic for term selection. For example, a term with a low document frequency has a high *idf* value as its weighting factor; but if the documents containing this term have a balanced distribution among all categories, this high weighting factor becomes unreasonable. Some attempts have been made to employ this category information, but they did not show uniform superiority with respect to *tfidf* (see [7, 10, 11, 12].

Further more, the $idf(x_i)$ term weighting factor cares only the total number of document which contains x_i, but not the *document information* — the relative significance of a term in each document. The more frequently term x_i occurs in document d_j, the more important x_i is to d_j as well as the category which d_j belongs to. In the de facto three-tier hierarchy "category ← document ← term", both χ^2 and *IG* only employ the relation "category ←-- term" in which the document information is lost.

The remainder of this paper is organized as follows: Sect. 2 discusses some term weighting constraints by intuition based on category information and document information; from these ideas, Sect. 3 implements a term weighting scheme through a probabilistic analysis; Sect. 4 presents some experiments to evaluate this scheme in detail; Sect. 5 gives a concluding discussion.

2   Intuitionistic Term Weighting Factor Constraints

Here we discuss the characteristics of distinctness metric. Good feature terms are those who have a great distinctness for one category and low distinctness for the other categories. One of the best feature selection criteria, $\chi^2_{\max}$ (see [9, 13]), is an implementation of this consideration. So, a term's distinctness for a category is a basic metric that will be used for calculating its global weight as a feature; it depends only of the term's distribution in the documents of that category. For a given term x_i, we discuss its relative distinctness for two categories C_1, C_2 in the three cases.

The slots in the figure stand for documents, placed in category C_1 or C_2; and the gray area in a slot stands for x_i's probability in the document (frequency proportion). **Case (a):** x_i has the same probability distribution in a subset of C_1's documents and a subset of C_2's documents; but C_1 has

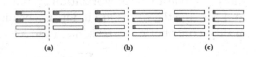

(a)   (b)   (c)

more documents than C_2. x_i should have a bigger distinctness for C_2. **Case (b):** C_1 and C_2 have the same amount of documents; but x_i's probability in each document is higher in C_1 than in C_2. x_i should have a bigger distinctness for C_1. **Case (c):** x_i has the same overall probability in C_1 and in C_2. While x_i is massed in fewer documents in C_1 than in C_2. x_i should have a bigger distinctness for C_1. The judgement in this case is not as evident as in case (a) and case (b), but it is a most important part of the idea in this study, as interpreted below.

The appearance of a given term in some document of a category is significant to the category, but the absence of the term (not the "negative evidence" in [14]) in some document is not significant to the category. When a category contains more than one topic, the above opinion is easy to understand. As a generalization of the *multi-topic* case, every document in a category could be treated as a component topic (named *micro-topic* in this paper) of the category. If a test document is very similar to a training document of some category, it should be judged to be very likely to belong to the category, despite how it is different from the other training documents of that category. Based on this consideration, if x_i is very frequent in a test document, that document is more likely to belong to the C_1 than belong to C_2 in case (c). On the contrary, current *df* based feature selection schemes (such as χ^2 and *IG*) are often *less* likely to select a term with a distribution like the one on C_1 in case (c).

3   A Partial Probability Model for Term Weighting

As discussed in Sect. 2, we analyzed the effect of a single term in a text categorization task, thus we present here a "partial probability model", which means only partial information of all terms is used to make the probability analysis.

3.1   Model Formulation

For brief, formulas presented here are the main steps of the partial probability modeling but not the fully detailed proof.

First, we define some common symbols: C_r for a category, D_j for a document of C_r, x_i for a term, X_i for a made-up document containing only x_i and $\omega_r(x_i)$ for the conditional weighting factor of x_i given C_r.

Notice that a document here (D_j or X_i) is not only an event but also a probability distribution of terms x_i ($i = 1, 2, \ldots, n$). That is why a document is also called a micro-topic.

Then we define the *conditional partial probability* $\mathfrak{P}_{x_i}(C_r|X_i)$ as the conditional probability of C_r given X_i considering only the information of x_i. Because most popular text categorization systems are based on the Bag-of-Words model and assume the terms are independent distributed, this concept of pseudo probability contribution is reasonable; so let

$$\sum_i \mathfrak{P}_{x_i}(C_r|D_j) = P(C_r|D_j) \tag{1}$$

Similarly to total probability formula, here we have

$$\mathfrak{P}_{x_i}(C_r|X_i) \triangleq \sum_j \mathfrak{P}_{x_i}(D_j|X_i)\mathfrak{P}_{x_i}(C_r|D_j) \tag{2}$$

And similarly to Bayes' formula, in (2)

$$\mathfrak{P}_{x_i}(D_j|X_i) \triangleq \frac{P(D_j) \cdot \mathfrak{P}_{x_i}(X_i|D_j)}{\sum_l P(D_l) \cdot \mathfrak{P}_{x_i}(X_i|D_l)} \tag{3}$$

Consider that all D_j have the same prior probability $P(D_j)$, and intuitively, $\mathfrak{P}_{x_i}(X_i|D_j) = P(x_i|D_j)$. Equation (3) becomes

$$\mathfrak{P}_{x_i}(D_j|X_i) = \frac{\mathfrak{P}_{x_i}(X_i|D_j)}{\sum_l \mathfrak{P}_{x_i}(X_i|D_l)} = \frac{P(x_i|D_j)}{\sum_l P(x_i|D_l)} \tag{4}$$

As $P(C_r|D_j)=1$ and (1), the other conditional partial probability in (2) can be calculated by

$$\mathfrak{P}_{x_i}(C_r|D_j) = \frac{P(x_i|D_j)\,\omega_r(x_i)}{\sum_k P(x_k|D_j)\,\omega_r(x_k)} \tag{5}$$

in which, "document information" is concretized. It describes how much x_i contribute to the "belongingness" between D_j and C_r.

By substituting (4) and (5) into (2), we obtain

$$\mathfrak{P}_{x_i}(C_r|X_i)=\sum_j \overbrace{\frac{P(x_i|D_j)}{\sum_l P(x_i|D_l)}}^{\mathcal{A}} \cdot \overbrace{\frac{P(x_i|D_j)\,\omega_r(x_i)}{\sum_k P(x_k|D_j)\,\omega_r(x_k)}}^{\mathcal{B}} \tag{6}$$

$$=\frac{\omega_r(x_i)}{\sum_l P(x_i|D_l)} \cdot \sum_j \frac{[P(x_i|D_j)]^2}{\sum_k P(x_k|D_j)\,\omega_r(x_k)} \tag{7}$$

Generally, $P(x_i|D_j)\,\omega_r(x_i) \ll \sum_k P(x_k|D_j)\,\omega_r(x_k)$. As a part of (6), we almost have $\mathcal{B} \propto \omega_r(x_i)$. So in the space spanned by the category conditional weighting factors $\boldsymbol{\omega_r}=[\omega_r(x_1),\ \omega_r(x_2),\ \omega_r(x_3),\ \ldots,\ \omega_r(x_n)]$, we insulate the implicit $\boldsymbol{\omega_r}$-unrelated part of $\mathcal{B}$ to together with $\mathcal{A}$ form a factor $\mathfrak{p}_r(x_i)$, and the other implicit part of $\mathcal{B}$ as another factor adjustable by $\boldsymbol{\omega_r}$; then we have an approximation

$$\mathfrak{P}_{x_i}(C_r|X_i) \simeq \mathfrak{p}_r(x_i)\frac{\omega_r(x_i)}{\sum_k \omega_r(x_k)} \tag{8}$$

where $\mathfrak{p}_r(x_i)$ is only related to C_r and x_i. Now we make a definition

$$\omega_r(x_i) \stackrel{\text{def}}{=\!=} \mathfrak{p}_r(x_i) \tag{9}$$

Then by (9), (8) and (7), $\omega_r(x_i)$ can be resolved by iteration

$$\omega_r^{[n+1]}(x_i) = \frac{\mathfrak{P}_{x_i}^{[n]}(C_r|X_i)}{\frac{\omega_r^{[n]}(x_i)}{\sum_k \omega_r^{[n]}(x_k)}} = \frac{\sum_k \omega_r^{[n]}(x_k)}{\sum_l P(x_i|D_l)}\sum_j \frac{(P(x_i|D_j))^2}{\sum_k P(x_k|D_j)\,\omega_r^{[n]}(x_k)} \tag{10}$$

3.2 Global Term Weighting Factor

By the model in Sect. 3.1, a term's conditional weight factors for each category can be figured out. Further more, they must constitute one *global weighting factor* in some way.

Before calculating that, a proportional assignment (normalization) needs to be performed over all categories' conditional partial probabilities $\mathfrak{p}_t(x_i)$, $p_r(x_i) = \frac{\mathfrak{p}_r(x_i)}{\sum_t \mathfrak{p}_t(x_i)}$, after which $p_r(x_i)$ satisfies $\sum_r p_r(x_i) = 1$.

Imitating the formula of *discrimination information*, we define here a quasi discrimination information as (in a two-category case)

$$I_{1,2}(x_i) = \left|\log\frac{p_1(x_i)}{p_2(x_i)} - \log\frac{P(C_1)}{P(C_2)}\right| = \left|\log\frac{p_1(x_i)}{P(C_1)} - \log\frac{p_2(x_i)}{P(C_2)}\right| = \left|\log\frac{p_1(x_i)}{P(C_1)}\right| + \left|\log\frac{p_2(x_i)}{P(C_2)}\right|$$

which is addible from information theory.

A little like χ^2_{avg} and χ^2_{max} for feature selection (see [13,3]), in multi-category case, we have two schemes to merge the pairwise discrimination informations —
$I(x_i) = \sum_r \left|\log\frac{p_r(x_i)}{P(C_r)}\right|$ and

$$I_{\text{max}}(x_i) = \max_r \left\{\log\frac{p_r(x_i)}{P(C_r)}\right\} \tag{11}$$

which actually stands for the largest positive discrimination x_i could provide for one category. These two quasi discrimination information formulae were both examined for being used as the global term weighting factor $\omega(x_i)$ in the experiments and "$\omega(x_i) \stackrel{\text{def}}{=\!=} I_{\text{max}}(x_i)$" performed better than "$\omega(x_i) \stackrel{\text{def}}{=\!=} I(x_i)$".

3.3   Relation with *idf*

In this subsection, we are going to deduct an asymptotical relation between $I_{\max}(x_i)$ and *idf* from some assumptions, that can be looked upon as another information theoretic perspective of *idf*.

First, we define $s = \arg\max_r \left\{ \log \frac{p_r(x_i)}{P(C_r)} \right\}$ and $idf(x_i) = \log \frac{N}{N_{x_i}}$, in which N stands for the total number of documents from all categories; N_{x_i} stands for the number of documents containing x_i. Considering a good feature term x_i, we define $\bar{P}(x_i|D_+)$ as the expected conditional probability of x_i given a document D_+ in C_s which contains x_i, and $\bar{P}(x_i|D_-)$ as the expected conditional probability of x_i given a document D_- not in C_s which contains x_i. Then, the fewer documents in C_s contain x_i, the bigger the ratio between $\bar{P}(x_i|D_+)$ and $\bar{P}(x_i|D_-)$ should be; otherwise, x_i could not be a good feature term. So we have

$$\frac{N_{C_s x_i}}{N_{C_s}} \sim \frac{\bar{P}(x_i|D_-)}{\bar{P}(x_i|D_+)} \tag{12}$$

in which, N_{C_s} stands for the number of documents of category C_s and $N_{C_s x_i}$ stands for the number of documents of category C_s which contain x_i.

If it is assumed that every category has almost the same "amount" of *positive terms* (x_i is "positive" to C_s by the definition of s) which means no category have too fewer training documents compared to the other categories, we have

$$\frac{\omega_s(x_i)}{\sum_k \omega_s(x_k)} \simeq \text{constant} \tag{13}$$

then $\frac{\omega_s(x_i)}{\sum_k P(x_k|D_j)\omega_s(x_k)} \simeq \text{constant}$. According to (7)

$$\mathfrak{P}_{x_i}(C_s|X_i) \tilde{\propto} \frac{\sum_j [P(x_i|D_j)]^2}{\sum_l P(x_i|D_l)} \simeq \bar{P}(x_i|D_+) \tag{14}$$

Similarly, for $r \neq s$,

$$\mathfrak{P}_{x_i}(C_r|X_i) \tilde{\propto} \bar{P}(x_i|D_-) \tag{15}$$

So, $\frac{\sum_r p_r(x_i)}{p_s(x_i)} \stackrel{(8),(13)}{=} \frac{\sum_r \mathfrak{P}_{x_i}(C_r|X_i)}{\mathfrak{P}_{x_i}(C_s|X_i)} \stackrel{(14),(15)}{\simeq} \sum_r \frac{\bar{P}(x_i|D_-)}{\bar{P}(x_i|D_+)} \stackrel{(12)}{\sim} \sum_r \frac{N_{C_r x_i}}{N_{C_s}} = \frac{N_{x_i}}{N_{C_s}}$.

Equally, $p_s(x_i) = \frac{p_s(x_i)}{\sum_r p_r(x_i)} \sim \frac{N_{C_s}}{N_{x_i}}$. Hence, $I_{\max}(x_i) = \log \frac{p_s(x_i)}{P(C_s)} \sim \log \frac{N_{C_s}/N_{x_i}}{N_{C_s}/N} = idf(x_i)$.

3.4   Statistical Characteristics

As presented in the subsections above, this partial probability model exploits as much information as possible from the training data to calculate term weighting factors more precisely. We discuss here some characteristics of the algorithm.

Leaning to small categories. In Sect. 3.3, an assumption was made that no category contains too fewer training documents than the others, with which we got the approximate equivalence to *idf*. However, if a category contains really fewer documents compare to the others, this model would lean to it, which means larger weighting factors for its positive terms.

Multi-topic category applicability. According to (7), the model encourages an asymmetric distribution of a term on the documents of a category (by a squared $P(x_i|D_j)$). More clearly in (2) and (6), none of the topics in a category loses its importance. The idea was addressed in Sect. 2.

Sensitiveness to sparseness. As a probabilistic model, by exploiting more detailed information, it is sensitive to the estimation error of term probabilities by term frequencies.

Computational time complexity. Experiments show that a small number of iterations are enough for (10) to converge, even for a large task. So the whole calculation of phase (10) and phase (11) has a time complexity $\mathcal{O}(N \cdot n)$, in which N is the document number and n is the term number.

In addition, the constraints (b) and (c) presented in Sect. 2 can easily be proved to be satisfied by (7), and (a) by (11).

4   Experiments

The main purpose of the experiments is to compare $tfidf(x_i, d_j) = \log(n(x_i, d_j) + 1) \cdot \log \frac{N}{N_{x_i}}$ and $tfI_{\max}(x_i, d_j) = \log(n(x_i, d_j) + 1) \cdot I_{\max}(x_i)$, as term weighting schemes.[1] The other phases of the experiment are done with the state-of-the-art approaches, but without meticulous tunings such as the cross-validation. Since the model is not a parametric one, only F_1 measure is used for evaluation.[2]

The main experiments were carried out on three data collections, Reuters-21578[3] and "TREC[4] 2005 Genomics Track[5]" for the *multilabel* case, and 20 Newsgroups[6] for the *single-label* case (see [3]). Stemming (by Porter's Stemmer[7]) and stopword removal are done in the preprocessing phase.

A feature selection by $\chi^2_{\max}$ (see [9,13]) is performed locally (see [3])[8] to reduce the dimensionality to various sizes on all data collections.

---

[1] Experiments show that the smoothed version of *tf* is better. And, in the conditional partial probability calculation, an initial value 1.0 is assigned to each conditional weight factor and the number of iterations of (10) is 5 (converged by observation).

[2] [15] reported a performance of 92% at BEP. Generally speaking, F_1 at BEP ought to be a little higher than at the other points for parametric approaches, but the difference is not significant. Nevertheless, nonparametric approaches are often more stable and easy to employ in practical applications.

[3] http://www.daviddlewis.com/resources/testcollections/reuters21578

[4] Text REtrieval Conference (http://trec.nist.gov).

[5] http://ir.ohsu.edu/genomics/

[6] http://people.csail.mit.edu/jrennie/20Newsgroups
http://www.gia.ist.utl.pt/~acardoso/datasets/ (preprocessed version)

[7] http://www.tartarus.org/~martin/PorterStemmer/

[8] According to [3], the distinction between local and global schemes usually does not impact on the choice of DR technique.

The LIBSVM (see [16]) implementation of SVMs is used in this study as the training and classifying program; the kernel type is set to linear. A local implemented Naïve Bayes classifier is also used as a secondary baseline for the single-label case. The performance is evaluated by *microaveraged* and *macro-averaged* F_1 measures (see [3,17]). The microaveraged values of *precision, recall)* and F_1 have the same value under single-label case.

Statistical significance test is performed on most result data to verify if the $tfI_{\max}$ scheme is superior than the *tfidf* scheme. Besides the term weighting scheme $\{tfidf, tfI_{\max}\}$, there are other variants effecting on the performance in these experiments, which are the dimensionality and the category. The *t*-test is not appropriate for this case, so we adopt the (*nonrepeated experimented*) multivariate Analysis of Variance (ANOVA) which works via F-test (equivalent to *t*-test in one-way case). It is reasonable to assume there is no intersection between the term weighting scheme and the dimensionality or between the term weighting scheme and the category, thus the *additive-effect model* can be adopted; and the main effect of the term weighting scheme is our concerning focus.

4.1   Results and Discussions

On Reuters-21578. Experiments on Reuters-21578 were mainly carried out on its "R(10)" category subset (see [17]) by "ModApté" split. First, the overall results on different dimensionalities are shown in Fig. 1, from which, we can see that the $tfI_{\max}$ scheme outperforms *tfidf* steadily on the macroaveraged F_1 measure and slightly on the microaveraged F_1 measure. The ANOVA on the data in Fig. 1 is shown in Table 1. In the table, D denotes the *degree of freedom*; the F-statistics, F_{scheme}, has the distribution $F_{(1,9)}$. In the microaveraging part, $p_{scheme} = P(F_{(1,9)} > 2.25) = 0.1677$ is the probability for the assumption "*scheme* $\in \{tfidf, tfI_{\max}\}$ has no apparent effect on F_1" to be true. Thus we have a $1 - 0.1667 = 83.33\%$ confidence to assert that $tfI_{\max}$ is superior to *tfidf* for getting a higher *microaveraged* F_1. The ANOVA for the macroaveraging part is similar, where the confidence is nearly 100%.

In the F_1 sub-figure of Fig. 1, dimensionality of 3,000 is the peak point for all four curves, so we list in Table 2 the performance details on this dimension-

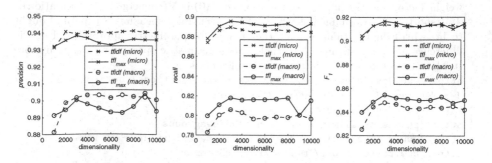

Fig. 1. R(10) — performance comparison on different dimensionalities

Table 1. R(10) — Two-way ANOVA significance test on the data in Fig. 1; source variables are *term weighting scheme* $\in \{tfidf, tfI_{max}\}$ and *dimensionality*

Dependent Var	Source	D	Sum of Squares	Mean Square	F-stat.	$p\|_{>F}$
	scheme	1	0.00000387	0.00000387	2.25	**0.1677**
micro F_1	*dim.*	9	0.00020089	0.00002232	12.98	0.0004
	Error	9	0.00001548	0.00000172		

ality to have a closer observation. The macroaveraged F_1 increases more than macroaveraged F_1, so tfI_{max} *does* help smaller categories more than bigger ones.

Table 2. R(10) — performance comparison at the coincident F_1 peak point (dimensionality of 3,000)

%		$tfidf$	tfI_{max}
micro	*precision*	**93.97**	93.87 (−0.10)
macro		**90.20**	90.06 (−0.14)
micro	*recall*	88.95	**89.56** (+0.61)
macro		80.60	**81.80** (+1.20)
micro	F_1	91.39	**91.66** (+0.27)
macro		84.80	**85.47** (+0.67)

On TREC 2005 Genomics Track. This document collection has four categories $\{A, E, G, T\}$, 5,837 documents for training and 6,043 documents for test; each document may belong to one or more categories. The four categories are very unbalanced in positive training documents; for A and G the numbers are 338 and 462, and for E and T the numbers are 81 and 36. Participants of the contest usually employ domain specific techniques or knowledge to yield acceptable performances. In this study, this document collection is only used as a additional common data set to examine the general effectiveness of the proposed approach adopting neither special techniques nor the official evaluation method.

The overall results are shown in Fig. 2. The curves of tfI_{max} are more smooth (stable) than the curves of $tfidf$ to some extent. The ANOVA on this data showed 99.97% and 99.49% confidences of tfI_{max}'s superiority in microaveraging case and macroaveraging case. In contrast to the results on R(10), this time the improvement of *macroaveraged* F_1 is slightly less significant than *microaveraged* F_1. According to Sect. 3.4, it is due to the over-sparseness of the small categories E and T which almost always get zero recalls.

On 20 Newsgroups. The "bypass" version of the collection which already had a standard split is used and the overall results are shown in Fig. 3, from which we can see tfI_{max} scheme yields quite stable improvements on all dimensionalities in all subfigures, and no significance test is needed.

Since the dimensionality of 10000 seems to be a good compromise between size and performance, we list in Table 3 the performance details on it, in which

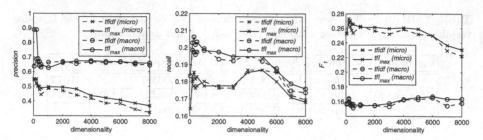

Fig. 2. TREC — performance comparison on different dimensionalities

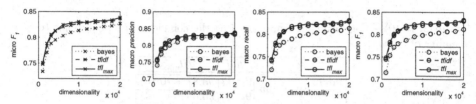

Fig. 3. 20 Newsgroups — performance comparison on different dimensionalities

Table 3. 20 Newsgroups — performance comparison at the dimensionality of 10000

%		Naïve Bayes	$tfidf$-SVM	$tfI_{\max}$-SVM
micro	F_1	81.35	82.73 (+1.38)	**83.06** (+0.33)
macro	*precision*	82.17	82.63 (+0.46)	**83.01** (+0.38)
	recall	80.03	81.98 (+1.95)	**82.37** (+0.39)
	F_1	79.86	82.08 (+2.22)	**82.50** (+0.42)

the Naïve Bayes classifier shows a quite good performance compared with SVMs, which is because of the non-sparseness of this document collection. Compared with the improvement between $tfidf$-SVM and Naïve Bayes, the improvement between $tfI_{\max}$-SVM and $tfidf$-SVM is fairly considerable, because the latter one is made only by improving the term weighting phase while the former one is made by replacing the entire process after dimensionality reduction.

4.2 Comprehensible Samples

For the sake of a manual observation on the difference between $I_{\max}$ and idf term weighting factor, some comprehensible sample terms is selected from the 20 Newsgroup document collection in a semi-automatic way. We first describe the sampling method and then carry on the observation and discussion.

First, a first-order mass normalization is performed on all the terms, i.e. $idf'(x_i) = \frac{idf(x_i)}{\sum_k idf(x_k)/n}$ and $I'_{\max} = \frac{I_{\max}(x_i)}{\sum_k I_{\max}(x_k)/n}$ for $i = 1, 2, ..., n$ where n is the total term number. Then they are sorted by $\left| I'_{\max}(x_i) - idf'(x_i) \right|$.

Table 4. Sample terms with apparently different idf' and I'_{max} values (from 20 Newsgroups)

	Term	tf	df	idf'	I'_{max}	Incre.	χ^2_{max} Rank	Category (max)
$idf' < I'_{max}$	"crypto"	262	141	0.592	1.210	**+0.618**	23	"sci.crypt"
	"armenian"	1333	132	0.601	1.168	**+0.567**	30	"soc.religion.christian"
	"spacecraft"	168	68	0.691	1.203	**+0.512**	108	"sci.space"
	"powerbook"	85	52	0.727	1.222	**+0.495**	154	"comp.sys.mac.hardware"
	"*messag*"	973	549	0.408	0.872	**+0.464**	1401	"rec.sport.hockey"
	"biker"	79	60	0.708	1.161	**+0.453**	132	"rec.motorcycles"
	"widget"	557	103	0.635	1.070	**+0.435**	61	"comp.graphics"
$idf' > I'_{max}$	"enlighten"	57	55	0.719	0.196	**−0.523**	24009	-
	"worthless"	66	60	0.708	0.249	**−0.459**	24597	-
	"slowli"	52	47	0.740	0.289	**−0.451**	26574	-
	"yep"	41	39	0.766	0.335	**−0.431**	28676	-
	"therebi"	32	29	0.806	0.392	**−0.414**	12713	-
	"resembl"	56	48	0.737	0.324	**−0.413**	24730	-
	"strang"	153	134	0.599	0.187	**−0.412**	19168	-
	"excess"	91	67	0.693	0.281	**−0.412**	9060	-
	"mulitpl"	281	164	0.572	0.240	**−0.332**	5581	-

From those with a big $\left|I'_{max}(x_i) - idf'(x_i)\right|$ value, we manually select[9] some samples and list them in Table 4.

Terms in the "$idf' < I'_{max}$" part are those with high frequencies (low idf) but good distinctness (except for "messag") which deserves a high I_{max}. Furthermore, for their high ranking by the χ^2_{max} term selection, this improvement is important.

Terms in the "$idf' > I'_{max}$" part of the figure have relatively low frequencies (high idf) but bad distinctness which deserves a low I_{max}. But this improvement is not significant, because 1) these terms have a fairly balanced distribution in the training set among all categories, and 2) relatively low χ^2_{max} ranks provide them less chances to be selected.

5   Conclusions

In this paper, we discussed the importance of category information and document information to improve text categorization, and introduced a partial probability model to make a tentative use of this information to improve the term weighting phase. It is nonparametric and stable; sufficient experiments showed

---

[9] (i) Hard-to-recognize abbreviations/stems are ignored. (ii) Terms that are similar or of the same kind are not all selected, such as { "crypto", "decrypt", "cryptograph", "crypt", "cryptosystem", ... } and { "armenia", "armenian", "turkish", "azerbaijian", ... }. (iii) *Bad* samples are *not* skipped on purpose, such as "messag" in Table 4; "Xxx Hockey Message Board" is a very frequent phrase in "rec.sport.hockey", but "message" should not be high-weighted.

its effectiveness. This study is hoped to provide inspiration for further studies on exploiting more information from the training data to boost text categorization performance.

References

1. Salton, G., Buckley, C.: Term weighting approaches in automatic text retrieval. Information Processing and Management: an International Journal **24** (1988) 513–523
2. Baeza-Yates, R.A., Ribeiro-Neto, B.A.: Modern Information Retrieval. ACM Press / Addison-Wesley (1999)
3. Sebastiani, F.: Machine learning in automated text categorization. ACM Computing Surveys (CSUR) **34** (2002) 1–47
4. Vapnik, V.: The Nature of Statistical Learning Theory. Springer Verlag (1999)
5. Joachims, T.: Text categorization with support vector machines: learning with many relevant features. In: Proceedings of ECML '98, Springer Verlag (1998) 137–142
6. Joachims, T.: A probabilistic analysis of the Rocchio algorithm with TFIDF for text categorization. In: Proceedings of ICML '97, Morgan Kaufmann Publishers (1997) 143–151
7. Debole, F., Sebastiani, F.: Supervised term weighting for automated text categorization. Text Mining and its Applications (2004) 81–98
8. Aizawa, A.: The feature quantity: An information theoretic perspective of tfidf-like measures. In: Proceedings of ACM SIGIR 2000, ACM Press (2000) 104–111
9. Yang, Y., Pedersen, J.O.: A comparative study on feature selection in text categorization. In: Proceedings of ICML '97, Morgan Kaufmann Publishers (1997) 412–420
10. Xue, D., Sun, M.: Select strong information features to improve text categorization effectiveness. Journal of Intelligent Systems, Special Issue (2002)
11. Xue, D., Sun, M.: A study on feature weighting in chinese text categorization. In: Proceedings of CICLing '03. (2003) 594–604
12. Li, J., Sun, M., Zhang, X.: A comparison and semi-quantitative analysis of words and character-bigrams as features in chinese text categorization. In: Proceedings of COLING-ACL '06, Association for Computational Linguistics (2006) 545–552
13. Rogati, M., Yang, Y.: High-performing feature selection for text classification. In: Proceedings of CIKM '02, ACM Press (2002) 659–661
14. Galavotti, L., Sebastiani, F., Simi, M.: Experiments on the use of feature selection and negative evidence in automated text categorization. In: Proceedings of ECDL '00, Springer-Verlag (2000) 59–68
15. Dumais, S., Platt, J., Heckerman, D., Sahami, M.: Inductive learning algorithms and representations for text categorization. In: Proceedings of CIKM '98, ACM Press (1998) 148–155
16. Chang, C.C., Lin, C.J.: LIBSVM: a library for support vector machines. (2001) Software available at http://www.csie.ntu.edu.tw/~cjlin/libsvm.
17. Debole, F., Sebastiani, F.: An analysis of the relative hardness of reuters-21578 subsets. Journal of the American Society of Information Science and Technology **56** (2005) 584–596

On the Impact of Lexical and Linguistic Features in Genre- and Domain-Based Categorization

Guillaume Cleuziou[1] and Céline Poudat[2]

[1] LIFO, Université d'Orléans, France
guillaume.cleuziou@univ-orleans.fr
[2] ERTIM, INALCO, Paris, France
celine.poudat@enst.fr

Abstract. Classification in genres and domains is a major field of research for Information Retrieval (scientific and technical watch, data-mining, etc.) and the selection of appropriate descriptors to characterize and classify texts is particularly crucial to that effect.

Most of practical experiments consider that domains are correlated to the content level (words, tokens, lemmas, etc.) and genres to the morphosyntactic or linguistic one (function words, POS, etc.). However, currently used variables are generally not accurate enough to be applied to the categorization task.

The present study assesses the impact of the lexical and linguistic levels in the field of genre and domain categorization. The empirical results we obtained demonstrate how important it is to select an appropriate tagset that meets the requirement of the task. The results also assess the efficiency of the linguistic level for both genre- and domain-based categorization.

1 Introduction

Text categorization (or classification), as any classification task, requires an appropriate set of descriptors. In the same way as it would be irrelevant to characterize the financial profiles of bank account users according to variables such as "size" or "eye color", it would be inappropriate to describe scientific texts thanks to variables such as "number of dialogue marks" as far as they are absent from scientific discourse.

Genre and domain classifications are today widely used in Information Retrieval (IR) systems and they also require appropriate descriptors. It is worth emphasizing that genres and domains are generally associated with distinct linguistic levels. On the one hand, domains, or subjects, are rather related to lexical features in practice: texts are often reduced to "bags of words" and each document is described on the basis of the whole corpus lexicon. The size of the latter calls for a necessary step of reduction of the description area: selection of the attributes thanks to statistical measures (number of occurrences in the corpus), interest measures (Mutual Information, Information Gain, chi-square measure,

A. Gelbukh (Ed.): CICLing 2007, LNCS 4394, pp. 599–610, 2007.

etc.), re-parameterisation of the space with methods like *Latent Semantique Indexing* (LSI) or feature clustering. These formalisms allow us to obtain efficient classifiers which can reach a precision of 90% on large corpora [Hof99, DMK03].

Genres are on the other hand generally classified thanks to morphosyntactic (or linguistic) variables which have proved to be quite efficient to validate of text typologies [KC94, KNS97, MR01].

Nevertheless, domain-based categorization is generally conducted on genre-homogene-ous corpora (*e.g.* Reuters[1] or Newsgroup[2]) whereas genres are most often classified on discourse-homogeneous ones (*e.g.* [KC94, KNS97, MR01]): this increases the classificatory power of the variables but prevents the joint use, and the evaluation of the scopes of the two levels.

The aim of the present study is to assess the impact of thematic and morphosyntactic variables on genre and domain classifications. The experiment will be conducted on a pilot-corpus that will allow us to determine the interest of a joint use of the two levels of description.

After a brief overview of the use of the notions of genres and domains in IR, we will discuss about the relation between the two concepts in Section 2. Section 3 presents the corpus and the methodology we adopted to evaluate the complementarity between linguistic and lexical features. The experimental aspects of this assessment and the obtained results are detailed respectively in Sections 4 and 5.

2   Genres and Domains

Although the notions of genres and domains are more and more common in IR, they are scarcely used conjointly as far as they are traditionally associated with variables or cues belonging to distinct linguistic levels. Indeed, domains are generally related in practice to lexical features whereas the notion of genre is rather connected to morphosyntactic variables.

Domains, or subjects, are indeed supposed to reflect particular fields of knowledge and are often described in terms of lexical relations, as in ontologies for instance. Different methods have been developed to characterize and classify texts in domains according to their contents. The most commonly used measures are computed from the basis of words, word clusters (unequally called topics, themes, etc.) or word stems frequencies which have turned out to be quite efficient in various applications. Word-based classification is still besides the most widespread because of its lower cost.

The notion of genre[3], which is traditionally philological and literary, is more and more common in IR and text categorization. Indeed genres can be identified and contrasted thanks to their specific linguistic properties: for instance, legal texts do not contain exclamation marks. Genre analysis and characterization are generally conducted according to a set of methods inherited from quantitative

---

[1] http://www.research.att.com/lewis/reuters21578.html

[2] http://people.csail.mit.edu/jrennie/20Newsgroups/

[3] Or "style", "register" or even "text type".

stylistics, *i.e.* using part-of-speech (POS) or function words categories. Besides, the morphosyntactic method, initiated by [Bib88], has been successful in various text and genre classification studies.

Since different domains can been retrieved inside different genres and vice versa, we are tempted to consider that domains and genre are not correlated. The associated descriptive levels (resp. lexical and linguistic) are then rarely used together in practice. Although some encouraging recent studies tried to use lexical features to improve genre-based categorization [WK99, LM02, PC03], the characterization of domains thanks to morphosyntactic variables is still undone, as far as we know. However, in the same way, domains might be properly classified thanks to linguistic variables or at least, this additional descriptive level may improve a word-based domain classification.

3   Methodology

3.1   Development of a Pilot Corpus

For our study, traditional benchmarks such as *Reuters* or *Newgroups* were excluded as they are generically homogeneous. Furthermore, since our goal is to evaluate the interests of two descriptive levels for genre- and domain-based categorization, we decide (for this study) to eliminate the discursive variability[4].

As genres and domains are key-notions for scientific discourse description and applications (scientific watch, document retrieval, etc.), we conducted the following experiments on scientific texts. As they are subjected to an important bureaucracy (peer reviewing, anonymity policy), scientific texts have to meet linguistic and structural constraints that might reduce variation.

We use a pilot corpus especially developed for this study : it is composed of 371 French scientific texts published about 2000, that is three different genres (articles, journal presentations[5] and reviews) and two scientific domains (linguistics and mechanics), described in Table 1.

Table 1. Presentation of the pilot corpus

	Linguistics	Mechanics
Articles	224	49
Journal presentations	45	
Reviews	53	

The relative small size of text collection is a common problem to all studies which requires such a specific corpus (*e.g.* [WK99]). Although the significance of

---

[4] Indeed, types of discourses seem to appear in first (before genres, domains or personal styles) with morphosyntactic characterizations [MR01].

[5] Or introductive articles, describing and presenting the topic of the journal issue, and the scientific articles it contains. Because of their specific purpose and design, journal presentations are clearly distinct from scientific articles.

the results is then limited, this first stage of experiments gives a crucial starting point for further experiments in wide corpus.

With regards to the following experiments, we will use the two following sub-corpora (in addition to the global corpus):

- *ART*-corpus refers to the text collection composed of *articles* only (first line in Table 1),
- *LING*-corpus refers to the collection which contains only the texts about *linguistics* (first column in Table 1).

Furthermore we will differentiate *local* and *global* corpora: *global* corresponds to the whole corpus whereas *local* refers to a subcorpus, homogeneous in genre (*ART*-corpus) or in domain (*LING*-corpus).

3.2 Feature Selection for Scientific Texts

Among the possible lexical variables, the choice of the most frequent substantives, or noun descriptors seems to be appropriate and quite economical, as they are potential scientific concepts rather than verbs, adverbs or adjectives. In that respect and as far as scientific domains are concerned, they are more discriminatory and have the advantage to be easily extracted. As singular and plural nouns might relate back to different concepts[6], the singular and plural forms of the nouns have been taken into account. About 10,000 singular nouns and 4,000 plural nouns are then extracted from the global corpus.

As far as they represent our generic descriptive hypothesis, the selection of morphosyntactic variables has been subjected to a precise linguistic expertise; indeed, it would be quite inappropriate to describe scientific texts according to features they do not possess, or with too general variables that would not include scientific texts properties. In addition to the traditional POS (nouns, verbs, adverbs, adjectives, prepositions, etc.), we selected a set of cues gathering the general descriptive hypothesis put forward in the literature focusing on scientific discourse. Table 2 describes these additional tags.

Finaly, a set of 136 variables is selected to describe the morphosyntax of the scientific texts. The tagging has been performed by learning with the tagger TnT (Trigrams'n'Tags) [Bra00] on the selected feature set.

3.3 Classifiers Used

Document classification (or categorization) has led to numerous works requering to machine learning technics. In this field of research, the most commonly used classifiers are : *Naïve Bayes* [LR94], SVM[7] [Joa98] and *Decision Trees* [CH98].

Because goals of the following experiments are two fold, we chose to use two methods very different in nature : texts will be classified with SVM in order

---

[6] "la langue" - language - and "les langues" - languages - are for instance different linguistic notions.

[7] Support Vector Machine.

Table 2. Description of the morphosyntactic descriptors

Tag	Description
ABR	Abbreviations
CON (+ attributes)	Connectives: addition, cause, consequence, conclusion, exemplification, disjunction, opposition, rephrasing, space, time, etc.
FGW	Foreign (non-French) elements
NUM (+ attributes)	Numerals: date, cardinal, ordinal + references in the text (e.g. "See in 12")
LS	Title cues and list marks
PON (+ attributes)	Punctuation marks : colon, square brackets, quotation marks, braces, slashs, etc.
VER:mod:[tense]	Modals
SIG	Acronyms
SYM	Symbols

to evaluate the accuracy rate obtained from various initial descriptions (lexical, linguistic or combined) and decision trees (DT) will help us to explain how lexical and linguistic features may be combined within the classifier.

The SVM method is acknowledged to outperform other methods in text categorization [DPHS98]. To simplify matters, it consists in learning a classifier in a new feature space, far more dimensioned than the original one. The new space is obtained from different kernel functions (*e.g.* linear, polynomial, rbf, etc.). As several studies showed that best accuracies were obtained with a linear SVM [Dum98], we decided to use this type of kernel in our experiments. For each classification task (genre or domain-based), it will then be possible to measure the relevance of each set of features: lexical features only ($\mathcal{L}$), morphosyntactic ones only ($\mathcal{M}$) and combined features ($\mathcal{L} \oplus \mathcal{M}$).

In contrast with the SVM numerical approach, DT proceeds in a more symbolic way. Although it usually provides less accurate results in text classification, the learned trees are easier to analyse and to interpret and the study of the trees enables us to bring out the role played by each of the features. In our experiments, we will use the well-known C4.5 method [Qui93].

3.4   Evaluation Framework

In this section we first give formal details about the feature vectors construction before describing the set of experiments.

Let $\mathcal{D}$ be a set of texts and $\mathcal{C}$ be a set of classes such that a unique class $c(d_i) \in \mathcal{C}$ is associated to each text $d_i \in \mathcal{D}$ (genre or domain). $\mathcal{D}$ is divided into a training set $\mathcal{D}_{train}$ and a test set $\mathcal{D}_{test}$.

$\mathcal{L}_{\mathcal{D}} = \{l_1, \ldots, l_{|\mathcal{L}|}\}$ denotes the ordered set of substantives (singular and plural) which occur within the texts from $\mathcal{D}_{train}$ (lexical description). In $\mathcal{L}_{\mathcal{D}}$, substantives are ordered by decreasing relevance for the given classification task $\mathcal{C}$ using the Mutual Information (MI):

$$\forall l_i \in \mathcal{L}, \ MI(l_i, \mathcal{C}) = \sum_{c_j \in \mathcal{C}} P(c_j).\log \frac{P(l_i|c_j)}{P(l_i)}$$

$\mathcal{M} = \{m_1, \ldots, m_{136}\}$ denotes the ordered set of 136 morphosyntactic (or linguistic) features described in section 3.2. We use the Information Gain (IG) coefficient to measure the interest of each descriptor according to the target classification function. Since features in $\mathcal{M}$ are continuous, a discretization step is necessary (cf. [Mit97]).

$\mathcal{L} \oplus \mathcal{M}$ corresponds to a mixture of the two feature sets $\mathcal{L}$ and $\mathcal{M}$ in the following order: $\mathcal{L} \oplus \mathcal{M} = \{l_1, m_1, l_2, m_2, \ldots, l_{136}, m_{136}, l_{137}, l_{138}, \ldots, l_{|\mathcal{L}|}\}$.

In order to determine the impact of the variables on genre and domain classification, it is necessary to observe the influence of each of the three feature sets ($\mathcal{L}$, $\mathcal{M}$ and $\mathcal{L} \oplus \mathcal{M}$) on local and global corpora. It is also interesting to observe the influence of the size of the feature vector ; in this way we will report results for different sizes : from 1 to 500.

The experimentations proposed in section 4 are the result of 2-fold cross-validations: $\mathcal{D}$ is splitted into two equal subcorpora, each of them being by turn used as test and training set. The reported values correspond to micro-averaging precisions[8] on 5 cross-validations.

For the SVM classifier, in case of multi-class problems, several binary classifiers are learned and combined.

4   Experimentations

The first experimentations are devoted to domain classification. They are based on "local" (*ART*-corpus) and "global" (whole corpus) corpora. The first set will be the basis of the discrimination of the two domains within the same genre whereas the second one will enable us to introduce a generic variation parameter.

Genre classification will then be conducted in the same way: first on the "local" corpus (*LING*-corpus), and next on the same "global" corpus.

4.1   Domain Classification

The results we obtained with the SVM method (figures 1 and 2) clearly show, against all expectations, that morphosyntactic variables are more discriminatory than lexical ones. Moreover, it is worth emphasizing that, for the same number of features, a combination of the two types of variables is on the whole more efficient than each of the two sets on their own.

The following precedence order is obtained (with or without generic variation):

$$\{\mathcal{L} \oplus \mathcal{M} - indexing\} > \{\mathcal{M} - indexing\} > \{\mathcal{L} - indexing\}$$

---

[8] Micro-averaging measures the proportion of well classified texts whatever the class. It differs from the macro-averaging which measures the average of the accuracies for each class separately.

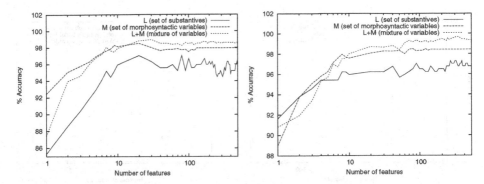

Fig. 1. Domain-based categorization with SVM on the ART-Corpus

Fig. 2. Domain-based categorization with SVM on the global Corpus

The same trends are noted with a decision tree classifier, although the accuracy rates are weaker than with SVM. The lexical indexation is also less efficient than the morphosyntactic and mixed ones.

The result is quite surprising as mechanics and linguistics are conceptually and lexically very different, or even opposed and scientific domains might be better discriminated thanks to morphosyntactic variables than with lexical features.

4.2   Genre Classification

The results we obtained with the SVM method (figures 3 and 4) confirm morphosyntactic variables are relevant to capture the genre dimension. The accuracy rate is higher using the feature sets containing morphosyntactic information than the lexical one. It must be emphasized that the domain differences do not disrupt this conclusion:

$$\{\mathcal{L} \oplus \mathcal{M} - indexing\} \approx \{\mathcal{M} - indexing\} \gg \{\mathcal{L} - indexing\}$$

Figures 5 and 6 report the results obtained with the decision tree classifier. The accuracy rates obtained are once again noticeably weaker than with SVM: 84% best rate *vs.* 88% with SVM. However, the precedence order obtained with C4.5 is rather different. Lexical cues are efficient on the global corpus (from 100 features) and this seems to corroborate the results obtained by [LM02] :

$$\{\mathcal{L} \oplus \mathcal{M} - indexing\} > \{\mathcal{M} - indexing\} \gg \{\mathcal{L} - indexing\}$$

Nevertheless the precedence order we obtain on the local corpus is quite similar to the one obtained with SVM.

From a technical point of view, the differences obtained between the two classifiers may be due to the different methods they are implemented on. Indeed,

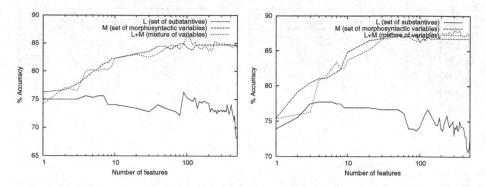

Fig. 3. Genre-based categorization with SVM on the LING-Corpus

Fig. 4. Genre-based categorization with SVM on the global Corpus

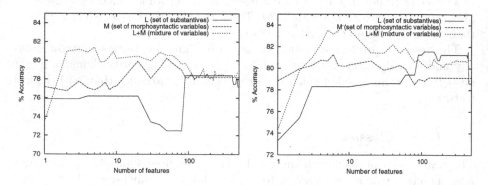

Fig. 5. Genre-based categorization with DT on the ART-Corpus

Fig. 6. Genre-based categorization with DT on the global Corpus

the SVM approach considers a new space of representation of the documents, with a high dimensionality and of which dimensions are defined by - linear - combinations of the initial descriptors. The method calls for the whole of the variables whereas the construction of a decision tree generally calls for a small set of precisely selected cues.

4.3   Further Analysis: Micro *vs.* Macro-precision

Before detailing the preceding results with the study of the decision trees, let us consider an intermediate synthesis of the experimentations we conducted so far.

Table 3 reports the macro and micro-precisions inducted by the decision trees learned from the global corpus for a defined number of descriptors. This is quite important because of the large size variations of the classes:

Table 3. Micro and macro-precisions on the global corpus with C4.5

Type of classification	Type of precision	Nature and size of the feature set		
		$\mathcal{M}_{136}$	$\mathcal{L}_{500}$	$\{\mathcal{M} \oplus \mathcal{L}\}_{500}$
Domain	micro	92.2%	93.3%	94.1%
	macro	**80.3%**	**80.4%**	**84.8%**
Genre	micro	79.9%	80.1%	81.1%
	macro	59.3%	61.9%	61.4%

The macro-precision analysis brings out phenomena that were hidden by the influence of the linguistic articles class (60% documents of the global corpus). Thereby, we can observe a clear emphasis of the relevance of the combined set for domain classification (+4.5%). A larger number of documents belonging to the mechanics domain is misclassified with the $\mathcal{M}$ or $\mathcal{L}$ descriptions than with a combined one. This observation reinforces once again the complementarity of the two levels in domain clustering.

5   Analysis of the Discriminatory Descriptors

5.1   Domain Descriptors

Table 4 reports the variables found in at least two decision trees out of the 10 obtained (five 2-fold cross-validations).

Table 4. Features retrieved from domain decision trees

Features		
Morphosyntactic	Lexical	Combined
References	*équation*	*équation*
Personal pronouns	*écoulement*	*vitesse*
Symbols, acronyms, abbreviations	*vitesse*	*écoulement*
Modal past participles	*coefficient*	*vitesses*
Adverbs and connectives	*déformation*	*laboratoire*
Reflexive pronouns	*amélioration*	Reflexive adjectives
	augmentation	Adverbial phrase
	courbes	Adverbs and connectives
	essais	Concessive connectives
	laboratoire	Nomber of "JE" ("I")
	mécanique	Prepositions
	vitesses	Punctuation (points)

The discriminatory lexical variables are all specific to mechanics. For instance, we observe in a sample that the term "écoulement" (*flow*) enables us to discriminate half of the texts of the training corpus belonging to mechanics. Linguistics texts are thus negatively differentiated: in the same sample, 90% of the linguistics corpus is correctly classified if the texts do not contain the term "écoulement" more than once and if they contain neither "mécanique" (*mechanics*), neither "vitesse" (*speed*) and nor "essais" (*test*). This discrimination is due to two reasons: (1) the more important size of the texts belonging to linguistics increases the number and the diversity of the descriptors and (2) mechanics articles seem to be more homogeneous in terms of lexicon.

On the contrary, the discriminatory morphosyntactic descriptors are more specific to the linguistic field: for instance, the number of prepositions enable us to differentiate up to 90% of the training corpus. In the same way, linguistics texts contain more personal pronouns and reference marks than mechanics ones.

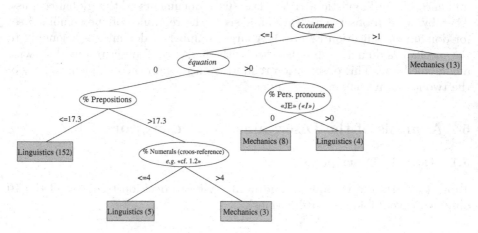

Fig. 7. Representative tree obtained with the combined feature set for domain-based categorization

Joint classifications use a higher number of morphosyntactic variables than lexical ones, in spite of the predominance of the lexical cues in the description space ($|\mathcal{L}| = 364 > |\mathcal{M}| = 136$). However, lexical cues are always the first used in the classification tree (cf. 7), morphosyntactic variables enable us to refine the classes. The morphosyntactic level seems to be discriminatory although it does not enable us to classify the documents in an acceptable way.

5.2   Genre Descriptors

Table 5 reports the variables found in at least three decision trees out of the whole of the trees. It is first to notice that the decision trees use more lexical variables to classify genres than domains. The substantives given in table 5 are characteristic of the reports and journal presentations. Most of the articles are correctly classified if the texts contain neither "contributions" (*contributions*), neither "chapitres" (*chapters*) and not more than one occurrence of

Table 5. Features retrieved from genre decision trees

Features		
Morphosyntactic	**Lexical**	**Combined**
Title cues (LS)	*chapitres*	Title cues (LS)
Proper nouns	*contributions*	*articles*
Passives/present perfect	*articles*	*chapitres*
Symbols	*presses*	*contributions*
Punctuation (colon)	*chapitre*	Passives/present perfect
Punctuation (points)	*bibliographie*	Concessive connectives
Consequence connectives	*journées*	Space connectives
Foreign elements	*linguistique*	Foreign elements
References	*numéro*	References
Reflexive "NOUS" ("WE")	*politique*	Reflexive "NOUS" ("WE")

"chapitre" (*chapter*). Lexical items are thus efficient to characterize genres, as [LM02] pointed out.

Morphosyntactic variables are particularly efficient to distinguish articles: title cues (LS) are indeed very discriminatory, as reviews are never structured and journal presentations far less than articles.

With regards to joint classification, it is worth emphasizing that three lexical items only are discriminatory: the substantives "articles", "chapitres" and "contributions", which are besides specific to articles. In the same way as in morphosyntactic classification, title cues are the first variables used in the classification tree.

6 Conclusion

In this paper we have presented an experimental assessment of the impact of the morphosyntactic and lexical variables to classify scientific genres and domains.

Although they were conducted on a small corpus, the results we obtained are quite encouraging as they not only corroborate the interest of linguistic features to classify genres, but illustrate the strong complementarity of the two levels in domain classification. Indeed, the joint use of the two sets of descriptors seems to be more efficient to discriminate domains, as morphosyntactic variables enable us to refine the partitions obtained with the lexicon. Moreover, it is worth emphasizing that genre classification are far better with the morphosyntactic level and the SVM classifier.

Further experiments will take into account additional genres and domains and will specify the impact of the two description levels. We also plan to assess the relevance of the descriptors we used: the morphosyntactic tagset we developed will be contrasted to the Penn TreeBank one [MSM94], and other lexical sets will be extracted to compare the relevance of the substantive-based approach we adopted.

References

[Bib88]   D. Biber. *Variation across Speech and Writing*. University Press, Cambridge, 1988.

[Bra00]   T. Brants. TnT - A Statistical Part-of-Speech Tagger. In *Proceedings of the Sixth Applied Natural Language Processing Conference (ANLP'00)*, Seattle, WA, 2000.

[CH98]   W.W. Cohen and H. Hirsh. Joins that generalize: text classification using WHIRL. In Rakesh Agrawal, Paul E. Stolorz, and Gregory Piatetsky-Shapiro, editors, *Proceedings of KDD-98,*, pages 169–173, New York, US, 1998. AAAI Press, Menlo Park, US.

[DMK03]   I. S. Dhillon, S. Mallela, and R. Kumar. A divisive information theoretic feature clustering algorithm for text classification. *Journal of Machine Learning Researches*, 3:1265–1287, 2003.

[DPHS98]   Susan Dumais, John Platt, David Heckerman, and Mehran Sahami. Inductive learning algorithms and representations for text categorization. In *Proceedings of CIKM'98*, pages 148–155. ACM Press, 1998.

[Dum98]   S. Dumais. Using svms for text categorization. *IEEE Intell. Systems*, 13(4), 1998.

[Hof99]   Thomas Hofmann. Probabilistic Latent Semantic Indexing. In *Proceedings of the 22nd Annual ACM Conference on Research and Development in Information Retrieval*, pages 50–57, Berkeley, California, August 1999.

[Joa98]   T. Joachims. Text categorization with support vector machines: learning with many relevant features. In Claire Nédellec and Céline Rouveirol, editor, *Proceedings of ECML-98*, number 1398, pages 137–142, Chemnitz, DE, 1998. Springer Verlag, Heidelberg, DE.

[KC94]   J. Karlgren and D. Cutting. Recognizing text genres with simple metrics using discriminant analysis. In *Proceedings of COLING 94*, Kyoto, 1994.

[KNS97]   B. Kessler, G. Nunberg, and H. Schültze. Automatic detection of text genre. In *Proceedings of the European Chapter of the Association for Computational Linguistics (EACL'97)*, pages 32–38, 1997.

[LM02]   Yong-Bae Lee and Sung Hyon Myaeng. Text genre classification with genre-revealing and subject-revealing features. In *Proceedings of the 25th annual international ACM SIGIR*, pages 145–150. ACM Press, 2002.

[LR94]   David D. Lewis and Marc Ringuette. A comparison of two learning algorithms for text categorization. In *Proceedings of SDAIR-94*, pages 81–93, Las Vegas, US, 1994.

[Mit97]   T. Mitchell. *Machine Learning*. McGraw Hill, New York, 1997.

[MR01]   D. Malrieu and F. Rastier. Genres et variations morphosyntaxiques. *Traitement Automatique des langues*, 42(2):548–577, 2001.

[MSM94]   M. P. Marcus, B. Santorini, and M. A. Marcinkiewicz. Building a large annotated corpus of english: The penn treebank. *Computational Linguistics*, 19(2):313–330, 1994.

[PC03]   C. Poudat and G. Cleuziou. Genre and Domain Processing in an Information Retrieval Perspective. In LNCS, editor, *Third International Conference on Web Engineering*, pages 399–402, Oviedo, Spain, 2003. Springer.

[Qui93]   J. R. Quinlan. *C4.5: Programs for Machine Learning*. Morgan Kaufmann, 1993.

[WK99]   Maria Wolters and Mathias Kirsten. Exploring the use of linguistic features in domain and genre classification. In *Proceedings of the ninth conference EACL'99*, pages 142–149, 1999.

Clustering Narrow-Domain Short Texts by Using the Kullback-Leibler Distance*

David Pinto[1,2], José-Miguel Benedí[1], and Paolo Rosso[1]

[1] Department of Information Systems and Computation,
UPV, Valencia 46022,
Camino de Vera s/n, Spain
{dpinto, jbenedi, prosso}@dsic.upv.es
[2] Faculty of Computer Science, BUAP, Puebla 72570,
Ciudad Universitaria, Mexico
dpinto@cs.buap.mx

Abstract. Clustering short length texts is a difficult task itself, but adding the narrow domain characteristic poses an additional challenge for current clustering methods. We addressed this problem with the use of a new measure of distance between documents which is based on the symmetric Kullback-Leibler distance. Although this measure is commonly used to calculate a distance between two probability distributions, we have adapted it in order to obtain a distance value between two documents. We have carried out experiments over two different narrow-domain corpora and our findings indicates that it is possible to use this measure for the addressed problem obtaining comparable results than those which use the Jaccard similarity measure.

1 Introduction

The clustering of narrow-domain short texts is an emergent area that has been not attended into detail by the computational linguistic community and only few works can be found in literature [1] [11] [15] [19]. This behaviour may be derived from the high challenge that this problem implies, since the obtained results are very unstable or imprecise when clustering abstracts of scientific papers, technical reports, patents, etc. Therefore, it is difficult to deal with this kind of data: if a term selection method is applied, this has to be done very carefully because term frequencies in the texts are very low. Generally only 10% or 20% of the keywords from the complete keyword list occur in every document and their absolute frequency usually is one or two, and only sometimes three or four [1]. In this situation, changing a keyword frequency by one can significantly change the clustering results.

However, most current digital libraries and other web-based repositories of scientific and technical information provide free access only to abstracts and not to the full texts of the documents. Evenmore, some repositories such as the

---

* This work has been partially supported by the MCyT TIN2006-15265-C06-04 project, as well as by the BUAP-701 PROMEP/103.5/05/1536 grant.

A. Gelbukh (Ed.): CICLing 2007, LNCS 4394, pp. 611–622, 2007.

well known MEDLINE[1], and the Conseil Européen pour la Recherche Nucléaire (CERN)[2], receive hundreds of publications every day that must be categorized on some specific domain, sometimes with an unknown number of categories a priori. This led to construct novel methods for dealing with this real problem. Although sometimes, keywords are provided by authors for each scientific document, it has been seen that this information is insufficient for conforming a good clustering [21]; evenmore, some of these keywords can lead to more confusion on the clustering process.

We have carried out a set of experiments and our results have been compared with those published earlier in this field. We have used the two corpora presented in [19] and the one suggested in [21], which we consider the most appropiate for our investigation because of their intrinsic characteristics: narrow-domain, short texts and number of documents. The two best hierarchical clustering methods reported in [19] were also implemented. Finally, we have used, as refered by [11], three different feature selection techniques in order to improve the clustering task.

The comparison between documents is performed introducing a symmetric Kullback-Leibler (KL) divergence. As the texts may differ in the terms, the frequency of many compared terms in the document will be zero. This causes problems in the KL distance computation when probabilities are estimated by frequencies of occurrence. In order to avoid this issue, a special type of back-off scheme is introduced. The next section explains into detail the use of the Kullback and Leibler distance as a similarity measure in the clustering task. In Section 3 we present the characteristics of every corpus used in our experiments, describing the use of feature selection techniques for selecting only the most valuable terms from each corpus. The description and the results obtained in our executions are presented in Section 4 and, finally the conclusions of our experiments are given.

2   The Kullback-Leibler Distance

In 1951 Kullback and Leiber studied a measure of information from the statistical aspect viewpoint; this measure involved two probability distributions associated with the same experiment [13]. The Kullback-Leibler divergence is a measure of how different two probability distributions (over the same event space) are. The KL divergence of the probability distributions P, Q on a finite set X is defined as shown in Equation 1.

$$D_{KL}(P||Q) = \sum_{x \in X} P(x) log \frac{P(x)}{Q(x)} \qquad (1)$$

Since this KL divergence is a non-symmetric information theoretical measure of distance of P from Q, then it is not strictly a distance metric. During the past

---

[1] http://www.nlm.nih.gov/
[2] http://library.cern.ch

years, various measures have been introduced in the literature generalizing this measure. We therefore have used the following different symmetric Kullback-Leibler divergences i.e., Kullback-Leibler Distances (KLD) for our experiments. Each KLD corresponds to the definition of Kullback and Leibler [13], Bigi [4], Jensen [10], and Bennet [2] [27], respectively.

$$D_{KLD1}(P||Q) = D_{KL}(P||Q) + D_{KL}(Q||P) \tag{2}$$

$$D_{KLD2}(P||Q) = \sum_{x \in X} (P(x) - Q(x)) \log \frac{P(x)}{Q(x)} \tag{3}$$

$$D_{KLD3}(P||Q) = \frac{1}{2} \left[D_{KL} \left(P||\frac{P+Q}{2} \right) + D_{KL} \left(Q||\frac{P+Q}{2} \right) \right] \tag{4}$$

$$D_{KLD4}(P||Q) = max \left(D_{KL}(P||Q) + D_{KL}(Q||P) \right) \tag{5}$$

KL and KLD have been used in many natural language applications like query expansion [8], language models [3], and categorization [4]. They have also been used, for instance, in natural language and speech processing applications based on statistical language modeling [9], and in information retrieval, for topic identification [5]. In this paper, we have considered to calculate the corpus document similarities in an inverse function with respect to the distance defined in Equations (2), (3), (4), or (5).

In the text clustering model proposed in this paper, a document j is represented by a term vector of probabilities $\vec{d_j}$ and the distance measure is, therefore, the KLD (the symmetric Kullbach-Leibler divergence) between a pair of documents $\vec{d_i}$ and $\vec{d_j}$.

A smoothing model based on back-off is proposed and, therefore, frequencies of the terms appearing in the document are discounted, whereas all the other terms which are not in the document are given an *epsilon* (ϵ) probability, which is equal to the probability of unknown words. The reason is that in practice, often not all the terms in the vocabulary (V) appear in the document d_j. Let $V(d_j) \subset V$ be the vocabulary of the terms which do appear in the documents represented in d_j. For the terms not in $V(dj)$, it is useful to introduce a back-off probability for $P(t_k, d_j)$ when t_k does not occur in $V(d_j)$, otherwise the distance measure will be infinite. The use of a back-off probability to overcome the data sparseness problem has been extensively studied in statistical language modelling (see, for instance [17]). The resulting definition of document probability $P(t_k, d_j)$ is:

$$P(t_k, d_j) = \begin{cases} \beta * P(t_k|d_j), & \text{if } t_k \text{ occurs in the document } d_j \\ \varepsilon, & \text{otherwise} \end{cases} \tag{6}$$

with:

$$P(t_k|d_j) = \frac{tf(t_k, d_j)}{\sum_{x \in d_j} tf(t_k, d_j)}$$

where: $P(t_k|d_j)$ is the probability of the term t_k in the document d_j, β is a normalisation coefficient which varies according to the size of the document; and ε is a threshold probability for all the terms not in d_j.

Equation 6 must respect the following property:

$$\sum_{k \in d_j} \beta * P(t_k|d_j) + \sum_{k \in V, k \notin d_j} \varepsilon = 1$$

and β can be easily estimated for a document with the following computation:

$$\beta = 1 - \sum_{k \in V, k \notin d_j} \varepsilon$$

3   Description of the Corpora

In the experiments we have carried out, three corpora with different characteristics with respect to their size and their balance were used. We consider that all these very narrow domain corpora are suitable for our experiments because of their average size per abstract and their narrow domain. In the following subsections we describe each corpus into detail.

3.1   The *CICLing-2002* Corpus

This corpus is made up by 48 abstracts from the *Computational Linguistics* domain, which corresponds to the conference *CICLing 2002*. This collection was used by Makagonov et al. [15] in their experiments on clustering short texts of narrow domains. We consider it a very small but a needed reference corpus, also for manually investigating the obtained results.

The topics of this corpus are the following ones: Linguistic (semantics, syntax, morphology, and parsing), Ambiguity (WSD, anaphora, POS, and spelling), Lexicon (lexics, corpus, and text generation), and Text Processing (information retrieval, summarization, and classification of texts). The distribution and the features of this corpus are shown in Tables 1 and 2, respectively.

Table 1. Distribution of the *CICLing-2002* corpus

Category	# of abstracts
Linguistics	11
Ambiguity	15
Lexicon	11
Text Processing	11

Table 2. Other features of the *CICLing-2002* corpus

Feature	Value
Size of the corpus (bytes)	23,971
Number of categories	4
Number of abstracts	48
Total number of terms	3,382
Vocabulary size (terms)	953
Term average per abstract	70.45

3.2 The *hep-ex* Corpus of CERN

This corpus is based on the collection of abstracts compiled by the University of Jaén, Spain [16], named *hep-ex*, and it is composed by 2,922 abstracts from the *Physics* domain originally stored in the data server of the CERN.

The distribution of the categories for each corpus is better described in Table 3; other characteristics are shown in Table 4. As can be seen, this corpus is totally unbalanced, which makes this task even more challenging.

Table 3. Categories of the *hep-ex* corpus

Category	# of abstracts
Particle physics (experimental results)	2,623
Detectors and experimental techniques	271
Accelerators and storage rings	18
Particle physics (phenomenology)	3
Astrophysics and astronomy	3
Information transfer and management	1
Nonlinear systems	1
Other fields of physics	1
XX	1

Table 4. Other features of the *hep-ex* corpus

Feature	Value
Size of the corpus (bytes)	962,802
Number of categories	9
Number of abstracts	2,922
Total number of terms	135,969
Vocabulary size (terms)	6,150
Term average per abstract	46.53

3.3 The *KnCr* Corpus of MEDLINE

This corpus, named KnCr, was created for the specific task of clustering short texts of a medical narrow domain [21]. It consists of 900 abstracts related with

Table 5. Categories of the *KnCr* corpus

Category	# of abstracts	Category	# of abstracts
blood	64	lung	99
bone	8	lymphoma	30
brain	14	renal	6
breast	119	skin	31
colon	51	stomach	12
genetic studies	66	therapy	169
genitals	160	thyroid	20
liver	29	Other (XXX)	22

Table 6. Other features of the *KnCr* corpus

Feature	Value
Size of the corpus (bytes)	834,212
Number of categories	16
Number of abstracts	900
Total number of terms	113,822
Vocabulary size (terms)	11,958
Term average per abstract	126.47

the "Cancer" domain. Table 5 and 6, show the complete characteristics of this new corpus.

3.4   Preprocessing

We have preprocessed all these collections by eliminating stop words and by applying the Porter stemmer [22]. The characteristics given in the above tables for each corpus were obtained after applying this preprocessing phase. The results reported in [19] show that better results can be obtained by using those terms which contribute to a better clustering (not noisy terms), instead of the complete vocabulary. This fact have led us to study this issue in order to apply it to our preprocessed corpora. Up to now, different Feature Selection Techniques (FSTs) have been used in the clustering task. However, clustering abstracts for a narrow domain implies the well known problem of the lackness of training corpora. This led us to use unsupervised term selection techniques instead of supervised ones. Following we describe briefly all the techniques employed in our experiments.

3.5   Description of the FSTs Used

The first two unsupervised techniques we are presenting in this sub-section have shown their value in the clustering [14] and categorization area [25]. Particulary, the document frequency technique is an effective and simple technique, and it is known that it obtains comparable results to the classical supervised techniques like χ^2 and Information Gain [26]. With respect to the transition point technique, it has a simple calculation procedure, which has been used in other areas of computational linguistic besides clustering of short texts: categorization of texts, keyphrases extraction, summarization, and weighting models for information retrieval systems (see [19]). Therefore, we consider that there exists enough evidence to use this technique as a term selection process.

1. *Document Frequency (DF)*: This technique assigns the value df_t to each term t, where df_t means the number of texts, in a collection, where t ocurrs. This technique assumes that low frequency terms will rarely appear in other documents, therefore, they will not have significance on the prediction of the class for this text.

2. *Term Strength (TS)*: The weight given to each term t is defined by the following equation:

$$ts_t = Pr(t \in T_i | t \in T_j), \text{with } i \neq j,$$

Besides, both texts, T_i and T_j must be as similar as a given threshold, i.e., $sim(T_i, T_j) \geq \beta$, where β must be tuned according to the values inside of the similarity matrix. A high value of ts_t means that the term t contributes to the texts T_i and T_j to be more similar than β. A more detailed description can be found in [25] and [18].

3. *Transition Point (TP)*: A higher value of weight is given to each term t, as its frequency is closer to a frequency named the transition point (TP_V) which can be found by an automatic inspection of the vocabulary frequencies of each text, identifying the lowest frequency (from the highest frequencies) that it is not repeated; this characteristic comes from the formulation of Booth's law for low frequency words [6] (see [19] for a complete explanation of this procedure). The following equation shows how to calculate the final value:

$$idtp(t, T) = \frac{1}{|TP_V - freq(t, T)| + 1}$$

where $freq(t, T)$ is the frequency of the term t in the document T.

The DF and TP techniques have a temporal linear complexity with respect to the number of terms of the data set. On the other hand, TS is computationally more expensive than DF and TP, because it requires to calculate a similarity matrix of texts, which implies this technique to be in $O(n^2)$, where n is the number of texts in the data set.

4   Experimental Results

Clustering very short narrow-domain texts, implies basically two steps: first it is necessary to perform the feature selection process and after the clustering itself. We have used the three unsupervised techniques described in Section 3.5 in order to sort the corpora vocabulary in non-increasing order, with respect to the score of each FST. Thereafter, we have selected different percentages of the vocabulary (from 20% to 90%) in order to determine the behaviour of each technique under different subsets of the vocabulary. The following step involves the use of clustering methods; three different clustering methods were employed for this comparison: Single Link Clustering (SLC) [12], Complete Link Clustering (CLC)[12], and KStar [23].

In order to obtain the best description of our experiments, we have carried out a v-fold cross validation evaluation [7]. This process implies to randomly split the original corpus in a predefined set of partitions, and then calculate the average F-measure (described in the next sub-section) among all the partitions results. The v-fold cross-validation allows to evaluate how well each cluster "performs" when is repeatedly cross-validated in different samples randomly drawn from the data. Consequently, our results will not be casual through the use of a specific clustering method and a specific data collection. In our case, we have used five partitions for the *CICLing-2002* corpus and, thirty for both, the *hep-ex* and the *KnCr* collections.

We have used the F-measure for determining the quality of clusters obtained, as it is described in the next sub-section. Thereafter the results are presented and discussed.

4.1   Performance Measurement

We employed the F-measure, which is commonly used in information retrieval [24], in order to determine which method obtains the best performance. Given a set of clusters $\{G_1, \ldots, G_m\}$ and a set of classes $\{C_1, \ldots, C_n\}$, the F-measure between a cluster i and a class j is given by the following formula.

$$F_{ij} = \frac{2 \cdot P_{ij} \cdot R_{ij}}{P_{ij} + R_{ij}}, \tag{7}$$

where $1 \leq i \leq m$, $1 \leq j \leq n$. P_{ij} and R_{ij} are defined as follows:

$$P_{ij} = \frac{\text{Number of texts from cluster } i \text{ in class } j}{\text{Number of texts from cluster } i}, \tag{8}$$

and

$$R_{ij} = \frac{\text{Number of texts from cluster } i \text{ in class } j}{\text{Number of texts in class } j}. \tag{9}$$

The global performance of a clustering method is calculated by using the values of F_{ij}, the cardinality of the set of clusters obtained, and normalizing by the total number of documents in the collection ($|D|$). The obtained measure is named F-measure and it is shown in equation 10.

$$F = \sum_{1 \leq i \leq m} \frac{|G_i|}{|D|} \max_{1 \leq j \leq n} F_{ij}. \tag{10}$$

5   Results

In the experiments we have carried out, the DF and TS techniques do not improve the results obtained by the transition point technique, which reinforces the hypothesis suggested by [19]. Besides, we have observed that there is not a significant difference between any of the symmetric KL distances. Therefore, we consider that in other applications, the simplest one should be used. Tables 7, 8 and, 9 show our evaluation results for all Kullback-Leibler approaches implemented, by using the *CICLing-2002*, *hep-ex* and, *KnCr* corpus, respectively. In each table, we have defined three sections, named (a), (b) and, (c), each one corresponding to the use of the TP, DF and, TS feature selection technique, respectively. In the first column we have named as *KullbackOriginal*, *KullbackBigi*, *KullbackJensen* and, *KullbackMax*, the KLD defined by Kullback and Leibler [13], Bigi [4], Jensen [10], and Bennet [2] [27], respectively.

Table 7. Results obtained by using the *CICLing-2002* corpus

	(a)-TP			(b)-DF			(c)-TS		
	SLC	CLC	KStar	SLC	CLC	KStar	SLC	CLC	KStar
KullbackOriginal	0,6	0,7	0,7	0,6	0,6	0,6	0,5	0,6	0,6
KullbackBigi	0,6	0,7	0,7	0,6	0,7	0,6	0,5	0,5	0,6
KullbackJensen	0,6	0,6	0,7	0,6	0,6	0,6	0,5	0,6	0,6
KullbackMax	0,6	0,7	0,7	0,6	0,7	0,6	0,5	0,6	0,6

Table 8. Results obtained by using the *hep-ex* corpus

	(a)-TP			(b)-DF			(c)-TS		
	SLC	CLC	KStar	SLC	CLC	KStar	SLC	CLC	KStar
KullbackOriginal	0,86	0,83	0,68	0,60	0,83	0,68	0,80	0,84	0,67
KullbackBigi	0,86	0,82	0,69	0,60	0,82	0,67	0,80	0,85	0,67
KullbackJensen	0,85	0,83	0,68	0,61	0,83	0,69	0,80	0,83	0,66
KullbackMax	0,86	0,83	0,69	0,61	0,83	0,68	0,80	0,85	0,67

Table 9. Results obtained by using the *KnCr* corpus

	(a)-TP			(b)-DF			(c)-TS		
	SLC	CLC	KStar	SLC	CLC	KStar	SLC	CLC	KStar
KullbackOriginal	0,52	0,38	0,39	0,51	0,37	0,38	0,49	0,36	0,38
KullbackBigi	0,52	0,38	0,39	0,51	0,37	0,38	0,49	0,36	0,38
KullbackJensen	0,52	0,36	0,40	0,52	0,36	0,39	0,48	0,34	0,38
KullbackMax	0,51	0,37	0,40	0,51	0,37	0,39	0,50	0,37	0,38

We have made a comparison among our results and those reported by Pinto et al. [20]. This evaluation is presented in Tables 10 and 11, where our best approach is compared with the results presented in [20], which we have named

Table 10. Comparison by using the *CICLing-2002* corpus

	(a)-TP			(b)-DF			(c)-TS		
	SLC	CLC	KStar	SLC	CLC	KStar	SLC	CLC	KStar
KullbackMax	0,6	0,7	0,7	0,6	0,7	0,6	0,5	0,6	0,6
PintoetAl	0,6	0,7	0,7	0,6	0,7	0,6	0,5	0,7	0,6

Table 11. Comparison by using the *hep-ex* corpus

	(a)-TP			(b)-DF			(c)-TS		
	SLC	CLC	KStar	SLC	CLC	KStar	SLC	CLC	KStar
KullbackMax	0,86	0,83	0,69	0,61	0,83	0,68	0,80	0,85	0,67
PintoetAl	0,77	0,87	0,69	0,59	0,86	0,68	0,74	0,86	0,67

PintoetAl. The comparison could be done only by using both, the *CICLing-2002* and the *hep-ex* corpora, because up to now, there are not published results with the characteristics needed for the *KnCr* corpus. We have observed that the use of KLD obtains comparable results, and we consider that this behaviour is derived from the size of each text. We are suggesting to use a smooth procedure, but the number document terms that does not appear in the corpus vocabulary can be extremely high. Further analysis will investigate this issue.

6   Conclusions

We have addressed the problem of clustering short texts of a very narrow domain with the use of a new measure of distance between documents, which is based on the symmetric Kullback-Leibler distance. We observed that there are very little differences in the use of any of the symmetric KL distances analysed. This fact led us to consider that in case of using this approach, the simplest implementation should be used.

Moreover, we have evaluated our approach with three different short-text narrow-domain corpora and, our findings indicates that it is possible to use this measure to tackle this problem, obtaining comparable results than those that uses the Jaccard similarity measure.

Despite we have implemented the KLD for using it in the short-text narrow-domain clustering task, we consider that this approach could be sucessfully implemented in other clustering tasks which involve the use of a more general domain and big size text corpora.

The use of a smooth procedure should be of more benefit as far as the vocabulary of each document would be more similar to the corpus vocabulary. Therefore, we consider that a performance improving could be obtained by using a term expansion method before calculating the similarity matrix with the analysed KLD. Further analysis will investigate this issue.

References

1. M. Alexandrov, A. Gelbukh, and P. Rosso: *An Approach to Clustering Abstracts*, In Proceedings of the 10th International Conference NLDB-05, volume 3513 of Lecture Notes in Computer Science, pages 275-285, Springer-Verlag, 2005.

2. C.H. Bennett, P. Gács, M. Li, P. Vitányi, and W. Zurek: *Information Distance*, IEEE Trans. Inform. Theory, 44:4, pages 1407–1423, 1998.

3. B. Bigi, Y. Huang, R. d. Mori: *Vocabulary and Language Model Adaptation using Information Retrieval*, In Proceedings of the ECIR-2003, volume 2633 of Lecture Notes in Computer Science, pages 305-319, Springer-Verlag, 2003.

4. B. Bigi: *Using Kullback-Leibler Distance for Text Categorization*, In Proceedings of the ECIR-2003, volume 2633 of Lecture Notes in Computer Science, pages 305-319, Springer-Verlag, 2003.

5. B. Bigi, R. d. Mori, M. El-Bèze, T. Spriet: *A fuzzy decision strategy for topic identication and dynamic selection of language models*, Special Issue on Fuzzy Logic in Signal Processing, Signal Processing Journal, 80(6):1085–1097, 2000.

6. A. D. Booth: *A Law of Occurrences for Words of Low Frequency*, Information and control, 10(4):386-393, 1967.

7. P. Burman, *A comparative study of ordinary cross-validation, v-fold cross-validation and the repeated learning-testing methods*, Biometrika 76(3):503-514, 1989.

8. C. Carpineto, R. d. Mori, G. Romano, B. Bigi: *An information-theoretic approach to automatic query expansion*, ACM Transactions on Information Systems, 19(1):1-27, 2001.

9. I. Dagan, L. Lee, F. Pereira: *Similarity-based models of word cooccurrence probabilities*, Machine Learning, 34(1–3):43-69, 1999.

10. B. Fuglede, F. Topse: *Jensen-Shannon Divergence and Hilbert space embedding*, IEEE Int Sym. Information Theory, 2004.

11. H. Jiménez, D. Pinto, and P. Rosso: *Uso del punto de transición en la selección de términos índice para agrupamiento de textos cortos*, Procesamiento del Lenguaje Natural, 35(1):114-118, 2005 (*in Spanish*).

12. S. C. Johnson: *Hierarchical Clustering Schemes*, Psychometrika, 2:241–254, 1967.

13. S. Kullback, R. A. Leibler: *On information and sufficiency*, Annals of Mathematical Statistics, 22(1):79–86, 1951.

14. T. Liu, S. Liu, Z. Chen, and W. Ma: *An evaluation on feature selection for text clustering*, In T. Fawcett and N. Mishra, editors, ICML, pages 488-495, AAAI Press, 2003.

15. P. Makagonov, M. Alexandrov, and A. Gelbukh: *Clustering Abstracts instead of Full Texts*, In Proceedings of the Seventh International Conference on Text, Speech and Dialogue (TSD 2004), volume 3206 of Lecture Notes in Artificial Intelligence, pages 129-135, Springer-Verlag, 2004.

16. A. Montejo-Ráez, L. A. Ureña-López, and R. Steinberger: *Categorization using bibliographic records: beyond document content*, Procesamiento del Lenguaje Natural, 35(1):119-126, 2005.

17. R. d. Mori: Spoken Dialogues with Computers, Academic Press, 1998.

18. V. Pekar, M. Krkoska, S. Staab. Feature Weighting for Co-occurrence-based Classification of Words, In Proceedings of the 20th Conference on Computational Linguistics, COLING-2004, 2004.

19. D. Pinto, H. Jiménez-Salazar, and P. Rosso: *Clustering abstracts of scientific texts using the transition point technique*, In Alexander F. Gelbukh, editor, CICLing, volume 3878 of Lecture Notes in Computer Science, pages 536-546. Springer-Verlang, 2006.

20. D. Pinto, P. Rosso, A. Juan, and H. Jiménez, : *A Comparative Study of Clustering Algorithms on Narrow-Domain Abstracts*, Procesamiento del Lenguaje Natural, 37(1):43–49, 2006.

21. D. Pinto, and P. Rosso: *KnCr: A Short-Text Narrow-Domain Sub-Corpus of Medline*, In Proceedings of TLH-ENC06, pages 266–269, 2006.

22. M. F. Porter: *An algorithm for suffix stripping*, In Program, 14(3), 1980.

23. K. Shin and S. Y. Han: *Fast clustering algorithm for information organization*, In A. F. Gelbukh, editor, CICLing, volume 2588 of Lecture Notes in Computer Science, pages 619-622, Springer-Verlang, 2003.

24. C. J. Van Rijsbergen: Information Retrieval, 2nd edition, Dept. of Computer Science, University of Glasgow, 1979.

25. Y. Yang: *Noise reduction in a statistical approach to text categorization*, In Proceedings of SIGIR-ACM, pages 256-263, 1995.

26. Y. Yang , J. O. Pedersen. A comparative study on feature selection in text categorization. In Proc. ICML, pages 412–420, 1997.

27. J. Ziv and N. Merhav: *A measure of relative entropy between individual sequences with application to universal classification*, IEEE Transactions on Information Theory, 39(4):1270–1279, 1993.

A Mixed Trigrams Approach
for Context Sensitive Spell Checking

Davide Fossati and Barbara Di Eugenio

Department of Computer Science
University of Illinois at Chicago
Chicago, IL, USA
dfossa1@uic.edu, bdieugen@cs.uic.edu

Abstract. This paper addresses the problem of real-word spell checking, i.e., the detection and correction of typos that result in real words of the target language. This paper proposes a methodology based on a mixed trigrams language model. The model has been implemented, trained, and tested with data from the Penn Treebank. The approach has been evaluated in terms of hit rate, false positive rate, and coverage. The experiments show promising results with respect to the hit rates of both detection and correction, even though the false positive rate is still high.

1 Introduction

Spell checking is the process of finding misspelled words in a written text, and possibly correct them. This problem has been widely studied, and spell checkers are probably among the first successful NLP applications widely used by the general public.

We can classify spelling errors in two main groups: *non-word errors* and *real-word errors*.

- *Non-word* errors are spelling errors that result in words that do not exist in the language. For example,
    * The *bok* is on the table.
  The word *bok* does not exist in English, and it probably derives from a typo of the noun *book*:
    The *book* is on the table.
- *Real-word* errors are errors that by chance end up to actual words. For example,
    * I saw *tree* trees in the park.
  The noun *tree* exists in English, but in this context it is most likely a typo of the numeral *three*:
    I saw *three* trees in the park.

According to Kukich, the problem of spell checking can be classified in three categories of increasing difficulty: non-word error detection, isolated-word error correction, and context-dependent word correction [1]. The real-word errors

A. Gelbukh (Ed.): CICLing 2007, LNCS 4394, pp. 623–633, 2007.

detection and correction task, focus of this paper, belongs to the third category. Such errors are the most difficult to detect and correct, because they cannot be revealed just by a dictionary lookup, but can be discovered only taking context into account.

Different approaches to tackle the issue of real-word spell checking have been presented in the literature. Symbolic approaches [2] try to detect errors by parsing each sentence and checking for grammatical anomalies. More recently, some statistical methods have been tried, including the usage of word n-gram models [3,4], POS tagging [5,6,7], Bayesian classifiers [8], decision lists [9], Bayesian hybrid methods [10], a combination of POS and Bayesian methods [7], and Latent Semantic Analysis [11].

The main problem with word n-grams is data sparseness, even with a fairly large amount of training data. In fact, a recent study [4] reported better performances using word bigrams rather than word trigrams, most likely because of the data sparseness problem. POS based methods suffer less of sparseness problems, but such approaches are unable to detect misspelled words that are of the same part of speech. Bayesian methods, on the other hand, are better able to detect this cases, but have worse general performance. These last two methods give better results when combined together [7].

A slightly different application area in which statistical contextual spell checking have been also studied is Optical Character Recognition (OCR). For this application, Markov Model based approaches using letter n-grams have been shown to be quite successful [12].

2   A Mixed Trigrams Approach

This paper proposes a statistical method based on a language model that is a combination of the word-trigrams model and the POS-trigrams model, called *mixed trigrams model*. The main linguistic motivation behind this model is to represent fine-grained lexical information at a local level, and summarize the context with syntactic categories. The main advantage of this model is a great reduction of the data sparsity problem. The following subsections formally define the model and the method to apply it to the spell checking problem.

2.1   Mixed Trigrams

Given a sentence, a *mixed trigram* is a sequence of three elements (e_i, e_{i+1}, e_{i+2}), where a generic element e_k is either the k-th word of the sentence or its part of speech. The particular type of mixed trigrams used in this work has the additional property that at most one of the elements can be a word. For example, consider the sentence:

The/DET kids/NOUN eat/VERB fresh/ADJ apples/NOUN

A complete set of mixed trigrams deriving from this sentence is the following:

(The, NOUN, VERB)
(NOUN, VERB, ADJ)
(VERB, ADJ, NOUN)
(DET, kids, NOUN)
(kids, VERB, ADJ)
(DET, NOUN, eat)
(NOUN, eat, ADJ)
(eat, ADJ, NOUN)
(DET, NOUN, VERB)
(NOUN, VERB, fresh)
(VERB, fresh, NOUN)

Additional trigrams can be considered by adding two "start of sentence" special words and two "end of sentence" special words, to capture the distinctions between words at the beginning, in the middle, or at the end of a sentence.

2.2 Confusion Sets

Another key definition is that of *confusion set*.

Given a dictionary W, a distance function d defining a metric on W, and a word $w \in W$, a confusion set $C(w) \subseteq W$ is a set of words such that $w_c \in C \Leftrightarrow |d(w, w_c)| \leq k$, where k is a constant.

In practice, the confusion set of a word contains all the words "similar enough" to that word. The main issue is then to define a reasonable distance function.

2.3 Levensthein Distance

The *Levensthein distance*, also known as *minimum edit distance* [13], is the minimum number of editing operations necessary to transform one word into another. An editing operation is either a character insertion, deletion, or substitution. The rationale behind the adoption of such a measure is that it reflects quite well some common typing mistakes, like pressing a key twice, typing two keys instead of one, skipping a key, and typing a key instead of another. Such mistakes lead to words with Levensthein distance of 1 from the original word. Another common mistake is switching two characters (e.g., typing *form* instead of *from*). In this case, the wrong word and the correct word will have a Levensthein distance of 2. These kind of mistakes have been found to represent the vast majority of typing errors [14,15,16]. So, it sounds reasonable to include in the confusion set of a word all the words with Levensthein distance less or equal than 2 from the original word.

2.4 Method

Consider the following problem.

Given a sentence $S = w_1 \dots w_k \dots w_n$, find the most likely sequence of elements $E = t_1 \dots w_k^c \dots t_n$, where:

- w_i, $1 \le i \le n$ are words;
- w_k is the *central word* (i.e., the word to be checked);
- t_i, $1 \le i \le n$, $i \ne k$ are part of speech tags;
- w_k^c is a word belonging to the confusion set of the central word w_k (ideally, it should be the correct word).

The observed word w_k is likely to be a spelling mistake of w_k^c if:

1. $w_k \ne w_k^c$, and
2. the probability of the sequence E is smaller than the probability of another sequence $\bar{E} = \bar{t}_1 \ldots \bar{w}_k^c \ldots \bar{t}_n$ such that $\bar{w}_k^c = w_k$. In other words, the sequence $\bar{E}$ is the most likely sequence of elements where the central word w_k is assumed to be correct. In practice, it is calculated by "forcing" the confusion set of the central word to contain only one element, equal to the central word itself.

The criterion above means that a word will be detected as a spelling mistake if another word in the confusion set has higher likelihood of fitting into the same context. In particular, the word in the confusion set belonging to the sequence with the highest probability will be selected by the correction algorithm. This maximization problem can be solved using the Markov Model approach traditionally applied to POS tagging, adopting the same simplifying assumptions, and using mixed trigrams instead of word trigrams. The resulting formula is:

$$\operatorname{argmax}_E \prod_{i=1}^{n} P(w_i|e_i)P(e_i|e_{i-1}e_{i-2})$$

In the previous formula, the variables w_i are words, and the variables e_i are either words or POS tags. The Viterbi algorithm [17] can be used to efficiently compute the sequence E. Figure 1 provides an intuitive example of how the detection process works.

2.5   Conditional Probability Estimation for the Central Word

In the previous formula, for $i = k$ (i.e., the index of the central word), the term $P(w_i|e_i) = P(w_k|w_k^c)$ means the probability of getting the word w_k from a misspelling of the word w_k^c. This probability cannot be easily estimated from a corpus. To estimate a value for this probability term, we define it as a function of the distance between the two words, such that the probability is lower if the distance between the words is greater. In other words, the assumption is that it is more likely to get a similar word, rather than a very different word, as result of a spelling mistake.

$$P(w_k|w_k^c) = \frac{\alpha(1-\alpha)^{d(w_k^c, w_k)}}{\operatorname{count}(\lambda \in W : d(\lambda, w_k) = d(w_k^c, w_k))}$$

The value of the parameter α should be tuned with empirical investigation.

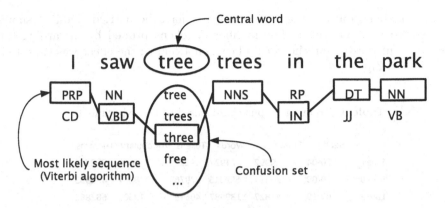

Fig. 1. Example of detection process

3   Experimental Settings

The method described in the previous section has been implemented and empirically evaluated. The following subsections present some details of the experimental settings.

3.1   Algorithm Training

Training the algorithm requires (a) creating a vocabulary, (b) gathering the probability estimations of the mixed trigrams and the conditional probabilities of each word given a POS, (c) calculating the distances among the words in the vocabulary, (d) calculating the conditional probability of each word given another word in its confusion set.

The vocabulary was created from the same corpus used to estimate trigrams and word-POS probabilities. Capitalization was removed, and the least frequent words (tokens with less than four occurrences) were not inserted in the vocabulary and their occurrences in the corpus were replaced with a special symbol for "unknown" words. The reasons are (1) to keep the dictionary and the probabilities table small, and (2) to gather good probability estimations to deal with real unknown words. In fact, even though the spell checking algorithm will check only the words present into the dictionary, the unknown words will be part of the surrounding context, so they have to be managed as well.

Trigrams and word-POS probabilities were estimated from portions of the WSJ section of the Penn Treebank corpus. Probabilities have been computed using the Maximum Likelihood Estimator (MLE) formula. The zero-probabilities were smoothed assigning a very small constant value to them. This smoothing method, however, introduces distortions in the probability space. The impact, hopefully small, of this distortion to the performance of the algorithm should be evaluated and corrected in future work; most likely, a more sophisticated smoothing technique should be used.

Three training data sets of increasing size have been tried. Table 1 shows some statistics about them. The number of tokens pruned by discarding the least frequent words from the vocabulary is noticeable; the effect was expected, and followed Zipf's law.

Table 1. Training corpus chunks used in the experiments

	Sections	Sentences	Words	Tokens	Vocabulary	Trigrams
Small	00-04	9992	274927	19225	5680	232758
Medium	00-09	20386	559315	27976	8857	403993
Large	00-19	41827	1139587	40689	13508	682868

The Levensthein distance measure was calculated for each pair of words in the vocabulary. This step is necessary for the determination of the confusion set of each word, that is computed at run-time looking for the words with Levensthein distance less or equal than 2 to the considered word.

The final training step is the calculation of the conditional probabilities that relate a word with its confusion set. To do that, the formula defined in the previous section was used, with three different values of α (0.25, 0.50, 0.75) for each of the three training sets. The total number of experimental settings was 9.

3.2 Test Data

A testing set of 500 sentences was collected from section 20 of the WSJ Penn Treebank. These sentences were randomly selected among the sentences with number of words between 10 and 30[1]. For each sentence in the test set, one spelling mistake was artificially inserted, by replacing a random word (among those words longer than two characters) with a word in its confusion set. This artificial insertion of spelling mistakes makes the test set ecologically invalid. However, this choice was considered appropriate for this first experimental stage, because choosing the test set in this way gives each "spelling mistake" a chance to be detected. In other words, the detection upper bound would be 100%, which makes it easier to interpret the final results.

3.3 Performance Measures

The following performance measures are considered relevant.

- *Detection hit rate.* It is the ratio between the number of typos detected and the total number of typos. The higher, the better.

---

[1] Since for each sentence in the WSJ corpus two special "start of sentence" tokens and two "end of sentence" tokens were added, the net number of "real" words in the test sentences actually ranges from 6 to 24 words.

- *Correction hit rate.* It is the ratio between the number of typos corrected and the total number of typos. This ratio is usually lower than the detection hit rate, because a spelling mistake can be rightly detected but corrected in a wrong way.
- *False positive rate on checked words.* It is the ratio between the number of false positives (i.e., correct words that are wrongly detected as typos) and the number of words checked by the algorithm. The lower, the better.
- *False positive rate on total words.* It is the ratio between the number of false positives and the total number of words in the tested sentences. Since not all the words are checked by the algorithm (see below), this ratio is usually lower than the false positive rate on checked words.
- *checked over unknown words ratio.* It is the ratio between the number of words checked and the number of words skipped by the algorithm because not in the vocabulary.
- *checked over short words ratio.* It is the ratio between the number of words checked and the number of words skipped because shorter than three characters. The reason why the words with less than three characters are skipped is that the confusion sets of short words were unmanageably high. In order to be able to check short words too, further research is needed in order to figure out how to prune the confusion set.
- *checked over skipped words ratio.* It is the ratio between the number of words checked and the total number of words skipped (unknown + short).
- *detected over false positive ratio.* It is the ratio between the number of detected typos and the number of false positives.

4   Experimental Results

4.1   Hit and False Positive Rates

Figure 2, Figure 3, and Figure 4 show the results of detection and correction hit rates (%), false positive rate on checked and total words (%), and the ratio between detected typos and false positives for the 9 possible combinations of the parameters (training corpus size and α value).

To put those numbers in perspective, the only results found in the literature that are somewhat comparable are those reported in [4]. Those experiments scored a maximum of 92% detection hit rate and 30% false positive rate with a word bigrams model; 55% detection hit rate and 18% false positive rate with a word trigrams model.

One might expect that the performance of the system would improve as the size of the training corpus increases, because a larger training corpus usually leads to a better estimation of the model's probability tables. In fact, Figure 3 shows a trend of reduction of the false positive rate as the corpus size gets larger. However, the results on hit rate do not display a similar positive trend. Also, both hit rate and false alarm rate show very little sensitivity with respect to the α parameter. This fact is interesting and unexpected.

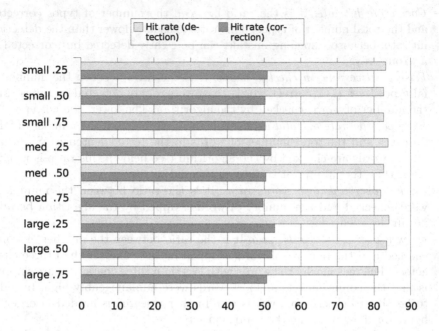

Fig. 2. Hit rates

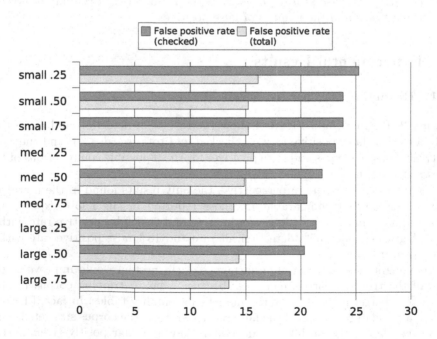

Fig. 3. False positive rates

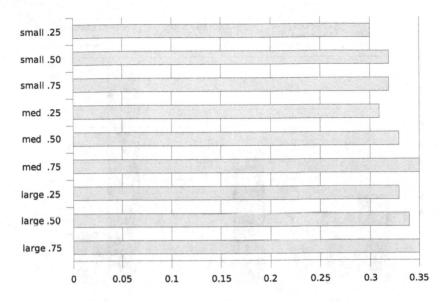

Fig. 4. Detected over false positive ratio

4.2 Coverage

Figure 5 shows the results for the coverage measures, i.e., checked over unknown, checked over short, and checked over skipped ratios. Those measures are independent on the values of α, as they depend only on the training corpus.

The coverage of the unknown words increases noticeably with the corpus size, because with a larger corpus more words are added to the vocabulary. However, the overall coverage is still depressed by the high amount of short words, that are skipped anyway.

5   Conclusions and Future Work

The results of these experiments are promising, and represent a good starting point for future research. Among the others, there are several points that would be worthy of further investigation:

- Improve the estimation of the probability tables, for example by using a more sophisticated smoothing technique.
- Deal with the problem of short words, that represent an important percentage of words that are now skipped.
- Explore the sensitivity of the algorithm to several other parameters, such as the threshold value to prune the vocabulary, and the length of the context to take into account.
- Run experiments on ecologically valid data.
- Explore the usage of alternative word distance measures and conditional probabilities estimations for words with respect to their confusion set.

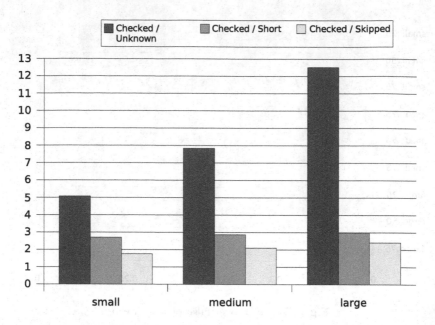

Fig. 5. Coverage of the spell checker

Acknowledgments

This work is supported by awards N00014-00-1-0640 from the Office of Naval Research, and awards IIS-0133123 and ALT-0536968 from the National Science Foundation. The authors thank Rajen Subba and Joel Booth for useful discussions.

References

1. Kukich, K.: Techniques for automatically correcting words in text. ACM Computing Surveys **24(4)** (1992) 377–439
2. Heidorn, G.E., Jensen, K., Miller, L.A., Byrd, R.J., Chodorow, M.S.: The EPISTLE text-critiquing system. IBM Systems Journal **21(3)** (1986) 305–326
3. Mays, E., Damerau, F.J., Mercer, R.L.: Context based spelling correction. Information Processing and Management **27(5)** (1991) 517–522
4. Berlinsky-Schine, A.: Context-based detection of real word typographical errors using markov models. Technical report, Cornell University, Ithaca, NY (2004) http://www.people.cornell.edu/ pages/arb36/typofinal.doc.
5. Marshall, I.: Choice of grammatical word-class without global syntactic analysis: tagging words in the lob corpus. Computers and the Humanities **17** (1983) 139–150
6. Garside, R., Leech, G., Sampson, G.: The Computational Analysis of English: a corpus-based approach. Longman (1987)
7. Golding, A., Schabes, Y.: Combining trigram-based and feature-based methods for context-sensitive spelling correction. In: 34th Annual Meeting of the Association for Computational Linguistics. (1996) http://acl.ldc.upenn.edu.

8. Gale, W.A., Church, K.W., Yarowsky, D.: A method for disambiguating word senses in a large corpus. Computers and the Humanities **26** (1993) 415–439
9. Yarowsky, D.: Decision lists for lexical ambiguity resolution: Application to accent restoration in spanish and french. In: Proceedings of the 32nd Annual Meeting of the Association for Computational Linguistics. (1994) 88–95
10. Golding, A.: A bayesian hybrid method for context-sensitive spelling correction. In: Proceedings of the Third Workshop on Very Large Corpora. (1995) 39–53
11. Jones, M.P., Martin, J.H.: Contextual spelling correction using latent semantic analysis. In: Fifth Conference on Applied Natural Language Processing. (1997) http://acl.ldc.upenn.edu.
12. Tong, X., Evans, D.A.: A statistical approach to automatic ocr error correction in context. In: Fourth Workshop on Very Large Corpora. (1996) http://acl.ldc.upenn.edu.
13. Jurafsky, D., Martin, J.H.: Speech and Language Processing. Prentice Hall (2000)
14. Damerau, F.J.: A technique for computer detection and correction of spelling errors. Communications of the A.C.M. **7** (1964) 171–176
15. Pollock, J.J., Zamora, A.: Automatic spelling correction in scientific and scholarly text. Communications of the A.C.M. **27(4)** (1984) 358–368
16. Mitton, R.: Spellchecking by computer. Journal of the Simplified Spelling Society **20(1)** (1996) 4–11 http://www.les.aston.ac.uk/simplspel.html.
17. Manning, C.D., Schutze, H.: Foundations of Statistical Natural Language Processing. MIT Press (1999)

Combining Methods for Detecting and Correcting Semantic Hidden Errors in Arabic Texts

Chiraz Ben Othmane Zribi, Hanene Mejri, and Mohamed Ben Ahmed

RIADI laboratory, National School of Computer Sciences, 2010,
University of La Manouba, Tunisia
{Chiraz.benothmane,Hanene.mejri,Mohamed.benahmed}@riadi.rnu.tn

Abstract. In this paper, we address the problem of semantic hidden errors in Arabic texts. These are spelling errors occurring in valid words and causing semantic irregularities. We first expose the different types of these errors. Then, we present and argue the adopted approach, which is based on the combination of several methods. Next, we describe the context of our work and show the multi-agent architecture of our system. Finally we present the testing framework used to evaluate the implemented system.

1 Introduction

Hidden errors are spelling errors that occur in valid words. The presence of such a word within an incorrect syntactic or semantic (even pragmatic) context makes the whole sentence incomprehensible. For instance:

Example: تطلع الشّمس علينا من الشّوق (the sun shines from <u>desire</u>).

In this example, the writer intended to write الشّرق (east) not الشّوق (desire) but a typographical error yielded a sentence that does not make sense.

Statistics mentioned in [1] show that hidden errors count for 40% of all spelling errors. This high number demonstrates the need for studying this kind of errors. In Arabic this problem is much more present because of the proximity of words. According to [2] the probability to encounter a hidden error is 14 times larger than in English and 10 times larger than in French.

Several researchers have taken an interest in this problem. Golding studied this kind of errors for the English language and proposed multiple correction methods such as the Bayesian method [3], the Trigram-based method [4] and the Winnow method [5]. Chinese was also studied by [6]. Swedish was the subject of a similar study by [7]. Bolshakov et al. studied a type of semantic errors called malapropisms. They were first interested in English [8] and Russian [9]. Then they studied and proposed a solution for the detection and the correction of these kind of errors for Spanish [10] [11].

Even though Arabic has characteristics that increase the probability of such errors occurring, there is only one research that we carried out earlier [12]. This work was concerned by the problematic of hidden errors in general and by the syntactic level in

A. Gelbukh (Ed.): CICLing 2007, LNCS 4394, pp. 634–645, 2007.

particular. Thus, the problem of hidden errors in Arabic is not yet resolved, and we hope to have a part in the solution by proposing a system for the detection and the correction of semantic hidden errors occurring in Arabic texts.

Due to the complexity of the problem, we made some assumptions to restrict the scope of our investigation: we first did not take into account the vowel marks in words. This is argued by the fact that the majority of texts (except of the didactic ones) are without vowels in spite of the importance of these marks in the process of reading. Second we assumed that there is only one hidden error at the most per sentence and that error results from one elementary typographical error such as: character insertion, deletion, substitution or transposition. Statistics have showed that only one of theses operations are at the origin of a spelling error in 90% of all cases [13].

The remainder of this paper is organized as follows: First, we present the concept of semantic hidden errors. Then we present our approach for detecting and correcting these errors. Next we explain the MAS (Multi –agent System) architecture of the implemented system. Finally, we describe the method we used to evaluate the efficiency of our system and the obtained results.

2 Semantic Hidden Errors

We call "semantic hidden" error every single-consonant spelling error which results in a correctly-spelled, but semantically incorrect word in a given context. This class of typographic mistakes cannot be detected by a simple spell checker, which is concerned only by the erroneous spelled words.

Semantic hidden errors can cause incomprehensive sentences or unfinished sentences. In the first case, the sentence is misinterpreted or completely absurd. The second case concerns sentences having a partial or incomplete meaning. We take an interest in this work only in errors giving incomprehensive sentences.

يعرضون عليه أموالا كبيرة (كثيرة)

They give him big (much) money

In this erroneous sentence, the adjective كبيرة (big) takes the place of the correct word كثيرة (much) due to the substitution of ب by ث.

3 Detecting Semantic Irregularities

To understand the meaning of a word, the computer (like human) must know the different representations of this word and its different contexts of use. This knowledge can be obtained by different resources as: thesaurus, ontologies, semantic networks or textual corpora.

In this work, we chose a method that obtains the words' meaning from textual corpora. This direction is based on the principle of the distributional linguistic that stipulates: "*the word's meaning can be determined statistically, from contexts (i.e., paragraphs, sentences, texts in which this word occurs* "[14]. For example, the word *plane* occurs often with words as: *take off, wing, airport*, and rarely with *lion* or *forest*.

For detecting semantic hidden errors, we propose to check the semantic validity of each word in the text. To this purpose we combine four methods (statistical and linguistic) making possible the representation of a word according its near and distant context and the comparison of this representation with the ones obtained from the textual corpora. The idea behind this combination is to profit from the advantages of each method. In addition, this involves the selection of only one error if there is a conflict. This decision is then taken by a process of voting that takes into account the results of the application of each method and chooses the most probable error.

A training phase is needed to obtain from the textual corpora all data which are used by the different proposed methods. These data are presented as linguistic information and statistical measures.

3.1 Co-occurrence-Collocation Method

This method verifies the contextual validity of a word by calculating its frequency of appearance in a given context using the following measures:

First, let:
$S = \{w_1, ..., w_i, ..., w_n\}$ be the input sentence to the semantic checker .
$L = \{l_1, ..., l_i, ..., l_n\}$ be the set of the words lemmas of the sentence.
$C = \{c_{-k}, ..., c_{-1}, c_1, ..., c_k\}$ be the set of k words surrounding the word to be analyzed.

- **Frequency of occurrence:** This frequency is calculated for each word w_i in the sentence to analyze, in a window of 10 words[1]. This is achieved by using Bayes' inversion formula:

$$p(w_i | C) = \frac{p(C | w_i) \times p(w_i)}{p(C)}.$$

(1)

The word w_i is closer to its surrounding words as the value of $p(w_i \backslash C)$ is higher.
- **Coefficient of collocation:** To determine this coefficient we first identify all collocations in a sentence by referring to a list of collocations obtained during the training phase. For this purpose, we used and adapted a part of the system accomplished by [15]. When a collocation is found in a sentence, a coefficient is given to each word in this expression. This coefficient is the Kulczinsky measure *(KUC)*, which is a criterion of association that identifies the degree of correlation between two lemmas l_i et l_j using the following formula:

$$KUC = \frac{a}{2}\left(\frac{1}{a+b} + \frac{1}{a+c}\right).$$

(2)

Where:
a: number of occurrences of the pair (l_i, l_j)
b: number of occurrences of the pairs where l_i is not followed by l_j
c: number of occurrences of the pairs where l_j is not followed by l_i

---

[1] This value can be adjusted easily.

The value of this coefficient varies from 0 to 1. When it is equal to 0.5 l_i is usually observed with l_j. Thus, an expression is considered as a collocation if the *KUC* coefficient is greater than 0.5.

- **Frequency of repetition:** This measure is used to know whether the lemma of the textual form to check repeats itself in the text. In fact, if a word is rare, one can suppose that it hides an error. This idea is based on the assumption that "Words (or more precisely lemmas of words) of a given text tend to repeat themselves" [16]. Indeed, according to research carried out by [16] on an Arabic textual corpus, it seems that a textual form can appear 5.6 times on average, whereas a lemma can appear 6.3 times on average in the same text.

For each lemma we calculate its frequency of occurrence within all text, using the following formula:

$$p(l_i) = \frac{\text{number of occurences of } l_i}{\text{total numbers of lemmas}}. \tag{3}$$

The word w_i whose lemma is l_i is closer to its distant context as the value of $p(l_i)$ is higher.

Finally, these three measures are combined by the following linear formula:

$$F(w_i) = \alpha * p(w_i | C) + \beta * KUC(w_i) + \delta * p(l_i). \tag{4}$$

Where $F(wi)$ is the total frequency of appearance of the word w_i in the text, and α, β and λ are three coefficients related to the three calculated contextual probabilities cited above. The values associated with these coefficients cannot be predicted, but must be obtained through several tests and comparisons of relevance. However, we estimate[2] that the value of α and β should be more important than that of λ because the context close to the target word is more relevant than its remote context. For each word, we calculate the $F(w_i)$ value which, compared with a threshold value, will validate the relevance of this word in its context.

3.2 Context-Vector Method

In this method we represent each word in a sentence by a vector representing its context. Therefore, a vector Vw_i is a vector representation of the probability of co-occurrence of a word w_i with all the words in the same sentence. If we consider the following sentence:

شرب الرجل كلبا(كأسا)

The men drunk a dog (glass)

The matrix below shows the co-occurrence probability of each word w_i in a sentence with its neighbours in the same context. The columns represent the words w_i and the rows represent the elements of the vector Vw_i. Thus, a cell contains the co-occurrence probability of the word w_i with the word w_j.

---

[2] After many tests we chose $\alpha = 2$ $\beta = 1$ and $\lambda = 0.5$.

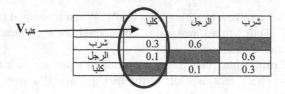

Fig. 1. Matrix of words' co-occurrences in a sentence

To represent the degree of correlation of each word w_i with the other words in the sentence, we propose to calculate the norm of each vector. Consequently, we evaluate the norm of each word's vector and we compare them to a threshold. The words having a norm lower to the threshold will be added to the list of probable errors.

In the last example, the norms of the words' vectors شرب, الرجل, كلبا are respectively equals to 0.67 ; 0.6 et 0.31 the word having the lower norm is كلبا (dog), it will be probably then suspected.

3.3 Vocabulary-Vector Method

The vocabulary relating to a text is a representative element for this later and a good indicator of its coherence. Consequently, we can study the semantic validity of a sentence by using the vector representation cited previously. Thus we propose to represent each word in the sentence using a vector according to its probability of occurrence with each word in the vocabulary. To evaluate the proximity between two vectors, we use the measure of angular distance expressed as following:

$$\text{Dist}(Vw_i, Vw_j) = \arccos(\text{Sim}(Vw_i, Vw_j)) . \tag{5}$$

$$\text{Sim}(Vw_i, Vw_j) = \cos(Vw_i, Vw_j) = \frac{Vw_i \, Vw_j}{\|Vw_i\| * \|Vw_j\|} = \frac{\sum_{t=1}^{x} Vw_{i_t} Vw_{j_t}}{\sqrt{\sum_{t=1}^{x} Vw_{it}^2 \sum_{t=1}^{x} Vw_{jt}^2}} .$$

We calculate the angular distance for each word's vector Vw_i regarding to all the words' vectors Vw_j of the sentence. The most distant vector to the context is the one which appears rarely with the words in the vocabulary. To select this vector, the sum of angular distances of each word's vector is calculated and then compared to a threshold. Those having a sum higher than the threshold will be suspected.

3.4 Latent Semantic Analysis Method

"*LSA* (Latent Semantic Analysis) is a method that makes possible the acquisition of knowledge by an automatically analysis of big textual corpora" [14]. Particularly, this method identifies the semantic similarity of two words, two textual segments or their combination even though these words or textual segments don't appear together.

The principle of *LSA* method consists on representing the words (terms) called lexical unities and the textual segments (documents: sentences, paragraphs or texts) called textual unities by vectors in a vector space of reduced dimensions in regards to the original space. The original space is represented by a matrix of co-occurrence (or matrix of words by context) $X(t, d)$ which represents the corpora of training, where the t

rows correspond to the lexical unities, and the *d* columns to the textual unities. A cell in this matrix contains the number of occurrences of a lexical unity in a textual unity.

The next step of *LSA* method consists, on expressing this matrix in a product of three other matrixes *T(t,r)*, *S(r,r)* et *D(r,d)* thanks to a sort of factorial analysis called *Singular Value Decomposition (SVD)*. The matrix *T* is orthogonal and represents the original term vectors, *S* is a diagonal matrix called also singular value matrix and *D* is an orthogonal matrix of original document vectors.

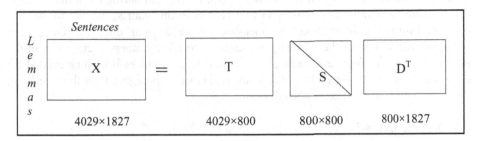

Fig. 2. Singular value decomposition of the matrix of co-occurrence

In our case, the matrix *X* is built during the training phase. The rows correspond to the lemmas of this corpus (we count **4029** lemmas), the columns represent the sentences (the corpus is composed of **1827** sentences).

The reduction of dimensions consists on the choice among the *n* dimensions the *k* ones that are the most pertinent and the most representative of the original space. This is done from the diagonal matrix *S* sorted according to the rank of its singular values. In this way, we obtain three matrixes *T (t,k)*, *S(k,k)* et *D(k,d)* of reduced dimensions (for us k=300, determined after some tests).

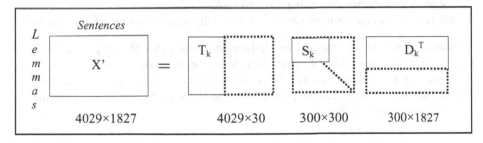

Fig. 3. Dimension reduction of the matrix of co-occurrence

However, before its decomposition in singular values, the initial matrix of co-occurrence undergoes a whole of transformations which consists in weighting each cell in order to highlight the importance of a word in a particular passage and its importance in the field of the speech in general. Therefore, we chose to apply the entropy to our initial matrix. This measurement is especially used in the field of the knowledge extraction and it qualifies the state of disorder of a source of information. It is thus calculated for each word of the matrix by the following formula:

$$\text{Entropy}(w_i) = 1 \sum_{j=1}^{n} \frac{f_{ij} \text{Log} f_{ij}}{\text{Log} n}. \tag{6}$$

Where n is the number of sentences in which the term w_i appears at least only once, f_{ij} is the frequency of appearance of the word w_i in the sentence.

The variant of the *LSA* method that we propose here verifies the semantic validity of words in a given sentence by comparing their semantic vectors which are extracted from the reduced matrix of co-occurrence which is obtained during the training stage. To measure the semantic proximity of two vectors in this matrix, we use, in the way of *Vocabulary-Vector* method, the measure of the angular distance. Thus, each semantic vector Vw_i of the word w_i is compared to all the others vectors Vw_j in the sentence using the angular distance. The sum of these distances is then calculated for each word and is compared to a threshold. If this value is higher than the threshold, the correspondent word is suspected.

3.5 Voting Method

Since our system is based on the assumption that there is one error at the most in a sentence and the suspected errors are sorted by a decreasing order of probability in each method we chose to apply a voting procedure of type *uninominal with classification* (the candidates are sorted and only one among them will be the winner). We present here the principle applied by this procedure.

1. We calculate the number of occurrences of the different hypothetical errors ranked first in each list, given by each method.
2. We select the errors having the biggest number of occurrences. If only one error obtains the biggest number of occurrences, this one is selected as being the most probable error in the sentence. Otherwise, we calculate once again the number of occurrences for errors but using the next rank.
3. We repeat this process until one error obtains the biggest number of occurrences.

However, this voting method can induce sometimes to a blocking situation when the number of occurrences of selected errors in the first rank never changes. In this case, we use a *confidence degree* that is attributed to each method, in order to select among the list of the retained errors, that one detected by the method having the highest confidence degree.

4 Correcting Semantic Errors

To correct semantic errors we proceed by generating all the forms close to the error. These forms are obtained through one editing error. They are then all added to a list, which contains the candidates for the correction. Because of lexical proximity of Arabic words, the number of these candidates can be excessively high and one could estimate that an average of 27 forms will be suggested for the correction of each error. In extreme cases, this number can reach 185 forms [2].

To reduce the number of candidates, we propose to substitute the erroneous word with each suggested correction and form thus a set of candidate sentences. These sentences are processed once more by the detection part of the system and sentences containing semantic anomalies are eliminated from the list. The remaining sentences are then sorted using the combined criteria of classification presented below:

- **Typographical distance criterion:** It measures the degree of resemblance between an erroneous word and a candidate correction of the word. [17] confers weights to the various operations of edition according to their relevance: 1.5 for adding a character, 1 for substituting two characters and 0.5 for deleting a character.
- **Proximity value criterion:** According to [2], there is a correlation between the classification of candidate corrections and the proximity values between character strings. Candidate corrections can be classified according to the value of their proximity to the form they aim to correct. This value is defined as: *"the sum of the squares of the sizes of the common maximum sub-strings"*.
- **Position of error criterion:** It gives more significance to the principal word of the sentence. This word is rarely incorrect since the writer is supposed to be more attentive when writing the beginning of the sentence rather than its end [18].

5 Context of Work

This work comes to complete the previous one [12] that was interested by the problem of hidden errors in Arabic texts. The system that we proposed for the treatment of these errors is based on a Multi-Agent-System (MAS). This system is composed principally of an agent for the correction and two groups of agents for detection: a group of syntactic agents responsible of the analysis of the syntactic anomalies and a group of semantic agents for the semantic inconsistencies. Only the agent correction and the group of syntactic agents were well studied and implemented, we thus supplement by this research the semantic part.

Accordingly, we implemented our semantic checker as a group of semantic agents, where each method suggested will be applied by a specific agent. Moreover, one *Supervisor* agent of the group is in charge of the activation of the different semantic analyzer agents. The semantic agents work, therefore, in parallel and communicate their results to the Supervisor which selects the most probable error among the lists of errors (given by each analyzer agent) thanks to the voting procedure.

The following figure illustrates the global architecture of the system using the two groups of syntactic and semantic agents in the two phases: detection and the correction. Because of the need of various linguistic information about the input text, a morpho-syntactic analysis [2] is performed at the beginning.

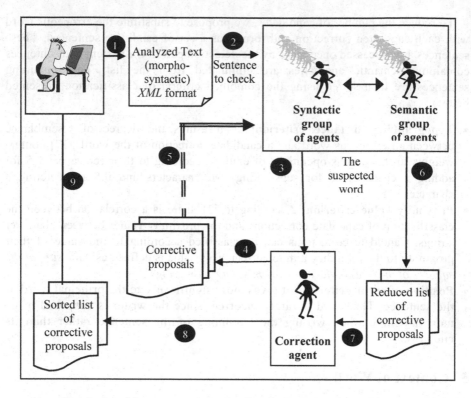

Fig. 4. A multi-agent system for the detection-correction of hidden errors

6 Testing and Results

We have built our own corpus of training in order to extract the data used by the various agents. This corpus is made of 30 economic texts (29 332 words) available on the Net, and which come from the corpus of contemporary Arabic, collected, treated and classified by category by [19]. We also chose a corpus of test of the same field counting 1 564 words and 50 hidden errors in 100 sentences.

6.1 Evaluation of the Detection Component

The following figure illustrates the performance of each agent and that one of the global system in term of accuracy.

The highest rate of accuracy for the semantic group agents is that of the Co-occurrence-Collocation agent with a value of 89.18%. This performance is explained by the complementarities of the phenomena of co-occurrence, collocation and repetition. On the other hand, the rate provided by *LSA* agent (82.92%) is weaker; this is certainly due to the modesty of our data of training which cause a high rate of sur-detection of errors. However, we think that *LSA* method remains always promising regarding the methods only based on the co-occurrences of the words. Indeed, the rate

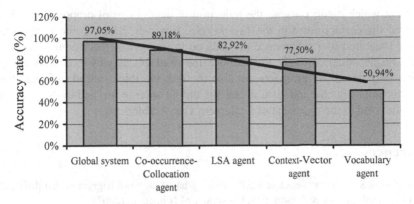

Fig. 5. Evaluation of the semantic group of agents

of precision of the agent *Context-Vector*, is low (77.5%) and that of the *Vocabulary-Vector* agent is not excellent (50.94%). The improvement of the results of the latter would require better corpora of training and strategy of extracting the vocabulary. Regarding the result of the evaluation of the total system, we can say that the rate of precision which is equal to 97.05% is very satisfactory. The performance of the voting system and its contribution for the selection of the most probable error in the sentence are thus confirmed.

6.2 Evaluation of the Correction Component

This phase was tested on two levels; initially after obtaining all the proposals for a correction, then after the reduction of the number of proposals. The obtained results are illustrated in the table hereafter.

Table 1. Evaluation of the correction agent

	Coverage	Accuracy	Ambiguity	Proposal	Rank
Initially	100%	100%	100%	46.67	13.82
After reduction	100%	80%	80%	5.98	3.43

We notice that our method of minimization of proposals decreases considerably, the average number of the proposals of 98% (from 46.67 to 5.98 proposals on average). Although, this reduction has reduced the ambiguity of our corrector of 20%, it did not occur without damage. In fact, it caused the fall of the precision (reduction of 20%).

7 Conclusion

Our system of detection of semantic hidden errors gave satisfactory results (97.05% of accuracy) in spite of the constraints and the restrictions related to the size and the non-diversity of our training corpora. We point out, also, the contribution of the process of correction which made possible the reduction of the number of proposals by 98% and advanced the correct form in the first ranks. However, because our solution uses a training stage and its performance depends on the quality of this training, we estimate that the results obtained can be furthermore improved specially by more tests and bigger training corpora. Other prospects are also in sight, we think indeed of integrating the two groups of syntactic and semantic agents unit in order to test and evaluate the global system devoted to the treatment of hidden errors in Arabic texts.

References

1. Verberne S.: Context sensitive spell checking based on word trigram probabilities. Master thesis Taal, Spraak & Informatica, University of Nijmegen, (2002)
2. Ben Othman C.: De la synthèse lexicographique à la détection et la correction des graphie fautives arabes. Thèse de doctorat, Université de Paris XI, Orsay, (1998)
3. Golding A.: A Bayesian hybrid method for context-sensitive spelling correction. In Proceedings of the third Workshop On Very Large Corpora, Cambridge, Massachuses, USA, (1995), 39-53
4. Golding A. and Schabes Y.: Combining trigram based and feature based methods for context sensitive spelling correction. In Proceedings of the 34th Annual Meeting of the Association for Computational Linguistics, Santa Cruz, (1996), 71-78
5. Golding A. R. et Dan Roth. A winnow-based approach to context-sensitive spelling correction. Machine Learning, (1999), 34(1-3), 107-130
6. Xiaolong W., Jianhua L. Combine trigram and automatic weight distribution in Chinese spelling error correction, Journal of computer Science and Technology, Volume 17 Issue 6, Province, China, (2001)
7. Bigert J., Knutsson O. Robust Error Detection : A Hybrid Approach Combining Unsupervised Error Detection and Linguistic Knowledge, in Proceedings of Robust Methods in Analysis of Natural Language Data (ROMAND'02), Frascati, Italie, (2002)
8. I. Bolshakov, A. Gelbukh.: On Detection of Malapropisms by Multistage Collocation Testing. NLDB-2003. Lecture Notes in Informatics, Bonner Kllen Verlag, (2003), 28–41
9. I. A. Bolshakov, A. Gelbukh. Paronyms for Accelerated Correction of Semantic Errors. International Journal on Information Theories and Applications, Vol.10, (2003), 11–19
10. A. Gelbukh, I. Bolshakov. On Correction of Semantic Errors in Natural Language Texts with a Dictionary of Literal Paronyms. AWIC-2004. Lecture Notes in Artificial Intelligence, N 3034, Springer (2004), 105–114
11. I.A. Bolshakov, S.N. Galicia-Haro, A. Gelbukh. Detection and Correction of Malapropisms in Spanish by means of Internet Search. TSD-2005. Lecture Notes in Artificial Intelligence, N 3658, Springer (2005), 115–122
12. Ben Othmane Z. C., Ben Fraj F., Ben Ahmed M.: A Multi-Agent System for Detecting and Correcting "Hidden" Spelling Errors in Arabic Texts. NLUCS 2005: 149-154
13. Ben Hamadou A. Vérification et correction automatique par analyse affixale des textes écrits en langue naturelle : le cas de l'arabe non voyellé. Thèse d'état en informatique, Faculté des Sciences de Tunis, (1993)
14. Landauer T.K., Foltz P.W. et Laham D., An introduction to Latent Semantic Analysis.Discourse Processes, Vol. 25, (1998), 259-284
15. Mlayeh I. Extraction de collocations à partir de corpus textuels en langue arabe. Mémoire de mastère, Ecole nationale des sciences informatiques, Université de la Manouba, 2004.

16. Ben Othmane Z. C. and Ben Ahmed M., le contexte au service des graphies fautives arabes. TALN 2003, Nantes, (2003), 11-14
17. Aloulou, C. Utilisation de l'approche multi-critère pour orienter un processus de correction des erreurs d'accord dans des phrases de la langue arabe non voyellée. Mémoire de DEA, Institut Supérieur de Gestion, Université de Tunis III, (1996)
18. Courtin J., Genthial D. et Menézo J. Intégration de strategies de correction dans un système de detection/correction d'erreurs, Colloque Informatique et Langue Naturelle (ILN93), Nantes, (1993)
19. Sulaiti L. Designing and Developing a Corpus of Contemporary Arabic. Master of Science, School of Computing, University of Leeds, United Kingdom, (2004)

Author Index